ISBN 978-0-260-45506-2
PIBN 10949345

FB &c Ltd, Dalton House, 60 Windsor Avenue, London, SW19 2RR.
Company number 08720141. Registered in England and Wales.

For support please visit www.forgottenbooks.com

JOURNAL OF THE PROCEEDINGS

OF THE

NINETY-FIRST CONVENTION

OF THE

Protestant Episcopal Church

IN THE

DIOCESE OF NEW-YORK,

WHICH ASSEMBLED IN

ST. JOHN'S CHAPEL, IN THE CITY OF NEW-YORK,

ON

WEDNESDAY, SEPTEMBER 30, A. D. 1874.

New-York:

PUBLISHED FOR THE CONVENTION,

BY POTT, YOUNG & CO., COOPER UNION, FOURTH AVENUE.

M.DCCC.LXXIV.

24

JOHN W. AMERMAN, PRINTER,
No. 47 Cedar Street, N. Y.

List of the Clergy

OF THE

DIOCESE OF NEW-YORK.

SEPTEMBER 30, 1874.

This List of Clergy, being that presented by the Bishop to the Convention, contains no note of changes which have since taken place.

This mark * designates the Alumni of the General Theological Seminary of the Protestant Episcopal Church in the United States.

THE RIGHT REV. HORATIO POTTER, D. D., LL. D., D. C. L., BISHOP OF THE DIOCESE.

The Rev. Charles C. Adams, rector of St. Mary's Church, Manhattanville, New-York.

The Rev. Samuel M. Akerly, missionary at Marlborough, Ulster county.

The Rev. John G. Ames, a Professor in the House of Evangelists, New-York.

The Rev. George B. Andrews, D. D., rector of Zion Church, Wappinger's Falls, Dutchess county.

The Rev. Edward Anthon, New-York.

*The Rev. Octavius Applegate, assistant minister of St. George's Church, Newburgh, Orange county.

*The Rev. Franklin Babbitt, rector of Grace Church, Nyack, Rockland county, and missionary.

*The Rev. Brady Electus Backus, St. Peter's Church, New-York.

The Rev. George W. Bacon, assistant minister of the Church of St. John Baptist, New-York.

The Rev. David F. Banks, rector of St. Paul's Church, Yonkers, Westchester county.

The Rev. Frederick A. P. Barnard, D. D., LL. D., President of Columbia College, New-York.

The Rev. James S. Barnes.

The Rev. John G. Barton, LL. D., deacon, Professor of the English Language and Literature in the College of the City of New-York.

*The Rev. Alfred B. Beach, D. D., rector of St. Peter's Church, New-York.

The Rev. Henry H. Bean, rector of St. Luke's Church, Rossville, Richmond county.

*The Rev. Wm. H. Benjamin, rector of St. Barnabas' Church, Irvington, Westchester county.

The Rev. John Blake, Chaplain in U. S. Navy.

The Rev. Cornelius W. Bolton, rector of St. Stephen's Church, North Castle, Westchester county.

The Rev. Robert Bolton, missionary at Lewisboro', Westchester county.

The Rev. Chauncey B. Brewster, rector of Christ Church, Rye, Westchester county.

The Rev. Wm. M. Atkinson Broadnax, New-York.

The Rev. John Brown, D. D., rector of St. George's Church, Newburgh, Orange county.

The Rev. J. Eastburn Brown, minister of St. George's Mission Chapel of Free Grace, New-York.

*The Rev. Thomas McKee Brown, minister of the Church of St. Mary the Virgin, New-York.

*The Rev. Clarence Buel, rector of Trinity Church, Mount Vernon, Westchester county.

*The Rev. Samuel Buel, D. D., Professor of Systematic Divinity in the General Theological Seminary, New-York.

The Rev. Edward C. Bull, Tarrytown, Westchester county.

The Rev. James S. Bush, rector of the Church of the Ascension, West Brighton, Richmond county.

*The Rev. Philander K. Cady, D. D., rector of Christ Church, Poughkeepsie, Dutchess county.

*The Rev. Charles Fobes Canedy, rector of St. John's Church, Monticello, Sullivan county, and missionary.

The Rev. Alexander Capron, rector of Grace Church, South Middletown, Orange county.

The Rev. Abraham Beach Carter, D. D., rector of the Chapel of the Holy Saviour, New-York.

The Rev. John Chamberlain, New-York.

*The Rev. George Alexander Chambers, officiating in New-Jersey.

The Rev. Elie Charlier, New-York.

*The Rev. Caleb Clapp, rector of the Church of the Nativity, New-York.

The Rev. James Starr Clark, D. D., Trinity Church, Madalin, Dutchess county, and missionary.

*The Rev. Augustus Vallete Clarkson, rector of the Church of St. Augustine, Croton, Westchester county. P. O., New-York.

The Rev. Lyman Cobb, Jr., deacon, (Note A.,) at St. John's Church, Yonkers, Westchester county.

*The Rev. William S. Coffey, rector of St. Paul's Church, Eastchester, Westchester county.

*The Rev. Charles B. Coffin, rector of Trinity Church, Haverstraw, Rockland county, and missionary.

*The Rev. Hiram H. Cole, New-York.

The Rev. Thomas K. Conrad, D. D., associate rector of the Church of the Heavenly Rest, New-York.

*The Rev. Samuel Cooke, D. D., rector of St. Bartholomew's Church, New-York.

*The Rev. William H. Cooke, an assistant minister of Trinity Church, New-York.

*The Rev. Nathaniel E. Cornwall, D. D., rector of St. Matthias' Church, New-York.

The Rev. Nathaniel E. Cornwall, Jr., New-York.

The Rev. Edward Cowley, New-York.

*The Rev. George Edward Cranston, deacon, New-York.

*The Rev. Algernon Sidney Crapsey, an assistant minister in Trinity Parish, New-York.

*The Rev. Robert Fulton Crary, rector of the Church of the Holy Comforter, Poughkeepsie.

*The Rev. Robert B. Croes, D. D.

*The Rev. Gouverneur Cruger, missionary at Montrose, Westchester county.

The Rev. J. Radcliff Davenport, New-York.

The Rev. Benjamin F. De Costa, New-York.

*The Rev. Joaquim De Palma, rector of the Church of Santiago, New-York.

*The Rev. Morgan Dix, D. D., rector of Trinity Church, New-York.

The Rev. Elijah Winchester Donald, deacon.

*The Rev. Zina Doty, deacon.

*The Rev. George William Douglas, deacon.

*The Rev. George B. Draper, D. D., rector of St. Andrew's Church, New-York.

The Rev. John Drisler, deacon, (Note A.,) Mission Chapel, Saw Mill Valley, Greenburgh, Westchester county.

*The Rev. Cornelius R. Duffie, D. D., rector of the Church of St. John Baptist, and chaplain of Columbia College, New-York.

*The Rev. Henry E. Duncan, D. D., Newburgh, Orange county.

The Rev. William N. Dunnell, rector of All Saints' Church, New-York.

The Rev. Heman Dyer, D. D., an assistant Minister of the Church of the Ascension, New-York.

*The Rev. Theodore A. Eaton, D. D., rector of St. Clement's Church, New-York.

*The Rev. John C. Eccleston, M. D., rector of St. John's Church, Clifton, Richmond county.

The Rev. Charles C. Edmunds, missionary at Ellenville, Ulster county.

*The Rev. William E. Eigenbrodt, D. D., Professor of Pastoral Theology in the General Theological Seminary, New-York.

*The Rev. William T. Egbert, rector of the Church of St. John the Evangelist, Memorial of Bishop Wainwright, New-York.

The Rev. Rufus Emery, rector of St. Paul's Church, Newburgh, Orange county.

The Rev. Ferdinand C. Ewer, D. D., St. Ignatius' Church, New-York.

The Rev. William Allen Fair, deacon.

*The Rev. Robert B. Fairbairn, D. D., Warden of St. Stephen's Training College, Annandale, Dutchess county.

The Rev. William V. Feltwell.

*The Rev. George W. Ferguson, rector of Trinity Church, Sing Sing, Westchester county.

The Rev. Augustus Fitch, residing in New-York.

The Rev. Edward O. Flagg, D. D., rector of the Church of the Resurrection, New-York.

The Rev. John C. Fleischhacker, minister of St. George's German Mission Chapel, New-York.

*The Rev. John Murray Forbes, D. D., New-York.

The Rev. Charles A. Foster, deacon.

The Rev. Edward K. Fowler, Monticello, Sullivan county.

*The Rev. William G. French, officiating for the New-York Protestant Episcopal City Mission Society, on Blackwell's Island.

The Rev. Thomas Gallaudet, D. D., rector of St. Ann's Church for Deaf Mutes, New-York.

The Rev. John N. Galleher, rector of Zion Church, New-York.

*The Rev. Walter Russell Gardner, deacon, rector elect of St. Thomas' Church, Amenia, Dutchess county.

The Rev. Ebenezer Gay, missionary at Stony Point, Rockland county.

*The Rev. G. Jarvis Geer, D. D., rector of St. Timothy's Church, New-York.

*The Rev. A. Herbert Gesner, Briar Cliff, Sing Sing, Westchester county.

*The Rev. J. Breckenridge Gibson, D. D., rector of St. John's School, Sing Sing, and of All Saints' Church, (Briar Cliff,) Ossining, Westchester county. P. O., Sing Sing.

*The Rev. Kingston Goddard, D. D., St. Andrew's Church, Richmond, Richmond county.

*The Rev. Alfred Goldsborough, rector of Christ Church, Warwick, Orange county, and missionary.

*The Rev. E. H. C. Goodwin, an officiating minister of Trinity Parish, New-York, at Fort Columbus, New-York harbor.

*The Rev. George S. Gordon, Peekskill, Westchester county.

*The Rev. William H. De L. Grannis, rector of St. James' Church, Goshen, Orange county.

*The Rev. Albert Zabriskie Gray, rector of St. Philip's Church in the Highlands, Philipsetown, Putnam county. P. O., Garrison's.

The Rev. Frederick M. Gray, rector of the Church of the Holy Comforter, (Eltingville,) Southfield, Richmond county.

The Rev. Horatio Gray.

*The Rev. Edmund Guilbert, rector of St. Mark's Church, Mount Pleasant, Westchester county.

*The Rev. Benjamin I. Haight, D. D., LL. D., assistant to the rector of Trinity Church, New-York.

*The Rev. Randall C. Hall, Clement C. Moore Professor of the Hebrew and Greek Languages in the General Theological Seminary, New-York.

The Rev. Alexander Hamilton, Jr., deacon, New-York, (Note A.)

The Rev. Robert George Hamilton, deacon.

*The Rev. Thomas R. Harris, rector of St. Paul's Church, Morrisania, New-York county.

*The Rev. A. Bloomer Hart, rector of the Church of the Advent, New-York.

*The Rev. Richard Miles Hayden, deacon.

The Rev. John G. B. Heath, officiating for the New-York Protestant Episcopal City Mission Society, in the Tombs and other public institutions, New-York.

The Rev. James I. Helm, D. D., rector of St. Paul's Church, Sing Sing, Westchester county.

The Rev. Francis A. Henry.

The Rev. Charles Higbee, rector of Christ Church, Pelham, Westchester county.

*The Rev. George H. Hinckle, deacon, Newburgh, Orange county.

*The Rev. Solomon G. Hitchcock, missionary at Piermont, Rockland county.

The Rev. Horace B. Hitchings, an assistant minister of Trinity Church, New-York.

*The Rev. John Henry Hobart, D. D.

The Rev. Charles Frederick Hoffman, All Angels' Church, New-York.

The Rev. William A. Holbrook, rector of the Church of St. James the Less, Scarsdale, Westchester county.

The Rev. Robert Holden, rector of Trinity School, New-York.

*The Rev. Samuel Hollingsworth, D. D., New-York.

The Rev. Stephen F. Holmes, officiating for the New-York Protestant Episcopal City Mission Society, as chaplain of St. Barnabas' House and Chapel, New-York.

The Rev. Montgomery R. Hooper, an assistant minister of St. Paul's Church, Yonkers, Westchester county.

*The Rev. George B. Hopson, Professor of the Latin Language in St. Stephen's Training College, Annandale, Dutchess county.

*The Rev. Edward C. Houghton, assistant minister of the Church of the Transfiguration, New-York.

*The Rev. George C. Houghton, an officiating minister in the Parish of Trinity Church, New-York.

The Rev. George H. Houghton, D. D., rector of the Church of the Transfiguration, New-York.

The Rev. George Howell, officiating in the Mission Chapel of the Atonement, New-York.

*The Rev. Robert S. Howland, D. D., rector of the Church of the Heavenly Rest, New-York.

The Rev. Ralph Hoyt.

The Rev. William Huckel, rector of St. Ann's Church, Morrisania, New-York county.

*The Rev. Albert S. Hull, rector of Trinity Church, Morrisania, New-York county.

The Rev. Pierre P. Irving, rector of Christ Church, New-Brighton, Richmond county.

The Rev. Theodore Irving, LL. D., residing in New-York.

*The Rev. Angus M. Ives, missionary at Tuckahoe and Wilmot, Westchester county.

*The Rev. Joseph Horsfall Johnson, missionary at Highland and Milton, Ulster county.

The Rev. Levi Johnston, Walden, Orange county.

*The Rev. Copeland Lea Jones.

*The Rev. William Marvin Jones.

*The Rev. Joseph F. Jowitt, an assistant minister of St. Thomas' Church, New-York.

The Rev. George T. Kaye, deacon, (Note A.)

The Rev. Melville C. Keith, deacon.

The Rev. Justin P. Kellogg, New-Windsor, Orange county.

The Rev. James E. Kenney, New-York.

The Rev. Edward H. Kettell, an assistant minister of the Church of the Holy Trinity, New-York.

The Rev. Arthur Clifford Kimber, an officiating minister in Trinity Parish, New-York.

The Rev. William Kirkus, an assistant minister of Grace Church, New-York.

*The Rev. Charles S. Knapp.

The Rev. John W. Kramer, M. D., an assistant minister of Grace Church, in charge of Grace Chapel, New-York.

The Rev. William S. Langford, rector of St. John's Church, Yonkers, Westchester county.

*The Rev. Francis E. Lawrence, D. D., pastor of the Church of the Holy Communion, New-York.

The Rev. Benjamin B. Leacock.

The Rev. John M. Leavitt, D. D., New-York.

*The Rev. Hamilton Lee, assistant minister of Christ Church, New-Brighton, Richmond county.

The Rev. Alexander S. Leonard, D. D., Fordham, New-York county.

The Rev. Robert W. Lewis, New-York.

*The Rev. William Fisher Lewis, rector of St. Peter's Church, Peekskill, Cortlandt, Westchester county.

The Rev. Charles S. Little, New-York.

*The Rev. John R. Livingston, Jr., rector of Trinity Church, Fishkill, Dutchess county, and missionary at Glenham. P. O., Glenham.

*The Rev. Robert Lowry, St. Thomas' Free Mission Chapel, New-York.

*The Rev. Nicholas F. Ludlum, missionary and financial agent of the New-York Protestant Episcopal City Mission Society, New-York.

*The Rev. William S. Ludlum, New-York.

The Rev. John P. Lundy, D. D., rector of the Church of the Holy Apostles, New-York.

The Rev. Lea Luquer, rector of St. Matthew's Church, Bedford, Westchester county.

*The Rev. Frederick N. Luson, missionary at Port Jervis, Orange county.

*The Rev. David H. Macurdy.

The Rev. Isaac Maguire, deacon, (Note A.,) missionary of the Protestant Episcopal Missionary Society for Seamen in the port and city of New-York, New-York.

*The Rev. Romaine S. Mansfield, missionary at Spring Valley, Rockland county, in charge also of St. John's Church, Clarkstown, Rockland county.

The Rev. Mytton Maury, St. James' Church, Fordham, New-York county.

The Rev. Dominick M. McCaffrey, officiating in New-York.

The Rev. John N. McJilton, D. D., New-York.

The Rev. Haslett McKim, Jr., rector of St. Thomas' Church, New-Windsor, Orange county.

*The Rev. Stephen A. McNulty, St. Mark's Church Mission, New-York.

*The Rev. William A. McVickar, D. D., officiating at Nice.

*The Rev. William N. McVickar, rector of Holy Trinity Church, Harlem, New-York.

The Rev. Alexander McWhorter, deacon.

*The Rev. Edward N. Mead, D. D., minister of St. Mary's Church, Beechwood, Westchester county. P. O., Scarborough, Westchester county.

The Rev. J. Austen Merrick, D. D., West Farms, New-York county.

The Rev. James Millett, rector of the Church of the Holy Martyrs, New-York.

The Rev. Benjamin F. Miller, rector of Grace Church, Milbrook, Dutchess county, and missionary.

The Rev. Henry E. Montgomery, D. D., rector of the Church of the Incarnation, New-York.

*The Rev. William White Montgomery, rector of St. Thomas' Church, Mamaroneck, Westchester county.

*The Rev. John W. Moore, minister of Christ Church, Red Hook, Dutchess county.

*The Rev. William Moore, missionary at Paterson, Putnam county.

*The Rev. Brockholst Morgan, rector of St. Peter's Church, Port Chester, Westchester county.

The Rev. James Hervey Morgan, New-York.

The Rev. John Morgan, New-York.

The Rev. Richard U. Morgan, D. D., residing at Stamford, Connecticut.

*The Rev. William F. Morgan, D. D., rector of St. Thomas' Church, New-York.

*The Rev. Charles W. Morrill, Church of the Intercessor, New-York.

The Rev. Lewis F. Morris, rector of St. Mary's Church, Yorktown, Westchester county.

The Rev. William Morris, LL. D., West Farms, New-York county.

*The Rev. Henry Mottet, Church of the Holy Communion, New-York.

The Rev. William A. Muhlenberg, D. D., Superintendent of St. Luke's Hospital, New-York.

The Rev. James Mulchahey, D. D., an assistant minister of Trinity Church, New-York.

The Rev. James Byron Murray, rector of the Church of the Holy Spirit, Rondout, Ulster county.

The Rev. Chester Newell, chaplain in the United States Navy.

The Rev. R. Heber Newton, rector of the Anthon Memorial Church, New-York.

*The Rev. Edwin A. Nichols.

The Rev. Samuel Nichols, residing at Greenfield, Connecticut.

*The Rev. Louis L. Noble, Professor of History and of the English Language and Literature in St. Stephen's College, Annandale, Dutchess county.

The Rev. McWalter B. Noyes, New-York.

The Rev. Frederick Oertel, in charge of Bethlehem Mission Chapel, under the direction of the New-York Protestant Episcopal City Mission Society, New-York.

*The Rev. Frederick Ogilby, D. D., an assistant minister of Trinity Church, New-York.

The Rev. Andrew Oliver, D. D., Professor of Biblical Learning and the Interpretation of Scripture in the General Theological Seminary, New-York.

The Rev. A. F. Olmsted, rector of the Church of the Messiah, Rhinebeck, Dutchess county.

The Rev. Charles T. Olmsted, an assistant minister of Trinity Church, New-York.

*The Rev. William W. Olssen, Professor of the Greek Language and Literature, and of Hebrew, in St. Stephen's College, Annandale.

The Rev. Samuel Osgood, D. D., LL. D., New-York.

The Rev. John William Paige, deacon, (Note A.,) at Anthon Memorial Church, New-York.

The Rev. Isaac Peck.

The Rev. Edward W. Peet, D. D, assisting at St. George's Church, New-York.

*The Rev. Thomas M. Peters, D. D., rector of St. Michael's Church, New-York.

The Rev. John Peterson, deacon, (Note A.,) assisting in St. Philip's Church, New-York.

The Rev. George L. Platt, rector of St. Paul's Church, Red Hook, Dutchess county. P. O., Madalin.

The Rev. Leon Pons, officiating minister of the French Church du St. Esprit, New-York.

The Rev. William M. Postlethwaite, rector of the Church of the Intercession, New-York.

The Rev. Henry C. Potter, D. D., rector of Grace Church, New-York.

*The Rev. John F. Potter, St. John's Church, Canterbury, Orange county, and missionary.

The Rev. Horace L. E. Pratt, rector of St. Mary's Church, Castleton, Richmond county.

The Rev. Joseph H. Price, D. D., rector of St. Stephen's Church, New-York.

The Rev. Thomas W. Punnett, rector of St. Paul's Memorial Church, Edgewater, Richmond county.

*The Rev. James S. Purdy, D. D., rector of St. James' Church, Hyde Park, Dutchess county.

*The Rev. Gustav Edmund Purucker, rector of Christ Church, Ramapo, Rockland county, and missionary. P. O., Suffern.

The Rev. D. Brainard Ray, Grace Church, Harlem, New-York.

The Rev. George B. Reese, Jr., rector of Zion Church, Greenburgh, Westchester county.

The Rev. George T. Rider, in charge of a female Seminary at Tarrytown, Westchester county.

The Rev. Henry C. Riley.

The Rev. H. Floy Roberts, missionary of the Floating Church of the Holy Comforter, New-York.

The Rev. John J. Roberts, officiating in New-York.

The Rev. J. J. Robertson, D. D., rector of Trinity Church, Saugerties, Ulster county.

The Rev. Charles F. Rodenstein, West Farms, New-York county.

The Rev. John Davidson Rockwell, deacon, (Note A.)

The Rev. R. Condit Russell, rector of St. James' Church, North Salem, and of St. Luke's Church, Somers, Westchester county, and missionary.

The Rev. Joseph Hine Rylance, D. D., rector of St. Mark's Church in the Bowerie, New-York.

*The Rev. William T. Sabine.

*The Rev. Henry Y. Satterlee, assistant minister of Zion Church, Wappinger's Falls, Dutchess county.

The Rev. Thomas S. Savage, M. D., officiating at Rhine Cliff, Dutchess county.

The Rev. Charles Schramm, D. D.

*The Rev. John F. Schroeder, deacon.

The Rev. Robert Scott, rector of Grace Church, West Farms, New-York.

The Rev. Uriah Scott, New-York.

*The Rev. William J. Seabury, rector of the Church of the Annunciation, and Ludlow Professor of Ecclesiastical Polity and Law in the General Theological Seminary, New-York.

The Rev. Francis M. Serenbez, missionary among the Germans, Newburgh, Orange county.

The Rev. William W. Sever.

*The Rev. Charles Seymour.

*The Rev. George F. Seymour, D. D., St. Mark's Church in the Bowerie Professor of Ecclesiastical History in the General Theological Seminary, New-York.

*The Rev. John W. Shackelford, rector of the Church of the Redeemer, New-York.

*The Rev. Frederick W. Shelton, LL. D., rector of St. Mark's Church, Carthage Landing, Dutchess county.

The Rev. Henry Beers Sherman, rector of the Church of the Ascension, Esopus, Ulster county.

The Rev. Frederick Sill, rector of St. Ambrose' Church, New-York.

*The Rev. Thomas H. Sill, an officiating minister in Trinity Parish, New-York.

*The Rev. Arthur Sloan, at St. Paul's Church, Yonkers, Westchester county.

*The Rev. Cornelius B. Smith, rector of St. James' Church, New-York.

*The Rev. Edward Bayard Smith, deacon.

*The Rev. George Henry Smith, rector of St. Paul's Church, Pleasant Valley, Dutchess county, and missionary.

*The Rev. James Tuttle Smith, rector of the Church of the Holy Sepulchre, New-York.

The Rev. John Cotton Smith, D. D., rector of the Church of the Ascension, New-York.

The Rev. Orsamus H. Smith, officiating at North Paterson, Putnam county.

*The Rev. William E. Snowden, rector of St. Andrew's Church, Walden, Orange county, and missionary.

*The Rev. James W. Sparks, rector of St. Mark's Church, New-Castle, Westchester county, and missionary.

*The Rev. Jesse A. Spencer, D. D., Professor of the Greek Language and Literature in the College of the City of New-York, New-York.

*The Rev. J. Selden Spencer, rector of Christ Church, Tarrytown, Westchester county.

The Rev. Constantine Stauder, officiating among Italians in New-York.

The Rev. William Staunton, D. D., New-York.

The Rev. John F. Steen, officiating in Missions of the Church of the Ascension, New-York.

*The Rev. Walter A. Stirling, New-York.

The Rev. Henry C. Stowell, New-York.

*The Rev. Francis Henry Stricker, deacon, China Mission.

*The Rev. Francis H. Stubbs, Church of the Beloved Disciple, New-York.

The Rev. Cornelius E. Swope, D. D., an assistant minister of Trinity Church, New-York.

The Rev. Edward W. Syle, officiating in Japan.

*The Rev. Stephen H. Synnott, rector of St. Paul's Church, Poughkeepsie, Dutchess county.

The Rev. John Clough Tebbets, Jr., deacon.

The Rev. Richard Temple.

The Rev. Charles C. Tiffany, rector of the Church of the Atonement, Madison Avenue, New-York.

The Rev. William B. Thomas, Poughkeepsie, Dutchess county.

*The Rev. William Reed Thomas, rector of the Church of the Holy Innocents, Cornwall, Orange county, and Missionary.

The Rev. Hugh Miller Thompson, D. D., rector of Christ Church, New-York.

*The Rev. Henry Martyn Torbert.

*The Rev. Uriah T. Tracy, officiating in New-York.

The Rev. Amos C. Treadway, residing in Watertown, New-York.

*The Rev. Isaac H. Tuttle, D. D., rector of St. Luke's Church, New-York.

The Rev. Alvi T. Twing, D. D., secretary and general agent of the Domestic Committee of the Board of Missions of the Protestant Episcopal Church, New-York.

The Rev. Stephen H. Tyng, D. D., rector of St. George's Church, New-York.

The Rev. Stephen H. Tyng, Jr., D. D., rector of the Church of the Holy Trinity, New-York.

*The Rev. Obadiah Valentine, deacon.

*The Rev. Frederick B. Van Kleeck, rector of Grace Church, White Plains, Westchester county.

*The Rev. Edward H. Van Winkle, deacon.

*The Rev. Isaac Van Winkle, rector of St. Mary's Church in the Highlands, Cold Spring, Putnam county.

The Rev. Peter Joseph Victor Von Roosbroeck, officiating for the New-York Protestant Episcopal City Mission Society, as chaplain of Bellevue Hospital, New-York.

*The Rev. Joseph M. Waite, at St. Bartholomew's Church, New-York.

The Rev. Robert J. Walker, missionary of the Floating Church of our Saviour for sailors in the port and city of New-York.

*The Rev. William D. Walker, assistant minister in charge of the Mission Chapel of Calvary Church, New-York.

*The Rev. William Walsh, Newburgh, Orange county.

*The Rev. Caleb T. Ward, deacon, New-York.

*The Rev. Arthur H. Warner, assistant minister of St. Luke's Church, New-York.

The Rev. Edward A. Washburn, D. D., rector of Calvary Church, New-York.

The Rev. John Henry Watson, Trinity Church, New-Rochelle, Westchester county.

*The Rev. Henry Nicoll Wayne, officiating in Trinity Parish, New-York.

*The Rev. Joshua Weaver, New-York.

The Rev. Henry Webbe.

*The Rev. George W. West, deacon, missionary at Stone Ridge, Ulster county.

The Rev. Sullivan H. Weston, D. D., an assistant minister of Trinity Church, New-York.

*The Rev. J. Bloomfield Wetherill, Philadelphia, Pennsylvania.

The Rev. E. S. Widdemer, in charge of the Mission Chapel of the Reconciliation, New-York.

The Rev. George D. Wildes, D. D., rector of Christ Church, Riverdale, New-York county.

*The Rev. James Henry Williams.

*The Rev. William T. Wilson, rector of the Church of the Mediator, South Yonkers, New-York county.

The Rev. Alvah Wiswall, deacon, New-York.

*The Rev. Curtiss T. Woodruff, Superintendent of the New-York Protestant Episcopal City Mission Society, New-York.

The Rev. D. G. Wright, in charge of the Poughkeepsie Academy, Poughkeepsie, Dutchess county.

*The Rev. Christopher B. Wyatt, D. D., rector of St. Peter's Church, Westchester, Westchester county.

The Rev. Henry L. Ziegenfuss, officiating temporarily at St. James' Church, Hyde Park, Dutchess county.

Number of Clergy present at this Convention,................			151
Number of Clergy absent,..................................			39
Number on the Roll of Convention,.........................			190
Number not entitled to seats,.............................			123
Number of Clergymen belonging to the Diocese,..............			313
Bishop, ...		1	
Priests,..		285	
Deacons, with full qualifications,.................	19		
" restricted, without full qualifications,...	8		
		27	
Whole number of Clergymen,................		313	

NOTE A.—This letter (A) designates deacons who have not passed the Examinations required by Canon 7, § II., and Canon 4, § V., Title I., of the Digest of the Canons of the Gen. Conv., and have been admitted to the restricted Diaconate.

A List of the Clergy

PRESENT AT THIS

CONVENTION.

The following Clergy of the Diocese, entitled to seats in the Convention, were present at its sittings:—

The Right Rev. Horatio Potter, D. D., LL. D., D. C. L.

Rev. C. C. Adams,
Samuel M. Akerly,
Octavius Applegate,
Franklin Babbitt,
David F. Banks,
Alfred B. Beach, D. D.,
Henry H. Bean,
William H. Benjamin,
Cornelius W. Bolton,
Robert Bolton,
J. Eastburn Brown,
T. McKee Brown,
Clarence Buel,
Samuel Buel, D. D.,
James S. Bush,
Philander K. Cady, D. D.,
Charles F. Canedy,

Rev. Alexander Capron,
A. B. Carter, D. D.,
Caleb Clapp,
A. Vallete Clarkson,
William S. Coffey,
William H. Cooke,
Nath'l E. Cornwall, D. D.,
Algernon S. Crapsey,
Robert F. Crary,
Joaquim De Palma,
George B. Draper, D. D.,
Cornelius R. Duffie, D. D.,
William N. Dunnell,
Theodore A. Eaton, D. D.,
John C. Eccleston, M. D.,
Charles C. Edmunds,
William T. Egbert,

Rev. Wm. E. Eigenbrodt, D. D.,
Rufus Emery,
Robert B. Fairbairn, D. D.,
George W. Ferguson,
Edward O. Flagg, D. D.,
John C. Fleischhacker,
Thomas Gallaudet, D. D.,
John N. Galleher,
Walter R. Gardner,
E. Gay,
George Jarvis Geer, D. D.,
J. Breckenridge Gibson, D. D.,
Kingston Goddard, D. D.,
Alfred Goldsborough,
H. C. Goodwin,
William H. De L. Grannis,
Albert Z. Gray,
Edmund Guilbert,
Randall C. Hall,
Thomas R. Harris,
James I. Helm, D. D.,
Charles Higbee,
Solomon G. Hitchcock,
Horace B. Hitchings,
William A. Holbrook,
George B. Hopson,
Edward C. Houghton,
George H. Houghton, D. D.,
Robert S. Howland, D. D.,
Albert S. Hull,
Angus M. Ives,
Joseph H. Johnson,
Joseph F. Jowitt,
Edward H. Kettell,
Arthur C. Kimber,
William Kirkus,
John W. Kramer, M. D.,
William S. Langford,
Hamilton Lee,
William Fisher Lewis,

Rev. John R. Livingston,
Lea Luquer,
Frederick N. Luson,
Haslett McKim,
W. Neilson McVickar,
Romaine S. Mansfield,
Mytton Maury,
James Millett,
H. E. Montgomery, D. D.,
Wm. W. Montgomery,
John W. Moore,
William Moore,
Brockholst Morgan,
L. F. Morris,
James Mulchahey, D. D.,
James B. Murray,
R. Heber Newton,
Louis L. Noble,
Frederick Oertel,
Frederick Ogilby, D. D.,
Andrew Oliver, D. D.,
A. F. Olmsted,
C. T. Olmsted,
William W. Olssen,
Thomas M. Peters, D. D.,
George L. Platt,
Henry C. Potter, D. D.,
John F. Potter,
Wm. M. Postlethwaite,
Horace L. E. Pratt,
Joseph H. Price, D. D.,
Thomas W. Punnett,
James S. Purdy, D. D.,
G. E. Purucker,
George B. Reese,
H. Floy Roberts,
J. J. Robertson, D. D.,
R. Condit Russell,
Joseph H. Rylance, D. D.,
Henry Y. Satterlee,

Rev. Robert Scott,
William J. Seabury,
George F. Seymour, D. D.,
Fred'k W. Shelton, LL. D.,
Henry B. Sherman,
Frederick Sill,
Thomas H. Sill,
Cornelius B. Smith,
George Henry Smith,
J. Cotton Smith, D. D.,
J. Tuttle Smith,
Orsamus H. Smith,
William E. Snowden,
James W. Sparks,
Jesse A. Spencer, D. D.,
J. Selden Spencer,
Stephen H. Synnott,
Charles C. Tiffany,

Rev. William R. Thomas,
Hugh M. Thompson, D. D.,
Isaac H. Tuttle, D. D.,
Stephen H. Tyng, Jr., D.D.,
Frederick B. Van Kleeck,
Isaac Van Winkle,
P. J. V. Von Roosbroeck,
Robert J. Walker,
William D. Walker,
Arthur H. Warner,
Edw'd A. Washburn, D. D.,
Henry N. Wayne,
George W. West,
Sullivan H. Weston, D. D.,
George D. Wildes, D. D.,
William T. Wilson,
Curtiss T. Woodruff,
Christop'r B. Wyatt, D. D.

A List of the Lay Delegates

TO THIS

CONVENTION.

THE following Delegates from the Churches of the Diocese, entitled to representation, presented the required certificates. The names of those who were present and sat in the Convention are printed in Roman letters. The names of those who were absent, or were not heard to answer to their names, are printed in Italics.

Counties.	*Churches.*	*Delegates.*
Dutchess,....	St. Thomas', Amenia,	William Nelson,
		David E. Lambert.
	St. Mark's, Carthage Landing,	*John Shurter,*
		Robert N. Verplanck,
		Samuel Verplanck.
	Trinity, Fishkill,	*Isaac E. Cotheal,*
		Oliver W. Barnes,
		John D. Fouquet.
	St. Luke's, Matteawan,	*John B. Seaman,*
		Henry E. Davies,
		Winthrop Sargent.
	Christ, Poughkeepsie,	Steph. M. Buckingham,
		Le Grand Dodge,
		George Cornwell.
	Holy Comforter, Po'keepsie,	William A. Davies,
		Samuel K. Rupley,
		William Harloe.

Counties.	*Churches.*	*Delegates.*
Dutchess,....	St. Paul's, Poughkeepsie,	*George B. Lent,*
		Robert Sanford,
		Guy C. Bailey, M. D.
	St. Paul's, Red Hook,	John Henry Livingston,
		Robert E. Livingston,
		Johnston Livingston.
	Messiah, Rhinebeck,	*Lewis Livingston,*
		Theophilus Gillender,
		James M. De Garmo.
	Zion, Wappinger's Falls,	Henry Mesier,
		Theodore R. Wetmore,
		Irving Grinnell.
New-York, ..	Annunciation, New-York,	George Shea,
		John D. Jones,
		Francis H. Weeks.
	Anthon Memorial,	William Tracy,
		John Wheeler,
		William H. Robinson.
	Ascension,	Frederick De Peyster,
		Fred. G. Foster,
		Francis Leland.
	Atonement, Madison Avenue,	J. D. Fitch,
		Wm. Graydon,
		John Proffat.
	Calvary,	James Emott,
		Samuel B. Ruggles,
		Frederick S. Winston.
	Christ,	*Edward A. Quintard,*
		Simeon Fitch,
		James Kent.
	Epiphany,	Benjamin C. Wetmore,
		John Mackey.
	Grace,	Adam Norrie,
		Michael Ulshoeffer,
		Lloyd W. Wells.
	Heavenly Rest,	*Montgom'ry H. Throop,*
		Watson J. Hildreth,
		Stephen Merrihew.

Counties.	*Churches.*	*Delegates.*
New-York,..	Holy Apostles, New-York,	William Borden,
		Robert H. Goff,
		Daniel B. Whitlock.
	Holy Martyrs,	James R. Mulligan,
		George T. Baldwin,
		John E. Ottiwell.
	Holy Sepulchre,	T. M. Cheesman, M. D.,
		John Pyne,
		John E. Hagler.
	Holy Trinity,	Robert Dumont,
		Effingham H. Nichols,
		Samuel W. Torrey.
	Incarnation,	Samuel M. Valentine,
		Lewis F. Therassen,
		Henry A. Oakley.
	Nativity,	John S. Smith,
		Charles O. Dowd,
		William Peasey.
	Resurrection,	*C. Y. Wemple,*
		Theodore C. Pohle,
		John G. Marshall.
	Santiago,	Jose Maria Mayorga,
		Frederico Martinez,
		Evaristo De Lamar.
	St. Ambrose,	John G. Barnard,
		Wm. S. Cutler,
		Joseph H. Buttenheim.
	St. Andrew's,	Edward H. Jacot,
		Alonzo C. Stewart,
		William H. Riblet.
	St. Ann's,	D. Colden Murray,
		Orlando L. Stewart,
		Henry I. Haight.
	St. Bartholomew's,	*James A. Roosevelt,*
		D. Henry Haight,
		George G. Kellogg.
	St. Clement's,	John Buckley,
		Geo. H. Romaine,
		Stephen T. Wygant.

Counties.	*Churches.*	*Delegates.*
New-York, . .	St. Esprit, New-York,	*John J. Burnier,*
		Lewis H. Pignolet,
		Thomas Verren.
	St. George's,	Charles Tracy,
		J. Pierrepont Morgan,
		William T. Blodgett.
	St. George the Martyr's,	Richard D. Perry,
		John Moulson,
		Robert Waller.
	St. Ignatius',	*Christian Zabriskie,*
		C. Dixon Varley,
		H. Sylvester Bosworth.
	St. John Baptist's,	*Thomas W. Clerke,*
		Charles Short,
		William B. Dixon.
	St. John Evangelist's,	*Hamilton R. Searles,*
		Daniel J. Coster,
		Thomas G. Pratt.
	St. Luke's,	A. B. McDonald,
		Francis Pott,
		Julian Botts.
	St. Mary's,	Richard L. Schieffelin,
		Peter C. Tiemann,
		George R. Schieffelin.
	St. Mary the Virgin's,	John W. Pirsson,
		John A. Beal,
		Edward C. Robinson.
	St. Michael's,	D. Tilden Brown,
		David H. Dick.
	St. Peter's,	George P. Quackenbos,
		E. H. Cushman,
		Edwin Young.
	St. Philip's,	*W. C. H. Curtis,*
		Aaron F. Potter,
		David Roselle.
	St. Thomas',	Lyman Denison,
		William H. Lee,
		George M. Miller.

Counties.	*Churches.*	*Delegates.*
New-York,..	St. Timothy's, New-York,	*Samuel R. Wells,*
		Hubbard G. Stone,
		W. G. Hitchcock.
	Transfiguration,	William C. Gilman,
		Sidney S. Harris,
		Nathaniel W. Chater.
	Trinity,	*John A. Dix,*
		George T. Strong,
		Stephen P. Nash.
	Zion,	George L. Jewett,
		Carlos Cobb,
		Howard Potter.
	Holy Trinity of Harlem,	*Benjamin P. Paddock,*
		Charles F. Alvord,
		Frederick Tinson.
	St. James', Fordham,	*G. L. Dashwood,*
		Moses Devoe,
		Fordham Morris.
	St. Ann's, Morrisania,	William H. Morris,
		J. Wm. Entz,
		Thomas H. Faile.
	St. Paul's,	T. J. Potter,
		Wash. Ritter, M. D.,
		Benjamin Saunders.
	Trinity,	William A. Bedell,
		Morris Wilkins,
		James Henry Welsh.
	Christ, Riverdale,	Francis M. Bacon,
		C. H. P. Babcock,
		Joseph J. Bicknell.
	Grace, West Farms,	William Simpson,
		Samuel M. Purdy,
		A. M. Campbell, M. D.
Orange,.....	St. John's, Canterbury,	Thomas P. Cummings,
		William J. Sherwood,
		Peter J. Hazen.
	Holy Innocents, Cornwall,	Robert W. Weir,
		Stephen R. Roe,
		Charles Tracy.

Counties.	*Churches.*	*Delegates.*
Orange,.....	St. James', Goshen,	*George C. Miller*,
		J. Francis Matthews,
		William T. Russell.
	St. John's, Greenwood,	Edward M. Parrott,
		Peter P. Parrott,
		Bernard De Witt.
	St. George's, Newburgh,	*Homer Ramsdell*,
		Henry Dudley,
		David B. St. John.
	St. Paul's,	*John S. Heard*,
		William E. Warren,
		Thomas S. Force.
	St. Thomas', New-Windsor,	Thomas W. Christie,
		Gethron Appleton.
	Grace, Port Jervis,	*Charles Cooper*,
		John Dutton,
		George A. Clement, Jr.
	Grace, South Middletown,	*Joseph W. Swalm*,
		Lewis Armstrong,
		Stoddard S. Draper.
	St. Andrew's, Walden,	George Weller,
		George Wellard,
		John C. Holbrow.
	Christ, Warwick,	Henry C. Weir,
		Samuel B. Dolsen,
		Grinnell Burt.
Putnam,.....	St. Mary's, Cold Spring,	*Gouverneur Kemble*,
		Robert B. Parrott,
		Fred'k D. Lent, M. D.
	St. Philip's, Philipsetown,	Hamilton Fish,
		Wil iam Moore,
		Henry W. Belcher.
Richmond,...	Ascension, Castleton, West Brighton,	Erastus Brooks,
		William H. Brown,
		Cornelius Dubois.
	St. Mary's, Castleton,	*William L. Wilson*,
		John L. Gratacap,
		Dallas B. Pratt.

Counties.	*Churches.*	*Delegates.*
Richmond,...	St. John's, Clifton,	*John A. Appleton,*
		George S. Scofield,
		Dwight Townsend.
	St. Paul's, Edgewater,	Albert Ward,
		Joseph R. Kearny,
		Alex. E. Outerbridge.
	St. Andrew's, Richmond,	Nathaniel Britton,
		Cornelius L. Perine,
		A. Hamilton Britton.
	St. Luke's, Rossville,	*D. A. Edgar,*
		H. S. Bidell,
		Henry H. Biddle.
Rockland,...	St. John's, Clarkstown,	*Benj. B. Barnes,*
		Henry Wylde,
		Cyrus F. Crum.
	St. Luke's, Haverstraw,	Hendrick D. Batchelder,
		John W. Babcock,
		John R. McKenzie.
	Grace, Nyack,	Daniel Ullman,
		Charles A. Brush,
		Wm. C. Moore.
	Christ, Piermont,	*Peter V. King,*
		James Weeks,
		Mason C. Weld.
	Christ, Ramapo,	*William G. Hamilton,*
		Theodore Haff,
		Henry R. Sloat.
Ulster,......	Ascension, Esopus,	Daniel Butterfield,
		E. Bergh Brown,
		Alexander Holland.
	St. John's, Kingston,	*Edmund Doremus,*
		Charles A. Fowler,
		William M. Hayes.
	Holy Spirit, Rondout,	*Claude V. Quilliard,*
		Wm. B. Litchfield,
		Hiram Roosa.
	Christ, Marlborough,	*Edward Jackson,*
		Gouvern'r Armstrong,
		James S. Knapp.

Counties.	*Churches.*	*Delegates.*
Ulster,......	All Saints', Milton,	*John Townshend,*
		Charles W. Weston,
		Charles E. Stott.
	Trinity, Saugerties,	*Aaron E. Vanderpoel,*
		William Mulligan.
Westchester,.	St. Matthew's, Bedford,	*John J. Banks,*
		Wm. H. Schieffelin,
		James M. Bates.
	St. Paul's, Eastchester,	John G. Fay,
		Edward Martin,
		Nathaniel Jarvis.
	Zion, Greenburgh,	*Shadrach Taylor,*
		Stephen Hyatt,
		William Vanderburgh.
	St. Barnabas', Irvington,	*George D. Morgan,*
		George W. Smith,
		Edward C. Gregory.
	St. John's, Lewisboro',	Ebenezer W. Raymond,
		Stephen L. Hoyt,
		Charles A. Raymond.
	St. Thomas', Mamaroneck,	Charles H. Burney,
		James Stringer,
		J. Knapp Purdy.
	St. Mark's, Mount Pleasant,	George S. Rice,
		Seabury Lawrence,
		Charles H. Currier.
	Trinity, Mount Vernon,	William A. Seaver,
		Gideon D. Pond,
		George H. Cameron.
	St. Mark's, New-Castle,	Robert S. Hart,
		Chauncey Smith,
		Lewis Tripp.
	Trinity, New-Rochelle,	Robert C. Fisher,
		Clarkson N. Potter,
		Robert R. Morris.
	St. Stephen's, North Castle,	B. A. Birdsall,
		William H. Creamer,
		Benjamin L. Creamer.

Counties.	*Churches.*	*Delegates.*
Westchester,	St. Peter's, Peekskill, Cortlandt,	Owen T. Coffin,
		E. H. Fairchild,
		Calvin Frost.
	Christ, Pelham,	*Frederic Prime*,
		Wm. H. De Lancey,
		H. W. Clark.
	St. John's, Pleasantville,	*J. T. Williams*,
		H. D. Lapaugh,
		H. J. Kinch.
	St. Peter's, Portchester,	Philip Rollhaus,
		A. W. Kelley,
		Charles Kelley.
	Christ, Rye,	Adam T. Sackett,
		Samuel K. Satterlee,
		Augustus Wiggin.
	St. James' the Less, Scarsdale,	William S. Popham,
		Alexander B. Crane,
		James Bleecker.
	All Saints', Briar Cliff, Sing Sing,	*John B. Church*,
		Russell Knowlton,
		Henry M. Brinckerhoff.
	St. Paul's,	Charles O. Joline,
		Samuel C. Nichols,
		John W. Mulholland.
	Trinity,	*George D. Arthur*,
		Marlborough Churchill,
		Benjamin Moore.
	Christ, Tarrytown,	George W. Morell,
		Edward Coles,
		William S. Wilson.
	St. John's, Tuckahoe,	Andrew Findlay,
		Samuel M. Raesbreck,
		Alexander Forbes.
	St. Peter's, Westchester,	*Rich. L. Morris, M. D.*,
		Robert H. Ludlow,
		John H. Screven.

Counties.	*Churches.*	*Delegates.*
Westchester,	Grace, White Plains,	M. M. Fisher,
		E. T. Prudhomme,
		S. Faile.
	St. John's, Wilmot,	Sylvester L. H. Ward,
		Clark Davis,
		Albert Archer.
	St. John's, Yonkers,	*Thomas Ludlow,*
		Levi P. Rose,
		Stephen H. Thayer, Jr.,
	St. Paul's,	W. H. C. Bartlett,
		J. Foster Jenkins,
		William C. Waring.

CLERGYMEN NOT MEMBERS OF THE CONVENTION PRESENT.

The Right Rev. George William Tozer, D. D., England.
The Right Rev. John Freeman Young, D. D., of the Diocese of Florida.
The Rev. Robert B. Croes, D. D.,
The Rev. John Morgan,
The Rev. Henry Mottet,
The Rev. William Staunton, D. D.,
The Rev. Henry C. Stowell,
The Rev. D. Brainerd Ray,
The Rev. Henry Ziegenfuss,
} of the Diocese of New-York.
The Rev. William A. Snively, of the Diocese of Long Island.
The Rev. James W. Stewart, of the Diocese of Albany.
The Rev. Charles A. Hale, of Central New-York.
The Rev. Vandervoort Bruce,
The Rev. James W. Coe,
} of the Diocese of New-Jersey.
The Rev. William P. Tenbroeck, of the Diocese of Wisconsin.

JOURNAL

OF

THE PROCEEDINGS

OF THE

CONVENTION.

New-York, Wednesday, September 30th, 1874.

This being the day fixed by the Constitution of the Protestant Episcopal Church in the Diocese of New-York for the meeting of the Annual Convention of the same, a number of the Clergy and Laity assembled for Divine Service, at ten o'clock in the morning, at St. John's Chapel in the City of New-York, the place appointed by the Bishop for the meeting.

Morning Prayer was said by the Rev. William Neilson McVickar, Rector of the Church of the Holy Trinity of Harlem, New-York, assisted by the Rev. Charles C. Tiffany, Rector of the Church of the Atonement, Madison Avenue, New-York, and the Rev. Albert Z. Gray, Rector of St. Philip's Church, Philipsetown, Putnam County, who read the Lessons. The Litany was said by the Rev. Samuel Cooke, D. D., Rector of St. Bartholomew's Church, New-York. The Ante-Communion Service was read by the Right Rev. Horatio Potter, D. D., LL. D., D. C. L., Bishop of the Diocese; the Rev. Joseph H. Price, D. D., rector of St. Stephen's Church, New-York, reading the Epistle, and the Right Rev. George William Tozer, D. D., retired Bishop of Central Africa, reading the Gospel. The Sermon was preached by the Rev. Robert B. Fairbairn, D. D., Warden of St. Stephen's College, Annandale. The Holy Communion was celebrated by the Right Reverend the Bishop of the Diocese, assisted by the Right Reverend Bishop Tozer, the Rev. Joseph H. Price, D. D., the Rev. Samuel Cooke, D. D., the Rev. Sullivan H. Weston, D. D., and the Rev. Theodore A. Eaton, D. D.

The Bishop of the Diocese took the Chair, and called the Convention to order.

The Secretary then proceeded, under the direction of the Bishop, to call the names of the Clergy of the Diocese entitled to seats, when one hundred and thirty* answered to their names, and took their seats as members.

The Churches entitled to representation were then called over, and the Lay Delegates presented their certificates; which were examined by the Secretary and a Committee of two members, appointed by the Presiding Officer, viz.: Hon. Hamilton Fish and Gen. George W. Morrell. The names of the Lay Delegates duly appointed were called, when Lay Delegates from eighty Parishes appeared and took their seats.†

A constitutional quorum being present, the Right Reverend the President declared the Convention organized for business.

The President announced the Seventh Rule of Order on the admission of persons not members to the sittings of the Convention.

On motion, the reading of the Rules of Order was unanimously dispensed with.

---

* A List of the Clergy who attended this Convention is prefixed to the Journal.

† A List of the Lay Delegates present in this Convention is prefixed to the Journal.

The Convention then proceeded, according to the Sixth Article of the Constitution, to the appointment of a Secretary and Treasurer.

On motion of the Rev. George F. Seymour, D. D., the vote by ballot was unanimously dispensed with; and the Rev. William E. Eigenbrodt, D. D., was elected Secretary.

On motion of Frederick De Peyster, Esq., the vote by ballot was unanimously dispensed with; and Edward F. De Lancey, Esq., was elected Treasurer.

The Secretary announced to the Convention, that he appointed the Rev. Theodore A. Eaton, D. D., the Assistant Secretary.

In compliance with Canon I. of the Diocese, the Bishop laid before the Convention a list of the Clergy of the Diocese.

The Right Rev. the President introduced the Right Rev. Bishop Tozer to the Convention, the Convention standing.

On motion of the Secretary, it was

Resolved, That the Right Rev. Bishop Tozer be invited to a seat beside the President during the sessions of this Convention.

The following Standing Committees, appointed by the Right Rev. the President, were then announced:

ON THE INCORPORATION AND ADMISSION OF CHURCHES.

The Hon. Hamilton Fish, the Rev. Alfred B. Beach, D. D., and the Hon. Michael Ulshoeffer.

ON THE DIOCESAN FUND.

The Rev. John N. Galleher, the Rev. Thomas Gallaudet, D. D., Francis Pott, Esq., Charles Tracy, Esq., and the Treasurer.

ON THE TREASURER'S REPORT.

David Clarkson, Esq., Frederick S. Winston, Esq., and Robt. H. Ludlow, Esq.

ON THE GENERAL THEOLOGICAL SEMINARY.

The Rev. James Mulchahey, D. D., the Rev. George Jarvis Geer, D. D., John Buckley, Esq., Cambridge Livingston, Esq., and Anthony B. McDonald, Esq.

ON CANONS.

The Rev. Benjamin I. Haight, D. D., LL. D., the Rev. Henry C. Potter, D. D., the Rev. Christopher B. Wyatt, D. D., the Hon. Hamilton Fish, George T. Strong, Esq., and Irving Paris, Esq.

INSPECTORS OF ELECTION.

For the Standing Committee: For the Clerical Votes—The Rev. Thomas Gallaudet, D. D., and Mr. Cornelius Dubois. For the Lay Votes—The Rev. Cornelius R. Duffie, D. D., and Gen. George W. Morrell.

For the Missionary Committee: For the Clerical Votes—The Rev. Thomas M. Peters, D. D., and Mr. W. H. C. Bartlett. For the Lay Votes—The Rev. Horace B. Hitchings and Mr. Charles Short.

The Report of the Committee on the Incorporation and Admission of Churches was presented and read, as follows:

Report

ON THE INCORPORATION AND ADMISSION OF CHURCHES.

The Committee on the Incorporation and Admission of Churches respectfully report:

That they have received, through the Secretary of the Convention, and have examined the papers presented by—

I. "*The Rector, Church Wardens and Vestrymen of the Holy Trinity Church* "*of Harlem, in the City and County of New-York.*"

The application is made in writing, according to Canon IV., and is accompanied by a duly certified and authenticated copy of a resolution of the

Vestry, agreeing to abide by and conform to and observe all the Canons of the Church, and all the rules, orders and regulations of the Convention; also by the requisite certificate of the Bishop, and by satisfactory evidence that not less than twenty-five persons, members of such Church, have habitually, for at least one year preceding the application, attended divine service in such Church or congregation

It is also accompanied by a copy of a paper purporting to be a Certificate of Incorporation, bearing date the 23d day of June, 1868, and recorded in the office of the Register of the City and County of New-York, in Liber 2 of Religious Incorporations, page 284; and also by a certified copy of an act of the Legislature of New-York, entitled "An Act for the Relief of the "Rector, Church Wardens and Vestrymen of the Holy Trinity Church of "Harlem, in the City and County of New-York," passed March 29, 1871, whereby, among other things, it is declared, that the "Certificate of Incorporation" of the said religious society, "and every act, deed, matter or thing "done or performed by such religious society since the recording of the said "certificate, are hereby ratified, confirmed and declared to be as valid in all "respects as if the said certificate and all other acts of said religious society "had been in conformity to the act passed May ninth, eighteen hundred and "sixty-eight."

A reference to the Report of the Committee on the Incorporation and Admission of Churches, made to the Convention in 1870, (Journal of Convention, pages 34, 35,) shows that this congregation made application for admission to union with the Convention at that time; it then submitted the same certificate of incorporation that is now presented; among the objections at that time was the absence of United States Revenue stamps.

They are still wanting on the papers now presented.

But the act of March 29, 1871, may be regarded as a special act of incorporation of this Church by the Legislature of New-York, and no United States Revenue stamps are required to such act.

The attention of the Committee has been directed to the absence from the certificate of incorporation of the declaration required by Canon IV., viz.: that the certificate of incorporation of every Church incorporated under any act of the Legislature of the State of New-York, *save the General Act of April 5, 1813, and the amendments thereto*, shall declare, upon its face, that the Church or congregation is a Protestant Episcopal Church, and that it is for ever to continue as such in communion with the Protestant Episcopal Church in the State of New-York.

The relieving act of 1871 recognises this congregation as incorporated under the acts "saved" from the operation of the Canon referred to, and the declaration is not by the Canon required of Churches incorporated under those acts.

The Committee, therefore, recommend the admission of this Church into union with the Convention.

II. "*The Society of the Free Church of St. Mary the Virgin.*"

The application is made in writing, and is accompanied by a duly authenticated copy of a Resolution of the congregation, agreeing to abide by and conform to and observe all the Canons of the Church, and all the rules, orders and regulations of the Convention. Also by the requisite Certificate of the Bishop, and by satisfactory evidence that not less than twenty-five persons, members of such Church, have habitually, for at least one year preceding the application, attended Divine-service in such Church or congregation.

The application of this Association has been before the Committee and the Convention on several previous occasions, when defects and omissions to comply with requirements of law, in order to constitute the Association an Incorporation, were indicated.

A reference to the accompanying letter from the Commissioner of Internal Revenue shows that the papers now presented are defective, and that the Association has failed to correct the omissions with regard to United States Revenue stamps, and consequently the Committee cannot report it as a duly incorporated body.

In the Report to the Convention of 1871, the Committee on the Incorporation and Admission of Churches expressed a doubt whether a Society incorporated itself under the act of April 13, 1854, (as this Association has attempted to do,) be a Church or Corporation, within the contemplation of the Constitution and Canons of this Church. Without repeating the argument or statement made in the Report of 1871, the Committee repeat the doubt then expressed.

If the Association had complied with the requirements of the United States Statutes, and were duly incorporated, there would still remain the objection (stated in the report of the Committee in 1873) of the absence from the paper, which purports to be a "Certificate of Incorporation," of the declaration required by the 4th Canon, (as amended in 1872,) viz., "that the Church or "congregation is a Protestant Episcopal Church, and that it is for ever to "continue as such in communion with the Protestant Episcopal Church in "the State of New-York."

The Committee recommend that the application be refused, and the papers be referred back to the applicants.

Since the drafting of the foregoing, and after the expiration of the time prescribed by the Canons for the presentation of papers of Churches applying for Admission, the Committee received a letter addressed to them in behalf of the Association above referred to, directing their attention to a decision of the Court of Appeals of the State of New-York, by virtue of which the letter claims that a United States Internal Revenue stamp was not necessary to the validity of the Certificate of Incorporation of this Association or Society. This letter accompanies the other papers of the Association submitted herewith.

Without raising the question as to how far the decision or opinion of a State court is conclusive in determining the constitutionality of an act of Congress, or in limiting the power of taxation of the Federal government, an examination of the decision referred to in the case of Moore *vs.* Moore, Vol.

47, (not 417, as stated in the letter,) N. Y. Reports, page 468, fails to change the opinion that the stamp is necessary.

The court in this case holds, "that it is not in the Constitutional power of "Congress to prescribe for the States a rule for the transfer of property "within them;" it proceeds to say: "Withont denying that it is within the "power of taxation, conferred upon it, for Congress to lay an excise tax upon "the business operations of communities, and to collect that tax by means of "stamps, to be placed upon the written instruments exchanged between "contracting parties, and to enforce the observance of the laws to that end, "by the imposition in it of penalties for its non observance, we are of opinion "that it is without that power to declare that a contract or conveyance "between citizens of a State, affecting the title to real estate, is void, for the "reason that such observance has been omitted."

The case before the court, upon which it gave this decision, turned upon the validity of two conveyances purporting to pass the title to real estate.

But the certificate of incorporation of an association under a general act of the State Legislature is not a contract or conveyance affecting the title to real estate, or to property of any kind. At the time of the proposed incorporation there is no property of any kind affected by the act of incorporation. All rights of property are in expectancy, to be acquired, if at all, after the completion of the act, which the certificate is designed to accomplish. The object is to give to several individuals an aggregate or corporate existence—to merge their individuality and personal responsibility into a new creation, called a body politic, or a corporation, with new functions and capacities. It is the fusion—the intermixture and combination of separate individual ingredients, into a compound with new and distinct powers and faculties, not possessed by any or all of the separate ingredients, but acquired only by the observance of the proper and prescribed rules of compounding. It is not a transfer of real estate, or of property of any kind, but a creation under a formula or prescription laid down by a statute.

The act under which this Association purports to be formed, does not profess to incorporate a Church, but a Building Society, whose object, in the language of the act, is to "found and continue one or more free Churches." The Society may found as many Churches of as many different denominations as its means may allow, but itself is not a Church.

It comes within that class of "business operations of communities" which the court, in the case cited, says it will not deny to be within the power of taxation conferred upon Congress.

The Committee, therefore, is obliged to adhere to the opinion, that the certificate of this Association is invalid, by reason of the want of properly affixed United States Revenue stamps. The letter of the Commissioner of Internal Revenue, which accompanies this report, indicates the manner in which this defect may yet be remedied.

The letter also claims that this Association, having made application for admission prior to the amendment of 1872 to Canon IV., such amendment is not applicable to their request for admission. The answer to this seems obvious.

I. It is competent to this Convention at all times to amend the Canons, and to prescribe to all Churches not admitted into union, such requirements as the Convention may think proper for the maintenance of its integrity and consistency as a Convention of Protestant Episcopal Churches, and for the exclusion from its body of associations not permanently and legally devoted to the doctrines of the Church.

II. This Association has never until this year presented papers sufficient to show its legal existence as a corporation, irrespective of any question as to the necessity of United States Revenue stamps.

The Committee are of opinion, therefore, that no equitable claim exists in its favor by reason of any informal or insufficient presentation of an application prior to the amendment of the Canon in 1872.

III. *The Rector, Church Wardens and Vestrymen of St. Ignatius' Church, in the City of New-York.*

The application is made in writing, and is accompanied by a duly authenticated copy of a resolution of the Vestry, agreeing to abide by and conform to and observe all the Canons of the Church, and all rules, orders and regulations of the Convention; also by the requisite certificate of the Bishop, and by satisfactory evidence that not less than twenty-five persons, members of such Church, have habitually, for at least one year preceding the application, attended divine service in such Church or congregation.

It is also accompanied by a duly certified copy of a certificate of incorporation of the Church under the acts amendatory of the act of April 5, 1813, bearing date the 11th day of December, 1871, and recorded in the office of the Register of the City and County of New-York, in Liber 2 of Religious Incorporations, page 311, on the 12th day of December, 1871.

The Committee, therefore, recommend the admission of this Church into union with the Convention.

Respectfully submitted.

HAMILTON FISH,
ALFRED B. BEACH,
M. ULSHOEFFER,
} *Committee.*

NEW-YORK, *September* 30, 1874.

TREASURY DEPARTMENT,
OFFICE OF INTERNAL REVENUE,
WASHINGTON, *September 9th*, 1874.

SIR: In your letter of the 7th instant, which I have the honor to acknowledge, you ask my opinion on a question presented in an accompanying statement, in regard to an Association in New-York, whether the requirements of law with regard to Revenue stamps have been duly complied with.

It appears from the statement that a Society, called "The Society of the

Free Church of St. Mary the Virgin," was organized in the City of New-York, under a general law of the State of New-York, the Certificate of Incorporation bearing date the 22d of October, 1868.

The Certificate of Incorporation was filed according to law in the County Clerk's Office of the County of New-York on the 3d December, 1868, and in the office of the Secretary of State on the 5th of December, 1868.

No United States Revenue stamps were on either of the Certificates when thus filed. But it would appear from certified copies of these Certificates, with memoranda to that effect on the margins, that stamps were subsequently affixed to the originals after filing.

The question is asked whether the stamps, which appear thus to have been affixed to these instruments, have been affixed in accordance with law, so as to make the Certificates and their filing legal and valid; and whether the fact that the stamps appear not to have been affixed within twelve months after the 1st of August, 1871, or within twelve months after making the instruments, or any irregularity as to the payment of a penalty, affect the validity of the instruments.

Referring to the accompanying "Statement," I reply with regard to the first stamping of the Certificate filed in the County Clerk's office, with a memorandum, signed by A. Williams, Collector, that it is defective, because there is no statement of the payment of a penalty, which was a condition precedent of the validity of such stamping. (Act of June 30, 1864, Section 158, amended.)

The second stamping of the same Certificate was invalid, because made by a Deputy Collector, who had no authority to stamp instruments unless when "Acting Collector."

The stamping of the Certificate in the Secretary of State's office was also invalid for the want of a penalty. The Collector at the date of his memorandum, September 30th, 1872, had no authority to remit the penalty on an instrument which had been issued more than twelve months, even in the absence of fraudulent intent. (Section 158, above referred to, amended by section 5, Act of July 14, 1870.) But there was no limit to the time in which an instrument might be stamped by a Collector on payment of the penalty.

After an instrument issued without stamps has been duly stamped by a Collector according to the provisions of said section 158 amended, it is as valid as if originally stamped, except as against rights acquired in good faith before the stamping of such instrument.

As regards the present case, the original Certificates of Incorporation on file can now be stamped without a penalty by any person having an interest therein, before some Judge or Clerk of a Court of Record, according to the provisions of an act to provide for the stamping of unstamped instruments, documents and papers, approved June 23d, 1874. (General Nature, No. 96.)

Very respectfully,

J. W. DOUGLASS,
Commissioner.

HON. HAMILTON FISH,
Washington, D. C.

Whereupon, according to the recommendation of this Committee,

> HOLY TRINITY CHURCH, of Harlem, New-York,
> THE CHURCH OF ST. IGNATIUS, New-York,

were received into union with this Convention.

On motion of S. P. Nash, Esq.,

> THE SOCIETY OF THE FREE CHURCH OF ST. MARY THE VIRGIN, New-York,

was received into union.

On motion of the Secretary, it was

Resolved, That the Standing Committee of this Convention on the General Theological Seminary report the number of Trustees to which, by the Constitution of the Seminary, this Diocese is entitled; the names of the present Trustees who represent this Diocese and are resident therein, and who, during the last three years, have served, or signified their willingness to serve; and the names of as many other suitable persons as may be necessary to fill the number secured by the Constitution of the Seminary to this Diocese, for nomination to the General Convention as Trustees from the Diocese of New-York.

The Convention adjourned until ten o'clock to-morrow morning.

THURSDAY, OCTOBER 1, TEN O'CLOCK, A. M.

The Convention met pursuant to adjournment.

Morning Prayer was said by the Rev. Thomas Gallaudet, D. D., rector of St. Ann's Church, New-York, assisted by the Rev. Edmund Guilbert, rector of St. Mark's Church, Mount Pleasant, North Tarrytown.

The Right Rev. the Bishop of the Diocese took the Chair.

The Minutes of yesterday's proceedings were read and approved.

Several Clergymen, not present yesterday, appeared and took their seats.*

Lay Delegates from several Parishes, from which no certificates were before received, presented certificates, which were examined by the Committee on the subject. On approval, the Delegates took their seats.†

The Rules of Order having been suspended for the purpose, on motion of the Secretary, it was

Resolved, That this Convention hereby expresses its gratification at the presence of the Right Reverend John Freeman Young, D. D., Bishop of Florida, and respectfully invites him to occupy a seat beside the President whenever he may please to attend its sessions.

The Right Reverend the President introduced the Bishop of Florida to the Convention.

---

* A List of the Clergy who attended this Convention is prefixed to the Journal.

† A List of the Lay Delegates present in this Convention is prefixed to the Journal.

The Bishop of the Diocese then delivered his

ANNUAL ADDRESS.

The Convention took a recess for half an hour.

The time of recess having expired, the Convention proceeded to the election of the Standing Committee, and of the Missionary Committee of the Diocese.

The names of the Clergy were called by the Secretary, and of the Churches by the Assistant Secretary. The members having deposited their ballots, the Tellers retired to count the votes.

The Rules of Order having been suspended for the purpose,

On motion of the Rev. Dr. Houghton, it was

Resolved, That 3,000 copies extra of the Bishop's Address be immediately printed for distribution.

The Convention proceeded to the election of the Trustees of the Fund for the Relief of Aged and Infirm Clergymen.

Ballot was unanimously dispensed with, and the following persons were chosen

TRUSTEES OF THE AGED AND INFIRM CLERGY FUND.

Cyrus Curtiss, Esq.,
William Betts, Esq.,
Edward F. De Lancey, Esq.

The Secretary of the Convention presented the following Report:

Report

OF THE SECRETARY OF THE CONVENTION.

The Secretary of the Convention begs leave respectfully to report:

That, in obedience to the order of the last Convention of this Diocese, the Journal of its Proceedings was printed and distributed in the usual manner under his direction; and that, according to the requirement of the Canons, sundry papers have from time to time been recorded by him, and others sent to the Clergymen and Parishes concerned in the same.

The Secretary takes this opportunity to inform the Convention, that during the last year he has caused such Journals of the Convention of this Diocese and of other Dioceses as for many years have been accumulating under his hand and remaining in his care, to be assorted and properly arranged, and a large number of the same to be bound into volumes for preservation and convenient reference. The Library Committee of the General Theological Seminary has kindly permitted him to deposit this collection under its own constant oversight on the shelves of its library, where access to the books can at any time be readily had under proper regulations by those who may wish to consult them. The labor of the work performed in this matter has been great, and therein he has been aided by Mr. Richard Sill. The çost, also, has been considerable; and there not having been authorized for a long time any appropriation for this purpose by the Convention, the expense has been defrayed by the Secretary to the amount, as appears from bills and receipts in his hands, of ($126 85) one hundred and twenty-six dollars and eighty-five cents. The whole number of bound volumes of Journals belonging to the Diocese and now in his care is about one hundred and forty.

Among these volumes it will be found that the Convention has one complete set of the Journals of the General Convention down to this day; two complete sets of the Journals of the Convention of the Diocese of New-York; three other sets of the New-York Journals nearly complete, and many sets, more or less perfect, of the Journals of the other Dioceses. One complete set of the New-York Journals belonging to the Convention, it has been ascertained, was destroyed some years ago by fire.

Appended to this Report is a list of all these volumes, and of all the Journals still unbound and belonging to this Convention. It includes ten sets completed from 1847 to 1873, ready for binding; and the Secretary ventures to recommend that, for preservation and to meet contingencies from possible loss, this be ordered by the Convention. He especially invites attention to this account of the several Journals still needed in order to complete certain partial sets bound, but otherwise to remain imperfect, of the Journals as well of this Diocese as of other Dioceses; and to the consideration of the greater value which will be added to this collection by such Churchmen as, having such copies and not caring otherwise to preserve them, will be so kind as to send them to him as a gift to the Diocese for this purpose.

These volumes deserve careful preservatión. Therein appear the struggles of the Church in this Diocese from its first organization for almost a century down to the present day; the hard work and wise counsels of its Episcopate; the foundation and expansion of its Parishes under its faithful Missionaries and Rectors; the formation of its laws and its plans of beneficence; the names and the acts of its Bishops, of its other Clergymen, and of its active and devoted Laymen in its behalf. Of these the greater part are at rest in Paradise. In most instances their memory might otherwise be lost among those now reaping goodly harvests from their self-denying labors. Like them, many of us, too, shall ere long have left behind us upon earth little open record of our toils beside that which is written in these annual Journals. In an endeavor to help in saving such pages from perishing, your Secretary has had much satisfaction.

All which is respectfully submitted.

WILLIAM E. EIGENBRODT,
Secretary of the Convention of the Protestant Episcopal Church, in the Diocese of New-York.

NEW-YORK, *September* 30, 1874.

APPENDIX.

Catalogue of Journals and other Documents belonging to the Diocese of New-York, in charge of the Secretary of the Convention.

NEW-YORK JOURNALS.

BOUND.

Two Sets, complete, from 1785 to 1871, say 20 vols.
One " from 1785 to 1871, with the exception of Journals for 1820, 1829, 1830, 11 vols.
One " from 1785 to 1871, with the exception of Journals for 1821, 1822, 1823, 1827, 1828, 1829, 1830, 11 vols.
One " from 1785 to 1871, with the exception of Journals from 1820 to 1830, inclusive, and 1844, 9 vols.
One Vol. from 1831 to 1840, except 1836, which has been torn out.
One " " 1839 to 1842, inclusive.
Two " " 1839 to 1840, "
Three " " 1850 to 1851, "
One " " each, 1839, 1854, 1855, 1856, 1857, 1858, 1859, 1860.

UNBOUND.

Ten Sets, complete, from 1847 to 1871, 63 vols. Wanted 7 Journals of 1865 to complete 7 vols. more. These are arranged ready for binding.

1835, 9; 1836, 12; 1837, 11; 1838, none; 1838, special, none; 1839, none; 1840, 2; 1841, 17; 1842, 8; 1843, 9; 1844, none; 1845, 13; 1846, none; 1847, 75; 1848, 34; 1849, 183; 1850, 62; 1850, special, 122; 1851, 173; 1852, 263; 1853, 84; 1854, 17; 1855, 33; 1856, 143; 1857, 260; 1858, 167; 1859, 26; 1860, 63; 1861, 73; 1862, 24; 1863, 22; 1864, 95; 1865, 1; 1866, 118; 1867, 22; 1868, 312; 1869, 308; 1870, 283; 1871, 68; 1872, 75; 1873, 111.

GENERAL CONVENTION JOURNALS.

BOUND.

One set, complete, from 1784 to 1871, 8 vols.
One vol. from 1832 to 1844, inclusive.

UNBOUND.

1841, 1; 1844, 3; 1847, 4; 1850, 2; 1853, none; 1856, 4; 1859, none; 1862, none; 1865, 1; 1868, 1; 1871, 1.

JOURNALS OF OTHER DIOCESES.

BOUND.

94 vols., to 1853, including in the same vols. General Convention Journals, beside those named above.

Alabama,	1 vol. from 1854 to 1870, inclusive.
Albany,	2 " " 1868 " 1872, "

California.	1 vol.	from	1853	to	1867,	inclusive.
Connecticut,	3 "	"	1854	"	1873,	"
Delaware,	1 "	"	1853	"	1862,	"
Georgia,	1 "	"	1853	"	1870,	"
Illinois,	1 "	"	1868	"	1873,	"
Indiana,	1 "	"	1854	"	1869,	"
Iowa,	1 "	"	1854	"	1869,	"
Kentucky,	1 "	"	1853	"	1873,	"
Long Island,	1 "	"	1868	"	1872,	"
Louisiana,	1 "	"	1853	"	1867,	"
Massachusetts,	2 "	"	1854	"	1860; 1869 to 1873, inclusive.	
Maine,	1 "	"	1853	"	1869, inclusive.	
Michigan,	2 "	"	1864	"	1873,	"
Minnesota,	1 "	"	1857	"	1872,	"
Missouri,	1 "	"	1866	"	1873,	"
Mississippi,	1 "	"	1853	"	1871,	"
New-Jersey,	2 "	"	1853	"	1860; 1868 to 1873, inclusive.	
N. Carolina,	2 "	"	1853	"	1873, inclusive.	
Ohio,	2 "	"	1860	"	1872,	"
Pennsylvania,	1 "	"	1853	"	1857,	"
Pittsburgh,	1 "	"	1865	"	1873,	"
S. Carolina,	2 "	"	1853	"	1873,	"
Tennessee,	1 "	"	1854	"	1873,	"
Texas,	1 "	"	1853	"	1873,	"
Virginia,	2 "	"	1854	"	1873,	"
West. New-York,	2 "	"	1863	"	1873,	"

UNBOUND.

Albany, 1873.
Alabama, 1871, 1872, 1873, 1874.
Arkansas, 1871.
California, 1871, 1872, 1873, 1874.
Central New-York, 1869, 1871, 1872, 1873, 1874.
Central Pennsylvania, 1871, 1872, 1873, 1874.
Dakota, 1874.
Delaware, 1869, 1870, 1871, 1872, 1874.
Easton, 1868, 1869, 1870, 1871, 1872, 1873, 1874.
Florida, 1853 to 1873, except 1856, 1858, 1859, 1867, 1868, 1871.
Georgia, 1871, 1872, 1873, 1874.
Illinois, 1853 to 1867, except 1854, 1862.
Indiana, 1865, 1870, 1871, 1872, 1873, 1874.
Iowa, 1870, 1871, 1872, 1873, 1874.
Kansas, 1869, 1870, 1871, 1872, 1873.
Kentucky, 1874.
Long Island, 1873, 1874.
Louisiana, 1872, 1873.
Maine, 1870, 1871, 1872, 1873.
Maryland, 1853 to 1874, except 1853, 1857, 1861, 1869.
Massachusetts, 1861 to 1868, inclusive, which completes the third vol.; also, 1874.
Michigan, 1853 to 1864, except 1858, 1859, 1860, 1862.
Minnesota, 1873, 1874.
Mississippi. 1871, 1873, 1874.
Missouri, 1853 to 1865, except 1855; also, 1874.
Nebraska, 1868, 1870, 1871, 1872, 1873.
New-Hampshire, 1853 to 1874, except 1871.
New-Jersey, 1861 to 1867, except 1866; besides 1874.
North Carolina, 1874.
Ohio, 1853 to 1859, except 1854.

Oregon and Washington, 1856 to 1873, except 1853, 1860, 1861, 1863, 1864, 1865, 1866, 1868, 1869, 1870.

Pennsylvania, 1853 to 1874, except 1858, 1860, 1866, 1867, 1871, 1872.

Rhode Island, 1853 to 1874, except 1859.

South Carolina, 1874.

Texas, 1870, 1871, duplicates.

Vermont, 1853 to 1874, except 1855, 1859, 1862, 1864.

Virginia, 1874.

Western New-York, 1853 to 1862, except 1853, 1854, 1859.

Wisconsin, 1874.

Journals of Rhode Island from 1790 to 1832, inclusive.

Journal of the General Council of the late Confederate States, 1865.

When completed, will make about 25 vols.

JOURNALS WANTED.

California, 1863.

Central New-York, 1870.

Florida, 1856, 1858, 1859, 1867, 1868, 1871.

Illinois, 1854, 1862.

Louisiana, 1868, 1870, 1871.

Maryland, 1853, 1857, 1861, 1862.

Michigan, 1558, 1859, 1860, 1862.

Mississippi, 1872.

Nebraska, 1869.

New-Hampshire, 1871.

New-Jersey, 1866.

Ohio, 1854.

Pennsylvania, 1858, 1860, 1866, 1867, 1871, 1872.

Rhode Island, 1859.

Vermont, 1855, 1859, 1862, 1864.

New-York, 1820 to 1830, inclusive, 1844, 1865.

Western New-York, 1853, 1854, 1859.

Oregon and Washington, 1853, 1860, 1861, 1863, 1864, 1865, 1866, 1868, 1869, 1870.

MISCELLANEOUS.

Trial of Bishop Onderdonk. 1 vol., bound.

Digest of the Canons and Constitution of the Protestant Episcopal Church. 2 vols., bound.

Sermon preached at the Consecration of Bishop Wainwright.

Several Sermons, Addresses and Charges by Bishops Potter, Vail, Doane, Littlejohn, Johns, Davis, Stevens, Clark, Eastburn, De Lancey, Whitehouse, Lee, Burges, Wilmer, Elliott and McCoskry. Drs. M. A. De Wolfe Howe, Coit, Bowman and Spencer.

Constitution and Canons, New-York Convention.

Rules of Order, " "

Proposed Code of Canons, 1860.

Report of Committee on Acts for Incorporation of Churches.

Report of the Training School, Annandale.

Proposed Act of Incorporation of Religious Societies.

Documents relating to Trinity Church.

MSS. Journal, Reports, &c., New-York Convention, 1847.

Bishop Bedell's Primary Charge.

Bishop Potter's Sermon before the Primary Convention of Long Island.

Bishop Stevens' Historical Discourse before the Convention of Georgia.

Bishop Atkinson's Charge on Sacramental Confession.

September, 1874.

On motion of S. P. Nash, Esq., it was

Resolved, That the thanks of this Convention be given to the Secretary for his care of the Journals belonging to the Diocese; and that the amount expended by him for this purpose be refunded to him by the Treasurer of the Convention out of the Diocesan Fund, and that a sum sufficient for binding the other Journals according to the recommendation in his Report be appropriated out of the same Fund, to that object.

The Report of the Missionary Committee of the Diocese was presented and read by the Rev. Alfred B. Beach, D. D.

Report

OF THE MISSIONARY COMMITTEE OF THE DIOCESE.

The Missionary Committee of the Diocese report that the receipts and disbursements for the past year have been as follows:

Balance on hand October 1, 1873,		$808 15
October 1, 1873, to October 1, 1874:		
Received from Churches,		4,798 25
" individuals,		1,792 00
" for interest,		505 94
" Trinity Church Corporation,		500 00
		$8,404 84
Payments:		
Stipends due October 1, 1873,	$1,575 00	
" for the year ending October 1, 1874,	6,545 00	
Circulars, Postages, &c.,	66 05	8,186 05
Balance on hand October 1, 1874,		$218 29

We have now thirty Missionaries upon our list.

It should be stated, that the increased receipts are not the result of any greater interest by the Church in the Missionary work of the Diocese, for, as matter of fact, the contributions from Parishes have fallen off nearly *one thousand* dollars from the amount received last year. The Bishop was twice obliged to make a special appeal in behalf of the fund, in order that the stipends over due might be paid. In answer to these appeals, a few individuals contributed $1,800, which alone enabled the Treasurer to meet the demands made upon him.

This kind offering enables us to enter upon the new Conventional year with a small balance on hand, and we now earnestly appeal to the members of the Church to continue to us their sympathy and aid, enlarging their contributions for the coming year, so that our Missionaries may be worthily sustained, and the work committed to our charge may be carried forward with greater vigor, and with more abundant success.

Additional means might be judiciously expended in building stations that are now struggling, and in opening new fields in regions where the services of the Church are greatly needed, and where they would be greatly valued.

We trust that our appeal will not be unheeded.

All which is respectfully submitted.

LIST OF MISSIONARIES IN THE DIOCESE OF NEW-YORK.

Counties.	*Stations.*	*Missionaries.*
Dutchess,........	Pleasant Valley,	The Rev. G. H. Smith.
	Madalin,	J. S. Clark, D. D.
	Glenham,	J. R. Livingston.
	Amenia Mission,	W. R. Gardner.
	Lithgow,	
	Pine Plains,	
	Millbrook,	B. F. Miller.
Orange,.........	Buttermilk Falls,	W. R. Thomas.
	Greenwood Iron Works,	
	Walden,	W. E. Snowden.
	Canterbury,	J. F. Potter.
	Port Jervis,	F. N. Luson.
	Monroe,	
	Newburgh,	F. M. Serenbez.
	Warwick,	Alfred Goldsborough.
Putnam,........	Patterson,	Wm. Moore.
Rockland, ...	Clarkstown,	
	Haverstraw,	C. B. Coffin.
	Nyack,	F. Babbitt.
	Piermont,	S. G. Hitchcock.
	Spring Valley,	R. S. Mansfield.
	Stony Point,	E. Gay, Jr.
	Sufferns,	G. E. Purucker.
Sullivan, ...	Monticello,	C. F. Canedy.
Ulster,..........	Marlboro',	S. M. Akerly.
	Ellenville,	C. C. Edmunds.
	Milton,	J. H. Johnson.
	Stone Ridge,	G. W. West.
Westchester,.....	Lewisboro',	R. Bolton.
	New Castle,	J. W. Sparks.
	North Castle,	
	Loomis,	
	Wilmot,	A. M. Ives.

Counties.	*Stations.*	*Missionaries.*
Westchester, ...	Montrose,	The Rev. G. Cruger.
	Croton,	*A. V. Clarkson.
	Pelhamville,	
	City Island,	

All which is respectfully submitted.

JAMES POTT, *Treasurer.*

NEW-YORK, *Sept.* 30, 1874.

The Report of the Education Committee was presented and read by the Rev. George F. Seymour, D. D.:

Report

OF THE SOCIETY FOR PROMOTING RELIGION AND LEARNING IN THE STATE OF NEW-YORK.

The Superintendent of the Society for Promoting Religion and Learning in the State of New-York, as the Canonical agent of the Diocese of New-York for distributing all funds for Theological Education, would most respectfully report:

That during the past Convention year, from October 1st, 1873, to October 1st, 1874, in discharging the duty with which it has been entrusted by the Convention, the Society has received and distributed the following sums:

Received by the Treasurer from the Diocese of New-York from October 1st, 1873, to October 1st, 1874,............	$773 21
" from other Dioceses during the same time,............	532 78
	$1,305 99

This entire amount has been applied directly to the object for which it was given. If any encouragement is needed to draw contributions into the treasury of the accredited Society of the Diocese, is it not to be found in the important practical consideration that there is no costly machinery between the donor and the recipient to absorb a larger or smaller amount of the offerings in the payment of salaries, commissions, &c., but that every farthing bestowed for the purpose of aiding young men in pursuing their theological studies goes to such young men in furtherance of the object for which it was designed? The Clergy and Laity of the Diocese of New-York are earnestly

* Without Stipend.

requested to remember the cause of theological education among their other benefactions. It has a special claim upon them, because the need is great, and a peculiar weight of obligation, because the Canon enjoins it as a specific duty.

In common with the Diocese of New-York and the Church at large, the Society for Promoting Religion and Learning has experienced a great loss during the past few months in the death of James F. De Peyster, Esq., for over thirty years its honored Treasurer. Few men have done more to make the influence of a high-toned Christian character and an unobtrusive, quiet life tell for good upon their fellow men than he. This he accomplished by natural gifts which predisposed him to the things which make for peace, but the Blessed Spirit wrought in him to elevate, and purify, and harmonize those gifts with which God originally endowed him, and the beautiful result was seen in him of a living embodiment of St. Paul's portraiture of Charity. It needs but to suggest the notes by which the Apostle delineates this crowning grace to bring to the recollection of all, who ever knew him, James F. De Peyster: "Charity suffereth long and is kind; charity envieth not; charity vaunteth not itself; is not puffed up; doth not behave itself unseemly; seeketh not her own; is not easily provoked; thinketh no evil, rejoiceth not in iniquity, but rejoiceth in the truth. Beareth all things, believeth all things, hopeth all things, endureth all things." Mr. De Peyster was among the Laity very much what the late Rev. Dr. Samuel R. Johnson, whose loss we were called upon to deplore last autumn, was among the Clergy, a representative of characteristics and qualities which are described by simplicity, amiability, guilelessness. The power of such a life and character was perhaps never better illustrated and demonstrated than in his position as Treasurer of this Society. The office in itself is simply perfunctory; it involves an immense amount of petty details, and the paying out small sums of money to a large number of beneficiaries at stated and frequently recurring intervals of time. To most men, especially if engaged in large and active business, such an office would have been regarded as a burdèn, as the merest drudgery, and if they could be induced to discharge its duties, it would be as a matter of real self-denial. But with Mr. De Peyster the giving out the quarterly payments to the scores of scholars, who waited upon him at his office, was a precious opportunity for becoming acquainted with the young men, and by showing them that he felt an interest in them, for winning their confidence and affection, so that they became fast friends, and ever after the spell of his influence was upon them for good. Hundreds of Clergy all over the land have the memory of Mr. De Peyster fixed deeply in their hearts, not as the Treasurer of the Society for Promoting Religion and Learning, but as the good man, the high-toned gentleman, the loving, sincere Christian, the generous, loyal friend, whose approval and good opinion they esteemed of great worth. When the worthy young men, who were recipients of the Society's benefactions, came to Mr. De Peyster to receive their quarterly payments, money was the least of the good gifts which he bestowed. He gave himself to them—something of his own lovely, gentle, high-toned character; something of his own noble, generous, large-hearted spirit—these were the precious gifts he bestowed; and no one, the while, was more unconscious of doing so than himself. Such is the loss which the Society for Promoting Religion and Learning deplores in the death of its Treasurer, and the Trustees beg, through their Superintendent, to place this brief tribute to Mr. De Peyster's memory upon the records of the Convention.

All of which is respectfully submitted.

GEORGE F. SEYMOUR,
Superintendent of the Society for Promoting Religion and Learning in the State of New-York.

GENERAL THEOLOGICAL SEMINARY, NEW-YORK,
October 1st, 1874.

The Report of the Trustees of the Episcopal Fund was presented and read:

Report

OF THE TRUSTEES OF THE EPISCOPAL FUND.

The Trustees of the "Episcopal Fund of the Diocese of New-York" report to the Convention as follows:

The capital of the Fund is $110,500, ($66 05 having been contributed by five Parishes since report of last year, and $1 51 for interest.) $102,500 is invested in bonds and mortgages on New-York City improved property at 7 per cent., and the balance, $8,000, is on deposit in the U. S. Trust Company at 3 per cent. awaiting a satisfactory permanent investment.

There are also belonging to the Fund 10 shares of the St. Louis and Iron Mountain R. R. stock, &c., mentioned in report of last year.

During the year $1,000 has been paid on account of a mortgage of Hochster on 79 St. Mark's Place, and a mortgage of Wm. B. Foster for $6,500 paid off.

The Income Account is as follows:

RECEIPTS.

Balance reported at last Convention,		$1,991 53
Interest on bonds and mortgages,		7,687 00
do. on other investments, (temporary,)		325 82
Sundry Parishes—assessment, viz.:		
On account 1873,	$709 97	
" " 1874,	2,583 08	
		3,293 05
		$13,297 40

PAYMENTS.

To Bishop Potter, to 1st October, 13 months,		$9,750 00
" City taxes, 1873, on Episcopal residence,		600 00
" Painting and Repairs, do. do.	$269 42	
" Croton Water Tax, do. do.	19 00	
" Premium of Fire Insurance, do.	33 75	
		322 17
" Circulars, Envelopes and Stamps,		27 94
" Deposit in U. S. Trust Co., &c.,		2,000 00
Balance of Cash in Phenix Bank,		597 29
		$13,297 40

Ditto also $5,000 New-York City stock.

The Trustees have also to report the decease of two of their number since the meeting of the Convention last year—George Merritt and Wm. E. Dunscomb.

These vacancies it becomes the duty of the Convention to fill.

All of which is respectfully submitted.

THOMAS P. CUMMINGS, *Treasurer*,
G. M. OGDEN,
FRED. G. FOSTER,
} *Trustees.*

NEW-YORK, *September 30th*, 1874.

The Convention proceeded to the appointment of two Trustees of the Episcopal Fund. Whereupon, balloting having been dispensed with, on motion of the Secretary, it was

Resolved, That George T. Strong, Esq., and Hugh Auchincloss, Esq., be and are hereby appointed Trustees of the Episcopal Fund, in the places of Wm. E. Dunscomb, Esq., and George Merritt, Esq., deceased.

The Report of the Special Committee on the Salary of the Bishop of the Diocese was presented and read;

Report

OF THE SPECIAL COMMITTEE ON THE SALARY OF THE BISHOP.

The Special Committee on the Salary of the Bishop report:

The deficiency of income of the "Episcopal Fund" has been supplied the past year by an apportionment among the Parishes of the Diocese by your Committee.

As the income of the Fund is still insufficient, an additional amount must be raised as heretofore.

Your Committee, therefore, offer the following resolution:

Resolved, That a Committee be appointed to make an equitable apportionment among the Parishes of the Diocese of a sum which, with the income of the "Episcopal Fund," will meet the amount pledged by this Convention for payment to the Bishop.

By order of the Committee.

THOS. P. CUMMINGS,
Secretary.

NEW YORK, *September* 30, 1874.

The Resolution recommended in this Report was adopted.

The Rev. Benjamin I. Haight, D. D., Rev. Isaac H. Tuttle, D. D., Cyrus Curtiss, Esq., Hon. John A. Dix, Frederick G. Foster, Esq., William Scott, Esq., Lloyd W. Wells, Esq., Frederick Prime, Esq., Thomas P. Cummings, Esq., and George M. Miller, Esq., were appointed this Committee.

The Report of the Trustees of the Aged and Infirm Clergy Fund was presented and read:

Report

OF THE TRUSTEES OF THE AGED AND INFIRM CLERGY FUND.

The Trustees of the Fund for the Relief of Aged and Infirm Clergymen of the Protestant Episcopal Church in the Diocese of New-York, respectfully report:

That since their report to the Convention of 1873, there have been received—

Contributions from 84 Churches,	$2,549 19
Interest,	1,564 76
Gift from James S. Bogert,	20 00
" " Henry K. Bogert,	20 00
" " Rev. H. McKim,	50 00
Legacy of Mrs. Sarah A. Barclay, from William Constable, Executor,	1,000 00
Principal of bond and mortgage paid off,	3,000 00
Balance fund at last Convention,	1,433 17
Total,	$9,637 12

There have been paid during the same period—

To beneficiaries,		$4,150 00
" Christ Church, Cherry Valley, for erroneous contribution sent in by mistake,		9 17
" expenses of four litigated foreclosures of mortgages, including insurance, taxes and assessments on the property bought in,		2,167 82
" contingent expenses for stamps, stationery, &c,		12 15
" principal awaiting re-investment,		1,832 18
		$8,171 32
Leaving a balance fund of		1,465 80
Total,		$9,637 12
Investments heretofore reported,		$44,650 00
Less four mortgages foreclosed—		
One of,	$5,800 00	
Two of $2,000 each,	4,000 00	
One of,	2,100 00	
Together,	$11,900 00	
And one mortgage paid off,	3,000 00	
		14,900 00
		$29,750 00
Add three dwelling houses and lots on Madison-street, Brooklyn, 18 ft. front by 100 ft. deep each; and one store, about 40 ft. by 56 ft., on the corner of Broadway and Quincy-street, Brooklyn, now rented for $600 a year, at the amount of the mortgages and expenses of foreclosure,		14,067 82
And principal awaiting re-investment on bond and mortgage,		1,832 18
Total permanent investments,		$45,650 00

The above real estate, which the present depressed state of affairs has compelled the Trustees to buy in on foreclosure, will be sold at the earliest practicable period.

The present number of regular stipendiaries is thirteen. Special appropriations have been made in five cases. One stipendiary has been added during the past year, and one has died.

HORATIO POTTER,
CYRUS CURTISS,
EDWARD F. DE LANCEY,
WILLIAM BETTS,
} *Trustees.*

Dated September 29th, 1874.

The Report of the Standing Committee on the Treasurer's Report was presented and read:

Report

OF THE TREASURER OF THE CONVENTION.

The Convention of the Diocese of New-York, in account current with EDWARD F. DE LANCEY, *Treasurer.*

September, 1873. DR.	
To paid the Rev. Clergy, mileage,	$123 83
" " back to Rev. H. E. Duncan amount paid by him to Diocesan Fund by mistake,	11 90
" " Secretary's salary,	600 00
" " Pott, Young & Co., printing,	37 10
" " J. W. Amerman, printing for Convention, 1873,	31 50
" " Pott, Young & Co., printing Journal of Convention, 1873,	1,068 20
" " J. W. Amerman, printing for the Bishop,	13 50
" " J. W. Amerman, printing forms, &c., for Convention of 1874,	40 75
" amount retained under Canon XII. for expenses of General Convention,	923 00
" contingent expenses,	7 00
	$2,856 78
Balance,	4,859 20
Total,	$7,715 98

CR.	
By balance from last year,	$3,735 82
" Contributions from 99 Parishes,	3,980 16
Total,	$7,715 98

October 1*st*, 1874.

The Committee on the Treasurer's Account have examined the same, and compared the payments with the vouchers and find them to correspond, and that there is now in the hands of the Treasurer forty-eight hundred and fifty-nine dollars and twenty cents.

ROBERT H. LUDLOW,
F. S. WINSTON, } *Committee.*

The Report of the Standing Committee on the General Theological Seminary was presented and read by the Rev. Dr. Mulchahey:

Report

OF THE STANDING COMMITTEE ON THE GENERAL THEOLOGICAL SEMINARY.

The Standing Committee on the General Theological Seminary respectfully report:

That the number of Trustees to which the Diocese is at this time entitled is 69.

The Diocese, as such, is entitled to 1. The number of Clergy is 313; the ratio of one Trustee for every eight Clergymen will give 39. The whole amount of money contributed by the Diocese is $253,842 37. The ratio of one Trustee for every $2,000 to the amount of $10,000, is 5. And one Trustee for every $10,000 above that sum will give 24.

The present number of Trustees who continue to reside in the Diocese and are willing to serve, as far as is known to the Committee, is 66; of whom 36 are Clergymen and 30 are Laymen, leaving 3 new nominations to be made. The Committee recommend as suitable persons to fill the vacancies the Rev. H. C. Potter, D. D., the Rev. Randall C. Hall and Mr. Geo. Montague.

The entire list of persons recommended to be nominated to the General Convention as Trustees of the General Theological Seminary on the part of the Diocese of New-York is as follows:

Rev. John Brown, D. D.,
Edward N. Mead, D. D.,
Joseph H. Price, D. D.,
Wm. E. Eigenbrodt, D. D.,
A. Bloomer Hart,
Isaac H. Tuttle, D. D.,
Jesse A. Spencer, D. D.,
Joshua Weaver,
Alfred B. Beach, D. D.,
Wm. F. Morgan, D. D.,
Theo. A. Eaton, D. D.,
Caleb Clapp,
Cornelius R. Duffie, D. D.,
Robt. S. Howland, D. D.,
Henry E. Duncan, D. D.,
Morgan Dix, D. D.,
Fred'k Ogilby, D. D.,
John M. Forbes, D. D.,
Edw. A. Washburn, D. D.,

Rev. Thomas M. Peters, D. D.,
Geo. H. Houghton, D. D.,
Henry E. Montgomery, D. D.,
Ferdinand C. Ewer, D. D.,
Sam'l Hollingsworth, D. D.,
Philander K. Cady, D. D.,
Thos. Gallaudet, D. D.,
Geo. J. Geer, D. D.,
Cornelius E. Swope, D. D.,
J. Breckinridge Gibson, D. D.,
Wm. W. Olssen,
Sullivan H. Weston, D. D.,
Sam'l Cooke, D. D.,
Clarence Buel,
Geo. F. Seymour, D. D.,
Sam'l Buel, D. D.,
Andrew Oliver, D. D.,
Henry C. Potter, D. D.,
Randall C. Hall,

Mr. John W. Mitchell,	Mr. Edw'd F. De Lancey,
Hamilton Fish, LL. D.,	Geo. M. Miller,
Cyrus Curtiss,	Wm. Kemble,
Rob't W. Weir,	Fred'k S. Winston,
Elias Butler,	Wm. A. Davies,
John Bard,	Harris C. Fahnestock,
Anthony J. Bleecker,	Cambridge Livingston,
Homer Ramsdell,	J. J. Astor,
Sam'l B. Ruggles, LL. D.,	Sam'l V. Hoffman,
Henry Drisler, LL. D.,	Wm. H. Guion,
Stephen P. Nash,	Wm. M. Kingsland,
Governeur M. Ogden,	Lloyd W. Wells,
Edward Haight,	John A. Dix, LL. D.,
A. B. McDonald,	Thomas W. Ogden,
John Buckley,	Wm. C. Gilman,

Mr. George Montague.

All which is respectfully submitted.

JAMES MUCHAHEY,
GEO. JARVIS GEER,
JOHN BUCKLEY,
C. LIVINGSTON,
A. B. MCDONALD.

On motion of the Secretary, it was

Resolved, That the persons named in the Report just read be and are hereby elected to be nominated to the General Convention as Trustees of the General Theological Seminary on the part of the Diocese of New-York.

The Report of the Trustees of the Parochial Fund was presented and read:

Report

OF THE TRUSTEES OF THE PAROCHIAL FUND.

The Trustees of the Parochial Fund respectfully report:

The lamented death of Mr. James F. De Peyster, so long the Trustee and the Treasurer of the Parochial Fund, leaves to the subscribers the duty of reporting to the Convention without his aid.

The account hereto annexed is taken from the book kept by the late Treasurer, and shows the balance on hand, and the stocks or securities in which the funds are now invested.

We call the attention of the Convention to the fact of there being a vacancy in the Board.

We are also informed that the will of Mr. De Peyster is not yet proved, in consequence of the absence of his son, who is now in Europe.

NEW-YORK, *Oct.* 1, 1874.

MURRAY HOFFMAN, *Chairman*,
WM. ALEX. SMITH.

Parochial Fund in account with JAMES F. DE PEYSTER, *Treasurer.*

DR.

1873.			
Dec.	To amount deposited with Savings Bank, $17 50 and $16 24,		$33 74
1874.			
Jan.	To amount deposited with Manhattan Savings Bank,..		104 08
" 1.	" deposit with Merchants' S. I., as credited on other side,		35 49
" "	" deposit with Manhattan Savings Bank,		17 07
March 28.	" deposit with Manhattan Savings Bank,		28 03
March 2.	" cash p'd J. F. De Peyster, Jr,		14 02
	Balance,		80 04
			$312 47

CR.

1873.			
Nov.	By cash for ½ year's interest on 5-20 Bond, $500,	$15 00	
	" " for prem. on gold,	1 24	16 24
	" " for interest, ½ year, due 1 July, on $500, with Greenwich S. B., cr. in last account.		
1874.			
Jan.	" " 5-20, $2,600, ½ year's interest,	78 00	
"	" " premium on gold,	8 58	86 58
" 1.	By cash for ½ year's interest, deposit G. S. Bank,		17 50
" 1	" " ½ year's interest on deposit with Merchants' C. S. B.,		17 50
" 1.	" " ½ year's interest on deposit with Manhattan S. Bank,		17 07
" 1	" " ½ year's interest on deposit with Merchants' Clerks',		35 49
March 1.	" " ½ year's interest on 10-40 U. S. Bond,	25 00	
	premium on gold,	3 03	28 03

March	2.	By interest coll'd on $500 U. S. 5 p. c., gold,	$12 50	
		prem. 112½, ...	1 52	
				$14 02
May	1.	By do. " $500 U. S. 6 p. c. gold @ 113,		16 95
July	9.	" cash rec'd pr. J. Ashton De Peyster,.......		35 00
Sept.	1.	" interest on U. S. 5 p. c. coupons, gold,....	25 00	
		prem. at 109⅝,.............	2 40	
				27 40
		Interest allowed on above,..................		69
				$312 47
		By balance,..		$80 04

ASSETS OF FUND, 1ST OCTOBER, 1873.

United States 5-20 Bond, Registered,..........................	$2,600 00
do. do. 5-20 " Coupons,..........................	500 00
do. do. 10 40 " do.	1,000 00
Amount deposited with Merchants' Clerks' Savings Institution,..	927 63
do. deposited with Manhattan Savings Bank,..............	569 82
do. deposited with Greenwich Savings Bank,.............	517 50
Making total assets,..................................	$6,114 95

1874.
Oct. 1. Cash on hand,.............................. $80 04

The Convention proceeded to fill two vacancies among the Trustees of the Parochial Fund, in consequence of the expiration of terms of office, and one occasioned by the death of Mr. James F. De Peyster.

Whereupon, ballot was unanimously dispensed with, and Hon. Murray Hoffman and Frederick S. Winston, Esq., were elected as such until October 1, 1877, and Adam Norrie, Esq., in place of Mr. De Peyster, until October, 1876.

The Report of the Trustees of the Sands' Fund was presented and read :

Report

OF THE TRUSTEES OF THE SANDS' FUND.

The Trustees of the Sands' Fund respectfully report :

That there has been received since their Report to the last Convention, for interest on the Fund,........................ $210 00

That there has been paid during the same period to the Bishop for the purposes of the Fund,.............................. $210 00

Principal invested, $3,000.

HORATIO POTTER, *Bishop of New-York,* WM. E. EIGENBRODT, *Secretary of the Convention of the Diocese of New-York,* EDWARD F. DE LANCEY, *Treasurer of the Convention,*	*Trustees.*

Dated NEW-YORK, *September* 30, 1874.

The Report of the Trustees of St. Stephen's College, Annandale, was presented and read :

Report

OF ST. STEPHEN'S COLLEGE, ANNANDALE.

The following report, on behalf of the Trustees of St. Stephen's College, is respectfully submitted to the Convention of the Diocese of New-York :

There have been in attendance, during the past academic year, sixty-seven students. At the commencement, held on the 17th of June, ten graduated Bachelors of Arts, and three completed their preparation, according to the requirements of the Canon, for entrance on the study of Theology. The College opened on the 9th inst. with 73 students.

Daily morning and evening prayer is said throughout the year. The Holy Communion is celebrated every Sunday. There is a sermon every Sunday morning preached by the College officers in rotation. At evening prayer on Sunday the Warden has delivered a course of lectures on the Church Catechism.

The young men have been actively engaged in ministering to the wants of the neighborhood. They have thus, with three sad exceptions, shown their zeal and loyalty for the Church, besides learning the work to which they have consecrated their lives. The most of these young men are persons of good ability, good scholarship and excellent character, and are thus giving promise of future usefulness in the ministry of the Church.

Of those who have received their classical education at St. Stephen's, about twenty are students of the General Seminary ; thirty have graduated from that Institution, and about sixty are now in orders.

R. B. FAIRBAIRN, *Warden, &c., &c.*

ANNANDALE, *Sept.* 29, 1874.

The Report of the Standing Committee on the Diocesan Fund was presented and read :

Report

OF THE STANDING COMMITTEE ON THE DIOCESAN FUND.

The Standing Committee on the Diocesan Fund respectfully recommend to the Convention the adoption of the following Resolution, viz.:

Resolved, That there be paid to the Clergy attending the Convention, who reside more than twenty miles from the place of meeting, and whose Parishes have contributed to the fund, as required by the Canon, seven cents per mile for every mile of the distance from their respective Parishes; and that the remainder be appropriated to paying for the printing of the Journal of this Convention, and the Canonical customary and prescribed expenses of the Diocese.

J. N. GALLEHER, *Chairman,*
THOMAS GALLAUDET,
CHARLES TRACY,
EDWARD F. DE LANCEY.

The Resolution recommended in this Report was adopted.

The Report of the New-York Protestant Episcopal City Mission Society was presented and read:

Report

OF THE NEW-YORK PROTESTANT EPISCOPAL CITY MISSION SOCIETY.

The Executive Committee of the New-York Protestant Episcopal City Mission Society respectfully report as follows:

That the official year ending March 31st, 1874, has been one of unusual activity and of peculiar interest and anxiety. During this period great financial troubles have befallen the country, seriously affecting all classes of the community. Thousands of industrious and worthy people have been suddenly thrown out of employment; labor of all kinds has been at a discount, and, as a necessary consequence, the demands upon the Society have been greater, while the pecuniary ability of many of its best friends has been more or less restricted.

ST. BARNABAS' HOUSE, 304 Mulberry-street, in charge of the "Sisterhood of the Good Shepherd," has continued its benign work in behalf of the homeless, the friendless and the destitute women and children applying at its ever open door, giving the care and comfort and assistance which their several needs required, either for a day or a week, *without fee or reward.* 1,746 persons have been admitted, of whom 547 were Americans, 965 Protestants, 778 Romanists, and 3 Jews. Situations have been obtained for 654; 648 have been sent to other institutions; 354 returned to their friends. During the year, 19,221 lodgings were furnished, and 94,358 meals given to the needy and destitute. Beside these, and the "House children," (16 in number,) the Sisters have had 105 children under their care in the Day Nursery.

So it appears that there were (including the Day Nursery children) 1,888 persons received into the House, against 1,611 last year, being an increase of 277; and that there were 1,208 lodgings and 12,716 meals more than the previous year. 154 visits were made to families in the neighborhood, and 2,474 individuals visited for purposes of relief, consolation and instruction.

Thanksgiving and Christmas are memorable for the means furnished to give so many families good dinners in their own homes, besides feasting 1,155 children and their friends in the House. The Christmas funds were never so abundant, (thanks to the loving givers,) and the Christmas tree not only rejoiced the hearts of the House and Day Nursery children, but made the mothers comfortable by substantial gifts of needed clothing.

The constant visitations among the sick poor make more and more evident the absolute necessity of a Dispensary in connection with the Home, and especially of an Infirmary for poor children who have contagious and infectious diseases. *There is no hospital in the city for children of this class.*

St. Barnabas' Chapel, 306 Mulberry-street, is growing steadily in importance and usefulness. It is really a large Parish, with its free Chapel, maintaining daily services at 9 A. M. and 5 P. M; Sunday services at 10.30 A. M. and 7.30 P. M.; a weekly lecture on Wednesday at 7.30 P. M.; Holy Communion every Thursday at 11 A. M., and on Holy Days at hours convenient for the Sisterhood.

The following statistics will give some idea of the work and its results:

Public services in the Chapel, 697; Baptisms, 68; Burials, 10; Marriages, 3; Holy Communion administered in public and in private, 122 times, to an aggregate of 1,494 persons; Parochial visits, 512; Worshippers from the House, 1,803; families, over 100; Sunday-School children, 313; Offertory, $355 81; Alms Chest, $5 09.

The great need of the region is a large and commodious and well appointed Church edifice, offering to the dense population *free sittings* as well as a free salvation.

St. Barnabas' Industrial Association, working in connection with the Chapel, has been blessed with most marked and unlooked for success. The ladies have furnished sewing to 59 women; have taught 165 children in the weekly Sewing School, against 97 last year; the children made 327 garments for their own benefit, besides much other work; 6,460 yards of material were used; 1,110 pieces of work cut out and made, and all but 12 sold, and 47 visits were made to families.

St. Barnabas' Free Reading Room Association, 308 Mulberry-street, are also working to increase the influences of the Chapel and the House. The Room is well lighted and comfortable, made attractive by a library of fair proportions, by illustrated papers, magazines and daily papers, and is open every evening except Sunday from 7 till 10 o'clock. 8,812 enjoyed the pleasures and the privileges of the Room the last year, being an average nightly attendance of over 28 boys and young men.

Such is a brief sketch of the work at St. Barnabas'; and if so much is now done with so little means, what might not be accomplished if the facilities were equal to the need!

Bethlehem Chapel, near the corner of 9th Avenue and 83d-street, is becoming more and more a power for good among the hundreds of German families who dwell in the rough district lying west of Central Park, between 60th and 90th streets.

The work and results of last year may be stated as follows:

98 public services, with an aggregate attendance of nearly 6,000 persons; families, 85; baptisms, 20; burials, 12; marriages, 4; confirmed, 22; present number of Communicants, 131; Day School, 142 scholars; Sunday-School, 165 scholars; Industrial School, 80 girls; Pastoral visits, 1,017; given to the very poor and needy, 1,052 meals; offertory, $307 20.

May God bless this work in the future as He has done so wondrously in the past!

Bellevue Hospital has received, as in former years, the almost entire labors of one Clergyman. He has held public service, with a sermon on every Sunday A. M., and on the great days of the Church, with an aggregate attendance of over 1,200 patients; baptized 76 infants and 8 adults; administered Holy Communion to 101 persons in the Chapel, and to 137 in the wards; read the burial service over 116 bodies; visits in the wards, 6,665; visits to families outside, 93; visits to the sick on Ward's Island, 936.

At the Tombs, Prisons, Homes, &c., of the City, public religious services have been held regularly, and visitations made as follows: Every Sunday A. M. at the Isaac Hopper Home at 10.30; every Sunday P. M. in the male department of the Tombs at 3 o'clock; every Tuesday in the female department at 10 o'clock, A. M.; every Thursday visit to the Nursery and Child's Hospital; every Friday at the Colored Home, public services at 10 A. M., and a Bible Class of over 50 inmates; twice a month, at least, service in the House of Detention; visit to the ten-day Station House, twice every week; the Boys' Prison as often as practicable, and also the Essex and Jefferson Markets, the Yorkville and Harlem prisons.

During the year 325 public services were held, with an aggregate attendance of 25,000 persons; 175 children were baptized; 6 persons were buried; Holy Communion was administered to 80 persons; 225 missionary visits were made, and religious conversation held with 2,500 individuals.

This one Missionary has, probably, preached the Gospel to as many persons as all our domestic Missionaries put together!

BLACKWELL'S ISLAND, with its five institutions, and constant population of 8,000 souls, has received the regular ministrations and constant care of one Missionary, with services as follows:

77 public services on Sunday, 98 on week days; total, 175; attendance on Sundays, 10,757; on week days, 3,210: total, 13,967; Baptisms, 28; Holy Communion administered 41 times to 774 persons; personal visitations in the wards, 1,536. In the library at the Lunatic Asylum there are now 400 volumes; at the Alms House, 630 volumes; and at the Charity Hospital, 150 volumes. 300 volumes have been taken from the one in the Lunatic Asylum by the patients, and 3,340 by persons in the Alms House. An united and successful effort has been made to supply abundant reading matter to all who wished for it, especially in the Penitentiary. The results have been most happy, and the demand is constantly increasing. 18,486 copies of daily and weekly religious and secular papers, besides large quantities of magazines, have been received and distributed during the year.

Besides all this, weekly services have been held in the New-York Orphan Asylum and in the Leake and Watts Orphan House. Also, Sunday services once or twice a month in the New-York Infant Asylum, occasional Sunday services in the Leake and Watts Orphan House, and regular Sunday visitations in the Roosevelt Hospital.

The whole work and its results may be thus summed up: Public and private services, 1,585; families under the care of the Society, 673; Baptisms, 375; Burials, 266; Confirmed, 23; present number of Communicants, 572; Holy Communion administered to distinct 752 persons in public and in private, Children taught in Sunday-Schools, 778; in Day Schools, 180; in Industrial Schools, 245; visits to families in need or sickness, 2,254; visits to individuals for relief and instruction, 15,391; different persons addressed at religious services, 36,500; persons reached and ministered unto in various ways, 83,300.

Such is the work which has been carried forward in the face of financial difficulties and numerous discouragements, arising from the increasing expenses and diminishing receipts.

The year was finished, however, *without incurring any debt* for necessary expenditures. It was only done, it must, in truth, be said, by drawing on the fund devoted to the canceling of the mortgages on the real estate.

The Committee are thankful to God, who enabled them by any means to meet the wants of so many of the needy and suffering, and preach the Gospel to so many who otherwise would not have heard the glad tidings of salvation; and they can but believe that the Clergy and Laity will realize, as never before, the absolute necessity of giving the Society the first place after the Parish in the list of their benefactions. A Society which is doing so much positive good, reaching so many of the deserving poor, carrying the Gospel to thousands whom no ordinary influences reach or can reach, ought to be free from any possibility of total or even partial suspension; ought, indeed, to be placed on a permanent basis.

For over 40 years it has been at work in the public, penal and charitable institutions of the city and adjacent islands, and out of it have grown many of the Homes and Hospitals which are an honor to the Church and the city, and it deserves to be better cared for, financially, than it has been or is at this moment cared for. The work commends itself to all as important and necessary; and yet, because, forsooth, it is a home work, which can be done at any time, it is put off, and either not done at all or crowded out of notice till outside, and more clamorous demands are satisfied. This is reversing the true order of things. The true order of Christian labor begins with the individual heart, each one making himself a centre of radiating influences, then combining with others in the Parish, the Diocese, the country and the world; ever working from within outward.

Instead of this, the city and Diocese receive the few thousands, while outside objects receive the ten and hundred thousands. If this work is not better sustained in future than it has been in the past, as a general thing, the Committee can see no other way but to *stop*, and they feel that the full responsibility of such a result must lie at the doors of Christian men and women of this city and country.

The Clergy in the employ of the Society are: the Rev. C. T. Woodruff, Superintendent; the Rev. S. F. Holmes, Chaplain of St. Barnabas'; the Rev. F. Oertel, Pastor of Bethlehem Chapel; the Rev. V. Van Roosbroeck, Chaplain at Bellevue Hospital; the Rev. J. G. B. Heath, Missionary to the Tombs, Homes, Prisons, &c.; the Rev. Wm. G. French, Missionary on Blackwell's Island; the Rev. N. F. Ludlum, Financial Agent and Visitor to the Roosevelt Hospital. Mr. John Schark is the teacher of the German Day School in connection with Bethlehem Chapel.

The officers of the Society are:—*President, (ex officio,)* the Right Rev. H. Potter, D. D., LL. D., D. C. L. *Vice-Presidents*, Rev. H. E. Montgomery, D. D., Rev. William F. Morgan, D. D., Mr. Fred. S. Winston, Mr. Thomas Egleston, Jr. *Executive Committee*, the Right Rev. the Bishop of the Diocese, Rev. H. E. Montgomery, D. D., Rev. Wm. F. Morgan, D. D., Rev. T. M. Peters, D. D., Rev. E. A. Washburn, D. D., Rev. Thomas Gallaudet, D. D., Rev. C. E. Swope, D. D., Rev. G. J. Geer, D. D., Rev. H. C. Potter, D. D., Messrs. Fred. S. Winston, Thomas Egleston, Jr., Wm. Alex. Smith, Clarence G. Mitchell, Robert S. Holt, James W. Elliott, M. D., George R. Schieffelin, William B. Clerke, Adam T. Sackett, Allen McLane, Isaac H. Holmes, Charles Spear, John H. Boynton, Peter G. Tiemann, Alfred M. Hoyt, Wm. Borden. *Secretary*, Mr. Isaac H. Holmes. *Treasurer*, Mr. Robert S. Holt. *Superintendent*, Rev. C. T. Woodruff. *Financial Agent*, Rev. N. F. Ludlum.

All of which is most respectfully submitted.

By order of the Committee of Direction.

CURTISS T. WOODRUFF,
Superintendent.

NEW-YORK, *September 25th*, 1874.

The Inspectors of the Votes for the Standing Committee o the Diocese presented their Reports.

Whereupon the following persons were declared duly electec by the concurrent votes of the Clergy and Laity, to be

THE STANDING COMMITTEE OF THE DIOCESE.

CLERGY.

REV. MORGAN DIX, D. D.,
WILLIAM E. EIGENBRODT, D. D.,
WILLIAM F. MORGAN, D. D.,
ISAAC H. TUTTLE, D. D.

LAITY.

STEPHEN P. NASH, Esq.,
LLOYD W. WELLS, Esq.,
HENRY DRISLER, LL. D.,
GEORGE MACCULLOCH MILLER, Esq.

The Inspectors of the Votes for the Missionary Committe presented their Reports.

Whereupon the following persons were declared duly electec by the concurrent votes of the Clergy and Laity, to be

THE MISSIONARY COMMITTEE.

CLERGY.

Rev. HENRY E. MONTGOMERY, D. D.,
ALFRED B. BEACH, D. D.,
CORNELIUS E. SWOPE, D. D.,
JAMES STARR CLARK, D. D.,
OCTAVIUS APPLEGATE.

LAITY.

GEORGE C. COLLINS, Esq.,
JAMES POTT, Esq.,
HAMILTON BRUCE, Esq.,
WILLIAM M. KINGSLAND, Esq.,
WILLIAM H. ASPINWALL, Esq.

On motion of the Secretary, it was

Resolved, That the thanks of this Convention be given to the Library Committee of the General Theological Seminary for the permission to deposit in the Library under its care the collections of the Journals of Conventions belonging to this Diocese and in charge of its Secretary.

On motion of the same, it was

Resolved; That this Convention laments the loss which it has sustained during the past year in the deaths of Floyd Smith, Esq., James F. De Peyster, Esq., George. Merritt, Esq., and William E. Dunscomb, Esq., all of whom had been for many years faithful officers of this body; and that it records upon its Journal its respect for their characters and its veneration for their memories.

On motion of the Rev. Henry C. Potter, D. D., it was

Resolved, That the Reverend the Secretary be requested to convey to the Rev. Dr. Haight the expression of regret on the part of this Convention at the occasion of his absence from this body, and of its hope that he may speedily be restored to health and to long-continued service in the Church.

On motion of the Secretary, it was

Resolved, That the thanks of this Convention be given to the Rector, Church Wardens and Vestrymen of Trinity Church, New-York, for the use of this Chapel by the Convention, and for their generous hospitality to its members.

On motion of the Rev. Frederick Sill, it was

Resolved, That 1,500 copies of the Journal of this Convention be published and distributed under the direction of the Secretary.

On motion of William Moore, Esq., it was

Resolved, That the thanks of this Convention be given to the Secretary, the Assistant Secretary and the Treasurer, for their labors.

On motion of the Rev. Stephen H. Tyng, Jr., D. D., the Convention standing, it was

Resolved, That this Convention do express, by rising, their eminent sympathy with the Bishop in the sorrows, domestic afflictions and anxieties through which in the Providence of God he has been called to pass, as they have abundantly offered for his consolation their fervent prayers.

On motion of the Secretary, it was

Resolved, That after the reading of the minutes and the usual devotions, this Convention adjourn *sine die.*

The Right Rev. the Bishop addressed the Convention.

The minutes of this day's proceedings were read and approved.

The Doxology was sung by the members; Prayers were said by the Rev. William D. Walker; the Blessing was pronounced by the Bishop of the Diocese:

And the Convention adjourned *sine die.*

HORATIO POTTER, D. D., LL. D., D. C. L.,
Bishop of New-York and President of the Convention.

Attest:

WILLIAM E. EIGENBRODT, D. D., *Secretary.*
THEODORE A. EATON, D. D., *Assistant Secretary.*

Annual Address

OF

THE BISHOP OF NEW-YORK.

My Brethren of the Clergy and Laity:

Just twenty years have passed away, since, on the Feast of St. Michael and All Angels, 1854, the assembled Clergy and Laity of the Diocese of New-York, then including the present Dioceses of Albany and Long Island, called upon him who now addresses you to undertake that most weighty and responsible office, which, then but a few days before, had been made vacant by death.

Twenty years in the life of a Diocese, especially when it is yet in the first century of its existence as a fully organized body, must needs be a history of great interest, full of pregnant lessons, and full of tokens of encouragement or discouragement for the future. And it must be confessed that twenty years in the life of a Christian Bishop, in a critical age, when the country has been developing with marvellous enterprise and energy, and has been passing through a great conflict—when the Church, in England, through all her vast possessions, and in this country, has been putting on her beautiful garments, has been vitalizing all her great principles and agencies, rising up in their might to something like a primitive zeal and self-devotion, twenty years, I say, in such an age, in the life of a Christian Bishop, in a large central Diocese, must needs be something very serious for him to look back upon! To review the pages that contain a record of his daily official life for so many years, to cast his eye over the complex and crowded scheme of annual duty, to try to recall one in a hundred of the anxious questions that necessarily presented themselves to him, one in a hundred of the critical and responsible situations in which the course of events placed him, to gaze back upon the whole vast checkered scene of care and labor, thinking less of what has been done than of what might and ought to have been done—such a retrospect cannot but humble any Chief Pastor under a sense of his grievous insufficiency, while yet it may awaken, as it certainly does in the present speaker, warmest thankfulness in view of numberless supports, preservations and blessings. And here, perhaps, I may be allowed to mention, as among the singular favors I have enjoyed in my official work—a thing which affects my mind strangely, as a kind of mystery: during my very nearly twenty years of service I have not lost or been obliged to postpone more than ten, I think not so many, strictly Episcopal services through indisposition.

It is but right that the Diocese should have an opportunity of seeing, so far as results may be represented in a general view, what has been the progress of the Church within its limits during the last twenty years, and what the enlargement of its work. Having first presented very briefly a general summary of the tokens of Church life and growth in the Diocese for the entire period, I shall then say a few words in regard to the state of the Diocese during the past Conventional year.

Dear Brethren of the Clergy and Laity, the results I

am about to present of a twenty years' stewardship are the fruits under the blessing of Almighty God of your joint prayers, labors and offerings. It is to the Clergy, supported by the zeal and liberality of the Laity, that we are indebted, through the divine goodness, for whatever increase we are privileged to behold in our Master's Vineyard.

I have then to report that during the past twenty years there have been Confirmed 56,598 persons. Of Ordinations, there have been 357 Deacons and 266 Priests—in all, 623. The larger number of Deacons ordained is manifestly due to the circumstance, that so many of the young men educated and ordained in this Diocese are called away, and are allowed to depart to labor in other fields before the time arrives for their admission to Priests' Orders. 76 new Parishes have been admitted into union with the Convention. Between 90 and 100 Corner-stones have been laid. 110 Churches have been Consecrated. And in addition to these, it must be mentioned that a considerable number of Churches, some of them large, substantial and costly structures, have been erected and occupied, but not yet consecrated, on account of some remaining incumbrance of debt, though it is believed that in no case is the debt of such magnitude as to render the property in the edifice insecure.

Of the Clergy there have been—

Received into the Diocese, . . .	481
Transferred to other Dioceses, . .	508
Instituted into Rectorships, . . .	40
Removed by death, ...	102
Deposed, ...	23
Baptisms, ...	123,048

Of which 15,044 were adults; a very remarkable and significant fact, as respects the state of religious things in this country.

Communicants admitted, (the reports throughout being imperfect in regard to this item,)	32,510
Contributions, ...	$11,808,294 22
The contributions reported for the year 1853-4, the year before my consecration, ...	158,138 84
Contributions for 1854-5, (all three Dioceses,)	208,084 58
Contributions reported for 1872-3, (two Dioceses off,)	949,061 75
The number of the Clergy in the Diocese of New-York twenty years ago, was .	304
The number in 1868, (just before the division,) was	446
The present number, after having surrendered to each of the Dioceses of Albany and Long Island about 70 Clergymen, is nearly the same that it was 20 years ago—about	310

As to the growth of Church life and work in the Diocese within the last twenty years, perhaps one of the most remarkable demonstrations of it may be seen in the development of Mission work among the Churches in this city. In my communication to the Diocese a year ago, I stated that "the Mission Chapels in this city had become at least fourfold what they were at the beginning of my Episcopate." But further investigation has convinced me that that statement was altogether inadequate. If we look at the magnitude of the work, the number of souls reached, the efficient means of influence employed, the abundance of the fruits gathered, we shall find it very safe to say, that within twenty years the work has increased more than tenfold. It has indeed risen up as almost a new work.

Let it not be thought invidious or indelicate if we present two or three examples. They are more impressive than general representations. In *Trinity Parish*, N. Y., the report of 1853 for the parent Church and two Chapels, St. Paul's and St. John's, includes daily services in Trinity, Communions monthly and on the great festivals, and a fair return of collections for Canonical objects, for the Missions of the Diocese, and for Seamen very good returns; but there is no mention of Schools for the Poor, or of Mission Chapels for the Poor. No doubt the corporation was doing much to assist feeble Churches of which no report was made. In 1855 the report was much the same, with the addition of Trinity Chapel. In 1873 the report of the same Parish shows a great enlargement of work; the addition of two free Chapels, St. Chrysostom and St. Augustine, besides St. Cornelius at Fort Columbus, weekly Communions in the Parent Church and two of the Chapels, an increase of Clergy for work among the poor, 229 Sunday-School teachers and Catechists, 2,764 scholars; daily Parish Schools, free: boys, 404; girls, 264. Industrial Schools: teachers, 123; scholars, 2,050; 504 Baptisms, against 174 in 1853; 323 Confirmed, against 61 in 1853; Communicants, 2,720, against 700 in 1853. Contributions from the people nearly ten-fold what they were in 1853. But the great and significant change is in Mission work in Schools and Chapels among the poor. In St. George's Parish the Sunday-School work was always large. The report of 1853 (the new Church having been completed, occupied, and being entirely filled) gives 700 Communicants, 1,100 children in the Sunday-Schools, a Missionary who visits extensively among the poor, though without a Chapel, a Dorcas Society, distributing garments very largely, a Sewing School, maintained by ladies on every Saturday, containing 170 girls, and a daily Parish School for the poor of 100 children. To these may be added the Rector's sermons and lectures at the average rate of four a week. The report for the same Parish in 1873 is brief, but it returns 2,000 Communicants, against

700 in 1853, 2,000 children in the schools, for the 1,100 in 1853, together with the very noteworthy addition of three Mission Chapels, one for Germans with German service, and two for English preaching and worship.

I might institute a similar comparison in the case of many other Parishes: St. Mark's, Calvary, St. Thomas', Grace, Ascension, Incarnation, St. Clement's, Holy Communion, St. Luke's, Holy Trinity, St. Ann's, St. Peter's, Transfiguration, Holy Apostles', St. John the Evangelist, St. Michael's, St. Mary's, and so of the rest, for they are all of one spirit. In each and all of these, and in many others, either by the addition of Mission Chapels or by the enlárgement of them, or by employing more Clerical force so as to work more extensively among the poor, or by the erection of free Churches, or by the opening of daily Schools, the preaching of the Gospel has been extended more largely to the poor, to those who had to be laboriously sought out and gathered in; ministrations for consolation and relief have been carried more widely among strangers, the dispersed and hidden children of sin and suffering, who only become known and accessible because sore distress has overtaken them.

And so year by year our Christian work has gone out more and more beyond the limits of the comfortable Parish. It has gone out to the highways and hedges. It has penetrated into the dark places of poverty, ignorance, sin. It has taken the friendless by the hand. The Church has sought to make her Ministry more like that of her blessed Master and Head, looking with especial compassion upon those who to the world seem most miserable and most absolutely lost. The Church and the Parish are less places for mere reputable preaching and a round of becoming ministrations. They are more and more centres of vast complex systems of all embracing Christian work, in which laymen and laywomen, the young and the old, bear their parts, setting no limits to their researches and efforts, and caring most for those who most need care.

It is under the influence of these larger and more loving views of Christian duty that new institutions have sprung up, that several feeble ones have rapidly developed into greatly increased importance, that new ventures of faith, new lines of Christian effort have been entered upon. St. Barnabas' House, (a part of the work of the City Mission,) the House of Mercy, the Midnight Mission, the Home for Incurables, the House of Rest for Consumptives, the Asylum for the Blind, St. Mary's Hospital for Children, the Sheltering Arms, the House of the Good Shepherd, Rockland County, the Hospitals at Poughkeepsie, Yonkers and Newburgh, the Home for Old Men and Aged Couples, the Church Mission to Deaf Mutes, are all new within the last twenty years; while St. Luke's Hospital, the Orphans' Home, and St. Luke's Home for Aged Indigent Christian Females, which twenty years ago were in their infancy, have now, by the blessing of God upon the loving zeal of our Christian people, risen up into large and well-established Institutions.

In the mean time the City Mission has been revived, and through its Chapels and the various Institutions visited, is carrying on a very useful work. The Sisters of St. Mary, at the House of Mercy, at St. Mary's School, N. Y., and at St. Gabriel's, Peekskill, and at the Orphanage at Memphis, Tennessee, where they last year braved the pestilence, the Sisters of the Holy Communion, and the Sisters of the Good Shepherd at St. Barnabas' House, have won all hearts that were near enough to understand them, by their patient endurance, their loving zeal and devotion.

Indeed, the rapid development and growth of woman's work in the Church in this Diocese within the last twenty years has been remarkable. Whether as associated in organized communities, or as separate, yet recognised and permanent helpers in Parishes under the direction of the Rector, after the manner of Deaconesses, or as Christian ladies, retaining their ordinary position and relations in society, yet, in a spirit of active beneficence availing themselves of leisure to speak for Christ in prisons and among the poor and suffering, they have in large numbers devoted themselves unobtrusively, unreservedly, to arduous Christian work, in a way which showed that they sympathized heart and soul with that more expansive, more far-reaching, more self-denying Christian spirit, the later manifestations of which I have been referring to.

On assuming the duties of the Episcopal office, one of my very first cares was the holding of a conference with a few Clergymen and Laymen at a friend's house on the subject of Mission work among the poor of this great city. It was a kind of work in which I had long been interested, and to which I had been led by my parochial experience to give much anxious thought. On the evening of that conference I pressed the general subject, and I also suggested a general scheme for large, organized City Mission work. It was warmly received. But I was never the devotee of theories and schemes; and as I looked around me in this city, and considered the position and relation of Clergy and Parishes, I preferred, instead of urging the establishment of the Central Mission House for a number of Missionaries, which I had suggested, to encourage that Mission work from strong parochial centres, which has since been so largely developed. There is, of course, room for general City Mission work under the auspices of a general City Mission Society. But by far the most extensive work has been carried on from parochial centres and under parochial direction.

From the evening of that first private conference, to which I have referred, down to the present time, *Mission work* among the poor and neglected has, perhaps, occupied a larger space in my addresses, conversations and sermons than any other branch of Christian duty. That the remarkable development of that kind of Christian work in the Diocese during the last twenty years is due in any considerable measure to the words of its Bishop

I am very far indeed from suggesting or supposing. In this city something is no doubt due to the circumstance that the influx of a large foreign population has created of late years an urgent demand for a kind of Christian agency which was not so much called for in former days. But increasing needs, arising silently in an unprecedented way, are not always met in a correspondingly increased spirit of love and devotion. It is the work of the good spirit of God. It is a part of that general movement toward deeper views of the ministry and of the work of the Church of God on earth, which has been stirring within the last thirty or forty years a large portion of the Church of England through all her borders, and a large portion of the Clergy and Laity of the Church in this country.

Every one will understand how consoling it must be to a Christian Bishop, how grateful to all zealous, loving members of the Church, that Christian work has been growing and not languishing in these past years—that Clergy and Laity—men and women have in so many cases risen to higher conceptions of the privilege and duty of living for Christ in the work of His Church. Most certainly, in looking back and around us we may recognise short comings enough to keep us humble; we may mark more than enough of deficiencies yet unprovided for to prevent us from relaxing in the fervency of our prayers and earnest endeavors. But we may well offer our thanksgivings for past blessings, and take courage for yet larger enterprises of love and mercy in the future.

While this Mission work and other Church work has been advancing in the city, the rural portions of the Diocese have by no means been idle or stationary. One county, which twenty years ago had two Missionaries but no Church edifice, has now seven Churches. In Richmond County, Staten Island, five new Churches have been erected; in Dutchess County, twelve, eight of them at new points; in Putnam, two; in Ulster, three; in Orange, seven; in Westchester, nineteen. Many of these, of course, were for Parishes existing previously. To these new Churches must be added a large number both in town and country that have been very considerably enlarged, and so far repaired and restored as to make them virtually new Churches. In several cases, in the interior of the Diocese, we have been indebted for an admirable Church edifice to the munificence of a single individual. One such, erected in Ellenville, Ulster County, by Mr. E. C. Humbert, of Brooklyn, as a memorial of a son, who departed this life in that village, I have consecrated within a few weeks. It is a beautiful edifice, in a region of country where it was much needed, and where I am persuaded it will exert with God's blessing a wide influence in refining and elevating the religious feelings of the people.

I cannot close this imperfect, and yet, as I fear, too extended review of Church work in the Diocese during the past twenty years without another brief reference to St. Stephen's Training College, Annandale—one of the most important Church Institutions in the country—whose Warden we had the pleasure of listening to yesterday. A very few words may be allowed, perhaps, especially at this crisis, in reference to its origin. It began in a small free Church school and mission, established by a large hearted Layman residing at Annandale, which from the first was under the charge of a young Clergyman then recently ordained. My first services there were held in the Chapel of the School House. On occasion of one of my early visits I went to one of the school rooms, to be present while one of the classes, composed of the larger boys, was receiving instruction by the young Clergyman, first in Latin, and then in some portions of early Church History. I was much struck by the beauty and thoroughness of the instruction given in the Latin language, but still more by the clearness, simplicity and beauty of the expositions given to these boys of the distinctions in principle between truth and error involved in the condemnations of heresy and vindications of the Truth of God in the early Councils of the Church. On my return to the house of my friend, the founder and supporter of that Church work, I stated to him the strong impression made upon me by the character of the instruction I had witnessed. And I observed that it would be nearly as easy to instruct twenty boys as five, and that without any very large outlay of money, without any very loud or ambitious professions, it would be possible to slowly establish a young *Nashotah*, an embryo Institution, which in time would become a thing of great importance to the Church. An enlargement of Church work speedily followed. A beautiful and costly Church was erected, and that having been laid in ruins by fire just as it was ready for consecration, another still more beautiful was erected in its place, to be a place of worship for the neighboring population, and a Chapel for the coming Institution. The work developed and grew and took shape, until St. Stephen's Training College, for the education of young men looking to the sacred ministry of the Church, had been duly organized and established under the charge of the young Clergyman to whom I have referred, as first Warden. That young instructor, that first Warden of St. Stephen's, has been now for several years Professor of Ecclesiastical History in the General Theological Seminary, for two or three years its Dean *ad interim*, the Rev. George F. Seymour, D. D., whom we must now speak of as the Bishop elect of the Diocese of Illinois.

St. Stephen's College has each year applicants for every room it can provide. A considerable number of its Alumni are already in Holy Orders, some 35, doing earnest work in the Church at various posts, all the way from the Atlantic to the Pacific. During the ensuing year some 26 of its graduates will be found pursuing the studies and training for the Ministry in the General Theological Seminary. It is an Institution for which we may well be grateful, and I have a good hope that its merits will be fully recognised, and that at some not very distant day large-minded Christian persons will be found to give it a liberal endowment.

But I promised at the outset, that after giving a general view of the progress of the Church and its work in this Diocese during the twenty years of my Episcopate, I would say a very few words respecting the aspects of Church life in the Diocese during the past year. The notice must necessarily be brief. One of the most obvious means of estimating the vigor of Church life, the efficiency and thoroughness of her ministrations, is to be found, of course, in the number and character of the Confirmations. In comparing the work of two given Parishes, an estimate formed merely from the numbers confirmed might be very fallacious and unjust, because, while the one Parish, from its position, might be constantly undergoing changes, receiving accessions of strangers, which furnish materials for large Confirmation classes, the other Parish, from its position, having a congregation which changes little, and which consists largely of persons who are already confirmed and Communicants, may have comparatively few to be called to that holy rite. But comparing the *whole Diocese* one year with another, the numbers confirmed will furnish an useful exponent of Church activity and progress. In the year 1853, my predecessor, after his first visitation of the Diocese, including all the Parishes but three, and when the Diocese had not been fully visited in the years immediately preceding, reported the then unprecedented number of 2,700. Some of these probably were accumulations of previous years, for in his second year, which he had nearly completed, the number confirmed was 1,427. In 1868, just previous to the division of the Diocese, the confirmations reported by me were 3,930, more than 1,200 above the confirmations reported under favorable circumstances in 1853. Since the division of the Diocese the confirmations have ranged not far from 25 and 2,600. Last year they were 2,485. This year they have been 3,083, nearly 500 in excess of any year since the division. The number would have been somewhat larger but for providential circumstances, which, for a time, forbade long and distant visitations. As it was, with the kind assistance of the Right Reverend the Bishop of Florida, who confirmed in two Churches for me, and of the Right Reverend Dr. Tozer, late of Central Africa, who made five visitations for me, including one ordination and several confirmations, all my actual appointments were duly met, and all actual requests for visitations were complied with. I would have made some further appointments had they seemed to be urgently required. A number of Parishes I shall hope to visit, God willing, after the close of the General Convention.

The natural desire of a large portion of the Clergy in and near the city to have their confirmations take place in the Lenten or Easter Season, leads to a crowding together of appointments in that portion of the year. In eight days, including Holy Week and Easter Sunday, there were 22 visitations, and 752 persons confirmed. In forty days, in portions of March and April, I had sixty visitations, and the number of persons confirmed was 1,693. I preached on an average about twice a week, and for the rest contented myself with somewhat extended addresses.

This rapid succession of visitations in one portion of the year has been in no way disagreeable or inconvenient to me. They never before were so thickly accumulated as during the late spring season, and I never passed through them with less wear and tear of body and mind, or with more satisfaction. It was enough for me that the wishes of the Clergy were met, and that my daily, hourly duties kept me constantly in the very thickest of Church life, in the very midst of her chiefest joys and triumphs. For what can be a higher or purer joy—what can be a more heart-cheering triumph, than to see multitudes of souls won for Christ, won to holy purposes, and to the solemn consecration of themselves to the Lord that bought them—to see them sealed, and blessed, and strengthened for a heavenly calling! What more animating and uplifting to the heart of a Chief Pastor, than to pass rapidly from one to another of Christ's ministering servants, to see them in the presence of their flocks, in the very act of gathering in the fruits of their labors, or the fruits of God's gracious work, and to note their loving zeal and devotion: sometimes, perhaps, the yearning of their hearts after some who had held back from the proffered blessing! It was a continual exhilaration, a course of duty and grateful service which any Christian Bishop might well be content to live and die in.

And here, my dear Brethren, is what I wished to say respecting the state of the Diocese during the past year. I have seen a great deal of hard clerical work in this Diocese during the past twenty years. But I never saw, and I never expect to see, during my remaining days, nobler examples of true Christian love and zeal, of intense devotion to ministerial duty, of painstaking care for the welfare of the flocks committed to their care, on the right hand and on the left, among men of all phases of theological thought, (no monopoly of zeal anywhere, in any corner,) than I saw made manifest by many tokens among the Clergy during my visitations in the past season. The whole Diocese seemed in a glow. Such a thing as clerical apathy, as an easy, superficial, perfunctory, professional tone, would have been an anomaly, very hard to find.

I might refer to many facts corroborative of what I myself saw and heard in my communications with the Clergy, but it would carry me too far. I content myself with speaking from the standpoints which I occupied in my visitations; and I do most fervently render thanks to Almighty God, Father, Son and Holy Ghost, that the great body of the Clergy, and so many laymen and women have been moved to such loving zeal and fidelity in the Master's service. No doubt the most zealous would acknowledge themselves unprofitable servants. No doubt the most grateful for mercies bestowed upon the Church would still proclaim that there are deficiencies and short comings—that there are works that need to be undertaken—important institutions and enterprises that deserve and ought to be better sustained. Nevertheless, we do feel bound to profess most thankfully our conviction that in this Diocese there has been, and is now advancing, a marked growth of spiritual life, an increase of energy in pious and charitable works.

I believe that other Dioceses in this country may say something of the same kind. And how is it, my dear Brethren, with our Mother Church of England? An able and well informed Clergyman of that Church declared recently that there never were so many earnest Communicants in the Church of England as at this present time. An eminent statesman of England, well acquainted at least with the general condition of the Church in that country, speaking certainly at that time without any party object to serve, declared, in reference to the idea of the Church being in danger, that a Church is in danger when there is little life in her—when she is languid and indolent, faithless to her great charge of souls—too much in love with the world; that, on the contrary, the Church of England was remarkably full of religious life and activity and good works, and that of such a Church there need be no fear. Another great statesman of England, an earnestly religious man, by his position thrown for many years into intimate relations with the Clergy and the Church, declared, within a few weeks, in his place in Parliament, that it was next to impossible for any young man to conceive of the change for the better which had taken place in the Church of England within the last forty years. He gave a dark picture of what the Church was before the beginning of that forty years; and then, speaking from his own intimate knowledge, he paid a glowing tribute to the devotion, the untiring zeal and fidelity of the great body of the Clergy of the Church. Indeed, it is no matter of opinion. Facts demonstrate the truth. In an hundred forms the activities of the Church of England make themselves apparent to every candid and intelligent eye; the Churches erected by single individuals, the labors among the Poor, the crowded and earnest Communions, the leading and active part taken by many of the nobility and gentry in all religious and charitable undertakings—these and other like evidences of spiritual life make England at this day a remarkable country.

In my first address to the Convention in 1855, being led by a case of discipline to touch the subject, I said, "it must, I think, be confessed by every enlightened observer, that the movement which has occurred in the Anglican Church within twenty years is the most energetic and the most important of any which has been witnessed in that branch of the Church since the period of the Reformation."

Having described the origin and character of the movement, and the living practical fruits it had produced, I added, "these are some of the abundant tokens, not that all which has been written is true; but that the Church, as a whole, has arisen and shaken herself from the dust, set herself to a new and more glorious warfare against the powers of darkness."

Care was taken in that address to recognise the obvious truth, that in every great movement in the Church, however legitimate and salutary in itself, there were likely to be tendencies to excess that would affect more or less a number of partial and unstable minds; and that while the great body of the Church might gain immeasurably from the movement, a few individuals, looking only at one side of truth, or one set of half truths, might be hurried into extremes, and borne away to revolve around a new and strange centre. I referred to certain secessions from the Church, and I said, "who, for one moment, would weigh her losses against her gains? Who that comprehends what the Anglican Church is now, and what she was thirty years ago, would be willing to carry her back to that state of comparative formalism and superficiality for the sake of having restored to her ten times the talent and learning which she has lost? What intelligent theologian can doubt that the Church, with her present expansion and moral energy, and her true appreciation of her own principles, is more than ever stable in her position, and the great bulwark of the truth of God against the errors and corruptions of Romanism?"

Since those words were spoken and placed on record nineteen years ago, the Church of England has gone on developing, deepening, extending her great work in the way I have briefly described. Her great Statesmen and her eminent Clergy gratefully recognise the fact. But, in the meantime, those tendencies to excess in a few minds which I have referred to as sure to accompany and follow every great movement in the Church, however salutary it may be in itself, have been appearing in the Church of England among a few men in the shape of high wrought statements on some points of doctrine, and in the shape of what may justly be termed excessive ceremonial. I say, "among a few men," for out of 15 or 20,000 Clergymen the number of these extremists is exceedingly small—so small that a well-informed person has significantly expressed it, by asserting that all their names might be written upon a very small sheet of note paper. And some of that small number are admitted to be singularly self-denying laborers in the most deplorably squalid and miserable portions of London and of other towns, and they are recognised as being peculiarly forcible and impressive Preachers of the great central vital truths of the Gospel.

In the meantime, such has been the effect of the earnest, affectionate, self-denying, pains-taking Ministry of the great body of the Clergy, that tens and hundreds of thousands of the people who had been alienated from the Church, or who had been born in the ranks of dissent, have been drawn by sympathy with her loving zeal into her fold, and are now worshipping with rejoicing hearts around her altars. Secessions from the Church are much rarer than they were twenty-five and thirty years ago, and where the Church is losing one she is gaining a hundred.

I do not wonder at the indignant exclamation of that great, that earnestly religious statesman, in the House of Commons of England, when vindicating the great body of the Clergy, when pointing out the extraordinary changes for the better which had taken place within forty years, he said, in that great assembly, in the face of the English nation: "I will never allow the eccentricities of a handful of Ritualists to make me forget the extraordinary merits of the great body of the Clergy of the Church of England."

The beneficed Clergy of the Church of England are in a very different position from the Clergy of the Church in this country. They have a legal title to their place and their living. They are independent of the people of the congregation, so far as any Rector can be said to be independent of the flock to which he ministers. They may, if so minded, (a thing not likely to occur often anywhere,) they may introduce services unacceptable to the majority of the congregation, with a degree of impunity not often possible with us. And so there may have been arguments in favor of restrictive legislation for the English Clergy, which have no application here. Whatever those arguments were, they seem not to have been satisfactory to many of the ablest of the Laity or to the great body of the Clergy. They did not think it right, for the sake of reaching a very few eccentric men, to enact a law which would render every Clergyman liable to be harassed by petty prosecutions whenever it should happen to please a few ignorant, evil-minded laymen, and suit the caprice of an intolerant Bishop. The question, however, lies beyond our province. That the Law was brought forward from the purest motives, no one can doubt who knows any thing of its authors. And that, in a greatly modified and improved form, it ultimately passed by a large majority, can surprise no one who considers the character of a Legislature, almost wholly secular, wholly so in one of its branches, and little conversant, a large portion of them, with just views of ecclesiastical subjects. Still less can the passage of such a bill, through such a Legislature, to control the action of a body of Clergy, in a peculiarly independent position, be deemed a matter of surprise by any one, who duly considers the extraordinary means employed in England to agitate the public mind and create alarm on the subject of supposed designs against the existing constitution of Church and State in that country. The whole history of the Church scarcely affords an example of disturbance, of acrimonious exaggeration so general, proceeding from causes so inconsiderable, as that which we have seen in England and in this country within the last few years. Notwithstanding the fact, to which I have referred, that secessions from the Church, in the direction of Rome, have been of late much fewer than they were twenty-five or thirty years ago, and that secessions have been more than counterbalanced by accessions, yet such has been the activity employed in selecting a few extreme statements, statements often capable of an innocent interpretation, but very liable to be misunderstood by ill-informed persons; such has been the activity in selecting such statements and others grossly offensive, often from writers who really represent nobody but themselves, (a half-dozen individuals,) activity in keeping those offensive statements passing and repassing before the public mind, along with partial and colored descriptions of ceremonial, in a very few Churches. (I have myself been reported as having officiated in Scarlet Robes!) such has been the unwearied perseverance and the bitterness with which many agents have helped to keep these chimeras before the world, before thousands of the quiet families of the Church, that no small number of ill-informed people have been persuaded that there was serious occasion for alarm.

Undoubtedly it is the imperative duty of the religious journalist, of the head of the parish, of the theological Professor, of the head of the Diocese, to expose errors which have invaded, or which threaten to invade the Church, and to vindicate the truth of God. But among considerate Church teachers of every class and degree, there will be a just proportion between the tone of those exposures and vindications, between the prominence given to them, the time and space allowed to them, and the magnitude of the peril. Because, while it is the duty of all who are in positions of influence or authority to warn the Church against error, it is also their duty, and a great and momentous duty it is, to protect the Church from being unnecessarily disturbed by idle or exaggerated alarms. The quiet devout families of the Church, the weary, overburdened members of our flock, who are trying, often in loneliness and sorrow, to do their duty, to serve God in peace, to find some comfort and rest for their souls, they have a right to demand of us that we feed them with food convenient for them, that we lift up their hearts above the perturbations of the world, and, above all, that we do not arouse their angry passions without cause, nor afflict them with anxieties and fears, when there is no need. Whenever we contribute beyond reason to fill the Church with suspicions and jealousies and acrimonious divisions, in just such proportion do we trouble the peace of her children, interfere with their spiritual edification and growth in grace, prevent them from dealing earnestly and truly with their own souls, in just such proportion do we cripple and vitiate the whole work of the Church, in preaching Christ at home and abroad, and in carrying on her warfare against the world, the flesh and the Devil. If the means and agencies employed in spreading criminations and recriminations—in sending far and wide unintentional misconceptions and misrepresentations—if these means and agencies were employed in pressing home the truth and love of Christ upon the hearts and consciences of men, in kindling a fire of love, zeal, devotion—in laying bare the corruption prevailing in glittering places—if they were employed with all their might in turning perishing souls away from the idolatry of wealth and pleasure and fashion, to the service of the Lord that bought them, and is soon to judge them—I say, if all the means and agencies now in large measure so cruelly misused, were used with a more heavenly wisdom and grace, what a mighty accession of power, and influence, and honor, would come to the Church of God.

And here is a consideration which it is hard to keep out of one's mind, but which it is by no means pleasant to dwell upon, either in public or in one's own thoughts in secret. This Church, of which, through the mercy of God, we have the privilege of being members, which we all profess to love, and no doubt do love fervently, is not alone on the earth. She is not speaking her words and doing her work with none but the eye of God upon her. If she were, it would still become her to take heed to her ways, and all her members to consider well what will be most conducive to her peace and edification. But our dear Church here on earth is not alone. She has to speak her words and to do her work in the presence of witnesses and spectators. On the right hand and on the left are religious bodies with their eyes upon us, their ears wide open to hear what we ourselves say of each other and of our own internal state. If we give ourselves a bad character beyond the truth of things, it is very doubtful whether those exterior bodies, on the one side or on the other, will have the knowledge or the disposition to reject our testimony against ourselves, or to reduce that testimony from what is exaggerated to what is real and true. If any member of this Church do allow himself, through passion, through prejudice and ignorance, through personal malevolence, to say what is untrue of another member of the Church or of a whole class of members, and so defame the Church, give her the character of having within her evils which she has not in any such measure as is vaguely conveyed, or distinctly asserted, then, besides other grievous injuries, he helps to lower his own Communion in the estimation of exterior bodies, and to lessen her influence for good, her power of winning those who need her guidance and her blessings.

I know it may be said that the most effectual way to still the loud voice of censure in the Church is to restrain the offences that provoke them. Yet the question will still return, whether many of the supposed offences are not imaginary, and whether those that really exist do not come very far short of forming any justification for the use that is made of them.

But, of course, what sort of statements respecting men and things, respecting opinions and practices in the Church shall be put forth, and made the staple of public discourse, must be left in large measure to individual judgment and conscience. No doubt there is room for much difference of opinion and practice in subordinate things, and that without any violation of essential unity.

And here, my dear Brethren, I must speak to you in a more personal way, though the first person has been already used more than suited the feelings of the speaker. Many persons in official positions have spoken in their respective spheres without reserve. In the place which I occupy, and at a moment like the present, I do not think it would become me, or be consistent with my duty, to keep silence as to my definite position and views. No one can be more sensible of the responsibility which attaches to his words and actions than I am. The responsibility is fully accepted, not without earnest prayer, that the feeblest and most unworthy of God's servants may be guided into all needful truth, and enabled to speak it in love.

As you may well suppose, my dear Brethren, there is nothing to tell which ought not to be already well known to the Diocese and to the Church at large, so far as the Church at large may choose to concern itself about the views of the present Bishop of New-York. From the first day of coming into the Episcopate unto this hour, I have spoken out in the plainest way in regard to the great fundamental principles of the Church and of the Gospel of our Lord and Saviour Jesus Christ. In my first Episcopal Address, some words of which have just now been recalled to your recollection, I said enough to make it clearly apparent what elements (including, of course, a true faith and a valid Ministry) I thought essential to the fullest spiritual life of the Church and to its best influence in the world.

On subsequent occasions, in times of agitation, (and when, with certain minds, has there not been agitation ?) I pointed out the absolute security under God for the unchangeableness and stability of the Church. Papal Rome on the one side might change, and had changed deplorably within our memory, because she guides herself by her living authorities, and so may add new articles to the faith whenever she pleases. The denominations on the other side might change, as many parts of Germany and Switzerland and New-England had changed, because they guide themselves by the prevailing individual opinion, and so may change the rule of faith whenever the majority of the congregation desire it. Far different from both of those conditions of existence the Church of our love, the whole Anglican Communion, remains, through the great goodness of God, through all revolutions of opinion around her, immovably fixed in her position, so far as her faith and order and her great leading principles are concerned, because she is pledged to an everlasting conformity to one and the same invariable standard: the eternal, immutable Word of God. She is pledged to conformity to the Word of God, not as that word may chance to be interpreted by one or another school of theologians in these later ages, interpreted in a sense unknown in the first ages; but she is pledged to conformity to the Word of God in the sense in which it was received and witnessed to, so far as vital matters were concerned, by the whole early undivided Church.

Very often reference has been made to the absolute certainty as well as stability thus given to the truth of God as it is held in the Church, ready for the use of all her children. It is quite wonderful, and yet not wonderful, how those who have been weary wanderers amid the wild conflicting opinions in the world, when they come intelligently into the Church, become at once conscious of a new feeling of repose and assurance of heart, in a great rest as to the certainty of the truth.

No doubt these unchangeable principles of the Church may be held in one spirit, or in another and very different spirit. The light and the associations spread over them and giving them character, may be of one tone or another. That tone may approach the spirit and temper of the sects, or it may partake more largely of the primitive *ethos*, deeper, broader, more genial—the visible absorbed into and filled with the supernatural, and invested with all the tender, soul-moving characters that come from the presence of our dear Lord on earth, and from the ages of martyrs and confessors. The truths and principles are unchanged; but the spirit in which they are held and used may vary, and has often varied. The visible Cross ever signifies the same thing; but under one set of circumstances it may move a multitude to tears, under another set of circumstances it may convert them into an angry mob.

In my Address of 1868 I referred to the great improvement which had taken place in the worship of the Church within twenty-five years; a tendency to greater outward reverence; to more becoming arrangements in the sacred edifice; to more tender care and order, and a more inspiring glow and animation in the services. Not a single principle had been in any way changed, but yet the whole worship of the Church had been made more what it ought to be.

At the time of the first separate organization of the Church in this country, the externals of public religious service had necessarily been in a very crude and neglected state. Scarcely any congregation in this Diocese would now be content with what was then very common. In those observations in 1868 I pointed out what a grievous injury it would have been to the Church in subsequent years; what an impediment to its life and growth; what discontent and violation of law would have risen up in the Church had our first General Conventions been so short-sighted and so unwise as to attempt, by a system of severe, minute, restrictive legislation, to fasten upon the Church for all time the crude, sordid forms and arrangements of that pioneer period. Nevertheless, while I exposed the fallacy of a somewhat popular notion, that much regard for the outward and visible things of Religion weakens our interest in the inward and spiritual, showing that the contrary is true, and that the maintainance of Religion in the heart of man, and in its place of influence in the world, depends largely upon the decency and becoming state observed in the public worship of Almighty God, I yet strongly deprecated excess in outward ceremonial, or the introduction of any novel forms of observance, which by their foreign aspects and associations might give unnecessary offence; might give rise to misconstructions; or by their too minute, mechanical details take off the thoughts of the worshippers from the supreme, spiritual realities of their appearing before God.

Finally, in the Address of 1871, in dealing with the important subject of woman's work in the Church, and especially with that work as carried on in organized associations of women, in sisterhoods—a thing which, although primitive, is now, within twenty or thirty years, only just springing up—after having been, for long years, or rather centuries, in abeyance in our branch of the Church, and which, therefore, is obnoxious prejudice in many quarters, which, indeed, may almost be said to be still on its trial; in doing this, I called attention to the obvious consideration, that, in a great movement and conflict like that of the Anglican Reformation, struggling to cast off Papal usurpation, and to sweep utterly away the onerous and corrupt additions to faith and practice of mediæval times, it would unavoidably happen, that some innocent and even useful things would, from the excitement of the contest, and the violence of the recoil, be condemned and cast off along with the really evil things, there would be a temporary loss of some good, which in time would be reclaimed. These incidental effects of the Reformation were much less serious in England than on the continent, where they were grievous and permanent. But even in the Anglican Church, for long years after the Reformation, we can recognise a state of feeling and practice with regard to certain things, which would not have been found in the primitive Church. These deficiencies and prejudices were not of such a nature as to make us regret the Reformation. No! a thousand times no! But those deficiencies and prejudices were of such a nature that any candid observer, comprehending the true spirit of Christianity and of the early Church, would say, the English Church would be none the worse, but much better, loftier in her spirit and tone, more efficient 'n her work, more secure in her position, if she would rise above her prejudices against innocent things, if she would, in a brave large spirit, supply to her living working system what she finds lacking in it, if she would judge of things less by their mere unlikeness to mediævalism, and more by their resemblance to the Gospel, as exemplified in the life and work of the Primitive Church. In a word, my leading thought was, that what we greatly needed to give us the dignity, the magnanimity, the freedom and efficiency of action, the assured confidence and repose of spirit of a true branch of the holy Apostolic Catholic Church of God, was an enlarged and liberal Christian spirit—along with inflexible devotion to the one immutable truth of God, inflexible opposition to false principles and dangerous practices on the one side and on the other—along with these a large, ingenuous tolerant spirit, averse to all narrow, acrimonious contentions, able to recognise good, and ever ready to employ it for the glory of God and the salvation of men. Without such a spirit we are little better than a sect. We are liable to spend our breath in unseemly belittling personal controversies, and we are little capable of seeing and knowing what we ought to do for the Church's weal in new emergencies, or of having power to do it.

The principles and order of this Church are unchangeable, because divine, and abundantly authenticated by the witness of the undivided early Church. It is as ridiculous to think that this Church, or any but an infinitesimal part of it, (eccentric, wayward, unstable spirits, always to be found in all ages in every religious body,) could ever be Romanized, mediævalized, as it would be to apprehend that the Church might be converted to Buddhism. But in regard to the spiritual life and work of the Church, if we have the enlarged Christian spirit of which I have spoken, we may perchance have occasion to see, from time to time, that there are ways and means by which, through the mercy of God, through the power of the Holy Ghost, we may as a Church do our work more thoroughly, and walk more nearly in the footsteps of our Lord and Saviour.

Such is the general spirit in which, during my Episcopate, I have ever spoken openly and frankly to the Church in this Diocese. My views and principles are precisely what they were thirty years ago. A deeper consideration of things may have enlarged the bounds of my toleration and sympathy—may have brought to me, as I hope it has, more of that enlarged and liberal Christian spirit of which I have spoken. A wider familiarity with the different modes and phases of worship used and allowable within the limits of our Church, may have taught me to see that things, which, once, with a narrower experience, I might have felt a repugnance to, are not only innocent, but in many cases useful. But in all other respects every succeeding year of my life has only confirmed previous impressions, and intensified, if possible, my devotion to the principles, the order and the ways of this Church.

And now what of the future? It would be superfluous, I hope, for me to say, here from this chair, that I am the friend of order in the Church, and of that measure of uniformity in worship and view, which it is reasonable to expect in a great ecclesiastical body. Absolute uniformity, in such a body, is a thing impossible, and a thing hardly to be desired, were it ever so easily attainable. In a vast ecclesiastical system, including, as it necessarily must, persons of widely differing tastes and mental habitudes, it can be no great effort of virtue in one Christian, to concede to another Christian the enjoyment of religious services, differing, in some minor respects, from those which he may prefer for himself.

Nevertheless, extravagant departures from what may justly be considered as the recognised order of the Church, whether they take place at one extreme, or at the other, are much to be regretted and deprecated. It is hard to relieve them from the imputation of a certain measure of self-will, and of a kind of indelicacy and disrespect toward the authorities of the Church, and toward the great body of her members. It were much to be wished, that members of the Church who engage in such courses, would consider seriously with themselves whether, upon a calm and severe examination, their line of conduct can be approved as altogether dutiful, and also, whether they are wise for themselves, or just toward the Church, when they persist in doing that which tends, reasonably or unreasonably, to provoke the intolerant and irritable, and so to bring down upon the Church a system of narrow restrictive legislation—legislation which, in some form, the Church barely escaped at the last General Convention, and which, were it to be adopted now, as it may be, would trouble the peace of the Church instead of promoting it, would cause many of the noblest spirits in our Household to hang their heads for very shame—not so much for any abridgment of their individual liberties, (though that might take a form that would be a grievance,) as for the exposure to all Christendom of a temper and a policy unworthy of an Apostolic Church. This latter class of persons, to whom I chiefly refer, as being averse to narrow restrictions, are themselves little inclined to any extreme views in Theology, or to any thing that can be fairly charged as excess in ceremonial. But they are strongly in favor of the utmost toleration and liberty that can be included within the limits of the Faith, and of that range of opinion and practice which, in the Primitive Church, and in the Anglican Church since the Reformation, has had examples abundantly sufficient to give it a claim to protection. Such persons (and the Church is full of them through all her borders) have no individual eccentricities to gratify—still less have they any party or personal views to indulge.

But without speaking for others, I may say for myself, that while I am far from being moved by any overweening anxiety touching the issue of several special questions now supposed to be pending in the Church, I must confess that I am profoundly interested in that great future which the Church in this country has before her, if she only have the wisdom and the courage to be true to herself, true to her Lord, true to her own divine constitution and order, true to that large, benignant, comprehensive spirit which should pervade and govern every true branch of the one Holy Catholic Church, true, in fine, to those great doctrines, full of Grace, Mercy, Truth, which cannot be confined within the narrow limits of any mere human system, doctrines which are as widely and graciously suited to the needs of suffering humanity as they are fitted to lift up the heart in adoring wonder and love toward their all-merciful Author.

Such a Church—a Church so grand and lofty in her spirit and proportions, a Church abounding in such names as Andrews and Herbert and Keble on the one hand, and in such names as Leighton and Simeon and Venn on the other; a Church which includes and deals gently, lovingly with such differing phases of mind and thought, such a Church is not to be served by a vehement dogmatism, by a narrow policy of proscription and denunciation worthy only of a sect.

And as to the preservation of peace and order, the great hope of the Church is not in a narrow, irritating system of restrictive legislation, which provokes disgust and conflict, while it is always tending to dwarf the mind of the Church to a familiarity with petty questions and ignoble views. The great hope is, first, in the steadfast, conservative habits of mind, in the modesty and delicacy of feeling which characterize the great body of the Church, and second, in the kindly paternal authority of her chief Pastors, an authority which becomes less gracious and less healing in proportion as it ceases to be paternal and discretionary, and comes to be obliged to make its appearance mainly in prescribed efforts to enforce arbitrary Canonical regulations. Of course, where clear, definite law is persistently violated, and where Canonical proceedings have been set in motion by parties having a right to act, it may become a necessity for the Ordinary to take steps toward discipline, however little suited it may be to his feelings to do so.

But it is believed that we may all take to ourselves this consoling assurance: Such is the moderate, considerate, steadfast temper of the great body of the Church, that eccentric and violently extreme people, whether of the Clergy or of the Laity, whether extreme and violent in one direction or in the other, will never establish a permanent influence in the Church, or succeed in commanding any considerable following. They may occasion a temporary noise and flurry in a very limited circle, but the noise and the flurry will pass away, and the disturbing name will speedily be forgotten.

There is a temper, a disposition of mind, an habitual way of acting in the Church, which I suppose all of us would agree in thinking most conducive to the peace, good order and well-being of the Church, and most becoming for those who have put on Christ, and become members of His Spiritual Body. It is when there is every where in the Church a prevalence of that spirit which makes the Chief Pastor for his part slow to restrict liberty of action, and the Clergy and people for their part slow to abuse it. And such I believe to be the spirit and habit which prevail almost universally throughout our Communion. And if, because of the infirmity of our nature, exceptional things must sometimes occur, there is still the great Christian remedy of patience, moderation, forbearance. We are ever prone to exaggerate the importance of passing events. There are people who seem to see a great crisis in the Church in every petty, eccentric movement of individuals. Their habits of judging and acting are formed amid the excitements and mutabilities of the world, rather than according to the unearthly, steadfast spirit of the Church, which, making little of the mere human agitations within her fold, moves on with an almost unseen but resistless power, swaying with her hidden influence both the one and the other of her contending factions, passing over and away from successive schools of human philosophy, yea, over and away from mere human inventions in theology, outlasts temporal kingdoms, as she will also survive the very earth itself, on which they have the beginning and the end of their being.

We are not to be indifferent to disorders or excesses in teaching and practice in the Church, if such unhappily should occur. Nor, on the other hand, are we to be impatient or violent or narrow in our methods of dealing with them. The sharp methods of criminal courts are little suited to the mysterious things of the Church of God. Above all, let us beseech the God of all grace and wisdom to save us, each one of us, from the wretched delusion of erecting our poor individual judgments into an infallible authority—to save us from the attempts to which self-confident men are so much prone—to reduce and circumscribe and compress all the manifold wisdoms and mysteries of the Church of God, until they can crowd them all into the nutshell of their own individual thinking.

And O! should it ever be our blessed privilege to recognise among our brethren, of whatever school of thought, a singular example of high and holy living, of pure devotion to God and to duty, of self-sacrifice in doing the work of the Lord, may the spirit of all grace keep us pure from the sin of admitting into our hearts the least feeling of envy, jealousy, or dislike—save us from using the coarse instruments of the world to beat down lofty characters in the Church of God, because they hold to one grain more or one grain less than suits with our theological code. The one "grain more," if it be so, may not be according to my views, or my way of speaking; but if it be within the limits of the Church's examples and the Church's toleration, then every attempt to disparage, to ostracize for such a cause, saddens me, and I say to myself in secret what I now say openly to my dear Brethren, "if such things are to be, so much the worse for the Church."

O, even at the best—even when the Church as a whole is in a spiritual glow—there is enough and more than enough of living at ease, of living for the world, enough and more than enough of those who live for what people will say of them. Let us cherish and protect every plant of true devotion in this vineyard of the Lord. Let us be forward to reverence and to use for the Church's service, for the Master's honor, whatever has been made, through His grace, most meet for a holy warfare against the powers of darkness.

As to supposed evils in the Church, we may remember, even if the evils were much greater than they are, that Time is a great Physician, and it may be added, a great Disciplinarian.

The grace and truth of God are great mediators and arbitrators in the things of the Church. There are great moral powers, which no man nor set of men may gainsay or resist. Whatever springs up in the Church as a work of God, must either grow and propagate itself, because it is a work of God, and good for the souls of men, suited to their needs, or else not growing, not propagating itself, because not a divine reality, not suited to man's need, it becomes a common thing of man's devising, loses its hold on Christian reverence, and so fades away and comes to nothing.

Within the memory of this generation, as before observed, a desire sprang up in the Church for a more reverent and becoming ordering of all outward things pertaining to the public worship of Almighty God—more goodly structures—more tender care for the decency, beauty, majesty of our spiritual sacrifices in the great congregation. It was to some extent criticized and opposed; but it rapidly grew and gained acceptance, for it was a work of God, needful for His honor and glory, and, if possible, still more needful for man's religious nature, and for the influence of divine things in the world.

But superadded to that recognised and accepted improvement in the ordering of divine services, widely, if not generally prevailing, there were, a few years since, introduced into some eight or ten churches in this country—in not more than eight or ten out of the whole 2,800 or 3,000 churches of the country—certain peculiar, more foreign, more exceptional features, especially in the celebration of the Holy Eucharist. Have those more foreign and exceptional features propagated themselves in the

Church in this country, and gained acceptance widely and rapidly as the really substantial improvements in public worship had done before them? I wish to be as little personal or invidious as possible. But I am exemplifying a great law for our special instruction at this time. And I venture to say, most confidently, that those more foreign and exceptional features have not propagated themselves—are not at this time propagating themselves in the Church in this country; they have not widely and rapidly touched and won men's hearts. They have not vindicated themselves by any inherent reality, or proved efficacy for good, by any appearance of their being necessary for the truth's sake, or for the soul's salvation. And not having grown, as a true plant of God, is it too much to say, that they are secretly losing a part of such hold as they had, in a limited sphere, on Christian reverence, and so preparing to fade away, rather than increase and spread abroad. And therefore, we say again, as to all exceptional things, we can afford to be patient, and we ought to be kind and sympathizing toward all the good we find in a servant of God, whether we fully approve of all his peculiarities or not. Time is a great Physician! Time is a great Disciplinarian!

One or two words more before leaving this general subject. I have spoken strongly in favor of administering the system of the Church in a large, tolerant, comprehensive spirit, and strongly against narrow restrictions. I have done so, looking chiefly to no special, temporary questions, to no limited objects, but desirous to place on record, with a full sense of responsibility in doing so, my deliberate, long-considered judgment, (to pass, when I am gone, for what it may be worth,) that a spirit, patient, sympathetic, largely tolerant and comprehensive, is the only administrative spirit that can ever conduce to the real well being of a great ecclesiastical body, or contribute to make this vast Communion of ours what it ought to be as a true branch of the One Holy Catholic Church of God.

But to administer the system of the Church in a comprehensive and tolerant spirit is one thing; to change the system itself at the expense of truth and consistency for the sake of making the Church acceptable to a greater number without, or more acceptable to some within, that is a very different thing. For one that would be pleased, a hundred would be not only displeased, but deeply wounded and wronged. To contrive a policy with a view to include the greatest number, is not the first or highest duty of the Church. The Church is the divinely authorized teacher of truth in the world, and her great duty, her imperative duty, (I might add, her wisest policy,) is to teach fundamental, well-authenticated truth positively in clear definite outlines, as God has taught it in His Holy Word, and abundantly attested in its true meaning, as to vital points, through the witness of His Primitive Saints. The light of the Church becomes dim whenever her teaching becomes vague, whenever it is lowered or softened to suit the popular taste. The teaching of the Most High is explicit, positive, in sharp outline, because that is to deal mercifully with fallen, sinful men, by setting up clearly in the world His full, absolute, exclusive truth. But because the Almighty Lord hath revealed in most definite and positive terms the truth we are to receive and believe to the saving of our souls, and hath told us what are the consequence of wilful unbelief, it does not, therefore, necessarily follow, that every human soul within the bounds of Christendom, within the light of the Gospel, is certainly lost unless it rise up to the full comprehension and acceptance of the whole truth precisely as revealed. The Lord is a God of mercy, and of infinite wisdom. He is our Maker; He knoweth whereof we are made; He makes allowance for our weakness, our slowness of heart, and even for our invincible prejudices. It is for us to speak the whole truth clearly; it is for all men in a Christian country to seek to know the whole truth clearly, and to try to live by it; but the final judgment of men who come short of the full, clear truth, that blessed be God! is for Him, and not for us.

But you have already been detained too long, and I must turn away from the crowd of reflections which offer themselves to my notice. From all that has been said, if these prolix observations have conveyed to you any clear and consistent impression, you will have perceived that he who has the duty and responsibility of addressing you to-day, while humble under a sense of his own unworthiness; while sensible that we of this Diocese, and all our brethren elsewhere, need increase of prayer and increase of devotion to our blessed Master's work, yet at the same time shows that the contemplation of the history of the Church during the last twenty years; during the last forty years, here and in England; its work and its progress; the contemplation of its present state and of its future prospects, is attended on his part with feelings of exceeding comfort, of devout thankfulness, of cheerful, unshaken confidence.

I hope it is not the apathy of a saddened heart, but I am free to say that I look forward to the approaching Council of the Church with the extreme of serenity. She will, I humbly trust, do the few things needful to facilitate and invigorate her work, and then for the most part leave new inventions and projects and impossible demands altogether untouched. Our position and powers in the Church as individuals, Bishops, Clergy, Laity, are, in many respects, analogous to our position in the natural world. In some lines of effort we can do great things. In other lines of effort we are absolutely impotent and helpless, and perverse effort is simply suicidal. In the natural world we are surrounded by great natural laws and powers. If we conform to those laws, and make a legitimate and skillful use of those powers, man can achieve mighty things. If he goes contrary to those laws and powers, or attempts to change them, he loses his labor, and injures, perhaps destroys himself. When he came into this world he found himself provided with those laws and powers, and subjected to them. He did not invent or create them, and he cannot change them. It is for him to obey them and use them aright.

Such in great measure is our position in the Church. Her great Truths, received from her Lord, her order and constitution, her doctrines, her sacraments, her ministry, are things determined and settled by divine authority, attested in the witness of primitive Saints. We come into the world, into the Church, and find ourselves encompassed and blessed by these great laws and powers, these supports of spiritual life, these means of achieving great things for our own good and for the good of our fellow-men. What part, then, shall we choose to act? We may accept and use these great laws and powers; we may labor and teach with them, working out everlasting blessings; or we may fight against them to our own great loss and to the great loss of others; but we have no power to change them. They are written, where the writing cannot be altered or effaced. Not all our declarations, not all the definitions of partial and local Synods, however venerable and imposing, can make one hair white or black. That such is the case may well be our exceeding great comfort. Amid all the varying policies and winds of doctrine that keep up agitation in some quarters, hurrying people this way and that way, we have the unspeakable consolation of knowing that ours is a heritage of truth and peace, of which, if we are only faithful to it, not all the powers of the world can deprive us.

Considering the position of the Church as having on either side of her great schools of thought, differing very much from her tone and her principles, it ought not greatly to surprise us, that, while vast numbers are coming from them to us, a few, through partial reading or partial associations, through morbid discontents and antipathies, having come under the influence of exterior ideas, should sometimes go away from us to them. We may regret the loss to them and to ourselves; but it is one of those things which, to some extent, will be always occurring in the religious world.

Against the eccentricities of individuals special arrangements afford no security. Our truest way to increase of peace, to still increasing life and power in the work of the Lord, is in striving to rise more above the world, more above its narrow divisions, to draw nearer to our Lord in true love and devotion, to become more like Him in real sanctity of heart, and then through Him to draw nearer to our Brethren in genuine sympathy and self-abnegation, so that we may labor and pray with them, and lose ourselves amid the joys of united affection and heavenly Communion.

Dearly beloved Brethren: When the Divine Sufferer, the Man of Sorrows, was just passing under the dark cloud of His passion, He did not hide Himself from the world; and in that wonderful address to His Brethren, (14th St. John,) He did not seek to draw chief attention to His own sorrows, but He employed the latest hours in consoling and instructing them, and preparing them for coming events.

The poorest and humblest of His servants, unworthy to be in any way referred to in such a connection, desires yet to place himself under the shadow of that great example. Instead of seeking privacy to brood over private griefs and anxieties, he wishes to employ himself still in doing his duty, and in shedding around him such light and comfort as he may. And therefore he appears as usual in his place, and he closes all with a heartfelt benediction, "Peace be unto you," and with an Apostolic word of exhortation, "Rejoice in the Lord alway, and again I say rejoice. Let your moderation be known unto all men. The Lord is at hand. Be careful for nothing; but in everything, by prayer and supplication with thanksgiving, let your requests be made known unto God; and the peace of God, which passeth all understanding, shall keep your hearts and minds, through Christ Jesus!"

DETAILED ACCOUNT OF VISITATIONS AND ACTS.

THE following is an account of the places visited and the Episcopal Acts performed by me since the last Convention:

1873. *Sept.* 28, *Sixteenth Sunday after Trinity*, A. M.—I officiated in St. Timothy's Church, New-York, and preached, the Rector being ill.

Evening.—I took part in the services in Calvary Free Chapel.

Sept. 29, *Monday, St. Michael and All Angels*, A. M.— I celebrated the Holy Eucharist in "Keble Hall," New-York, on the opening of the School year.

P. M.—I attended a meeting of the Domestic Committee in reference to the death of Bishop Randall.

Oct. 5, *Seventeenth Sunday after Trinity*, A. M.—In the Chapel of St. Chrysostom, at a special ordination, the Right Rev. Dr. Tozer preaching, I advanced to the Priesthood the Rev. Algernon Sidney Crapsey, A. M.

P. M.—In the Cathedral Church of St. Peter and St. Paul, Chicago, the Rev. Samuel Moran, Deacon, was advanced to the Priesthood, at my request, by the Right Rev. the Bishop of Illinois.

Evening.—I took part in services in Calvary Chapel, New-York, the Right Rev. Dr. Tozer preaching.

Oct. 7, *Tuesday*, Evening.—In Grace Church, Nyack, I confirmed *ten*, and addressed them.

Oct. 8, *Wednesday*.—I attended and officiated at the funeral of Mr. George Merritt, in St. Barnabas' Church, Irvington.

Oct. 12, *Eighteenth Sunday after Trinity*, A. M.—In St. John's Church, Clarkstown, Rockland County, I preached, confirmed *four*, and addressed them.

P. M.—In St. Paul's Church, Spring Valley, I preached, confirmed *five*, and addressed them.

Oct. 13, *Monday*.—I presided at a meeting of the Standing Committee of the General Theological Seminary.

Oct. 14, *Tuesday*, A. M.—In St. John's Church, Yonkers, I met the Southern Convocation, celebrating the Holy Eucharist, and after the service presiding at a business meeting of the Convocation. The sermon was by the Right Rev. Dr. Tozer, late of the Central African Mission.

Evening.—In Christ Church, Riverdale, *eight* were confirmed by the Right Rev. Bishop Clark, of Rhode Island, at my request.

Oct. 16, *Thursday*, Evening.—In St. John's Church, Kingston, I presided at a service held on occasion of the meeting of the Western Convocation, and addressed the congregation, which was also addressed by the Rev. Dr. Haight, by several of the Clergy of the Western Convocation, and by the Right Rev. Dr. Tozer, late of Central Africa.

Oct. 17, *Friday*, A. M.—In the Church of the Messiah, Rhinebeck, the Right Rev. Dr. Tozer preaching, I admitted to the Diaconate Mr. Henry L. Ziegenfuss, late a Minister of the Lutheran Body.

Evening.—In St. John's Church, Kingston, I presided at a service largely attended by the Clergy, in which addresses were made in support of various branches of Church work.

Oct. 18, *Saturday, St. Luke's Day*, A. M.—In St. John's Church, Kingston, the Right Rev. Dr. Tozer preaching, I instituted the Rev. Walter Delafield into the Rectorship of said Church, and at the same time confirmed *three* persons.

Oct. 21, *Tuesday*, Evening.—I presided at a meeting of the Executive Committee of the New-York City Mission Society.

Oct. 22, *Wednesday*.—I presided at a meeting of the Foreign Committee.

Oct. 24, *Friday*.—I attended a meeting of the House of Bishops for the election of a Missionary Bishop, to succeed the lamented Bishop Randall, in the jurisdiction of Colorado, &c.

Oct. 26, *Twentieth Sunday after Trinity*, A. M.—In Christ Church, New-Brighton, Staten Island, at a special ordination, I preached, and advanced the Rev. Hamilton Lee to the Priesthood.

Oct. 27, *Monday*, Evening.—In Trinity Church, Mount Vernon, I preached, confirmed *nineteen*, and addressed them.

Oct. 28, *Tuesday*, A. M.—In St. Mark's Church, New-Castle, I baptized *two* adults and *one* child, preached, and confirmed *seven*, and addressed them. The work in this Parish has been much aided by Mr. Gardner, a Candidate for Holy Orders.

Oct. 29, *Wednesday*.—Was devoted to the Board of Missions.

Oct. 31, *Friday*. A. M.—I consecrated Calvary Free Chapel, New-York, the Rev. Dr. Washburn, the Rector of the Parent Parish, preaching.

Nov. 1, *All Saints, Saturday*, A. M.—In St. Ann's Church, New-York, I received a Probationer into the Sisterhood of the Good Shepherd, and celebrated the Holy Eucharist, and I confirmed in private a sick person connected with St. Barnabas' House.

Evening.—In All Saints' Church, New-York, I confirmed *twenty-two*, and addressed them.

Nov 2, *Sunday*, Evening.—In the Church of the Holy Communion, New-York, I presided at a service on occasion of the Anniversary of the New-York Bible and Common Prayer-Book Society. Sermon by the Rev. Dr. Potter, of Grace Church.

Nov. 4, *Tuesday*, Evening.—In St. Peter's Church, Portchester, I preached, confirmed *thirty-one*, and addressed them; the second confirmation within a year.

Nov. 6, *Thursday*, A. M.—I had the pleasure of consecrating the "Church of the Beloved Disciple," New-York. Sermon by the Rev. Dr. Dix. This beautiful Church has been erected at the sole cost of one Christian lady, Miss Caroline Tallman. It stands by the side of the Home for Indigent Christian Females, and is designed, among other uses, to serve as a Chapel for the inmates of that Institution.

Nov. 9, *Twenty-second Sunday after Trinity*, A. M.—I preached in St. Paul's Church, Poughkeepsie.

P. M.—In the Church of the Holy Trinity, Highland, Ulster County, I confirmed *ten*, and addressed them and the congregation.

Nov. 12, *Wednesday*, Evening.—I met the Board of Trustees of St. Stephen's College. Later in the evening I met the Trustees of the Society for Promoting Religion and Learning.

Nov. 13, *Thursday*, P. M.—I met the Trustees of the House of Mercy, New-York.

Nov. 14, *Friday*, P. M.—In the Church of the Transfiguration, New-York, at a special confirmation, I confirmed *one* person.

Nov. 16, *Twenty-third Sunday after Trinity*, A. M.—In St. Mary's Church, Manhattanville, New-York, I preached, confirmed *ten*, addressed them, and celebrated the Holy Eucharist.

P. M.—I presided at the anniversary of St. Luke's Hospital, New-York, and made a few remarks.

Nov. 18, *Tuesday*, A. M.—In the Church of Divine Love, Montrose, I confirmed *two*, and addressed them.

P. M.—In St. Augustine's Church, Cortlandt, (Croton,) I confirmed *six*, and addressed them.

Evening.—I presided at a meeting of the Executive Committee of the City Mission Society, New-York.

Nov. 20, *Thursday*.—I presided at the first anniversary of the Home for Old Men and Aged Couples, New-York, and found much cause for thankfulness in the work done in the first year.

Nov. 23, *Sunday before Advent*, A. M.—In Calvary Free Chapel, New-York, at a special ordination, the Rev. Dr. Seymour preaching, I advanced the Rev. Charles Fobes Canedy, A. B., to the Priesthood.

Nov. 29, *Saturday*, A. M.—In St. Peter's Church, Peekskill, I instituted the Rev. William Fisher Lewis into the Rectorship of said Church, and preached.

Nov. 30, *St. Andrew's Day, and First Sunday in Advent*, A. M.—I officiated at the opening of St. Andrew's Church, Harlem, preaching and celebrating the Holy Eucharist, assisted by the Rector. This is a noble edifice.

Dec. 2, *Tuesday*.—In Christ Church, Suffern, I confirmed *nine*, and addressed them.

Dec. 7, *Second Sunday in Advent*, Evening.—I preached in the temporary Church of the Holy Trinity, New-York.

Dec. 14, *Third Sunday in Advent*, Evening.—I presided at the anniversary service for the House of Mercy in Trinity Chapel, New-York. Report read by the Chaplain, the Rev. Dr. Seymour, and the sermon by the Rev. Dr. Dix.

Dec. 15, *Monday*, Evening.—I presided at a meeting of the Domestic Committee, New-York.

Dec. 16, *Tuesday*, Evening.—I presided at a meeting of the Executive Committee of the City Mission Society, New-York.

Dec. 18, *Thursday.*—I opened the new Church of St. Paul, Spring Valley, Rockland County, and preached, and celebrated the Holy Eucharist.

Dec. 21, *St. Thomas' Day, Fourth Sunday in Advent*, A. M.—This being the first anniversary of the consecration of St. Thomas' Chapel, New-York, I preached in the Chapel.

Dec. 22, *Monday.*—I attended a meeting of the Trustees of Columbia College, New-York.

Dec. 23, *Tuesday*, Evening.—I presided at a meeting of the Foreign Committee.

Dec. 28, *Sunday after Christmas*, A. M.—I attended in St. Thomas' Church, New-York, the semi-centennial of the Parish, and took part in the services; the sermon by the Bishop of New-Jersey.

1874. *Jan.* 13, *Tuesday.*—I received the Southern Convocation for business and for dinner, addressing them at the business meeting on some aspects of the Church at the present time.

Jan. 18, *Second Sunday after the Epiphany*, Evening.—In the Church of the Reformation, New-York, I preached, confirmed *seventeen*, and addressed them.

Jan. 19, *Monday*, Evening.—Met the Domestic Committee.

Jan. 25, *Third Sunday after the Epiphany, Conversion of St. Paul*, P. M. —In the Floating Chapel of our Saviour, New-York, I confirmed *twenty-nine*, and addressed them.

Feb. 8, *Monday.*—Presided at a meeting of the Standing Committee of the General Theological Seminary.

Feb. 15, *Quinquagesima Sunday*, P. M.—In the Anthon Memorial Church, New York, at a service chiefly for the young, after sermon by the Rector, I addressed the congregation and children.

Evening.—In Trinity Chapel, New-York, I presided at a service in the interest of the House of the Good Shepherd. Sermon by the Rev. Mr. Galleher, Rector of Zion Church.

Feb. 18, *Ash-Wednesday*, A. M.—I preached in the Church of the Transfiguration, New-York.

Evening.—I preached in the Church of the Heavenly Rest, New-York.

March 1, *Second Sunday in Lent*, A. M.—In Grace Church, New-York, I advanced the Rev. William Kirkus, A. M., LL. B., to the Priesthood. Sermon by the Rev. Dr. Rylance, of St. Mark's Church, New-York.

Evening.—In the Mission Chapel of the Rev. Mr. McCaffrey, (for the Holy Trinity Church,) I preached, confirmed *twelve*, and addressed them.

March 3, *Tuesday.*—I received the Committee on the Cathedral for this Diocese.

March 8, *Third Sunday in Lent*, A. M.—In St. Clement's Church, New-York, I preached, confirmed *twenty-seven*, and addressed them. This Church has been restored and much improved.

Evening.—In the Church of the Annunciation, New-York, I confirmed *twelve*, and addressed them.

March 10, *Tuesday*, P. M.—I attended a meeting of the Trustees of the House of Mercy, New-York.

Evening.—I presided at a joint meeting of the Domestic and Foreign Missionary Committees, and afterwards of the Trustees of Seamen's Mission.

March 11, *Wednesday*, P. M.—At the Church Hospital, (St. Barnabas',) Poughkeepsie, I confirmed *two* sick persons.

March 12, *Thursday*, A. M.—In the Church of the Holy Comforter, Poughkeepsie, I preached, and admitted to the Diaconate William Charles Grubbe; and, afterwards, in the same place, presided at a meeting of Dutchess County Convocation.

March 13, *Friday*, P. M.—In St. George's Church, Newburgh, I confirmed *twenty nine*, and addressed them.

March 15, *Fourth Sunday in Lent*, A. M.—In the Church of St. John Baptist, New-York, I preached, confirmed *twenty-six*, and addressed them, (*eight* of them from the Orphan's Home.)

Evening.—In the Church of the Redeemer, New-York, I confirmed *thirty-three*, and addressed them.

March 17, *Tuesday*, Evening.—In Trinity Church, Mount Vernon, I preached, confirmed *nineteen*, and addressed them.

March 22, *Fifth Sunday in Lent*, A. M.—In the Church of the Holy Apostles, New-York, I preached, confirmed *twenty*, and addressed them.

P. M.—In the Church of the Heavenly Rest, New-York, I confirmed *thirteen*, and addressed them.

Evening.—In St. Peter's Church, New-York, I confirmed *thirty-four*, and addressed them.

March 23, *Monday*, Evening.—In St. George's Mission Chapel, New-York, ("Bread of Life,") I confirmed *thirteen*, and addressed them, and at my request they were addressed by the Rev. Dr. Tyng.

March 24, *Tuesday*, Evening.—In St. George's German Mission Chapel, New-York, I confirmed *fifty-five*, and addressed them. They were also addressed by the Rev. Dr. Tyng and the Rev. Mr. Fleischhacker, the Minister of the Chapel.

March 25, *Wednesday*, *Feast of the Annunciation*, P. M.—In the Church of the Transfiguration, New-York, at a special confirmation, I confirmed *twelve*.

Evening.—In Grace Church Chapel, New-York, I confirmed *twenty nine*, and addressed them.

March 26, *Thursday*, Evening.—In St. George's English Mission Chapel, I confirmed *thirty-seven*, and addressed them; and they were also addressed by the Rev. Dr. Tyng.

March 27, *Friday*, P. M.—In St. Peter's Church, Peekskill, I preached, confirmed *fifteen*, and addressed them.

March 29, *Sunday before Easter*, A. M.—In St. Thomas' Church, New-York, I confirmed *fifty-four*, and addressed them, the Rector preaching.

P. M.—In Calvary Church, New-York, I confirmed *fourteen*, and briefly addressed them.

Evening.—In the Anthon Memorial Church, New-York, I confirmed *twenty-six*, and addressed them.

March 30, *Monday before Easter*, P. M.—In Trinity Church, Sing Sing, I confirmed *thirty-six*, and addressed them.

Evening.—In St. Paul's Church, Sing Sing, I confirmed *eleven*, and addressed them.

March 31, *Tuesday*, A. M.—In Grace Church, New-York, I confirmed *seventeen*, and addressed them.

P. M.—In St. Paul's Church, Eastchester, I confirmed *twelve*, and addressed them.

Evening.—In St. Luke's Church, New-York, I confirmed *fifty-eight*, and addressed them.

April 1, *Wednesday*, A. M.—In the Church of St. Bartholomew, New-York, I confirmed *twenty-six*, and addressed them.

Evening.—In St. Timothy's Church, New-York, I preached, confirmed *thirty-three*, (*one* being from St. James' Church, Goshen,) and addressed them.

April 2, *Thursday*, A. M.—In the Church of the Ascension, New-York, I confirmed *thirty-six*, and addressed them.

P. M.—In the Church of the Atonement, New-York, I confirmed *twenty*, and briefly addressed them, and celebrated the Holy Eucharist, assisted by the Rector.

Evening.—In St. Paul's Chapel, New-York, I briefly addressed the Candidates, and confirmed *fifty-nine*.

April 3, *Good Friday*, A. M.—In St. George's Church, New-York, I confirmed *thirty-two*, and addressed them, the Rev. Dr. Tyng kindly preaching at my desire.

P. M.—In St. John's Church, Clifton, Staten Island, I confirmed *twenty-five*, and addressed them.

Evening.—In the Church of the Holy Trinity, New-York, I confirmed *forty-nine*, and addressed them, and at my request they were addressed by the Rev. Dr. Tyng, Sen.

April 4, *Easter Even*, A. M.—In the Church of the Holy Communion, New-York, I confirmed *fifty-four*, (*one* of them from St. Ann's Church,) and addressed them.

P. M.—In Trinity Church, New-York, I confirmed *fifty-two*, and addressed them.

Evening.—In St. John's Church, Yonkers, I confirmed *forty-two*, and addressed them.

April 5, *Easter Sunday*, A. M.—In the Church of the Holy Saviour, New-York, I confirmed *fifteen*, and addressed them and the congregation, and celebrated the Holy Eucharist, assisted by the Rector.

P. M.—In the Church of the Holy Trinity, Harlem, I confirmed *twenty-six*, and addressed them.

Evening.—In the Church of St. John the Evangelist, New-York, I confirmed *fifty-five*, and addressed them.

April 6, *Easter Monday*, Evening.—In the Church of the Intercession, New-York, I confirmed *fourteen*, and addressed them.

April 7, *Easter Tuesday*, Evening.—In St. Mary's Church, Mott Haven, I preached, confirmed *sixteen*, and addressed them.

April 8, *Wednesday*, Evening.—In the Church of St. Ignatius, New-York, I preached, confirmed *twenty-five*, and briefly addressed them.

April 9, *Thursday*, A. M.—In the Church of the Annunciation, New-York, I took part in the services at the funeral of that good and faithful man, Floyd Smith, long a member of the Standing Committee of the Diocese, and a devoted servant of the Church in many ways.

April 10, *Friday*, Evening.—In the Chapel of the Shepherd's Flock, New-York, I confirmed *thirty-three*, and addressed them and the congregation.

April 12, *Sunday after Easter*, A. M.—In St. John's Chapel, New-York, I confirmed *ninety-eight*, and addressed them.

P. M.—In St. Alban's Church, New-York, I confirmed *eleven*, and addressed them.

Evening.—In Trinity Chapel, New-York, I confirmed *forty-two*, (*one* of them from the Church of the Transfiguration,) and addressed them.

April 13, *Monday*, P. M.—I presided at a meeting of the Standing Committee of the General Theological Seminary.

Evening.—In St. Philip's Church, New-York, I confirmed *sixty-one*, and addressed them.

April 14, *Tuesday*, A. M.—In St. Barnabas' Chapel, New-York, I held an anniversary service for the Sisterhood of the Good Shepherd, this being the fifth anniversary of their institution by me. I made a short address and celebrated the Holy Eucharist.

P. M.—I presided at a meeting of the Trustees of the House of Mercy.

April 15, *Wednesday*, Evening.—In St. Chrysostom's Chapel, (of Trinity Parish,) New-York, I confirmed *fifty-two*, and addressed them.

April 16, *Thursday*, Evening.—In the Church of St. Ambrose, New-York, I confirmed *thirty-three*, and addressed them; also, in two separate private confirmations, I confirmed *two* sick persons; making in all *thirty-five*.

April 17, *Friday*, Evening.—In St. Mary's Church, Cold Spring, I confirmed *sixteen*, and addressed them.

April 19, *Second Sunday after Easter*, A. M.—In Christ Church, Poughkeepsie, I preached, confirmed *thirty-two*, and addressed them.

P. M.—In St. Paul's Church, Poughkeepsie, I preached, confirmed *ten*, and addressed them.

Evening.—In the Church of the Holy Comforter, Poughkeepsie, I confirmed *thirty-eight*, and addressed them.

April 20, *Monday*, A. M.—In St. Paul's Church, Poughkeepsie, at a special ordination, I preached, and advanced the Rev. Henry L. Ziegenfuss to the Priesthood, and celebrated the Holy Eucharist, assisted by the Rector.

April 21, *Tuesday*, Evening.—In Zion Church, Wappinger's Falls, I preached, confirmed *sixteen*, and addressed them.

April 22, *Wednesday*, P. M.—In St. Luke's Church, Matteawan, I preached, confirmed *eleven*, and addressed them.

Evening.—In the Church of St. John Baptist, Glenham, I preached, and confirmed *fifteen*.

April 23, *Thursday*, Evening.—In St. Thomas' Mission Chapel, New-York, I preached, confirmed *twenty-nine*, and addressed them.

April 24, *Friday*, Evening.—In St. Augustine's Chapel, (of Trinity Parish,) New-York, I confirmed *twenty-six*, and addressed them.

April 26, *Third Sunday after Easter*, A. M.—In Christ Church, New-York, I preached, confirmed *twenty*, and briefly addressed them.

P. M.—In St. Ann's Church, New-York, I spoke to the children, confirmed *forty-seven* persons, (*one* of them from the Church of St. John the Evangelist,) and addressed them.

Later in the P. M.—In the Church of the Holy Sepulchre, New-York, I confirmed *eight*, and addressed them.

Evening.—In Calvary Free Chapel, New-York, I confirmed *thirty-nine*, and addressed them.

April 27, *Monday*, P. M.—I met a number of Clergymen on Church business.

Evening.—In Grace Church, White Plains, I preached, confirmed *nineteen*, and addressed them.

April 28, *Tuesday*, A. M.—In Christ Church, Paterson, I met the Southern Convocation, the Rev. Dr. Wyatt, Dean, preaching, and at the close of the Holy Communion I briefly addressed the Clergy and congregation.

Evening.—At the Mission at Brewster's Station, I preached.

May 3, *Fourth Sunday after Easter*, A. M.—In St. James' Church, New-York, I preached, and admitted Elijah Winchester Donald to the Diaconate, also confirmed *forty-four*, (*three* of them from the St. Thomas' Mission Chapel,) and addressed them.

P. M.—In St. Mark's Church, New-York, I confirmed *ninety-two*, (*fifty-eight* of them from St. Mark's Mission Chapel,) and addressed them.

Evening.—In Zion Church, New-York, I confirmed *thirteen*, and addressed them.

May 4, *Monday*, Evening.—In the Church of the Resurrection, New-York, I preached, confirmed *seventeen*, and addressed them.

May 6, *Wednesday*, Evening.—In St. Barnabas' Chapel, New-York, I confirmed *twenty-five*, and addressed them. A very interesting work is done in St. Barnabas' House and Chapel, and the only regret is that both of them are not far more ample in their accommodations.

May 8, *Friday*, Evening.—In Bethlehem Mission Chapel, New-York, I confirmed *seventeen*, and addressed them. This is an interesting and useful German Mission.

May 10, *Fifth Sunday after Easter*, A. M.—In the Church of the Transfiguration, New-York, I confirmed *twenty-eight*, (*one* of them from St. Mary the Virgin, and *two* of them from St. Chrysostom's Church,) and addressed them.

Also in the A. M.—I officiated at a funeral in Trinity Chapel, New-York.

P. M.—In Grace Church, Harlem, I preached, confirmed *fifteen*, (*one* of them from the Church of the Resurrection, New-York, and addressed them.

Evening.—In St. Andrew's Church, Harlem, I confirmed *twenty-five*, and addressed them.

May 12, *Tuesday*, Evening.—In the Church of the Ascension, West Brighton, Staten Island, I confirmed *twenty-five*, and addressed them.

May 14, *Thursday, Ascension Day*, Evening.—In the Church of the Incarnation, New-York, I confirmed *twenty*, and addressed them.

May 15, *Friday*, A. M.—In St. Luke's Church, New-York, officiated at the funeral of the wife of the Rector.

May 16, *Saturday*, A. M.—In Christ Church, Pelham, I preached, confirmed *seven*, and addressed them.

P. M.—In the Chapel in Pelhamville, I confirmed *seven*, (*one* of them in private,) and addressed them.

May 17, *Sunday after Ascension*, A. M.—In Christ Church, Rye, I preached, confirmed *sixteen*, (*one* of them in private,) and addressed them.

P. M.—In St. Thomas' Church, Mamaroneck, I confirmed *eight*, and addressed them.

Evening.—In Trinity Church, New-Rochelle, I preached, confirmed *sixteen*, and addressed them.

May 20, *Wednesday*, Evening.—In St. Paul's Church, Edgewater, Staten Island, I confirmed *twenty*, and addressed them.

May 21, *Thursday*, Evening.—In the Church of the Epiphany, New-York, I confirmed *seventeen*, and addressed them.

May 24, *Whitsun-Day*, A. M.—In St. James' Church, Goshen, I preached, confirmed *twenty*, addressed them, and celebrated the Holy Eucharist, assisted by the Rector.

Evening.—In Grace Church, Middletown, I preached, confirmed *sixty-five*, and addressed them.

May 25, *Monday*, Evening.—In Grace Church, Port Jervis, I preached, confirmed *eleven*, and addressed them. This Parish, through the zeal and devotion of the Rector, aided by many friends, has erected a beautiful and commodious Church edifice.

May 26, *Tuesday*, P. M.—In St. John's Church, Greenwood, I confirmed *ten*, and addressed them.

May 27, *Wednesday*, P. M.—I visited the Sheltering Arms at their annual festival, and made a brief address to some of the children.

Evening.—In All Saints' Church, New-York, it being the semi-centennial jubilee of the Parish, I confirmed *thirty-seven*, (*eight* of them being from Madison-street Chapel,) and addressed them.

May 29, *Friday*, A. M.—In the Chapel of St. Mary Magdalen of the House of Mercy, New-York, at a special ordination, the Rev. Dr. Seymour preaching, I advanced the Rev. Joseph Horsfall Johnson and the Rev. Henry Martyn Torbert to the Priesthood.

Evening.—In the Church of St. Mary the Virgin, I confirmed *sixteen*, and addressed them.

May 30, *Saturday*, Evening.—In the Church of the Holy Trinity, New-York, at a special and second confirmation, I confirmed *nine*, and briefly addressed them.

May 31, *Trinity Sunday*, A. M.—In the Church of the Holy Communion, New York, the Rev. Dr. Lawrence preaching, I advanced the Rev. Henry Mottet and the Rev. Brady Electus Backus to the Priesthood.

2½ P. M.—In St. Philip's Church, New-York, I officiated at the funeral of the Rector, the Rev. Wm. J. Alston, whose death is a sad loss to his flock and to the Church at large. I addressed the congregation, as did the Rev. Dr. Potter, of Grace Church, at my request.

4 P. M.—In the Church of the Nativity, New-York, I preached, confirmed *twenty-three*, and addressed them.

June 2, *Tuesday*, Evening.—In Trinity Chapel, New-York, I solemnized a marriage, assisted by the Rev. Dr. Tyng, Jr.

June 3, *Wednesday*, A. M.—I solemnized a marriage.

Evening.—I presided at a meeting of the Society for Promoting Religion and Learning.

June 4, *Thursday*.—I solemnized a marriage.

Evening.—In the Chapel on Governor's Island, I confirmed *four*, and addressed them.

June 5, *Friday*, Evening.—In Christ Church, Tarrytown, I confirmed *nine*, and addressed them.

June 7, *First Sunday after Trinity*, A. M.—In St. Ann's Church, Morrisania, I preached, confirmed *eleven*, and addressed them.

P. M.—In Trinity Church, Morrisania, I confirmed *nineteen*, and addressed them.

June 10, *Wednesday*, Evening.—In St. Paul's Church, Newburgh, I confirmed *fourteen*, and addressed them.

June 12, *Friday*, Evening.—In St. Mark's Church, Tarrytown, I confirmed *eleven*, and addressed them.

June 14, *Second Sunday after Trinity*, A. M.—In St. James' Church, Fordham, I confirmed *twenty one*, (*two* of them from the Home for Incurables,) and addressed them, and also celebrated the Holy Eucharist, assisted by the Rector.

Evening.—In St. Peter's Church, Westchester, I preached, confirmed *sixteen*, and addressed them.

June 15, *Monday*, Evening.—In St. Paul's Church, Morrisania, I confirmed *eight*, and addressed them.

June 16, *Tuesday*, P. M.—In the Church of the Holy Innocents, Cornwall, I confirmed *ten*, and addressed them.

June 17, *Wednesday*, A. M.—I attended a meeting of the Trustees of St. Stephen's College, Annandale.

Evening.—In the Chapel of St. Stephen's College, Annandale, I confirmed *seven*, and addressed them.

June 18, *Thursday*, A. M.—I attended the Commencement of St. Stephen's College, Annandale.

Evening.—In St. John's Church, Kingston, I confirmed *eight*, and addressed them.

June 19, *Friday*, A. M.—In the Chapel at Stone Ridge, I confirmed *four*, and addressed them, and celebrated the Holy Eucharist.

P. M.—In the Church of the Holy Spirit, Rondout, I confirmed *thirteen*, and addressed them.

June 20, *Saturday*, A. M.—I visited the School at Keble Hall, at the close of the year, delivering the premiums, and making a brief address. The School is in a very satisfactory condition.

On the same A. M.—I attended the closing services of St. Mary's School, making a brief address in the Chapel, and afterwards in the School-room delivering the prizes and making a short address.

June 21, *Third Sunday after Trinity*, A. M.—In St. Michael's Church, New-York, I confirmed *thirty-nine*, and addressed them, and celebrated the Holy Eucharist, assisted by the Rector.

June 23, *Tuesday*.—I attended a special meeting of the Board of Trustees of the General Theological Seminary.

June 24, *Wednesday*, A. M.—In St. Ann's Church, New-York, at a re-union of the Alumni of the General Theological Seminary, I celebrated the Holy Eucharist, assisted by the Rector. Afterwards I presided at a breakfast of the Alumni.

M.—I attended the Commencement of Columbia College.

June 25, *Thursday*.—I attended the annual meeting of the Trustees of the General Theological Seminary.

June 26, *Friday*, A. M.—I attended the Commencement of the General Theological Seminary, and celebrated the Holy Eucharist. The sermon by the Bishop of North Carolina.

June 28, *Fourth Sunday after Trinity*, A. M.—In the Church of the Transfiguration, New-York, the Rev. Francis Harison, Rector of St. Paul's Church, Troy, preaching, I admitted to the Diaconate Walter Russell Gardner, A. B., George William Douglas, A. B., Edward Bayard Smith, A. B., Obadiah Valentine, A. B., Edward H. Van Winkle, A. M., John Clough Tebbets, Jr., A. B., Richard Miles Hayden, A. B., Zina Doty, LL. B., John Lightner Egbert, John William Paige, A. B., William Allen Fair, A. B., Robert George Hamilton, and Robert Ritchie, by request of the Ecclesiastical Authority of Wisconsin. At the time I advanced to the Priesthood the Rev. George Alexander Chambers.

P. M.—I administered the Holy Communion to a sick person in private.

Evening.—In the Church of the Beloved Disciple, New-York, I confirmed *twelve*, (*three* of them from St. Luke's Church, New-York,) and addressed them.

June 29, *Monday*, Evening.—In the Church of the Reconciliation, Mission Chapel of the Church of the Incarnation, New-York, I confirmed *fifteen*, (*one* of them from the Church of the Incarnation,) and addressed them.

June 30, *Tuesday*, A. M.—In the Church of St. James the Less, Scarsdale, I preached, instituted the Rev. William A. Holbrook as Rector, confirmed *ten*, and addressed them.

P. M.—In St. John's Church, Wilmot, I confirmed *six*, and addressed them. This Church has been much improved.

Evening.—In St. John's Church, Tuckahoe, I confirmed *fifteen*, and addressed them.

July 5, *Fifth Sunday after Trinity*, A. M.—In St. Paul's Church, Yonkers, the Right Reverend Bishop Tozer, late of the Central African Mission, kindly acting at my request, preached, and advanced the Rev. Arthur Sloan, the Assistant Minister of the Parish, to the Priesthood, and also confirmed *thirty-seven*, and addressed them.

P. M.—In Zion Church, Greenburgh, the Right Rev. Dr. Tozer, at my request, confirmed *ten*, and addressed them.

Evening.—In St. Barnabas' Church, Irvington, he preached, and confirmed *six*.

July 8, *Wednesday*, P. M.—At the Chapel of the House of Mercy, New-York, the Chaplain, the Rev. Dr. Seymour, having administered the Holy Baptism to *six* persons, I confirmed *seven*, (*six* inmates, and *one* person from without, a near relative of one of the Sisters,) and addressed them.

July 12, *Sixth Sunday after Trinity*, A. M.—In St. Andrew's Church, Richmond, the Right Reverend the Bishop of Florida, at my request, preached, and confirmed *seventeen*.

P. M.—In the Church of the Holy Comforter, Southfield, he preached, and confirmed *fourteen*.

July 14, *Tuesday*, A. M.—I consecrated the Church of the Holy Trinity, Highland, Ulster County, preaching and celebrating the Holy Eucharist.

July 24, *Friday*, Evening.—In St. Peter's Church, Portchester, the Right Rev. Bishop Tozer, at my request, preached, and confirmed *thirty-two*.

July 28, *Tuesday*, Evening.—At Chapel, the Right Rev. Dr. Tozer, at my request, confirmed *six*.

August 14, *Friday*, Evening.—In Christ Church, Warwick, I preached, confirmed *eleven*, and addressed them.

Aug. 16, *Eleventh Sunday after Trinity*, A. M.—In St. John's Church, Monticello, I preached, confirmed *twelve*, and addressed them.

Evening.—In the same Church, I preached.

Aug. 17, *Monday*, I confirmed a sick person in private, connected with St. John's Church.

Aug. 18, *Tuesday*, A. M.—In Ellenville, Ulster County, I consecrated the new and beautiful edifice, St. John's Memorial Church, erected at the sole cost of Mr. E. C. Humbert, of Brooklyn, Long Island. Sermon by the Rev. Mr. Homer, of Brooklyn.

Evening.—In the same Church, after a sermon by the Rev. Professor Seymour, I confirmed *thirteen*, and addressed them and the congregation.

Aug. 20, *Thursday*, A. M.—In the Church of the Transfiguration, New-York, I received *two* Probationers into the Sisterhood of St. Mary, and celebrated the Holy Eucharist.

Aug. 30, *Thirteenth Sunday after Trinity*, A. M.—In Christ Church, Red Hook, I preached, confirmed *nine*, and addressed them.

Sept. 6, *Fourteenth Sunday after Trinity*, A. M.—I preached in the Church of the Transfiguration, New-York.

Sept. 15, *Tuesday*, P. M.—In the Church of the Divine Love, Crugers, I confirmed *seven*, and addressed them.

Sept. 20, *Seventeenth Sunday after Trinity*, Evening.—In the Mission Chapel of the Church of the Atonement, New-York, I preached, confirmed *eighteen*, and addressed them.

CANDIDATES FOR HOLY ORDERS.

The following is a complete List of the Candidates for Holy Orders in this Diocese, with the dates of their admission respectively; being in all, 29.

I.—CANDIDATES FOR DEACON'S AND PRIEST'S ORDERS.

Dan Marvin, A. M., December 6, 1866.
Charles Sumner Moor Stewart, December 2, 1869.
George B. Johnson, A. B., June 1, 1871.
William Henry Conover, A. B., August 3, 1871.
Henry Stoughton Tracy, A. B., { C. D. O., September 27, 1871. C. P. O., November 2, 1871. }
Alfred Evan Johnson, A. B., November 2, 1871.
Floyd William Tompkins, A. B., September 5, 1872.
Henry D. Jardine, October 3, 1872.
Edgar Snyder, A. B., December 5, 1872.
Amos Turner Ashton, A. B., March 6, 1873.
Charles Lancaster Short, A. B., April 3, 1873.
John Sword, August 4, 1873.
John Punnett Peters, A. B., September 4, 1873.
Clarence E. Woodman, A. B., September 16, 1873.
Henry Van Rensselaer, September 18, 1873.
G. Arnolt Carstensen, A. B., September 18, 1873.
William H. Tomlins, A. B., September 18, 1873.
Frederick H. T. Horsfield, A. B., October 2, 1873.
George Love, A. M., October 2, 1873.
William Oliver Embury, November 6, 1873.
Oliver Perry Vinton, A. B., November 6, 1873.
George F. Behringer, A. B., December 4, 1873.
Henry Townsend Scudder, A. B., June 4, 1874.
George H. Wilson, A. B., September 30, 1874.
Victor C. Smith, A. B., September 30, 1874.—24.

II.—CANDIDATES FOR DEACON'S ORDERS.

Not having passed any Literary Examination:

John Pickavant Crawford, November 5, 1868.
Henry Homer Washburn, June 5, 1873.
Gilbert B. Hendrickson, October 2, 1873.
Benjamin Haight, May 7, 1874.
Charles Tileston Whittemore, September 30, 1874.—5.

CANDIDATES FOR HOLY ORDERS ORDAINED DEACONS.

I. The Candidates for Deacon's and Priest's Orders, named below, have passed the examination required by Canon VIII., Section 3, and Section 7, Title I., of the Digest of the Canons of the General Convention, and have been ordained to the Diaconate:

1873.	October	17.	Henry L. Ziegenfuss, A. M.
1874.	March	12.	William Charles Grubbe.
"	May	3.	Elijah Winchester Donald, A. B.
"	June	28.	Zina Doty, LL. B.
"	"	"	Obadiah Valentine, A. B.
"	"	"	George William Douglas, A. B.
"	"	"	Edward H. Van Winkle, A. M.
"	"	"	Walter Russell Gardner, A. B.
"	"	"	Richard Miles Hayden, A. B.
"	"	"	John Lightner Egbert.
"	"	"	Edward Bayard Smith, A. B.
"	"	"	John Clough Tebbets, Jr., A. B.
"	"	"	William Allen Fair, A. B.

I. Also, by request of the Ecclesiastical Authority of the Diocese of Wisconsin, Robert Ritchie, A. B.

II. The Candidates named below have not passed the three examinations required for Priest's Orders, and have been admitted to the restricted Diaconate:

1874.	June	28.	Robert George Hamilton.
"	"	"	Julius W. Paige.—16.

DEACONS ADVANCED TO THE PRIESTHOOD.

The Deacons named below have been ordained to the Holy Order of Priests:

1873.	October	5.	The Rev. Algernon Sidney Crapsey.
"	"	26.	The Rev. Hamilton Lee.
"	November	23.	The Rev. Charles Fobes Canedy.
1874.	March	1.	The Rev. William Kirkus.
"	April	20.	The Rev. Henry L. Ziegenfuss.
"	May	29.	The Rev. Joseph Horsfall Johnson.
"	"	"	The Rev. Henry Martyn Torbert.
"	"	31.	The Rev. Henry Mottet.
"	"	"	The Rev. Brady Electus Backus.
"	June	28.	The Rev. George Alexander Chambers.
"	July	5.	The Rev. Arthur Sloan, by the Right Rev. Bishop Tozer, at my request.—11.

RESIGNATION OF PARISHES.

I have received Notice of the Resignation, by the Clergymen named below, of the Parishes or Cures respectively mentioned:

The Rev. C. W. Camp, as an Assistant Minister of Christ Church, New-York.

The Rev. Henry E. Duncan, D. D., of the Rectorship of St. Luke's Church, Matteawan.

The Rev. William V. Feltwell, of the Rectorship of Grace Church, West Farms.

The Rev. Charles A. Foster, Deacon, of the Professorship of History and of the English Language and Literature in St. Stephen's College.

The Rev. Francis Harison, of the Rectorship of St. Peter's Church, Peekskill.

The Rev. Charles Frederick Hoffman, of the Rectorship of St. Philip's Church in the Highlands, Philipsetown.

The Rev. George Howell, of the Rectorship of Grace Church, City Island.

The Rev. Levi Johnston, of the Rectorship of St. Andrew's Church, Walden.

The Rev. Charles S. Knapp, of the Rectorship of St. Mary's Church, Mott Haven.

The Rev. David Macurdy, of the Rectorship of St. John's Church, Canterbury.

The Rev. Richard U. Morgan, D. D., of the Rectorship of Trinity Church, New-Rochelle.

The Rev. Frank L. Norton, as an Assistant Minister of St. Thomas' Church, New-York.

The Rev. William W. Olssen, of the Professorship of Mathematics and Natural Philosophy in St. Stephen's College.

The Rev. Charles Carroll Parsons, of the Rectorship of St. Mary's Church in the Highlands, Cold Spring, Putnam County.

The Rev. J. Rambo, of the Rectorship of the Church of the Epiphany, New-York.

The Rev. William T. Sabine, of the Rectorship of the Church of the Atonement, Madison Avenue, New-York.

The Rev. John I. Roberts, as an Assistant Minister of St. Thomas' Church, New-York.

The Rev. Dudley D. Smith, as an Assistant Minister of the Church of the Holy Trinity, New-York.

The Rev. James W. Sparks, of the Rectorship of All Saints' Church, Milton.

The Rev. Alvah Wiswall, as Deacon in Trinity Parish, New-York.

The Rev. John F. Potter, of the Rectorship of St. John's Church, Greenwood Iron Works.—21.

CLERGYMEN APPOINTED TO CURES.

In behalf of the Clergymen named below, I have received the Canonical Certificate of the election or appointment to the Cures or offices respectively mentioned. In each case I have certified that the person so chosen is a qualified Minister of this Church, and transmitted the certificate to the Secretary of the Convention for record by him, according to the requirements of the Canon.

The Rev. Frederick M. Gray, to the Rectorship of the Church of the Holy Comforter, Eltingville.

The Rev. Edward H. Kettell, as an Assistant Minister of the Church of the Holy Trinity, New-York.

The Rev. Albert Z. Gray, to the Rectorship of St. Philip's Church in the Highlands, Philipsetown.

The Rev. William Fisher Lewis, to the Rectorship of St. Peter's Church, Peekskill.

The Rev. William W. Olssen, to the Professorship of the Greek Language and Literature, and of the Hebrew Language, in St. Stephen's College, Annandale.

The Rev. James Mulchahey, D. D., as an Assistant Minister of Trinity Church, New-York.

The Rev. Hamilton Lee, as Assistant Minister of Christ Church, New-Brighton.

The Rev. Benjamin I. Haight, D. D., LL. D., as Assistant to the Rector of Trinity Church, New-York.

The Rev. William Kirkus, as an Assistant Minister of Grace Church, New-York.

The Rev. Robert Scott, to the Rectorship of Grace Church, West Farms.

The Rev. William Augustus Holbrook, to the Rectorship of the Church of St. James the Less, Scarsdale.

The Rev. William E. Snowden, to the Rectorship of St. Andrew's Church, Walden.

The Rev. Lewis L. Noble, to the Professorship of History, and of the English Language and Literature in St. Stephen's College, Annandale.

The Rev. Charles C. Tiffany, to the Rectorship of the Church of the Atonement, Madison Avenue, New-York.

The Rev. Charles B. Coffin, to the Rectorship of Trinity Church, Haverstraw.

The Rev. Walter R. Gardner, to the Rectorship of St. Thomas' Church, Amenia.

The Rev. James W. Sparks, to the Rectorship of St. Mark's Church, New-Castle.

The Rev. Isaac Van Winkle, to the Rectorship of St. Mary's Church in the Highlands, Cold Spring, Putnam County.

The Rev. Algernon S. Crapsey, as an Assistant Minister of Trinity Church, New-York.

The Rev. Leon Pons, as Officiating Minister of the French Church du St. Esprit, New-York.

The Rev. Henry N. Wayne, as an Officiating Minister in Trinity Parish, New-York.

The Rev. Thomas McKee Brown, as Minister of the Free Church of St. Mary the Virgin, New-York.

The Rev. John F. Potter, to the Rectorship of St. John's Church, Canterbury, Cornwall, Orange County.—23.

CLERGYMEN RECEIVED INTO THE DIOCESE.

The Clergymen named below have been received into the Diocese upon Letters Dimissory of the Ecclesiastical Authority of the Dioceses respectively mentioned. I have given to them the Canonical Certificate of their reception.

The Rev. Frederick M. Gray, from the Diocese of New-Jersey.
The Rev. Edward H. Kettell, from Colorado.
The Rev. Theodore Irving, LL. D., from the Diocese of Huron.
The Rev. Albert Zabriskie Gray, from the Diocese of New-Jersey.
The Rev. William Fisher Lewis, from the Diocese of Albany.
The Rev. Francis H. Stubbs, from the Diocese of Albany.
The Rev. Constantine Stauder, from the Diocese of Ohio.
The Rev. Robert Lowry, from the Diocese of New-Jersey.
The Rev. John Henry Watson, from the Diocese of Pennsylvania.
The Rev. Francis A. Henry, from the Diocese of Connecticut.
The Rev. James S. Barnes, from the Diocese of Long Island.
The Rev. William A. Holbrook, from the Diocese of New-Jersey.
The Rev. James Mulchahey, D. D., from the Diocese of Ohio.
The Rev. George H. Hincle, deacon, from the Diocese of Central Pennsylvania.
The Rev. Robert Scott, from the Diocese of Massachusetts.
The Rev. William E. Snowden, from the Diocese of Maryland.
The Rev. George W. West, deacon, from the Diocese of Albany.
The Rev. Louis L. Noble, from the Diocese of New-Jersey.
The Rev. Charles C. Tiffany, from the Diocese of Massachusetts.
The Rev. Charles H. Coffin, from the Diocese of Maryland.
The Rev. William Kirkus, from the Diocese of Manchester, England.
The Rev. Leon Pons, from the Diocese of Albany.—22.

ALSO, THE CANDIDATES FOR DEACON'S AND PRIEST'S ORDERS NAMED BELOW.

Elijah Winchester Donald, A. B., (admitted February 17, 1872,) from the Diocese of Rhode Island.

Clarence E. Woodman, A. B., (admitted September 16, 1873,) from the Diocese of Connecticut.

John Lightner Egbert, from the Diocese of Kentucky.

LETTERS DIMISSORY GRANTED.

I have granted Letters Dimissory, at their request, to the Clergymen named below, and have received notice of the acceptance of the same from the respective Ecclesiastical Authorities, viz.:

The Rev. Francis Harison, to the Diocese of Albany.
The Rev. Frank Hallam, deacon, to Maryland.
The Rev. Alfred B. Leeson, deacon, to Maryland.
The Rev. Robert Boyd Van Kleeck, deacon, to the Diocese of Albany.
The Rev. John B. Morgan, to Pennsylvania.
The Rev. H. Warren Fay, deacon, to Massachusetts.
The Rev. Arthur Ritchie, to Maryland.
The Rev. Dudley D. Smith, to Delaware.
The Rev. Jacob Rambo, to Ohio.
The Rev. Hobart Chetwood, to California.
The Rev. Merritt H. Wellman, to New Jersey.
The Rev. Charles B. Coffin, to Maryland.
The Rev. Samuel Moran, deacon, to New-Jersey.
The Rev. Frank L. Norton, to Massachusetts.
The Rev. C. W. Camp, to New-Jersey.
The Rev. George D. Silliman, to California.
The Rev. William C. Grubbe, deacon, to the Diocese of Albany.
The Rev. Benjamin F. Newton, deacon, to Massachusetts.
The Rev. John L. Egbert, deacon, to Massachusetts.
The Rev. Walter Delafield, to the Diocese of Albany.
The Rev. Charles C. Parsons, to New-Jersey.
The Rev. James M. La Tourette, to the jurisdiction of the Missionary Bishop of Colorado, &c.
The Rev. William R. Carroll, to Pennsylvania.
The Rev. Anthony Ten Broeck, D. D., to New-Jersey.—24.

ALSO, THE CANDIDATES FOR DEACON'S AND PRIEST'S ORDER NAMED BELOW.

William Henry Weibel, A. B., (admitted December 7, 1871,) to the Diocese of Central New-York.

Ingram N. W. Irvine, (admitted March 13, 1873,) to the Diocese of Long Island.

George Edward Hand, A. B., (admitted October 8, 1872,) to the Diocese of Tennessee.

Henry Mason Smythe, (admitted November 7, 1871,) to the Diocese of Albany.—4.

CLERGYMEN DECEASED.

Since the last Convention, the following Clergymen of the Diocese have departed this life:

The Rev. Samuel G. Appleton, November 29, 1873.
The Rev. William J. Alston, May 26, 1874.
The Rev. Benjamin Evans, May 21, 1874.
The Rev. William Henry Josephus, November, 1873.
The Rev. William Wood Seymour, January 5, 1874.
The Rev. Antoine Verren, D. D., March 17, 1874.
The Rev. Eastburn Benjamin, September 8, 1874.—7.

ALSO, THE FOLLOWING CANDIDATE FOR DEACON'S AND PRIEST'S ORDERS.

David Wilkinson Olmsted.

RECTORS INSTITUTED.

1873.	October	18.	The Rev. Walter Delafield, into the Rectorship of St. John's Church, Kingston.
"	November	29.	The Rev. William Fisher Lewis, into the Rectorship of St. Peter's Church, Peekskill.
1874.	June	30.	The Rev. William A. Holbrook, into the Rectorship of the Church of St. James the Less, Scarsdale.—3.

CHURCHES CONSECRATED.

Since the last Convention, the following Churches have been consecrated by me:

1873.	October	1.	Calvary Free Chapel, New-York.
"	November	6.	The Church of the Beloved Disciple, New-York.
1874.	July	14.	The Church of the Holy Trinity, Highlands, Ulster County.
"	August	18.	St. John's Memorial Church, Ellenville, Ulster County.—4.

SUMMARY.

The following is a Summary of Episcopal Acts in the Diocese since the last Convention:

Number of Persons Confirmed,		3,083
Candidates Ordained to the Diaconate,	16	
Candidates Ordained to the Priesthood,	11	

Ordinations, total, ...	27
Churches Consecrated, ...	4
Clergymen received from other Dioceses, ...	23
" transferred to " "	24
" instituted into Rectorships, ...	3

HORATIO POTTER, D. D., LL. D., D. C. L.,

Bishop of New-York.

Appendix:

No. I.

PAROCHIAL, MISSIONARY AND OTHER CLERICAL REPORTS.

The following portions of the Parochial, Missionary and other Clerical Reports, made to the Bishop of the Diocese, are published by his direction, in accordance with the following section, to which attention is respectfully requested, of

CANON 15, TITLE I.,

OF DIGEST OF THE CANONS OF THE GENERAL CONVENTION.

Of the Mode of securing an accurate View of the State of the Church.

§ I. As a full and accurate view of the state of the Church, from time to time, is highly useful and necessary, it is hereby ordered that every Minister of this Church, or, if the Parish be vacant, the Wardens, shall present, or cause to be delivered, on or before the first day of every Annual Convention, to the Bishop of the Diocese, or, when there is no Bishop, to the President of the Convention, a statement of the number of baptisms, confirmations, marriages and funerals, and of the number of Communicants in his Parish or Church; also the state and condition of the Sunday-Schools in his Parish; also the amount of the

Communion alms, the contributions for missions, diocesan, domestic and foreign, for parochial schools, for Church purposes in general, and of all other matters that may throw light on the same. And every Clergyman, not regularly settled in any Parish or Church, shall also report the occasional services he may have performed; and, if he have performed no such services, the causes or reasons which have prevented the same. And these Reports, or such parts of them as the Bishop shall think fit, may be read in Convention, and shall be entered on the Journals thereof.

DUTCHESS COUNTY.

St. Thomas' Church, Amenia; the Rev. WALTER R. GARDNER, Deacon and Rector elect.

Families, 40. Individuals, 150. Baptisms, (ad. 6, inf. 5,) 11. Communicants, 39. The Holy Communion celebrated, beginning with July, 1874, once each month. Catechists and Sunday-School teachers, 5. Catechumens: Sunday scholars, 52; total number of young persons instructed, 52. Celebration of Divine Service: Sundays, morning service and sermon.

Contributions.—Episcopal Fund, $2; Diocesan Fund, $10; Church purposes in general, $100—total, $112.

This Parish has been without a Clergyman for the most of the year last past. Services have been maintained, however, through the self denying efforts of Mr. Elisha Risley, who, by permission of the Bishop of the Diocese, has acted as lay reader.

The present incumbent entered upon his work July 5, 1874. In addition to the morning service at the Parish Church, he holds an afternoon mission service in the school house at Ameniaville, (a village on the rail-road, five miles away,) with an average congregation of twenty.

The seats in this Church are free, all expenses being met by subscription.

The subscriptions for this year have not yet been obtained, hence the small sum under the head "Contributions."

Chapel of St. Stephen's College, Annandale; the Rev. R. B. FAIRBAIRN, D. D, the Rev. G. B. HOPSON, the Rev. W. W, OLSSEN and the Rev. L. L. NOBLE, Ministers in charge.

Families, about 40. Individuals, about 250. Baptisms, inf. 6. Burials, 4. Confirmed, 7. Communicants: added, 14; present number, about 150. Sermons twice on Sunday during term, once during long vacations, on great festivals, and on other important occasions. Communion has been celebrated each Sunday during term, the long vacation, first Sunday in each month.

The Parish School has been maintained. There has been an attendance of 85 children. They have been frequently instructed in the Catechism by the Warden of the College. There is also a Sunday-School, in which about 50 children have been instructed in their religious duties.

Contributions.—Aged and Infirm Clergy, $123; Society for the Increase of the Ministry, $47 42; Diocesan Missions, $42 10; St. Mark's School, Salt Lake City, $40; Ladies' Sewing Society, $59 27, which Society contributed a large amount of clothing for the House of the Good Shepherd, Tompkins' Cove; Parish Library, $12 54; Society for the Promotion of Religion and Learning, $40 66—total, $364 99.

The usual service has been maintained at Barrytown, under the auspices of the St. Peter's Brotherhood, which association continues to render important service in parochial work.

For the services at Barrytown a Chapel has been built by Mrs. J. L. Aspinwall, as a memorial of her late husband, John Lloyd Aspinwall, who always took a deep interest in the religious instruction of his neigborhood. The Chapel is named St. John the Evangelist.

St. Mark's Church, Carthage Landing; the Rev. F. W. SHELTON, LL. D., Rector.

Families, 17. Individuals, 71. Baptisms, inf. 5. Burials, 2. Communicants: present number, 25. The Holy Communion celebrated on the first Sunday of every month, and on the principal festivals. Catechists and Sunday-School teachers, 6. Catechumens: Children taught the Catechism openly in the Church, 25; times, 12; total number of young persons instructed, 25. Celebration of Divine Service: Sundays, 92; Holy Days, 4; other days, 7—total, 103.

Contributions.—Episcopal Fund, $2; Diocesan Fund, $5; Parish purposes, $535—total, $542.

Trinity Church, Fishkill; the Rev. JOHN R. LIVINGSTON, Rector.

Burials, 4. Communicants: admitted, 8; removed into the Parish, 1; died, 1; present number, 34. The Holy Communion celebrated on the first Sunday of the month and upon the chief festivals, and several times in private. Catechists and Sunday-School teachers, 4. Catechumens, 12. Celebration of Divine Service: Sundays, morning service, evening service monthly; Holy Days, Thanksgiving, Christmas, Ash-Wednesday, Good Friday; other days, Wednesdays in Lent, and a weekly service.

Contributions.—Episcopal Fund, $7; Diocesan Fund, $5; Missionary Committee of the Diocese, $11; Theological Education Fund, $5 32; Fund for Aged and Infirm Clergymen, $14; in aid of the sufferers at Memphis, Tenn., $18; New-York Bible and Common Prayer-Book Society, $7; Colored people, $4 50; Mission to the Indians, $5; Board of Missions P. E. Church, U. S.: Domestic Committee, $7 50; Foreign Committee, $5; Highland Hospital, Matteawan, Dutchess County, $10; the Poor, $10; Parish purposes, $90; Church purposes in general, $15—total, $214 32.

Free Church of St. John Baptist, Glenham; the Rev. JOHN R. LIVINGSTON, Rector and Missionary.

Baptisms, (ad. 9, inf. 27,) 36. Confirmed, 15. Marriages, 3. Burials, 5. Communicants: admitted, 11; removed from the Parish, 16; died, 1; present number, 30. The Holy Communion celebrated on the third Sunday in the month, Sunday after Christmas, Thursday evening in Passion Week, Sunday after Easter, and on St. John Baptist Day. Catechists and Sunday-School teachers, 6. Catechumens, 40; times, monthly; total number of young persons instructed, 40. Daily Parish School, free; Scholars, 20. Celebration of Divine Service: Sundays, morning and evening; Holy Days, most of the Saints' Days, early service Christmas and Easter; other days, Thanksgiving Day, Ember and Rogation Days, twice a week during Lent, daily in Passion Week.

Contributions.—Episcopal Fund, $2; Diocesan Fund, $2; Theological Education Fund, $2; Fund for Aged and Infirm Clergymen, $4; New-York Bible and Common Prayer-Book Society, $5; Sunday-School offering on St. John Baptist Day, $50 85; Mission to the Indians, $2; Board of Missions P. E. Church, U. S.: Domestic Committee, $11 25; Foreign Committee, $2 50; the Poor, $50; Parish purposes, $25—total, $146 10.

The failure of our manufacturing interests has greatly affected this Parish during the past year. Many have moved, and are moving from their temporal and spiritual home here.

Those who have remained have shown diligence in the service of their Lord. The Canonical collections have been mostly made from the Sunday-School offerings. May the good Lord cause a brighter day to dawn upon us.

St. James' Church, Hyde Park; the Rev. JAMES S. PURDY, D. D., Rector; the Rev. HENRY L. ZIEGENFUSS, Assistant Minister, *pro tem.*

Families, 51. Individuals, 166. Baptisms, (ad. 2, inf. 18,) 20. Marriages, 2. Burials, 12. Communicants: died, 4; present number, about 100. The Holy Communion celebrated on the first Sunday in every month, and on all great festivals. Catechists and Sunday-School teachers, 8. Catechumens: Children taught the Catechism openly in the Church, 90; times, every Sunday. Celebration of Divine Service: Sundays, three times; Holy Days, once; other days, Wednesday and Friday evenings—total, 137, (including services in the Chapel at Staatsburgh.)

Contributions.—Diocesan Fund, $30; Missionary Committee of the Diocese, $34 88; Theological Education Fund, $16 84; books for Sunday-School, $26 20; Bishop's Salary, $30; Board of Missions P. E. Church, U. S.: Domestic Committee, $40 03; Missions in the county, $67 21; House of Mercy, $15 30; the Poor, $171 03; Parish purposes, $981 15 —total, $1,412 64.

On account of the Rector's absence in Europe, a full report cannot be given. That presented above covers a period of not quite six months.

Trinity Church, Madalin; the Rev. JAMES STARR CLARK, D. D., Rector and Missionary.

Individuals, 200. Baptisms, (ad. 1, inf. 4,) 5. Burials, 5. Communicants: admitted, 2; removed into the Parish, 6; removed from the Parish, 6; present number, 52. The Holy Communion celebrated the first and third Sundays in each month, and on all high festivals. Catechists and Sunday-School teachers, 6. Catechumens: Children taught the Catechism openly in the Church, 85; total number of young persons instructed, 85. Celebration of Divine Service: Sundays, 104; Holy Days, 10; other days, 14—total, 128.

Contributions.—Episcopal Fund, $2; Missionary Committee of the Diocese, $5; Fund for Aged and Infirm Clergymen, $2; the Poor, $15; Parish purposes, $302; Church purposes in general, $50—total, $376.

Trinity School—a Church boarding-school for boys—of which the Bishop is Visitor, has been successfully carried on during the past year by the Rector and his assistants. It was begun seven years since to meet a want generally and deeply felt, *i. e.*, the combination of home influence with thorough mental, moral and religious training.

The school offers special advantages to boys looking forward to the Sacred Ministry and to the sons of the Clergy.

Grace Church, Millbrook; the Rev. B. F. MILLER, Rector and Missionary.

Families, 17. Individuals, 55. Baptisms, inf. 2. Marriages, 2. Burials, 3. Communicants: removed from the Parish, 7; present number, 27. The Holy Communion celebrated first Sunday in every month, Christmas and Whitsun-day. Catechists and Sunday-School teachers, 4. Catechumens: Sunday scholars, 20. Celebration of Divine Service: Sundays, 52; Holy Days, 4; other days, 1—total, 57.

Contributions.—Parish purposes, $50.

I have rectified the list of Communicants. Last year there were thirty-four upon the roll; I find only twenty-seven that it will answer to retain upon the Register. There are only eighteen actually present, and I can report only fifteen who come to the Holy Communion.

St. Paul's Church, Pleasant Valley; the Rev. GEO. HENRY SMITH, Rector and Missionary.

Baptisms, inf. 4. Marriage, 1. Burials, 2. Communicants: as last reported, 22; removed into the Parish, 1; removed from the Parish, 6; present number, 17. The Holy Communion celebrated first Sunday in the month and greater feasts, 14 times, and 171 individual receptions—average 12 3-14. Catechist and Sunday-School teacher, the Rector. Catechumens, about 20. Celebration of Divine Service: Sundays, 46; Holy Days, 10; other days, 5—total, 61. In Manchester, 12; in Rochdale, 4. Total, 77.

Contributions.—Missionary Committee of the Diocese, $2 24; Fund for Aged and Infirm Clergymen, $1 57; Mission to Jews, $1 85; Board of Missions P. E. Church, U. S.: Freedmen, $2 84; Domestic Committee, $2 48; Foreign Committee, $3; Indian Commission, $1 44; Parish purposes, $347 70—total, $362 62.

St. Paul's Church has suffered much by removals and by the illness of the Rector during the past year. The Village of Pleasant Valley contains 500 people, and the Presbyterians, Methodists and Friends have each a place of worship, centrally located; while the Church is on one side, where a lot was unfortunately donated.

As often as his health permits the Rector holds services at Rochdale, a hamlet of about 100 inhabitants, three miles from Pleasant Valley, and at Manchester, about seven miles distant; at each place is a good Sunday-School.

Christ Church, Poughkeepsie; the Rev. PHILANDER K. CADY, D. D., Rector.

Baptisms (ad. 4, inf. 43,) 47. Confirmed, 32. Marriages, 8. Burials, 25. Communicants: present number, about 300. The Holy Communion is celebrated on the first Sunday in each month, on the great festivals, and weekly from the first Sunday in Advent to Trinity Sunday, inclusive. Catechists and Sunday-School teachers, 35. Catechumens, 250. Daily Parish Schools: 2, free; Scholars. (males, 60, females, 65,) 125. Celebration of Divine Service: Sundays, twice; on all the Holy Days, daily during Lent, and five times a week during the rest of the year.

Contributions.—Episcopal Fund, $13 08; Diocesan Fund, $40; Missionary Committee of the Diocese, $61 11; Theological Education, $25; Fund for Aged and Infirm Clergymen, $20; New-York City Church Charities, $4 75; Church schools in the West, $36; New-York Bible and Common Prayer-Book Society, $31 65; Memphis orphans, $75 68; Church in Highland, Ulster County, N. Y., $161 17; St. Barnabas' Hospital, Poughkeepsie, $914 64; Missions: Domestic Committee, $206 50; Foreign Committee, $141 27; Dutchess County Convocation, $177 80; Parochial Schools, $930; the Poor, $665 17; Parish purposes, $275; Children's offerings, $206 06—total, $3,984 38.

St. Barnabas' Hospital, Poughkeepsie.

This Institution, under the management of the three Parishes of Poughkeepsie, has been successfully administered during the past year. At the present date, 14 patients are cared for within its walls; 76 have been received since the last report in the Journal of 1873, of whom 7 died, 4 were discharged incurable, and 56 were dismissed recovered.

Church of the Holy Comforter, Poughkeepsie; the Rev. ROBERT F. CRARY, Rector.

Baptisms, (ad. 9, inf. 98,) 107. Confirmed, 40. Marriages, 7. Burials, 19. Communicants: admitted, 32; removed from the Parish, 26; died, 3; present number, 291. The Holy Communion celebrated on the first Sunday in each month and on the greater festivals, and eight times in private. Catechists and Sunday-School teachers, 24. Catechumens, 269. Children taught the Catechism openly in the Church, all the school. Industrial School: Scholars, females, 103. Celebration of Divine Service: Sundays, twice every Sunday, three times on the first Sunday of each month, and once a Sunday for four months of the year at St. Barnabas' Hospital; Holy Days, all; other days, every Friday throughout the year, daily during Lent, and twice on Wednesdays and Fridays.

Contributions.—Episcopal Fund, $8; Diocesan Fund, $30; Missionary Committee of the Diocese, $88; Convocation of Dutchess County, $55 10; Theological Education Fund, $17 78; Fund for Aged and Infirm Clergymen, $7; New-York City Mission to the Jews, $17 57; Church of the Holy Trinity, Highland, Ulster County, $50; St. Barnabas' Hospital, Poughkeepsie, $158 77; Scholarship Salt Lake City, Bp. Tuttle, $40; Bp. Seabury Divinity School, Bp. Whipple, $30; Indian Mission, Bp. Hare, $20; Colorado Mission, Bp. Spalding, $20; Pacific Coast Mission, Dr. Breck, $50; Nashotah Mission, Dr. Cole, $30; Church Aid Society, $54 08; Ladies' Association, $40 88; Men's Association, $89 14; Board of Missions P. E. Church, U. S.: Domestic Committee, $62 86; Foreign Committee, $30; Sunday-School, $146 56; Industrial School, $21 08; the Poor, $215 98; Parish purposes, $1,261 79; Church purposes in general, $91 89—total, $2,535 48.

St. Paul's Church, Poughkeepsie; the Rev. S. H. SYNNOTT, Rector.

Baptisms, (ad. 2, inf. 20,) 22. Confirmed, 10. Marriages, 10. Burials, 15. Communicants: present number, about 180; total number of young persons instructed, 150. Celebration of Divine Service, 220 times.

Contributions.—About $4,000.

Christ Church, Red Hook; the Rev. JOHN W. MOORE, Rector.

Families and parts of families, 24. Individuals, about 90. Baptisms, (ad. 1, inf. 11,) 12. Confirmed, 9. Marriages, 2. Burial, 1. Communicants: admitted, 8; removed into the Parish, 6; removed from the Parish, 11; present number, 35. The Holy Communion celebrated monthly and on the chief festivals. Children taught the Catechism openly in the Church, 26; times, every Sunday. Celebration of Divine Service: Sundays, morning and evening; Holy Days, all the principal Holy Days; other days, Fridays in Lent, daily during Holy Week, Thanksgiving and Day of Intercession; and some extra services during the month of August, with Lectures on Confirmation, preparatory to the Bishop's visit.

Contributions.—Episcopal Fund, (including assessment, $5,) $11; Diocesan Fund, $16; Missionary Committee of the Diocese, $20 75; Theological Education Fund, $10 40; Fund for Aged and Infirm Clergymen, $10; New-York Bible and Common Prayer-Book Society, $5 72; Protestant Episcopal Tract Society, $4 28; Board of Missions: Domestic Committee, $21 71; Foreign Committee, $28 10; Indian Commission, $20; Home Mission to Colored People, $12 23; Jewish Mission in New-York, $5; the Poor, Parish purposes and Church purposes in general, $358 61—total, $523 80.

St. Paul's Church, Red Hook, (Tivoli); the Rev. G. LEWIS PLATT, Rector. P. O. Madalin.

Families, about 25. Baptisms, inf. 2. Marriages, 2. Burials, 6. Communicants: admitted, 4; removed into the Parish, 1; present number, 35. The Holy Communion celebrated once a month. Catechists and Sunday-School teachers, 14. Catechumens: Children taught the Catechism openly in the Church, about 120. Celebration of Divine Service: every Sunday morning, Ash-Wednesday, Good Friday and on Thanksgiving Day—total, 55.

Contributions.—Fund for Aged and Infirm Clergymen, $5; Diocesan Fund, $1; Offerings for charity, $60 60; Am. Ch. Miss. Soc., chiefly for Mexico, $186; S. S. Miss. Contributions for Mexico, $35 20; Ladies' Benevolent Soc. St. Paul's Ch., $45 23; for Sunday-School purposes, $121 50; Parish purposes, $207—total, $661 53.

There is an increasing interest in our Christian work in the Parish. The Rector and his family have been the recipients of many attentions, kindnesses and generous gifts, in times of joy, affliction and illness, for which it is but fitting there should be this recorded expression of gratitude. Disabled during the winter and early spring for three months, the Rector was kindly relieved in his Church services by the aid of the Clergy of St. Stephen's College, Annandale.

The Services and the Sunday-School at the Clermont Chapel, north of our Church, on the Sunday afternoons, for eight months in the year, have been continued, as before, with considerable interest.

Church of the Messiah, Rhinebeck; the Rev. A. F. OLMSTED, Rector.

Families, 27. Baptisms, inf. 2. Marriage, 1. Burials, 4. Communicants: removed into the Parish, 2; removed from the Parish, 6; present number, 63. The Holy Communion celebrated on first Sunday of every month, and on Easter Sunday and Christmas Day. Catechists and Sunday-School teachers, 5. Sunday-School scholars, about 30. Bible Class, instructed by the Rector, 18; total, 48. Celebration of Divine Service: 53 Sundays, 100 times; 8 Holy Days, 8 times; 13 other days, 13 times—total, 74 days, 121 times.

Contributions.—Diocesan Fund, $20; Fund for Aged and Infirm Clergymen, $7 50; Board of Missions P. E. Church, U. S.: Dakota Hall, $23 40; Foreign Committee, $13 92; Com. Alms and other Sunday collections, $168 98; the Poor, Parish purposes, (including Salary,) about $2,100—total, $2,333 80.

Church of the Ascension, Rhinecliff; the Rev. THOMAS S. SAVAGE, Minister.

Families, 20. Individuals, 90. Marriage, 1. Communicants: admitted, 6; removed into the Parish, 4; removed from the Parish, 1; present number, 33. The Holy Communion celebrated once every month, and on prominent festivals. Catechists and Sunday-School teachers, 7. Catechumens, 2. Members of other classes for religious instruction, about 12; Sunday Scholars, 42. Daily Parish School: 1, paid in part; Scholars, females, 30.

Contributions.—Episcopal Fund, $2; Board of Missions P. E. Church, U. S.: Domestic Missions, $3 65; Foreign Committee, $17 66; Parochial Schools, $53; the Poor, (Communion Alms,) $23 92; Parish purposes, $58 06; Memorial Church of Bishop Auer, at Monrovia, $18—total, $176 29.

A Society has been formed among the ladies of the congregation for aiding our Missions to the Indians. The Rector attends and opens the meeting with prayer, and reading reports and letters of the Missionaries, and giving such facts as are calculated to enhance the interest of the Society in the work.

One box, valued at about eighty dollars, has been forwarded, and another is ready.

The Church edifice is undergoing repairs, to which liberal contributions have been gained. The expenses of the Parish are defrayed mostly by Mrs. M. R. Miller, whose interest and active benevolence continue.

Our congregations gradually increase, and the state of the Parish is encouraging.

Congregation of the Church, Pawling; the Rev. ORSAMUS H. SMITH, officiating.

Burials, 2. Communicants: present number, 5. The Holy Communion celebrated once. Celebration of Divine Service: Once in four weeks at Hurd's Corners, and in other places on several occasions, preaching, assisting at Holy Communion and reading prayers.

I have been enabled to continue my work at Hurd's Corners, in Pawling, as in the past, with considerable regularity. The number which assembles for worship is undiminished, harmonious and apparently devout. I am comforted and encouraged by the hope and trust that I am yet able to do something for Christ and the Church. I believe that a foundation will be laid on which some younger and stronger hand will build a Church and congregation in the village of Pawling.

Zion Church, Wappinger's Falls; the Rev. GEORGE B. ANDREWS, D. D., Rector; the Rev. HENRY Y. SATTERLEE, Assistant Minister, with Pastoral charge.

Families and parts of families, 298. Individuals, about 1,125. Baptisms, (ad. 4, inf. 38,) 42. Confirmed, 18. Marriages, 9. Burials, 14. Communicants: admitted, 20; removed into the Parish, 19; removed from the Parish, 12; died, 2; present number, 275. The Holy Communion celebrated on the first Sunday in the month, and on the greater festivals, 16 times, in private, 5 times—total, 21 times. Catechists and Sunday-School teachers, 30. Catechumens, 402; Children taught the Catechism openly in the Church, all the school; times, 12; members of other classes for religious instruction, 39. Celebration of Divine Service: Sundays, three times every Sunday, except in July and August, when the afternoon service was omitted; Holy Days and other days, fifty times—total, 206 times.

Contributions.—Episcopal Fund, $10; Diocesan Fund, $35; Missionary Committee of the Diocese, $15; Theological Education Fund, $5; Fund for Aged and Infirm Clergymen, $11 83; New-York Bible and Common Prayer-Book Society, $5; Protestant Episcopal Tract Society, $5; General P. E. S. S. Union and Church Book Society, $5; General Theological Seminary, $5; Board of Missions P. E. Church, U. S.: Domestic Committee, $20; Foreign Committee, $13 70; the Poor, $167 60; Parish purposes, (including all departments of Parish work,) $2,353 59; Church purposes in general, $230 99—total, $2,887 71.

NEW-YORK COUNTY.

Church of All Angels, New-York; the Rev. CHARLES FREDERICK HOFFMAN, Rector; the Rev. BENJAMIN WEBB, Rector's Assistant and Principal of the Parish School.

Families and parts of families, 40. Individuals, 150. Burial, 1. Communicants: admitted, 1, removed into the Parish, 16; removed from the Parish, 5; present number, 60 The Holy Communion celebrated on Christmas, Ash-Wednesday, Thursday before Easter, Easter, Ascension, Whitsun-Day, Trinity Sunday, all Sundays in Lent, first Sunday in the months, and other Sundays; total 25 times. Catechist, the Rector; Sunday-School teachers, 9. Catechumens, 58. Children taught the Catechism openly in the Church, all that come to the Rector's catechisings; times, 9; total number of young persons instructed, 58. One Daily Parish School, paid and free; number small. Celebration of Divine Service: all Sundays and many other days; total, 190.

Contributions.—Episcopal Fund, $1; Diocesan Fund, $6; Missionary Committee of the Diocese, $1 50; Theological Education Fund, $1; Fund for Aged and Infirm Clergymen, $1 50, New-York City Mission Society, 50 cts.; Church Missionary Society for Seamen, $1 50; General Theological Seminary, $25; Board of Missions P. E Church, U. S.: Niobrara League, $13; Parochial School, the Poor, Parish purposes and Church purposes in general, $1,612 17—total, $1,663 17.

This report is somewhat approximate. The present Rector resigned his former charge (St. Philip's Church in the Highlands, opposite West Point) the twenty-third of October, A. D 1873, and, after officiating at different places occasionally, took charge of All Angels' Church last Christmas. The field in which it is situated is a hard one, and we may require about four thousand dollars to pay off assessments, &c., besides much patience, perseverance, diligence and endurance. During the past year, however, comparatively speaking, much has been accomplished. The Church has been painted inside and outside, a new chancel window inserted, the chancel newly furnished to a considerable extent, the Church repaired, otherwise furnished, and provided with prayer-books and hymnals. The Rectory has been re-roofed, painted outside, and repaired; our fence and ground put in better condition; circulars and cards have been issued, house to house visiting done, a community of gatherers for All Angels' Church founded, a Church Furnishing Society brought into life, the envelope system introduced, and a Parish School started.

The Rev. Benjamin Webb has assisted the Rector for several months, rendering faithful service.

The above amount of contributions includes two hundred dollars from Trinity Church, private gifts, and the sum received as rent for the Rectory. Our Church is a free Church.

All Saints' Church, New-York; the Rev. WILLIAM N. DUNNELL, Rector.

Families, 160. Individuals, about 800. Baptisms, (ad. 10, inf. 73,) 83. Confirmed, 53. Marriages, 36. Burials, 49. Communicants: admitted, 20; removed into the Parish, 12; removed from the Parish, 11; died, 3; present number, 212. The Holy Communion celebrated first Sunday of each month, and on greater festivals. Catechists and Sunday-School teachers, 37. Catechumens, 407; times, 56; total number of young persons instructed, 407. Celebration of Divine Service: Sundays, twice or three times; Holy Days, once; other days, daily in Lent, and Wednesdays throughout the year--total, 204.

Contributions.—Episcopal Fund, $5; Diocesan Fund, $60; Missionary Committee of the Diocese, $4 23; Theological Education Fund, $5; Fund for Aged and Infirm Clergymen, $4 60; Board of Missions P. E. Church, U. S.: Domestic Committee, $12 91; the Poor, $218; Parish purposes, $823; Church purposes in general, $1,350—total, $2,482 73.

Church of the Annunciation, New-York; the Rev. WILLIAM J. SEABURY, Rector.

Families, 89. Individuals, 272. Baptisms, (ad. 4, inf. 14,) 18. Confirmed, 12 Marriages, 8. Burials, 17. Communicants: admitted, 8; removed into the Parish, 4; removed from the Parish, 5; died, 3; present number, 187. The Holy Communion celebrated on every Lord's Day and on the other Holy Days, twice on Christmas, Easter and Whitsun-Day. Catechists and Sunday-School Teachers, 11. Catechumens: Children taught the Catechism openly in the Church, about 100; times, 49. Celebration of Divine Service: Sundays, 7½ A. M., 10½ A. M., 3½ or 5 P. M., (7½ A. M. omitted on first Sunday in the month;) Holy Days, 7 A. M., 9 A. M. and 5 P. M.; other days, 9 A. M. and 5 P. M.; total number of services held under the above rule, 678; number of individual receptions of the Holy Communion, 1,751.

Contributions.—Episcopal Fund, $20; Diocesan Fund, $42; Missionary Committee of the Diocese, $72 50; Fund for Aged and Infirm Clergymen, $26 70; Board of Missions P. E. Church, U. S.: Foreign Committee, $13 05; the Poor, $625 36; Parish purposes, $4,722 12; Church purposes in general, (Memphis sufferers and Mission to Jews,) $75 06—total, $5,596 79.

For several years past, as opportunity offered, the Vestry have secured to the Church the titles of the pews, which were originally vested in individual owners, and during the past year all private rights to the exclusive use of pews have been given up to the Church, and since Whitsun-Day the Church has been declared free for the use of all who desire to worship God according to the order of the Book of Common-Prayer. The Church depends solely upon the offertory for its support.

During the past winter a deputation of Sisters from the Community of St John Baptist at Clewer, in England, having established a charitable work in this city, subject to the visitation of the Bishop of the Diocese, have attended Sunday services at this Church with the objects of their charity. At the request of these Sisters, and by permission of the Bishop, the Rector of this Church has officiated in the Chapel of their House, celebrating the Holy Eucharist on week days on fifteen occasions; the total number of individuals present and receiving at such services having been sixty-one.

Anthon Memorial Church, New-York; the Rev. R. HEBER NEWTON, Rector.

Families, 108, (pew renting.) Baptisms, inf. 21. Confirmed, 26. Marriages, 2. Burials, 14. Communicants: admitted, 27; removed into the Parish, 30; removed from the Parish, 40; died, 4; present number, 310. The Holy Communion celebrated Christmas, Holy Thursday, Easter, (twice,) Trinity Sunday and the first Sunday in each month. Catechists and Sunday-School teachers, 42. Catechumens, 315. Industrial School: Teachers, 12; scholars, 112. Celebration of Divine Service: Sundays, 105; Holy Days, 23; other days, 46—total, 175.

Contributions.—Parochial: Sunday-Schools, $378 67; Works amongst the Poor, $7,950 15, $280 72; Miscellaneous Parish purposes, $1,121 67; Special Parish purposes, $3,148 50—$12,879 71. *Extra-Parochial:* Foreign Missions, $283 08; Domestic Missions, $270 55; Miscellaneous, $227 23—$780 81. Total, $13,660 52.

Church of the Atonement, Madison Avenue, New-York; the Rev. C. C. TIFFANY, Rector.

Baptisms, (ad. 1, inf. 13,) 14. Confirmed, 20. Marriages, 4. Burials, 9. The Holy Communion celebrated on the first Sunday in each month, and on the festivals of our Lord. Celebration of Divine Service: Sundays, 10½ A. M. and 7½ P. M.; Holy Days, the greater festivals; other days, prayers and lectures from Advent to Easter.

Contributions.—Fund for Aged and Infirm Clergymen, $20; Board of Missions P. E. Church, U. S.: Domestic Committee, (Am. Ch. Miss. Soc.,) $116; Parochial Schools, Mission Chapel and S. School, $2,705 96; the Poor, (by the Communion alms,) $916 50; Parish purposes, (Col. for Parish work,) $1,008 75; Church purposes in general, Mission work in Kentucky, $120; Ev. Education Soc., $213 32; Col. for the Jews, $111—total, $5,273 53.

The late Rector of the Church of the Atonement resigned his charge in May last, and at the same time left the ministry of the P. E. Church. The present Rector took charge of the Church in June, when a large number of the remaining congregation were leaving the city for their country homes, and he now sends in the report to the Convention while many are still away. He is therefore unable at present to report with any accuracy the statistics of the Church. Some of those leaving it have applied for letters, and as the pew rental runs to November 1st, no pews are legally vacated. It has been thought better, then, to make no report, rather than an erroneous or imperfect one, with the simple statement that there remains the nucleus of a good congregation and Sunday-School.

Chapel of the Atonement, New-York; the Rev. GEORGE HOWELL, A. M., Assistant Minister of the Church of the Atonement, and in charge of the Chapel of the Atonement.

Families, 120. Individuals, 230. Baptisms, inf. 12. Marriages, 3. Communicants: died, 2; present number, 104. The Holy Communion celebrated the third Sunday in each month. Sunday-School teachers and catechists, 30; scholars, 450. Services: Children's service, each Sunday, at 9 A. M. Sunday-School, 3 P. M.

The regular morning and evening Church services; two other services during the week, and in addition, the Winter Women's meeting and Girls' Sewing School.

The present incumbent came into the charge of the Chapel February, 1874. Class awaiting confirmation.

Church of the Beloved Disciple, New-York; the Rev. ISAAC H. TUTTLE, D. D., Rector; the Rev. F. H. STUBBS, Assistant Minister.

Families, 18. Individuals, 136. Baptisms, (ad. 1, inf. 9,) 10. Confirmed, 9. Burials, 3. Communicants: admitted, 7; removed into the Parish, 24; removed from the Parish, 1; died, 2; present number, 95. The Holy Communion celebrated on all Sundays and Holy Days. Catechists and Sunday-School teachers, 5. Catechumens, 46. Celebration of Divine Service: Sundays, 92; Holy Days, 41; other days, 387--total, 520.

Contributions.—Missionary Committee of the Diocese, $13 36; Church Mission to the Jews, $9; St. Luke's Home for Indigent Christian Females, $21 75; Board of Missions P. E. Church, U. S.: Domestic Committee, $31 76; Sunday-School, $36 33; the Poor, $79 54; Parish purposes, $561 31—total, $753 05.

The gift of the Church by Miss Tallman, about $100,000.

The Church of the Beloved Disciple is a beautiful edifice, located at 89th-street and Madison Avenue, and is the gift of Miss Caroline Tallman in memory of her parents.

The noble donor has secured the pews on the side wall nearest to St. Luke's Home for Indigent Christian Females, for the free use of the inmates of this Institution.

On the sixth of November last this Church was consecrated by the Bishop of New-York, assisted by Bishop Tozer, Bishop Neely, Bishop Vail and a large number of the Clergy.

The Rev. Francis H. Stubbs, the Minister in charge, entered on duty soon after the consecration of the Church, and his acceptable labors have been attended with favorable results, considering the check on up-town building and the terrible crossings in this vicinity caused by the Fourth Avenue improvements.

Calvary Church, New-York; the Rev. E. A. WASHBURN, D. D., Rector; the Rev. W. D. WALKER, Assistant and Missionary; the Rev. F. A. HENRY, Assistant to Rector.

Families, 280. Baptisms, (ad. 2, inf. 10,) 12. Confirmed, 15. Marriages, 6. Burials, 15. Communicants, 470. The Holy Communion celebrated each fourth Sunday, Christmas, Easter and Trinity Sundays. Catechists and Sunday-School teachers, 10. Catechumens, 80. Daily Parish Schools: See Report of Calvary Free Chapel. Celebration of Divine Service: Sundays, twice throughout the year, except August; Holy Days, all feasts and fasts, and daily in Lent; other days, Wednesday and Friday mornings.

Contributions.—Episcopal Fund, $140; Diocesan Fund, $120; Aid for Aged and Infirm Clergymen, $285 15; New-York City Mission Society, $971; Church Missionary Society for Seamen, $211 60; New-York Bible and Common Prayer-Book Society, $500; Board of Missions P. E. Church, U. S.: Domestic Committee, $2,373 54; Foreign Committee, $652 15; Completion of new Chapel, $20,000; the Poor, $3,183; Support of Free Mission Chapel, $6,000; City charities, $1,428 30; Increase of Ministry, $559; Legacy to St Luke's Hospital, $10,000; Legacy to St. Ann's Church for Deaf Mutes, $10,000; Missions to Colored people and Indians, $323; Western Missions, $2,990; Lent offering for Missionary Clergy, $500; two Scholarships for Philada. Divinity School, $10,000; for the Evangelical Alliance, $400—total, $71,136 74.

Calvary Free Chapel, New-York; the Rev. WILLIAM DAVID WALKER, in charge.

Families, about 300. Individuals, over 1,000. Baptisms, (ad. 5, inf. 47,) 52. Confirmed, 41. Marriages, 22. Burials, 46. Communicants: about 400; admitted, 30; removed into the Parish, 26; removed from the Parish, 40; died, 11. The Holy Communion celebrated twice each month, and on each of the great festivals. Catechists and Sunday-School teachers, 59. Catechumens: Sunday-School scholars, 600 to 700; Children taught the Catechism openly in the Church, 600 to 700; times, 15; members of other classes for religious instruction, 50; Industrial School, 175. Daily Parish School: scholars, males 20, females, 30. A school receiving instruction in singing weekly, about 200. Celebration of Divine Service: Sundays, morning and evening; also a third service on the first Sunday of the month; Holy Days, once; other days, Wednesday and Friday evenings, twice daily during Lent—total, 310 times.

Contributions.—Missionary Committee of the Diocese, $55 66; Building fund of a Church in Virginia, $37 12; Fund for Aged and Infirm Clergymen, $14 85; New-York City Mission Society, $18 85; Support of Reading Room, $80: New-York Bible and Common Prayer-Book Society, $18 45; Mission to the Jews, $15; Home Missions to Colored people, $20 75; Board of Missions P. E. Church, U. S.: Domestic Committee, $79 52; Foreign Committee, $5 25; Parochial Schools, $70; the Poor, $50; Parish purposes, $590; Weekly Offertory, $1,327 11. Sunday-School contributions: For Bishop Tuttle's Schools, Salt Lake City, $40; Orphan's Home, New-York, $50; Sheltering Arms, New-York, $25; Bishop Hare's Indian Schools, $60; Mission work in Haiti, $25—total, $2,582 56.

In connection with the Chapel is a Free Reading Room for men, open during the winter, spring and autumn, which does a very useful work. There is also a young men's debating society, meeting weekly, in one of the rooms of the new Chapel, which is also helpful to many a youth. Our Benevolent Society is very fruitful in good works, providing garments for the needy, visiting sick and aged people, burying the dead in Christ with a decent and reverent respect. Its membership is quite large.

Christ Church, New-York; the Rev. HUGH MILLER THOMPSON, D. D., Rector.

Families, 120. Baptisms, inf. 13. Confirmed, 20. Marriages, 11. Burials, 9. Communicants: admitted, 46; removed into the Parish, 20; removed from the Parish, 56; died, 2; present number, 408. The Holy Communion celebrated every Sunday and Holy Day. Catechists and Sunday-School teachers, 36. Catechumens: Children taught the Catechism openly in the Church, 360; times, 9; total number of young persons instructed, 360. Celebration of Divine Service: Sundays, 110; Holy Days, 30; other days, 288—total, 428.

Contributions.—Parochial Schools, Sunday-School and Industrial School, $720; the Poor, $600; Parish purposes, $7,000; Church purposes in general, $320—total, $8,320.

Church of the Epiphany, New-York; [no Rector.]

Families, 73. Individuals, 293. Baptisms, (ad. 8, inf. 9,) 17. Confirmed, 18. Marriages, 2. Burials, 9. Communicants: admitted, 18; removed into the Parish, 3; removed from the Parish, 11, died, 5; present number, 175. The Holy Communion celebrated the first Sunday in each month and on Christmas Day. Catechists and Sunday-School teachers, 38. Catechumens: members of other classes for religious instruction, 120; Sunday scholars, 1,090, total number of young persons instructed, 1,200 Daily Ragged School: free; Scholars, (males, 52, females, 41,) 93. Celebration of Divine Service. Sundays, 10½ A M. and 7½ P. M.; Holy Days, Christmas, Good Friday, Ascension Day and Thanksgiving Day, and every Friday evening at 8 o'clock—total, 160.

Contributions.—Domestic Missions, $30; Foreign Committee, (Mexico, $18; Africa, $21 64,) $39 64; Parochial Schools, ragged, $866 66; the Poor, &c., $817 42; Parish purposes. $1,867 84—total, $3,618 56.

There have been contributed also for female Missionaries other than our own Church workers, $760.

We have a Mission Home in which a variety of Christian work is carried on, to which there have been contributed $3,000.

The contributions above mentioned to the Ragged School, the poor, and to Parish purposes, and also to the female Missionaries and Mission Home, include not only Church collections and offerings by the people of the congregation, but from others who do not attend our Church, although the Church is in a Mission field.

Grace Church, New-York; the Rev. HENRY C. POTTER, D. D., Rector; the Rev. JOHN W. KRAMER, M. D., and the Rev. WILLIAM KIRKUS, LL. B., Assistant Ministers.

Families, about 850. Individuals, 2,000. Baptisms, (ad. 2, inf. 87,) 89. Confirmed, 46. Marriages, 22. Burials, 35. Communicants: present number, 850. The Holy Communion celebrated on the first and second Sundays of the month, and on the greater festivals. Catechists and Sunday-School teachers, 28. Catechumens, 461. Parish School: free 1; Scholars: females, 500. Celebration of Divine Service: Sundays, thrice on all Sundays; all Holy Days; other days, daily in Lent, and semi-weekly in Advent.

Contributions.—Episcopal Fund, (Bishop's Salary,) $150; Diocesan Fund, $150; New-York Orphan Asylum, $436 48; Jewish Missions, $200 77; Missionary Committee of the Diocese, $453 56; Education Fund, $50,000; for Aged and Infirm Clergymen, $542 14; New-York City Mission Society, $1,145 82; Church Missionary Society for Seamen, $210; St. Luke's Hospital, $51,208 83; St. Luke's Home, $840 01; New-York Bible and Common Prayer-Book Society, $780 60; Home for Incurables, $893 20; Home Mission to Colored People, $400 95; Sheltering Arms, $1,166; Midnight Mission, $800; Domestic Missions, $31,693 34; Foreign Missions, $11,013 36; Parochial Building Fund, $27,573 93; the Poor, $9,225 47; Parish purposes, $2,635 05; Church purposes in general, $1,006 07—total, $191,977 61.

Of the above statistics, the following are those of Grace Chapel: Families, 126. Baptisms, adult, 1, infants 23. Marriages, 15. Burials, 25. Communicants, 192. S. School Catechumens, 461. Contributions, $1,006 07. Concerning these, the report of the Minister in charge remarks:

"The statistics show that our work has not yet recovered from the embarrassing results of the fire of last year. We are worshipping in a locality that is not convenient for the attendance of our people, and, unfortunately, this hindrance to more successful work cannot be immediately remedied. The large number of poor and suffering persons who have demanded the attention of the Pastor during the year would seem to indicate that the congregation will come together in its aforetime numerical strength whenever it may be possible to offer it a Church edifice in our old neighborhood."

Grace Church, Harlem; the Rev. D. BRAINERD RAY, Rector.

Baptisms, (ad. 4, inf. 26,) 30. Confirmed, 18. Marriages, 11. Funerals, 21. Divine Service every Sunday in the year except one. Sunday-School, every Sunday.

Not having received a report of the financial affairs up to date, owing to the absence of the Treasurer from the city, I am unable to give an account of the receipts and expenditures, but can report the Parish as entirely free from debt, and enjoying a fair degree of material prosperity for the times.

Church of the Holy Apostles, New-York; the Rev. JOHN P. LUNDY, D. D., Rector.

Baptisms, (ad. 4, inf. 67,) 71. Confirmed, 20. Marriages, 17. Funerals, 33. Communicants: admitted, 32; removed into the Parish, 4; removed from the Parish, 7; died, 7; present number, about 370. Services: Sundays, 114; Holy Days, 12; other days, 67—total, 193. The Communion celebrated once a month, and on all the high festivals. Children catechised once a month in the Church, except during the summer. Sunday, Infant and Industrial schools as heretofore.

Contributions.—Episcopal Fund, $15; Missionary Committee of the Diocese, $78 63; Fund for Aged and Infirm Clergymen, $58 63; New-York City Mission Society, $38 25; Church Mission Society for Seamen, $38 25; Board of Missions P. E. Church, U. S.: Domestic Committee, $92 05; special for Indian Missions, $185; Sheltering Arms, $58; the Poor, $524 62; Parish purposes, $5,428 91—total, $6,816 84.

The larger part of the Parochial contributions was an Easter offering towards the liquidation of a debt on our School building.

Church of the Heavenly Rest, New-York; the Rev. R. S. HOWLAND, D. D., Rector; the Rev. THOMAS K. CONRAD, D. D., Associate Rector.

Baptisms, (ad. 4, inf. 18,) 22. Confirmed, 13. Marriages, 6. Burials, 11. Communicants: present number, about 300. The Holy Communion celebrated second Sunday of the month, All Saints' Day, Holy Thursday and greater festivals. Catechists and Sunday-School teachers, 27. Catechumens: Children taught the Catechism openly in the Church, 290. Celebration of Divine Service: Sundays, every Sunday of the year; Holy Days, all principal Holy Days; other days, every day in Lent, once a week during the autumn and winter.

Contributions.—Missionary Committee of the Diocese, $100; Easter, $10,000; the Poor, $972 05; Parish purposes, $2,708 90; Church purposes in general, $720 12—total, $14,501 07.

The Easter collection of $10,000 is the last payment of the sum of $53,233 83, constituting the floating debt of the Church, which has now been entirely liquidated.

Floating Church of Our Saviour, New-York; the Rev. ROBERT J. WALKER, Missionary.

Families, about 50. Individuals, 500. Baptisms, (ad. 2, inf. 25,) 27. Confirmed, 29. Marriages, 11. Burials, 12. Communicants: admitted, 29; removed into the Parish, 6; removed from the Parish, 8; died, 3; present number, 94. The Holy Communion celebrated the first Sunday of each month, Christmas and Easter Day. Catechists and Sunday-School teachers, 7. Catechumens, 50. Celebration of Divine Service: Sundays, 106; Holy Days, 3; other days, 78—total, 187.

Contributions.—Board of Missions P. E. Church, U. S.: Domestic Committee, $2; the Poor, $135 84; Books for Seamen, $14 23—total, $152 07.

Some thousands of seamen from nearly every maritime country have attended the services of the Floating Church during the past year. All who desired it have been supplied with testaments, books and tracts in their own languages. The interest shown by these strangers during the celebration of Divine Service has been very remarkable, and numbers have doubtless been greatly benefited by the ample provision made for their spiritual wants by the "Protestant Episcopal Church Missionary Society for Seamen in the City and Port of New-York."

Church of the Holy Comforter, New-York; the Rev. HENRY FLOY ROBERTS, Missionary.

Families, 15. Individuals, indefinite. Baptisms, inf. 4. Marriages, 2. Burial, 1. Communicants: present number, 20. The Holy Communion celebrated first Sunday in each month, and on Christmas and Easter. Catechumens: there is no Sunday-School. Celebration of Divine Service: Sundays, 104; Holy Days, 2; other days, 18—total, 124.

Contributions.—Fund for Aged and Infirm Clergymen, $4; the Poor, $52 28; for books for distribution, $10 27—total, $66 55.

Our work is almost entirely among seamen and boatmen who have no fixed habitation, so that we have no report of various items which constitute the reports of regular Parishes, and for this reason our report will appear meagre.

But what we are able to report in the way of statistics can give but little, if any, idea of the nature of our work or the success which attends it. We gather the men who are scattered about the wharves and in the vessels in our vicinity into our Chapel. and preach to them the Gospel of the Redeemer, and distribute among them bibles, testaments, prayer-books and religious books of various kinds and in different languages, and we often learn that these instrumentalities are the means of the reformation or conversion of the men of the sea. During the past year our encouragement has been greatly increased, and we look forward to still greater success in the future.

Free Church of the Holy Martyrs, New-York; the Rev. JAMES MILLETT, Rector.

Families, 180. Individuals, 450. Baptisms, 90. Marriages, 28. Burials, 60. Communicants, 100. The Holy Communion celebrated on the first Sunday of each month, also Christmas, Easter, Whitsun-Day and Trinity Sunday. Sunday-School teachers, 14; scholars, 100.

If we had the means of attracting the children by clothing and gifts of other kinds, we could easily number 300. Our services are well attended, considering the obstacles by which we are beset—the lager beer saloons and tenement houses, which rarely furnish any Church goers. In a large city like New-York, (which gives a tone to the rest of the cities of the Union,) there is a wide field for Missionary effort. Let us each endeavor to do what we can in our sphere, and the gracious Lord of the harvest will bring about the wished for result in His own good time, while we, His ministering servants, go on "waiting and hoping." The repairs of our Church last spring and half the summer prevented the administration, as well as preparation for our "Annual Confirmation."

Church of the Holy Saviour, New-York; the Rev. ABRAHAM BEACH CARTER, D. D., Rector.

Baptisms, inf. 4. Confirmed, 15. Marriages, 15. Burials, 12. Communicants: present number, average 150. The Holy Communion celebrated on first Sunday of every month, and principal festivals. Celebration of Divine Service: one hundred and sixty-five full services have been held by the Rector during the year.

The attendance has largely increased during the past year, and the signs of spiritual life are most encouraging. During the winter months, a service in the French language was conducted by the Rev. C. Miel every Sunday afternoon, which was well attended. The Rector still continues to give two services each week at the Ludlow-street Prison, where there have been results most gratifying and encouraging in the numbers who have been brought to ask, in all sincerity of purpose, "What must I do to be saved?"

Church of the Holy Sepulchre, New-York; the Rev. J. TUTTLE SMITH, Rector.

Families, 54. Individuals, 250. Communicants: present number, 75. The Holy Communion celebrated on all feasts for which there is a Proper Preface, on Epiphany and Maundy Thursday, on the last Sunday of every month, and weekly during Lent and Advent. Catechists and Sunday-School teachers, 15. Catechumens: Children taught the Catechism openly in the Church, 90; times, 14. Celebration of Divine Service: Sundays, morning and afternoon; Holy Days, all the principal Holy Days; other days, Tuesdays, Wednesdays, Thursdays and Fridays.

Contributions.—Episcopal Fund, $3.

All the seats in this Church are free, and the offertory is the sole support.

Church of the Holy Trinity, New-York; the Rev. STEPHEN H. TYNG, Jr., D. D., Rector; the Rev. D. M. MCCAFFREY, and the Rev. E. H. KETTELL, Assistant Ministers.

Statistics of Parish Church and five Mission Chapels.—Baptisms, 124. Confirmed, 88. Marriages, 67. Funerals, 110. Sunday-School Teachers and Scholars, 1,900.

The Lay-Workers in the House of the Evangelists report the following Missionary statistics for the year: Services conducted or assisted in, 691. Prayer Meetings, or assisted in, 1,012. Addresses, 1,035. Average attendance on Sunday services or meetings, 1,572. Average attendance on week services or meetings, 278. Superintending Sunday-School, average 4. Teaching in Sunday-School, average 6. Scholars under care as Superintendent or teacher, 776. Average attendance, 506. Visits, 7,774. Scriptures read to families or individuals, 1,230. Families or individuals prayed with, 1,521. Bibles sold or given, 58. Prayer-Books sold or given, 7. Pages of tracts and papers distributed, 109,150. Average attendance at mothers' meetings, 56. Average attendance at sewing school, 203. Conversed with on the subject of religion, 1,643. Invited to Church or Sunday-School, 1,096. Induced to attend Church, 158. Induced to attend Sunday-School, 26. Children placed in institutions, 28. Persons relieved, 826. Funerals, 16.

Contributions.—Home Mission work in the Parish, $30,000; other benevolent purposes, including subscriptions to new Church, about $70,000. Total, $100,000.

The institutions supported by the congregation are: Four Mission Chapels, with connected societies or schools; House of the Evangelists, a training school, and associate Mission of lay-workers; Dispensary and Infirmary for the sick poor; Dorcas and Employment Society, to provide garments for the poor; Orphanage for wards of the Church; Home for Christian Care, which owns a farm of forty acres near Sing Sing, with buildings for benevolent uses; three Sunday-Schools in the Parish Church and five in the Chapels.

The statistics for the first ten years of the history of this Parish are as follow: Total Contributions, $636,340 16. Baptisms, 897. Confirmations, 597. Funerals, 536. Marriages, 268. Communicants, about 1,400

The above report embraces the period from Easter, 1873, to Easter, 1874.

Holy Trinity Church of Harlem; the Rev. W. NEILSON MCVICKAR, Rector.

Families or representatives, circ., 150. Baptisms, (ad. 11, inf. 4.) 15. Confirmed, 24. Marriages, 6. Burials, 21. The Holy Communion celebrated first Sunday in month, Christmas and Easter and Whitsun-Day. Sunday scholars, circ., 350. Celebration of Divine Service: Sundays, twice; Holy Days, Good Friday, Ash-Wednesday, Christmas, Ascension; other days, Wednesday evening lectures, during Holy Week, four times a week during Lent.

Contributions.—Episcopal Fund, $5; Diocesan Fund, $80—total, $85.

Church of the Incarnation, New-York; the Rev. HENRY E. MONTGOMERY, D. D., Rector.

Families, same as last report. Baptisms, (ad. 3, inf. 28,) 31. Confirmed, 20. Marriages, 23. Burials, 21. Communicants, same as before. Children taught the Catechism openly in the Church, all. Celebration of Divine Service: as usual.

Contributions.—Total contributions and receipts of Parish, $28,000.

The Mission of this Church, known as the "Church of the Reconciliation," is in a prosperous condition.

Church of the Reconciliation, (Mission of the Church of the Incarnation,) New-York; the Rev. E. S. WIDDEMER, Minister in charge.

Families, 123. Individuals, 500. Baptisms, (ad. 1, inf. 36,) 37. Confirmed, 15. Marriages, 15. Burials, 11. Communicants, 140. The Holy Communion celebrated second Sunday in each month. Catechists and Sunday-School teachers, 35; Sunday scholars, 300. Sewing School, 150.

Church of the Intercession, New-York; the Rev. W. M. POSTLETHWAITE, Rector.

Families, 98. Individuals, 490. Baptisms, inf. 9. Confirmed, 14. Marriages, 2. Burials, 8. Communicants: admitted, 16; present number, 102. The Holy Communion celebrated first Sunday in each month. Catechists and Sunday-School teachers, 24. Sunday scholars, 195.

Contributions.—Missionary and charitable objects, $2,981 34.

On Sunday, September 20th, 1874, we dedicated our new Church building, corner of 158th-street and the Grand Boulevard.

Church of the Nativity, New-York; the Rev. C. CLAPP, Rector.

Families, 130. Individuals, 350. Baptisms, (ad. 3, inf. 39,) 42. Confirmed, 23. Marriages, 20. Burials, 24. Communicants: present number, 110. The Holy Communion celebrated on the first Sunday of each month, and on Christmas, Easter, Whitsun-Day and Trinity Sunday. Catechists and Sunday-School teachers, 7. Catechumens, 150; times, every Sunday. Total number of young persons instructed, 150. Daily Parish Schools: mostly free; Scholars, males, nearly equal; females, 90. Celebration of Divine Service: Sundays, at 10½ A. M., Catechetical exercises, 3 P. M., and at Lent, 7½ P. M.; Holy Days, at 9 A. M.; other days, daily morning Prayer at 9; Friday evenings, half-past 7.

Contributions.—Diocesan Fund, $24; Fund for Aged and Infirm Clergymen, $3; New-York Bible and Common Prayer-Book Society, $15; Parochial Schools, $250; the Poor, $150; Parish purposes, $300; offerings of the children of the schools for missions, $180; other charitable institutions of the Church, in sums of $10 each, $842.

Church of the Resurrection, New-York; the Rev. EDWARD O. FLAGG, D. D., Rector.

Families, 100. Individuals, 350. Baptisms, (ad. 4, inf. 14,) 18. Confirmed, 20. Marriages, 8. Burials, 23. Communicants: admitted, 15; removed into the Parish, 20; removed from the Parish, 9; present number, 80. The Holy Communion celebrated first Sunday in the month and greater festivals. Catechists and Sunday-School teachers, 16. Catechumens: Sunday scholars, 150. Celebration of Divine Service: Sundays, morning and evening; Holy Days, greater festivals and fasts.

Contributions.—Church purposes in general, $4,000.

This Parish is in a promising condition.

Spanish Church of Santiago, New-York; the Rev. JOAQUIM DE PALMA, Rector.

Families, 54. Individuals, 282. Baptisms, inf. 14. Marriages, 17. Burials, 5. Communicants: admitted, 4; removed from the Parish, 10; died, 2; present number, 57. The Holy Communion celebrated first Sunday in the month and on Christmas Day. Catechists and Sunday-School teachers, 3. Catechumens: members of other classes for religious instruction, 40; Sunday scholars, 35; total number of young persons instructed 60. Celebration of Divine Service: Sundays, service at 12½ P. M.; Holy Days, Good Friday and Christmas Day; other days, Thanksgiving Day.

Contributions.—The Poor, $60.

Notwithstanding the pecuniary difficulties with which this Missionary work has to contend, God has blessed my efforts, and new converts are slowly but steadily joining our fold. The number of baptisms, and especially of marriages, is a proof of the success of this Mission, when it is remembered that I have to work among Roman Catholics. Not all the Cubans that belong now to my Church can come regularly to our Sunday services, because they are scattered all over the city, and some are living in Fordham, Harlem and Brooklyn. For this reason I continue my Evangelical lectures in Brooklyn every Wednesday evening, with a congregation of from 30 to 40 Cubans.

St. Ambrose' Church, New-York; the Rev. FREDERICK SILL, Rector.

Baptisms, (ad. 23, inf. 118,) 141. Confirmed, 32. Marriages, 122. Burials, 140. Communicants, 175; admitted, 47; removed into the Parish, 6; removed from the Parish, 19; died, 19; present number, 190. The Holy Communion celebrated on the first and third Sundays of every month, the latter an early celebration at 7 A. M., several times in private, and twice on each of the three high festivals. Celebration of Divine Service: Sundays, twice a day throughout the year, lacking two Sundays, closed for repairs; Holy Days, nearly all, including all the Ember and Rogation Days; Wednesday evenings, full service and lecture from October to May; Friday evenings, Litany service from May to October. The holy season of Lent is likewise observed, with daily services through the great week thereof. On Thanksgiving Day, Easter, P. M., and Christmas Eve, festivals of the children are held.

Contributions.—Episcopal Fund, $2; Diocesan Fund, $18; Missionary Committee of the Diocese, $6 44; Theological Education Fund, $5; Berkeley Divinity School, $10; Fund for Aged and Infirm Clergymen, $5 60; Orphan's Home, $7 26; House of the Good Shepherd, $23; New-York Bible and Common Prayer-Book Society, $2 52; Church Fund $58 82, Rector, in addition to salary, $310 53; reduction of mortgage on Church property, $100; Board of Missions P. E Church, U. S.: Foreign Committee, Joppa, $3; Domestic Committee, $10 84; Bishop Morris, $10; Rev. Mr. Love, $21; other colored people $37 21; Sunday-School, $136; the Aged, through the Friendly Society, $192; the Poor, $456 82; Revered Brethren, $7 25; Parish purposes, $9 50; Church purposes in general, $2,644 88; toward interments, $244 20—total, $4,321 90.

Requisite repairs have been put upon the Parish Church in compliance with the positive directions of the Building Department. Parts of the outer stone work have been newly pointed, and some necessary painting done within, whereby the Parish has incurred a debt of $690 15.

The Church has been the recipient of several valuable gifts the past year, among which was a set of purple altar coverings and a piece of silver plate, whereby the Communion set is rendered complete.

The work of the Parish is heavy, while the means at the disposal of the Rector are very limited and inadequate.

St. Andrew's Church, New-York; the Rev. GEORGE B. DRAPER, D. D., Rector.

Families, about 200. Baptisms, (ad. 7, inf. 61,) 68. Confirmed, 27. Marriages, 13. Burials, 38. Communicants: admitted, 35; removed into the Parish, 79; removed from the Parish, 22; died, 2; present number, 323. The Holy Communion celebrated on first Sunday of every month, St. Andrew's Day, Christmas Day, Easter, Ascension, Whitsun-

Day and Trinity Sunday. Catechists and Sunday-School teachers, 28. Catechumens, 328. Children taught the Catechism openly in the Church, every month. Celebration of Divine Service: Sundays, morning and evening, and children's service on the last Sunday P. M. of the month; Holy Days, morning; other days, evening prayer on Fridays throughout the year, and daily services in Lent.

Contributions.—Missionary Committee of the Diocese, $33 90; New-York City Mission Society, $63; City Mission to Jews, $22 91; Board of Missions P. E. Church, U. S.: Mission to Colored People of the South, $59 53; Domestic Committee, $128 70; Foreign Committee, $51 70; Industrial School of Parish, $80 42; the Poor, $411 56; Sunday-School of Parish, $135 91; Parish purposes, $1,798 56; Easter Flowers, $44; Church purposes in general, $870 50—total, $3,699 69.

The new Church building, the corner-stone of which was laid on the second day of November, 1872, was completed at the time specified in the contract, and opened for Divine Service on St. Andrew's Day, 1873.

For beauty and adaptedness to use, the new St. Andrew's Church can hardly be excelled by any structure of the same dimensions and no greater cost. It has sittings for over 900 persons, and could easily be made to accommodate one or two hundred more. Its arrangements for the ingress and egress of the congregation, and for the proper performance of every service, are admirably convenient. The building is well lighted and ventilated, comfortably warm in winter, and in summer cool. Its acoustic qualities are perfect, and that, without the least departure from the old and accepted types of Church arrangement in quest of concert hall advantages.

The whole cost of the building, organ and furniture has been not far from $100,000. Other expenses were incurred in connection with the enterprise, amounting to at least $15,000 more, but we have not considered them as fairly chargeable to the building account. The Parish and its friends have raised nearly one-half of the whole amount expended, and they have no doubt of their ability to carry the burden thus assumed, with the prospect of relief, which, in this portion of the city they enjoy, from the constant and rapid increase of the population. We report a number of communicants nearly one-third more than that we had last year.

St. Ann's Church for Deaf Mutes, New-York; the Rev. THOMAS GALLAUDET, D. D., Rector; the Rev. JOHN CHAMBERLAIN, Assistant.

Families, upwards of 150. Individuals, about 1,000. Baptisms, (ad. 14, (7 deaf mutes,) inf. 49,) (1 deaf mute, and 2 children of deaf mutes,) 63. Confirmed, 44, (20 deaf mutes.) Marriages, 38, (5 deaf mutes.) Burials, 39. Communicants: admitted, 46; removed into the Parish, 8; removed from the Parish, 46; died, 5; present number, 517, (about 75 deaf mutes.) The Holy Communion celebrated every Sunday, at 7 A. M., on the first Sunday of the month and high festivals, at 10.30 A. M., and on other Holy Days at 9 A. M. Catechists and Sunday-School teachers, 25. Catechumens: Children taught the Catechism openly in the Church, 100; times, 12; members of other classes for religious instruction, 20; Sunday Scholars, 50; total number of young persons instructed, 170. Daily Parish School: one, free; Scholars: males, 10, females, 25. Sewing School: upwards of 100. Boys' Thursday evening meeting in Chapel, 40. Celebration of Divine Service: Sunday, six, one being for deaf mutes; Holy Days and other days, twice, and on some days in Lent, three times.

Contributions.—Episcopal Fund, $10; Diocesan Fund, $60; Missionary Committee of the Diocese, $101 54; Fund for Aged and Infirm Clergymen, $40; New-York City Mission Society, (St. Barnabas' House, $26 50,) $68; New-York Bible and Common Prayer-Book Society, $15 75; Board of Missions P. E. Church, U. S.: Domestic Committee, $47 50; Indian Commission, $16 25; Foreign Committee, $55 84; Freedmen Commission, $18; Parochial Schools, Sunday-Schools and the Poor, $2,735 71; Parish purposes, offerings and donations, ($1,000 from Trinity Church, $4,830 99, balance of the legacy of Mrs. Mary C. C. Van Horne, $6,207 91, legacy with interest of Mr. G. R. Jackson.) $17,153 62; Church purposes in general, $240 54; Church Mission to Deaf Mutes, $371 29—total, $20,929 04.

In carrying on the special Mission to Deaf Mutes, St. Ann's Church is thankful for the aid which has been extended by the recently incorporated Society, known as "The Church Mission to Deaf Mutes." It is very desirable that the remaining mortgage of $15,000 upon St. Ann's Church and Rectory should be paid. It is hard for a Church with free seats to pay interest on a mortgaged debt. We trust that the time is not far distant when we shall be able to report the payment of this mortgage.

Midnight Mission; the Rev. THOMAS GALLAUDET, D. D., Chaplain.

Confirmed, 1. Marriage, 1. Frequent services, in which the Chaplain has been kindly assisted by quite a number of his brethren of the Clergy.

St. Bartholomew's Church, New-York; the Rev. SAMUEL COOKE, D. D., Rector; the Rev. JOSEPH M. WAITE, Assistant Minister.

Families, 250. Individuals, 1,200. Baptisms, (ad. 2, inf. 10,) 12. Confirmed, 26. Marriages, 11. Burials, 18. Communicants: present number, 450. The Holy Communion celebrated monthly.

St. Clement's Church, New-York; the Rev. THEODORE A. EATON, D. D., Rector.

Baptisms, (ad. 5, inf. 82,) 87. Confirmed, 27. Marriages, 5. Burials, 7. Communicants: admitted, 13; removed into the Parish, 10; removed from the Parish, 11; died, 5; present number, about 150. The Holy Communion celebrated on the first Sunday in every month, and on the festivals for which a Special Preface is provided. Sunday-School teachers, 13; Sunday Scholars, 150. Public Catechising in Church every month for nine months of the year. Celebration of Divine Service: twice every Sunday; on every festival and Saint's Day, daily in Lent, and every Wednesday and Friday for nine months of the year.

Contributions.—Episcopal Fund, $5; Diocesan Fund, $25; Missionary Committee of the Diocese, $75; Burial Fund, $41; Fund for Aged and Infirm Clergymen, $69; Parish Mission of St. Clement's, $952 23; for Organ for Sunday-School, $120; for Thanksgiving for the Poor, $46, for Christmas Festival, $69, St. Mary's Hospital for Children, $45; Flower Fund, $92 75; Board of Missions P. E Church, U. S.: Domestic Committee, $187 30; Foreign Committee, $51; Indian Missions, $30; Freedmen, $25, the Poor, by Communion Alms, $425 65; Parish purposes, Sunday offerings, $1,394 28, Christmas offering, $1,710 10; Easter offering, $457 91—total, $5,840 22.

The repairs of the Church edifice, which were in progress when the Parochial report of last year was made, were completed at the close of November, 1873. By the generous aid of Trinity Church, and the liberal offerings of the congregation of St. Clement's, the cost of these repairs, amounting to nearly $4,000, was defrayed within less than three months.

The "Parish Mission" continues its work among the poor and the sick, and has been the instrument, it is believed, of much good, both temporal and spiritual, to many people. With a Mission house, which is greatly needed, and one or more Christian "Sisters" or "Deaconesses" to co-operate with the faithful and earnest "Sister" now in charge, the work of the Mission could be much enlarged, and its benefits more widely extended.

Church Du St. Esprit, New-York; (no Rector,) the Rev. LEON PONS, Minister elect.

Baptisms, inf. 6. Marriages, 20. Burials, 6. Communicants: died, 6. The Holy Communion celebrated Christmas, Easter, Whitsuntide and September. Catechists and Sunday-School teachers, 2. Catechumens, 10; Children taught the Catechism openly in the Church, 25; times, once. Celebration of Divine Service: 48 Sundays, every Sunday once, 10½ A. M.; 4 Holy Days, one service—total, 52.

Contributions.—Episcopal Fund, $2; Diocesan Fund, $48; Theological Education Fund, $2; Fund for Aged and Indigent Clergymen, $3; Board of Missions P. E. Church, U. S.: Domestic Committee, $2; Foreign Committee, $3—total, $60.

On the seventeenth day of March, 1874, Rev. Antoine Verren, D. D., Rector of this Church, died, at the age of 73 years, after a pastorate of 47 years in this Church. From February to July the pulpit was supplied by the Rev. J. de Palma, Rector of the Church of Santiago.

On the 24th day of September instant the Rev. Leon Pons was elected Minister of said Church, provisorily, for one year.

The death of the Rector and interruptions or changes in the officiating Minister are the causes of the imperfections of the foregoing report. We have no means to supply the deficiencies therein.

By order of the Vestry.

J. Burnier, *Clerk.*

St. George's Church, New-York; the Rev. Stephen H. Tyng, D. D., Rector. *St. George's Chapel of Free Grace;* the Rev. J. Eastman Brown, Minister. *St. George's Chapel of Bread of Life;* ————, Minister. *St. George's German Chapel;* the Rev. J. C. Fleischhacker, Minister.

Communicants: St. George's Church, 1,400; Chapel of Free Grace, 250; German Chapel, 300—1,950. Baptisms: St. George's Church, 35; St. George's Chapels, 125—160. Confirmations: St. George's Church, 34; Chapel of Free Grace, 50; Chapel of Bread of Life, 13; German Chapel, 55—152. Sunday-Schools: Teachers, 130; Scholars, 2,050—2,180.

Benevolent contributions, $55,227 16.

I give the statistics of my Parish reports.

The general history of old Parishes like St. George's changes but little from year to year. Our poor multiply—our wealthy members diminish. Demands upon us are constantly increasing—means of supply lessen. Thus difficulties are multiplied, and labors enlarged.

Church of St. George the Martyr, New-York; the Rev. Frederick Sill, Minister in charge.

The Holy Communion celebrated on the third Sunday of every month, at 7 A. M.; on the three high festivals and St. George's Day in the Parish Church of St. Ambrose.

Contributions.—Episcopal Fund, $2; Diocesan Fund, $5; the Poor, (in response to 27 applications from poor English people,) $79 19; Parish purposes, $36 50; Church purposes in general, $293 67—total, $415 36.

A floating debt of nearly $300 was generously paid by a parishioner in February last. A portion of it was due the Minister in charge, previous to his relinquishment of all claim to salary.

The St. George's Society is an organization distinct from the Church of St. George the Martyr, having originated previous to the American Revolution. It has a Permanent Fund of $35,000, the interest of which is wholly applied to the relief of the poor English. On the first of May, 1872, it appointed the Rector or Minister in charge of the "Martyr" one of its Chaplains ex officio at a salary of $250 per annum, and payable out of a Contingent Fund, which appointment still continues. During the past year 24 patients have been admitted to the free use of the Beds of the Church in St. Luke's Hospital; one remained two days, one five days, and the remainder from three weeks to five months and upwards.

The extensive arrangements made in the city last winter to relieve the distressed, materially lessened the number of applicants upon the charity of the Church.

St. James' Church, New-York; the Rev. CORNELIUS B. SMITH, Rector.

Baptisms, (ad. 6, inf. 38,) 44. Confirmed, 41. Marriages, 6. Burials, 19. Communicants: present number, 291. The Holy Communion celebrated on all high festivals, on the first Sunday in the month, and on Thursday evening in Holy Week. Catechists and Sunday-School teachers, 34. Catechumens, 366. Celebration of Divine Service: Sundays, 96 times; also on all chief Holy Days, and every day of Lent, and Rogation days, and ordinarily on Fridays.

Contributions.—Episcopal Fund, $8; Diocesan Fund, $50; Missionary Committee of the Diocese, $65 10; Theological Education, by Society for Increase of Ministry, $101 04; St. Luke's Home, $55 06; St. James' Free Chapel, $960 88; Children's Fold, $55 49; American Bible Society, $60 16; Memphis and Louisiana Sufferers, $119 22; Decorations and repairs of the Church, $2,117 18; Board of Missions P. E Church, U. S.: Colored Freedmen, $54 81; Indians, $34 90; Domestic Committee, $346 04; Foreign Committee, $310 52; Parochial Schools, $387 29; the Poor, $432 68; Ladies' Association, $69 25; Church purposes in general, $44 25--total, $5,321 87.

The interior of the Church has been decorated. At the Mission, in Second Avenue, there have been constant services and Sunday-School sessions; also, Mothers' meetings, weekly readings, and a Sewing School.

Church of St. John Baptist, New-York; the Rev. CORNELIUS ROOSEVELT DUFFIE, D. D., Rector; the Rev. GEORGE W. BACON, M. D., LL. B., Assistant Minister.

Baptisms, (ad. 9, inf. 12,) 21. Confirmed, 25. Marriages, 9. Burials, 10. Communicants: admitted, 10; removed into the Parish, 19; removed from the Parish, about 25, died, 4; present number, about 200. The Holy Communion celebrated on chief festivals, and on the second Sunday of each month.

Contributions.—Episcopal Fund, Bishop's Salary, $5; Diocesan Fund, $16; Missionary Committee of the Diocese, $30; Theological Education Fund, $5 45; New-York City Mission Society, $5; Church Missionary Society for Seamen, $5; Board of Missions P E. Church, U. S.: Freedmen's Com., $27 75; Domestic Committee, (including Mite Chests, $20 37,) $76 37; Foreign Committee, $27 80; Indian Commission, $27 75; the Poor, and Parish purposes, $2,238 56; Church purposes in general, $41—total, $2,505 68.

Church of St. John the Evangelist, New-York; the Rev. WILLIAM TODD EGBERT, Rector.

Families, 425. Individuals, 1,500. Baptisms, (ad. 23, inf. 55,) 78. Confirmed, 58. Marriages, 16. Burials, 28. Communicants: admitted, 50; removed into the Parish, 60; removed from the Parish, 40; died, 20; present number, about 500. The Holy Communion celebrated on first Sunday in every month, and on the great festivals. Catechists and Sunday-School teachers, 35. Catechumens: Children taught the Catechism openly in the Church, 300; times, 9; members of other classes for religious instruction, 40; total number of young persons instructed, 340. Celebration of Divine Service: Sundays, 104; Holy Days, 5; other days, 80—total, 127.

Contributions.—Episcopal Fund, $8; Diocesan Fund, $20; Missionary Committee of the Diocese, $10; Theological Education Fund, $3; Fund for Aged and Infirm Clergymen, $3; New-York City Mission Society, $3; Church Missionary Society for Seamen, $3; Education of two young men for the Ministry, $400; Board of Missions P. E. Church, U. S.: Domestic Committee, $25; Foreign Committee, $25; for Rev. Walter Moore, work in Colorado, $131 50; for Rev. Abiel Leonard's work in Missouri, $112 21; the Poor, $1,462 33; Parish purposes, $5,049 73; Church purposes in general, $325—total, $7,580 77.

St. Luke's Church, New-York; the Rev. ISAAC H. TUTTLE, D. D., Rector; the Rev. A. H. WARNER, Assistant.

Baptisms, (ad. 5, inf. 85,) 90. Confirmed, 61. Marriages, 37. Burials, 52. Communicants, about 320. The Holy Communion celebrated weekly, and on all festivals. Catechists and Sunday-School teachers, 41. Catechumens, 480. Children taught openly in the Church, generally every Sunday. Daily Parish School: 1; partly pay, for females. Celebration of Divine Service: Daily throughout the year; Sundays, three services generally every Sunday.

Contributions.—Episcopal Fund, $7; Diocesan Fund, $50; Missionary Committee of the Diocese, $62 20; Aid to Students, $125; Fund for Aged and Infirm Clergymen, $35 36; New-York City Mission Society, $72 82; Church Missionary Society for Jews, $44 72; Rev. Mr. Love, colored Clergyman, South, $45; Mite Society for Church objects, $250; for Tracts, $31; Rev. Mr. Cowan, California, $50 14; Education of Indian boy, Isaac H. Tuttle, by Infant Class, $100; Board of Missions P. E. Church, U. S.: Rev. J. J. Enmigahbough, $35; Domestic Committee, $150; Foreign Committee, $152; St. Luke's Home for Indigent Christian Females, $248 22; Parochial School, $100; Relief Society for the Poor, $226 79; Sunday-School offerings for Dr. Breck and others, $226; Church improvements, $989 60; Communion and other offerings for the Poor, $1,161 37; Church purposes in general, (Penny Collections,) $707 97; Support of Sunday Schools, $175 70—total $5,340 89.

St. Mark's Church and Mission Chapel, New-York; the Rev. J. H. RYLANCE, D. D., Rector; the Rev. S. A. MCNULTY, Assistant.

Families, 275. Individuals, about 900. Baptisms, (ad. 5, inf. 56,) 61. Confirmed, 92. Marriages, 15. Burials, 37. Communicants: admitted, 50; removed into the Parish, 7; removed from the Parish, 15; died, 5; present number, about 402. The Holy Communion celebrated monthly at both Church and Chapel, and all festivals of the Church. Catechumens: total number of young persons instructed, 700. Daily Parish School: one, free; Teachers, 2; Scholars, 120. Celebration of Divine Service: Sundays, 52; Holy Days, 15; other days, 26—total, 93.

Contributions.—Missionary Committee of the Diocese, $158 70; Aged and Infirm Clergymen, $112 33; Church Missionary Society for Seamen, $88 95; New-York Bible and Common Prayer-Book Society, $10; Board of Missions P. E. Church, U. S.: Domestic Committee, $828 37; Foreign Committee, $250; Parochial Schools, $950; the Poor and Mission expenses, $4,716 17; Parish purposes, $560 54; Church purposes in general, $1,218 26; Evangelical Knowledge Society, $73 95; American Church Missionary Society, $400; American Church Missionary Society, City Committee, $300: Evangelical Education Society, $300; Missions to Colored People, $110 20; Indian Missions, $184 65; Indian Missions, Parochial Aid Society, $308 35—total, $10,655 52.

St. Mary's Church, New-York; the Rev. CHARLES C. ADAMS, Rector.

Families, 55. Individuals, 350. Baptisms, (ad. 1, inf. 15,) 16. Confirmed, 12. Marriages, 8. Burials, 6. Communicants: admitted, 15; removed into the Parish, 2; removed from the Parish, 10; died, 2; present number, 142. The Holy Communion celebrated every Lord's Day, (weekly,) and on the chief Holy Days, Catechumens, 12. Children taught the Catechism openly in the Church, 80; times, 12; Sunday scholars, all Sunday scholars above included; total number of young persons instructed, 100. Celebration of Divine Service: Sundays, 10½ A. M., 7½ P. M.; Holy Days, 10 A. M., 4 P. M.; other days, daily, 8½ A. M., 4 P. M.; total prayers said, 700 times; sermons preached, 104.

Contributions.—Episcopal Fund, $5; Diocesan Fund, $14; Missionary Committee of the Diocese, $7; Fund for Aged and Infirm Clergymen, $25; New-York City Mission, $7; Church Missionary Society for Jews, $10; Board of Missions P. E. Church, U. S.: Domestic Committee, $63 63; Foreign Committee, $22; Parish purposes, $847 50; Church purposes and offertory, $963 90—total, $1,965 03.

St. Mary's is a free Church, supported chiefly by the offertory, without pew rents, envelopes or subscriptions.

Within the year a new furnace and organ have been put in the Church, pavements put in the yard, and fences painted.

December 18th, 1873, was the fiftieth year since the Parish was organized, and the Rev. Dr. Peters preached a sermon on the occasion, which has been published.

Church of St. Mary the Virgin, New-York; the Rev. THOMAS MCKEE BROWN, Minister in charge; the Rev. MCWALTER BERNARD NOYES, Assisting.

Families, 39. Individuals, about 300. Baptisms, (ad. 4, inf. 29,) 33. Confirmed, 18. Marriages, 5. Burials, 7. Communicants: admitted, 18; removed into the Parish, 14; removed from the Parish, 17; died, 2; present number, 184. The Holy Communion celebrated daily throughout the year, and twice each Sunday, and on chief Holy Days. Catechists and Sunday-School teachers, 12. Catechumens: total number of young persons instructed, 100. Celebration of Divine Service: Sundays, 289; Holy Days, 85; other days, 441—total, 815.

Contributions.—Episcopal Fund, $10; Church purposes in general, $6,500—total, $6,510.

The Reverend Beverly R. Betts has rendered valuable assistance on Sundays and other days, throughout the year.

St. Matthias' Church, New-York; the Rev. N. E. CORNWELL, D. D., Rector.

Families, about 50. Baptisms, (ad. 1, inf. 7,) 8. Marriages, 13. Burials, 10. Communicants: present number, about 50. The Holy Communion celebrated on the first Sunday of each month, and the festivals of Christmas Day, Easter Sunday and Whitsun-Day.

Until the month of May, I continued the services of the Free Church of St. Matthias as usual. Since that time, at the request of the Rev. Dr. Muhlenberg, I have discharged the duties of Pastor of St. Luke's Hospital; holding two services in the Chapel on Sundays, and the morning and evening services in the Wards and the Chapel on other days of the week.

St. Michael's Church, New-York; the Rev. T. M. PETERS, D. D., Rector; the Rev. C. T. WARD, Assistant.

Families, 83, besides Asylums. Individuals, 870 Baptisms, (ad. 5, inf. 39,) 44. Confirmed, 39. Marriages, 5. Burials, 39. Communicants: admitted, 38; removed into the Parish, 8; removed from the Parish, 32; died, 3; present number, 179. The Holy Communion celebrated twice a month on Sunday, and also on high festivals. Catechists and Sunday-School teachers, 18; Sunday scholars, 177. Total number of young persons instructed, 452. Celebration of Divine Service: Sundays, always thrice, often four, occasionally five times; Holy Days, once, twice or thrice: other days, every morning, with occasional interruptions.

Contributions.—Missionary Committee of the Diocese, $16 86; Fund for Aged and Infirm Clergymen, $11 92; New-York City Mission Society, $73 98; Church Missionary Society for Seamen, $6 60; Board of Missions P. E. Church, U. S: Domestic Committee, $21 85; Foreign Committee, $26 70; Freedmen's Mission, $16 85; Indian Missions, $42 66, the Poor, $1,239 54; Parish purposes, $1,533 85; Church purposes in general, $1,208 80—total, $4,199 11.

Seats free. All offerings included in foregoing report.

This Parish mourns the death of its Senior Warden for forty-two, and its Treasurer for fifty-six years, the late James F. De Peyster, under whose prudent management the resources of the Church have greatly increased.

St. Peter's Church, New-York; the Rev. ALFRED B. BEACH, D. D., Rector; the Rev. BRADY E. BACKUS, A. M., Assistant.

Baptisms, (ad. 9, inf. 133,) 142. Confirmed, 34. Marriages, 27. Burials, 40. Communicants: present number, about 400. The Holy Communion celebrated on the first Sunday in every month, and on the great festivals. Catechists and Sunday-School teachers, 74. Catechumens: Children taught the Catechism openly in the Church, all in the Parish who will come, being invited to do so; times, monthly; members of other classes for religious instruction, 75; Sunday Scholars, 657; total number of young persons instructed, 731. Celebration of Divine Service: Sundays, 112; on all Holy Days, and daily, morning and evening, through Lent.

Contributions.—Episcopal Fund, $15; Diocesan Fund, $40; Diocesan Missions, $118 20; Fund for Aged and Infirm Clergymen, $41 66; New-York Bible and Common Prayer-Book Society, $40; Domestic Missions, $60 13; Sunday-School at Mooer's Forks, (from S. S.,) $7 50; Sufferers at Memphis, ($30 from S. S.,) $88 50; Orphan's Home, ($66 05 from S. S.,) $92 05; Sheltering Arms, (from S. S.,) $57 12; St. Luke's Home, $211; Parish Mission, ($280 from S. S.,) $1,300; Charity Fund of Young Men's Association, $293 25; Dorcas Society, $100 50; Sewing School, $84; Christmas Festival, for S. S., $234 45; Additional in S. S., for various objects, $241 97; Parish general Fund, $1,822 27; Communion Alms and other offerings for the Poor, $420 21—total, $5,367 81.

St. Philip's Church, New-York; (Rectorship vacant.)

Families, 125. Individuals, 450. Baptisms, (ad. 34, inf. 14,) 48. Confirmed, 62. Marriages, 8. Burials, 23. Communicants, 200; removed from the Parish, 2; died, 28; present number, 198. The Holy Communion celebrated on the first Sunday in each month, Christmas Day, Easter and Whitsun-Day, Holy Thursday. Catechists and Sunday-School teachers, 10. Catechumens, 15; Children taught the Catechism openly in the Church, 75; times, 46; total number of young persons instructed, 90. Daily Parish School: scholars, males, 30, females, 60. Celebration of Divine Service: Sundays, 48, two services; Holy Days, Christmas, Ash Wednesday, Good Friday, Epiphany; other days, once a week to Lent, then twice a week; Passion Week daily, and National Thanksgiving Day—total, 117.

Contributions.—Episcopal Fund, $3; Diocesan Fund, $30; Fund for Aged and Infirm Clergymen, $16 25; New-York Bible and Common Prayer-Book Society, $10; Freedmen, $27; Mission to the Jews, $14 50; Auer Memorial, $23; the Poor, $308 26; Parish purposes, $452 74; Church purposes in general, $2,650—total, $3,534 75.

During the past year our Parish has been severely afflicted with much sickness, and many deaths of our members. Financially we had many and pressing demands upon us. By the monetary panic of 1873 we suffered a loss of $700, deposited in one of the banking houses for current expenses. And lastly, the hand of Divine Providence has been sorely laid upon us, in the death of our beloved Rector, the Rev. William J. Alston, which occurred upon the 26th of May, 1874. We still have with us the Rev. John Peterson, Deacon; who, though having nearly reached his threescore and ten, is still active in the Church work.

St. Stephen's Church, New-York; the Rev. J. H. PRICE, D. D., Rector; the Rev. A. B. HART, Associate.

Families, 60. Baptisms, (ad. 3, inf. 9,) 12. Marriages, 5. Burials, 7. Communicants: present number, 60. The Holy Communion celebrated on the first Sunday in the month, and on the high festivals. Catechists and Sunday-School teachers, 12. Catechumens, 100. Celebration of Divine Service: Sundays, 52, 10.30 A. M. and 4 P. M.; Holy Days, all Holy Days, at 11 A. M.

Contributions.—Fund for Aged and Infirm Clergymen, $30 50; New-York City Mission Society, $32; for Africa, $25; the Poor, $50; Parish purposes, $2,898 53—total, $2,536 03.

St. Thomas' Church, New-York; the Rev. WILLIAM F. MORGAN, D. D., Rector; the Rev. JOSEPH F. JOWITT, Assistant Minister; the Rev. ROBERT LOWRY, Minister in charge of St. Thomas' Chapel.

Families, 325. Individuals, 1,800. Baptisms, (ad. 9, inf. 27,) 36. Confirmed, 56. Marriages, 12. Burials, 11. Communicants, 800. The Holy Communion celebrated first Sunday in every month, and on all high festivals. Catechists and Sunday-School teachers, 35. Catechumens, 155. Children taught the Catechism openly in the Church, 250; Bible Classes, numbering 76. Celebration of Divine Service: Sundays, all; Holy Days, all; other days, Wednesdays.

Contributions.—Sunday-School, $218 64; Church Book Society, $141 58; House of Rest for Consumptives, $194 09; Bible and Common Prayer-Book Society, $109; House of Mercy, $295 11; Shepherd's Fold, $383 62; Theological Learning, $62 25; Church Mission to Jews, $76; Mission to Seamen, $169 75; Communion offerings, $1,665 33; Church Fund, $1,073 11; Domestic Missions, $423; Foreign Missions, $139 64; Dr. and Mrs. Hill, Athens, $157 69; City Missions, $960 91; Diocesan Missions, $245; Employment Society, $210; Mission to French People, $184 13; St. Thomas' Chapel, $2,374 56; Orphan's Home, $223; St. Luke's Home, $122; other collections, special, $491 17; Episcopal Fund in full; Diocesan Fund in full; Contributions to the Tower, $30,000; Contributions for decorating St. Thomas' Chapel, $400; aggregate of Contributions, $41,446; Pew rents, $42,000—total, $83,476.

Notwithstanding the financial depression of the country, and its effect upon Church resources and offerings, this Parish has prosecuted and accomplished the work it had in hand. The tower is finished, the chime of ten bells in its place, and the interior of St. Thomas' Chapel most tastefully decorated. This latter work is largely due to the energy and liberality of Joseph M. Cooper, Esq., a valued member of the Parish.

The prospects of St. Thomas' Chapel were never so encouraging. Under the pastoral charge of the Rev. Robert Lowry, every department of Church life and activity is advancing. The Sunday-School is especially prospered, and under the superintendence of Mr. Alexander C. Morgan and his noble band of helpers, is to be ranked among the largest in the city. Appended is the report of the Rev. Minister in charge.

St. Thomas' Chapel, New-York; the Rev. WILLIAM F. MORGAN, D. D., Rector; the Rev. ROBERT LOWRY, Minister in charge.

Public Services, 150. Holy Communion administered 10 times. Baptisms, (ad. 9, inf. 30,) 39. Confirmed, 32. Marriages, 3. Funerals, 8. Communicants, 115. Sunday Scholars, (school, 187, infants, 132,) 319 on record. Families, 121. Parochial visits, 762.

Contributions.—December, 1873, $41 28; January, 1874, $56 67; February, $100 47; March, $132 81; April, $127 81; May, $73 40; June, $48; July, $56 67; August, $47 95; September, $52 68—total, $742 80. Deduct Holy Communion Alms, $154 11—for Pastor's salary, $587 89. Diocesan Missions, $3 70; Foreign Missions, $7 63; for the Jews, $5; for Communion wine, $10; for Chapel Decoration, $50; for Cushions for Chapel, $440—total, $519 33. Add weekly offerings, $742 80—total, $1,261 63.

The above report embraces a period from St. Thomas' Day, December 21st, 1873, to October 1st, 1874.

St. Timothy's Church, New-York; the Rev. GEORGE JARVIS GEER, D. D., Rector.

Baptisms, (ad. 8, inf. 41,) 49. Confirmed, 33. Marriages, 13. Burials, 24. Communicants: admitted anew, 32; removed into the Parish, 30; removed from the Parish, 40; died, 9; present number, 278. The Holy Communion celebrated on the first and third Sundays in the month and on the principal Holy Days. Catechists and Sunday-School teachers, 45. Catechumens: total number of young persons instructed, 325. Celebration of Divine Service: Sundays, morning and evening throughout the year; Holy Days, those set forth in the calendar; other days, Wednesday evening service and lecture from November 1 to May 1; Prayers Wednesday and Friday, daily morning and evening in Lent.

Contributions.—Episcopal Fund, $4; Diocesan Fund, $27 70; Missionary Committee of the Diocese, $23 10; Fund for Aged and Infirm Clergymen, $7 40; Mission to Jews, $18; Indian Commission, $18; Home Mission to Colored Persons, $12; Domestic Missions, $34 21; Foreign Committee, $15; Clergymen's Insurance League, $18; Parish Mutual, $15; Communion Alms, including Alms Chest, $239 57; Parish purposes, $7,532 88; Church purposes in general, $48 85—total, $8,027 71.

Church of the Transfiguration, New-York; the Rev. GEORGE H. HOUGHTON, D. D., Rector; the Rev. EDWARD C. HOUGHTON, Assistant Minister.

Baptisms, (ad. 13, inf. 54,) 67. Confirmed, 37. Marriages, 42. Burials, 25. Communicants: present number, 450. The Holy Communion celebrated Sundays and other Holy Days. Catechumens: total number of young persons instructed, 100. Celebration of Divine Service: Daily.

Contributions.—$13,102 49.

Trinity Church, New-York, including St. Paul's, St. John's and Trinity Chapels, the Mission Chapels of St. Chrysostom and St. Augustine, and the Chapel of St. Cornelius, Fort Columbus, on Governor's Island; the Rev. MORGAN DIX, D. D., Rector; the Rev. BENJAMIN I. HAIGHT, D. D., LL. D., Assistant Rector; the Rev. SULLIVAN H. WESTON, D. D., the Rev. CORNELIUS E. SWOPE, D. D., the Rev. JAMES MULCHAHEY, D. D., the Rev. FREDERICK OGILBY, D. D., the Rev. WM. H. COOKE, the Rev. CHARLES T. OLMSTED, the Rev. HORACE B. HITCHINGS and the Rev. ALGERNON SIDNEY CRAPSEY, Assistant Ministers; the Rev. THOS. H. SILL, Mission Priest at St. Chrysostom's Chapel; the Rev. ARTHUR C. KIMBER, Mission Priest at St. Augustine's Chapel; the Rev. H. N. GOODWIN, Chaplain at Fort Columbus; and the Rev. GEO. C. HOUGHTON, the Rev. JOHN H. HOUGHTON and the Rev. HENRY N. WAYNE, temporarily officiating.

I.—GENERAL STATEMENT.

BAPTISMS: *Adults*, 42; *Infants*, 449—*total*, 491.
CONFIRMED, 336.
MARRIAGES, 146.
BURIALS, 252.
COMMUNICANTS, 2,789.
CATECHISTS AND SUNDAY-SCHOOL TEACHERS, 222.
CATECHUMENS AND SUNDAY SCHOLARS, 3,124.
DAILY PARISH SCHOOLS, free—*Boys*, 435; *Girls*, 274—*total*, 709.
INDUSTRIAL SCHOOLS—
Teachers, ... 112
Scholars, ... 2,171
CONTRIBUTIONS OF THE PEOPLE, $28,672 92.

II.—SPECIFICATIONS.

TRINITY CHURCH—

Baptisms: Adults, 12; *Infants*, 97—*total*, 109.
Marriages,....... 43
Confirmed,........ 51
Burials, ... 30
Communicants—
Added,........................ 49
Died or removed,............ 10
Present number,............. 643
Catechumens—
Sunday-School: Teachers,.................................. 34
Scholars,.................................. 498
Industrial School: Teachers,..................................
Scholars,. ....
Daily School for Boys: Teachers,.......................... 5
Scholars, ... 275

ST. PAUL'S CHAPEL—

Baptisms: Adults, 3; *Infants*, 43—*total*, 46.
Marriages,....... 19
Confirmed,....... 58
Burials,.......... 21
Communicants—
Added,...................... 29
Died or removed,......uncertain.
Present number,.......about 400
Catechumens—
Sunday-School: Teachers,.................................. 20
Scholars,.................................. 252
Industrial School: Teachers,.............................. ...
Scholars, ...all in the Parish School.
Daily Parish School for Girls: Teachers,.............. 3
Scholars,.................. 117

ST. JOHN'S CHAPEL—

Baptisms: Adults, 9; *Infants*, 144—*total*, 153.
Marriages,........ 33
Confirmed,........ 98
Burials,........... 76
Communicants—
Added, ... 47
Died or removed,............ 98
Present number, ... 663
Catechumens—
Sunday-School: Teachers,.............. 67
Scholars,........................ 900
Industrial School: Teachers,.............................. 40
Scholars,..... 1,200
Daily Parish School for Boys and Girls: Teachers,.......... 2
Scholars,.......... 75

TRINITY CHAPEL—

Baptisms: Adults, 1; *Infants*, 29—*total*, 30.
Marriages, ... 10
Confirmed,........ 44
.... 27

Communicants—
Added, ... 29
Died or removed, ... 11
Present number, ... 667

Catechumens—
Sunday-School: Teachers, ... 41
Scholars, ... 482
Industrial School: Teachers, ... 29
Scholars, ... 284
Daily Parish School for Boys: Teachers, ... 2
Scholars, ... 85

ST. CHRYSOSTOM'S FREE MISSION CHAPEL—

Baptisms: Adults, 16; *Infants*, 101—*total*, 117.
Marriages, ... 27
Confirmed, ... 55
Burials, ... 72

Communicants—
Added, ... 45
Died or removed, ... 73
Present number, ... 324

Catechumens—
Sunday-School: Teachers, ... 40
Scholars, ... 490
Industrial School: Teachers, ... 18
Scholars, ... 184
Daily Parish School for Girls: Teachers, ... 2
Scholars, ... 157

ST. AUGUSTINE'S FREE MISSION CHAPEL—

Baptisms: Adults, 3; *Infants*, 82—*total*, 85.
Marriages, ... 12
Confirmed, ... 26
Burials, ... 27

Communicants—
Added, ... 26
Died or removed, ... 23
Present number, ... 72

Catechumens—
Sunday-School: Teachers, ... 17
Scholars, ... 475
Industrial School: Teachers, ... 22
Scholars, ... 386

ST. CORNELIUS' CHAPEL, *Fort Columbus, Governor's Island*—

Baptisms: Infants, 4
Marriages, ... 3
Confirmed, ... 4
Burials, ... 3

Communicants—
Added, ... 5
Removed, ... 4
Present number, ... 20

CELEBRATION OF DIVINE SERVICE.—*Trinity Church:* daily, twice, throughout the year. *St. Paul's Chapel:* Sundays, thrice; also on high feast days and Litany days; and daily in Holy Week. *St. John's Chapel:* Sundays, thrice; and daily during Lent. *Trinity Chapel:* daily, throughout the year, twice; Sundays, four times, and from Advent to

Easter, five times; four services daily in Holy Week. *St. Chrysostom's Chapel:* Sundays, five services; week days, two; Holy Days, five; and during Lent, daily. *St. Augustine's Chapel:* Sundays, twice; Holy Days, once; occasional week day services, and Wednesday evening lectures. *St. Cornelius' Chapel:* Sundays, twice; chief Holy Days, once; Wednesdays and Fridays in Advent and Lent, once; on Friday evenings in Lent, short service and lectures for men only.

THE HOLY COMMUNION—When celebrated:

Trinity Church: Every Sunday and Holy Day, except Good Friday; two celebrations on the greater feasts, at 7 A. M. and 10½ A. M.

St. Paul's Chapel: Every Sunday, at 7 A. M., and on the second Sunday in the month, and on the high feast days, also at 10½ A. M. From Advent to Trinity, every Thursday, at 12 M.

St. John's Chapel: Every Sunday and high feast day.

Trinity Chapel: Every Sunday, at 7 A. M.; also on the first and third Sundays, a second celebration, at 10½ A. M.; also every Saints' Day and Holy Day.

St. Chrysostom's Chapel: Two celebrations every Sunday and Holy Day, except on Good Friday; on Christmas, Easter Day and Whitsun-Day, four celebrations; daily celebration, at 7 A. M., during Advent and Lent, and throughout the Octaves of the greater feasts.

St. Augustine's Chapel: First and third Sundays in each month; weekly during Lent, and on Christmas, All Saints' Day and other high feast days.

St. Cornelius' Chapel: The first Sunday in every month and the principal festivals.

COLLECTIONS AND CONTRIBUTIONS IN THE PARISH OF TRINITY CHURCH IN THE CITY OF NEW-YORK.

	Trinity Church.	*St. Paul's Chapel.*	*St. John's Chapel.*	*Trinity Chapel.*	*St. Chrysos. Chapel.*	*St. Augus. Chapel.*	*St. Corne. Chapel.*	*Total.*
Missionary Committee of the Diocese,	$855 81	$76 64	$30 78	$844 53	$24 93	$22 47	....	$1,854 94
New-York City Mission,	228 99	61 92	16 94	342 75	13 33	....	....	663 93
Theological Education Fund,	36 77	18 75	....	....	....	20 53	....	76 05
Fund for Aged and Infirm Clergymen,	85 63	54 30	....	....	13 63	34 50	$6 30	194 36
Church Missionary Society for Seamen,	32 34	32 37	3 72	39 90	5 65	....	....	113 98
New-York Bible and Common Prayer-Book Society,	36 76	18 75	12 19	380 09	5 13	....	....	452 92
Board of Missions : Domestic Committee,	1,130 51	175 91	70 00	2,596 52	68 93	13 47	....	4,055 14
Foreign Committee,	164 44	103 84	....	465 17	....	....	....	733 45
Home African Mission,	108 86	61 00	20 40	327 91	9 96	....	....	528 13
Indian Missions,	24 95	26 81	7 77	56 95	10 28	....	....	126 76
Orphan's Home,	88 55	57 21	38 68	94 66	14 87	....	....	293 91
House of Mercy,	55 61	....	....	....	14 27	....	....	69 88
The Poor, including Communion Alms,	2,673 93	1,015 74	606 53	2,479 51	967 65	597 19	....	8,340 55
Other Contributions and Offerings,*	2,587 36	742 97	21 29	6,846 22	1,097 78	312 63	61 61	11,669 86
	$6,306 51	$2,486 21	$828 30	$14,424 21	$2,246 40	$1,000 79	$67 91	

* Additional reported as collected through St. John's Guild before its withdrawal from the Parish, about $24,000.

COLLECTIONS AND CONTRIBUTIONS IN THE PARISH OF TRINITY CHURCH IN THE CITY OF NEW-YORK.

By the Vestry:		
Special Contributions to the Salary of the Bishop,		$1,800 00
Diocesan Fund,		1,100 00
Parochial Schools: at Trinity Church,	$3,865 00	
St. Paul's Chapel,	1,740 00	
St. John's Chapel,	2,300 00	
Trinity Chapel,	2,060 00	
St. Chrysostom's Chapel,	1,100 00	
		11,065 00
Industrial Schools: Trinity Church,	$1,000 00	
St. Paul's Chapel,	250 00	
St. John's Chapel,	1,000 00	
St. Augustine's Chapel,	150 00	
		2,400 00
Sunday-School Festivals,		2,425 00
Alms to the Poor,		3,000 00
		$21,790 00

Zion Church, New-York; the Rev. JOHN N. GALLEHER, Rector.

Families, 83. Baptisms, (ad. 2, inf. 5,) 7. Confirmed, 13. Marriages, 5. Burials, 5. Communicants: admitted, 17; removed into the Parish, 71; removed from the Parish, 9; died, 4; present number, 143. The Holy Communion celebrated on first Sunday in each month, and on greater festivals. Catechists and Sunday-School teachers, 12. Catechumens: Sunday Scholars, 65; total number of young persons instructed, 65. Celebration of Divine Service: Sundays, 98 times; Holy Days, 42 times; other days, 116 times—total, 256 times.

Contributions.—Episcopal Fund, $10; Diocesan Fund, $100; Missionary Committee of the Diocese, $98 77; Fund for Aged and Infirm Clergymen, $57 40; New-York City Mission Society, $326 54; Board of Missions P. E. Church, U. S.: Domestic Committee, $599 65; the Poor, $648 68; Parish purposes, $2,923 23; Church purposes in general, $2,364 81—total, $7,429 08.

Chapel of Bellevue Hospital, New-York; the Rev. P. T. VICTOR VON ROOSBROECK, Missionary.

Baptisms, (ad. 8, inf. 76,) 84. Confirmed, 2. Burials, 116. Communicants, 238. The Holy Communion celebrated on the third Sunday of every month, Christmas, Easter, St. Luke's Day, and Thanksgiving. Celebration of Divine Service: Sundays, every Sunday, at 10½ A. M.; Holy Days, Christmas, St. Luke's Day and Thanksgiving; other days, the first day in Lent, Fridays during Lent, and Good Friday; all the Fridays in Advent.

Bethlehem Chapel, New-York; the Rev. FR. OERTEL, Missionary.

Families, 88. Individuals, 197. Baptisms, inf. 29. Confirmed, 18. Marriages, 6. Burials, 10. Communicants: admitted, 24; removed from the Parish, 14; died, 5: present number, 138. The Holy Communion celebrated on all festivals. Catechists and Sunday School teachers, 7. Catechumens: Children taught the Catechism openly in the Church, 76; times, 26; members of other classes for religious instruction, 32; Sunday Scholars, 130; total number of young persons instructed, 36. Daily Parish School: free; scholars, males, 70, females, 48. Industrial School: Females, 82. Celebration of Divine Service: Sundays, morning and evening, 104 times; Holy Days, six times; other days, 12 times; total, 122 times.

Contributions.—The Poor, $92 43; Parish purposes, $125; Church purposes in general, $59 17—total, $276 60.

The Industrial School is entirely supported by the ladies of the Industrial Society, and their expenses are not included in this report. The congregation being poor, I never have been able, to my regret, to take up collections for other purposes. It is for the wants of the Parish itself, which is never sufficient for meeting all demands, and leaves us generally at the end of the year with a small debt.

St. James' Church, Fordham, New-York; the Rev. MYTTON MAURY, Rector.

Families, 70. Individuals, 250. Baptisms, 9. Confirmed, 21. Marriages, 2. Burials, 4. Communicants: present number, 115. The Holy Communion celebrated first Sunday in every month, and great festivals. Catechists and Sunday-School teachers, 13; Catechumens, 80. Celebration of Divine Service: Every Sunday, A. M., and great festivals.

Contributions.—Episcopal Fund, $8; Missionary Committee of the Diocese, $10; Theological Education Fund, $7; Fund for Aged and Infirm Clergymen, $17 57; the Poor, $195 99; Parish purposes, $16,000; Church purposes in general, $57—total, $16,295 56.

Church of the Mediator, Kingsbridge, New-York; the Rev. W. T. WILSON, Rector.

Families, 39. Individuals, 190. Baptisms, (ad. 7, inf. 10,) 17. Burials, 8. Communicants: admitted, 5; removed into the Parish, 3; removed from the Parish, 17; died, 2; present number, 68. The Holy Communion celebrated on the first Sunday of every month, and on all the principal festivals. Catechists and Sunday-School teachers, 14. Catechumens: Children taught the Catechism openly in the Church, 110; total number of young persons instructed, 110.

Contributions.—Episcopal Fund, $10; Diocesan Fund, $40; Missionary Committee of the Diocese, $45 75; Theological Education Fund, $21 25; Fund for Aged and Infirm Clergymen, $30 31; Parochial Schools, $808; the Poor, $341 99; Parish purposes, $2,149; Church purposes in general, $310—total, $3,256 30.

Christ Church, Riverdale, New-York; the Rev. GEORGE D. WILDES, D. D., Rector.

Families, 50. Individuals, 250. Baptisms, inf. 9. Confirmed, 8. Marriages, 2. Burials, 6. Communicants: admitted, 8; removed into the Parish, 7; present number, 110. The Holy Communion celebrated on the first Sunday of every month, and on the greater festivals. Sunday Scholars, 50; teachers, 8. Celebration of Divine Service: Sundays, twice; Holy Days, greater festivals, and occasional lectures.

Contributions.—Episcopal Fund, $40: Diocesan Fund, $20; Missionary Convocation, $100; Midnight Mission, $25; St. Barnabas' Home, $25; New-York City Missions, $600; Society for Increase of Ministry, $25; Fair for Hospital, $1,000; Sheltering Arms, $25; Indian Commission, $160; Domestic Missions, $211 90; Special, for Church in Virginia, $25; German Missions, $150; the Poor, $421 28; Parish purposes, $1,150; Church purposes in general, $3,600—total, $7,578 78.

In addition to the foregoing report of contributions, it is to be said, that various sums, in large aggregate amount, have been collected within the limits of the Parish from individuals for unreported Church purposes.

St. Ann's Church, Morrisania, New-York; the Rev. WILLIAM HUCKEL, Rector.

Families, 60. Individuals, about 250. Baptisms, (ad, 3, inf. 11,) 14. Confirmed, 11. Marriages, 2. Burials, 14. Communicants: admitted, 5; removed from the Parish, 10; died, 5; present number, 90. The Holy Communion celebrated on the first Sunday of each month, and on the chief festivals. Sunday-School teachers, 14; Scholars, 200. Celebration of Divine Service: Sundays, 100; other days, 40—total, 140.

Contributions.—Episcopal Fund, $7; Diocesan Fund, $10; Foreign Committee, $87; Domestic Committee, $34; Home Missions to Colored people, $16 64; Education Soc., $30; Home for Incurables, $65; Sunday-Schools, $200; Ladies' Benevolent Society of St. Ann's, $147; the Poor, $175; Easter offering for Parish purposes, $1,300; Contributions of Sunday-Schools for benevolent objects, $146 79—total, $2,168 43.

The Church edifice, during the year, has been neatly painted, and the grounds enclosed with a new fence.

The Ladies' Benevolent Society, the past winter, gave weekly employment to twenty-eight deserving poor women.

St. Paul's Church, Morrisania, New-York; the Rev. THOMAS R. HARRIS, Rector.

Families and parts of families, 54. Individuals, about 250. Baptisms, (ad. 5, inf. 8,) 13. Confirmed, 9. Marriages, 8. Burials, 8. Communicants: present number, 90. The Holy Communion celebrated the first Sunday of each month, fortnightly in Advent, weekly in Lent, and on all the greater festivals. Catechists and Sunday-School teachers, 12. Catechumens, about 100.

Contributions.—Diocesan Fund, $12; Missionary Committee of the Diocese, $8 85; Board of Missions P. E. Church, U. S.: Domestic Committee, $58 26; Freedmen and Indians, $13 09; the Poor and Sunday-School, $84 14; Parish purposes, from Offertory, $917 96; Parish purposes, from donations, &c., $400—total, $1,482 30.

Trinity Church, Morrisania, New-York; the Rev. ALBERT S. HULL, Rector.

Families, 50. Individuals, 265. Baptisms, (ad. 8, inf. 21,) 29. Confirmed, 19. Marriages, 4. Burials, 10. Communicants, 125. The Holy Communion celebrated every Lord's Day and Holy Day. Catechists and Sunday-School teachers, 13. Catechumens, 100. Celebration of Divine Service: Sundays, three times; Holy Days, once; other days, Wednesdays and Fridays.

Contributions.—Episcopal Fund, $3; Diocesan Fund, $8; Fund for Aged and Infirm Clergymen, $11 63; the Poor, $300 74; Parish purposes, $682 70; House of the Good Shepherd, $30—total, $1,038 07.

Grace Church, West Farms, New-York; the Rev. ROBERT SCOTT, Rector.

Families, 31. Individuals, 140. Baptisms, inf. 7. Marriage, 1. Burials, 3. Communicants: admitted, 1; removed into the Parish, 1; present number, 69. The Holy Communion celebrated first Sunday in every month. Catechists and Sunday-School teachers, 14. Catechumens: Children taught the Catechism openly in the Church, 140; times, 12. Celebration of Divine Service: Sundays, twice every Sunday; Holy Days, all Holy Days; other days, second Sunday in month at Home for Incurables.

Contributions.—Episcopal and Diocesan Funds, $18 45; Parish purposes, $3,000.

Having but recently become Rector of the Parish, I am unable to present a very satisfactory report of its condition. The absence of any report of offertories for charitable and religious purposes connected with the Church, is due partly to our weak financial condition, and also my very recent connection with the Parish. We hope, D. V., during the coming ecclesiastical year, to take up offertories for all or most of the objects named in the report. We are also planning for Missionary work among the Germans in our place, of whom we have a large number.

ORANGE COUNTY.

St. John's Church, Canterbury; (Rectorship vacant at the time of making this report. Reported by the Clerk of the Vestry.)

Families, 34. Individuals, 153. Baptisms, inf. 4. Marriage, 1. Burials, 2. Communicants: admitted, 3; removed into the Parish, 8; removed from the Parish, 6; died, 1; present number, 55. The Holy Communion celebrated monthly, and on chief festivals. Catechists and Sunday-School teachers, 5. Catechumens, 32. Children taught the Catechism openly in the Church, 32; times, 6. Celebration of Divine Service: Sundays, 98; Holy Days, 5; other days, 12—total, 115.

Contributions.—Episcopal Fund, $2; Diocesan Fund, $12; Sunday-School, $27 95; Parish purposes, (offerings, $500 07; subscriptions, &c., $456 44,) $956 51—total, $998 46.

The "Parsonage Fund," by accumulation of interest, &c., now amounts to $2,175.

The Parish has been "vacant" since May last, but save on one Sunday, there has been no interruption of the services.

Church of the Holy Innocents, Cornwall, P. O. Highland Falls; the Rev. WILLIAM REED THOMAS, M. A., Rector.

Families, 52. Individuals, 215. Baptisms, (ad. 2, inf. 26,) 28. Confirmed, 10. Marriages, 5. Burials, 16. Communicants: admitted, 10; removed into the Parish, 2; removed from the Parish, 2; died, 2; present number, 80. The Holy Communion celebrated on the first Sunday of every month, and on the chief festivals, and six times in private. Catechists and Sunday-School teachers, 8. Catechumens: Children taught the Catechism openly in the Church, 90; times, 12; members of other classes for religious instruction, 10; total number of young persons instructed, 100. Celebration of Divine Service: Sundays, morning and afternoon; during the winter and Lenten season frequently in the evening; Holy Days, 25; other days, 35—total, 164.

Contributions.—Episcopal Fund, $3; Diocesan Fund, $20; Missionary Committee of the Diocese, $25; Theological Education Fund, $10; Fund for Aged and Infirm Clergymen, $13 50; Church of the Holy Trinity, Highland, Ulster County, $100; "House of the Good Shepherd," $72 18; General Theological Seminary, $10; Board of Missions P. E. Church, U. S.: Domestic Committee, $5 75; the Poor, $165; Parish purposes, $150; Church purposes in general, $250—total, $824 38.

During the winter a very successful series of Mission services was held among the private soldiers and non-commissioned officers at West Point. Lenten services were also conducted at the Post Chapel, by request of the Chaplain and resident Professors and officers.

St. James' Church, Goshen; the Rev. WILLIAM H. DE L. GRANNIS, Rector.

Baptisms, (ad. 8, inf. 13,) 21. Confirmed, 21. Marriages, 8. Burials, 5. Communicants: present number, 225. The Holy Communion celebrated the first Sunday in every month, on the high festivals, and on St. James' Day. Catechists and Sunday-School teachers, 20. Catechumens: Children taught the Catechism openly in the Church, 120. Celebration of Divine Service: Sundays, twice, and at the County House once a month; Holy Days, once; other days, Fridays.

Contributions.—Episcopal Fund, $8; Diocesan Fund, $40; the Western Convocation, $200; Theological Education Fund, $15 79; Fund for Aged and Infirm Clergymen, $37 50; Home Mission to Colored People, $129; Indians, $159 09; Board of Missions P. E. Church, U. S.: Domestic Committee, $75 50; Foreign Committee, $72 50; "St. James' Guild," $100; the Poor, applied to various purposes, $99 65; Parish purposes, $1,000; Christmas Tree and Sunday-School, $150; Church purposes in general, Faribault, $45 25—total, $1,856 78.

St. John's Church, Greenwood Iron Works; the Rev. JOHN F. POTTER, A. M., late Rector and Missionary.

Families, 40. Individuals, 200. Baptisms, inf. 32. Confirmed, 10. Marriages, 3. Burials, 7. Communicants: admitted 10; present number, 70. The Holy Communion celebrated on the first Sunday of each month, the greater feasts, Thanksgiving Day, and weekly in Advent and Lent. Catechists and Sunday-School Teachers, 5. Catechumens, 70. Daily Parish School, 1; tuition nominal; for boys and girls, with an average attendance of about 30. Celebration of Divine Service: Sundays, 101; Holy Days, 34; other days, 31—total, 166.

Contributions.—Episcopal Fund, $3; Diocesan Fund, $4 50; Missionary Committee of the Diocese, $15; Theological Education Fund, $11 28; for an aged and infirm Clergyman, $5; New-York Bible and Common Prayer-Book Society, $3: Protestant Episcopal Tract Society, $2 50; General P. E. S. S. Union and Church Book Society, $3 50; General Theological Seminary, $7 08; Parochial Schools, $382; the Poor and other alms, $45 72; Parish purposes, including Rector's salary and Church purposes in general, $1,176 61; Mission to the Jews, $6 47; University of the South, $1 50; St. Luke's Hospital, $3; Rev. J. Hardin George, $27 50; Memphis Sufferers, $9 50—total, $1,709 11.

There is a debt of about $3,400 now held against the Church, which has not been materially changed since the past Rectorate. A new organ has been placed in the Church, and paid for. A communicant (not resident in the Parish) has materially aided us in the past as in preceding years. Baptism has been administered at the Clove and O'Niel mines, also at Southfield and Monroe, and the number included in the foregoing report. The seats in the Church are free.

St. George's Church, Newburgh; the Rev. JOHN BROWN, D. D., Rector; the Rev. OCTAVIUS APPLEGATE, Assistant Minister.

Families, 200. Individuals, 800. Baptisms, (ad. 11, inf. 101,) 112. Confirmed, 29. Marriages, 13. Burials, 31. Communicants: admitted 31; removed into the Parish, 18; removed from the Parish, 43; died, 8; present number, 401. The Holy Communion celebrated first Sunday, and days having Proper Preface; in public, 28, in private, 7; total, 35. Catechists and Sunday-School teachers, 50. Catechumens, 350. Celebration of Divine Service: in the Church, 267, in the Chapel, 114—total, 381.

Contributions.—Episcopal Fund, $18; Diocesan Fund, $60; Missionary Committee of the Diocese, $123 57; Theological Education Fund, $103; Fund for Aged and Infirm Clergymen, $47 92; New-York Bible and Common Prayer-Book Society, $70; Board of Missions P. E. Church, U. S.: Domestic Committee, $149 03; Foreign Committee, $92; the Poor, $479 06; Parish purposes, $1,565 20; Church purposes in general, $552 21; Indian Missions, $68 75; Mission to Colored People, $68 75; Jews Mission, $32; St. Mark's School, Salt Lake City, $80; Bishop Tuttle, $20; Bishop Clarkson, $100; Nashotah, $37; Midnight Mission, $46 16; Western Convocation, $500; Highland Church Building Fund, $100; German Mission in Newburgh, $75; Sunday-School Library, $100; St. George's Mission, $1,468 89; Benevolent Association, $81 05; Industrial School, $25; Altar Society, $95 66—total, $6,158 85.

Rev. George W. Hinckle, Deacon, officiates in St. George's Mission.

Two hundred dollars of the above amount contributed to St. George's Mission are a present of a Communion service, and the sum of $418 41 has been given in collections by the congregation worshipping in the Chapel.

St. Paul's Church, Newburgh; the Rev. RUFUS EMERY, Rector.

Families, 119. Individuals, about 400. Baptisms, inf. 19. Confirmed, 15. Marriages, 2. Burials, 10. Communicants: admitted, 11; removed into the Parish, 20; removed from the Parish, 7; died, 5; present number, 144. The Holy Communion celebrated on the first Sunday in every month, and every day with Proper Preface. Catechists and Sunday-School teachers, 17. Catechumens: Children taught the Catechism openly in the Church, 120; times, 6. Celebration of Divine Service: Sundays, twice; Holy Days, once; other days, every Wednesday—total, 170.

Contributions.—Episcopal Fund, $3; Diocesan Fund, $15; Missionary Committee of the Diocese, $2; Theological Education Fund, $1; Fund for Aged and Infirm Clergymen, $10; Western Convocation, $25; S. S. Library, $40; Memphis Sufferers, $10; Parish Library, $20; Sewing School, $21; Society for the Increase of the Ministry, $25; Mission to the Jews, $4 63; Christmas Tree, $100; Rev. A. B. Flower, $6; the Poor, $20; Parish purposes, $3,069 05; Church purposes in general, $50—total, $3,421 68.

During the past year an Organ has been procured, and the indebtedness of the Paris reduced by the gift of "Building Fund Bonds" of the Corporation, amounting to t thousand dollars.

St. Thomas' Church, New-Windsor; the Rev. HASLETT MCKIM, Rector.

Families, 34. Individuals, 103. Baptisms, inf. 3. Burials, 4. Communicants: remov from the Parish, 4; died, 1; present number, 44. The Holy Communion celebrated fi Sunday of each month, Easter and Christmas. Catechists and Sunday-School teachers, Catechumens: Sunday scholars, 65. Celebration of Divine Service: Sundays, 104; Hol Days, Christmas, Passion-Week, Ash-Wednesday, Ascension; other days, every Frida in Lent, Thanksgiving—total, 120.

Contributions.—Episcopal Fund, $3; Diocesan Fund, $20; Missionary Committee of th Diocese, $15; Theological Education Fund, $8; Fund for Aged and Infirm Clergymen $6 79; the Poor, $67 75—total, $120 54.

Other contributions of the Church go towards the Rector's salary.

Since June there have been afternoon services in St. Thomas', instead of the Sunday School exercises and evening service at Moodna.

Grace Church, Port Jervis; the Rev. F. N. LUSON, Rector and Missionary.

Families, 45. Individuals, 157. Baptisms, (ad. 4, inf. 26,) 30. Confirmed, 11. Marriage, 1. Burials, 3. Communicants: admitted, 12; removed into the Parish, 2; removed from the Parish, 3; present number, 65. The Holy Communion celebrated the first Sunday of the month and on all festivals. Catechists and Sunday-School teachers, 9. Catechumens, 75; Children taught the Catechism openly in the Church, 40; times, 8. Celebration of Divine Service: Sundays, twice; Holy Days, once; other days, Wednesdays and Fridays.

Contributions.—Diocesan Fund, $8 25. Missionary Committee of the Diocese, $5; Western Convocation, Auxiliary Diocesan Missions, $18 75; Foreign Committee, $4; Parish purposes, $2,450—total, $2,489.

Since the last report the Church interior has been completed. This has added very much to the strength of the Mission. There is still a debt of some five thousand dollars against the Church and ground. We trust to obtain help to remove this before long. Some members of Trinity Chapel contributed $550, and a bell costing nearly $400. With the debt removed, a self-supporting and permanent Parish would at once come into existence in this important centre. We very much need a hospital and dispensary for the benefit of the Rail-Road men, who so largely make up the population of the place.

Grace Church, South Middletown; the Rev. ALEX. CAPRON, Rector.

Families, about 210. Individuals, 850. Baptisms, (ad. 44, inf. and children, 55,) 99. Confirmed, 64. Marriages, 6. Burials, 23. Communicants: present number, about 225. The Holy Communion celebrated the first Sunday of each month, and on the chief festivals. Catechists and Sunday-School teachers, 28. Catechumens: Children taught the Catechism openly in the Church, 289; times, monthly: total number of young persons instructed, about 300. Celebration of Divine Service: Sundays, 104; other days, 60—total, 164.

Contributions.—Episcopal Fund, $2. Diocesan Fund, $30; Sunday-School, about $400. the Poor, $133 43. Parish purposes, say $1,100—total, $1,675 43.

St. Andrew's Church, Walden ; the Rev. WILLIAM E. SNOWDEN, Rector.

Families, 52. Individuals, 200. Baptisms, (ad. 2, inf. 17.) 19. Marriages, 3. Burials, 6. Communicants: present number, 66. The Holy Communion celebrated on the first Sunday in every month, and whenever there is a Proper Preface. Catechists and Sunday-School teachers, 9. Catechumens: Children taught the Catechism openly in the Church, 18.

Contributions.—Episcopal Fund, $2; Missionary Committee of the Diocese, $13 41; Fund for Aged and Infirm Clergymen, $3; New-York Bible and Common Prayer-Book Society, $3; Parish purposes, $404 19—$425 60.

The present Rector took charge in the middle of July last, when the Parish had been without ministerial oversight for three months and a half. The record of official acts includes those of his predecessor since the Convention of 1873.

Christ Church, Warwick ; the Rev. ALFRED GOLDSBOROUGH, Rector.

Families, 35. Individuals, 100. Baptisms, (ad 9, inf. 12,) 21. Confirmed, 11. Burial, 1. Communicants: admitted, 15; removed into the Parish, 4; removed from the Parish, 5; present number, 50. The Holy Communion celebrated on the first Sunday of each and every month, and on the greater festivals. Catechists and Sunday-School teachers, 8. Catechumens: Children taught the Catechism openly in the Church, 40; times, 12. Celebration of Divine Service: All Sundays in the year, and the greater festivals and fasts, and twice per week through Lent.

Contributions.—Episcopal Fund, $2; Diocesan Fund, $12; Missionary Committee of the Diocese, $10; Convocation, $15; Fund for Aged and Infirm Clergymen, $5; the Poor, $6; Parish purposes, $400; Church purposes in general, not including Salary, $200—total, $650.

The Church is growing in numbers and strength, and the Rector feels very much encouraged in his work. He has continued the services again this summer over at Greenwood Lake, (seven miles distant,) every Sunday afternoon, during the months of July, August and September.

PUTNAM COUNTY.

St. Mary's Church in the Highlands, Cold Spring ; the Rev. ISAAC VAN WINKLE, Rector.

Baptisms, (ad. 6, inf. 28,) 34. Confirmed, 16. Marriages, 4. Burials, 6. Communicants: admitted, 11; removed into the Parish, 1; removed from the Parish, 1; died, 2; present number, 148. The Holy Communion celebrated every Sunday and Holy Day up to August 1, 1874; since that date, on first Sunday in the month, and on Holy Days; in private, 2. Catechists and Sunday-School teachers, 21. Catechumens: Children taught the Catechism openly in the Church, 149; times, 12. Celebration of Divine Service: Sundays, 146; Holy Days, 66; other days, 80—total, 292.

Contributions.—Diocesan Fund, $42; Missionary Committee of the Diocese, $11 50; Theological Education Fund, $12; Fund for Aged and Infirm Clergymen, $19 93; Society for Conversion of Jews, $5 41; Sufferers from yellow fever, $100; House of the Good Shepherd, $36 12; special objects, $11; Board of Missions P. E. Church, U. S : Domestic Committee, $43 50; Sunday-School purposes, $133 35; the Poor, $231 54; Parish purposes, $1,275 92—total, $1,922 27.

The former Rector, the Reverend C. C. Parsons, resigned the Rectorship August 1st. This report is, therefore, mainly his. The present Rector entered upon his duties on the last Sunday in August.

A very beautiful and substantial stone Chapel for the Sunday-School has been recently completed and thoroughly furnished with every thing requisite for the school. This costly and noble gift has been made to the Parish by a member of the Vestry, Mr. Frederick P. James, and is a memorial to his two sons, Frederick P. and Julian James.

Christ Church, Paterson ; the Rev. WILLIAM MOORE, Missionary.

Families, 3. Individuals, 18. Communicants: present number, 8. The Holy Communion celebrated on 11th Sunday after Trinity, 1874. Catechists and Sunday-School teachers, 2. Catechumens: Children taught the Catechism openly in the Church, 6; times, 40; Sunday scholars, 6. Celebration of Divine Service: Sundays, 15; other days, 1—total, 16.

Paterson has but few children, consequently it has but few young people. It does not increase in population.

I have two other Missions; one at Kent Cliffs, where I officiate twice a month, the other at Brewsters, where there are held sometimes more services than one in a month.

Our services at the former have been remarkably well attended since their commencement there. Twenty-four persons have been publicly baptized since the last report to the Diocesan Convention, ten of whom are now ready to be confirmed. The Sunday-School connected with this Mission is in a very flourishing condition.

Our services at the latter have been also, we are thankful to say, well attended. This Mission has a Sunday-School but three months old, which now numbers about forty scholars. Two infants have been baptized at this Mission station.

We are also sorry to report that the effects of the late panic have caused quite a number of persons well disposed towards the Church to leave Brewsters, a town chiefly supported by trade, in pursuit of suitable employment.

I have only received through my three Missions the sum of $120 within the Conventional year, which is a very small sum indeed towards my support.

St. Philip's Church in the Highlands, Philipsetown ; the Rev. ALBERT ZABRISKIE GRAY, Rector.

Families, about 50. Individuals, about 225. Baptisms, (ad. 2, inf. 16.) 18. Burials, 2. Communicants: present number, about 60. The Holy Communion celebrated first Sunday of each month, and on all festivals. Catechists and Sunday-School teachers, 8. Catechumens, 65; Children taught the Catechism openly in the Church, monthly. Celebration of Divine Service: Sundays, twice at Church, and once at Mission Chapel of St. James; Holy Days, all Holy Days; other days, according to season—always Wednesdays and Fridays.

Contributions.—Episcopal Fund, $13; Diocesan Fund, $24; Missionary Committee of the Diocese, $48; Southern Missionary Convocation, $63 25; Theological Education Fund, $28 20; Fund for Aged and Infirm Clergymen, $15 55; special Mission gifts, &c., $236 02; New-York Bible and Common Prayer-Book Society, $17 79; Protestant Episcopal Tract Society, $16 55; General P. E. S. S. Union and Church Book Society, $16 55; General Theological Seminary, $22 85; Board of Missions P E. Church, U. S.: Domestic Committee, $457 68; Foreign Committee, $52 80; Indian Missions, $31 44; to the Jews, $7 28; Memphis Sufferers, $43 54; the Poor, $280 77; Parish purposes, $1,087 88; total, $2,462 65, including pew rents, etc., $4,213 02.

The present Rectorship began on the first Sunday of November last.

A large sum has been subscribed for repairs and alteration of the Rectory.

Regular services are maintained at the Mission Chapel of St. James, thanks to the kind assistance of the Rev. James A. Upjohn.

RICHMOND COUNTY.

Church of the Ascension, (West Brighton,) Castleton; the Rev. JAMES S. BUSH, Rector.

Families, 130. Individuals, 721. Baptisms, (ad, 8, inf. 68,) 76. Confirmed, 25. Marriages, 4. Burials, 8. Communicants: admitted, 25; died, 1; present number, 283. The Holy Communion celebrated monthly, and on Easter, Whitsun-Day and Christmas. Catechists and Sunday-School teachers, 50. Catechumens, 229; Catechised monthly by the Rector. Celebration of Divine Service: Sundays, twice every Sunday; Holy Days, Christmas, Easter and Ascension; other days, in Lent three times a week.

Contributions.—Diocesan Fund, $52; Fund for Aged and Infirm Clergymen, $24 80; the Poor. $678 53; Parish purposes, $604 94; Church purposes in general, $2,745 74—total, $4,054 01.

The Rector has also ministered occasionally to the inmates of the Nursery and Child's Hospital, Staten Island. His Assistant, Mr. Charles Congdon, has held a Church service there every Sunday through the year.

St. Mary's Church, Castleton; the Rev. HORACE L. EDGAR PRATT, Rector.

Families, 29. Individuals, 200. Baptisms, inf. 9. Marriages, 4. Burials, 4. Communicants: admitted, 3; died, 2; present number, 59. The Holy Communion celebrated on the first Sunday of each month, and other days for which there is a "Proper Preface." Celebration of Divine Service: Sundays, twice; Holy Days, Wednesdays and Fridays in Lent, and every day in Passion-Week.

Contributions.—Diocesan Fund, $7; the Poor, $101 55; Parish purposes, $234; Church purposes in general, $379 50—total, $722 05.

Through the liberality of one member of the Vestry, the Church building has been greatly improved, by a new roof of slate, and otherwise renovated, at a cost of $1,900. The Rectory has also been newly painted and much repaired the present year.

St. John's Church, Clifton; the Rev. JOHN C. ECCLESTON, D. D., Rector.

Baptisms, inf. 24. Confirmed, 25. Marriage, 1. Burials, 8. Communicants, 250. Catechists and Sunday-School teachers, 15. Catechumens, 182; Children taught the Catechism openly in the Church, 200; times, 12. St. Simon's Mission Sunday-School: pupils. 100; teachers, 10. Rector's Friday evening Bible Class for laboring people, 65. Rector's Sunday morning Bible Class for young persons, 23.

Contributions.—Diocesan Fund, $19 27; Missionary Committee of the Diocese, 100; Charitable contributions of "Pas. Aid Soc.," $269; Sufferers by flood in Louisiana, $30; Ladies' Dorcas Soc., $151; Evangelical Education Soc., $14 85; Sunday-School Missions, $101 40; Indian Missions, $50; American Bible Soc., $127 97; "S. R. Smith" Infirmary, $356; Domestic Committee, $150 63; Church Hospital on Long Island, $25; St. John's Guild, $45; the Poor, $401 27; Sunday-School purposes, $550; Liquidation of Church debt, $2,000—total, $4,389 27.

St. Paul's Memorial Church, Edgewater; the Rev. THOMAS W. PUNNETT, Rector.

Families, about 130. Baptisms, (ad. 6, inf. 38,) 44. Confirmed, 20. Marriages, 17. Burials, 18. Communicants: present number, 212. The Holy Communion celebrated weekly during Advent and Lent, and the months of May, June and July; also on Christmas, Easter, Ascension Day, Whitsun-Day, the Feast of Trinity, and the first Sunday in the month. Catechists and Sunday-School teachers, 15. Catechumens, 190; times, 10;

Scholars, 190. Celebration of Divine Service: all Sundays, Holy Days and other days—total, 325.

Contributions.—Bishop's Salary, $8; Diocesan Fund, $10; "Annandale" Student, $220; Fund for Aged and Infirm Clergymen, $25 62; Tennessee, $2; Louisiana, $20; Rev. Patrick, $45; "S. I. Infirmary," $40 23; Board of Missions P. E. Church, U. S.: Domestic and Foreign Committee and Indian, $185 43; the Jews, $9 11; the Poor, $184 17; Parish purposes, $2,857 25; Church purposes in general, $730 17—total, $4,346 98.

We have not sold the old Church building, but have laid out between $1,100 and $1,200 in adapting it to Sunday-School purposes.

Christ Church, New-Brighton; the Rev. PIERRE P. IRVING, Rector.

Baptisms, (ad. 1, inf. 20,) 21. Marriages, 6. Burials, 17. Communicants, 110. The Holy Communion celebrated on the first Sunday in every month, and on Easter and Christmas. Catechists and Sunday-School teachers, 15. Catechumens, 125; Children taught the Catechism openly in the Church, 100. Celebration of Divine Service: Sundays, 104; Holy Days, 20; other days, 6—total, 130.

Contributions.—Fund for Aged and Infirm Clergymen, $40 91; Board of Missions P. E. Church, U. S.: Domestic Committee, $75 18; Foreign Committee, $29 55; the Poor, $61 81; Parish purposes, $918 55; Church purposes in general, $1,113 48—total, $3,194 75.

St. Luke's Church, Rossville; the Rev. HENRY H. BEAN, Rector.

Families, 30. Individuals, 75. Baptisms, inf. 7. Burials, 2. Communicants: present number, 30. The Holy Communion celebrated on the first Sunday of each month, and on high festivals. Catechists and Sunday-School teachers, 4; Catechumens: Children taught the Catechism openly in the Church, 25; times, 12.

Contributions.—Board of Missions P. E. Church, U. S.: Domestic Committee, for Bp. Hare, from S. S., $15.

Church of the Holy Comforter, (Eltingville,) Southfield; the Rev. FREDERICK M. GRAY, Rector.

Families, 45. Individuals, 175. Baptisms, (ad. 1, inf. 5,) 6. Confirmed, 14. Marriages, 2. Burials, 2. Communicants: present number, 40. The Holy Communion celebrated on the first Sunday in every month, and on Christmas Day and Whitsun-Day. Catechists and Sunday-School teachers, 6. Catechumens: Children taught the Catechism openly in the Church, 48; times, 8. Celebration of Divine Service: Sundays, 94; Holy Days, 4; other days, 13—total, 111.

Contributions.—Fund for Aged and Infirm Clergymen, $6 76; Board of Missions P. E. Church, U. S.: Domestic Committee, $1 50; Parish purposes, $1,632 73; Church purposes in general, $30 02—total, $1,671 01.

ROCKLAND COUNTY.

St. John's Church, Clarkstown; the Rev. ROMAINE S. MANSFIELD, Rector and Missionary.

Families, 31. Individuals, 150. Baptism, inf. 1. Confirmed, 4. Communicants: admitted, 8; removed into the Parish, 1; removed from the Parish, 5; present number, 25. Catechumens: total number of young persons instructed, 50. Celebration of Divine Service: Sundays, once each Sunday; Holy Days, high festivals.

Contributions.—Diocesan Fund, $5; Missionary Committee of the Diocese, $5; House of Good Shepherd, $10; weekly offerings, (including Rector's salary,) $556 10—total, $576 10.

Trinity Church, Haverstraw; the Rev. CHARLES B. COFFIN, Rector.

Families, 57. Individuals, 309. Baptisms, inf. 2. Burials, 4. Communicants: admitted, 6; removed into the Parish, 5; removed from the Parish, 9; died, 2; present number, 73. The Holy Communion celebrated about eight times during the past year. Catechists and Sunday-School teachers, 8. Catechumens, 80. Daily Parish School: one, paid; Scholars: males, 3, females, 9. Celebration of Divine Service: Sundays, morning and evening.

Contributions.—Episcopal Fund, $4; Diocesan Fund, $11 20; Missionary Committee of the Diocese, $3; Theological Education Fund, $2; Fund for Aged and Infirm Clergymen, $3 53—total, $23 73.

For nearly the entire Conventional year the Parish has been without a Rector.

Grace Church, Nyack; the Rev. FRANKLIN BABBITT, Rector and Missionary.

Families, 66. Baptisms, (ad. 1, inf. 3,) 4. Confirmed, 10. Marriages, 8. Burials, 11. Communicants: present number, 125. The Holy Communion celebrated monthly. Catechists and Sunday-School teachers, 8; Sunday scholars, 70. Celebration of Divine Service: Twice every Sunday, and on the principal Holy Days.

Contributions.—Diocesan Fund, $3 55; Missionary Committee of the Diocese, $12 68; Fund for Aged and Infirm Clergymen, $16 59; Weekly offertory, $652 29; House of the Good Shepherd, $11; Building fund for the new Church, $2,836 48; Board of Missions P. E. Church, U. S.: Domestic Committee, $66 93; Sunday-School, $53 the Poor, $100 20—total, $3,753 62.

Christ Church, Piermont; the Rev. SOL. G. HITCHCOCK, Rector and Missionary.

Families, 40. Baptisms, inf. 21. Marriages, 9. Burials, 11. Communicants: removed into the Parish, 9; removed from the Parish, 3; died, 2; present number, 70. The Holy Communion celebrated from Advent to Trinity Sunday, on the Church festivals; during the remainder of the year on the first Sunday of the month. Sunday School teachers, 12; Scholars, 132. Celebration of Divine Service: Sundays, A. M., P. M., and occasionally evenings; Holy Days, those of general observance; other days, only occasional.

Contributions.—Episcopal Fund, $2; Diocesan Fund, $5; Missionary Committee of the Diocese, $14 47; Orphan's Home Asylum, $10; Indian Commission, $6 79; House of Good Shepherd, $5; Church Mission to Jews, $2; Home Mission to Colored people, $2; New-York Bible and Common Prayer-Book Society, $9; Protestant Episcopal Tract Society, $6; General P. E. S. S. Union and Church Book Society, $4 90; General Theological Seminary, $1; Southern Convocation, $11 41; Board of Missions P. E. Church, U. S.: Domestic Committee, (Mr. and Mrs. Smith, $100,) $112 70; Foreign Committee, (Mr. and Mrs. Smith, $50,) $68 90; Sunday-School, 12 vols. for library, and (Mrs. S. $25, others, $8,) $68 48; Christmas Tree, $93; the Poor, besides clothing from J. F. De P. and several ladies, $49 02; Parish purposes, $680 27; towards Salary, $55 80; Church purposes in general, $25 48; Ministerial gifts and perquisites, ($20 from Ringwood,) $107—total, $1,335 17.

On Thanksgiving Day, choice productions of the orchard, the garden, the field, the slaughter-house and the wardrobe, were placed at the head of the Church aisle, and after service distributed among the poor.

The Christmas gift of a new Surplice, made by the daughter of the late C. N. S. Rowland, Esq., who was formerly a visitant attendant upon our services, was presented to the Rector by several ladies of the congregation.

The most noteworthy item of Parochial expenditure for the past year has been the purchase of a Sunday-School organ, at a cost of $200.

The loss sustained by our Parish through the death, on June 12th, of James F. De Peyster, Esq., who had spent his last eleven summers in Piermont, will be as readily understood, as the wide sphere of usefulness which he had filled in the Church and in the world, rendered him well and favorably known.

Christ Church, (Ramapo,) Suffern ; the Rev. GUSTAV E. PURUCKER, Rector and Missionary.

Families, 60. Individuals, 193. Baptisms, (ad. 6, inf. 6,) 12. Confirmed, 9. Marriage, 1. Communicants: admitted, 12: removed into the Parish, 2; removed from the Parish, 7; present number, 48. The Holy Communion celebrated on the first Sunday in the month; all the high festivals of the Church; also on Ash-Wednesday and Good Friday. Catechists and Sunday-School teachers, 8. Catechumens, 55. Children taught the Catechism openly in the Church, 45; times, 12; Sunday scholars, 10; total number of young persons instructed, 55. Daily Parish School: 1, free; Scholars, (males, 12, females, 23,) 35. Celebration of Divine Service: Sundays, twice every Sunday; Holy Days, once; other days, once on all Saint's Days, and during Lent every day once, Wednesdays and Fridays twice—total, 172.

Contributions.—Episcopal Fund, $8; Diocesan Fund, $30; Missionary Committee of the Diocese, $7; Theological Education Fund, $3; Fund for Aged and Infirm Clergymen, $5; New-York City Mission Society, for the Jews, $3 70; General Theological Seminary, $4; the Poor, and Church purposes in general, $83 09; Parish purposes, $1,616 68; Furniture for Parish School and teacher's salary, since April 15th, $500—total, $2,255 47.

Through the generosity of a lady of the Parish, a Parochial School was opened on the 15th of April last, with good promise of success.

A fair, for the benefit of the Church, was lately held by the ladies of the Sewing Society, who realized a little above $500 from their sales. This sum is to be devoted to the purchasing of a furnace for the Church.

Mission services have been occasionally held at different points by the Missionary, especially at Darlington, (N. J.,) a place three miles distant.

Also, the colored people of the mountains around us are under our care, and they, in many instances, evince a deep sense of their Christian duty and privileges.

St. Paul's Church, Spring Valley ; the Rev. ROMAINE S. MANSFIELD, Rector and Missionary.

Baptisms, (ad. 2, inf. 3,) 5. Confirmed, 5. Marriages, 3. Burial, 1. Communicants: admitted, 5; removed into the Parish, 2; removed from the Parish, 10; present number, 32. Catechists and Sunday-School teachers, 6. Catechumens, 40. Children taught the Catechism openly in the Church, 50; times, 12. Celebration of Divine Service: Sundays, once each; Holy Days, all the high festivals.

Contributions.—Weekly offerings, $504 17; Building Fund, $1,062—total, $1,566 17.

The first service was held in our new Church on the 18th of last December. The Bishop of the Diocese was present, and preached and celebrated the Holy Eucharist.

Church of the Holy Child Jesus, Stony Point ; the Rev. EBENEZER GAY, Jr., Missionary.

Baptisms, inf. 3. Marriages, 2 Burials, 3. Communicants: present number, 16. The Holy Communion celebrated frequently. Celebration of Divine Service: Sundays, twice; Holy Days, twice; other days, daily from Advent to Easter

Contributions.—Missionary Committee of the Diocese, $9 04; Fund for Aged and Infirm

Clergymen, $3 63; New-York City Mission Society to Jews, $2 97; Board of Missions P. E. Church, U. S.: Domestic Committee, $7 79; Parish purposes, building of the Church, $99 02—total, $122 45.

The Rector would report that the general interest of the Church in the House of the Good Shepherd, Rockland County, seems to be much increased, and this opportunity is embraced to acknowledge with gratitude the kind offices and aid of very many of the Clergy and Laity of the Diocese

SULLIVAN COUNTY.

St. John's Church, Monticello; the Rev. CHARLES FOBES CANEDY, Rector and Missionary.

Families, 78. Individuals, 315. Baptisms, (ad. 7, inf. 21,) 28. Confirmed, 13. Marriages, 3. Burials, 10. Communicants: admitted, 8; removed into the Parish, 2; died, 7; Present number, 143. The Holy Communion celebrated on the first and third Sundays of every month, and on the chief festivals. Catechists and Sunday-School teachers, 10. Catechumens, 98. Children taught the Catechism openly in the Church, 98; times, 12; members of other Classes for religious instruction, 6; total number of young persons instructed, 104. Celebration of Divine Service: Sundays, 134; Holy Days, 29; other days, 69—total, 232.

Contributions.—Episcopal Fund, $2; Diocesan Fund, $16; Missionary Committee of the Diocese, $15; Theological Education Fund, $7 44; Fund for Aged and Infirm Clergymen, $10 40; Easter, special offering, Building Fund, $100; Mission to Jews, $3 25; Board of Missions P. E. Church, U. S.: Foreign Committee, $6 70; Western Convocation, $5 29; the Poor, $32 96; Parish purposes, $658 65—total, $857 69.

A font of handsome design has been imported from England and placed in the Church. The expense was met by the offerings of the Sunday-School, reserved for this purpose during the incumbency of the immediate predecessor of the present Rector.

Services have been maintained at White Lake during the summer. Mr. R. B. Drane, of the General Theological Seminary, acted as Lay Reader.

The Rev. E. K. Fowler, whose active labors here extended over a period of forty-three years, is still blessed with a measure of health, and is enabled, though with great difficulty, to attend Divine Service regularly.

The above report of the number of celebrations of Divine Service includes services at St. Mary's Mission in Thompsonville, and at White Lake.

ULSTER COUNTY.

Church of the Ascension, Esopus; the Rev. HENRY BEERS SHERMAN, Rector.

Baptisms, inf. 2. Burials, 2. Communicants: died, 1; present number, 6.

The congregation is made up for the most part of summer residents, whose parochial relations are in the Cities of New-York and Brooklyn. Attendance upon the services is encouraging during the summer months, and the number of Communicants at the monthly celebration is from 20 to 30—of whom six only may be classed in the local enumeration.

Church of the Holy Spirit, (Rondout,) Kingston; the Rev. JAMES BYRON MURRAY, Rector.

Baptisms, (ad. 6, inf. 15,) 21. Confirmed, 13. Marriages, 3. Burials, 15. Communicants: admitted, 8; removed into the Parish, 4; died, 2; present number, 136. The Holy Communion celebrated on the first Sunday of every month, on all the high festivals, and ten times with the sick. Catechists and Sunday-School teachers, 12. Catechumens, 109;

Children taught the Catechism openly in the Church, 80; times, 13. Celebration of Divine Service: Sundays, twice, with occasionally a missionary service; Holy Days, once on each Holy Day and Saint's Day; other days, Thanksgiving, twice a day during Lent, and Friday evening from Advent to the end of the Epiphany season. With most of these services there has been a Lecture or Sermon. There was a special service held in December in accordance with the request of the Bishop.

Contributions.—Episcopal Fund, $2; Diocesan Fund, $20; Missionary Committee of the Diocese, $5; Fund for Aged and Infirm Clergymen, $5; Sunday-School, $41 08; the Poor, $26 31; Parish purposes, $755 52; Church purposes in general, $18—total, $872 91.

St. John's Church, Kingston ; (Rectorship now vacant.)

Families, 130. Individuals, 517. Baptisms, (ad. 12, inf. 39,) 51. Marriages, 2. Burials, 10. Communicants: present number, 189. The Holy Communion celebrated the first Sunday in each month and Holy Days. Catechists and Sunday-School teachers, 15. Catechumens, 10; Children taught the Catechism openly in the Church, 50; total number of young persons instructed, 80. Daily Parish School: Scholars: males, 30, females, 50.

Contributions.—Diocesan Fund, $24; Fund for Aged and Infirm Clergymen, $30 60; the Poor, $70; Church purposes in general, $2,600—total, $2,724 60.

Christ Church, Marlborough ; the Rev. SAMUEL M. AKERLY, Rector and Missionary.

Families, 24. Individuals, 80. Burials, 4. Communicants: died, 1; present number, 35. The Holy Communion celebrated once a month. Catechists and Sunday-School teachers, 7. Catechumens: all Children taught the Catechism in the Sunday-School; Sunday scholars, 70. Celebration of Divine Service: Sundays, twice; Holy Days, Christmas, Ash-Wednesday, Good Friday; other days, Thanksgiving, weekly service in Lent, also in summer.

Contributions.—Episcopal Fund, $3; Diocesan Fund, $5; Missionary Committee of the Diocese, $21; Fund for Aged and Infirm Clergymen, $10; Sunday-School Collections for Indian Missions, $10 34; American Church Mission Society, by boxes, $29 78; Domestic Committee, $5; Foreign Committee, $8; Auer Memorial, Africa, $10; Garments for the Poor, also for Church, by Ladies' Society, $65; Parish purposes, $158—total, $325 12.

All Saints' Church, Milton ; the Rev. JOSEPH H. JOHNSON, Missionary.

Families, 23. Individuals, 96. Baptisms, (ad. 4, inf. 7,) 11. Confirmed, 12. Marriage, 1. Burial, 1. Communicants, 25; removed into the Parish, 1; removed from the Parish, 2; present number, 16. The Holy Communion celebrated the first Sunday of the month at Milton, and once every two weeks at Highland. Catechists and Sunday-School teachers, 8. Catechumens, 45. All the Communicants meet on Friday evenings for instruction in the principles of the faith; total number of young persons instructed, 45. Celebration of Divine Service: Sundays, All Saints', Milton, morning service each Sunday; Holy Trinity, Highland, Holy Communion every second Sunday, and evening prayer every Sunday afternoon; Holy Days, evening prayer at Highland; other days, instruction service on Friday evenings throughout the year; through Lent, evening prayer and sermon on Wednesday evenings, occasional extra service at Milton; Holy Week, Litany, and lecture every evening; two extra services at Milton; total, 158.

Contributions.—Episcopal Fund, $3 50; Diocesan Fund, $2 75; Missionary Committee of the Diocese, $3 50; Fund for Aged and Infirm Clergymen, $2; Church purposes in general, $125—total, $136 25.

The annual report includes that for Holy Trinity, Highland. Besides the sum of

$135 25 raised by the offertory, $510 have been given to the Milton Parish by the ladies of the congregation. This donation was the result of a fair.

Through the kindness of our friends, and especially by the untiring efforts of Rev. Dr. Cady, Rector of Christ Church of Poughkeepsie, the debt of $2,850 upon the Church of the Holy Trinity, Highland, has been been paid, and the Church edifice consecrated.

A generous friend, a summer resident in the Parish, has presented to the Parish a Communion service of silver, and a pair of candelabras for the purpose of lighting the Church at the evening services.

Trinity Church, Saugerties; the Rev. J. J. ROBERTSON, D. D., Rector.

Families, about 43. Individuals, about 185. Baptisms, inf. 12. Marriage, 1. Burials, 8. Communicants: removed into the Parish, 2; removed from the Parish, 4; died, 1; present number, 68. The Holy Communion celebrated first Sunday in each month, and festivals with Preface, except Ascension Day. Catechists and Sunday-School teachers, 8. Catechumens, 68; Children taught the Catechism openly in the Church, Sunday scholars; times, 8; total number of young persons instructed, 68. Celebration of Divine Service: Sundays, 101; Holy Days, 8; other days, 17—total, 126.

Contributions.—Salary of Bishop, $4; Episcopal Fund, $5 52; Diocesan Fund, $18; Missionary Committee of the Diocese, $81 59; Theological Education Fund, $42 15; Fund for Aged and Infirm Clergymen, $23 22; Home Missions to Colored People, $27 48; Western Convocation, $50; New-York Bible and Common Prayer-Book Society, $21 12; Protestant Episcopal Tract Society, $9 26; General P. E. S. S. Union and Church Book Society, $3 79; Indian Commission, $29 09; Sunday-School Collections for Missions to Indians under Bishop Hare, $15 74; Board of Missions P. E. Church, U. S.: Domestic Committee, $53 10; Foreign Committee, $57 94; Church Mission to Jews, $8 79; the Poor, $113 69; Parish purposes, $4,462 37—total, $5,030 85.

Since last report the edifice of Trinity Church, Saugerties, has undergone extensive and expensive improvements. The whole interior has been reconstructed (in harmony with the beautiful Chancel erected last year, with its exquisite stained glass window, at the cost of Mrs. Vanderpoel,) and stained glass inserted in the side windows. Besides the complete renewal of ceiling, interior walls and flooring, and the introduction of a new set of pews without doors; the floor has been newly carpeted, and the approach to the altar made more Churchlike. A furnace has been constructed under the Church. And, besides painting the exterior, a gilded cross now surmounts the spire, visible from a great distance, instead of its predecessor, the weather-cock. Were the zealous and devoted founders of the Church, Barclay and Kearny, (whose monuments grace the walls,) still on earth, how it would delight them to gaze on the improvements introduced by a succeeding generation! The cost of the whole thus far has been $4,078 63. Female Communicants, especially the wife of the Senior Warden, Mrs. Battelle, have done much in aiding to secure the pecuniary means and in encouraging the work, and with their own hands have laid the carpets. This renewal of the interior of the Church has made it necessary for us to worship in a private building with contracted space, and thus smaller congregations, for about three months. This, together with the expense of refitting the Church, and that at a season of depression in the money market, must account for a decrease of liberality to Missionary and other extra Parochial Church operations. May the congregation, as a spiritual edifice, be so renewed in "the beauty of holiness," that henceforth they may increase in every good word and work. So prays their grateful pastor, who has continued to be favored with their liberal kindness to himself and family.

St. Peter's Church, Stone Ridge; the Rev. GEORGE W. WEST, Deacon and Missionary.

Families, 12. Individuals, 30. Baptisms, (ad. 4, inf. 3,) 7. Confirmed, 4. Burials, 2. Communicants: present number, 11. The Holy Communion celebrated All Saint's Day, A. D. 1873, by the Rev. Walter Delafield; June 19th, A. D. 1874, by the Bishop, and on the

15th Sunday after Trinity by the Rev. J. H. Johnson. Catechumens, 13; times, 50. Celebration of Divine Service: Sundays, morning and evening prayer at Stone Ridge, and evening prayer at Rosendale; other days, every Saturday evening at Stone Ridge—total, about 200.

Contributions.—The Poor, $8; Parish purposes, $19; Church purposes in general, $600—total, $627.

Two Missions have been started near the village of Stone Ridge—St. Paul's Mission at High Falls, and St. John's at Rosendale. Services are suspended for the present at High Falls, but we hope to begin them again as soon as a suitable room or hall can be procured. The services at Rosendale are well attended.

The Missionary takes this opportunity of saying, that the Church here is indebted almost for its existence to the Hon. H. Abeel and his sister, who have, for upwards of twelve years, carefully kept the Church in order and in good repair.

St. Peter's Church school for boys opened on September 16th with twelve pupils. A school for girls is in contemplation, a house having already been offered.

A bell and fence for the Church are greatly needed, and $140 have been contributed.

WESTCHESTER COUNTY.

St. Matthew's Church, Bedford; the Rev. LEA LUQUER, Rector.

Families, about 45. Baptisms, inf. 2. Burials, 3. Communicants: present number, 70. The Holy Communion celebrated on the first Sunday of every month and on the chief festivals of the Church. Catechumens: total number of young persons instructed, 26.

Contributions.—Episcopal Fund, $4; Diocesan Fund, $12; Board of Missions P. E. Church, U. S.: Domestic Committee, $5 10; Foreign Committee, $58 69; Parish purposes, $1,300; Church purposes in general, $171 64—total, $1,551 43.

The Church and Rectory have been thoroughly repaired and painted at an expense of about $1,200, which was readily and cheerfully contributed by the members of the congregation.

Church of the Divine Love, (Montrose,) Cortlandt; the Rev. GOUVERNEUR CRUGER, Rector and Missionary.

Baptisms, inf. 13. Confirmed, 9. Burials, 2. Communicants: admitted, 3; removed from the Parish, 1; died, 1; present number, 19. The Holy Communion celebrated on first Sunday of each month, and on all the great festivals. Catechists and Sunday-School teachers, 13; Catechumens: Children taught the Catechism openly in the Church, 133; times, 52; members of other classes for religious instruction, 2; total number of young persons instructed, 135. Celebration of Divine Service: Sundays, all, 104; Holy Days, all, 35—total, 139.

Contributions.—Episcopal Fund, $4; Diocesan Fund, $3 87; Missionary Committee of the Diocese, $3 87; Theological Education Fund, $3 87; Fund for Aged and Infirm Clergymen, $3 87; Parish purposes, $382 77—total, $402 25.

Class numbering two, prepared last year, were confirmed too late to be mentioned in last report.

St. Paul's Church, East Chester; the Rev. WILLIAM SAMUEL COFFEY, Rector.

Families, 70. Individuals, 280. Baptisms, inf. 20. Confirmed, 12. Marriages, 10. Burials, 22. Communicants: admitted, 11; removed into the Parish, 13; removed from the Parish, 5; died, 1; present number, 110. The Holy Communion celebrated on the first Sunday in the month and the greater festivals. Catechists and Sunday-School teachers, 6. Total number of young persons instructed, 50. Celebration of Divine Service: Sundays, twice on Sundays, and three times in the week.

Contributions.—Episcopal Fund, $8; Diocesan Fund, $14; Missionary Committee of the Diocese, $22 17; Fund for Aged and Infirm Clergymen, $5; New-York Bible and Common Prayer-Book Society, $18 56; General Theological Seminary, $17 26; Board of Missions P. E. Church, U. S.: Domestic Committee, $28 80; Jews, $6 54; the Poor and Parish purposes, $347 58; Church purposes in general, $19—total, $482.

The stone wall around the Church-yard, spoken of in our report of 1868, is now in course of erection, but of much better quality than then contemplated. The corner-stone of this structure was laid with brief but appropriate ceremony on St. Bartholomew's Day. The cost of this work will be about $3,000.

Zion Church, Greenburgh; the Rev. George Bickham Reese, Rector.

Baptisms, (ad. 1, inf. 11,) 12. Confirmed, 10. Burials, 9. Communicants: present number, 100. The Holy Communion celebrated on the first Sunday of every month and principal feast days. Catechumens, 150. Children taught the Catechism openly in the Church, every Sunday; total number of young persons instructed, 150. Celebration of Divine Service, 150 times.

Contributions.—Episcopal Fund, $10; Diocesan Fund, $20; Missionary Committee of the Diocese, $10; Fund for Aged and Infirm Clergymen, $17; Board of Missions P. E. Church, U. S.: Foreign Committee, $35; Sunday-Schools, $100; the Poor, $286; Parish purposes, (exclusive of pew rents,) $3,043; Church purposes in general, (House of the Good Shepherd, $100; A Church Missionary Society, $20; St. John's Riverside Hospital, $80,) $200—total, $3,721.

St. Paul's Mission Chapel, Greenburg; the Rev. John Drisler, Deacon and Missionary.

Families, 10. Individuals, 30. Baptisms, (ad. 2, inf. 2,) 4. Confirmed, 4, and 2 elsewhere. Communicants: admitted, 3; present number, 16. The Holy Communion celebrated second Sunday in the month. Catechists and Sunday-School teachers, 5. Catechumens, 20; Children taught the Catechism openly in the Church, 20; times, once a month; Sunday scholars, 25; total number of young persons instructed, 20. Daily Parish School: mostly free; Scholars: males, 6, females, 6. Celebration of Divine Service: Sundays, morning and evening; Holy Days, principal Holy Days; other days, every Friday during Lent, every day through Passion Week.

Contributions.—Episcopal Fund, $1 75; Diocesan Fund, $1 75; Fund for Aged and Infirm Clergymen, $2; New-York Bible and Common Prayer-Book Society, $4—total, $9 50. One dollar and twenty-five cents were given by the children of Sunday-School for Bishop Auer Memorial Church, African Mission.

During the present year a Parish School has been opened, with an attendance of 12 scholars. Several of the children who have attended Sunday-School have removed from the place; some others have been added, which keeps the number about the same.

Four* persons have been confirmed, and three added to the Holy Communion; otherwise there has been very little change since the last year's report.

---

* Two other members of the Parish have been confirmed—one at White Plains, one at Carmansville; both have become Communicants.

St. Barnabas' Church, Irvington on Hudson; the Rev. WILLIAM HENRY BENJAMIN, Rector.

Families, 55. Baptisms, (ad. 2, inf. 10.) 12. Confirmed. 6. Marriages, 4. Burials, 3. Communicants: died, 2; removed from the Parish, 1; removed into the Parish, 5; present number, 101. The Holy Communion celebrated monthly, and on the great festivals. Catechists and Sunday-School teachers, 11; Scholars, 56; Children taught the Catechism openly once a month in Church, 70. Celebration of Divine Service: Sundays, twice; in Lent, three times; Holy Days, on the great festivals and fasts; other days, in Lent six times a week, with two lectures, in Holy Week twice daily, with a sermon, once weekly during portions of year.

Contributions.—Episcopal Fund Assessment, $10; Diocesan Fund, $20; Aged and Infirm Clergy Fund, $21 51; New-York City Mission, $127 26; County Missions, (Saw Mill Valley Chapel,) $130; St. John's Hospital, Yonkers, $46 52; Board of Missions P. E. Church, U. S.: Domestic Missions, $387 14; Children's Aid Society, $28; the Poor, $350; Christmas Tree, $122 25; through a lady of the Parish for the South, $600; gift to the Rector, $975; Parish purposes, excluding pew rents, $1,450—total, $4,267 68; pew rents for the year, $3,200—total, $7,467 68.

Since my last report this Parish has lost one of its most devoted members and liberal benefactors, Mr. George Merritt, who died October 5th, 1873. "The righteous and their works are in the hands of God."

A stained glass window, of exceeding beauty, erected to his memory by his wife and children, adorns the southern transept of the Church.

In addition to my own Church services, I officiated once a week in Lent for Rev Mr. Drisler, and have administered the Holy Communion on frequent occasions in his Chapel.

St. John's Church, Lewisboro'; the Rev. ROBERT BOLTON, A. M., Rector.

Families, 22. Individuals, 77. Marriage, 1. Burials, 2. Communicants, 31; removed into the Parish, 1; died, 1; present number, 30. The Holy Communion celebrated first Sunday in the month and on all the great festivals, also every third Sunday in the month at the Rectory school-room. Catechist and Sunday-School teacher, 1. Catechumens, 14: member of other classes for religious instruction, 1; Sunday scholars, 6; total number of young persons instructed, 20. Daily Parish School: 1; paid. Scholars: males, 12, females, 6. Celebration of Divine Service: twice every Lord's Day; Sundays, fifty; Holy Days, four—total, 54.

Contributions.—Episcopal Fund, $1; Diocesan Fund, 50c.; Missionary Committee of the Diocese, $1 50; Theological Education Fund, 50c.; Fund for Aged and Infirm Clergymen, 50c.—total, $4.

St. Thomas' Church, Mamaroneck; the Rev. WM. WHITE MONTGOMERY, Rector.

Baptisms, inf. 17. Confirmed, 8. Marriages, 6. Burials, 5. Communicants: admitted, 6; removed into the Parish, 7; removed from the Parish, 6; present number, 130. The Holy Communion celebrated 16 times in public, including Christmas, Maundy-Thursday, Easter Day, Ascension Day, Whitsun-Day and Trinity Sunday; in private, once. The Sunday-School held in the Church, under the charge of the Rector, with ten teachers, and an average attendance of 63 pupils. The School catechised frequently. Celebration of Divine Service: Sundays, 100; Holy Days and other days, 40—total, 140.

Contributions.—Episcopal Fund, $9; Diocesan Fund, $30; Missionary Committee of the Diocese, $29 10; Fund for Aged and Infirm Clergymen, $30 60; New-York Bible and Common Prayer-Book Society, $12; Board of Missions P. E Church, U. S.: Domestic Committee, $39 43; Foreign Committee, (from Sunday-School,) $40 58; Indian Missions, (from S. S., $6 50,) $28; Nebraska Divinity School, $57 25; Missions to Colored People, $3 13; Bp. Auer Memorial, $13; House of Good Shepherd, $20; for the Poor, $172 20; Parish purposes, including Sunday-School, $986 12—total, $1,469 41.

St. Mark's Church, Tarrytown, Mount Pleasant; the Rev. EDMUND GUILBERT, Rector.

Families, 70. Individuals, 400. Baptisms, (ad. 5, inf. 21,) 26. Confirmed, 11. Marriages, 12. Burials, 15. Communicants: present number, 135. The Holy Communion celebrated weekly on the Lord's Day, on all Saints' Days, on all the chief festivals, six times in private. Catechumens, 125. Daily Parish School: 1; paid; Scholars, males, 30. Celebration of Divine Service: Sundays, three times each Sunday, and on the chief festivals; daily in Holy Week; other days, all Saints' days, and every Wednesday and Friday throughout the year.

Contributions.—Episcopal Fund, $4; Diocesan Fund, $7 75; Sunday-School, $233 72; General Theological Seminary, $25; Board of Missions P. E. Church, U. S.: Domestic Committee, $35 97; Foreign Committee, $40; Church Mission to Deaf Mutes, $7 88; the Poor, $286 57; Parish Church Building Fund, $1,756; Parish purposes in general, $1,834—total, $4,250 89.

Trinity Church, Mount Vernon; the Rev. CLARENCE BUEL, Rector.

Families, 90. Individuals, 350. Baptisms, (ad 5, inf. 19,) 24. Confirmed, 33. Marriages, 3. Burials, 8. Communicants: admitted, 33; removed into the Parish, 15; removed from the Parish, 5; died, 2; present number, 150. The Holy Communion celebrated on every Sunday during Advent and Lent, and thereafter until Trinity Sunday, and always on the first Sunday in each month; also on the greater festivals, and on several of the Saints' days and other Holy Days during the year. Catechists and Sunday-School teachers, 20. Catechumens: Children taught the Catechism openly in the Church, 177; times, 12; members of other classes for religious instruction, 38; total number of young persons instructed, 212. Celebration of Divine Service: Sundays, twice on each, and on each first Sunday in the month three times; Holy Days, on nearly all, one service on each; other days, on Fridays throughout the year; also daily during Lent, and on Wednesday evenings during Advent and Lent; also on days for which special services were appointed by ecclesiastical authority.

Contributions.—Episcopal Fund, $3; Diocesan Fund, $36; Missionary Committee of the Diocese, $24 84; Theological Education Fund, $17 30; Fund for Aged and Infirm Clergymen, $21 15; Sisters of St. Mary at Memphis, Tennessee, $10; Children's Fold, New-York, $12 50; for St. John's Guild, New-York, $5; St. Mary's Hospital for Children, New-York, $27 82; Church of the Advent, Nashville, $4; Church Mission to the Jews, $7 88; Board of Missions P. E. Church, U. S.: Domestic Committee, $29 37; Foreign Committee, $19 91; Home Missions for Colored People, $4 22; the Poor, $140 70; Parish purposes, $4,329 68—total, $4,693 37.

The encouraging state of the Parish, to which allusion was made in the last previous report, has continued during the past year. Its numerical increase has been very considerable, and much has also been accomplished in the way of reducing its financial burdens.

With respect to offerings it is proper to add, that besides those above enumerated, the ladies contributed a valuable Christmas box of clothing and provisions to the Children's Fold in the City of New-York.

St. Mark's Church, New Castle; the Rev. JAMES WILLIAM SPARKS, Rector and Missionary.

Families, 43. Individuals, 170. Baptisms, (ad. 3, inf. 3,) 6. Confirmed, 7. Marriages, 2. Burials, 2. Communicants: admitted, 7; present number, 68. The Holy Communion celebrated monthly and Holy Days. Catechists and Sunday-School teachers, 4. Catechumens, 40. Celebration of Divine Service: Sundays, three services, (full,) including one at Chappaqua; Holy Days, all, one service; other days, during Lent, three weekly services.

Contributions.—Episcopal Fund, $2; Diocesan Fund, $10; Missionary Committee of the Diocese, $4 22; Theological Education Fund, $3 25; Fund for Aged and Infirm Clergymen, $8; the Poor, $41 86; Parish purposes, $1,041 93—total, $1,106 26.

The foregoing list of Communicants includes six at Chappaqua, where I hold Divine Service, and a Sunday-School (of 20 children) every Sunday afternoon.

Trinity Church, New Rochelle.

Families, 115. Individuals, 450. Baptisms, (ad. 4, inf. 22,) 26. Confirmed, 16. Marriages, 8. Burials, 12. Communicants: admitted, 18; removed into the Parish, 14; removed from the Parish, 10; died, 4; present number, 145. The Holy Communion celebrated first Sunday in each month and the chief festivals, and six times in private. Catechists and Sunday-School teachers, 10. Catechumens, 91. Children taught the Catechism openly in the Church, all; times, 5. Celebration of Divine Service: Sundays, twice; Holy Days, morning service generally; other days, Fridays, evening prayer, Lent services, Wednesdays once, Fridays twice; Holy Week, daily, twice—total, 158.

Contributions.—Episcopal Fund, $15; Diocesan Fund, $32; Board of Missions P. E. Church, U. S.: Domestic Committee, $129 53; Foreign Committee, $24 55; Sunday-School, $63; Woman's Missionary Aid Society, $220; Offertory Collections, $1,020; Bishop Neely, $56 75; Church debt, $410—total, $1,970 83.

The former Rector, the Rev. R. U. Morgan, D. D., retired from his connection with the Parish in September last.

The Rev. J. Henry Watson, officiating in the Parish since January, presents the above report.

St. Stephen's Church, North Castle; the Rev. C. W. Bolton, Rector.

Families, 36. Individuals, 150. Baptisms, (ad. 1, inf. 4,) 5. Marriages, 6. Burials, 8. Communicants: present number, 60. The Holy Communion celebrated every month. Catechists and Sunday-School teachers, 5. Catechumens, 40.

Contributions.—Board of Missions P. E. Church, U. S.: Domestic Committee, $16 41; Foreign Committee, $36 41—total, $52 82.

St. Peter's Church, (Cortlandt,) Peekskill; the Rev. Wm. Fisher Lewis, Rector.

Families and parts of families, 81. Baptisms, (ad. 2, inf. 10,) 12. Confirmed, 15. Marriage, 1. Burials, 8. Communicants: admitted, 13; removed into the Parish, 7; removed from the Parish, 5, died, 2, present number, 101. The Holy Communion celebrated every Sunday, All Saints' Day, Christmas Day, Feast of Circumcision, and of the Epiphany and Ascension Day; and in private, five times. Catechists and Sunday-School teachers, 14. Catechumens, 100; Children taught the Catechism openly in the Church, 100; times, 12. Celebration of Divine Service: Sundays, Parish Church, 8; St. Peter's Chapel, 146—total, 154; Holy Days, 30, other days, 105—total, 289.

Contributions.—Episcopal Fund, $7; Diocesan Fund, $30; Missionary Committee of the Diocese, $21 65; Fund for Aged and Infirm Clergymen, $16 69; Southern Miss. Convocation, $52; St Mary's Hospital, $22 75, General Theological Seminary, $12; Board of Missions P. E. Church, U S.: Indian Miss., $7 77; Domestic Committee, $20; Colored Missions, $20; Parochial Schools, $117 75; the Poor, $35 68; Parish purposes, $697 74; House of Good Shepherd, $21 60; Nashotah, $19 50; Jews, $9 50—total, $1,111 58.

Christ Church, Pelham; the Rev. CHARLES HIGBEE, Rector.

Baptisms, inf. 6. Funerals, 3. Confirmations, 7. Communicants: present number, 59. Services twice each Sunday. Sunday-School: scholars, 50; teachers, 4. The Rector being superintendent, public Catechism first Sunday of month.

Collections for poor of the Parish and other charitable objects about $353.
Pews all taken.

St. John's Church, Pleasantville; the Rev. JAMES WILLIAM SPARKS, Missionary.

Families, 3. Individuals, 26. Communicants, 11. Catechists and Sunday-School teachers, 2. Catechumens, 6. Celebration of Divine Service: Sundays, every Sunday afternoon.

Contributions.—Parish purposes, $115 55.

As a Missionary of the Church, I visited this Parish, and found that its Church had been closed for nearly twelve months; it had no Vestry. I organized a Vestry, and held afternoon services, and when unable to be present myself, undertook to supply the congregation with Lay services.

A subscription list is now started, and the Missionary thinks, with outside aid, services can be maintained. The attendance so far has been good.

St. Peter's Church, Portchester; the Rev. BROCKHOLST MORGAN, Rector.

Families, 141. Individuals, 564. Baptisms, (ad. 27, inf. 37,) 64. Confirmed, 63. Marriages, 14. Burials, 15. Communicants: admitted, 21; removed into the Parish, 6; removed from the Parish, 2; died, 3; present number, 172. The Holy Communion celebrated on the first Sunday in every month, and on the great festivals. Catechumens: Children taught the Catechism openly in the Church, 250; total number of young persons instructed, 250. Celebration of Divine Service: Sundays, 100; other days, 52—total, 152.

Contributions.—Episcopal Fund, $9; Diocesan Fund, $40; Missionary Committee of the Diocese, $15 35; Southern Missionary Convocation, N. Y., $16 91; Board of Missions P. E. Church, U. S.: Foreign Committee, $23 68; the Poor, $212 19; Parish purposes, $1,095 23; Mission to Jews, $7 10—total, $1,419 46.

The above statistics will show to what a high state of prosperity, under God, this Parish has attained during the past year. In addition to these things, numerous other ways of promoting the Church's work have been successfully carried on, in the way of Sewing Schools, Singing Schools, &c. The Parish Church has been enlarged and beautifully remodelled at a considerable expense, and a commodious Chapel erected for the constantly increasing Sunday-School. Two Confirmations have been necessary this year; one by the Bishop of the Diocese, and the other, at his request, by the Right Rev. Dr. Tozer. The offerings of the Parish for Church enlargements, etc., have been about $10,000.

Christ Church, Rye; the Rev. CHAUNCEY B. BREWSTER, Rector.

Families, about 150. Baptisms, (ad. 2, inf. 10,) 12. Confirmed, 16. Marriage, 1. Burials, 11. Communicants: admitted, 16; removed into the Parish, 7; removed from the Parish, 1; died, 3; present number, about 200. The Holy Communion celebrated the first Sunday in each month and the greater festivals. Catechists and Sunday-School teachers, 18. Catechumens, 153, including 30 in Mission Sunday-School; Children taught the Catechism openly in the Church, 123; times, 11; members of other classes for religious instruction, 10; total number of young persons instructed, 153. Celebration of Divine Service: Sundays, twice; Holy Days, once; other days, Fridays throughout the year. In the Chapel at Milton Divine Service celebrated regularly on alternate Sunday evenings, and every Sunday during a large portion of the year.

Contributions.—Episcopal and Diocesan Funds, $80; Missionary Committee of the Diocese, $54 15; Theological Education Fund, $83 70; Fund for Aged and Infirm Clergymen, $43 65; Southern Convocation, $58 51; Indian Missions, $50; New-York Bible and Common Prayer-Book Society, $52 24; Mission to Jews, $34 65; House of Good Shepherd, $32 10; sundry Western Missions, $38 75; Board of Missions P. E. Church, U. S.: Domestic Committee, $232 29; Foreign Committee, $105 10; Woman's Missionary Society, Auxiliary, $678 85; the Poor. $477 09; Parish purposes, $499 21; sundry outside purposes, $94 55; amount raised by Ladies' Sewing Society, $1,200; appropriated and subscribed for Music, $500; contributed by Sunday-School to Missions, $118 88; raised for Sunday-School expenses, $228 50; donated for improvements at the Chapel, $379 30; offerings at the Chapel in Milton, $58 49—total, $5,045 01.

Church of St. James the Less, Scarsdale; the Rev. WILLIAM AUGUSTUS HOLBROOK, Rector.

Families, 44. Individuals, 300. Baptisms, inf. 8. Confirmed, 10. Marriages, 3. Burials, 2. Communicants: admitted, 11; removed into the Parish, 16; removed from the Parish, 20; died, 1; present number, 80. The Holy Communion celebrated first Sunday of each month and five great feasts. Catechists and Sunday-School teachers, 8. Catechumens: Children taught the Catechism openly in the Church, 50; times, 12; Sunday scholars, 40; total number of young persons instructed, 70. Celebration of Divine Service: Sundays, once A. M., once P. M., once at night during summer; Holy Days, all; other days, Thanksgiving Day, Institution—total, 176.

Contributions.—Episcopal Fund, $2; Diocesan Fund, $30; Missionary Committee of the Diocese, $18 24; New-York Bible and Common Prayer-Book Society, $12 10; Protestant Episcopal Tract Society, $2 58; General P. E. S. S. Union and Church Book Society, $5 06; Board of Missions P. E. Church, U. S.: Domestic Committee, $32 22; Parochial Schools, $52; the Poor, $20; Parish purposes, $2,086 29; Church purposes in general, $139 33—total, $2,399 82.

Prior to the present incumbency, no provision had been made the past year for Canonical offerings, in consequence of which some of these not here represented must be postponed to the next report. Under Church purposes in general are included: Mission to Colored People, $8 77; Mission to the Jews, $4 50; Mission of Bp. Tuttle, $27 10; Indian Scholarship, $18 96, two scholarships in Utah, $80. The Sewing Society has sent to Bp. Tuttle's school two barrels of clothing, valued at over $100.

All Saints' Church, Briar Cliff, (Sing Sing;) the Rev. J. BRECKENRIDGE GIBSON, D. D., Rector.

Families, 12. Individuals, about 50. Baptisms, inf. 1. Burial, 1. Communicants: present number, 30. The Holy Communion celebrated monthly and on all the greater festivals. Catechists and Sunday-School teachers, 2. Catechumens, 16. Celebration of Divine Service: Sundays, throughout the year, twice each Sunday; Holy Days, Christmas, Ash-Wednesday, Good Friday; other days, Wednesdays and Fridays in Lent, Holy Week—total, 123.

Contributions.—Episcopal Fund, $2; Diocesan Fund, $8; Missionary Committee of the Diocese, $15 33; Theological Education Fund, $12 25, New-York Bible and Common Prayer-Book Society, $13 13; Board of Missions P. E Church, U. S.: Domestic Committee, $28 21; Foreign Committee, $35 29; the Poor, $51 27; Parish purposes, $811 53; Church purposes in general, $38 45—total, $1,015 46

The Senior Warden of the Parish, Mr. Peter R Brinckerhoff, was called to his rest in Paradise on Friday, September 5, 1874.

His loss to the Parish seems, to human judgment, to be irreparable. He has left a sacred memory of quiet, earnest devotion to the Church's work and to the duties of the Christian life.

St. Paul's Church, Sing Sing ; the Rev. JAMES I. HELM, D. D., Rector.

Baptisms, (ad. 5, inf. 15,) 20. Confirmed, 11. Marriages, 2. Burials, 12. Communicants: present number, 133. The Holy Communion celebrated first Sunday in every month, on great festivals, and with the sick in private. Celebration of Divine Service: Sundays, twice; Holy Days, once; other days, in Lent, Wednesdays and Fridays, twice; twice daily in Holy Week, at other times on Fridays, and on Thanksgiving—total, 200.

Contributions.—Episcopal Fund, $8; Diocesan Fund, $30; Missionary Committee of the Diocese, $25; Fund for Aged and Infirm Clergymen, $33 65; New-York Bible and Common Prayer-Book Society, $22; Board of Missions P. E. Church, U. S.: Domestic Committee, $60; Foreign Committee, $20; the Poor, $250; Parish purposes, $1,000; Church purposes in general, $50—total, $1,418 65.

During Lent the ladies of the Parish prepared and forwarded to one of our Missionaries in the South a box of clothing and useful articles, valued at $300.

There is a Ladies' Aid Society, which provides, by dues and contributions, a fund for the various wants of the Parish.

Also a Guild of the young male members, and one of the young female members for associated Parish work.

Trinity Church, Sing Sing ; the Rev. GEO. W. FERGUSON, Rector.

Baptisms. (ad. 13, inf. 38,) 51. Confirmed, 35. Marriages, 2. Burials, 7. Communicants: admitted, 23; removed into the Parish, 2; removed from the Parish, 10: present number, 159. The Holy Communion celebrated on the first Sunday in each month, weekly during Advent and Lent, on the great festivals, and on Ash-Wednesday and Thanksgiving Day. Catechists and Sunday-School teachers, 18. Catechumens: Children taught the Catechism openly in the Church, 135; times, 12. Celebration of Divine Service: Sundays, 114; Holy Days, 41; other days, 110—total, 265.

Contributions.—Episcopal Fund, $8 59; Diocesan Fund, $50; Missionary Committee of the Diocese, $48 78: Southern Missionary Convocation of the Diocese, $30 64; Fund for Aged and Infirm Clergymen, $26; House of the Good Shepherd, Tompkins' Cove, $100; Home Missions to Colored people, $43 46; Mission to Jews, $8 74; New-York Bible and Common Prayer-Book Society, $18 67; Board of Missions P. E. Church, U. S.: Domestic Committee, $138; Foreign Committee, $38 97; the Poor, $562 13; Parish purposes, (new building site, $12,621 09; other objects, $1,148 43,) $13,769 52; Church purposes in general, $395 52—total, $15,239 02.

Of the number confirmed at the Bishop's visitation, fourteen were pupils of the Rev. Dr. Gibson's school, (St. John's.) This school and the students of Mt. Pleasant Academy attend regularly the services of the Church in this Parish. Among the students of St. John's there are about 35 communicants not included in the number reported.

The Vestry of this Church have lately bought, and paid for, a piece of ground on Highland Avenue, 180 feet by 200, costing $14,500, three members of the Vestry having given $4,000 each. Plans and estimates for the erection of a new stone Church are being prepared, and we hope at an early day to begin the work of building.

The Parish is entirely free from debt.

Christ Church, Tarrytown ; the Rev. J. SELDEN SPENCER, Rector.

Families, about 80. Individuals, about 400. Baptisms, (ad. 3, inf. 18,) 21. Confirmed, 9. Marriages, 4. Burials, 5. Communicants: present number, about 120. The Holy Communion celebrated on the first Sunday of every month, and on the greater festivals.

Catechists and Sunday-School teachers, 12; Sunday scholars, 90. Celebration of Divine Service: Sundays, morning and evening; Holy Days, great festivals; other days, Wednesday and Friday in Lent, daily in Holy Week, and Wednesday mornings in the week.

Contributions.—Episcopal Fund, $20; Diocesan Fund, $50; Missionary Committee of the Diocese, $29 83; Fund for Aged and Infirm Clergymen, $31 87; New-York Bible and Common Prayer-Book Society, $19 05; Board of Missions P. E. Church, U. S.: Indian Commission, $11; Domestic Committee, ($99 52; Mite Chests, $18 27,) $117 79; Foreign Committee, ($28 85; Bishop Auer's Memorial, $60 86,) $89 71; Mite Chests, $2 30; Sunday-School purposes, festivals, &c., $145; the Poor, $157 05; received for building a Rectory, $2,300; for House of Good Shepherd, $20—total, $2,996 60.

The Parish has just entered upon the work of building a Rectory.

St. John's Church, Tuckahoe, (Yonkers;) the Rev. ANGUS M. IVES, Minister.

Families, 49. Individuals, 198. Baptisms, (ad. 1, inf. 7,) 8. Marriages, 4. Burials, 4. Communicants: admitted, 10; removed from the Parish, 3; died, 2; present number, 67. The Holy Communion celebrated monthly, and on the principal festivals. Catechists and Sunday-School teachers, 6. Catechumens: Children taught the Catechism openly in the Church, 41. Celebration of Divine Service: Sunday mornings throughout the year, and on the greater festivals.

Contributions.—Episcopal Fund, $7 61; Diocesan Fund, $13 21; Missionary Committee of the Diocese, $8 32; Fund for Aged and Infirm Clergymen, $4 55; New-York Bible and Common Prayer-Book Society, $4; Board of Missions P. E. Church, U. S.: Domestic Committee, $7 61; Foreign Committee, $3 80; Mission to the Jews, $5 35; Parish purposes, $1,239 44—total, $1,293 89.

St. Peter's Church, Westchester; the Rev. CHRISTOPHER B. WYATT, D. D., Rector.

Families, about 120. Individuals, about 650. Baptisms, (ad. 1, inf. 24,) 25. Confirmed, 16. Marriages, 7. Burials, 16. Communicants: present number, about 125. The Holy Communion celebrated the first Sunday of each month and on all chief festivals. Catechists and Sunday-School teachers, 17. Catechumens: Children taught the Catechism openly in the Church, all the Sunday-School children; times, 12; members of other classes for religious instruction, 12. Sunday scholars, 150. Celebration of Divine Service: Sundays, all, twice; Holy Days, all, once; other days, twice in every week.

Contributions.—Episcopal Fund, $25; Diocesan Fund, $61; Missionary Committee of the Diocese, $242 57; Diocesan Missions, through Southern Convocation, $140; Theological Education Fund, $[illegible]; Fund for Aged and Infirm Clergymen, $72 76; "House of the Good Shepherd," Tompkins' Cove, $25[illegible]; New-York Bible and Common Prayer-Book Society, $[illegible]; Board of Missions P. E. Church, U. S.: Domestic Committee, $268 75; Missions in Texas, $[illegible] 02; Missions in Rockland County, $79; the Poor, $[illegible]; Parish purposes, $[illegible]; Sunday School, $[illegible]; Church purposes in general, $[illegible]—total, $[illegible].

[illegible] Church, White Plains; the Rev. FREDERICK B. VAN KLEECK, Rector.

[illegible] parts of families, 1[illegible]. Baptisms, (ad. 4, inf. 17,) 21. Confirmed, 19. Marriages, [illegible]. Burials, 20. Communicants: removed from the Parish, 4; died, 2; present number, [illegible]. The Holy Communion celebrated first Sunday in the month, the greater festivals, Christmas, Easter and Whitsun-Day twice; weekly noon celebration Thursdays in Advent and Lent. Catechists and Sunday-School teachers, 21. Catechumens, 150. Children taught the Catechism openly in the Church, 150; times, 12; total number of young persons instructed, 150. Celebration of Divine Service: Sundays, twice in the Parish Church, first Sunday in the month. Children's service and Catechetical instruction in the afternoon; evening service and sermon each alternate Sunday at Rosedale Mission; Holy Days, morning service; other days, Wednesdays, afternoon; Fridays, morning; in Lent, daily evening service, with meditation; Friday nights, with lecture; Wednesdays, Thursdays, Fridays, morning service.

Contributions.—Episcopal Fund, $10; Diocesan Fund, $40; Missionary Committee of the Diocese, $41 18; Theological Education Fund, $18 05; Fund for Aged and Infirm Clergymen, $24 09; New-York City Mission Society to the Jews, $18; Life Membership Society for Increase of the Ministry, gift of Parishioner, $25; Day of Intercession, Alms for Bishop Tuttle, $10; New-York Bible and Common Prayer-Book Society, $20 07; House of Good Shepherd, Rockland County, $44 17; Diocesan Missions in Maine, $33 06; Indian Missions, $52 26; Board of Missions P. E. Church, U. S.: Domestic Committee, (Offerings, $108 30; Mite Chests, $35 19,) $143 49; Foreign Committee, (Offerings, $42 40; savings in Lent, $22 75,) $65 15; Home Missions to Colored People, $20 20; the Poor, $177 87; Parish purposes, $1,476 15; Church purposes in general, $682 53—total, $2,901 27.

St. John's Church, Wilmot, New-Rochelle; the Rev. ANGUS M. IVES, Missionary.

Families, 26. Individuals, 108. Baptisms, (ad. 2, inf. 3,) 5. Confirmed, 6. Marriage, 1. Burials, 5. Communicants: admitted, 4; died, 2; present number, 25. The Holy Communion celebrated on the third Sunday of every month and on the greater festivals. Catechists and Sunday-School teachers, 7. Catechumens: Children taught the Catechism openly in the Church, 27. Celebration of Divine Service: Sunday afternoons throughout the year, on the greater festivals, and on the morning of the third Sunday every month.

Contributions.—Episcopal Fund, $2; Diocesan Fund, $5; Missionary Committee of the Diocese, $4; Theological Education Fund, $3; Fund for Aged and Infirm Clergymen, $5; Board of Missions P. E. Church, U. S.: Domestic Committee, $1 83; Foreign Committee, $1 05; Parish purposes, $260—total, $281 88.

St. John's Church, Yonkers; the Rev. WM. S. LANGFORD, Rector.

Baptisms, (ad. 2, inf. 50,) 52. Confirmed, 29. Marriages. 18. Burials, 28. Celebration of Divine Service: Sundays, twice, and third Sunday in each month, three times; Holy Days, principal; other days, Wednesdays, and daily during Lent.

Contributions.—Episcopal Fund, $20; Diocesan Fund, $30; Missionary Committee of the Diocese, $15 26; Fund for Aged and Infirm Clergymen, $20; Board of Missions P. E. Church, U. S.: Foreign Committee, $140; on account Church improvement, $18,184; the Poor, $1,041 17; Parish purposes, $1,098 86; various objects, $3,640 95—total, $24,590 24.

St. John's Church, Yonkers; the Rev. WM. S. LANGFORD, Rector.

[Report for the year 1873–74.]

Baptisms, (ad. 5, inf. 59,) 64. Confirmed, 43. Marriages, 10. Burials, 22. Communicants, 350. The Holy Communion celebrated first Sunday in each month, Christmas, Easter, Whitsun-Day and Trinity Sunday. Sunday-School: 40 teachers; 500 scholars. Divine Service: Sundays, twice, and on third Sunday in each month, three times; Holy Days, principal; other days, Wednesdays, and daily during Lent—total, about 200.

Contributions.—Episcopal Fund, $18; Diocesan Fund, $34 79; Missionary purposes in the Diocese, $32 08; Aged and Infirm Clergy Fund, $23 26; Foreign Committee, Board of Missions, $79 82; on account Church Building Improvement, $10,500; the Poor, $785 01; Parish purposes, $485 72; various objects, $5,040 20—total, $16,998 88.

St. Paul's Church, Yonkers; the Rev. D. F. BANKS, Rector; the Rev. M. R. HOOPER and the Rev. ARTHUR SLOAN, Assistant Ministers.

Families, 154. Individuals, 845. Baptisms, (ad. 2, inf. 53,) 55. Confirmed, 35. Marriages, 4. Burials, 5. Communicants: admitted, 34; removed into the Parish, 15; removed from the Parish, 6; died, 1; present number, 269. The Holy Communion celebrated on the first Sunday in the month and greater festivals. Catechumens, 24. Total number of young persons instructed, 285. Celebration of Divine Service: Sundays, twice; other days, daily.

Contributions.—Diocesan Fund, $50; Missionary Committee of the Diocese, $20 38; New-York City Mission Society, $20; Board of Missions P. E. Church, U. S.: Domestic Committee, $281 10; Foreign Committee, $5; the Poor, $621 08; Parish purposes, $1,789 43; Church purposes in general, $1,078 84—total, $3,865 83.

FROM THE FOLLOWING PARISHES NO REPORTS HAVE BEEN RECEIVED.

St. Peter's Church, Lithgow, Dutchess County.

St. Luke's Church, Matteawan, Dutchess County.

Church of the Regeneration, Pine Plains, Dutchess County.

Church of the Ascension, New-York, the Rev. John Cotton Smith, D. D., Rector.

Church of the Holy Communion, New-York, the Rev. F. E. Lawrence, Pastor.

Church of the Intercessor, New-York.

Church of the Mediator, New-York.

Church of the Redeemer, New-York, the Rev. J. W. Shackelford, Rector.

Church of St. Ignatius, New-York, the Rev. F. C. Ewer, D. D., Rector.

St. Andrew's Church, Richmond, Richmond County, the Rev. Kingston Goddard, D. D., Rector.

St. Luke's Church, Haverstraw, Rockland County.

St. Paul's Church, Ellenville, Ulster County, the Rev. C. C. Edmunds.

St. Mary's Church, Mott Haven, New-York, vacant.

St. Mary's Church, Beechwood, Westchester County, the Rev. E. N. Mead, D. D., Rector.

St. Augustine's Church, Croton, the Rev. A. V. Clarkson, Rector.

St. Mary's Church, North Castle, Westchester County.

St. Luke's Church, Somers, Westchester County.

St. Mary's Church, Yorktown, Westchester County.—18.

Also from the following, which have been admitted into union with the Convention, but which maintain no services:

St. Mary's Church, Beekman, Dutchess County.
Church of the Advent, New-York.
Church of the Crucifixion, New-York.
Emmanuel Church, New-York.
Free Church of St. George's, Beekman-street, New-York.
Church of the Good Shepherd, New-York.
Church of the Holy Evangelists, New-York.
Church of the Holy Light, New-York.
Church of the Redemption, New-York.
St. Barnabas' Church, New-York.
St. Jude's Church, New-York.
St. Matthew's Church, New-York.
St. Paul's Church, 12th Ward, New-York.
St. Sauveur's Church, New-York.
St. Saviour's Church, New-York.
St. Simon's Church, New-York.—16.

OTHER CLERICAL REPORTS.

The Bishop of the Diocese has also received Reports, according to the Canon, from the following Clergymen of the Diocese, not having Parochial or Missionary charge:

The Rev. J. S. BARNES respectfully reports:

That for the last year he has been laboring as Missionary at St. John's Church and Hospital, Yonkers, under the direction of the Rector, and that any official acts performed are incorporated in the Rector's report.

The Rev. W. M. A. BRODNAX reports as follows:

During the past year I have supplied vacant pulpits, as opportunities offered.

The Rev. SAMUEL BUEL, D. D., Professor of Systematic Divinity and Dogmatic Theology in the General Theological Seminary, respectfully reports:

That since his last report he has been engaged in the performance of his duties as Professor of Systematic Divinity and Dogmatic Theology in the General Theological Seminary, and that he has officiated occasionally, in Divine service, in preaching, and in celebrating the Holy Communion, in the Church of the Annunciation, in the City of New-York; in St. George's Church, in the same city; in St. John's Church, Brooklyn; in Trinity Church, Mt. Vernon; in St. Ann's Church, Brooklyn, and in Christ Church, Ramapo, and in the Chapel of the General Theological Seminary.

The Rev. EDWARD COWLEY respectfully reports:

That in addition to his duties in charge of "The Children's Fold," he has assisted several of the Clergy in their respective Parishes, preaching, baptizing and administering the Holy Communion; the records being made where they severally belonged. He has also baptized one infant, and officiated at one burial, not otherwise than hereby registered.

The whole amount raised for "The Children's Fold," and not elsewhere acknowledged, during the past Conventional year, has been about $4,000. Cordial thanks are hereby expressed to all who have aided in this interesting work of caring for the lambs of Christ.

Something also has been done towards the "Building Fund," notwithstanding the general disturbance in the financial affairs of our country. That fund now amounts to a little over $1,200. That these hundreds may soon be increased to as many thousands is my sincere prayer.

The Rev. HENRY E. DUNCAN, D. D., respectfully reports:

That soon after his resignation in May of St. Luke's Parish, Matteawan, he received a unanimous invitation to the Rectorship of St. Paul's Church, Rahway, New-Jersey, which, after careful consideration, he deemed it best to decline. He has officiated once in New-Jersey, once in Connecticut, and on several occasions in this Diocese. His temporary place of residence is Newburgh.

The Rev. WILLIAM E. EIGENBRODT, D. D., Professor of Pastoral Theology in the General Theological Seminary, respectfully reports:

That during the last year, besides the regular discharge of his duties in the General Theological Seminary, he has officiated in various Churches in the Dioceses of New-York and of Long Island, by saying prayers, preaching, baptizing, and administering the Holy Communion.

The Rev. RANDALL C. HALL respectfully reports as follows:

In addition to his duties in the General Theological Seminary, he has officiated and preached almost every Sunday.

Since the first of May he has taken temporary charge of St. John's Church, Dover, New-Jersey, during the absence of the Rector in Europe.

The Rev. ALEXANDER HAMILTON, deacon, respectfully reports:

That during the past year he has been engaged in the duties of his office in Westchester County, New-York City, and past summer frequently assisting at Christ Church, West Islip, Diocese of Long Island.

The Rev. LEVI JOHNSTON reports as follows:

I have to report that my official acts between the meeting of last Convention, 1873, and the 1st of April, 1874, are contained in the report of the Rector of St. Andrew's Church, Walden, N. Y., having resigned the Rectorship of the Parish at the latter date.

Since April I have officiated at St. James' Church, Goshen, St. John's Church, Greenwood, and St. Andrew's Church, Walden.

The Rev. WILLIAM KIRKUS reports as follows:

From September 1st to October 31st, 1873, I performed the services required of me as Assistant Minister of the Parish of St. John Baptist, New-York City, Rev. Dr. Duffie, Rector.

From November 1st to the present time, I performed the services required of me as Assistant Minister of Grace Church, New-York City, Rev. H. C. Potter, D. D., Rector.

I have also preached thirty-three times in other Churches in this Diocese, and in the Dioceses of Long Island, New-Jersey and Rhode Island.

The Rev. R. U. MORGAN, D. D., reports as follows:

Since my retirement from the Rectorship of Trinity Church, New-Rochelle, I have attended public worship on Sundays, the higher festivals, several "Holy Days" and week days.

I have performed the services of the Church 12 times, administered the Holy Communion 6 times, and also once in private; preached 15 times.

I have assisted in reading service 54 times, and assisted in celebrating the Holy Communion 28 times.

Read the burial service twice; married one couple.

The Rev. WILLIAM W. OLSSEN, A. M., Professor of the Greek Language and Literature, and of the Hebrew Language in St. Stephen's College, Annandale, N. Y., reports as follows:

During the past year I have performed the duties of the above named professorship, and have taken part in the daily services of the College Chapel. In addition I have elsewhere read service, in whole or in part, 31 times, preached 27 times, celebrated the Holy Communion in public 4 times, in private once, baptized 4 infants, and read the burial service over the bodies of 3 persons.

The Rev. SAMUEL OSGOOD, D. D., reports:

Baptisms, (ad. 2, inf. 19,) 21; marriage, 1; burials, 4.

Dr. Osgood has kept his position in the Diocese as before, and generally preached on Sundays and other Church days. He has lived part of the year as usual at his home in Fairfield, Connecticut, and rendered religious services in that neighborhood. His longest term of service in one pulpit was four months, in the Church of the Ascension, Staten Island, during the Rector's (the Rev. J. S. Bush) absence. He preached on Whitsun-Day and Trinity Sunday at St. Thomas', in this city; at King's Chapel, Boston, on Quinquagesima Sunday, and at Appleton Chapel, Cambridge, the Sunday after Easter, after advising the Bishop of Massachusetts of his intention. He has given a number of literary lectures for Church charities, and he has acted as a member of the Italian Commission, attended many meetings and raised some money for its service. He has written much for Church periodicals, and been a student of Christian literature and a friend of generous methods of education within the measure of his ability and opportunity. Imperative circumstances require him to live in or near this city, and he desires regular pulpit occupation, with the usual labors of teaching the young and visiting the afflicted.

The Rev. JOHN H. ROGERS reports as follows:

I would most respectfully present to you the following report of my official acts during the past year:

Assisted sundry Clerical brethren in morning or evening service on 75 occasions.

This assistance has been largely rendered to the Rector of St. Paul's Church, Tompkinsville, Staten Island; to the Rector of the Church of St. John Baptist, and to the Rector of St. Thomas' Church, New-York City.

Read morning or evening service in vacant Parishes, or during the temporary absence of the Rector, 47 times. Celebrated the Holy Communion, 12 times. Preached 61 sermons. Attended 3 funerals; baptized 2 infants.

During the past three months I have had temporary charge of the Church of the Redeemer, New-York City, the Rector having been absent in Europe for this period. This charge will expire on his return, which is expected about the 5th of October.

The Rev. CHARLES SEYMOUR, A. M., respectfully reports:

That since the last Convention until Easter he has officiated on every Sunday, (except one, and that at Christ Church, Pelham,) for a part of the time, at the Church of the Holy Apostles, and for the remainder of the time at the Church of St. John Baptist, New-York City; that since Easter and to this date he has had temporary charge of Grace Church, Westfield, New-Jersey, which was duly admitted last May into union with the Convention of the Diocese of New-Jersey; that in Westfield, he has publicly celebrated the Holy Communion on the first Sunday of the month, and also on Whitsun-Day and Trinity Sunday. Baptisms, 7; marriages, 3.

Residence for the present, Mt. Vernon, N. Y.

The Rev. GEORGE F. SEYMOUR, S. T. D., Professor of Ecclesiastical History in the General Theological Seminary, respectfully reports:

That since the last Convention, in addition to his duties as Professor in the General Theological Seminary, and Acting Dean of the Institution, he has continued to hold the position of Chaplain of the House of Mercy, New-York, at the foot of West 86th-street.

In this Institution, which has for its object the reclamation of fallen women, he has officiated on 219 occasions; he has baptized 7 adults, admitted 12 to the Holy Communion, and attended 3 funerals.

The Bishop of New-York visited the House of Mercy on Wednesday, July 8th, and confirmed seven candidates. The Sisters of St. Mary, who have been in charge of this Institution since 1863, still continue their labors of self-denying love with a larger measure of success than ever before. The number of inmates at present in the House is 76. Increased subscriptions in amount and number are earnestly solicited to defray the larger outlay which is required to support so numerous a family.

Outside of the House of Mercy the Professor has baptized 4 infants, preached 50 times, and attended 5 funerals.

Summary.—Baptisms, (ad. 7, inf. 4,) 11. Confirmed, 7. Burials, 5. New Communicants admitted, 12.

The Rev. J. A. Spencer, S. T. D., reports as follows:

That since the last Convention he has been constantly occupied in the duties of his position as Professor of the Greek Language and Literature in the College of the City of New-York. In addition, he has officiated in the various services of the Church, in preaching, administering the Holy Communion, etc., on 17 occasions. He has also solemnized one marriage.

The Rev. A. C. Treadway reports as follows;

I returned from California, where I have been living and laboring as occasions offered and my health permitted, for the last few years, to my home in Oswego, in the month of May. Since this date I have rendered similar services in this city. I would be glad to continue these labors, but can scarcely expect it; and yet I thank God, most heartily, for the measure of health and strength I yet enjoy.

The Rev. Edward H. Van Winkle, deacon, respectfully reports as follows:

That since his ordination to the Diaconate, on the Fourth Sunday after Trinity, A. D. 1874, he has performed the following services:

He has assisted twice at the celebration of the Holy Communion, and attended one funeral.

He has preached once in Calvary Church, Pamrapo, N. J.; has read service on twelve occasions, and preached eleven times in St. John's Church, Jersey City; has read service and preached four times in St. Peter's Church, Stone Ridge; has read service on eight occasions, and preached six times in Trinity Church, Hoboken, N. J.

He has performed the above duties, for the most part, during the absence of the Rectors.

He has resided at No. 25 West Ninth-street, New-York City.

The Rev. Obadiah Valentine, deacon, reports as follows:

I would respectfully report, that since my ordination last June, I have been engaged as the Assistant Minister of the Church of the Holy Apostles, in this city. My ministerial acts will be embraced in the report of that Parish.

The Rev. William Walsh, residing at Newburgh, reports as follows:

During the year past I have been almost continuously engaged in the duties of the ministry, chiefly in the Parishes of Orange County, either by supplying Parishes during vacancies in the Rectorships or in assisting in regular Parochial ministrations. My distinct official acts have been registered in the Parishes where they respectively took place.

The Rev. Joshua Weaver reports as follows:

During the past year I have read morning or evening prayer 35 times, and assisted in the same 110 times. Have preached on 37 different occasions. Have celebrated the Holy Communion 23 times, and assisted in its celebration 21 times. Baptized 1 infant, and read the burial service at 3 funerals.

San Francisco, September 14, 1874.

Appendix:

No. II.

A Table,—Showing the names of the Churches and Chapels in the Diocese of New-York, with the numbers in each, respectively, of BAPTISMS, CONFIRMATIONS, COMMUNICANTS, MARRIAGES and BURIALS, so far as reported to the Bishop, for the year ending September 30, 1874. Prepared and published at the request of the Convention by the Secretary, in compliance with a Resolution recorded on p. 94 of the Journal of 1866. In those cases where all the columns are blank, there is no Parochial Report from the Parish for the past year.

Churches and Chapels.	Baptisms.	Confirmations.	Communicants.	Marriages.	Burials.
Dutchess County.					
Amenia, St. Thomas'..	11	..	39	..	..
Annandale, St. Stephen's College Chap	6	7	150	..	4
Beekman, St. Mary's,	..	..	..	..	..
Carthage Landing, St. Mark's,	5	..	25	..	2
Clinton, Apostle's,	..	..	..	..	..
Fishkill, Trinity,	..	..	84	..	4
Glenham, St. John Baptist,	36	15	30	3	5
Hyde Park, St. James',	20	.	100	2	12
Lithgow, St. Peter's,	1	2	14	..	3
Madalin, Trinity,	5	..	52	..	5
Matteawan, St. Luke's,	39	13	186	3	28
Millbrook, Grace,	2	..	27	2	3
Pawling,	..	..	5	..	2
Pine Plains, Regeneration,	..	..	..	..	..
Pleasant Valley, St. Paul's,	4	..	17	1	2
Poughkeepsie, Christ.	47	32	300	8	25
Holy Comforter,	107	40	291	7	19
St. Paul's,	22	10	180	10	15
Red Hook, Christ,	12	9	85	2	1
St. Paul's,	2	..	35	2	6
Rhinebeck, Messiah.	2	..	63	1	4
Rhinecliff, Ascension,	..	..	33	1	..
Wappinger's Falls, Zion,	42	18	275	9	14
New-York County.					
New-York, Advent,	..	..	..	..	..
All Angels',	..	..	50	..	1
All Saints',	83	53	212	86	49
Annunciation,	18	12	137	8	17
Anthon Memorial,	21	26	310	2	14

Churches and Chapels.	Baptisms.	Confirmations.	Communicants.	Marriages.	Burials.
New-York, Ascension,	..	..	..	..	..
Ascension Miss. Chapel,	..	..	..	..	..
Atonement,	..	..	..	..	..
Atonement, Madison Av.,	14	20	225	4	9
Atonement Chapel,	12	..	104	8	..
Bellevue,	84	2	238	..	116
Beloved Disciple,	10	9	95	..	3
Bethlehem Chapel,	29	18	133	6	10
Calvary,	12	15	470	6	15
Calvary Free Chapel,	52	41	450	22	46
Christ Church,	13	20	408	11	9
Crucifixion,	..	..	..	..	..
Emmanuel,	..	..	..	..	..
Epiphany	17	18	175	2	9
Free Church of Saint George's Chapel,	..	..	..	..	..
Our Saviour,	..	..	..	..	..
Floating Chapel of Our Saviour,	27	20	94	11	12
Good Shepherd,	..	.	..	..	..
Grace, / Grace Chapel,	39	46	850	22	85
Heavenly Rest,	22	13	8	6	11
Holy Apostles,	71	20	370	17	33
Holy Communion,	..	.	..	..	..
Holy Comforter,	4	..	20	2	1
Holy Evangelists,	..	..	..	..	..
Holy Innocents,	..	..	..	..	..
Holy Light,	..	..	..	..	..
Holy Martyrs,	90	..	100	28	60
Holy Saviour,	4	15	150	15	12
Holy Sepulchre,	..	..	75	..	..
Holy Trinity,	124	88	1,400	67	110
House of Mercy,	7	7	..	..	3
Incarnation,	31	20	400	23	21
Intercession,	9	14	102	2	8
Intercessor or St Alban's	..	..	..	..	..
Mediator,	..	..	..	..	..
Nativity,	42	23	110	20	24
New-York City Mission, (including Bellevue and Bethlehem Chapels,)	875	23	201	6	266
Reconciliation,	87	15	140	15	11
Redeemer, Yorkville,	..	..	..	..	..
Redemption,	..	..	..	..	..
Reformation,	..	..	..	..	..
Resurrection,	18	20	80	8	23
Santiago,	14	..	57	17	5
St. Ambrose,	141	32	175	122	140
St. Andrew's,	68	27	323	13	38
St. Ann's,	63	44	517	38	39
St. Barnabas',	..	..	..	..	.
St. Bartholomew's,	12	26	450	11	18
St. Clement's,	37	27	150	5	7
St. Esprit,	6	..	100	20	6
St. George's and Chapels,	160	152	1,950	..	..
St. George the Martyr's,	..	..	..	..	..
St. James',	44	41	291	6	19
St. John Baptist,	21	25	200	9	10
St. John Evangelist,	78	58	500	16	28
St. Jude's	..	..	..	..	..
St. Luke's,	90	61	320	37	52
St. Mark's, / St. Mark's Mission,	61	92	402	15	37
St. Mary's	16	12	142	8	6
St. Mary the Virgin,	83	18	184	5	7
St. Matthew's,	..	..	..	..	..
St. Matthias',	8	..	50	13	10
St. Michael's	44	39	179	5	39
St. Paul's in 12th Ward,	..	..	..	..	..

Churches and Chapels.	Baptisms.	Confirmations.	Communicants.	Marriages.	Burials.
New-York, St. Peter's,	142	34	400	27	40
St. Philip's,	48	62	198	8	23
St. Saviour's,	..	..	..	..	..
St. Sauveur's,	..	..	..	..	..
St. Simon's,	..	..	..	..	..
St. Stephen's,	12	..	60	5	7
St. Thomas',	36	50	800	12	11
St. Thomas' Miss. Chap.,	39	32	115	3	8
St. Timothy's,	49	33	278	13	24
Transfiguration,	67	37	450	42	25
Trinity Church, St. Paul's Chapel, St. John's Chapel, Trinity Chapel, St. Chrysostom, St. Augustine, (Miss. Cha.,) St. Cornelius', Governor's Island,	491	336	2,789	146	252
Zion Church,	7	13	143	5	5
Harlem, Grace,	30	18	..	11	21
Fordham, St. James',	9	21	115	2	4
Morrisania, St. Ann's,	14	11	90	2	14
St. Paul's,	13	9	90	8	8
Trinity,	29	19	125	4	10
Mott Haven, St. Mary's,	..	..	..	..	..
Riverdale, Christ,	9	8	110	2	6
Kingsbridge, South Yonkers, Mediator,	17	..	68	..	8
West Farms, Grace,	7	..	69	1	8
Orange County.					
Canterbury, St. John's,	4	..	55	1	2
Cornwall, Holy Innocents,	28	10	80	5	16
Goshen, St. James',	21	21	225	3	5
Greenwood Iron Works, St. John's,	32	10	70	3	7
Newburgh, St. George's,	112	29	401	18	31
St. Paul's,	19	15	144	2	10
New-Windsor, St. Thomas',	3	..	44	..	4
Port Jervis, Grace,	30	11	65	1	3
South Middletown, Grace,	99	61	225	6	23
Walden, St. Andrew's,	19	..	66	3	6
Warwick, Christ,	21	11	50	..	1
Monroe, Grace,	..	..	..	..	..
Putnam County.					
Cold Spring, St. Mary's,	34	16	148	4	6
Paterson, Christ,	.	..	8	..	..
Philipsetown, St. Philip's,	18	..	60	..	2
Richmond County.					
Castleton, West-Brighton, Ascension,	76	25	283	4	8
St. Mary's,	9	..	50	4	4
Clifton, St. John's,	24	25	250	1	8
Edgewater, St. Paul's,	38	20	212	17	18
New-Brighton, Christ,	21	..	110	6	17
Richmond, St. Andrew's,	..	..	..	..	..
Rossville, St. Luke's,	7	..	30	..	2
Southfield, Holy Comforter,	6	14	40	2	2
Rockland County.					
Clarkstown, St. John's,	1	4	25	..	..
Haverstraw, Holy Trinity,	2	..	73	..	[illegible]

Churches and Chapels.	Baptisms.	Confirmations.	Communicants.	Marriages.	Bu
Haverstraw, St. Luke's,	..	..	..	..	
Nyack, Grace,	4	10	125	8	
Piermont, Christ,	21	..	70	9	
Ramapo, Christ,	12	..	48	1	
Spring Valley, St. Paul's,	5	5	82	3	
Stony Point, Holy Child Jesus,	3	..	16	2	
Sullivan County.					
Monticello, St. John's,	28	13	143	8	
Ulster County.					
Ellenville, St. Paul's,	.	..	..	..	
Esopus, Ascension,	2	..	6	..	
Kingston, St. John's,	51	..	189	2	
(Rondout,) Holy Spirit,	21	13	136	8	
Marlborough, Christ,	.	..	35	..	
Milton, All Saints',	11	12	25	1	
Saugerties, Trinity,	12	..	68	1	
Stone Ridge, St. Peter's,	7	4	11	..	
Westchester County.					
Bedford, St. Matthew's,	2	..	70	..	
Beechwood, St. Mary's,	..	..	..	..	
Briar Cliff, All Saints',	1	..	30	..	
City Island, Grace,	..	..	..	..	
Cortlandt, Divine Love,	13	9	19	..	
Croton, St. Augustine's,	..	..	..	..	
East Chester, St. Paul's,	20	12	110	10	
Greenburgh, Zion,	12	10	100	..	
Mission Chapel,	4	4	16	.	
Irvington, St. Barnabas',	12	6	101	4	
Katonah, St. Mark's,	..	..	.	..	
Lewisborough, St. John's,	..	..	31	1	
Mamaroneck, St. Thomas',	17	8	130	6	
Mount Pleasant, St. Mark's,	26	11	135	12	
Mount Vernon, Trinity,	24	38	150	3	
New-Castle, St. Mark's,	6	7	63	2	
New-Rochelle, Trinity,	26	16	145	3	
North Castle, St. Mary's,	..	..	..	..	
St. Stephen's,	5	..	60	6	
North Salem, St. James',	1	..	40	2	
Peekskill, (Cortlandt,) St. Peter's,	12	15	101	1	
Pelham, Christ,	6	7	59	..	
Pleasantville, St. John's,	..	..	11	..	
Portchester, St. Peter's,	64	63	172	14	
Rye, Christ,	12	16	200	1	
Scarsdale, St. James the Less,	8	10	80	3	
Sing Sing, St Paul's,	20	11	133	2	
Trinity,	51	35	150	2	
Somers, St. Luke's,	.	..	.	..	
Tarrytown, Christ,	21	9	120	4	
Tuckahoe, St. John's,	8	..	67	4	
Westchester, St. Peter's,	25	16	125	7	
White Plains, Grace,	21	19	193	7	
Wilmot, St. John's,	5	6	25	1	
Yonkers, St. John's,	64	43	350	10	
St. Paul's,	55	35	269	4	
Yorktown, St. Mary's,	..	..	..	..	

Appendix:—No. III.

A Table,—Showing the names of the Churches and Chapels of the Diocese of New-York, with the sums contributed by each to the EPISCOPAL, DIOCESAN, EDUCATION and MISSIONARY FUNDS, respectively, for the year 1873–74, in compliance with Canons xiii., xiv. and xv.; prepared and published by order of the Convention, by the Secretary of the same, with the aid of the Treasurers of the Funds; to which are added, the Contributions to the FUND FOR AGED AND INFIRM CLERGYMEN, required by Canon xvi. The apportionment for the Salary of the Bishop, when paid, appears in the columns of the Episcopal Fund.

Counties.	Churches and Chapels.	Clergymen.	Episcopal.	Diocesan.	Education.	Missionary.	Aged and Inf. Clergy.
Dutchess,........	Amenia, St. Thomas'................	Rev. W. R. Gardner.........	$2 00	$12 (0	....	....	....
	Annandale, Holy Innocents.........	R. B. Fairbairn, D. D....	7 00	20 00	....	$32 10	$123 00
	Beekman, St. Mary's................	....	....	....	....	....	....
	Carthage Landing, St. Mark's.......	F. W. Shelton, LL. D...	2 00	5 00	....	17 00	....
	Fishkill, Trinity....................	J. R. Livingston.........	7 00	5 00	$5 32	8 00	14 00
	Glenham, St. John Baptist...........	J. R. Livingston.........	2 00	2 00	2 00	8 00	4 00
	Hyde Park, St. James...............	J. S. Purdy, D. D.......	30 00	30 00	16 84	34 88	31 20
	Lithgow, St. Peter's................	....	....	....	....	1 50	....
	Madalin, Trinity....................	J. S. Clark, D. D.......	....	....	....	5 00	....
	Matteawan, St. Luke's..............	....	8 18	....	14 07	25 70	10 00
	Millbrook, Grace....................	B. F. Miller............	....	....	....	....	....
	Pine Plains, Regeneration..........	....	....	....	....	....	....
	Pleasant Valley, St. Paul's.........	G. H. Smith............	2 00	1 05	....	2 24	1 57
	Poughkeepsie, Christ...............	P. K. Cady, D. D.......	13 08	40 00	....	61 11	20 00
	Holy Comforter......	R. F. Crary............	8 00	30 00	17 78	38 00	7 00
	St. Paul's...........	S. H. Synnott..........	....	20 00	....	26 39	36 68

Counties.	Churches and Chapels.	Clergymen.	Episcopal.	Diocesan.	Education.	Missionary.	Aged and Inf. Clergy.
Dutchess........	Red Hook, Christ..................	Rev. J. W. Moore...........	$5 00 } 6 00 }	$8 32	$10 40	$20 75	$10 00
	St. Paul's, (Tivoli,)......	G. L. Platt.............	....	1 00	....	....	5 00
	Rhinebeck, Messiah...............	A. F. Olmsted.........	....	20 00	....	....	7 50
	Rhine Cliff, Ascension............	T. S. Savage, M. D....	2 00	....	....	....	....
	Wappinger's Falls, Zion...........	G. B. Andrews, D. D....	10 00	35 00	5 00	15 00	11 83
New-York,......	New-York, Advent..................	....	....	....	....	....	....
	All Angels'............	C. F. Hoffman.........	1 00	6 00	1 00	1 50	1 50
	All Saints'............	W. N. Dunnell.........	5 00	60 00	....	....	....
	Annunciation	W. J. Seabury.........	15 00	42 00	....	29 60	....
	Anthon Memorial.......	R. H. Newton..........	12 00	....	....	....	80 31
	Ascension..............	J. Cotton Smith, D. D...	50 00	110 00	....	23 00	23 00
	Atonement..............	....	....	....	....	....	....
	Atonement, Madison Av.	C. C. Tiffany..........	15 00	....	....	....	....
	Beloved Disciple........	I. H. Tuttle, D. D......	....	....	....	13 36	....
	Calvary	E. A. Washburn, D. D..	120 00	120 00	....	....	....
	Calvary Free Chapel....	W. D. Walker..........	....	....	....	20 64	....
	Christ	H. M. Thompson, D. D..	20 00	....	....	....	....
	Crucifixion............	....	....	....	....	....	....
	Emmanuel...............	....	....	....	....	....	....
	Epiphany	....	....	....	....	....	....
	Free St. George's Chapel	....	....	....	....	....	....
	Good Shepherd..........	....	....	....	....	....	....
	Grace..................	H. C. Potter, D. D......	125 00	150 00	....	353 16	50 00
	Heavenly Rest..........	R. S. Howland, D. D....	....	....	....	75 00	....
	Holy Apostles..........	J. P. Lundy, D. D......	15 00	....	....	58 63	58 63
	Holy Communion.........	F. E. Lawrence, D. D...	30 00	....	....	200 00	....
	Holy Comforter.........	H. F. Roberts..........	....	....	....	....	4 00
	Holy Evangelists'......	....	....	....	....	....	....
	Holy Light.............	....	....	....	....	....	....
	Holy Martyrs...........	James Millett..........	....	....	....	....	....

Counties.	Churches and Chapels.	Clergymen.	Episcopal.	Diocesan.	Educa ion.	Missionary.	Aged and Inf. Clergy.
New-York, ...	New-York, Holy Saviour...........	Rev. A. B. Carter, D. D.......	....	....	....	....	....
	Holy Sepulchre.........	J. Tuttle Smith.........	$3 00	....	....	....	....
	Holy Trinity...........	S. H. Tyng, Jr., D. D....	....	$100 00	....	....	....
	Holy Trinity of Harlem.	W. N. McVickar........	5 00	80 00	....	....	....
	Incarnation............	H. E. Montgomery, D. D.	45 00	70 00	$10 00	$50 00	....
	Intercession............	W. M. Postlethwaite...	....	....	....	....	....
	Intercessor, or St. Alban's	C. W. Morrill..........	20 00	....	....	50 00	....
	Mediator	....	....	....	....	....	....
	Nativity..............	Caleb Clapp...........	....	24 00	....	....	....
	Reconciliation	E. S. Widdemer........	....	....	....	....	....
	[illegible]er	J. W. Shackelford......	3 00	....	....	50 00	$27 76
	Redemption............	....	....	....	....	....	....
	Reformation	....	....	....	....	....	....
	Resurrection...........	E. O. Flagg, D. D......	....	....	....	....	....
	Santiago	J. De [illegible]a..........	....	....	....	....	....
	St. [illegible]e	Frederick Sill.........	2 00	18 00	5 00	6 44	....
	St. Andrew's..........	G. B. [illegible]er, D. D.....	....	....	....	32 90	....
	St. Ann's.............	T. [illegible]det, D. D.....	8 00	60 00	....	101 54	40 00
	St. Augustine's.........	A. C. Kimber..........	....	....	....	22 47	34 50
	St. Bartholomew's......	S. Cooke, D. D.........	80 00	'73, $160 '74, $160	....	....	252 60
	St. Chrysostom's	T. H. Sill.............	....	....	5 13	29 72	13 63
	St. Clement's..........	T. A. Eaton, D. D......	5 00	25 00	....	75 00	69 00
	St. Esprit	....	....	48 00	2 00	....	3 00
	St. George's...........	S. H. Tyng, D. D......	....	80 00	....	....	....
	St. George the Martyr's.	Frederick Sill.........	2 00	5 00	....	....	....
	St. Ignatius'...........	F. C. Ewer, D. D......	....	....	....	....	....
	St. James'............	C. B. Smith..........	'73, 5 00 5 00	50 00	....	65 10	....
	St. John Baptist........	C. R. [illegible]e, D. D......	5 00	16 00	5 45	30 00	....
	St. John Evangelist.....	W. T. Egbert..........	11 00	13 21	3 00	10 00	3 00

Counties.	Churches and Chapels.	Clergymen.	Episcopal.	Diocesan.	Education.	Missionary.	Aged and Inf. Clergy.
New-York.......	New-York, St. J[illegible]n's...............	....	....	....	....	....	....
	St. Luke's............	Rev. I. H. Tuttle, D. D.	$7 00	$50 00	....	$62 20	$35 36
	St. Mark's............	J. H. Rylance, D. D....	70 00	....	....	153 70	....
	St. Mary's............	C. C. Adams...........	4 00	....	....	....	25 00
	St. Mary the Virgin's...	T. M. Brown...........	10 00	....	....	....	....
	St. Matthew's..........	....	....	....	....	....	....
	St. [illegible]thias'...........	N. E. Cornwall, D. D...	....	....	....	....	....
	St. M[illegible]'s...........	T. M. Peters, D. D......	20 00	100 00	....	10 56	11 92
	St. Paul's, 12th Ward...	....	....	....	....	....	....
	St. Peter's	A. B. Beach, D. D.......	15 00	40 00	....	124 50	41 66
	St. [illegible]p's	....	2 00	30 00	....	....	16 25
	St. Sauveur's..........	....	....	....	....	....	....
	St. Saviour's..........	....	....	....	....	....	....
	St. Simon's...........	....	....	....	....	....	....
	St. Stephen's..........	J. H. Price, D. D........	....	50 00	....	....	30 50
	St. Thomas'...........	W. F. Morgan, D. D....	75 00	200 00	....	269 19	....
	Chapel.....	....	....	....	....	6 70	....
	St. Timothy's..........	Geo. J. Geer, D. D.......	5 00	27 70	....	23 60	7 40
	Transfiguration........	Geo. H. Houghton, D. D.	45 00	160 00	$150 00	220 00	150 00
	Trinity, with	Morgan Dix, D. D.......	....	....	36 77	825 81	85 63
	St. Paul's, ...	....	1,800 00	1,100 00	....	67 37	....
	St. John's and	....	....	....	....	91 92	....
	Trinity Chapels, ...	....	....	....	180 00	849 53	224 09
	Zion	J. N. Galleher.........	10 00	100 00	....	98 27	57 40
	Grace, Harlem.........	D. B. Ray............	....	....	....	....	....
	St. Cornelius', Governor's Island	....	....	....	....	....	....
	St. James', Fordham....	Mytton Maury.........	10 00 8 00	....	6 00	18 00	'73, 81 95 '74, 17 57
	St. Ann's, Morrisania...	Wm. Huckell..........	6 00	10 00	....	....	....
	St. Paul's, Morrisania...	T. R. Harris...........	....	12 00	....	8 85	....

Counties.	Churches and Chapels.	Clergymen.	Episcopal.	Diocesan.	Education.	Missionary.	Aged and Inf. Clergy.
New-York,	New-York, Trinity, Morrisania	Rev. A. S. Hull	....	$8 00	....	....	....
	St. Mary's, Mott Haven	....	....	15 00	....	....	....
	Christ, Riverdale	Geo. D. Wildes, D. D.	$20 00	40 00	....	....	....
	Grace, West Farms	Robert Scott. 1873,	{ 5 00 3 00 }	18 50	....	....	$7 71
	Mediator, Kingsbridge	W. T. Wilson	10 00	40 00	$21 24	$45 75	30 31
Orange	Canterbury, St. John's	J. F. Potter	2 00	12 00	....	....	....
	Cornwall, Holy Innocents	W. R. Thomas	3 00	20 00	10 00	25 00	13 50
	Goshen, St. James'	W. H. De L. Grannis	7 00	30 00	16 50	....	37 50
	Greenwood Iron Works, St. John's	....	3 00	4 50	{ 3 40 4 25 3 58 }	14 83	....
	Monroe, Grace,	....	....	....	....	....	....
	Newburgh, St. George's	John Brown, D. D.	18 00	60 00	103 00	123 57	48 00
	St. Paul's	Rufus Emory......1873,	5 00	'73, $14 '74, $36	....	7 00	....
	New-Windsor, St. Thomas'	H. McKim	3 00	20 00	8 00	15 00	6 79
	Port Jervis, Grace	F. N. Luson	....	8 00	....	5 00	....
	South Middletown, Grace	A. Capron	2 00	30 00	....	....	....
	Walden, St. Andrew's	W. E. Snowden	2 00	3 00	....	13 41	....
	Warwick, Christ	Alfred Goldsborough	2 00	12 00	....	10 00	5 00
Putnam	Cold Spring, St. Mary's	Isaac Van Winkle	18 00	42 00	12 00	11 50	19 92
	Patterson, Christ	William Moore	....	....	....	....	....
	Philipsetown, St. Philip's,	Albert Z. Gray	13 00	24 00	28 20	48 00	15 55
Richmond	Castleton, West Brighton, Ascension	James S. Bush	....	52 00	....	....	24 50
	St. Mary's	H. L. E. Pratt	....	7 00	....	....	....
	Clifton, St. John's	J. C. Eccleston, M. D.	9 00	19 62	....	....	....
	Edgewater, St. Paul's Memorial	T. W. Punnett	8 00	36 00	....	6 11	25 62
	New-Brighton, Christ,	P. P. Irving	13 00	60 00	....	....	40 94
	Richmond, St. Andrew's	K. Goddard, D. D.	....	....	....	....	....
	Rossville, St. Luke's	H. H. Bean	....	12 00	....	2 10	....

Counties.	Churches.	Clergymen.	Episcopal.	Diocesan.	Education.	Missionary.	Aged and Inf. Clergy.
Richmond	Southfield, (Eltingville,) Holy Comforter,	Rev. F. M. Gray	....	....	....	....	$7 00
Rockland	Clarkstown, St. John's	R. S. Mansfield	....	....	....	....	....
	Haverstraw, Trinity	C. B. [illegible]	....	....	....	....	....
	St. Luke's	....	....	....	....	....	....
	Nyack, Grace	F. Babbitt	....	$3 55	....	$26 15	16 59
	Piermont, Christ	S. G. Hitchcock	$3 00	5 00	....	1 00	....
	Ramapo, Christ,	G. E. Purucker	3 00	30 00	....	7 00	....
	Spring Valley, St. Paul's	R. S. [illegible]	....	....	....	5 00	....
	Stony Point, Holy Child Jesus	....	....	....	....	....	3 63
Sullivan	Monticello, St. John's	C. F. [illegible]	2 00	16 00	$7 45	15 00	10 40
	Thompsonville, St. Mary's	....	....	....	....	....	....
Ulster	Ellenville, Trinity	C. C. Edmunds	....	....	....	....	....
	Esopus, Ascension	H. B. Sherman	....	....	....	....	....
	Kingston, St. John's	....	....	24 00	....	8 00	30 60
	Rondout, Holy Spirit	J. B. Murray	2 00	20 00	....	5 00	5 00
	Marlborough, Christ	S. M. Akerly	3 00	5 00	....	21 00	10 00
	Milton, All Saints'	J. H. [illegible]	....	....	....	15 33	....
	Saugerties, Trinity	J. J. Robertson, D. D.	{ 5 52 4 00 }	18 00	....	81 59	23 22
	Stone Ridge, St. Peter's	G. W. West	....	....	....	....	....
Westchester	Bedford, St. Matthew's	Lea Luquer	4 00	12 00	....	5 10	....
	Beechwood, St. Mary's	E. N. Mead, D. D	3 00	....	11 00	....	....
	City Island, Grace	....	....	....	....	....	....
	Croton, (Cortlandt,) St. Augustine's	A. V. Clarkson	....	....	....	....	....
	Eastchester, St. Paul's	W. S. Coffey	8 00	14 00	....	22 17	5 00
	Greenburgh, Zion	Geo. B. Reese	10 00	20 00	....	10 00	17 00
	Irvington, St. Barnabas'	W. H. Benjamin	10 00	20 00	....	20 00	21 50
	Katonah, St. Mark's	....	....	....	....	....	....
	Lewisboro', St. John's	Robert Bolton	....	....	....	2 00	....
	Mamaroneck, St. Thomas'	W. W. Montgomery	9 00	30 00	....	29 10	30 60

Counties.	Churches and Chapels.	Clergymen.	Episcopal.	Diocesan.	Education.	Missionary.	Aged and Inf. Clergy.
Westchester.....	Montrose, Divine Love............	Rev. G. M. Cruger..........	$4 00	$3 75	....	....	....
	Mount Pleasant, St. Mark's........	Ed. Guilbert...........	4 00	7 75	....	....	....
	Mount Vernon, Trinity......	Clarence Buel..........	3 00	36 00	$17 31	$25 00	$21 15
	New Castle, St. Mark's............	....	2 00	10 00	3 25	4 22	3 00
	New Rochelle, Trinity.............	J. H. Watson..........	14 00	30 00	....	....	....
	North Castle, St. Mary's...........	....	....	....	....	....	....
	St. Stephen's.........	C. W. Bolton.........	....	....	....	....	....
	North Salem, St. James'...........	R. C. Russell..........	2 00	6 00	....	....	....
	Peekskill, (Cortlandt,) St. Peter's...	W. F. Lewis...........	7 00	30 00	....	....	16 69
	Pelham, Christ....................	Chas. Higbee..........	....	20 00	....	....	....
	Pleasantville, St. John's..........	....	....	....	....	....	....
	Port Chester, St. Peter's..........	Brockholst Morgan.....	9 00	40 00	....	15 35	....
	Rye, Christ......................	C. B. Brewster.........	18 00	60 00	33 70	54 15	43 65
	Saw Mill Valley, St. Paul's........	J. Drisler.............	....	3 50	....	2 00	3 00
	Scarsdale, St. James the Less.......	....	....	30 00	....	18 24	....
	Sing Sing, Briar Cliff, All Saints'...	J. B. Gibson, D. D......	2 00	8 00	12 25	....	....
	St. Paul's....	J. I. Helm, D. D........	8 00	30 00	....	25 00	33 65
	Trinity	G. W. Ferguson........	8 59 9 00	50 00	....	48 78	25 00
	Somers, St. Luke's...............	R. C. Russell..........	3 00	6 00	....	....	....
	Tarrytown, Christ................	J. S. Spencer..........	20 00	50 00	....	29 83	31 87
	Tuckahoe, St. John's..............	A. M. Ives.............	7 61	18 21	....	8 50	4 55
	Westchester, St. Peter's...........	1873, C. B. Wyatt, D. D.......	25 00 19 05 22 00	60 00	28 05	240 47	72 75
	White Plains, Grace..............	F. B. Van Kleeck.......	8 00	....	....	41 18	....
	Wilmot, St. John's...............	A. M. Ives.............	2 00	5 00	....	4 00	5 00
	Yonkers, St. John's...............	W. S. Langford........	18 00	34 79	....	22 42	23 26
	St. Paul's...............	D. F. Banks............	....	....	....	10 00	....
	Yorktown, St. Mary's.............	Lewis F. Morris........	....	....	....	....	....

SUMMARY

FOR THE YEAR ENDING AT THE CONVENTION, 1874.

*Episcopal Fund, from — Churches,			$3,293 05
Diocesan " " 99 "			3,980 16
Education " " 44 "			773 21
Missionary " Collections from — "		$4,798 25	
	Interest,	505 94	
	Donations,	1,792 00	
	Trinity Church Corporation,	500 00	7,596 19
Aged and Infirm Clergy Fund :			
	Contributions from 84 Churches,	$2,549 19	
	Interest on investments,	1,564 76	
	Donations and Legacy,	1,090 00	5,203 95
	Total,		$20,846 56

NOTE.—In some instances, contributions sent to the Treasurer immediately after the Convention of 1873, but before the preparation of the Table for 1872–73, being included in that year's Table, are not repeated in the Table which is above. The fact of the contributions will, in such case, appear by reference to such items in the Parochial Reports of this Journal in 1874. In this Table appear some contributions handed to the Treasurers since their official Reports to the Convention, This will account for any seeming discrepancy in a few instances between this Table and Parochial Reports.

* This includes the apportionment for the Salary of the Bishop

Appendix:

No. IV.

NOTE.—According to a Resolution recorded on page 94 of the Journal of 1866, there is included in the following List of Churches of this Diocese the date of the admission into its Convention of such Churches as are in union with the same. It is to be observed that such date is not always that of the origin or incorporation of the Parish.

A. Of these Parishes, some existed under Royal Charter, or otherwise, prior to the first Convention of the Diocese in 1785. This class is denoted by the letter A, placed after the date of admission into union.

B. A few others seem to have been admitted by the Conventions in which they respectively appeared for the first time by their delegates, although mention of the admission seems to have been omitted by the Journal. Such are designated by the letter B.

C. The few incorporated under the law of April 13, 1854, are marked by the letter C.

List of Churches in the Diocese of New-York.

Counties.	Towns.	Churches.	Admitted.
Dutchess..........	Amenia,	St. Thomas',	1849
	*Annandale,	*Holy Innocents,	
	Beekman,	St. Mary's,	1850
	Carthage Landing,	St. Mark's,	1868
	*Clinton,	*Apostles,	
	Fishkill,	Trinity,	1787 A
	*Glenham,	*St. John Baptist,	
	Hyde Park,	St. James',	1812
	Lithgow,	St. Peter's,	1834 A
	Madalin,	Trinity,	1866
	Matteawan,	St. Luke's,	1833
	*Millbrook,	Grace,	
	Pine Plains,	Regeneration,	1860
	Pleasant Valley,	St. Paul's,	1837
	Poughkeepsie,	Christ,	1785
		Holy Comforter,	1866 C
		St. Paul's,	1835
	*Red Hook,	*Christ,	

Towns.	Churches.	Admitted.
.... Red Hook,	St. Paul's,	1817
Rhinebeck	Messiah,	1852
*Rhinecliff,	*Ascension,	
Wappinger's Falls,	Zion,	1834
.... New-York,	Advent,	1847
	All Angels',	1859
	All Saints',	1824
	Annunciation,	1838
	Anthon Memorial,	1861
	Ascension,	1827
	*Ascen. Miss. Chapel,	
	Atonement,	1860
	Atonement, Madison Avenue,	1867
	*Beloved Disciple,	
	Calvary,	1836
	*Calvary Miss.Chap'l	
	Christ,	1802
	Crucifixion,	1846
	Emmanuel,	1845
	Epiphany,	1845
	Heavenly Rest,	1870
	*Holy Comforter,	
	*Our Saviour,	
	Free Church of St. George's,	1864 c
	Good Shepherd,	1846
	Grace,	1809
	Holy Apostles,	1845
	*Holy Communion,	
	Holy Evangelists,	1845
	Holy Innocents,	1854
	Holy Light,	1870
	Holy Martyrs,	1847
	Holy Saviour,	1866
	Holy Sepulchre,	1866
	Holy Trinity,	1865
	†Holy Trinity of Harlem,	1874
	Incarnation,	1852
	Intercession,	1849
	Intercessor,	1861
	Mediator,	1862
	Nativity,	1834
	Reconciliation,	1863
	Redeemer,	1853
	Redemption,	1843
	*Reformation,	
	Resurrection,	1862
	Santiago,	1867
	St. Ambrose,	1867
	St. Andrew's,	1829
	St. Ann's,	1854
	St. Barnabas',	1846
	St. Bartholomew's,	1835

Counties.	Towns.	Churches.	Admitted.
[illegible]w-York	New-York,	*St. Chrysostom's,	
		St. Clement's,	1830
		*St. Cornelius',	
		St. Esprit,	1804 B
		St. George's,	1812
		St. George the Martyr's,	1845
		†St. Ignatius',	1874
		St. James',	1810
		St. John Baptist's,	1848
		St. John Evangelist's,	1853
		St. Jude's,	1843
		St. Luke's,	1821
		St. Mark's,	1801
		St. Mary's, *b*,	1824
		†St. Mary the Virgin's,	1874 C
		St. Matthew's,	1846
		St. Matthias',	1864
		St. Michael's, *a*,	1807
		St. Paul's, 12th Ward	1862
		St. Peter's,	1831
		St. Philip's,	1853
		St. Sauveur's,	1844
		St. Saviour's,	1864
		St. Simon's,	1844
		St. Stephen's,	1805
		St. Thomas',	1824
		St. Timothy's,	1854
		Transfiguration,	1849
		Trinity,	1785 A
		with St. Paul's, St. John's and Trinity Chapels,	
		Zion,	1810
	*Harlem,	*Grace,	
	Fordham,	St. James',	1855 A
	Morrisania,	St. Ann's,	1841
		St. Paul's,	1853
		Trinity,	1869
	Mott Haven,	St. Mary's,	1857
	Riverdale,	Christ,	1866
	West Farms,	Grace,	1848 B
Orange	Canterbury,	St. John's,	1858
	Cornwall,	Holy Innocents,	1850
	Goshen,	St. James',	1803
	Greenwood,	St. John's,	1868 C
	*Monroe,	*Grace,	
	Newburgh,	St. George's,	1785 A
		St. Paul's,	1860
	New-Windsor,	St. Thomas',	1818
	Port Jervis,	Grace,	1854

(*a*.) Incorporated Aug. 17, 1807.

(*b*.) Incorporated Dec. 8, 1823.

Counties.	Towns.	Churches.	Admitted.
Orange,..............	South Middletown,	Grace,	1845
	Walden,	St. Andrew's,	1785 A
	Warwick,	Christ,	1866
Putnam..............	Cold Spring,	St. Mary's,	1840
	Paterson,	Christ,	1821 B
	Philipsetown,	St. Philip's,	1840
Richmond	Castleton, (W. Brighton,)	Ascension,	1870
	Castleton,	St. Mary's,	1851
	Clifton,	St. John's,	1843
		*St. Simon's Chapel,	
	Edgewater,	St. Paul's Memorial,	1833
	New-Brighton,	Christ,	1851
	Richmond,	St. Andrew's,	1785
	Rossville,	St. Luke's,	1843
	Southfield,	Holy Comforter,	1866
Rockland..........	Clarkstown,	St. John's,	1867
	Haverstraw,	Trinity,	1847
		St. Luke's,	1871
	Nyack,	Grace,	1862
	Piermont,	Christ,	1848
	Ramapo,	Christ,	1860
	*Spring Valley,	*St. Paul's,	
Sullivan	Monticello,	St. John's,	1817
	*Thomsonville,	*St. Mary's,	
Ulster	Ellenville,	St. Paul's,	1853
	Esopus,	Ascension,	1842
	*Highland,	*Holy Trinity,	
	Kingston,	St. John's,	1832
	Marlborough,	Christ,	1837
	Milton,	All Saints',	1850
	Rondout,	Holy Spirit,	1850
	Saugerties,	Trinity,	1831
	Stone Ridge,	St. Peter's,	1846
Westchester	Bedford,	St. Matthew's,	1787 A
	*Beechwood,	*St. Mary's,	
	Briar Cliff,	All Saints',	1869
	*City Island,	*Grace,	
	Cortlandt, (Croton,)	St. Augustine's,	1855
	East Chester,	St. Paul's,	1787
	Greenburg,	Zion,	1834
	Irvington,	St. Barnabas',	1859
	Katonah,	St. Mark's,	1853
	Lewisboro',	St. John's,	1853
	Mamaroneck,	St. Thomas',	1817
	*Montrose,	*Divine Love,	
	Mount Pleasant,	St. Mark's,	1864
	Mount Vernon,	Trinity,	1857
	New Castle,	St. Mark's,	1851 A
	New-Rochelle,	Trinity,	1785
	North Castle,	St. Mary's,	1853 A
		St. Stephen's,	1844
	North Salem,	St. James',	1792 A

* Not in Union with the Convention.

Counties.	Towns.	Churches.	Admitted.
Westchester	Peekskill,	St. Peter's,	1791 A
	Pelham,	Christ,	1843
	Pleasantville,	St. John's,	1853
	Portchester,	St. Peter's,	1852
	Rye,	Christ,	1786 A
	Scarsdale,	St. James the Less,	1849
	Sing Sing,	St. Paul's,	1834
	Sing Sing,	Trinity,	1869
	Somers,	St. Luke's,	1839
	Tarrytown,	Christ,	1836
	Tuckahoe,	St. John's,	1853
	Westchester,	St. Peter's,	1790 A
	White Plains,	Grace,	1824 A
	Wilmot,	St. John's,	1861
	Yonkers,	Mediator,	1858 B
		St. John's,	1787 A
		St. Paul's,	1859
	Yorktown,	St. Mary's,	1870

Number of Churches and Chapels represented by certificates of Lay Delegates,.. 113
Number of Churches not represented,........................ 53

Number do. entitled to representation,.................... 166
Number do. not in union with the Convention,............. 26

Number of Churches and Chapels in the Diocese,.................. 192

Three Churches were admitted into union at this Convention.

* Not in union with the Convention.
† Admitted at this Convention.

Appendix:

No. V.

Officers of the Diocese.

THE DIOCESAN CONVENTION.

The Rt. Rev. HORATIO POTTER, D. D., LL. D., D. C. L., *President.*
The Rev. WILLIAM E. EIGENBRODT, D. D., *Secretary.*
The Rev. THEODORE A. EATON, D. D., *Assistant Secretary.*
EDWARD F. DE LANCEY, Esq., *Treasurer.*

THE STANDING COMMITTEE.

The Rev. MORGAN DIX, D. D., *President.*
The Rev. WILLIAM E. EIGENBRODT, D. D., *Secretary.*
The Rev. WILLIAM F. MORGAN, D. D.,
The Rev. ISAAC H. TUTTLE, D. D.,
STEPHEN P. NASH, Esq.,
LLOYD W. WELLS, Esq.,
HENRY DRISLER, LL. D.,
GEORGE MACCULLOCH MILLER, Esq.

THE DEPUTIES TO THE GENERAL CONVENTION.

The Rev. BENJAMIN I. HAIGHT, D. D.,
The Rev. SAMUEL COOKE, D. D.,
The Rev. ALFRED B. BEACH, D. D.,
The Rev. PHILANDER K. CADY, D. D.,
The Hon. SAMUEL B. RUGGLES,
The Hon. HAMILTON FISH,
CAMBRIDGE LIVINGSTON, Esq.,
WILLIAM A. DAVIES, Esq.

THE PROVISIONAL DEPUTIES.

The Rev. George J. Geer, D. D.,
The Rev. Henry C. Potter, D. D.,
The Rev. Theodore A. Eaton, D. D.,
The Rev. Christopher B. Wyatt, D. D.,
The Hon. John A. Dix,
The Hon. James Emott,
Prof. T. Eccleston,
Prof. Henry Drisler, LL. D.

THE MISSIONARY COMMITTEE.

*The Rev. Henry E. Montgomery, D. D.,
The Rev. Alfred B. Beach, D. D.,
The Rev. Cornelius E. Swope, D. D.,
The Rev. James Starr Clark, D. D.,
The Rev. Octavius Applegate,
George C. Collins, Esq.,
James Pott, Esq.,
Hamilton Bruce, Esq.,
William M. Kingsland, Esq.,
William H. Aspinwall, Esq.

TRUSTEES OF THE EPISCOPAL FUND.

Gouverneur M. Ogden, Esq.,
Thomas P. Cummings, Esq., *Secretary and Treasurer.*
Frederick G. Foster, Esq.,
George T. Strong, Esq.,
Hugh Auchincloss, Esq.

THE TRUSTEES OF THE AGED AND INFIRM CLERGY FUND.

The Rt. Rev. Horatio Potter, D. D., LL. D., D. C. L.,
Cyrus Curtiss, Esq.,
William Betts, Esq.,
Edward F. De Lancey, Esq.

THE TRUSTEES OF THE PAROCHIAL FUND.

The Right Rev. The Bishop of the Diocese, *ex-officio.*
John Jay, William Alexander Smith, } Until October, 1875.
Adam Norrie, Robert B. Parrott, } Until October, 1876.
Murray Hoffman, Frederick S. Winston, } Until October, 1877.

* Deceased since the Convention.

The Committee

ON THE INCORPORATION AND ADMISSION OF CHURCHES.

The Hon. HAMILTON FISH,
The Rev. ALFRED B. BEACH, D. D.,
The Hon. MICHAEL ULSHOEFFER.

Special Committees of the Convention.

ON THE SALARY OF THE BISHOP.

(See Journal of 1874, pp. 50, 51.)

The Rev. Benjamin I. Haight, D. D.; the Rev. Issaac H. Tuttle, D. D.; Cyrus Curtiss, Esq.; Hon. John A. Dix; Frederick G. Foster, Esq.; William Scott, Esq.; Lloyd W. Wells, Esq; Frederick Prime, Esq.; Thomas P. Cummings, Esq., and George Macculloch Miller, Esq.

ON A CATHEDRAL.

(See Journal of 1872, pp. 89, 111.)

The Rt. Rev. Horatio Potter, D. D., LL. D., D. C. L.; the Rev. Morgan Dix, D. D.; Henry C. Potter, D. D.; John Cotton Smith, D. D.; George H. Houghton, D. D.; Philander K. Cady, D. D.; Hon. Hamilton Fish; Messrs. John J. Cisco, Stephen P. Nash, Mr. Guion, Mr. Duncan; Hon. S. B. Ruggles; Messrs. William Scott, George M. Miller, Howard Potter, Wm. T. Blodgett.

*** *The* STANDING COMMITTEE *of the Diocese meets statedly on the* FIRST THURSDAY *of every month. Papers requiring the action of the Committee should be sent prior to this date, and addressed to the Secretary.*

Appendix:

No. VI.

STATISTICS OF THE DIOCESE, 1873-74.

From the Episcopal Address, the Parochial and Missionary Reports, etc.

Clergymen canonically resident in the Diocese,....................	313
Churches and Chapels,....................................	192
Ordinations : Deacons, 16 ; Priests, 11,..........................	27
Clergymen instituted into Rectorships,..........................	8
" received into the Diocese,..........................	22
" transferred to other Dioceses,..........................	24
" died,..	7
Candidates for Orders,....................................	29
Churches consecrated,....................................	4

The following statistics are derived from 143 Parochial Reports :

Baptisms : Adults, 613 ; Infants, 4,168—total,....................		4,781
Confirmed,..		3,083
Marriages,..		1,248
Burials,..		2,369
Catechumens,..		27,299
Catechists, or Sunday-School teachers,..........................		2,092
Communicants : admitted, as reported from 72 Parishes,..........		1,158
present number, as reported from 143 Congregations,......................	27,959	
add as estimated from 18 Parishes not reporting,........................	1,000	
	——	28,959

CANONICAL COLLECTIONS AND FOR OTHER OBJECTS.

For the Episcopal Fund, Salary of the Bishop, &c., from — Churches,..........		$3,293 05
" Education " — "		773 21
" Diocesan " 99 "		3,980 16
" Missionary " — "	$4,798 25	
" " Donations,.............	2,292 00	
" " Interest on Investments,.	505 94	
	———	7,596 19
For the Aged and Infirm Clergy, 84 Churches,.......	$2,549 19	
" " " Int. on Investments,	1,564 76	
" " " Donations, &c.,......	1,090 00	
	———	5,203 95
Total,....................		$20,846 56

TOTAL CONTRIBUTIONS FROM 143 PAROCHIAL REPORTS,.......$938,408 01

There being no reports from 18 living and working Churches on the List of this Diocese, these statistics do not present a complete view of the Diocese in these respects during the past year.

Difference in the dates of making the calculations severally will account for any discrepancy between the foregoing statement of the Contributions and those given in the preceding Table.

STATISTICAL SUMMARY

For the years since the last General Convention, 1871–72, 1872–73, 1873–74.

Number of Churches entitled to representation in the Convention of the Diocese, ... 166
" not in union with the Convention, ... 26

" and Chapels in the Diocese, ... 192

Churches and Chapels consecrated: In 1871–72, 2; in 1872–73, 1; in 1873–74, 4; total, ... 7

	1871–'72.	1872–'73.	1873–'74.	Total.
CLERGYMEN:				
Received into the Diocese,	25	14	22	61
Transferred to other Dioceses,	25	24	24	73
Deceased,	3	3	7	13

CANONICALLY BELONGING TO THE DIOCESE SEPTEMBER 30, 1874.

Bishop,		1
Priests,		285
Deacons, with full qualifications, three examinations,	19	
" without " one examination,	8	
		27
Whole number of Clergymen,		313

ORDINATIONS.

	1871–'72.	1872–'73.	1873–'74.	Total.
DEACONS:				
With full qualifications, three examinations,	14	11	14	39
Without full qualifications, one examination,	3	0	2	5
Total Deacons,	17	11	16	44
PRIESTS,	7	9	11	27
Total Ordinations,	24	20	27	71

	1871–'72.	1872–'73.	1873–'74.	Total.
BAPTISMS: Infants,	3,437	3,633	4,168	11,238
Adults,	482	466	613	1,561
Total,	3,919	4,099	4,781	12,799
CONFIRMED,	2,601	2,485	3,083	8,169
MARRIAGES,	1,231	1,255	1,248	3,734
BURIALS,	2,102	2,067	2,369	6,628
COMMUNICANTS ADMITTED,	750	918	1,158	2,826

Present number, as reported in 148 Parochial reports,............ 27,959
Add as estimated in 18 Parishes not reporting,.................... 1,000

Total,... 28,959

Catechumens or Sunday Scholars, as reported in 1874, in 127 Parochial reports,... 27,299

Catechists or Sunday-School teachers, as reported in 1874, in 112 Parochial reports,... 2,092

CONTRIBUTIONS:

(*So far as reported to the Convention of the Diocese during the last three years.*)

	1871-'72.	1872-'73.	1873-'74.	
EDUCATION FUND,...	$737 25	$593 56	$773 21	$2,104 02
EPISCOPAL FUND,....	3,906 69	3,667 90	3,293 05	10,867 64
DIOCESAN FUND,....	4.375 23	3.900 20	3,980 16	12,255 5[illegible]
MISSIONARY FUND,..	5,590 71	6,267 32	7,596 19	19,454 2[illegible]
AGED AND INFIRM CLERGY FUND,..	7,436 37	6,909 80	3,639 19	17,985 3[illegible]
TOTAL CONTRIBUTIONS, stated in Parochial reports,	734,352 73	940,061 75	938,408 01	$2,616,822 4[illegible]

The Contributions from this Diocese to the Board of Missions of the General Convention during the last three years have been as follows:

	1871-'72.	1872-'73.	1873-'74.	
Foreign Committee,..	$20,988 43	$21,733 15	$16,302 93	$59,024
Domestic Committee,.	34,555 25	35,718 24	35,319 23	105,592
Home Missions to Colored People,..	3,066 40	2,539 43	2,996 45	8,602
Indian Department,..	....	18,738 34	12,540 23	31,278
Total,...........	$58,610 08	$78,729 16	$67,158 84	$204,498

NEW-YORK, *October*, 1874.

JOURNAL OF THE CONVENTION:

1874.

CONTENTS.

JOURNAL OF THE PROCEEDINGS

OF THE

INETY-SECOND CONVENTION

OF THE

Protestant Episcopal Church

IN THE

DIOCESE OF NEW-YORK,

WHICH ASSEMBLED IN

'. JOHN'S CHAPEL, IN THE CITY OF NEW-YORK,

ON

WEDNESDAY, SEPTEMBER 29, A. D. 1875.

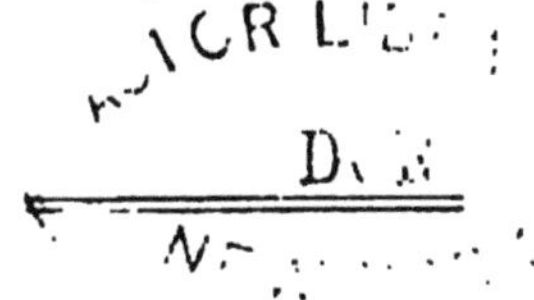

New-York:

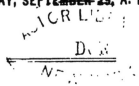

PUBLISHED FOR THE CONVENTION,

BY POTT, YOUNG & CO., COOPER UNION, FOURTH AVENUE.

M.DCCC.LXXV.

John W. Amerman, Printer,
47 Cedar-street, N. Y.

List of the Clergy

OF THE

DIOCESE OF NEW-YORK.

SEPTEMBER 29, 1875.

This List of Clergy, being that presented by the Bishop to the Convention, contains no note of changes which have since taken place.

This mark * designates the Alumni of the General Theological Seminary of the Protestant Episcopal Church in the United States.

THE RIGHT REV. HORATIO POTTER, D. D., LL. D., D. C. L., BISHOP OF THE DIOCESE.

The Rev. Charles C. Adams, rector of St. Mary's Church, Manhattanville, New-York.

*The Rev. Samuel M. Akerly.

*The Rev. John G. Ames, a Professor in the House of Evangelists, New-York.

*The Rev. Edward Anthon, New-York.

*The Rev. Octavius Applegate, assistant minister of St. George's Church, Newburgh, Orange county.

*The Rev. Amos Turner Ashton, deacon, rector elect of St. Thomas' Church, Amenia, Dutchess county, and missionary. P. O., Amenia Union.

*The Rev. Joseph Atwell, rector of St. Philip's Church, New-York.

*The Rev. Franklin Babbitt, rector of Grace Church, Nyack, Rockland county, and missionary.

*The Rev. David F. Banks, rector of St. Paul's Church, Yonkers, Westchester county.

*The Rev. Frederick A. P. Barnard, D. D., LL. D., President of Columbia College, New-York.

*The Rev. James S. Barnes, Brooklyn, Long Island.

*The Rev. Edward T. Bartlett, rector of St. Luke's Church, Matteawan, Dutchess county.

*The Rev. John G. Barton, LL. D., deacon, Professor of the English Language and Literature in the College of the City of New-York.

*The Rev. Alfred B. Beach, D. D., rector of St. Peter's Church, New-York.

*The Rev. Henry H. Bean, rector of St. Luke's Church, Rossville, Richmond county.

John W. Amerman, Printer,
47 Cedar-street, N. Y.

*The Rev. William H. Cooke, an assistant minister of Trinity Church, New-York.

*The Rev. Nathaniel E. Cornwall, D. D., rector of St. Matthias' Church, New-York.

The Rev. Nathaniel E. Cornwall, Jr., New-York.

The Rev. Edward Cowley, New-York.

*The Rev. Algernon Sidney Crapsey, an assistant minister in Trinity Parish, New-York.

*The Rev. Robert Fulton Crary, rector of the Church of the Holy Comforter, Poughkeepsie.

*The Rev. Robert B. Croes, D. D., Yonkers, Westchester county.

*The Rev. Gouverneur Cruger, missionary at Montrose, Westchester county.

The Rev. J. Radcliff Davenport, New-York.

The Rev. Benjamin F. De Costa, New-York.

*The Rev. Joaquim De Palma, rector of the Church of Santiago, New-York.

*The Rev. Morgan Dix, D. D., rector of Trinity Church, New-York.

The Rev. Elijah Winchester Donald, deacon, rector elect of the Church of the Intercession, New-York.

*The Rev. Zina Doty.

*The Rev. George William Douglas, deacon.

*The Rev. Henry A. Dows, Missionary at Monroe, Orange county.

*The Rev. George B. Draper, D. D., rector of St. Andrew's Church, New-York.

The Rev. John Drisler, deacon, (Note A.,) Mission Chapel, Saw Mill Valley, Greenburgh, Westchester county.

*The Rev. Cornelius R. Duffie, D. D., rector of the Church of St. John Baptist, and chaplain of Columbia College, New-York.

*The Rev. Henry E. Duncan, D. D.

The Rev. William N. Dunnell, rector of All Saints' Church, New-York.

The Rev. Heman Dyer, D. D., an assistant minister of the Church of the Ascension, New-York.

*The Rev. Theodore A. Eaton, D. D., rector of St. Clement's Church, New-York.

*The Rev. John C. Eccleston, M. D., rector of St. John's Church, Clifton, Richmond county.

*The Rev. William E. Eigenbrodt, D. D., Professor of Pastoral Theology in the General Theological Seminary, New-York.

*The Rev. William T. Egbert, rector of the Church of St. John the Evangelist, Memorial of Bishop Wainwright, New-York.

The Rev. Rufus Emery, rector of St. Paul's Church, Newburgh, Orange county.

The Rev. Ferdinand C. Ewer, D. D., St. Ignatius' Church, New-York.

*The Rev. Robert B. Fairbairn, D. D., Warden of St. Stephen's Training College, Annandale, Dutchess county.

*The Rev. George W. Ferguson, rector of Trinity Church, Sing Sing, Westchester county.

The Rev. Edward O. Flagg, D. D., rector of the Church of the Resurrection, New-York.

The Rev. John C. Fleischhacker, minister of St. George's German Mission Chapel, New-York.

*The Rev. John Murray Forbes, D. D., New-York.

The Rev. Edward K. Fowler, Monticello, Sullivan county.

*The Rev. William G. French, officiating for the New-York Protestant Episcopal City Mission Society, on Blackwell's Island.

The Rev. Thomas Gallaudet, D. D., rector of St. Ann's Church for Deaf Mutes, New-York.

The Rev. John N. Galleher, D. D., rector of Zion Church, New-York.

*The Rev. Walter Russell Gardner.

The Rev. Ebenezer Gay, missionary at Stony Point, Rockland county.

*The Rev. G. Jarvis Geer, D. D , rector of St. Timothy's Church, New-York.

*The Rev. J. Breckenridge Gibson, D. D., rector of St. John's School, Sing Sing, and of All Saints' Church, (Briar Cliff,) Ossining, Westchester county. P. O., Sing Sing.

*The Rev. Kingston Goddard, D. D., St. Andrew's Church, Richmond, Richmond county.

*The Rev. Alfred Goldsborough, rector of Christ Church, Warwick, Orange county, and missionary.

*The Rev. E. H. C. Goodwin, an officiating minister of Trinity Parish, New-York, at Fort Columbus, New-York harbor.

*The Rev. George S. Gordon, Peekskill, Westchester county.

*The Rev. William H. De L. Grannis, rector of St. James' Church, Goshen, Orange county.

*The Rev. Albert Zabriskie Gray, rector of St. Philip's Church in the Highlands, Philipsetown, Putnam county. P. O., Garrison's.

The Rev. Frederick M. Gray, rector of the Church of the Holy Comforter, (Eltingville,) Southfield, Richmond county.

The Rev. Horatio Gray.

*The Rev. Edmund Guilbert, rector of St. Mark's Church, Mount Pleasant, Westchester county.

*The Rev. Benjamin I. Haight, D. D., LL. D., assistant to the rector of Trinity Church, New-York.

The Rev. Charles R. Hale, New-York.

*The Rev. Randall C. Hall, Clement C. Moore Professor of the Hebrew and Greek Languages in the General Theological Seminary, New-York.

The Rev. Alexander Hamilton, Jr., deacon, New-York, (Note A.)

The Rev. Robert George Hamilton, deacon.

*The Rev. Thomas R. Harris, rector of St. Paul's Church, Morrisania, New-York.

*The Rev. A. Bloomer Hart, rector of the Church of the Advent, New-York.

The Rev. John G. B. Heath, officiating for the New-York Protestant Episcopal City Mission Society, in the Tombs and other public institutions, New-York.

The Rev. James I. Helm, D. D., rector of St. Paul's Church, Sing Sing, Westchester county.

The Rev. Francis A. Henry.

The Rev. Charles Higbee, rector of Christ Church, Pelham, Westchester county.

*The Rev. George H. Hinckle, officiating at Newburgh, Orange county.

*The Rev. Solomon G. Hitchcock, missionary at Piermont, Rockland county.

The Rev. Horace B. Hitchings, an assistant minister of Trinity Church, New-York.

*The Rev. John Henry Hobart, D. D.

The Rev. Charles Frederick Hoffman, rector of All Angels' Church, New-York.

The Rev. William A. Holbrook, rector of the Church of St. James the Less, Scarsdale, Westchester county.

The Rev. Robert Holden, rector of Trinity School, New-York.

The Rev. Stephen F. Holmes, officiating for the New-York Protestant Episcopal City Mission Society, as chaplain of St. Barnabas' House and Chapel, New-York.

The Rev. Montgomery R. Hooper, an assistant minister of St. Paul's Church, Yonkers, Westchester county.

*The Rev. William Berrian Hooper, rector of Trinity Church, Mount Vernon, Westchester county.

*The Rev. George B. Hopson, Professor of the Latin Language in St. Stephen's Training College, Annandale, Dutchess county.

*The Rev. Edward C. Houghton, assistant minister of the Church of the Transfiguration, New-York.

*The Rev. George C. Houghton, an officiating minister in the Parish of Trinity Church, New-York.

The Rev. George H. Houghton, D. D., rector of the Church of the Transfiguration, New-York.

The Rev. George Howell, officiating in the Mission Chapel of the Atonement, New-York.

*The Rev. Robert S. Howland, D. D., rector of the Church of the Heavenly Rest, New-York.

The Rev. Ralph Hoyt.

The Rev. William Huckel, rector of St. Ann's Church, Morrisania, New-York.

*The Rev. Albert S. Hull, rector of Trinity Church, Morrisania, New-York.

The Rev. Pierre P. Irving, New-Brighton, Richmond county.

The Rev. Theodore Irving, LL. D., residing in New-York.

*The Rev. Angus M. Ives, missionary at Tuckahoe and Wilmot, Westchester county.

*The Rev. Alfred Evan Johnson, deacon.

*The Rev. Joseph Horsfall Johnson, missionary at Highland and Milton, Ulster county.

The Rev. Edward O. Flagg, D. D., rector of the Church of the Resurrection, New-York.

The Rev. John C. Fleischhacker, minister of St. George's German Mission Chapel, New-York.

*The Rev. John Murray Forbes, D. D., New-York.

The Rev. Edward K. Fowler, Monticello, Sullivan county.

*The Rev. William G. French, officiating for the New-York Protestant Episcopal City Mission Society, on Blackwell's Island.

The Rev. Thomas Gallaudet, D. D., rector of St. Ann's Church for Deaf Mutes, New-York.

The Rev. John N. Galleher, D. D., rector of Zion Church, New-York.

*The Rev. Walter Russell Gardner.

The Rev. Ebenezer Gay, missionary at Stony Point, Rockland county.

*The Rev. G. Jarvis Geer, D. D , rector of St. Timothy's Church, New-York.

*The Rev. J. Breckenridge Gibson, D. D., rector of St. John's School, Sing Sing, and of All Saints' Church, (Briar Cliff,) Ossining, Westchester county. P. O., Sing Sing.

*The Rev. Kingston Goddard, D. D., St. Andrew's Church, Richmond, Richmond county.

*The Rev. Alfred Goldsborough, rector of Christ Church, Warwick, Orange county, and missionary.

*The Rev. E. H. C. Goodwin, an officiating minister of Trinity Parish, New-York, at Fort Columbus, New-York harbor.

*The Rev. George S. Gordon, Peekskill, Westchester county.

*The Rev. William H. De L. Grannis, rector of St. James' Church, Goshen, Orange county.

*The Rev. Albert Zabriskie Gray, rector of St. Philip's Church in the Highlands, Philipsetown, Putnam county. P. O., Garrison's.

The Rev. Frederick M. Gray, rector of the Church of the Holy Comforter, (Eltingville,) Southfield, Richmond county.

The Rev. Horatio Gray.

*The Rev. Edmund Guilbert, rector of St. Mark's Church, Mount Pleasant, Westchester county.

*The Rev. Benjamin I. Haight, D. D., LL. D., assistant to the rector of Trinity Church, New-York.

The Rev. Charles R. Hale, New-York.

*The Rev. Randall C. Hall, Clement C. Moore Professor of the Hebrew and Greek Languages in the General Theological Seminary, New-York.

The Rev. Alexander Hamilton, Jr., deacon, New-York, (Note A.)

The Rev. Robert George Hamilton, deacon.

*The Rev. Thomas R. Harris, rector of St. Paul's Church, Morrisania, New-York.

*The Rev. A. Bloomer Hart, rector of the Church of the Advent, New-York.

The Rev. John G. B. Heath, officiating for the New-York Protestant Episcopal City Mission Society, in the Tombs and other public institutions, New-York.

The Rev. James I. Helm, D. D., rector of St. Paul's Church, Sing Sing, Westchester county.

The Rev. Francis A. Henry.

The Rev. Charles Higbee, rector of Christ Church, Pelham, Westchester county.

*The Rev. George H. Hinckle, officiating at Newburgh, Orange county.

*The Rev. Solomon G. Hitchcock, missionary at Piermont, Rockland county.

The Rev. Horace B. Hitchings, an assistant minister of Trinity Church, New-York.

*The Rev. John Henry Hobart, D. D.

The Rev. Charles Frederick Hoffman, rector of All Angels' Church, New-York.

The Rev. William A. Holbrook, rector of the Church of St. James the Less, Scarsdale, Westchester county.

The Rev. Robert Holden, rector of Trinity School, New-York.

The Rev. Stephen F. Holmes, officiating for the New-York Protestant Episcopal City Mission Society, as chaplain of St. Barnabas' House and Chapel, New-York.

The Rev. Montgomery R. Hooper, an assistant minister of St. Paul's Church, Yonkers, Westchester county.

*The Rev. William Berrian Hooper, rector of Trinity Church, Mount Vernon, Westchester county.

*The Rev. George B. Hopson, Professor of the Latin Language in St. Stephen's Training College, Annandale, Dutchess county.

*The Rev. Edward C. Houghton, assistant minister of the Church of the Transfiguration, New-York.

*The Rev. George C. Houghton, an officiating minister in the Parish of Trinity Church, New-York.

The Rev. George H. Houghton, D. D., rector of the Church of the Transfiguration, New-York.

The Rev. George Howell, officiating in the Mission Chapel of the Atonement, New-York.

*The Rev. Robert S. Howland, D. D., rector of the Church of the Heavenly Rest, New-York.

The Rev. Ralph Hoyt.

The Rev. William Huckel, rector of St. Ann's Church, Morrisania, New-York.

*The Rev. Albert S. Hull, rector of Trinity Church, Morrisania, New-York.

The Rev. Pierre P. Irving, New-Brighton, Richmond county.

The Rev. Theodore Irving, LL. D., residing in New-York.

*The Rev. Angus M. Ives, missionary at Tuckahoe and Wilmot, Westchester county.

*The Rev. Alfred Evan Johnson, deacon.

*The Rev. Joseph Horsfall Johnson, missionary at Highland and Milton, Ulster county.

*The Rev. Copeland Lea Jones.

*The Rev. William Marvin Jones.

*The Rev. Joseph F. Jowitt.

The Rev. Justin P. Kellog, New-Windsor, Orange county.

The Rev. James E. Kenney, New-York.

The Rev. Arthur Clifford Kimber, an officiating minister in Trinity Parish, New-York.

*The Rev. Charles S. Knapp, officiating at Aspinwall.

The Rev. John W. Kramer, M. D., an assistant minister of Grace Church, in charge of Grace Chapel, New-York.

*The Rev. Edward H. Krans, an assistant minister at St. Ann's Church for Deaf Mutes, New-York.

*The Rev. Francis E. Lawrence, D. D., pastor of the Church of the Holy Communion, New-York.

*The Rev. Hamilton Lee.

The Rev. Alexander S. Leonard, D. D., Fordham, New-York county.

The Rev. Robert W. Lewis, New-York.

The Rev. S. Seymour Lewis, officiating at Yonkers, Westchester county.

*The Rev. William Fisher Lewis, rector of St. Peter's Church, Peekskill, Cortlandt, Westchester county.

The Rev. Charles S. Little, New-York.

*The Rev. John R. Livingston, Jr., rector of Trinity Church, Fishkill, Dutchess county, and missionary at Glenham. P. O., Glenham.

The Rev. George Love, deacon.

*The Rev. Robert Lowry, St. Thomas' Free Mission Chapel, New-York.

*The Rev. Nicholas F. Ludlum, missionary and financial agent of the New-York Protestant Episcopal City Mission Society, New-York.

*The Rev. William S. Ludlum, New-York.

The Rev. John P. Lundy, D. D., rector of the Church of the Holy Apostles, New-York.

The Rev. Lea Luquer, rector of St. Matthew's Church, Bedford, Westchester county.

*The Rev. David H. Macurdy.

The Rev. Isaac Maguire, deacon, (Note A.,) missionary of the Protestant Episcopal Missionary Society for Seamen in the port and city of New-York, New-York.

*The Rev. Romaine S. Mansfield, missionary at Spring Valley, Rockland county, in charge also of St. John's Church, Clarkstown, Rockland county.

The Rev. Mytton Maury, New-York.

The Rev. Dominick M. McCaffrey, officiating in New-York.

The Rev. Haslett McKim, Jr., rector of St. Thomas' Church, New-Windsor, Orange county.

*The Rev. Stephen A. McNulty, officiating minister at St. Mark's Church Mission, New-York.

*The Rev. William A. McVickar, D. D., officiating at Nice.

*The Rev. William N. McVickar, New-York.

The Rev. Alexander McWhorter, deacon.

*The Rev. Edward N. Mead, D. D., minister of St. Mary's Church, Beechwood, Westchester county. P. O., Scarborough, Westchester county.

The Rev. J. Austen Merrick, D. D., West Farms, New-York county.

The Rev. James Millett, rector of the Church of the Holy Martyrs, New-York.

The Rev. Benjamin F. Miller, rector of Grace Church, Milbrook, Dutchess county, and missionary.

*The Rev. William White Montgomery, rector of St. Thomas' Church, Mamaroneck, Westchester county.

*The Rev. John W. Moore, minister of Christ Church, Red Hook, Dutchess county.

*The Rev. William Moore.

*The Rev. Samuel Moran, rector of St. John's Church, Greenwood Iron Works, Orange county, and missionary.

*The Rev. Brockholst Morgan, rector of St. Peter's Church, Port Chester, Westchester county.

The Rev. James Hervey Morgan, New-York.

The Rev. Richard U. Morgan, D. D., residing at Stamford, Connecticut.

*The Rev. William F. Morgan, D. D., rector of St. Thomas' Church, New-York.

*The Rev. Charles W. Morrill, Church of the Intercessor, New-York.

The Rev. Lewis F. Morris.

The Rev. William Morris, LL. D., West Farms, New-York county.

The Rev. Joshua Morsell, D. D., rector of Grace Church, City Island, New-York county, and missionary.

*The Rev. Henry Mottet, Church of the Holy Communion, New-York.

The Rev. William A. Muhlenberg, D. D., Superintendent of St. Luke's Hospital, New-York.

The Rev. James Mulchahey, D. D., an assistant minister of Trinity Church, New-York.

The Rev. James Byron Murray.

The Rev. Chester Newell, chaplain in the United States Navy.

The Rev. R. Heber Newton, rector of the Anthon Memorial Church, New-York.

*The Rev. Edwin A. Nichols.

The Rev. Samuel Nichols, residing at Greenfield, Connecticut.

*The Rev. Louis L. Noble, Professor of History and of the English Language and Literature in St. Stephen's College, Annandale, Dutchess county.

The Rev. McWalter B. Noyes, New-York.

The Rev. Frederick Oertel, in charge of Bethlehem Mission Chapel, under the direction of the New-York Protestant Episcopal City Mission Society, New-York.

*The Rev. Frederick Ogilby, D. D., an assistant minister of Trinity Church, New-York

The Rev. Andrew Oliver, D. D., Professor of Biblical Learning and the Interpretation of Scripture in the General Theological Seminary, New-York.

The Rev. A. F. Olmsted, rector of the Church of the Messiah, Rhinebeck, Dutchess county.

The Rev. Charles T. Olmsted, an assistant minister of Trinity Church, New-York.

*The Rev. William W. Olssen, Professor of the Greek Language and Literature, and of Hebrew, in St. Stephen's College, Annandale.

The Rev. Samuel Osgood, D. D., LL D., New-York.

The Rev. John William Paige, deacon, New-York.

The Rev. Isaac Peck.

The Rev. Edward W. Peet, D. D., assisting at St. George's Church, New-York.

*The Rev. Thomas M. Peters, D D., rector of St. Michael's Church, New-York.

The Rev. John Peterson, deacon, (Note A.,) assisting in St. Philip's Church, New-York.

The Rev. George L. Platt, rector of St. Paul's Church, Red Hook, Dutch County. P. O., Madalin.

The Rev. Leon Pons, rector of the French Church du St. Esprit, New-York.

The Rev. Henry C. Potter, D. D., rector of Grace Church, New-York.

*The Rev. John F. Potter, St. John's Church, Canterbury, Orange county, and missionary.

The Rev. Horace L. E. Pratt, rector of St. Mary's Church, Castleton, Richmond county.

The Rev. Joseph H. Price, D. D., rector of St. Stephen's Church, New-York.

*The Rev. James S. Purdy, D. D., rector of St. James' Church, Hyde Park, Dutchess county.

*The Rev. Gustav Edmund Purucker, rector of Christ Church, Ramapo Rockland county, and missionary. P. O., Suffern.

The Rev. D. Brainard Ray, Grace Church, Harlem, New-York.

The Rev. George B. Reese, Jr., rector of Zion Church, Greenburgh, Westchester county.

The Rev. George T. Rider, in charge of a female Seminary at Nyack, Rockland county.

The Rev. Henry C. Riley, officiating in Mexico.

The Rev. H. Floy Roberts, missionary of the Floating Church of the Holy Comforter, New-York.

The Rev. John J. Roberts, New-York.

The Rev. J. J. Robertson, D. D., rector of Trinity Church, Saugerties, Ulster county.

The Rev. N. Frazier Robinson, deacon, Trinity Church, New-York.

The Rev. N. Thayer Robinson, deacon.

The Rev. Charles F. Rodenstein, West Farms, New-York county.

*The Rev. John Gardner Rosencrantz, Grace Church, Port Jervis, Orange county, and missionary.

The Rev. R. Condit Russell, rector of St. James' Church, North Salem, and of St. Luke's Church, Somers, Westchester county, and missionary.

The Rev. Joseph Hine Rylance, D. D., rector of St. Mark's Church in the Bowerie, New-York.

*The Rev. Henry Y. Satterlee, rector of Zion Church, Wappinger's Falls, Dutchess county.

*The Rev. Erastus Huntington Saunders, assistant minister at the Church of the Heavenly Rest, New-York.

The Rev. Thomas S. Savage, M. D., officiating at Rhine Cliff, Dutchess county.

The Rev. Charles Schramm, D. D.

*The Rev. John F. Schroeder, deacon

The Rev. Robert Scott, rector of Grace Church, West Farms, New-York.

The Rev. Uriah Scott, New-York.

*The Rev. William J. Seabury, rector of the Church of the Annunciation, and Ludlow Professor of Ecclesiastical Polity and Law in the General Theological Seminary, New-York.

The Rev. Francis M. Serenbez, missionary among the Germans, Middletown, Orange county.

*The Rev. Charles Seymour.

*The Rev. George F. Seymour, D. D., St. Mark's Church in the Bowerie Professor of Ecclesiastical History in the General Theological Seminary, New-York.

*The Rev. John W. Shackleford, rector of the Church of the Redeemer, New-York.

*The Rev Frederick W. Shelton, LL. D., rector of St. Mark's Church, Carthage Landing, Dutchess county.

*The Rev. Henry Beers Sherman, rector of the Church of the Ascension, Esopus, Ulster county.

*The Rev. George F. Siegmund, assistant minister of the Church of the Annunciation, New-York.

*The Rev. Thomas H. Sill, an officiating minister in Trinity Parish, New-York.

*The Rev. Cornelius B. Smith, rector of St. James' Church, New-York.

*The Rev. George Henry Smith, rector of St. Paul's Church, Pleasant Valley, Dutchess county, and missionary.

*The Rev. James Tuttle Smith, rector of the Church of the Holy Sepulchre, New-York.

*The Rev. John Cotton Smith, D. D., rector of the Church of the Ascension, New-York.

*The Rev. Orsamus H. Smith, officiating at North Paterson, Putnam county.

*The Rev. William E. Snowden, rector of St. Andrew's Church, Walden, Orange county, and missionary.

*The Rev. Jesse A. Spencer, D. D., Professor of the Greek Language and Literature in the College of the City of New-York, New-York.

*The Rev. J. Selden Spencer, rector of Christ Church, Tarrytown, Westchester county.

The Rev. Constantine Stauder, officiating among Italians in New-York.

The Rev William Staunton, D. D., New-York.

The Rev. John F. Steen, officiating in Missions of the Church of the Ascension, New-York.

The Rev. Christopher S. Stephenson, rector of St. Mary's Church, Mott Haven, New-York.

*The Rev. Walter A. Stirling, New-York.

The Rev. Henry C. Stowell, New-York.

*The Rev. Francis Henry Stricker, deacon, China Mission.

*The Rev. Francis H. Stubbs, Church of the Beloved Disciple, New-York.

The Rev Cornelius E. Swope, D. D., an assistant minister of Trinity Church, New-York.

The Rev. Edward W Syle, officiating in Japan.

*The Rev. Stephen H. Synnott, rector of St. Paul's Church, Poughkeepsie, Dutchess county.

The Rev. John Clough Tebbets, Jr., Grace Church, New-York.

The Rev. Richard Temple.

The Rev. Charles C. Tiffany, rector of the Church of the Atonement, Madison Avenue, New-York.

The Rev. William B. Thomas, Poughkeepsie, Dutchess county.

*The Rev. William Reed Thomas, rector of the Church of the Holy Innocents, Cornwall, Orange county, and missionary.

The Rev. Hugh Miller Thompson, D. D , rector of Christ Church, New-York.

*The Rev. Henry Martyn Torbert.

*The Rev. Uriah T. Tracy, rector of the Church of the Epiphany, New-York.

The Rev. Amos C. Treadway, residing in Watertown, New-York.

The Rev. John W. Trimble.

*The Rev Isaac H. Tuttle, D D , rector of St Luke's Church, New-York

The Rev. Alvi T Twing, D. D , secretary and general agent of the Domestic Committee of the Board of Missions of the Protestant Episcopal Church, New-York.

The Rev. Morris Ashurst Tyng, New-York.

The Rev. Stephen H. Tyng, D. D., rector of St. George's Church, New-York.

The Rev. Stephen H. Tyng, Jr., D. D., rector of the Church of the Holy Trinity, New-York.

*The Rev. James A. Upjohn.

*The Rev. Obadiah Valentine, missionary at Ellenville, Ulster county.

*The Rev. Frederick Van Kleeck, rector of Grace Church, White Plains, Westchester county.

The Rev. Peter Joseph Victor Van Roosbroeck, officiating for the New-York Protestant Episcopal City Mission Society, as chaplain of Bellevue Hospital. New-York.

*The Rev. Edward H. Van Winkle, deacon, New-York.

*The Rev. Isaac Van Winkle, rector of St Mary's Church in the Highlands— Cold Spring, Putnam county.

*The Rev. Joseph M. Waite, at St. Bartholomew's Church, New-York.

The Rev. Robert J. Walker, missionary of the Floating Church of our Saviour— for sailors in the port and city of New-York.

*The Rev. William D. Walker, assistant minister in charge of the Mission Chapel of Calvary Church, New-York.

*The Rev. William Walsh, Newburgh, Orange county.

*The Rev. Caleb T. Ward, deacon, New-York.

*The Rev. Arthur H. Warner, assistant minister of St. Luke's Church, New-York.

The Rev. Edward A. Washburn, D. D., rector of Calvary Church, New-York.

The Rev. John Waters, D. D., Kingston, Ulster county.

The Rev. John Henry Watson, Trinity Church, New-Rochelle, Westchester county.

*The Rev. Joshua Weaver, New-York.

The Rev. Benjamin Webb, New-York.

The Rev. Henry Webbe,

*The Rev. George W. West, missionary at Haverstraw, Rockland county.

The Rev. Sullivan H. Weston, D. D., an assistant minister of Trinity Church, New-York.

The Rev. E. S. Widdemer, in charge of the Mission Chapel of the Reconciliation, New-York.

The Rev. Howard T. Widdemer, rector of St. Ambrose' Church, New-York.

The Rev. George D. Wildes, D. D., rector of Christ Church, Riverdale, New-York.

*The Rev. James Henry Williams.

*The Rev. William T. Wilson, rector of the Church of the Mediator, South Yonkers, New-York. P. O., Kingsbridge, New-York.

The Rev. Alvah Wiswall, deacon, New-York.

The Rev. Allan Sheldon Woodle, B. D., assistant minister at Christ Church, New-York.

*The Rev. Curtiss T. Woodruff, Superintendent of the New-York Protestant Episcopal City Mission Society, New-York.

The Rev. D G. Wright, in charge of the Poughkeepsie Academy, Poughkeepsie, Dutchess county.

*The Rev. Christopher B. Wyatt, D. D., rector of St. Peter's Church, Westchester, Westchester county.

The Rev. Joseph H. Young, deacon, at St. Mark's Church, New-Castle, Westchester county, and missionary. P. O., Mount Kisco.

The Rev. Henry L. Ziegenfuss, rector of Christ Church, Poughkeepsie, Dutchess county.

Number of Clergy present at this Convention,...............	150
Number of Clergy absent,..............................	34
Number on the Roll of Convention,........................	184
Number not entitled to seats,.............................	120
Number of Clergymen belonging to the Diocese,............	304

Bishop,		1
Priests,		281
Deacons, with full qualifications,	17	
" restricted, without full qualifications,	5	
	——	22
Whole number of Clergymen,		304

NOTE A.—This letter (A) designates deacons who have not passed the Examinations required by Canon 7, § II., and Canon 4, § V., Title I., of the Digest of the Canons of the Gen. Conv., and have been admitted to the restricted Diaconate.

CLERGY LIST :—CORRECTIONS.

Page 3, line 20, read The Rev. Joseph S. Attwell.
" 4, line 10, read The Rev. W. M. Atkinson Brodnax.
" " line 35, read The Rev. Elie Charlier.
" 5, line 15, strike out 'asterisk.'
" 10, line 1, read The Rev. A. F. Olmstead.
" 11, line 8 from bottom, strike out 'asterisk.'
" 12, line 11, add—and Professor in the Imperial College, Yedo.
" " line 36, read *The Rev. Frederick B. Van Kleeck.
" 13, line 8, read The Rev. George Waters, D. D.

A List of the Clergy

PRESENT AT THIS

ONVENTION.

lowing Clergy of the Diocese, entitled to seats in the n, were present at its sittings:—

3HT REV. HORATIO POTTER, D. D., LL. D., D. C. L.

vius Applegate,
s T. Ashton,
ph Atwell,
klin Babbitt,
d F. Banks,
ard T. Bartlett,
ed B. Beach, D. D.,
ry H. Bean,
iam H. Benjamin,
ielius W. Bolton,
ert Bolton,
incey B. Brewster,
iur Brooks,
. H. Brown,
IcKee Brown,
uel Buel, D. D.,
es S. Bush,

Rev. C. William Camp,
Charles F. Canedy,
Alexander Capron,
A. B. Carter, D. D.,
John Chamberlain,
Caleb Clapp,
A. Vallete Clarkson,
William S. Coffey,
William H. Cooke,
Nath'l E. Cornwall, D. D.,
Algernon S. Crapsey,
Robert F. Crary,
Joaquim De Palma,
Morgan Dix, D. D.,
E. W. Donald,
H. A. Dows,
George B. Draper, D. D.,

Rev. Cornelius R. Duffie, D. D.,
William N. Dunnell,
Theodore A. Eaton, D. D.,
John C. Eccleston, M. D.,
William T. Egbert,
Wm. E. Eigenbrodt, D. D.,
Rufus Emery,
Robert B. Fairbairn, D. D.,
George W. Ferguson,
Edward O. Flagg, D. D.,
John C. Fleischhacker,
Thomas Gallaudet, D. D.,
John N. Galleher, D. D.,
E. Gay,
George Jarvis Geer, D. D.,
J. Breckenridge Gibson, D. D.,
Kingston Goddard, D. D.,
Alfred Goldsborough,
H. C. Goodwin,
William H. De L. Grannis,
Albert Z. Gray,
Frederick W. Gray,
Edmund Guilbert,
Randall C. Hall,
Thomas R. Harris,
J. G. B. Heath,
James I. Helm, D. D.,
Charles Higbee,
Solomon G. Hitchcock,
Horace B. Hitchings,
Charles F. Hoffman,
William A. Holbrook,
Samuel F. Holmes,
George B. Hopson,
Edward C. Houghton,
George C. Houghton,
George H. Houghton, D. D.,
Albert S. Hull,
Angus M. Ives,
Joseph H. Johnson,

Rev. Arthur C. Kimber,
John W. Kramer, M. D.,
Edward H. Krans,
William Fisher Lewis,
John R. Livingston,
Lea Luquer,
Haslett McKim,
Stephen A. McNulty,
Romaine S. Mansfield,
James Millett,
Wm. W. Montgomery,
John W. Moore,
Samuel Moran,
Brockholst Morgan,
Joshua Morsell, D. D.,
James Mulchahey, D. D.,
R. Heber Newton,
Louis L. Noble,
Frederick Oertel,
Frederick Ogilby, D. D.,
Andrew Oliver, D. D.,
A. F. Olmsted,
C. T. Olmsted,
William W. Olssen,
Thomas M. Peters, D. D.,
George L. Platt,
Leon Pons,
John F. Potter,
Horace L. E. Pratt,
Joseph H. Price, D. D.,
James S. Purdy, D. D.,
G. E. Purucker,
George B. Reese,
H. Floy Roberts,
J. J. Robertson, D. D.,
J. G. Rosencrantz,
R. Condit Russell,
Joseph H. Rylance, D. D.,
Henry Y. Satterlee,
E. H. Saunders,

ev. Robert Scott,
William J. Seabury,
George F. Seymour, D. D.,
Fred'k W. Shelton, LL. D.,
Henry B. Sherman,
George F. Siegmund,
Thomas H. Sill,
Cornelius B. Smith,
J. Tuttle Smith,
Orsamus H. Smith,
William E. Snowden,
Jesse A. Spencer, D. D.,
J. Selden Spencer,
Christopher S. Stephenson,
Stephen H. Synnott,
C. E. Swope, D. D.,
Charles C. Tiffany,
William R. Thomas,

Rev. Hugh M. Thompson, D. D.,
Isaac H. Tuttle, D. D.,
Obadiah Valentine,
Frederick B. Van Kleeck,
P. J. V. Van Roosbroeck,
Isaac Van Winkle,
Robert J. Walker,
William D. Walker,
Arthur H. Warner,
Edw'd A. Washburn, D.D.,
George W. West,
Sullivan H. Weston, D. D.,
H. T. Widdemer,
George D. Wildes, D. D.,
William T. Wilson,
Allan H. Woodle,
Curtiss T. Woodruff.

A List of the Lay Delegates

TO THIS

CONVENTION.

The following Delegates from the Churches of the Diocese, entitled to representation, presented the required certificates. The names of those who were present and sat in the Convention are printed in Roman letters. The names of those who were absent, or were not heard to answer to their names, are printed in Italics.

Counties.	*Churches.*	*Delegates.*
Dutchess,....	St. Thomas', Amenia,	William Nelson,
		Charles T. Lovell.
	St. Mark's, Carthage Landing,	*John H. Shurter,*
		Robert N. Verplanck,
		Samuel C. Verplanck.
	Trinity, Fishkill,	Alexander Bartow,
		Oliver W. Barnes,
		John D. Fouquet.
	St. James', Hyde Park,	N. A. Pendleton Rogers,
		James Roosevelt.
	St. Luke's, Matteawan,	*Henry W. Sargent,*
		Henry E. Davies,
		George K. Seaman.
	Christ, Poughkeepsie,	Steph. M. Buckingham,
		Le Grand Dodge,
		George Cornwell.
	Holy Comforter,	William A. Davies,
		Samuel K. Rupley,
		Benjamin Van Loan.

Counties.	*Churches.*	*Delegates.*
Dutchess,....	St. Paul's, Poughkeepsie,	*George B. Lent,*
		Robert Sanford,
		Guy C. Bailey, M. D.
	St. Paul's, Red Hook,	John Henry Livingston,
		Johnston S. De Peyster,
		Charles C. Champlin.
	Messiah, Rhinebeck,	*David P. Sipperly,*
		Edward Jones,
		Richard J. Garretson.
	Zion, Wappinger's Falls,	Abraham S. Mesier,
		Francis R. Rives,
		Everett P. Wheeler.
New-York, ..	All Angel's, New-York,	*James L. Adams,*
		W. C. Wannenberg,
		T. H. Bainton.
	All Saints',	Wilson Small,
		John H. Betts,
		John Blake.
	Annunciation,	John D. Jones,
		George Shea,
		James Weeks.
	Anthon Memorial,	William Tracy,
		John Wheeler,
		William H. Robinson.
	Ascension,	Frederick De Peyster,
		Fred. G. Foster,
		Francis Leland.
	Atonement, Madison Avenue,	Wm. Graydon,
		Phineas W. Kingsland,
		Frederick Neilson.
	Calvary,	James Emott,
		Samuel B. Ruggles,
		Frederick S. Winston.
	Epiphany,	*Robert Betty,*
		Edw. G. Black,
		Chas. Treichell.
	Grace,	Adam Norrie,
		Lloyd W. Wells,
		Charles G. Landon.

unties.	*Churches.*	*Delegates.*
r-York, . .	Heavenly Rest, New-York,	*Benj. A. Willis,*
		Elbridge T. Gerry,
		Charles S. Fisher, Jr.
	Holy Martyrs,	James R. Mulligan,
		George T. Baldwin,
		John E. Ottiwell.
	Holy Sepulchre,	T. M. Cheesman, M. D.,
		John Pyne,
		John E. Hagler.
	Holy Trinity,	Robert Dumont,
		Effingham H. Nichols,
		Samuel H. Hurd.
	Incarnation,	Samuel M. Valentine,
		Edgar M. Crawford,
		Charles B. Fosdick.
	Nativity,	John S. Smith,
		Thomas N. Smith,
		William Peasey.
	Redeemer,	*Elias J. Pattison,*
		Charles A. Acton,
		Geo. D. Blythinge.
	Resurrection,	*C. Y. Wemple,*
		James M. Boyd.
	Santiago,	José Joaquin Govantes,
		Francis V. Mendoza,
		Domingo Ferrer.
	St. Ambrose,	Wm. S. Cutler,
		Andrew Robinson,
		Wm. W. Crossley.
	St. Andrew's,	Edward H. Jacot,
		Alonzo C. Stewart,
		William H. Riblet.
	St. Ann's,	D. Colden Murray,
		Orlando L. Stewart,
		Henry I. Haight.
	St. Bartholomew's,	*D. Henry Haight,*
		George G. Kellogg,
		George D. H. Gillespie.

Counties.	*Churches.*	*Delegates.*
New-York,..	St. Clement's, New-York,	John Buckley,
		Stephen T. Wygant,
		Geo. H. Romaine.
	St. Esprit,	John P. Schlumpf,
		Lewis H. Pignolet,
		Frederick Renaud.
	St. George's,	Charles Tracy,
		J. Pierrepont Morgan,
		William T. Blodgett.
	St. George the Martyr's,	E. W. Canning,
		John Moulson,
		Robert Waller.
	St. Ignatius',	Christian Zabriskie,
		H. Sylvester Bosworth,
		John V. Hecker.
	St. James',	Andrew D. Letson,
		Thomas Rutter,
		John McDonald.
	St. John Baptist's,	Thomas W. Clerke,
		John Dewsnap,
		William B. Dixon.
	St. John Evangelist's,	Hamilton R. Searles,
		Thomas G. Pratt,
		Edward Buss.
	St. Luke's,	A. B. McDonald,
		Francis Pott,
		Julian Botts.
	St. Mark's,	William Remsen,
		P. J. Schuyler,
		Evert A. Duyckinck.
	St. Mary's,	Richard L. Schieffelin,
		Peter C. Tiemann,
		George R. Schieffelin.
	St. Mary the Virgin's,	John W. Pirsson,
		Edward H. Clarke,
		James Burt.
	St. Michael's,	D. Tilden Brown,
		Benj. F. Tieman,
		Wm. F. Chester.

Counties.	*Churches.*	*Delegates.*
[N]ew-York,..	St. Peter's, New-York,	George P. Quackenbos,
		E. H. Cushman,
		Edwin Young.
	St. Philip's,	Philip H. White,
		Jeremiah W. Bowers,
		Ezekiel Dias.
	St. Stephen's,	*James Blackhurst,*
		George Ashforth,
		S. M. Pike.
	St. Thomas',	Lyman Denison,
		George M. Miller,
		William J. Peake.
	St. Timothy's,	Elam O. Potter,
		Archibald Turner,
		L. P. Williams.
	Transfiguration,	Gerardus B. Docharty,
		Edwin T. Butler,
		David B. Williamson.
	Trinity,	John A. Dix,
		Cambridge Livingston,
		Stephen P. Nash.
	Zion,	John M. Stuart,
		D. C. Calvin,
		David Clarkson.
	Holy Trinity of Harlem,	*Benjamin P. Paddock,*
		Charles F. Alvord,
		Frederick Tinson.
	St. James', Fordham,	G. L. Dashwood,
		Moses Devoe,
		Fordham Morris.
	St. Ann's, Morrisania,	William H. Morris,
		J. Wm. Entz,
		Thomas H. Faile.
	St. Paul's,	T. J. Potter,
		James W. White,
		Benjamin Saunders.
	Trinity,	*Morris Wilkins,*
		James Henry Welsh,
		Francis H. Nash.

Counties.	*Churches.*	*Delegates.*
New-York,..	St. Mary's, Mott Haven,	*George Briggs*,
		William R. Beal,
		Andrew A. French.
	Christ, Riverdale,	Francis M. Bacon,
		Bowie Dashe,
		Joseph H. Bicknell.
	Mediator, South Yonkers,	Maturin L. Delafield,
		Joseph H. Godwin,
		John L. Berrien.
	Grace, West Farms,	Samuel M. Purdy,
		A. M. Campbell, M. D.
		James L. Wells.
Orange,.....	St. John's, Canterbury,	Thomas P. Cummings.
	Holy Innocents, Cornwall,	Robert W. Weir,
		Stephen R. Roe,
		Charles Tracy.
	St. James', Goshen,	George C. Miller,
		J. Francis Matthews,
		William T. Russell.
	St. George's, Newburgh,	*Francis Scott*,
		Henry Dudley,
		David B. St. John.
	St. Paul's,	*John S. Heard*,
		Eugene B. Noe,
		R. V. K. Montfort.
	St. Thomas', New-Windsor,	Thomas W. Christie,
		Gethron Appleton.
	Grace, South Middletown,	Joseph B. Swalm,
		John Wilkins,
		Stoddard S. Draper.
	St. Andrew's, Walden,	George Weller,
		George Weller, Jr.,
		George C. Wooster.
	Christ, Warwick,	Henry C. Weir,
		Samuel B. Dolsen,
		Grinnell Burt.
Putnam,.....	St. Mary's, Cold Spring,	Robert P. Parrott,
		Robert B. Hitchcock,
		Fredk. P. James.

ounties.	*Churches.*	*Delegates.*
nam,.....	St. Philip's, Philipsetown,	*Hamilton Fish*,
		William Moore,
		Henry W. Belcher.
hmond,...	Ascension, Castleton, West Brighton,	Erastus Brooks,
		William H. Brown,
		Cornelius Dubois.
	St. Mary's, Castleton,	John L. Gratacap,
		Dallas B. Pratt,
		Charles E. Wemple.
	St. John's, Clifton,	*John A. Appleton*,
		George S. Scofield,
		Dwight Townsend.
	St. Paul's, Edgewater,	*Albert Ward*,
		Roland Thomas,
		Alex. E. Outerbridge.
	Christ, New-Brighton,	H. Eugene Alexander,
		John Q. Jones,
		Beverly Robinson.
	St. Luke's, Rossville,	*D. A. Edgar*,
		H. S. Bidell,
		Henry H. Bidel.
kland,...	St. John's, Clarkstown,	*Benj. B. Barnes*,
		Henry Wylde,
		Clayton T. Platt.
	St. Luke's, Haverstraw,	Hendrick D. Batchelder,
		John W. Babcock,
		John Oldfield.
	Grace, Nyack,	Wm. C. Moore,
		O. E. Hosmer,
		Jas. B. Simonson.
	Christ, Ramapo,	William G. Hamilton,
		Theodore Haff,
		Henry R. Sloat.
ivan,....	St. John's, Monticello,	Israel P. Tremaine,
		Wm. H. Cady,
		Abraham Olmstead.
ter,......	Ascension, Esopus,	Daniel Butterfield,
		E. Bergh Brown,
		Alexander Holland.

Counties.	*Churches.*	*Delegates.*
Ulster,......	St. John's, Kingston,	Charles D. Bruyn,
		Newton Frien,
		Augustus W. Reynolds.
	Holy Spirit, Rondout,	*Claude V. Quilliard,*
		Clifford Coddington,
		Hiram Roosa.
	Trinity, Saugerties,	*Aaron E. Vanderpoel,*
		Cornelius Battele.
Westchester,.	St. Matthew's, Bedford,	John Jay,
		John J. Banks,
		James M. Bates.
	Zion, Greenburgh,	Shadrach Taylor,
		Alex. Vanderburgh,
		Edward R. Satterlee.
	St. John's, Lewisboro',	Ebenezer W. Raymond,
		Stephen L. Hoyt,
		Charles A. Raymond.
	St. Thomas', Mamaroneck,	Charles H. Burney,
		James Stringer,
		J. Knapp Purdy.
	St. Mark's, Mount Pleasant,	George S. Rice,
		Charles H. Currier,
		John Webber.
	Trinity, Mount Vernon,	William A. Seaver,
		Gideon D. Pond,
		Alfred Starr.
	St. Mark's, New-Castle,	Robert S. Hart,
		James S. Hawley,
		Edwin Snyder.
	Trinity, New-Rochelle,	Robert C. Fisher,
		Robert R. Morris,
		Wm. E. Burnett.
	St. Stephen's, North Castle,	Wm. A. Carr,
		William H. Creamer,
		Charles Raymond.
	St. Peter's, Peekskill, Cortlandt,	Calvin Frost,
		Owen T. Coffin,
		James H. Robertson.

unties.	*Churches.*	*Delegates.*
stchester,	Christ, Pelham,	Robert W. Edgar,
		A. Newbold Morris,
		Wm. H. De Lancey.
	St. Peter's, Portchester,	Philip Rolhaus,
		Augustus W. Kelley,
		Augustus Abendroth.
	Christ, Rye,	John C. Jay,
		Adam T. Sackett,
		G. H. Van Wagenen.
	St. James the Less, Scarsdale,	William S. Popham,
		James Bleecker,
		Alexander B. Crane.
	All Saints', Briar Cliff, Sing Sing,	*Russell Knowlton*,
		Charles C. Clarke,
		Henry M. Brinckerhoff.
	St. Paul's,	*M. L. Cobb*,
		Charles O. Joline,
		Gilbert M. Todd.
	Trinity,	Marlborough Churchill,
		George D. Arthur,
		Wm. W. Benjamin.
	Christ, Tarrytown,	Nathaniel B. Holmes,
		George W. Morell,
		Ambrose C. Kingsland.
	St. John's, Tuckahoe,	Andrew Findlay,
		Samuel M. Raesbreck,
		Alexander Forbes.
	St. Peter's, Westchester,	Robert H. Ludlow,
		Rich. L. Morris, M.D.,
		John H. Screven.
	Grace, White Plains,	E. T. Prudhomme,
		William H. Dearman,
		Daniel J. Tripp.
	St. John's, Wilmot,	Sylvester L. H. Ward,
		Clark Davis,
		Zalmon Bonnett.

Counties.	*Churches.*	*Delegates.*
Westchester,.	St. John's, Yonkers,	Henry Anstice.
		Levi P. Rose,
		John P. Groshen.
	St. Paul's,	William Iles,
		J. Foster Jenkins,
		John P. Ritter.
	St. Mary's, Yorktown,	*Henry S. Bollinge,*
		James C. Nicoll,
		Charles D. Morris.

CLERGYMEN NOT MEMBERS OF THE CONVENTION PRESENT.

The Right Rev. Thomas Atkinson, D. D., of the Diocese of North Carolina.

The Rev. Robert B. Croes, D. D.,
The Rev. Alvi T. Twing, D. D.,
The Rev. David H. Macurdy,
The Rev. Wm. A. M. Broadnax,
The Rev. George W. Hinckle,
The Rev. Samuel Osgood, D. D., LL. D.,
The Rev. James Byron Murray,
The Rev. Joshua Weaver,
The Rev. R. G. Hamilton, deacon,
The Rev. Alfred E. Johnson, deacon,
The Rev. N. Frazier Robinson, deacon,
The Rev. William Staunton, D. D.,
The Rev. Henry C. Stowell,
The Rev. D. Brainerd Ray,
} of the Diocese of New-York.

The Rev. Samuel M. Haskins, D.D.,
The Rev. Henry M. Beare,
} of the Diocese of Long Island.

The Rev. James W. Stewart, of the Diocese of Albany.

The Rev. Vandervoort Bruce,
The Rev. James W. Coe,
} of the Diocese of New-Jersey.

The Rev. William P. Tenbroeck, of the Diocese of W sconsin.

The Rev. Josiah P. Tustin, D. D., of the Diocese of Michigan.

The Rev. George S. Mallory, of the Diocese of Connecticut.

The Rev. Wellington E. Webb, of the Diocese of Ohio.

JOURNAL

OF

THE PROCEEDINGS

OF THE

CONVENTION.

New-York, Wednesday, Feast of St. Michael and All Angels, September 29th, 1875.

This being the day fixed by the Constitution of the Protestant Episcopal Church in the Diocese of New-York for the meeting of the Annual Convention of the same, a number of the Clergy and Laity assembled for Divine Service, at ten o'clock in the morning, at St. John's Chapel in the City of New-York, the place appointed by the Bishop for the meeting.

Morning Prayer was said by the Rev. Arthur Brooks, Rector of the Church of the Incarnation, New-York, assisted by the Rev. Theodore A. Eaton, D. D., Rector of St. Clement's Church, New-York, and the Rev. Samuel Osgood, D. D., LL. D., who read the Lessons. The Litany was said by the Rev. William T. Wilson, Rector of the Church of the Mediator, Kingsbridge, New-York. The Ante-Communion Service was read by the Right Rev. Horatio Potter, D. D., LL. D., D. C. L., Bishop of the Diocese; the Rev. Stephen H. Synnott, rector of St.

Paul's Church, Poughkeepsie, reading the Epistle, and the Rev. Morgan Dix, D. D., rector of Trinity Church, New-York, reading the Gospel. The Sermon was preached by the Rev. Joseph H. Rylance, D. D., Rector of St. Mark's Church in the Bowerie, New-York. The Holy Communion was celebrated by the Right Reverend the Bishop of the Diocese, assisted by the Rev. Morgan Dix, D. D., the Rev. Sullivan H. Weston, D. D., the Rev. Stephen H. Synnott, the Rev. George B. Draper, D. D., and the Rev. William S. Coffey.

The Bishop of the Diocese took the Chair, and called the Convention to order.

The Secretary then proceeded, under the direction of the Bishop, to call the names of the Clergy of the Diocese entitled to seats, when one hundred and twenty-two* answered to their names, and took their seats as members.

The Churches entitled to representation were then called over, and the Lay Delegates presented their certificates; which were examined by the Secretary and a Committee of two members, appointed by the Presiding Officer, viz.: Hon. Samuel B. Ruggles and Gen. George W. Morell. The names of the Lay Delegates duly appointed were called, when Lay Delegates from eighty-two Parishes appeared and took their seats.†

A constitutional quorum being present, the Right Reverend the President declared the Convention organized for business.

The President announced the Seventh Rule of Order on the admission of persons not members to the sittings of the Convention.

On motion, the reading of the Rules of Order was unanimously dispensed with.

---

* A List of the Clergy who attended this Convention is prefixed to the Journal.

† A List of the Lay Delegates present in this Convention is prefixed to the Journal.

The Convention then proceeded, according to the Sixth Article of the Constitution, to the appointment of a Secretary and Treasurer.

On motion of Lloyd W. Wells, Esq., the vote by ballot was unanimously dispensed with; and the Rev. William E. Eigenbrodt, D. D., was elected Secretary.

On motion of the same, the vote by ballot was unanimously dispensed with; and Edward F. De Lancey, Esq., was elected Treasurer.

The Secretary announced to the Convention, that he appointed the Rev. Theodore A. Eaton, D. D., the Assistant Secretary.

In compliance with Canon I. of the Diocese, the Bishop laid before the Convention a list of the Clergy of the Diocese.

The following Standing Committees, appointed by the Right Rev. the President, were then announced:

ON THE INCORPORATION AND ADMISSION OF CHURCHES.

Charles Tracy, Esq., the Rev. Alfred B. Beach, D. D., and the Hon. John A. Dix.

ON THE DIOCESAN FUND.

The Rev. Thomas Gallaudet, D. D., the Rev. John N. Galleher, D. D., Francis Pott, Esq., Charles Tracy, Esq., and the Treasurer.

ON THE TREASURER'S REPORT.

David Clarkson, Esq., Frederick S. Winston, Esq., and Robt. H. Ludlow, Esq.

ON THE GENERAL THEOLOGICAL SEMINARY.

The Rev. Morgan Dix, D. D., the Rev. George Jarvis Geer, D. D., John Buckley, Esq., Cambridge Livingston, Esq., and Anthony B. McDonald, Esq.

ON CANONS.

The Rev. Benjamin I. Haight, D. D., LL. D., the Rev. Henry C. Potter, D. D., the Rev. Christopher B. Wyatt, D. D., the Hon. Hamilton Fish, Hon. Samuel B. Ruggles and Irving Paris, Esq.

INSPECTORS OF ELECTION.

For the Standing Committee: For the Clerical Votes—The Rev. William White Montgomery and Mr. Cornelius Dubois. For the Lay Votes—The Rev. Robert F. Crary and Gen. George W. Morell.

For the Missionary Committee: For the Clerical Votes—The Rev. Thomas M. Peters, D. D., and Mr. N. B. Holmes. For the Lay Votes—The Rev. Horace B. Hitchings and Mr. Gerritt H. Van Wagenen.

The Report of the Committee on the Incorporation and Admission of Churches was presented and read, as follows:

Report

ON THE INCORPORATION AND ADMISSION OF CHURCHES.

The Committee on the Incorporation and Admission of Churches respectfully report:

That they have received but one application for admission into union with the Church in this Diocese.

This application has come from the Society of "The Church of the Holy Trinity in Highland, town of Lloyd, county of Ulster," a Society incorporated under the act of April 13, 1854, entitled "An Act for the Incorporation of Societies to establish Free Churches."

The Committee in their reports in former years have fully expressed their doubt as to whether a Society of this description be a Church or congregation within the intent of the constitution and Canons of this Church. Without now repeating what they have said upon this point, and contenting themselves with simply renewing the expression of that doubt, they have to report, with reference to the present application, that the certificate of incorporation is defective, in that it fails to declare upon its face that the Society incorporated is a Protestant Episcopal Church, and that it is for ever to continue as such in communion with the Protestant Episcopal Church in the State of New-York, as is required by section 1 of Canon IV. of this Diocese.

Respectfully submitted.

M ULSHOEFFER, ALFRED B. BEACH, } *Committee*

Whereupon, it was

Ordered, That the papers of the Society of the Church of the Holy Trinity, Highland, Ulster county, be referred back to the applicants for remedy.

The Secretary informed the Convention, That there was upon the table a communication addressed to this House, from the Diocese of Albany.

On motion of the same, it was

Ordered, That this communication be received.

COMMUNICATION FROM THE DIOCESE OF ALBANY.

To the Convention of the Diocese of New-York:

At the last Convention of the Diocese of Albany, held at Troy, Jan. 15th, 1875, the following resolution was passed:

"*Resolved,* That a Committee of five be appointed to memorialize the next Annual Convention of the Diocese of New-York to assist, in whatever way it may deem best, the Diocese of Albany in completing its Episcopal Endowment."

The undersigned, as the Committee under this resolution, respectfully represent:

That the Episcopal Fund of the Diocese of Albany is $37,500. This sum was raised when the Diocese was organized. It was contributed entirely by Churchmen within this Diocese, and was regarded at the time as unexpectedly liberal and large, considering our numbers and our means.

The efforts which then proved so successful were greatly stimulated by expectations that the Diocese of New-York would supplement what we should raise with a generous, if not an equal amount. Those expectations were based not only upon the natural and reasonable feeling that the Mother Diocese would not allow her young daughter to go forth without some provision for her needs, but also upon repeated representations to that effect, made in your Convention, and actual measures there inaugurated.

Our hopes, however, were doomed to disappointment. Nothing has been received from the Diocese of New-York towards our Episcopal Fund. In consequence, the income from that Fund pays only about one-half of the Bishop's salary, while the deficiency has to be made up by assessments upon the Parishes. These assessments are a burden more grievous to be borne, because we fondly expected to be freed from it by your promised aid. And, what is worse, they divert from the Parishes offerings which would otherwise go to our Missionary work.

This work is very heavy upon us. About one-half of the Parishes and Clergy of the Diocese are dependent on Missionary aid. There is, besides, a large field for new operations, if we could command the means. Of all this responsibility the New Diocese relieved the Old; and that responsibility has been nobly borne. We are now contributing annually to Diocesan Missions five times as much as before the division. But yet all our increased efforts are insufficient for the constantly increasing necessities. We are unable to undertake much work which is pressing upon us; and, at times, we have been compelled, for want of means, to reduce the number and stipends of our Missionaries. It is highly important that the contributions of the Diocese should be turned still more into this channel; and such would be the case, if the Episcopal Fund were made sufficient to enable us to do away with the assessments, which are now drawing largely upon the resources of our Parishes.

To help us attain this most desirable object, we make our petition to your honorable body. All of us feel that we are at least equitably entitled to a portion of your Episcopal Fund. But there is among us a no less general repugnance to enforce any claims, however persuaded we are of their validity; or to resort to any methods, except those of friendly solicitation. We would fain believe that it is enough to remind you of the assurances of help, which were kindly held out to us at the time of the division; and we would earnestly beg that they may now be redeemed. We would ask for our Diocese what was done for Western New-York, what Western New-York did for Central, and what has become customary on the erection of a new Diocese from an old one. We would appeal to the generosity of our brethren of the strong and richly-favored Diocese of New-York, to your sense of propriety and justice, and above all, to those cords of love which ever did, and, we trust, ever will bind us together in Christ and His Church.

WM. PAYNE, *St. George's, Schenectady.*
J. IRELAND TUCKER, *Holy Cross, Troy.*
NATHAN B. WARREN, *Troy.*
H. R PIERSON, *Albany*
JNO. TAYLOR COOPER, *Albany.*

On motion of the Secretary, it was

Resolved, That the Communication from the Diocese of Albany be referred to a Committee of Five, to consider the same, and report to this Convention.

Charles Tracy, Esq., Hon. James Emott, Rev. Edward A. Washburn, D. D., Rev. Morgan Dix, D. D., and Cambridge Livingston, Esq., were appointed this Committee.

The Secretary presented a Report from the Treasurer of sundry subscriptions, formerly received by a Committee of this Convention, for aid in enlargement of the Episcopal Fund of the Diocese of Albany.

Report

OF THE TREASURER OF THE SUBSCRIPTIONS FOR THE ENLARGEMENT OF THE ENDOWMENT OF THE EPISCOPATE OF ALBANY.

EDWARD HAIGHT, *Treasurer, in account with the* COMMITTEE ON SUBSCRIPTIONS FOR THE DIOCESE OF ALBANY.

Balance on hand, as per last report, Sept. 30, 1874, ...		$1,438 72
Invested in receipts of the United States Trust Co.,...	$1,433 72	
Cash on hand,....................................	5 00	
		$1,438 72

E. E.

EDWARD HAIGHT,
Treasurer.

NEW-YORK, *Sept.* 29, 1875.

On motion of the Secretary, it was

Ordered, That this Report be referred to the Special Committee on the Communication from the Diocese of Albany.

The Convention adjourned until ten o'clock to-morrow morning.

THURSDAY, SEPTEMBER 30, TEN O'CLOCK, A. M.

The Convention met pursuant to adjournment.

Morning Prayer was said by the Rev. William E. Snowden, rector of St. Andrew's Church, Walden, assisted by the Rev. John R. Livingston, rector of Trinity Church, Fishkill, and the Rev. John G. Rosencrantz, rector of Grace Church, Port Jervis.

The Right Rev. the Bishop of the Diocese took the Chair.

The Minutes of yesterday's proceedings were read and approved.

Several Clergymen, not present yesterday, appeared and too their seats.*

Lay Delegates from several Parishes, from which no certi cates were before received, presented certificates, which we examined by the Committee on the subject. On approval, t Delegates took their seats.†

The Committee on Credentials reported, That a certifica presented from St. Andrew's Church, Richmond, was defecti from want of the signature of the Rector of the Parish, a of declaration of the right of those claiming to have been pointed Delegates to vote for Wardens and Vestrymen in Parish.

The Bishop of the Diocese then delivered his

ANNUAL ADDRESS.

On motion of the Secretary, it was

Resolved, That the Clergy of the Diocese in charge of Parishes be and hereby are requested by this Convention to

---

* A List of the Clergy who attended this Convention is prefixed to the Journal.

† A List of the Lay Delegates present in this Convention is prefixed to the Journal.

read to their congregations, on the next annual Thanksgiving Day, or on the Sunday preceding, so much of the Bishop's Address as relates to the Fund of the Diocese of New-York for the Relief of Aged and Infirm Clergymen.

Ordered, That a copy of this Resolution and such portion of the Bishop's Address be transmitted, prior to that period, to the Parochial Clergy of the Diocese.

The Right Reverend the President introduced the Bishop of North Carolina to the Convention.

Whereupon, it was unanimously

Resolved, That this Convention hereby expresses its gratification at the presence of the Right Reverend Thomas Atkinson, D. D., Bishop of North Carolina, and respectfully invites him to occupy a seat beside the President, whenever he may please to attend its sessions.

The Convention proceeded to the election of the Standing Committee, and of the Missionary Committee of the Diocese.

The names of the Clergy were called by the Secretary, and of the Churches by the Assistant Secretary. The members having deposited their ballots, the Tellers retired to count the votes.

The Convention proceeded to the election of the Trustees of the Fund for the Relief of Aged and Infirm Clergymen.

Ballot was unanimously dispensed with, and the following persons were chosen

TRUSTEES OF THE AGED AND INFIRM CLERGY FUND.

Cyrus Curtiss, Esq.,
William Betts, Esq.,
Edward F. De Lancey, Esq.

The Secretary of the Convention presented the following Report:

Report

OF THE SECRETARY OF THE CONVENTION.

The Secretary of the Convention begs leave respectfully to report:

That, according to the order of the Convention in 1874, the Journal of its proceedings was printed and distributed, as usual, under his direction. In compliance with the Canons, he has also, during the past year, recorded various documents, which have been sent to him for the purpose, and he has transmitted all other documents and papers, as required, to such Clergymen and Parishes in the Diocese as were concerned in the same.

The work of putting the Journals of the Conventions of this Diocese and of other Dioceses, and belonging to this Diocese, into a state proper for their security and preservation, as referred to in his last report, has been continued from that until the present time. During this year 106 new volumes of these Journals have been bound and added to the collection, which was then reported to be deposited in the Library of the General Theological Seminary, nnder the care of its Committee, as the property of this Convention, and accessible to any one for reference, and subject to the order of your Secretary. The whole number of these bound volumes, belonging to the Diocese, is now 250. From surplus copies of some Journals in his care he has been able to supply several Dioceses and individuals with what they have wanted, in order to complete their series; and from several he has received copies needed by him for filling up the numbers not otherwise to be found in our own files.

Under authority of the resolution on page 45 of the Journal of the New-York Convention of 1874, the expense of this binding, and of boxes for the Journals yet unbound, has been defrayed from the Diocesan Fund. Two members of this Convention, who are interested in historic records, have provided whatever else was needed for this work, without expense to the Diocese, to the amount of about one hundred dollars.

In an Appendix will be found a catalogue of this collection as it appears in its present state.

All which is respectfully submitted.

WILLIAM E. EIGENBRODT,
Secretary of the Convention of the Protestant Episcopal Church in the Diocese of New-York.

NEW-YORK, *Sept.* 28, 1875.

The Report of the Missionary Committee of the Diocese was presented and read by the Rev. Cornelius E. Swope, D. D.

Report

OF THE MISSIONARY COMMITTEE OF THE DIOCESE.

The Missionary Committee of the Diocese begs leave to present its Annual Report as follows:

The number of Missionary stations is 36.

The number of Missionaries, 27.

The Report of the Treasurer will show that, at the beginning of the current year, there was a balance in the Treasury of $218 29. Since that time the receipts from all sources have been $6,767 46, making the gross amount available for the uses of the Committee, $6,985 75.

The expenditures of the Committee thus far have been $5,757 77, leaving at this date a balance in the Treasury of $1,227 98.

There will be due, however, to the Missionaries on the 1st of October next, $1,550. This payment the Committee have every reason to believe they will be able to meet promptly.

In presenting this Report, your Committee feel that they have cause for gratitude in the result of their year's labors. They have a band of faithful, energetic Missionaries now in the field, and the work being accomplished is of a solid and enduring character, while the stipends of the Missionaries have been promptly paid. There is, of course, abundant room for more extended operations, and these your Committee are ready and anxious to undertake so soon as the necessary means are provided. If the many Parishes of the Diocese which hitherto, from oversight or from a mistaken impression that their co-operation is not needed, have failed to make offerings for this work, would contribute to the Treasury of your Committee in the same proportion as those who have always regularly and liberally aided us, the sphere of our operations might be greatly enlarged and much useful work might be done.

Your Committee, therefore, confidently express the hope, that in the coming year a still greater interest may be manifested in their work, and that the cause of Diocesan Missions may take that place which it deserves in the sympathies and kindly co-operation of all the members of the Church in our Diocese.

All of which is respectfully submitted.

C. E. SWOPE,
Secretary.

NEW-YORK, *Feast of St. Michael and All Angels*, 1875.

LIST OF MISSIONARIES IN THE DIOCESE OF NEW-YORK.

Counties.	*Stations.*	*Missionaries.*
Dutchess, ...	Pleasant Valley,	The Rev. G. H. Smith.
	Madalin,	J. Starr Clark, D. D.
	Glenham,	J. R. Livingston.

Counties.	*Stations*	*Missionaries.*
Dutchess,........	Amenia Station,	The Rev. A. T. Ashton.
	Lithgow,	
	Pine Plains,	
	Millbrook,	B. F. Miller.
Orange,.........	Buttermilk Falls,	W. R. Thomas.
	Greenwood Iron Works,	S. Moran.
	Walden,	W. E. Snowden.
	Canterbury,	J. F. Potter.
	Port Jervis,	J. G. Rosencrantz.
	Monroe,	H. A. Dows.
	Middletown,	F. M. Serenbez.
	Warwick,	Alfred Goldsborough.
Putnam,........	Patterson,	
Rockland,........	Clarkstown,	
	Haverstraw,	G. W. West.
	Nyack,	F. Babbitt.
	Piermont,	S. G. Hitchcock.
	Spring Valley,	R. S. Mansfield.
	Stony Point,	E. Gay, Jr.
	Sufferns,	G. E. Purucker.
Sullivan,........	Monticello,	C. F. Canedy.
Ulster,..........	Marlboro',	
	Ellenville,	O. Valentine.
	Milton,	J. H. Johnson.
	Stone Ridge,	
Westchester,....	Lewisboro',	R. Bolton.
	New Castle,	J. W. Young.
	North Castle,	
	Loomis,	
	Wilmot,	A. M. Ives.
	Montrose,	G. Cruger.
	Croton,	
	Pelhamville,	
	City Island,	J. Morsell, D. D.

REPORT OF THE TREASURER OF THE MISSIONARY COMMITTEE.

RECEIPTS

Balance on hand, October 1, 1874,...........................	$218	29
1875 —Received from Churches,....	5,480	26
" individuals,..........................	1,055	00
" interest,....	338	28
	$7,091	83

PAYMENTS.

Stipends paid in 1874,	$200 00
" to October 1, 1875,	6,823 86
Circulars, &c.,	32 40
Balance,	35 57
	$7,091 83

Balance on hand September 30, 1875,	$35 57
Received from estate of George Merritt, for investment,	5,000 00

All which is respectfully submitted.

JAMES POTT, *Treasurer*.

NEW-YORK, *Sept.* 30, 1875.

The Convention took a recess for half an hour.

The time of recess having expired, and the Convention having re-assembled ;

The Report of the Education Committee was presented and read by the Rev. George F. Seymour, D. D.:

Report

OF THE SOCIETY FOR PROMOTING RELIGION AND LEARNING IN THE STATE OF NEW-YORK.

The Superintendent of the Society for Promoting Religion and Learning in the State of New-York, as the Canonical agent of the Diocese of New-York for distributing all funds for Theological Education, most respectfully submits the following report :

That during the past Convention year, from October 1st, 1874, to October 1st, 1875, in discharging the duty with which it has been entrusted by the Convention, the Society has received and distributed the following sums :

Received by the Treasurer from the Diocese of New-York from October 1st, 1874, to October 1st, 1875,	$902 05
Received from other Dioceses during the same time,	263 05
Total amounts received,	$1,165 10

This entire sum has been devoted to the objects for which it was bestowed.

The Society for Promoting Religion and Learning has been in existence for more than seventy years. Its record is a remarkable one. Owing to judicious management and faithful administration of its property it has not only kept steadily on in the path of usefulness during all this period, but it has from year to year increased its power for doing good. Notwithstanding all the vicissitudes and disasters in trade and monetary affairs which have occurred since the beginning of the present century, this Society has never failed, as each year closed, to have its tale to tell of admirable works accomplished, of benefits scattered far and wide with a liberal hand. And now, when for many months our country has been checked in its career of material prosperity, when the wealthy feel the need of restraint in expenditure, and numbers who have never dreamed of straitened circumstances for themselves and those dependent upon them, are forced to endure hard self-denial, this Society, by God's blessing, is enabled to report a larger amount of benefactions given than ever before.

Over one hundred and twenty young men, representing almost every section of the United States, have been kept at their books in preparation for the Sacred Ministry. Among these are cases which illustrate the great service which the Society renders the Church in such seasons of depression as the present. Several Students who, at the outset of their career, were in affluent circumstances, would now be forced to abandon study, and forego, at least for the present, the prospect of taking Orders, owing to the loss of means, were it not for the helping hand of the Society for Promoting Religion and Learning.

Such an agency for doing good ought to be liberally supported by the Clergy and Laity, not only of the Diocese of New-York, but of the whole State and country. Two or three among the many reasons which might be named, which give it a just claim upon the confidence and sympathy of Churchmen, may be concisely stated:

First. The Society for Promoting Religion and Learning in its distribution of Scholarships is administered by the Trustees upon principles as broad and comprehensive as those of the Church herself; all are aided, without distinction or difference as to theological bias or school of thought, who are otherwise qualified to receive assistance.

Second. The management of the business of the Society is such that no unnecessary expense is incurred. The comparatively small amount which is expended in taking care of the property is derived from the income of the estate; and hence,

Third. All collections, and offerings and donations which are made to the funds of the Society are sacredly devoted, without the diminution of a single farthing, to the object for which they are given.

All of which is respectfully submitted.

GEO. F. SEYMOUR,
Superintendent of the
Society for Promoting Religion and Learning in the State of New-York.

GENERAL THEOLOGICAL SEMINARY,
September 30*th*, 1875.

The Report of the Trustees of the Episcopal Fund was presented and read:

Report

OF THE TRUSTEES OF THE EPISCOPAL FUND.

The Trustees of the Episcopal Fund of the Diocese of New-York report to the Convention as follows:

The capital of the Fund is $110,507 50, ($7 50 having been especially contributed by two Parishes during the year.)

$110,500 is invested in bonds and mortgages on improved City property, at seven per cent., and $7 50 in cash in bank. There is also belonging to the Fund 12 shares of St. Louis Iron Mountain and Southern Rail-Road stock, of the par value of $100 each, and fractional scrip for $40, received in exchange for the 10 shares mentioned in the report of last year.

During the year a bond and mortgage of Ely & Judson, for $7,500, has been paid off; $500 received on account of a bond and mortgage of A. M Fanning; the deposit of $8,000 withdrawn from the U. S. Trust Company, and investments made as follows:

$10,000 on bond and mortgage of A. Journeay, on house and store No. 76 South 5th Avenue.

$6,000 on bond and mortgage of Herman Philips, on house and lot, Bedford Avenue, Brooklyn

Both for three years at seven per cent.

The Income Account is as follows:

RECEIPTS.

Balance reported at last Convention,		$597 29
Interest on bonds and mortgages,		7,316 95
" on N. Y. City stocks,		345 00
" from U. S. Trust Company,		215 87
Sundry Parishes—Assessments, viz.:		
On account 1874,	$682 61	
" " 1875,	2,647 20	
		3,329 81
Withdrawn from U. S. Trust Company,		2,000 00
		$13,804 92

PAYMENTS.

To Bishop Potter, to 1st October,		$9,000 00
" City taxes, 1874, on "Episcopal Residence,"		672 00
" Croton Water Tax, do.	$19 00	
" Prem. of Fire Insurance, do.	31 88	
" Painter's repairs to do. including relaying sidewalk, new range, &c.,	485 37	
		536 25
" Circulars, Envelopes and Stamps,		23 46
" Counsel fee for examining title for investment,		65 00
" Paid for $1,000 N. Y. City stock,		962 50
" Temporary investment on bond and mortgage,		2,500 00
" Balance of cash in Bank,		45 71
		$13,804 92

Ditto, $6,000 N. Y. City stock.

The Trustees have also to report the decease of one of their number—George Templeton Strong, Esq.—who was elected a Trustee at the meeting of the Convention last year. It becomes the duty of this Convention to fill the vacancy.

All of which is respectfully submitted.

THOMAS P. CUMMINGS, *Treasurer*,
G. M. OGDEN,
FRED. G. FOSTER,
HUGH AUCHINCLOSS,
} *Trustees.*

NEW-YORK, *September* 29, 1875.

The Convention proceeded to the appointment of one Trustee of the Episcopal Fund. Whereupon, balloting having been unanimously dispensed with, on motion of the Secretary, it was

Resolved, That the Hon. John A. Dix be and is hereby appointed Trustee of the Episcopal Fund, in the place of George T. Strong, Esq., deceased.

The Report of the Special Committee on the Salary of the Bishop of the Diocese was presented and read:

Report

OF THE SPECIAL COMMITTEE ON THE SALARY OF THE BISHOP.

The Special Committee on the Salary of the Bishop report:

The deficiency of income of the "Episcopal Fund" has been supplied the past year by an apportionment among the Parishes of the Diocese by your Committee.

As the income of the Fund is still insufficient, an additional amount must be raised as heretofore.

Your Committee, therefore, offer the following resolution:

Resolved, That a Committee be appointed to make an equitable apportionment among the Parishes of the Diocese of a sum which, with the income of the "Episcopal Fund," will meet the amount pledged by this Convention for payment to the Bishop.

By order of the Committee.

THOS. P. CUMMINGS,
Secretary.

NEW-YORK, *September* 30, 1875.

The Resolution recommended in this Report was adopted.

The Rev. Benjamin I. Haight, D. D., Rev. Isaac H. Tuttle, D. D., Cyrus Curtiss, Esq., Hon. John A. Dix, Frederick G. Foster, Esq., William Scott, Esq., Lloyd W. Wells, Esq., Frederick Prime, Esq., Thomas P. Cummings, Esq., and George M. Miller, Esq., were appointed this Committee.

The Report of the Trustees of the Aged and Infirm Clergy Fund was presented and read:

Report

OF THE TRUSTEES OF THE AGED AND INFIRM CLERGY FUND.

The Trustees of the Fund for the Relief of Aged and Infirm Clergymen of the Protestant Episcopal Church in the Diocese of New-York, respectfully report:

That since their report to the Convention of 1874 there have been received—

Contributions from 91 Churches,	$3,324 85
Interest and rents,	2,023 60
Gift from James L. Bogert,	25 00
" " Henry K. Bogert,	25 00
" " a member of Trinity Chapel, by Rev. C. T. Olmsted,	20 00
" " "Mrs. H. W.,"	50 00
" Lent offering of "Y.," by Dr. Ogilby,	40 00
Legacy of George Merritt,	5,000 00
Principal awaiting re-investment at date of last report,	1,832 18
Balance fund at last Convention,	1,465 80
Total,	$13,809 43

There have been paid during the same period—

To beneficiaries,	$4,698 00
For investment in U. S. 5-20 bonds and accrued interest,	2,485 00
For repairing and putting in order three houses in Madison-street, and one on Broadway, Brooklyn, bought in on foreclosure,	3,932 90
Contingent expenses for stationery, printing, stamps, &c.,	28 61
	$11,144 51
Leaving a balance fund of	2,664 92
	$13,809 43

Investments heretofore reported,		$45,650 00
Less amount of principal awaiting re-investment at date of last report,		1,832 18
		$43,817 82
Add amount expended for the four houses bought in on foreclosure, as above reported,	$3,932 90	
Add amount paid for new investment in U. S. 5-20 bonds, as above reported,	2,485 00	
		6,417 90
Total permanent investments,		$50,235 72

On account of the existing depression, the Trustees have not yet been able to sell the real estate in Brooklyn bought in on foreclosure. The store on Broadway has been rented for $650 a year. The three dwelling houses

on Madison-street will also be rented if not disposed of during the coming season.

The present number of regular stipendiaries paid quarterly is thirteen. Special appropriations have been made in eight cases. One stipendiary has died during the year, and one has been added to the list.

HORATIO POTTER,
CYRUS CURTISS,
WILLIAM BETTS,
EDWARD F. DE LANCEY, } *Trustees.*

NEW-YORK, *September 29th*, 1874.

The Report of the Standing Committee on the Treasurer's Report was presented and read:

Report

OF THE TREASURER OF THE CONVENTION.

The Convention of the Diocese of New-York, in account current with EDWARD F. DE LANCEY, *Treasurer.*

September, 1874. DR.

To paid Rev. Clergy, mileage to Convention of 1874,...........	$100 00
" " Canonical quota of expenses of General Convention,....	923 00
" " Secretary's Salary,..................................	600 00
" " Pott, Young & Co., for printing for the Bishop,........	11 57
" " Pott, Young & Co., for printing Journal of Convention,	1,096 94
" " J. W. Amerman, printing envelopes, &c., for Diocesan Fund,...	17 25
" " J. W. Amerman, printing Forms, &c., for Standing Committee,......................................	31 00
" " J. W. Amerman, printing pastoral for the Bishop,.....	92 13
" " binding Journals, pursuant to resolution of Convention of 1874,..	236 65
" " Treasurer General Convention, extra assessment for expenses of last General Convention,................	313 00
" " amount retained under Canon XIV. towards expenses of next General Convention,........................	305 00
" " contingent expenses, (stamps, bad money, &c.,)........	8 28
	$3,734 82
Balance,..	6,466 62
Total, ...	$10,201 44

CR.

By balance from last year, ...	$4,859 20
" contributions from 110 Parishes, ...	5,342 24
Total, ...	$10,201 44

EDWARD F. DE LANCEY,
Treasurer of the Convention of the Diocese of New-York.

Dated September 29th, 1875.

SEPTEMBER 29TH, 1875.

The Committee on the Treasurer's account have examined the same, and compared the payments with the vouchers, and find them to correspond, and that there is now in the hands of the Treasurer sixty-four hundred and sixty-six $\frac{62}{100}$ dollars, ($6,466 $\frac{62}{100}$.)

D. CLARKSON,
ROBERT H. LUDLOW,
F. S. WINSTON,
} *Committee.*

The Report of the Standing Committee on the General Theological Seminary was presented and read by the Rev. Dr. Dix:

Report

OF THE STANDING COMMITTEE ON THE GENERAL THEOLOGICAL SEMINARY.

The Standing Committee on the General Theological Seminary respectfully report:

That there is a vacancy in the number of the Trustees to which this Diocese is entitled, caused by the removal of the Rev. Samuel Hollingsworth, D. D., to the Diocese of Massachusetts. The Committee recommend the Rev. James Mulchahey, D. D., as, in their judgment, a suitable person to fill the said vacancy, and they therefore offer for adoption the following resolution:

Resolved, That the Rev. James Mulchahey, D. D , be, and is hereby nominated by the Convention of this Diocese, to the Board of Trustees of the General Theological Seminary, to fill the vacancy in the representation from the Diocese of New-York, caused by the removal of the Rev. Dr. Hollingsworth from that Diocese.

All which is respectfully submitted.

MORGAN DIX,
GEO. JARVIS GEER,
CAMBRIDGE LIVINGSTON,
ANTHONY B. MCDONALD.

On motion of the Rev. Dr. Dix,

The Resolution recommended in this Report was adopted.

On motion of the same, it was

Ordered, That the Secretary of this Convention send a copy of this Resolution to the Board of Trustees of the General Theological Seminary.

The Report of the Trustees of the Parochial Fund was presented and read:

Report

OF THE TRUSTEES OF THE PAROCHIAL FUND.

The Trustees of the Parochial Fund respectfully report:

That the account of the Treasurer hereto annexed shows the situation of the funds, the cash on hand, and the securities in which the funds are invested.

In reference to the amount of eight thousand dollars stated to be invested on a bond and mortgage, they report:

That several years past a considerable sum of money was collected in England and placed in the hands of Trustees there, to be remitted to Trustees in New-York for the benefit of the Church of the Messiah. Such remittance was made, invested in stocks of the United States, and the dividends paid to and for the benefit of such Church.

The said Church, whose members were colored persons, became extinct as an organization, and has, by a general consent, been merged in the Church of St. Philip's, also of colored persons.

A consent was signed by the surviving Trustees, both in England and this country, that the funds be placed in charge of the Trustees of the Parochial Fund in the Diocese of New-York, to be applied to the use and benefit of the Church of St. Philip's in New-York, and the support of the officiating Minister thereof.

In consequence the stocks and cash were transferred to the former Treasurer of this Board. They have been sold, and the proceeds invested in the bond and mortgage of D. Maguire for $8,300, mentioned in the Treasurer's account. The interest has been paid to or for the use of the Minister of such Church.

Respectfully submitted.

MURRAY HOFFMAN, *President*,
WM. ALEX. SMITH, *Secretary*,
F. S. WINSTON,
} *Trustees.*

NEW-YORK, *September 29th*, 1875.

The Parochial Fund in account with WM. ALEX. SMITH, *Treasurer.*

1874.	DR.	
Nov. 6.	To cash paid for $500 U. S. 5 per cent. 10-40 bond, 112¼,	$562 50
1875.		
April 28.	" " St. Philip's Church, New-York, amount of interest on mortgage,................	297 25
July 6.	" " " " "	290 50
	Balance,..	291 27
		$1,441 52

1874.	CR.		
Sept. 30.	Balance per last report,........................		$44 57
Nov. 2.	By cash rec. for $500 U. S. 5-20 coupons of 1862, called in,		541 25
1875.			
Jan. 4.	" " interest, 6 months, on bond and mortgage of D. Maguire for $8,300,..........	$290 50	
	Balance of interest due from estate of J. F. De Peyster,..............	6 75	297 25
March 1.	" " interest on $1,500 U. S. 5 per cent. 10-40 bonds, $37 50, gold, at 114⅝,............		43 03
June 1.	" " interest, 6 months, on mortgage, $8,300,.....		290 50
Sept. 8.	" " " on $1,500 U. S. 5 per cent. 10-40 bonds, $37 50, gold, at 114⅛,............		42 80
29.	" " interest on $2,600 U. S. 6 per cent. 5-20 of 1867, 12 months, $156, gold, at 116⅝,.....		182 12
			$1,441 52

Sept. 30. Balance,.. $291 27

On hand:

$1,500 U. S. 5 per cent. 10-40 bonds.

$2,600 U. S. 6 per cent. 5-20 registered bonds of 1867.

Deposited in Greenwich Savings Bank, $544 33.

Deposited in Manhattan Savings Institution, $785 18.

Deposited in Institution for Savings of Merchants' Clerks, $1,078 69.

Bond and mortgage of D. Maguire, (the interest of which is appropriated to St. Philip's Colored Church, New-York,) $8,300.

WM. ALEX. SMITH,
Treasurer.

NEW-YORK, *September 30th*, 1875.

The Convention proceeded to fill two vacancies among the Trustees of the Parochial Fund, in consequence of the expiration of terms of office.

Whereupon, ballot was unanimously dispensed with, and Hon. John Jay and William Alexander Smith, Esq., were elected as such until October 1, 1878.

The Report of the Trustees of the Sands' Fund was presented and read:

Report

OF THE TRUSTEES OF THE SANDS' FUND.

The Trustees of the Sands' Fund respectfully report:

That there has been received since their Report to the last Convention, for interest on the Fund,...........................	$210 00
That there has been paid during the same period to the Bishop for the purposes of the Fund,..................	$210 00

Principal invested, $3,000.

HORATIO POTTER, *Bishop of New-York*,
WM. E. EIGENBRODT, *Secretary of the Convention of the Diocese of New-York*,
EDWARD F. DE LANCEY, *Treasurer of the Convention*, } *Trustees.*

Dated NEW-YORK, *September* 29, 1875.

The Report of the Trustees of St. Stephen's College, Annandale, was presented and read:

Report

OF ST. STEPHEN'S COLLEGE, ANNANDALE.

The following report is submitted to the Convention of the Diocese of New-York in behalf of the Trustees of St. Stephen's College:

There were seventy-three Students in attendance the last academic year. Eight graduated at the Commencement, June 17th. The new year began on the 8th of this month. There are now in attendance 76 young men; all of whom are communicants but three, and about 70 of whom are preparing for the sacred ministry.

R. B. FAIRBAIRN,
Warden, &c.

ANNANDALE, *Sept.* 27, 1875.

The Report of the Standing Committee on the Diocesan Fund was presented and read:

Report

OF THE STANDING COMMITTEE ON THE DIOCESAN FUND.

The Standing Committee on the Diocesan Fund respectfully recommend to the Convention the adoption of the following Resolution, viz.:

Resolved, That there be paid to the Clergy attending the Convention, who reside more than twenty miles from the place of meeting, and whose Parishes have contributed to the fund, as required by the Canon, seven cents per mile for every mile of the distance from their respective Parishes; and that the remainder be appropriated to paying for the printing of the Journal of the Convention, and the Canonical customary and prescribed expenses of the Diocese.

THOMAS GALLAUDET, *Chairman*.
J. N. GALLEHER, S. T. D.,
CHARLES TRACY,
EDWARD F. DE LANCEY.

The Resolution recommended in this Report was adopted.

The Report of the New-York Protestant Episcopal City Mission Society was presented and read:

Report

OF THE NEW-YORK PROTESTANT EPISCOPAL CITY MISSION SOCIETY.

The Executive Committee of the New-York Protestant Episcopal City Mission Society respectfully report as follows:

That the official year ending March 31, 1875, has been rich in God's manifold blessings upon the work done in His name. In no preceding year has so much been accomplished, so much real charity bestowed, so much sickness and suffering alleviated, especially among children. The position of the Society to-day is one of which the Church should be proud; and the review of what has been done, and is now doing, should rouse the members thereof to most vigorous efforts to sustain it fully, and make it the rallying centre of the noblest and best work among those whom no other Christian influence reaches.

1. Look at its field. It goes among the poorest and most ignorant; it visits the sick in Bellevue, Charity, Roosevelt, the Woman's and Ward's

Island Hospitals; it goes to the Tombs, the County Jail, the Essex, Yorkville and Harlem Prisons; to the Colored Home and the House of Detention; to the Penitentiary and Work House, and speaks of repentance and hope; it cheers and comforts the inmates of the Alms House, the Lunatic, Orphan and Infant Asylums, and the Leake and Watts Orphan House; at Bethlehem Chapel it relieves the destitute, and instructs the Germans ignorant of the Church and the way of salvation by Jesus Christ; at St. Barnabas' House it shelters the homeless women and children, feeds the hungry, clothes the naked, is a friend to the friendless, and every where labors to lift up the fallen and save the lost. It is the work of all others which we, as Churchmen and as citizens, ought to be the least willing to neglect; work at our own doors, which, if we do neglect, will be left undone, and which is especially commended to us by that most gracious of all sanctions: "Inasmuch as ye have done it unto one of the least of these My brethren, ye have done it unto Me."

Only $30,000 are required to do it.

2. Look at the means we have had to do with.

From all sources,—collections in churches, collections by the financial agent and voluntary contributions,—we have received for all purposes outside of St. Barnabas' House, $12,172 79; for St. Barnabas' House, $5,828 60; making the sum total, $18,001 39.

To sustain seven missionaries, who devote their whole time and strength to the work of the Society, to keep open St. Barnabas' Chapel for regular Sunday and daily and week-day Services, and for its flourishing Sunday-School of 300 scholars; to provide Sunday Services at Bethlehem Chapel for the Germans west of Central Park, and for its Sunday and regular Day Schools, and to pay the expenses of the Day Nursery at St. Barnabas', required $18,151 81; to meet the wants of St. Barnabas' House required $8,057 40; to pay interest on bonds, $1,610; to defray the incidental expenses of repairs, insurance, printing, burials, &c., required $1,567 32; making a total of $29,386 53, leaving a deficiency of $11,385 14.

Providentially we had a balance from the legacies of Mr. and Mrs. Van Horne, which had been laid aside as a fund towards rebuilding 306 Mulberry-street, and we were compelled, with great reluctance, to draw upon that balance in order to meet the deficiency and avoid a floating debt.

Now the fact which gives special significance to this report is this: an annual deficiency is not a new thing in the history of the Society; it has been a stubborn fact to contend with for many years; and, in consequence thereof, notwithstanding all our appeals in Churches and to individuals, we have, from time to time, been forced to mortgage the property of the Society, which is valued at $52,000, in order to avoid an increasing debt, or very largely to reduce the work.

We did not dare to shut our ears to the cry of the 154,000 spiritually destitute, the outcasts of society, annually found in the prisons and hospitals and almshouse; we did not dare to turn away from the door of St. Barnabas' House the homeless and friendless women and children constantly applying there for refuge and relief; we did not dare to turn our faces away from the sick and the needy begging for care and good nursing; and we flattered ourselves, year by year, that our brethren, and through them, our fellow-citizens, would see and feel the urgent necessity and the practical bearings of this work, and would adequately support us in doing it. But we were mistaken.

We are now bankrupt! We have drained every possible resource, and yet we are in debt for August's expenses, and have nothing to pay the bills maturing on the first of September next.

This is a most mortifying report to make to a Convention like this, especially when we consider the numbers, the great influence and the vast wealth of the Church in this city, and the immense sums of money which are annually given by our own people to outside objects. The fault is not in the giving to these objects, but in neglecting to give, first, to sustain this Christ-like work at our own doors.

The Church and the world about us would be justly amazed and shocked if we should suspend operations, and we should doubtless be censured for abandoning such a charitable work But does the whole responsibility rest upon us? Can it be reasonably expected that we, as the Executive Committee, shall carry on this enterprise? It cannot be! It ought not to be, were it possible, for it is a field for all to labor in; it is a toil for Christ in His own chosen sphere, and among those whom He came specially to seek and to save.

The following summary tells what has been done from April 1, 1874, to March 31, 1875: 1,498 public and private services, with an aggregate attendance of 106,071 persons; Holy Communion administered to 868 distinct individuals; 341 baptisms; 65 persons confirmed: 297 bodies received Christian burial; an average attendance of 145 at the Sunday-School in St. Barnabas' Chapel, and of 94 in Bethlehem Chapel; an average of 87 children present in the Day School at Bethlehem Chapel, and of 28 in St. Barnabas' and the Day Nursery; an average of 112 girls present in the Industrial School held in St. Barnabas' Chapel and Free Reading Room, and of 60 at Bethlehem Chapel; an average of 41 women supplied with sewing weekly by the St Barnabas' Industrial Association; 2 200 families visited, and more or less assisted; 19,505 individuals visited, conversed and prayed with, and relieved, when needy, in tenement houses and institutions; an average of 305 books drawn weekly from the libraries on Blackwell's Island, and an aggregate of 16,436 papers distributed; an average of 50 books drawn from the "Gilbert Library" in the Tombs, and papers and magazines without count distributed weekly in all the institutions under the charge of our Missionaries.

The number of women and children received into St. Barnabas' House from April 1, 1874, to March 31, 1875, was 1,663, and the number of children received into the Day Nursery, 102, making a total of 1,763. The amount paid by the mothers who go out to work daily while their children are cared for and fed and instructed in the Day Nursery, was $137 98. 106,865 free meals, and 20,548 free lodgings were furnished, being an increase over last year of 12,507 meals, and 1,327 lodgings.

And what shall we say more? It were easy enough to go into most interesting detail regarding each department of labor, and give abundant evidence of encouraging results, but it is not necessary now. It will all appear in good time in the printed Annual Report.

The work is going on—must go on; to stop, to reduce, would be shameful! For the honor of God and His Church, and the salvation of priceless souls, let us all who are here present—Clergy and Laity—take hold of it in earnest, and go forth to urge our brethren to take hold of it, till the whole Church is so aroused and warmed as to resolve, that whatever else is done or left undone, this City Mission, this essentially home work, shall henceforth be done, and well done!

The Clergy in the employ of the Society are the Rev. C. T. Woodruff, Superintendent; the Rev. S F. Holmes, Chaplain of St. Barnabas' Chapel; the Rev. F. Oertel, Pastor of Bethlehem Chapel; the Rev. V. Van Roosbroeck, Chaplain at Bellevue Hospital; the Rev. J. G. B Heath, Missionary to the Tombs, Homes, Prisons, &c.; the Rev. Wm. G. French, Missionary on Blackwell's Island; the Rev. N. F. Ludlum, Financial Agent and Visitor to the Roosevelt Hospital; Mr. John Schark is the teacher of the German Day School in connection with Bethlehem Chapel.

The officers of the Society are: *President*, (*ex-officio*,) the Rt. Rev. Horatio Potter, D. D., LL. D., D. C. L. *Vice-Presidents*, Rev. T. M. Peters, D. D., Rev. William F. Morgan, D. D., Mr. Frederick S. Winston, Mr. Thomas Eggleston. *Secretary*, Mr. Isaac H. Holmes. *Treasurer*, Mr. Robert S. Holt.

Executive Committee.—The Rt. Rev. the Bishop of the Diocese, Rev. T. M. Peters, D. D., Rev. Wm. F. Morgan, D. D., Rev. E. A. Washburn, D. D., Rev. Thomas Gallaudet, D. D., Rev. G. J. Geer, D. D., Rev. Henry C. Potter, D. D., Rev. C. C. Tiffany, Rev. Arthur Brooks, Messrs. Frederick S. Winston, Thomas Eggleston, Wm. Alex. Smith, Robert S. Holt, James W. Elliott, M. D., Geo. R. Schieffelin, Adam T. Sackett, Isaac H. Holmes, Charles Spear, John H. Boynton, Peter G. Tiemann, Alfred M. Hoyt, William Borden, Henry E. Pellew, James Pott.

The Rev. N. F. Ludlum is the *Financial Agent*.

All of which is respectfully submitted.

By order of the Executive Committee.

CURTISS T. WOODRUFF,
Superintendent of the New-York Protestant Episcopal City Mission Society.

NEW-YORK, *September* 30, 1875.

Mr. Charles Tracy, from the Special Committee on a communication from the Diocese of Albany, presented and read the following Report:

Report

OF SPECIAL COMMITTEE ON COMMUNICATION FROM THE DIOCESE OF ALBANY.

To the Convention of the Diocese of New-York:

The Special Committee, to which were referred the Communication from the Diocese of Albany, and also the Account rendered by Mr. Edward Haight, Treasurer, of funds raised by subscription in its aid, respectfully report as follows:

The subject of the communication is not new. It has been considered carefully and disposed of by former Conventions of this Diocese.

When the division of the Diocese, by setting off the Dioceses of Albany and Long Island, first was proposed, it was distinctly declared here in Convention and fully understood, that, if the proposal was carried into effect, the Episcopal Fund should be left intact, and be held entire for the support of the Episcopate in this Diocese. All that followed, to and including the creation of the new Dioceses, was upon that understanding; and the consent to the division, given here, did not express or imply any interference with that fund.

This Convention has no right or legal authority to divert the Fund to the use of another Diocese

In short, there is no foundation for any claim of the Diocese of Albany to a division of the Fund.

The Journals of the Convention in past years contain reports and proceedings which your Committee deem conclusive on this subject.

The Convention of 1869 adopted the following resolution:

"*Resolved*, That, in the opinion of this Convention, the Episcopal Fund of "this Diocese is solemnly and inalienably pledged to the support of the "Episcopate of New-York, and may not be diverted to the maintenance of "the Episcopate of Long Island or the Episcopate of Albany."

Your Committee see no cause for reconsidering that resolution, or disturbing the final decision then carefully and deliberately made and recorded

Nor has the Convention come short of its duty in respect to any reasonable expectations of voluntary aid arising from the former unity of the several Dioceses, and from sympathy, fraternity and common Christian aims and pursuits of them all, and the proprieties of good neighborhood. This Convention, in 1867, appointed a Committee "on the enlargement of the endowment for the Diocese of Albany," which Committee was renewed in 1868; and by its Chairman, Rev Dr. W. F Morgan, made a report in 1869, showing their diligent efforts to obtain subscriptions for that purpose from the laymen of this Diocese, and that the sum of $1,325 had been thus raised; and at its own request, that Committee was discharged. The same Convention appointed a new Committee, of which Rev. Dr. A. B. Beach was Chairman, to prosecute still further efforts to obtain moneys for the endowment of the Episcopate of the Albany Diocese. The second Committee presented to the Convention in 1870 a report, signed by three Clergymen and three laymen, showing that they had made great efforts, but that only $155 had been received by the Treasurer during the year; and the Committee, at its own request, was discharged.

The Convention of 1871 received a report from Mr. Edward Haight, Treasurer, showing that the whole amount which had come to his hands from this source was $1,428 72, and that the same, except a very small item, stood invested in the United States Trust Company. Yearly reports from Mr. Haight have been presented from time to time to and including the present year, showing the same state of things.

Your Committee find an account in the United States Trust Company in the name of "Edward Haight, Treasurer for funds of the Diocese of Albany," which stands credited with $1,283 72, deposited February 21, 1870, and $150 deposited March 9, 1870; total, $1,433 72. The amount draws interest at four per cent. a year, and the interest accrued on this amount has so increased the fund that it now amounts to $1,759 97.

This money, the gift of individuals, has been offered to the Diocese of Albany, as your Committee are informed.

The Convention of this Diocese never promised to assist the Diocese of Albany in this regard, but it endeavored to do so by seeking contributions among the laity; and this it has tried in the most faithful manner through the labors of two Committees zealous in the cause. The Convention never guaranteed success in the attempt. It gave no assurance of aid. Not having power to require contributions to this object by assessing the Parishes, it has done its utmost in the proper direction, and now is under no further obligations in the matter.

Your Committee therefore recommend that no further action be had on the communication so referred; and that a copy of this report be transmitted to the Diocese of Albany.

All which is respectfully submitted.

CHARLES TRACY,
JAMES EMOTT,
E. W. WASHBURN,
MORGAN DIX,
CAMBRIDGE LIVINGSTON.

NEW-YORK, *September* 30, 1875.

On motion of Mr. Tracy, it was

Resolved, That this Report be accepted, and the recommendation contained therein approved by this Convention.

Ordered, That a copy of this Report be transmitted by the Secretary of this House to the Diocese of Albany.

The Inspectors of the Votes for the Missionary Committee presented their Reports.

Whereupon the following persons were declared duly elected by the concurrent votes of the Clergy and Laity, to be

THE MISSIONARY COMMITTEE.

CLERGY.

Rev. ALFRED B. BEACH, D. D.,
CORNELIUS E. SWOPE, D. D.,
JAMES STARR CLARK, D. D.,
OCTAVIUS APPLEGATE,
CHRISTOPHER B. WYATT, D. D.

LAITY.

HAMILTON BRUCE, Esq.,
ANTHONY B. McDONALD,
WILLIAM M. KINGSLAND, Esq.,
JAMES POTT, Esq.,
C. A. HIGGINS, Esq.

The Inspectors of the Votes for the Standing Committee of the Diocese presented their Reports.

Whereupon the following persons were declared duly elected by the concurrent votes of the Clergy and Laity, to be members of

THE STANDING COMMITTEE OF THE DIOCESE.

CLERGY.

Rev. MORGAN DIX, D. D.,
WILLIAM E. EIGENBRODT, D. D.,
ISAAC H. TUTTLE, D. D.

LAITY.

STEPHEN P. NASH, Esq.,
LLOYD W. WELLS, Esq.,
HENRY DRISLER, LL. D.

The Convention proceeded to the election of one Clerical and of one Lay member of the Standing Committee.

The names of the Clergy were called by the Secretary, and of the Churches by the Assistant Secretary. The members having deposited their ballots, the Tellers retired to count the votes.

The Secretary informed the Convention, That he had received from the Secretary of the House of Deputies of the General Convention of the Protestant Episcopal Church in the United States the following communication, viz.:

THE GENERAL CONVENTION OF THE PROTESTANT EPISCOPAL CHURCH.

To the Secretary of the Convention of the Diocese of New-York:

Sir: In compliance with the requirements of Article 9 of the Constitution of the Church, I would hereby officially make known, through you, to the Diocesan Convention of New-York, the following proposed changes in the Constitution of the Protestant Episcopal Church in the United States of America, recommended by the General Convention of 1874, and to be finally acted upon by the General Convention of 1877, to wit:

I. It was, by concurrent action of the two Houses of the General Convention of 1874,

Resolved, That it be recommended and proposed that the following alteration be made in Article 5 of the Constitution, to wit: Insert at the end of the Article the words:

"The General Convention may, upon the application of the Bishop and Convention of an organized Diocese, setting forth that the territory of the Diocese is too large for due Episcopal supervision by the Bishop of such Diocese, set off a portion of such Diocesan territory, which shall thereupon be placed within, or constitute, a Missionary jurisdiction, as the House of Bishops may determine."

II. It was further

Resolved, That the following be proposed and made known to the several Dioceses as an amendment to Article 8 of the Constitution, to be added at the end of the Article as it now stands, to wit, the words:

"*Provided,* That the General Convention may by Canon arrange and set forth a shortened form of Morning and Evening Prayer, to be compiled wholly from the Book of Common Prayer."

III. It was further

Resolved, That the following be proposed as an amendment, by way of addition, to the 8th Article of the Constitution, to wit:

"*Provided, however*, That the General Convention shall have power, from time to time, to amend the Lectionary; but no act for this purpose shall be valid which is not voted for by a majority of the whole number of Bishops entitled to seats in the House of Bishops, and by a majority of all the Dioceses entitled to representation in the House of Deputies."

Resolved, second, That the Secretary of the House of Deputies cause the foregoing proposed amendment of the Constitution to be made known to the several Dioceses, according to the Constitution and Canons of the Church.

In testimony whereof, I have this day hereunto affixed my name,

WILLIAM STEVENS PERRY,

Secretary of the House of Deputies of the General Convention of the Protestant Episcopal Church.

GENEVA, N. Y., *January* 1, 1875.

On motion of the Secretary, it was

Resolved, That the proposed changes, recommended by the General Convention of 1874, to be made in the Constitution of the Protestant Episcopal Church in the United States, be referred to a Special Committee of Five, to report to the next Convention of the Church in this Diocese; and that the attention of the Committee is more especially requested to the proposed alteration in regulation of the Lectionary.

The Rev. Alfred B. Beach, D. D., the Rev. Hugh Miller Thompson, D. D., the Rev. Wm. E. Eigenbrodt, D. D., the Hon. Hamilton Fish and the Hon. Samuel B. Ruggles were appointed this Committee.

On motion of the Secretary, the following preamble and resolution were adopted, viz.:

Whereas There are now in this Diocese several Parishes, which, because of a change in the civil names of their several localities, have been obliged to take legal measures for a corresponding change of designation in their Acts of Incorporation; and other instances of this kind are likely to occur in the future; therefore, it is

Resolved, That all incorporated Parishes in union with this Convention, which are now or hereafter may be in this condition, lay before the Committee on the Incorporation and Admission of Churches evidence to show whether all the requirements of the law of the State of New-York, in order to such change, have or have not been complied with; and that, on the delivery of a Certificate from this Committee to the Bishop that the evidence is satisfactory, and its endorsement by him and transmission to the Secretary of the Convention, that Officer shall change accordingly the designation of such Parishes in the List of the Churches of this Diocese.

Ordered, That the Secretary report to the Convention all such Certificates from this Committee as may be so received by him; and that the same be printed in an Appendix to the Journal.

The Inspectors of the Votes for one Clerical and one Lay member of the Standing Committee of the Diocese presented their Reports.

Whereupon,

GEORGE MACCULLOUGH MILLER, Esq.,

was declared duly elected by the concurrent votes of the Clergy and Laity to be a member of the STANDING COMMITTEE OF THE DIOCESE.

The Convention proceeded to the election of one Clerical member of the Standing Committee of the Diocese.

Ballot was unanimously dispensed with.

Vote was taken by Orders; and

The Rev. WILLIAM F. MORGAN, D. D.,

was declared duly elected by the concurrent votes of the Clergy and Laity to be a member of the STANDING COMMITTEE OF THE DIOCESE.

On motion of the Rev. Alfred B. Beach, D. D., it was

Resolved, That the Form of Certificate of the Incorporation of Churches, formed and organized under the Act of April, 1854, laid before the Convention of 1873 by the Committee on Canon be referred to that Committee, with instructions to make it conform with the requirements of Sec. 1 of Canon IV. of 1872, and report the same at the next Convention.

On motion, it was

Resolved, That this Convention expresses hereby its thanks to the Hon. Hamilton Fish, for the laborious and valuable services which for many years he has given to the Church in this Diocese, as Chairman of the Committee on the Incorporation and Admission of Churches into union with this Convention; and that it deeply regrets that he has declined again to accept that office at the present session.

On motion of the Rev. Curtiss T. Woodruff, it was

Resolved, That the Rev. the Secretary be requested to convey to the Rev. Dr. Haight the expression on the part of this Convention of its regret at his continued absence from this body, its deep thankfulness to God for His great goodness in restoring him to some degree of his former health, praying also that he may yet live many days to bless the Church he has so long and faithfully served.

On motion of the Rev. Dr. Dix, it was

Resolved, That this Convention laments the loss sustained during the past year in the death of George Templeton Strong, Esq., long known for his devotion to the cause and the interests of the Church in this city and elsewhere, and appointed last year to a position of trust in this body, and that it records upon its Journal its respect for his character and its veneration for his memory.

On motion of the same, it was

Resolved, That this Convention has heard with deep regret the deaths of the Rev. Dr. H. E. Montgomery, and Messrs. George C. Collins, Wm. H. Aspinwall and Gouverneur Kemble, all of them distinguished in past years for their services to the Church in this Diocese, and places on record this testimony of its reverence for their memory and its sorrow for their loss.

On motion of the Secretary, it was

Resolved, That the thanks of this Convention be given to the Rector, Church Wardens and Vestrymen of Trinity Church, New-York, for the use of this Chapel by the Convention, and for their generous hospitality to its members.

On motion of the Rev. William T. Egbert, it was

Resolved, That 1,500 copies of the Journal of this Convention be published and distributed under the direction of the Secretary.

On motion of the Rev. John W. Kramer, M. D., it was

Resolved, That the thanks of this Convention be given to the Secretary, the Assistant Secretary and the Treasurer, for their labors.

On motion of the Secretary, it was

Resolved, That after the reading of the minutes and the usual devotions, this Convention adjourn *sine die*.

The minutes of this day's proceedings were read and approved.

The Doxology was sung by the members; Prayers were said by the Rev. Morgan Dix, D. D.; the Blessing was pronounced by the Bishop of the Diocese:

And the Convention adjourned *sine die*.

HORATIO POTTER, D. D., LL. D., D. C. L.,
Bishop of New-York and President of the Convention.

Attest:

WILLIAM E. EIGENBRODT, D. D., *Secretary*.
THEODORE A. EATON, D. D., *Assistant Secretary*.

Annual Address

OF

THE BISHOP OF NEW-YORK.

MY BRETHREN OF THE CLERGY AND LAITY:

Once more we are allowed the precious privilege of meeting in the Holy Place for united prayer and praise, for the word of godly counsel, for loving fellowship in the reception of the Holy Communion of the Body and Blood of our Lord, for a renewed clasping of fraternal hands, drawing heart nearer to heart, and for those duties of consultation and co-operative action, which we hope may contribute, with the blessing of Almighty God, to the furthering of our work in His Church. And surely, my dear brethren, to meet together for loving communion, and for the interchange of cordial greetings, as being all one body in Christ, could not be altogether in vain, even though there were no business to engage our attention. May God the Holy Ghost be with us and bless us in our reunion in His service, causing our hearts to warm toward each other, guiding us in our deliberations, and so breathing upon our spirits, that all our thoughts and words may be in keeping with the sanctity of the place, and with the religious importance of the duties in which we are here engaged!

On the present occasion it is not my purpose to detain you with any very extended communication. In my last annual Address, as I was then completing the twentieth year of my Episcopate, I took occasion to review the work and progress of the Diocese during that period, comparing the record of 1874 with that of 1854, and entering into details with regard to the present status of the Diocese. Those details, so recently given, supersede the necessity of much particularity on the same subjects at the present time.

The late session of the General Convention, at a season of the year favorable to Episcopal visitations, was so far extended as to diminish materially the portion of time which could be given to Diocesan engagements. A providential hindrance, also, arrested official duty for a brief period. Nevertheless, I was able to offer several visitations for which the Clergy were not prepared, or, to speak more properly, for which the Clergy saw no present need. Instead of arranging the visitations of the Diocese in a mere arbitrary and mechanical way, I have endeavored to meet, as far as possible, the wishes of the Clergy, going to them at those times when the visitation would be most useful.

And at the close of another Conventional year, it is with very especial thankfulness that I again find myself able to record, that in the midst of crowded appointments, and often rapid and extended journeys, no engagement has been interfered with through indisposition.

Among the latest official acts which I had the pleasure of reporting last year was the consecration of a memorial free Church, erected at the sole cost of one loving Christian parent, who thus made an offering unto the Lord, and set up a memorial to the departed in the place where the pious, affectionate young son had been called to be with his Saviour.

And immediately after the last Convention I had the very great pleasure of consecrating another free memorial Church—the Church of St. John the Evangelist—erected at Barrytown, Red Hook, by the widow, in memory of her departed husband. Mr. John Aspinwall, a faithful, loving Christian man, held in high esteem throughout the Diocese, and very extensively out of the Diocese. He had been for several years a Trustee and the Treasurer of St. Stephen's College, Annandale, and an annual munificent contributor to its current expenses. One of his very last acts previous to his sudden attack of indisposition, was to explain to the Rev. the Warden of the College every minute detail in his accounts as Treasurer, and in the business of the College; so that the Warden was able to proceed at once with the temporary charge of the duties of Treasurer, having every paper in its place, and every account adjusted—an example worthy of all imitation, and not without its use in these days.

Present at that consecration, among many friends of the departed and of his family, was his elder brother, Mr. William H. Aspinwall, then in delicate health, and since gone to his rest. He, too, was an earnest Christian man, whose faith was known by his works, everywhere known and honored throughout the country. I think I may be excused for the mention of one characteristic incident. Two or three years before his death, and when he appeared in perfect health, I had occasion to accompany him on a visit to some property left by the late Robert B. Minturn for religious and Church purposes in the neighborhood of Tarrytown, from which visit we returned to his country house, Highwood, north of that village. Soon after our arrival I found him writing in an account book, in a small apartment which he used as his office. On my offering to retire he requested me to remain and be seated, as he had nothing of importance to engage his attention. And then, in a very gentle, quiet way, and as if saying something which he would not mention to every one, he explained that it was his habit to make a record of all his contributions, great and small, as without such a precaution he would be unable at the end of the year to judge whether he had given what it was his duty to give, and that it was some time since he had made his usual entries. And then turning to me with a smile, he added, "I do not content myself with *one-tenth*—I do not think it enough." Most of you have heard of some of his numerous and very large contributions. Of such examples I shall speak further in a few moments.

The Free Memorial Church of St. John, erected by Mrs. John Aspinwall, is placed at a point where it is likely to be particularly useful, as it offers the privileges of the Church to many who, on account of the difficulty of reaching other places of worship, would have been liable to live in neglect of the saving influences and comforts of religion. The church is well attended, and is favored with the excellent ministrations of Prof. Hopson of St. Stephen's College. On the evening of the 17th of June, after having attended the Commencement exercises at St. Stephen's College, I visited St. John's Memorial Church for the first Confirmation held in it since its consecration. It was a touching, soothing service, something to be deeply thankful for, awakening grateful, loving thoughts of the past, as well as bright, heart-cheering hopes for the future.

I am tempted to indulge in one further incident. At the close of the service, and as I was about to leave the church, I was accosted by a young man, who modestly introduced himself, saying—what is often mentioned to me by strangers in various parts of the Diocese, and what always gives me lively pleasure—that many years before he had been confirmed by me; that it was in a distant place, and when he was quite young; and that he had always remembered and had thought much of one observation I had made to the confirmed. Seeing, I suppose, that there were some quite young persons among them, at least this one, who now stood before me a Christian young man, I had reminded them (as I have others) that "our Blessed Lord, our great Pattern in all things, was found at twelve years of age in the Temple, already earnestly engaged about His Father's business"—an observation, no doubt, thrown out as an encouragement and incentive to *them*, as well as a slight hint to Christian parents not to be too slow in encouraging and instructing their children to come to their Heavenly Father in Confirmation, to seal their devotion to Him, to have Him seal His love and mercy to them—come to the Divine Helper for the grace and strength which alone can enable them to "fight the good fight of faith," enable them to keep themselves in peace and purity, and at last to win the crown of righteousness. It was a gentle hint to Christian parents not to be too backward in "bringing their children" (to use the words of the Church in her injunction to parents and sponsors:) "Ye shall *take care* that this child *be brought to* the Bishop to be confirmed by him so soon"—and so on: meet care in preparation previously being, of course, presupposed. And the *thought* of his blessed Lord in the temple at twelve years of age, already feeling that He "*must* be about His Heavenly Father's business," had been year after year, in the heart of that child, that young man, on whom I had long ago, in a distant place, laid my unworthy hands, and who now stood before me, grateful for the step he had been moved to take, grateful for the blessing he had received. And I asked, "Where are you now, and how are you engaged?" He said, "I am in the General Theological Seminary, endeavoring to prepare for the sacred ministry of the Church." And so the grace of God had, as we trust, led on that young disciple through tender years, through the perils of opening youth, until he had separated himself for the work of the ministry! Surely there never was more need than now that we seek with God's help to turn the hearts of the fathers to the children, and the hearts of the children to their fathers, above all to *Him* who is God and Father of all, that they may be made meet for His service in every sphere where they are to move, and especially, if it may be so, meet for His service in the ministry of His Church. The thought of my meeting with that young man will always be associated in my mind along with many other touching and instructive things with my first Confirmation in that Free Memorial Church of St. John the Evangelist, Barrytown. Having spoken of one Confirmation because of the interesting and instructive circumstances connected with it, let me be excused for referring to another, which had peculiar features of interest, and which, if I mistake not, is well fitted to convey both encouragement and admonition. On Tuesday, the 13th day of April last, I found myself in the midst of a heavy snow storm, and eight miles distant from the rural church in which I had appointed Confirmation for that evening, and which I was to reach by a private conveyance. In the afternoon, when I had to decide on my movements, the snow was deep, still falling thickly, and with no prospect of speedy abatement. There could be little hope of finding many of the congregation or of the class for Confirmation present on such an evening, when no carriages seemed to be moving, and no paths could have been broken. There was some reason for judging that it would better for the Parish, and especially for the candidates, to postpone the visitation to a more favorable evening But I had other engagements for the following days, and besides I had, through all my Episcopate, made it an inflexible rule to be punctual in keeping my appointments, unless hindered by insurmountable obstacles Through the kindness of my host, in sending his carriage, I made my way through the storm, and along the deep, unopened ways, reaching the house of friends, near the church, an hour or two before the service. The friend who welcomed me said he "knew I would come," and assured me that I "would have a full church." I confess I was a little incredulous, for I saw no paths broken and many of the congregation and of the candidates had to come considerable distances, and the storm was unabated.

Well! the church *was* filled to its utmost capacity with an attentive, earnest-looking congregation; and there were forty-five candidates for confirmation, most of them of full age, every one of whom was present. It is true there were factories within the limits of the Parish, which, through the kindness of the proprietors, had continued in operation through the hard winter, employing many workmen, a portion of whom, with their families, attended the church, and were evidently taking care of themselves. But what brought them to church on that stormy night, through that deep snow? What brought those forty-five candidates with such brave resolution and such absolute punctuality? The numbers were large for a moderate sized Parish, even with a factory in it. Some of them were, no doubt, attached to the Church through early education. But what brought so many of them to prefer the Church to the other religious bodies, which are not apt to be inactive?

Would mere preaching, however able and earnest, have done it? Would cold perfunctory visiting have wrought such a miracle?—for it was a miracle of grace and mercy. We know how stolid and apathetic and passive and worldly poor human beings can be. We know how long they can even come to church, and hear preaching and Holy Scripture, and be in the midst of strong cries and supplications for grace and mercy, in the midst of swelling voices of praise and adoration, and yet for years and years hardly once think of their own salvation, hardly once think of *doing any thing*, taking *any step* toward a really religious life, hardly once open their souls to a more solemn view of their own inward state, of judgment and eternity, of their true duty to God and to their neighbor. It seems, at times, as if nothing but an earthquake would awaken them—no! and not even an earthquake! It must be the still small voice from Heaven, and a *revelation*, in some way, by some means, of the love and goodness and holiness of God. Ah! it must be love and goodness and holiness Incarnate. It must come near in human form! It was when God the Son took upon Him our flesh, and appeared among us in our likeness, and showed us of His love and pity, weeping over us and suffering for us, making the way of truth and duty and life plain before our faces, rekindling hope and courage by offering mercy and help, and by pointing to the opening heavens, it was then, that the flinty hearts softened and grew warm and full of love, and sprang up from the death apathy of sin to the life of righteousness.

No; if divine love and goodness are to touch and win human hearts, and especially hearts which are, as it were, *afar off* through hard labor and weary cares and rude neglect and coarse and debasing associations, if they are to be effectually reached by such high things as divine love and goodness, the love of goodness must appear not only in words, not only in abstract propositions, but they must appear incarnate, in human form, speaking, looking, acting, *loving and serving* in a way not to be mistaken or resisted. "Ye have not chosen Me,"* said our blessed Lord, "but *I* have chosen *you*," "and ordained you, that ye should go and bring forth fruit," "and that your fruit should remain." And the loving St. John said, "We love *Him* because He *first* loved us."† Yes; and it is ever so. Alienated souls—souls afar off from God, whether through worldy mindedness and senseless frivolity, or through weary exile in poverty and blinding misery, they are most surely won to the love of God and divine things, to the love of the Church and the means of grace, to the love of the Christian people and minister *in* the Church, *when love first goes out to them*—goes out to them tenderly, unmistakably in the sermon—goes out to them in more searching,

* John xv 16. † 1 John iv. 19

far-reaching ways in private through the minister and his loving lay-helpers in personal, individual manifestations of interest among the people, an interest which unobtrusively seeks to cheer and elevate the temporal life and almost insensibly to win them to the life eternal.

Yes! my dear brethren, those candidates, and others with them, flocked to the church on that, to them, memorable evening; toiling through the untrodden snow, and regardless of the blinding storm, because they knew and felt that in that holy place there was something warmer than the artificial warmth that was to comfort the body, something brighter than the natural light that was to make material forms visible to the eye of sense! There was *love* there—love human and divine; love which had found them out in their homes; love, which by the gentlest, tenderest ministries, had made many things bright around them, and above them, which were never bright before; a love which imperceptibly led them into more hopeful and peaceful ways, and brought them with a new longing into the House of God, that in the wilderness of this weary world they might be fed with bread from heaven! They had been lovingly led to "taste and see that the Lord was gracious," and they hastened on that night to worship with the friends they had learned to love, and to make a final offering of themselves unto their Father in Heaven, seeking increase of His grace, to live to Him and in Him for ever! I never looked upon a scene of more real living interest, or one in which there appeared to be a more tender Christian sympathy on the one side and on the other.

Pardon me, my dear brethren, for lingering so long over what may strike many as ordinary and commonplace. I wish it were more ordinary and familiar than it is. My dear brethren, you will utterly mistake my thought and my motive in putting this one case so much forward, if you suppose my words to involve any thing invidious, as if I were making comparisons, or suggesting that the signally good work done here was due to superior ability and unusual Christian faithfulness; nothing of the kind. I select the example because it brings out in clear strong relief what cannot be made so palpable in ordinary cases: the blessed results which come from a ministry, both clerical and lay, which, not confining itself to congregations or masses of people, deals discreetly, lovingly with individuals, and which aims, after the example of our Lord, to do good, if need be, in things temporal, both because that is in itself right, and because it opens the way for doing good more effectually in spiritual things.

No doubt the circumstances of this Parish were in some respects exceptional, and peculiarly favorable for the kind of work that was done there. There was, if I may say so, a large mass of material: laboring people, many of them new comers in the neighborhood, with loose and uncertain relations with the Church,—material which might be earnestly, lovingly dealt with, or shall we say it, almost wholly *let alone!* There was a Clergyman there, and there were a few lay people who could not, and would not, let *them alone!* They went among the laboring people, not to patronize them, but to help them, in a delicate sympathizing way, to make their hard life a little brighter, and with God's blessing, a little better. There was a lay gentleman of leisure, who gave up much of his time to contrive ways and means of making things cheerful and improving for them during the long dreary Winter. A reading-room was opened, and lecturers were brought in occasionally to fill a week evening with bright, fresh, cheery, animating things, things entertaining, something to make a pleasant change in the dull routine of life, and at the same time fitted to enlarge and improve the mind. That gentleman and his wife, along with other lay people of a similar spirit, were to be found in the Sunday-School and in the choir, and all this kindly, cheering intercourse was interpenetrated with a delicate, loving, religious influence, which, accompanied by that of the Rector and his wife, prepared the way for such a consummation and such a scene as that which I witnessed on the evening of my visitation. It is needless to add that the layman, who, with his wife, had all along shown so much interest and taken so much pains, and who resided some distance from the village, did not fail to come through the storm, were in their places, assisting in the music, and seemed to take as tender an interest in the *confirmed* as if they had been brothers and sisters in the flesh, as they were brothers and sisters in the Lord. So much may be done *by love*, where there is the opportunity, which does not often happen in the same measure. So much may be done by *painstaking*, *loving attention to individuals*, *when they are accessible;* done by the Clergy, and if there be the heart and the time for it, done by some of the Laity.

Happy the Rector of a Parish who has such an arm of strength at his side: Lay people, men and women, so loving, so willing, so discreet! And happier still, if possible, the Lay people who have such "a mind to work," to work for their Lord, and for the souls which He hath redeemed with His own most precious blood. Again I say, pardon this prolix narrative. I did not wish to put it in the shape of a barren generality. And if it should happen that any of the persons to whom I have referred are present, and incline to feel that I have in my statement approached too near to the indelicate, they too must pardon me. I have not spoken to flatter any one, much less to impeach or disparage any; but I have spoken so much at length, and with so much of particularity with the wish to *emphasize*, to bring forward into the very forefront of this day's argument a *form of Church work*, which I trust is far from being uncommon in the Church, which has been often inculcated with the highest authority, but which I think can never be too highly estimated, or too frequently or too earnestly recommended. My dear brethren, on this subject my convictions are profound and earnest, growing out of the very reason of things, and confirmed by the experience and observation of a long life, a life not deficient in opportunities for knowing and judging. The transcendent importance of preaching, preaching in public, setting forth the truth of God in the great congregation, reasoning of righteousness, temperance, and judgment to come, upholding and animating the faith and hope of the Christian, comforting the mourners, whether mourners for sin, or for nearest ones removed out of sight, exposing the fallacies of sin and unreason, keeping the whole social atmosphere filled with images of truth and duty, the importance of such preaching, such addresses in public assemblies of people, no one will be so weak as to call in question. But there are two kinds of preaching, public and private. Public expositions of divine truth and appeals to the conscience, which serve to keep up the general moral and religious tone of the community, and to prepare the way for addresses, which are more private, personal, pointed. The members of a congregation may be again and again interested, impressed by the representations of the preacher. Their religious sensibilities may be kept alive. But if they are to be moved to break away from their passive habits, if they are to be moved to take some positive forward step toward a religious life, it must generally be by the persuasive power of that preaching which comes to them in *private* in the form of a friendly, pointed, personal address, an address which, as being personal and friendly, touches the heart and the conscience, and can go into particulars, solving doubts, removing groundless scruples, strengthening the feeble knees, and like the Apostle, taking the impotent man "*by the hand and lifting him up!*" And this impotent, passive soul, which might have remained for years immovable in spite of the most able public preaching, being taken by the hand in private, may be seen in a few days delivered from the thraldom of old passive habits, and walking, and leaping, and praising God, as he enters joyfully into the temple, to do what he would have done years ago, had he been sooner spoken to in private, as he has been now. He would have become an active and useful Christian man; he would have found comfort and strength for his soul, for he would have been living within the inner circle of God's blessing; would have been complying with the conditions on which, through Christ Jesus, comfort and strength are freely given to the children of men. I fully believe that in the Church in this country there are at this moment thousands and tens of thousands of baptized Christian people living in a passive, unfruitful way, strangers to the Holy Communion, and to the comforts of religious hope and blessing, who would have been living, fruitful branches of the Vine, active Christians, had they been duly spoken to in private by their beloved pastors. I say not this as faulting your earnest and laborious ministry, but only to express strongly my sense of the *infinite importance of that private personal communication* which so readily goes to the heart, and moves to definite and decisive action.

During the last year or two the financial condition of the country has been greatly disturbed and depressed. The causes of this state of things are not far to seek—are involved in no mystery. In an internal war of four or five years, conducted on a gigantic scale, no small portion of the wealth of the nation must needs be absolutely extinguished; and then if trade be stimulated to excess by artificial excitements, and the people, under the influence of these excitements, rush into mad extravagance of living, and into adventurous speculative modes of doing business, a day of reckoning will be sure to come.

We must meet these trying circumstances in a brave, Christian spirit of faith and love. The dimensions of our Church work cannot be reduced and enlarged by turns to suit the ebb and flood of our temporal prosperity. The things that have been undertaken cannot be abandoned, or left without adequate support. Our missionaries, at home and in distant fields, are at their posts, and must be sustained and encouraged, unless we would incur discredit, and expose them to personal loss and mortification. Now, if ever, is a time for Christian people of wealth to give freely—to give for themselves, and also for *others*, who, though willing, are for the time unable to give.

In ordinary times Christian people of moderate means are not to be encouraged in laying the whole duty of giving upon the rich. All are to give. Giving for Christian purposes, to send the Gospel and the Church to the spiritually destitute, is a *duty* and a *privilege* for all. It is a means of grace, a part of our stewardship; and not to give, even out of our poverty, is to come short of duty and of blessing. "If ye have not been faithful in the unrighteous mammon, who shall commit unto you the true riches?" But these *are* times when those having an abundance may well hear an especial call. We hear it said that there are large sums lying unemployed, locked up from lack of confidence to let them go out for use. But *here* in *religious work* is a safe *investment* for all such hidden treasure: lay it up in heaven; lend it unto the Lord! And He will most surely repay. The good seed sown will spring up in an abundant harvest—some thirty, some sixty, some an hundred-fold of blessing to needy souls, blessing to the giver in this life and in the life eternal. Let us look unto Him who in His high estate emptied Himself of His glory, made Himself poor, that we, through His poverty, might be rich, rich in grace and peace here; rich in ineffable glory and blessedness among His saints and angels in heaven.

The Missions of the Diocese have, on the whole, been well sustained, and I have good hope that the close of the Convention year will find the Treasury without any deficit—the missionaries will not depart on their return to their labors without the very moderate sum which they will then be entitled to carry with them.

I cannot say so much for the treasury of the *City Mis-*

sion, one of the most useful and necessary works which the Church in this Diocese is prosecuting. "To the *poor* the Gospel must be preached," if we are to vindicate our *title* to the Christian name we bear. *St. Barnabas' House*—where so much good is done, so much misery relieved, where the hungry are fed, and where the unhappy wanderer finds Christian shelter and care until she can be sent back to her friends in safety; *St. Barnabas' House* and *Chapel* both need enlargement, in order to render *comfortably* the blessed service to which they are appointed. The tender, self-denying Sisters of the Good Shepherd, and the faithful Chaplain, do their work bravely and nobly, as do the missionaries who go to the institutions on the islands and to the prisons of the city. The executive officers who have the main charge of the affairs of the City Mission Society, ought not to spend anxious hours wasting their spirits in plans for securing the necessary means of prosecuting the work. Ample streams of supply ought to flow into their treasury almost without appeal from them. The wealth among the members of the Church in this city is ample for all such purposes, and cannot be devoted to more useful ministries.

Since our last Convention a service in Italian has been undertaken. It met with a most cordial welcome from a portion of the Italian-speaking population, and the attendance has been rapidly increasing in numbers and interest. Another priest of the same nationality is seeking admission into our ministry. He will find an ample sphere for the exercise of his office, either here or in the neighboring cities. Our Church services in German, in French and in Spanish are well conducted, and are increasing in interest, though they are not yet so well known or so well supported as they deserve to be.

My dear brethren, are we fully awake to the peculiar composition of this great central city of the Diocese, and of the country, and to the *duties* which it imposes upon us? It is *cosmopolitan* in its population. It draws its citizens from all nations. It has families from all countries, speaking the languages and worshipping, if they *do* worship, according to the customs of their old foreign homes. Their children will grow up speaking the tongue of their adopted country, and will in due time become incorporated in our English-speaking congregations unless, through our neglect, they have, in the mean season, lost their interest in religous things, and become alienated from religious observances. They ought to be provided with pastors who can speak to them in their own beloved tongue, who can familiarize them with the pure principles and simple forms of our worship, and so bring them to recognise the great truth, that, in the country of their adoption, there is a religion—a Church which is primitive and Apostolic, without being *mediæval*, without having the corrupt additions in doctrine and practice of the Middle Ages. It is to be hoped that the religious interests of these foreign-speaking people in our city will be duly borne in mind by our people of wealth, and that our endeavors to provide pastors and places of worship for these strangers will command their sympathy and support. When attending these foreign Churches or Chapels for confirmation, where the children and youth are kept for many months under a course of instruction and training, I have often been struck with the intelligent, cultivated air of the candidates, who, for the most part, were the children of poor laboring people, and I have been pleased in thinking how much this long course of instruction and training must have done, not only to establish them in good religious principles and dispositions, but also at the same time to raise them up for life to a higher plane of intelligence and cultivation of manners, in other words, to humanize and refine them, and so increasing the hope, that in future years they would be kept *above* those coarse and degrading habits, so injurious to themselves and to the community in which they live. It is estimated that, in the City of New-York alone, there is a population of about 250,000 Germans. In that part of the city south of Canal-street, there is a German peaking population of over 80,000, (more in number than he population of Detroit,) and yet, among them there re but two places of worship, where there is public rayer and preaching in their own language; and other arts of the city are scarcely better provided. Of thirty laces of worship in the city where alone there are serices, that can be understood by the Germans, but two re furnished by our Church. It has been thought that mportant aid might be rendered to the Church in this natter by some organized effort; and accordingly "The Church German Society" has been established, with the ope of securing the co-operation of such of the clergy nd laity of New-York and other Dioceses as might be nterested in the objects which it has in view. The purose of the Church German Society is,

1. To provide Hymnals, Service Books, and suitable ermons in the German Language for such American lergymen or lay readers as may be able and willing to onduct German services.

2. To search out young Germans of good education and bilities to be educated for the ministry in our Church.

3. To assist such young men in acquiring the necessary reparation for ministerial work in both languages, so hat they may be able to act as assistants in our American parish churches and missions.

4. To aid in the publication and circulation of such periodicals, books and tracts, as will lead the Germans n this country and abroad, to a better understanding of he position and principles of our Church: and on the other hand to the dissemination among our own people, of sound German literature, original and translated.

5. To act as a medium of communication between those Churchmen who are interested in the spiritual welfare of our German fellow-citizens, and to interest others.

Those who are interested in these important objects, are recommended to apply to, or communicate with the Rev. Mr. Siegmund, Corresponding Secretary of the Church German Society, at the office of the Society, No. 140 West 14th-street, New-York; a clergyman as well qualified to speak of German liturgies in their different phases and of German work in this country as any person in our Church.

Renewed acknowledgments are due for the good done by *woman's work* in the past year. I have already referred to the severe labors of the Sisters of the Good Shepherd in St. Barnabas' House. The *Sisters of Mercy* of the Holy Communion have a *Dispensary*, open daily, where about 6,000 prescriptions have been put up. Also a *Shelter* for respectable girls, where 437 homeless, but worthy, women have been received and placed in situations; sixteen aged women cared for. Also a Babies' Shelter and Day Nursery, where eighty little ones received the tender care of the Sisters—forty-seven in Shelter permanently, and thirty-three in Day Nursery. *School for Girls*, fifty-three scholars. Sisters' Bible Class have had eighty and ninety on the roll, besides inmates of the Shelter who always attend. Visits have been made to at least 800 families, and many meals given away.

There are now *three ladies' auxiliary associations* in the city. One auxiliary to the Domestic Committee has been engaged for three or four years in sending relief to missionaries and their families who are at work in remote parts of our own country. Another association of ladies, more recently formed, sends aid to our foreign missionaries and their families; and still another, "The Niobrara League," forwards aid and comfort to the missionaries among the Indians.

These associations of ladies do good, not only in the special way which they had in view in uniting for work, but by their frequent meetings and by the communications they receive from the distant missionaries whom they have cheered by their offerings and by their loving messages, their interest in mission work is kept alive and active, and naturally extends itself in the circles in which they move, thus helping to keep the whole Church well informed and deeply interested in Home and Foreign Mission work. Nor, in speaking of Woman's Work, must I omit to mention the satisfaction I have found in visiting the House in the Second Avenue occupied by the Sisters of the Community of St. John Baptist, chiefly sustained from the private property of one of the community. In the House they have a middle class school of girls, who receive a good English education, and are trained in housework and needlework. In the last few months some of them have been filling situations, where they have given entire satisfaction. The Sunday evening services in the Chapel in the House have been attended by friends and by the children and parents from the German Parish, who have thus been led to know and value the Church services. Since last October their works have been an *Industrial School* amongst the German population in the neighborhood of the Church of the Nativity, with an average attendance of over ninety girls; a *Sunday-School*, with an average attendance of between fifty and sixty; an Employment Society, which provided sewing for nearly forty women in the Parish; a daily *Infant School*, with an average attendance of twenty; a weekly Singing Class of about thirty children. The Sisters visit in the Parish daily, aid the sick, prepare candidates for the Sacraments, and urge a regular attendance on the German Church services, which have proved attractive to that people. All this work is carried on in a very quiet, noiseless way, and cannot but enlist the sympathy of those who come to know it. The Sisters of St. Mary are going on with their work in the two schools, in the House of Mercy and in the Child's Hospital. The Sisters of St. Mary were organized for work among all classes of people, the rich as well as the poor. And so, while some are engaged in works of charity and mercy among the poor and wretched, others of their number are employed in the work of education, in training the daughters of the higher classes for their future responsibilities in the Church of God. At the urgent desire of the Bishop of Tennessee, a number of the Sisters were sent to Memphis two years ago. They now have a flourishing school, numbering between ninety and a hundred pupils, occupying a large and commodious house, with garden and play-ground adjoining the Cathedral and Bishop's house; while they still continue the work begun at the fearful time of the yellow fever epidemic of visiting the sick and poor, caring for their wants both bodily and spiritual. They have kept no record of the number of families visited; but they have brought between forty and fifty children and adults to baptism.

In the Diocese of New-York they have two schools, both in the most prosperous condition, where a hundred and fifty young girls or more come under their instruction. They have a *Hospital* for children, which is asking now for more room, where little patients are received entirely free of charge. They have the care of the House of Mercy, with its seventy or eighty inmates, and of Trinity Infirmary. And one of their number devotes all her time to visiting the city Institutions: prisons and asylums on the Islands in the East River and the poor in their own homes.

I cannot close this communication without reminding you that there is a Fund for the Relief of the Aged and Infirm Clergy of the Diocese.* Recent appeals made to me by some of my afflicted brethren for aid from that Fund have much touched my feelings, as they would yours, were you cognizant of the cases. Sure I am that no year will be allowed by you to pass without a contribution to that Fund. The day usually appropriated to that grateful duty is the day of our annual Thanksgiving, a very suitable one for such an offering, an offering which should worthily express our sense of the great mercies we have received, and also our affectionate esteem and veneration for the spiritual pastors who minister in heavenly things.

---

* It deserves to be stated that, during the past year, the sum expended on beneficiaries has been $4,698, while the sum received from the Parishes has been $3,324 85, and that there have been *no expenses for management.*

DETAILED ACCOUNT OF VISITATIONS AND ACTS.

The following is an account of the places visited and the Episcopal Acts performed by me since the last Convention:

1874. *Oct.* 4, *Eighteenth Sunday after Trinity*, A. M.—I consecrated the Free Memorial Church of St. John the Evangelist at Barrytown, Red Hook, and delivered an address. This Church is erected by Mrs. John L. Aspinwall in memory of her late husband.

P. M.—In the Holy Innocents' Chapel of St. Stephen's College, Annandale, I confirmed *four* persons, and briefly addressed them.

Oct. 6, *Tuesday*, P. M.—I laid the corner-stone of Trinity Church, Morrisania, and made a brief address. An address was also delivered by the Rev. Dr. Seymour.

Oct. 7, *Wednesday*.—I took part in the opening services of the General Convention, and continued my attendance up to the closing services, Tuesday evening, Nov. 3d.

Oct. 20, *Tuesday*, Evening.—In Christ Church, New-York, I presided at a meeting called to consider the subject of an Evangelization Society.

Oct. 21, *Wednesday*, A. M.—In Grace Church, New-York, I celebrated the Holy Communion for the Association of the Alumni of the General Theological Seminary, and afterwards presided at their re-union at breakfast

P. M., 4½ o'clock.—In the Chapel of Calvary Church, New-York, I presided at a meeting of the Clergy called to take action in memory of the late Rev. Henry E. Montgomery, D. D., Rector of the Church of the Incarnation, New-York

Evening.—In the Church of the Transfiguration, New-York, I presided at a meeting called in behalf of the University of the South, and made a brief address.

Oct. 25, *Sunday*, Evening—In the Church of the Transfiguration, New-York, I presided at a meeting called to consider the subject of forming a Church Building Society.

Oct. 27, *Tuesday*, P. M.—In Grace Church, New-York, I presided at the Anniversary of the Ladies' Domestic Missionary Relief Association.

Nov. 1, *All Saints', and Twenty-second Sunday after Trinity*, A. M.—In St. Thomas' Church, Amenia Union, I preached, confirmed *twelve*, and addressed them.

P. M.—In Amenia Village I preached, and confirmed *one* person.

Nov. 4, *Wednesday*, Evening.—I presided at a joint meeting of the Domestic and Foreign Missionary Committees.

Nov. 8, *Twenty-third Sunday after Trinity*, A. M.—In Grace Church, New-York, I assisted at the consecration of the very Rev. the Dean of Haiti, the Rev. James Theodore Holley, D. D , uniting in the laying on of hands, &c.

Nov. 20.—In St. George's Church, Newburgh, at a special ordination, the Rev. Dr. Seymour, of the General Theological Seminary, preaching, I admitted to the Diaconate Mr. George Love, A. B., and I advanced to the Priesthood the Rev. Walter R. Gardner, the Rev. George W Hinckle and the Rev. John C. Tebbetts. After the service there was a very pleasing re-union of the large number of the Clergy present, and of the Parishioners and visitors, amounting in all to 200 or more, at a luncheon in one of the school rooms adjacent to the Church. All hearts, the givers and receivers alike, seemed cheered by the services and the social enjoyments of the day.

P M.—I presided at a business meeting of the Western Convocation.

Evening.—In the same Church, I preached, confirmed *six* at a special confirmation, (the second of the year,) and addressed them.

Nov. 21, *Saturday*, P. M.—In Trinity Church, Fishkill, I confirmed *six*, and addressed them and the congregation.

Nov. 22, *Twenty-fifth Sunday after Trinity*, Evening.—In Zion Church, New-York, the Rev. Dr. Seymour preaching, I presided at the annual meeting of the Sunday-School Association.

Nov. 24, *Tuesday*, Evening.—In St. Paul's Church, Spring Valley, I preached, confirmed *three*, and briefly addressed them.

Nov. 27, *Friday*, Evening.—In St. Andrew's Church, Walden, I preached, confirmed *eleven*, and addressed them.

Nov. 30, *St. Andrew's Day*, *Monday*, A. M.—In the Chapel of the General Theological Seminary, New-York, on occasion of the Annual Matriculation of the Junior Class, I addressed the Students of the Seminary, and celebrated the Holy Eucharist.

Dec. 3, *Thursday*, A. M.—In Trinity Chapel, New-York, I officiated at the funeral of the Rev. Francis C. Wainwright.

Dec. 5, *Saturday*, A. M —In the Chapel of the Alms House on Blackwell's Island, I confirmed *twelve*, and addressed them. I afterwards confirmed *three* in the Infirmary, making *fifteen* in all.

Dec. 6, *Second Sunday in Advent*, A. M —In St. Mary's Church, Manhattanville, New-York, I preached, confirmed *nine*, and addressed them, and celebrated the Holy Eucharist, assisted by the Rector

Dec. 7, *Monday*, Evening.—Presided at a meeting of the Foreign Committee.

Dec. 8, *Tuesday*, P. M.—I presided at a meeting of the Trustees of the House of Mercy, New-York.

Dec 10, *Thursday*, A. M —In St Paul's Church, Poughkeepsie, I met the Convocation of Dutchess County, and after A. M. prayer and a sermon by the Rev. the Warden of St Stephen's College, Annandale, I celebrated the Holy Eucharist, assisted by the Rector, and presided at a business meeting of the Convocation.

Dec. 13, *Third Sunday in Advent*, A. M.—In St. Ann's Church, New-York, I preached, and at a Special Confirmation confirmed *one* person from the Diocese of Massachusetts.

Dec. 14, *Monday*, P. M.—I presided at a stated meeting of the Standing Committee of the General Theological Seminary, New-York.

Dec. 15, *Tuesday*, Evening.—I presided at a meeting of the Executive Committee of the City Mission Society, New-York.

Dec. 16, *Wednesday*, A. M.—In the Church of St. Ambrose, New-York, I took part in the funeral services for the late Rector, the Rev. Frederick Sill. The character of the attendance and the feeling of the people bore witness to his services and worth.

P. M.—I attended the Anniversary of the Home for Old Men and Aged Couples, New-York, and made a short address. The Institution is one of touching interest, and is well sustained.

Dec. 20, *Fourth Sunday in Advent*, A. M.—In the Church of St. Esprit, New-York, I addressed the congregation on the encouraging prospects opening before them under the ministrations of their recently settled minister, the Rev. Mr. Pons, and then spoke to them on some of the Lessons of the Season of Advent.

Evening.—In St. Chrysostom's Chapel, New-York, I preached, in place of the Rev. Frederick Sill, late Rector of St. Ambrose Church, who was to have preached on this evening for a particular purpose in St. Chrysostom's Chapel.

Dec. 23, *Wednesday*, A. M.—In St. Ann's Church, New-York, I preached, and advanced the Rev. Zina Doty to the Priesthood, assisted in the service by the Rev. Dr. Tyng and the Rector.

Dec. 25, *Christmas Day*, A. M.—In Trinity Church, Morrisania, I preached, on occasion of the first opening of the new edifice for Divine Service.

1875. *Jan.* 17, *Second Sunday after the Epiphany*, A. M —I preached in St. Michael's Church, Bloomingdale, N. Y.

Evening.—I preached in St. Barnabas' Chapel, New-York.

Jan. 18, *Monday*, Evening.—I presided at the stated meeting of the Domestic Committee.

Jan. 19, *Tuesday*, Evening —I received a number of the Clergy of the city to consult on a portion of our Christian work.

Jan. 24, *Septuagesima Sunday*, A. M.—I preached in St. Luke's Church, New-York, and celebrated the Holy Eucharist, assisted by the Rector and Assistant Minister, and visited the admirable Sunday-Schools of the Parish.

Jan. 25, *Monday*, *Conversion of St. Paul*, A M.—In St. Ann's Church, New-York, I received a Probationer into the Sisterhood of the Good Shepherd, celebrating the Holy Eucharist, and addressed a few words of sympathy and encouragement to the Sisters, who are leading a laborious and exceedingly useful life.

Jan. 27, *Wednesday*, Evening.—I met a Committee on business connected with Columbia College, New-York

Jan. 31, *Sexagesima Sunday*, A. M.—I preached in Calvary Free Chapel, New-York.

Evening.—I presided at the Anniversary Service for the House of Mercy in Trinity Chapel, New-York

Feb. 2, *Tuesday, Purification,* A. M.—In St. Mary's Church, Burlington, N. J., I acted as Consecrator at the Consecration of the Right Rev. John Scarborough, D. D., as Bishop of the Diocese of New-Jersey, the Bishops of Pennsylvania, Long Island, Albany, Massachusetts and Central Pennsylvania present and assisting. Sermon by the Right Rev. the Bishop of Pittsburgh.

Feb 14, *First Sunday in Lent,* A. M.--In the Church of the Holy Trinity, New-York, I preached.

P. M.—In the Floating Chapel of our Saviour for Seamen, New-York, I preached, confirmed *twenty,* and addressed them. This Chapel is doing a very interesting work.

Feb. 28. *Third Sunday in Lent,* Evening —In the Chapel of Calvary Church, New-York, I presided at a meeting on City Missions, and made a brief address.

March 7, *Fourth Sunday in Lent,* A. M.—In St. Peter's Church, New-York, I preached, and administered the Holy Communion.

Evening.—In the Church of the Redeemer, New-York, I confirmed *fifteen,* and addressed them

March 11, *Thursday,* A. M —In the Church of the Holy Comforter, Poughkeepsie, I met the Convocation of Dutchess County, and at a Special Ordination advanced the Rev. John Gardner Rosencrantz to the Priesthood, the Rev Mr. Gardner, of Amenia Union, preaching.

Evening.—In the Church of the Mediator, New-York, (Mission Chapel of the Holy Trinity, New-York,) I confirmed *nine,* and addressed them and the congregation At my request, they were also addressed by the Rev. Dr Tyng, Jr , Rector of the Church of the Holy Trinity.

March 14, *Fifth Sunday in Lent,* A. M —In the Church of the Holy Apostles, New-York, I addressed the congregation, and confirmed *twenty-seven,* and also made an address to them, and celebrated the Holy Eucharist, assisted by the Rector

P. M —In the Church of St. John the Baptist, New-York, I addressed the congregation ; then confirmed *thirteen,* and addressed them

Evening.—In St. Peter's Church, New York, I confirmed *thirty-three,* and addressed them

March 16, *Tuesday,* Evening —In St. George's English Mission Chapel, New-York, I confirmed *twenty seven,* and addressed them, and, at my request, they were addressed by the Rector of St George's.

March 18, *Thursday,* Evening —In St. George's German Mission Chapel, New-York, I confirmed *sixty-one,* and addressed them. They were also addressed, at my request, by the Rector of St. George's.

March 19, *Friday,* Evening —In St Peter's Church, Peekskill, I preached, confirmed *thirteen,* (*one* of them in private,) and addressed them.

March 21, *Sunday before Easter,* A M.—In St. Thomas' Church, New-York, I confirmed *thirty-six,* and addressed them.

P. M.—In the Church St. Esprit, New-York, I confirmed *eleven*, and addressed them.

P. M., (later.) In Grace Church Chapel, New-York, I confirmed *eighteen*, and addressed them.

Evening.—In the Anthon Memorial Church, New-York, I confirmed *thirteen*, and addressed them.

March 22, *Monday*, P. M.—In Trinity Church, Sing Sing, I confirmed *seventeen*, (*three* of them in private.) and addressed them.

Evening.—In St. Paul's Church, Sing Sing, I confirmed *eight*, and addressed them.

March 23, *Tuesday*, A. M.—In Grace Church, New-York, I confirmed *fourteen*, and addressed them.

Evening.—In St. Luke's Church, New-York, I confirmed *thirty nine*, and addressed them.

March 24, *Wednesday*, P. M.—In the Church of the Transfiguration, New-York, at a Special Confirmation, I confirmed *nine*, and briefly addressed them

Evening.—In St. Timothy's Church, New-York, I preached, confirmed *twenty*, and addressed them.

March 25, *Thursday*, *Feast of the Annunciation*, A. M.—In the Church of the Ascension, New-York, I confirmed *thirty-two*, and addressed them.

Evening.—In St. Paul's Chapel, New-York, I confirmed *thirty-six*, and addressed them.

March 26, *Good Friday*, A. M.—In St. George's Church, New-York, the Rector preaching, I confirmed *twenty*, and addressed them.

P. M.—In St. John's Church, Clifton, S. I., I confirmed *sixteen*, and addressed them.

March 27, *Easter Even*, A. M.—In the Church of the Holy Communion, New-York, I confirmed *sixty*, and addressed them.

P. M.—In Trinity Church, New-York, I confirmed *sixty-one*, and addressed them.

March 28, *Easter Day*, A. M.—In All Saints' Church, New-York, I confirmed *thirty-nine*, and addressed them, and celebrated the Holy Eucharist, assisted by the Rector.

P. M.—In the Church of the Holy Trinity, Harlem, I confirmed *thirteen*, and addressed them.

Evening.—In the Church of St. John the Evangelist, New-York, I confirmed *forty-four*, and addressed them.

March 30, *Tuesday*, A. M.—In the House of Mercy, New-York, I received two Probationers into the Sisterhood of St. Mary, and celebrated the Holy Eucharist, assisted by the Chaplain of the House, the Rev. Dr. Seymour, and by the Pastor of the Sisterhood, the Rev. Dr Houghton.

Evening.—In St. Mary's Church, Mott Haven, I preached, confirmed *ten*, and addressed them

April 2, *Friday*, P. M.—I presided at a meeting of the Foreign Committee.

Evening.—In the Chapel of the Church of the Ascension, (Shepherd's Flock,) New-York, I confirmed *thirty-eight*, and addressed them.

April 4, First Sunday after Easter, A. M.—In St. John's Chapel, New-York, I confirmed *ninety-nine*, and addressed them.

P. M.—In St. Alban's Church, New-York, I confirmed *eleven*, and addressed them.

Evening.—In Trinity Chapel, New-York, I confirmed *forty-five*, (*one* of them from St. John's Chapel,) and, at my request, they were addressed by the Right Rev. the Bishop of Maine.

April 6, Tuesday, A. M.—In St. Barnabas' Chapel, New-York, I presided at the Anniversary Service of the Sisterhood of the Good Shepherd, making a few remarks, and celebrating the Holy Eucharist, assisted by the Pastor of the Sisterhood, the Rev. Dr. Gallaudet.

Evening.—I solemnized a marriage.

April 7, Wednesday, A. M.—In Trinity Church, Mount Vernon, I met the Southern Convocation, made a brief address in the absence of the appointed Preacher, celebrated the Holy Eucharist, assisted by the Dean, and presided at a business meeting.

Evening.—In the Chapel of St. Chrysostom, (of Trinity Parish,) New-York, I confirmed *forty*, and addressed them.

April 9, Friday, Evening.—In St. Mary's Church in the Highlands, the Rev. Dr. Seymour preaching, I confirmed *four*, and addressed them.

April 10, Saturday, A. M.—In St. Mary's Church in the Highlands, the Rev. Dr. Seymour preaching, I instituted the Rev. Isaac Van Winkle as Rector.

April 11, Second Sunday after Easter, A. M.—In Christ Church, Poughkeepsie, I preached, confirmed *seven*, and addressed them.

P. M.—In St. Paul's Church, Poughkeepsie, I preached, confirmed *twenty*, and addressed them.

Evening.—In the Church of the Holy Comforter, Poughkeepsie, I confirmed *eighteen*, and addressed them.

April 12, Monday, P. M.—In St. James' Church, Hyde Park, I confirmed *seventeen*, and addressed them.

April 13, Tuesday, Evening.—In Zion Church, Wappinger's Falls, I preached, confirmed *forty-five*, and addressed them. This is a very interesting and earnest Parish.

April 14, Wednesday, P. M.—In St. Luke's Church, Matteawan, I confirmed *five*, and addressed them.

April 15, Thursday, P. M.—In Trinity Church Infirmary, New-York, I confirmed *seven* sick persons, adding a few words of consolation and encouragement.

April 18, Third Sunday after Easter, A. M.—In Christ Church, New-York, I confirmed *twenty-nine*, (*one* of them from the Church of the Holy Trinity, New-York,) and addressed them, and celebrated the Holy Eucharist, assisted by the Rector.

P. M.—In St. Ann's Church for Deaf Mutes, New-York, I confirmed *fifty-one*, (*one* of them, a mute, in private,) and addressed them. *Fourteen* of them were mutes.

Evening.—In Calvary Free Chapel, New-York, I confirmed *twenty-four*, and addressed them.

April 19, *Monday*, Evening.—In the Church of the Atonement, New-York, I confirmed *seven*, and addressed them.

April 20, *Tuesday*, Evening.—In St. Philip's Church, New-York, I confirmed *twenty-two*, and addressed them.

April 21, *Wednesday*, A. M.—I officiated at the funeral of a Clergyman's daughter.

Evening.—In St. Barnabas' Chapel, New-York, I confirmed *thirty-seven*, and addressed them; good evidence, along with other tokens, of excellent work going on in that Mission.

April 22, *Thursday*, Evening.—In St. Thomas' Free Chapel, New-York, I confirmed *thirty-three*, (*two* of them from St. Barnabas' Chapel,) and addressed them.

April 23, *Friday*, Evening.—In St. Augustine's Chapel, (of Trinity Parish,) New-York, I confirmed *thirty-three*, and addressed them.

April 25, *Fourth Sunday after Easter, and St. Mark's Day*, A. M.—In St. Mark's Church, New-York, I confirmed *seventy-three*, (*fifty-two* of them from the Mission Chapel of the Parish,) and addressed them.

P. M.—In the Church of the Heavenly Rest, New-York, I confirmed *twenty-eight*, and addressed them.

Evening.—In St. James' Church, New-York, I confirmed *twenty-two*, and addressed them.

April 28, *Wednesday*, A. M.—In the Church of the Holy Trinity, Philadelphia, I took part in the Consecration of the Rev. Thomas Augustus Jaggar, D. D., late Rector of that Church, and Bishop elect of the Diocese of Southern Ohio, acting with the Bishop of Pennsylvania in presenting the Candidate, and uniting in the laying on of hands.

May 2, *Fifth Sunday after Easter*, A. M.—In the Church of the Transfiguration, New-York, I confirmed *nineteen*, and addressed them, this being the second Confirmation of the year.

P. M.—In Grace Church, Harlem, I preached, confirmed *eight*, and addressed them.

Evening.—In St. Andrew's Church, Harlem, I confirmed *twenty-seven*, (*one* of them from the Church of the Holy Trinity, Harlem,) and addressed them.

May 3, *Monday*, P. M.—In St. Mary's Church, Beechwood, I confirmed *two*, and briefly addressed them.

Evening.—In St. Mark's Church, Tarrytown, I confirmed *twelve*, and addressed them.

May 4, *Tuesday*, P. M.—I officiated at the funeral of a venerable Layman of the Church.

Evening.—In the Church of the Resurrection, New-York, I confirmed *nine*, and addressed them.

May 5, *Wednesday*, Evening.—In the Bethlehem Mission Chapel of the City Mission, (German,) New-York, I confirmed *twenty-three*, and addressed them.

May 6, *Thursday, Ascension Day,* A. M.—I consecrated the Church of the Ascension, West Brighton, Staten Island, and preached, and I celebrated the Holy Eucharist, assisted by the present and former Rectors.

Evening.—In St. John's Church, Yonkers, I confirmed *thirty-six*, and addressed them.

May 7, *Friday*, Evening.—In the Chapel of the Reconciliation, (Chapel of the Church of the Incarnation,) New-York, I confirmed *forty*, and addressed them.

May 9, *Sunday after the Ascension,* A. M.—In the Church of the Holy Sepulchre, New-York, I confirmed *twelve*, and addressed them.

P. M.—In the Church of the Annunciation, New-York, I confirmed *eight*, and briefly addressed them.

Evening.—In the Church of the Holy Trinity, New-York, I confirmed *one hundred and six*, and addressed them, and, at my request, they were also addressed by the Rev. Dr. Tyng, Sen

May 10, *Monday*, Evening.—In the Church of St. Ignatius, New-York, I preached, confirmed *thirteen*, and addressed them.

May 11, *Tuesday*, Evening.—In Trinity Church, Mount Vernon, I confirmed *nineteen*, and addressed them.

May 15, *Saturday*, A. M.—In Christ Church, Pelham, I preached, confirmed *four*, and briefly addressed them.

May 16, *Whitsun-Day*, A. M.—In Christ Church, Rye, I preached, confirmed *thirteen*, and addressed them, and celebrated the Holy Eucharist, assisted by the Rector.

Evening.—In Trinity Church, New-Rochelle, I preached, confirmed *twenty-five*, and addressed them.

May 18, *Tuesday*, Evening.—In St. Peter's Church, Portchester, I preached, confirmed *twenty eight*, and addressed them.

May 19, *Wednesday*, Evening —In the Church of the Epiphany, (50th-street,) New-York, I confirmed *ten*, and addressed them.

May 21, *Friday*, Evening.—In the Church of St. Mary the Virgin, New-York, I confirmed *twenty*, and addressed them.

May 23, *Trinity Sunday*, A. M.—In Zion Church, New-York, the Rector preaching, I advanced to the Priesthood the Rev. George W. West, the Rev. Obadiah Valentine, and the Rev. William Allen Fair. On the same occasion I confirmed *eleven*, and briefly addressed them.

Evening.—In the Church of the Holy Martyrs, New-York, I confirmed *twenty*, and addressed them.

May 29, *Saturday*, P. M.—In Christ Church, Marlboro', I preached, confirmed *six*, and addressed them.

May 30, *First Sunday after Trinity*, A. M —In St. Paul's Church, Pleasant Valley, I preached, confirmed *seven*, and addressed them.

P M —In the Church of the Holy Trinity, Highland, Ulster County, I preached, confirmed *fourteen*, and addressed them.

June 2, *Wednesday*, Evening.—In the Church of the Incarnation, New-York, I confirmed *eleven*, and addressed them.

June 3, *Thursday*, P. M.—In St. Peter's Church, Westchester, I confirmed *seven*, and briefly addressed them.

Evening.—In Grace Church, White Plains, I preached, confirmed *fourteen*, and addressed them.

June 4, *Friday*, A. M.—In St Mark's Church, New-Castle, I preached, confirmed *four*, and addressed them.

June 6, *Second Sunday after Trinity*, A. M.—In the Church du St. Esprit, New-York, I instituted the Rev. Leon Pons as Rector, and preached, and celebrated the Holy Eucharist.

Evening.—In St. Ambrose' Church, New-York, I confirmed *twelve*, and addressed them and the congregation.

June 8, *Tuesday*, A. M —In St. Paul's Church, East Chester, on occasion of a commemorative service in memory of the Rev. Thomas Standard, A. M., M. D., Rector of the Parish for thirty-three years, and who departed this life in 1760, the Rev. Mr. Coffey, the present respected Rector read an historical paper and delivered a discourse on the early history of the Church in this country. The immediate occasion of this interesting service was the dedication of a monumental tablet, recently erected in the Church to the memory of the former Rector, the Rev. Thomas Standard, whose remains rest beneath the Altar.

June 14, *Monday*, P. M.—I attended a meeting of the Standing Committee of the General Theological Seminary, New-York.

June 15, *Tuesday*, P. M.—In Christ Church, Poughkeepsie, at a second and Special Confirmation, I confirmed *twenty-two*, and addressed them.

June 16, *Wednesday*, P. M.—I attended a meeting of the Trustees of St. Stephen's College, Annandale.

Evening.—In the Church of the Holy Innocents, (the Chapel of the College,) I presided at the Annual Missionary Meeting. Sermon by the Rev. Dr. Mulchahey, of Trinity Parish, New-York.

June 17, *Thursday*, A. M.—I attended an adjourned meeting of the Trustees, and afterwards the Commencement exercises of the College, which were particularly interesting and encouraging.

Evening.—In the Memorial Church of St. John the Evangelist, Barrytown, I confirmed *nine*, and addressed them. This interesting Church is making itself very useful.

June 20, *Fourth Sunday after Trinity*, A. M.—In St. Michael's Church, New-York, I confirmed *eighteen*, (*one* of them from the Church of the Nativity,) and addressed them.

P. M.—In the House of Mercy, New-York, at a Special Confirmation, I confirmed *two* persons.

P. M., (later.)—In the Church of All Angels, New-York, I preached, confirmed *eleven*, and addressed them.

June 23, *Wednesday*, A. M.—At the Commencement of Union University, Schenectady, I delivered the Chancellor's Address.

June 24, *Thursday*.—I attended the Annual Meeting of the Trustees of the General Theological Seminary, New-York.

June 25, *Friday*.—I presided at the Commencement of the General Theological Seminary, New-York, and after the address of the Right Rev. the Bishop of Maine, presented the Testimonials to the graduating class, with a few words of sympathy and counsel, and celebrated the Holy Eucharist, assisted by the Bishop of Maine.

June 26, *Saturday*, A. M.—I was occupied with the concluding examination of the candidates for Deacons' Orders.

June 27, *Fifth Sunday after Trinity*, A. M.—In Trinity Church, New-York, the Rev. Dr. Dix, the Rector, preaching, I admitted to the Diaconate Amos Turner Ashton, A. B., Henry David Jardine and Floyd William Tomkins, B. A.

P. M.—In the Church of the Beloved Disciple, New-York, I confirmed *twelve*, (*one* from All Angels' Church,) and addressed them.

June 29, *Tuesday*, A. M.—I solemnized a marriage in Trinity Chapel, New-York.

P. M.—I officiated at a funeral.

June 30, *Wednesday*, P. M.—In St. Luke's Church, Somers, I preached, confirmed *four*, and addressed them.

P. M.—In St. James' Church, North Salem, I preached, confirmed *nine*, and addressed them.

July 1, *Thursday*, A. M.—In St. John's Church, Lewisboro', I preached, confirmed *five*, and addressed them.

July 2, *Friday*, A. M.—In St. Matthew's Church, Bedford, I preached, confirmed *five*, and addressed them.

July 4, *Sixth Sunday after Trinity*, A. M.—In the Church of the Ascension, West Brighton, S. I., I preached, confirmed *eleven*, and addressed them, and celebrated the Holy Eucharist, assisted by the Rector.

P. M.—In Christ Church, New-Brighton, I confirmed *fourteen*, and addressed them.

July 11, *Seventh Sunday after Trinity*, A. M.—In St. George's Church, Newburgh, I confirmed *fifty-four*, (*twenty* of them from the Mission Chapel,) and addressed them.

P. M.—In St. Thomas' Church, New Windsor, I preached, confirmed *sixteen*, and addressed them.

Evening.—In St. Paul's Church, Newburgh, I confirmed *ten*, (*one* of them in private,) and addressed them.

July 13, *Tuesday*, A. M.—In St. Paul's Church, Spring Valley, I met the Southern Convocation, the Rev. Mr. Hooper, of Mount Vernon, preaching, and I celebrated the Holy Eucharist, and consulted with the Clergy on Church business.

July 14, *Wednesday*, A. M.—In the Church of the Transfiguration, New-York, I preached, and at a Special Ordination admitted Mr. George F. Behringer to the Diaconate.

P. M.—In the House of Mercy, New-York, after the Baptism of two of the inmates, I confirmed *five*, and addressed them.

July 18, *Eighth Sunday after Trinity*, A. M.—In Zion Church, Greenburgh, I preached, confirmed *eight*, and addressed them.

P. M.—In St. Barnabas' Church, Irvington, I preached.

Evening.—In the Chapel at Hastings, I preached.

July 19, *Monday*, P. M.—In the Church of the Transfiguration, New-York, at a Special Confirmation, I confirmed *four* persons.

July 25, *Ninth Sunday after Trinity and St. James*, A. M.—In St. Philip's Church, New-York, I preached, and admitted Mr. Wm. Heuston Morris, (colored,) of the Diocese of Northern New-Jersey, to the Diaconate, acting at the request of the Bishop of that Diocese.

July 26, *Monday*, Evening.—In Grace Church, Nyack, I confirmed *seventeen*, and addressed them.

July 27, *Tuesday*, A. M.—In Christ Church, Piermont, I preached, confirmed *seven*, and addressed them.

July 28, *Wednesday*, A. M.—In the Church of St. James the Less, Scarsdale, I preached, confirmed *seven*, and addressed them.

July 29, *Thursday*, P. M.—In St. John's Church, Greenwood Iron Works, I confirmed *ten*, and addressed them.

Evening.—In Christ Church, Warwick, I preached, confirmed *six*, and addressed them.

July 30, *Friday*, Evening.—In Grace Church, Port Jervis, I preached, confirmed *eighteen*, and addressed them.

Aug. 4, *Wednesday*, Evening.—In St. John's Church, Canterbury, I preached, confirmed *four*, and addressed them.

Aug 5, *Thursday*, A. M.—I consecrated St. John's Church, Canterbury, and preached.

Aug. 24, *Tuesday*, P. M.—At Rosendale, Ulster County, I confirmed *twelve*, and addressed them, and afterwards addressed an interesting congregation.

Aug. 25, *Wednesday*, P. M.—I attended and officiated at the funeral of the Rev. George B. Andrews, D. D, late Rector of Zion Church, Wappinger's Falls, Dutchess County. Dr. Andrews was in years, though not by Ordination, the Senior Presbyter of the Diocese, and pre-eminent for his sweet, engaging Christian character.

Aug. 26, *Thursday*, A. M.—In St. Paul's Mission Chapel, in Saw Mill Valley, Greenburgh, I preached, confirmed *three*, and addressed them.

Aug. 29, *Fourteenth Sunday after Trinity*, A. M.—I preached in the Church of the Transfiguration, New-York.

Aug. 30, *Monday*, A. M.—In the Church of the Divine Love, Montrose, I preached, confirmed *two*, and addressed them.

Sept. 9, *Thursday*, P. M.—I laid the corner-stone of St. Mary's Church, Mott Haven, and made a brief address. Addresses were also made by the Rev. Dr. Seymour and by the Rev. Dr. Flagg.

Sept. 13, *Monday*, Evening.—In Grace Church, City Island, I preached, confirmed *fourteen*, and addressed them.

Sept. 16, *Thursday*, A. M.—In St. James' Church, Hyde Park, I met the Dutchess County Convocation, celebrating the Holy Eucharist, &c. Sermon by Prof. Olssen.

P. M.—In the Chapel at Staatsburgh, I confirmed *seven* persons, and addressed them. The services of Mr. Parks here as Lay Reader have been very useful.

Sept. 18, *Saturday.*—In St. Mary's Church in the Highlands, I officiated at the funeral of a venerable and much respected and beloved Layman of the Church.

Sept. 19, *Seventeenth Sunday after Trinity,* A. M.—In the Church of the Redeemer, New-York, the Rector, the Rev. Mr. Shackelford, preaching, I admitted Alfred Evan Johnson, an Alumnus of the General Theological Seminary, to the Diaconate.

Sept. 24, *Friday,* A. M.—In the Church of the Transfiguration, New-York, at a Special Confirmation, I confirmed *one* person.

Sept. 27, *Monday* —I presided at a meeting of the Society for Promoting Religion and Learning.

CANDIDATES FOR HOLY ORDERS.

The following is a complete List of the Candidates for Holy Orders in this Diocese, with the dates of their admission respectively ; being in all, 33.

I.—CANDIDATES FOR DEACON'S AND PRIEST'S ORDERS.

Dan Marvin, A. M., December 6, 1866.
George B. Johnson, A. B., June 1, 1871.
William Henry Conover, A. B., August 3, 1871.
Henry Stoughton Tracy, A. B., { C. D. O., September 27, 1871. / C. P. O , November 2, 1871. }
Edgar Snyder, A B., December 5, 1872.
Charles Lancaster Short, A. B., April 3, 1873.
John Sword, August 4, 1873.
John Punnett Peters, A. B., September 4, 1873.
Henry Van Rensselaer, September 18, 1873.
G. Arnolt Carstensen, A. B., September 18, 1873.
William H. Tomlins, A. B , September 18, 1873.
Frederick H. T. Horsfield, A. B., October 2, 1873.
William Oliver Embury, November 6, 1873.
Oliver Perry Vinton, A. B., November 6, 1873.
Henry Townsend Scudder, A. B., June 4, 1874.
George H. Wilson, A. B., September 30, 1874.
Victor C. Smith, A. B , September 30, 1874.
Edwin C. Alcorn, A. B , November 5, 1874.
John Quick Archdeacon, A. B , November 5, 1874.
Samuel M. C. Orpen, January 7, 1875.
Richard Hamilton, A. B., February 4, 1875.
Charles Sanford Olmsted, May 6, 1875.
Le Grand Randall, May 6, 1875.
Charles Robert Stroh, A. B , June 10, 1875.

Harry J. Bodley, A. B., July 1, 1875.
Benjamin M. Bradin, A. B., September 24, 1875.
William Montague Geer, A. B., October 8, 1875.
Henry Robert Percival, A. B., October 8, 1875.—28.

II.—CANDIDATES FOR DEACON'S ORDERS.

Not having passed any Literary Examination:

John Pickavant Crawford, November 5, 1868.
Henry Homer Washburn, June 5, 1873.
Benjamin Haight, May 7, 1874.
Charles Tileston Whittemore, September 30, 1874.
James R. F. Nisbett, October 8, 1875.—5.

CANDIDATES FOR HOLY ORDERS ORDAINED DEACONS.

I. The Candidates for Deacons and Priest's Orders, named below, have passed the examination required by Canon VIII., Section 3, and Section 7, Title I., of the Digest of the Canons of the General Convention, and have been ordained to the Diaconate:

1874.	November	30.	Mr. George Love, A. B.
1875.	June	27.	Mr. Amos Turner Ashton, A. B.
"	"	"	Mr. Henry David Jardine.
"	"	"	Mr. Floyd William Tomkins.
"	July	14.	Mr. George F. Behringer.
	"	25.	Mr. William Heuston Morris, by the request of the Ecclesiastical Authority of the Diocese of Northern New-Jersey.
"	September	19.	Mr. Alfred Evan Johnson, A. B.—7.

DEACONS ADVANCED TO THE PRIESTHOOD.

The Deacons named below have been ordained to the Holy Order of Priests:

1874.	November	20.	The Rev. Walter R. Gardner.
"	"	"	The Rev. George W. Hinckle.
"	"	"	The Rev. John C. Tebbets.
"	December	23.	The Rev. Zina Doty.
1875.	March	11.	The Rev. John G. Rosencrantz.
"	May	23, (Trinity Sunday.)	The Rev. George W. West.
"	"	" " "	The Rev. Obadiah Valentine.
	"	" " "	The Rev. William Allen Fair.—8.

RESIGNATION OF PARISHES.

I have received Notice of the Resignation, by the Clergymen named below, of the Parishes or Cures respectively mentioned:

The Rev. Samuel M. Akerly, as Minister of Christ Church, Marlborough.

The Rev. Brady Electus Backus, as Assistant at St. Peter's Church, New-York.

The Rev. Clarence Buel, of the Rectorship of Trinity Church, Mount Vernon.

The Rev. Charles B. Coffin, of the Rectorship of Trinity Church, Haverstraw.

The Rev. Thomas K. Conrad, D. D., as Associate in the Church of the Heavenly Rest, New-York

The Rev. Charles C. Edmunds, as Minister of St. Paul's Church, Ellenville.

The Rev. Campbell Fair, of the Rectorship of St. Ambrose Church, New-York.

The Rev. Walter R. Gardner, of the Rectorship of St. Thomas' Church, Amenia.

The Rev. Pierre P. Irving, of the Rectorship of Christ Church, New-Brighton.

The Rev. Edward Kettell, as Assistant Minister of the Church of the Holy Trinity, New-York.

The Rev. Hamilton Lee, as Assistant Minister of Christ Church, New-Brighton.

The Rev. Frederick N. Luson, as Minister of Grace Church, Port Jervis.

The Rev. Mytton Maury, of the Rectorship of St. James' Church, Fordham.

The Rev. James Byron Murray, of the Rectorship of the Church of the Holy Spirit, Rondout, Kingston.

The Rev. Thomas W. Punnett, of the Rectorship of St. Paul's Memorial Church, Edgewater, S. I.

The Rev. James W. Sparks, of the Rectorship of St. Mark's Church, Newcastle.

The Rev. Obadiah Valentine, as Assistant Minister of the Church of the Holy Apostles, New-York.

The Rev. Philander K. Cady, D. D., of the Rectorship of Christ Church, Poughkeepsie.—18.

CLERGYMEN APPOINTED TO CURES.

In behalf of the Clergymen named below, I have received the Canonical Certificate of the election or appointment to the Cures or offices respectively mentioned. In each case I have certified that the person so chosen is a qualified Minister of this Church, and transmitted the certificate to the Secretary of the Convention for record by him, according to the requirements of the Canon.

The Rev. Edward H. Krans, as an Assistant Minister of St. Ann's Church, New-York.

The Rev. John Chamberlain, as an Assistant Minister of St. Ann's Church, New-York.

The Rev. Christopher S. Stephenson, to the Rectorship of St. Mary's Church, Mott Haven, New-York.

The Rev. Joshua Morsell, D. D., to the Rectorship of Grace Church, City Island.

The Rev. William Berrian Hooper, to the Rectorship of Trinity Church, Mount Vernon.

The Rev. Obadiah Valentine, as Assistant Minister of the Church of the Holy Apostles, New-York.

The Rev. Allan S. Woodle, as Assistant Minister of Christ Church, New-York.

The Rev. Philip A. H. Brown, as an Assistant Minister in Trinity Parish, New-York.

The Rev. Campbell Fair, to the Rectorship of St. Ambrose Church, New-York.

The Rev. Charles Frederick Hoffman, to the Rectorship of the Church of All Angels, New-York.

The Rev. Leo Pons, to the Rectorship of the French Church du St. Esprit, New-York.

The Rev. Samuel Moran, to the Rectorship of St. John's Church, Greenwood Iron Works.

The Rev. Joseph H. Atwell, to the Rectorship of St. Philip's Church, New-York.

The Rev. Howard T. Widdemer, to the Rectorship of St. Ambrose' Church, New-York.

The Rev. C. William Camp, to the Rectorship of St. John's Church, Kingston.

The Rev. Amos Turner Ashton, to the Rectorship of St. Thomas' Church, Amenia.

The Rev. U. T. Tracy, to the Rectorship of the Church of the Epiphany, New-York.

The Rev. Arthur Brooks, to the Rectorship of the Church of the Incarnation, New-York.

The Rev. E. Winchester Donald, to the Rectorship of the Church of the Intercession, New-York.

The Rev. Erastus Huntington Saunders, as Assistant Minister at the Church of the Heavenly Rest, New-York.

The Rev. Henry Y. Satterlee, to the Rectorship of Zion Church, Wappinger's Falls.

The Rev. Henry L. Ziegenfuss, to the Rectorship of Christ Church, Poughkeepsie.

The Rev. Stephen A. McNulty, as Officiating Minister at St. Mark's Mission Chapel, New-York.

The Rev. George F. Siegmund, as Assistant Minister at the Church of the Annunciation, New-York.

The Rev. Edward T. Bartlett, to the Rectorship of St. Luke's Church, Matteawan.—25.

CLERGYMEN RECEIVED INTO THE DIOCESE.

The Clergymen named below have been received into the Diocese upon Letters Dimissory of the Ecclesiastical Authority of the Dioceses respectively mentioned. I have given to them the Canonical Certificate of their reception.

The Rev. Charles R. Hale, from the Diocese of Central New-York.

The Rev. Christopher S. Stephenson, from the Missionary Jurisdiction of Nevada.

The Rev. Henry A. Dows, from the Diocese of Connecticut.

The Rev. Joshua Morsell, D. D., from the Diocese of Massachusetts.

The Rev. Edward T. Bartlett, from the Diocese of Albany.

The Rev. Erastus H. Saunders, from the Diocese of Albany.

The Rev. James A. Upjohn, from the Diocese of Albany.

The Rev. Edward H. Krans, from the Diocese of Massachusetts.

The Rev. Allan Sheldon Woodle, B. D., from the Diocese of Wisconsin.

The Rev. William Berrian Hooper, from the Diocese of Central Pennsylvania.

The Rev. Joseph L. Tucker, from the Diocese of Mississippi.

The Rev. Philip A. H. Brown, from the Diocese of Albany.

The Rev. John Gardner Rosencrantz, from the Diocese of Long Island.

The Rev. John Waters, D. D., from the Diocese of Albany.

The Rev. Campbell Fair, from the Diocese of Louisiana.

The Rev. Joseph Atwell, from the Diocese of Georgia.

The Rev. Arthur Brooks, from the Diocese of Illinois.

The Rev. S. Seymour Lewis, from the Diocese of Central New-York.

The Rev. Samuel Moran, from the Diocese of Northern New-Jersey.

The Rev. Morris A. Tyng, from the Diocese of Ohio.

The Rev. Howard T. Widdemer, from the Diocese of Albany.

The Rev. Joseph H. Young, deacon, from the Diocese of Massachusetts.

The Rev. John W. Trimble, from the Diocese of Albany.

The Rev. N. Thayer Robinson, deacon, from the Diocese of Pennsylvania.

The Rev. Benjamin Webb, from the Diocese of Albany.

The Rev. N. Frazier Robinson, deacon, from the Diocese of Pennsylvania.

The Rev. C. William Camp, from the Diocese of New-Jersey.

The Rev. George F. Siegmund, from the Diocese of Western New-York.—28.

LETTERS DIMISSORY GRANTED.

I have granted Letters Dimissory, at their request, to the Clergymen named below, and have received notice of the acceptance of the same from the respective Ecclesiastical Authorities, viz. :

The Rev. Thomas K. Conrad, to the Diocese of Pennsylvania.

The Rev. E. Bayard Smith, (deacon,) to the Diocese of Central New-York.

The Rev. John D. Rockwell, (deacon,) to the Diocese of Central Pennsylvania.

The Rev. Richard Miles Hayden, (deacon,) to the Diocese of Central New-York.

The Rev. Brady Electus Backus, to the Diocese of Albany.

The Rev. Frederick N. Luson, to the Diocese of Illinois.

The Rev. J. Bloomfield Wetherell, to the Diocese of Northern New-Jersey.

The Rev. Thomas W. Punnett, to the Diocese of Maryland.

The Rev. Henry N. Wayne, to the Diocese of Maryland.

The Rev. Clarence Buel, to the Diocese of Long Island.

The Rev. William Kirkus, to the Diocese of Maryland.

The Rev. Levi Johnston, to the Diocese of Northern New-Jersey.

The Rev. Arthur Sloan, to the Diocese of Connecticut.

The Rev. E. H. Kettell, to the Diocese of Rhode Island.

The Rev. A. Herbert Gessner, to the Diocese of Central Pennsylvania.

The Rev. James W. Sparks, to the Diocese of Long Island.

The Rev. Campbell Fair, to the Diocese of Maryland.

The Rev. John H. Rogers, to the Diocese of Albany.

The Rev. Floyd W. Tompkins, (deacon,) to the Missionary jurisdiction of Colorado.

The Rev. George E. Cranston, to the Diocese of Maryland.

The Rev. William Allen Fair, to the Missionary jurisdiction of Cape Palmas.

The Rev. Joseph L. Tucker, to the Diocese of Western New-York.

The Rev. Henry D. Jardine, (deacon,) to the Diocese of Missouri.

The Rev. Wm. S. Langford, to the Diocese of New-Jersey.

The Rev. Samuel Hollingsworth, D. D , to the Diocese of Massachusetts.

The Rev. John M. Leavitt, D D , to the Diocese of Pennsylvania.

The Rev. Charles C. Edmunds, to the Diocese of Albany.—27.

ALSO, THE CANDIDATE FOR DEACON'S AND PRIEST'S ORDER NAMED BELOW.

Charles Sumner Stewart, to the Diocese of Rhode Island.

CLERGYMEN DECEASED.

Since the last Convention, the following Clergymen of the Diocese ha departed this life:

The Rev Henry Eglinton Montgomery, D. D., at New-York, October 1 1874.

The Rev. Augustus Fitch, at New-York, November 19, 1874.

The Rev. Frederick Sill, at New-York, December 13, 1874.

The Rev. George W. Bacon, LL. B., M. D., at Flushing, N. Y., Decem 25, 1874

The Rev. John Morgan, at Rossville, N. Y., January 22, 1875.

The Rev. John N. McJilton, D. D., at New-York, April 13, 1875.

The Rev Charles Bouton Coffin, at Edgewater, N. Y., July 9, 1875.

The Rev. George B. Andrews, D. D., at Wappinger's Falls, N. Y., Aug 22, 1875.—8.

RECTORS INSTITUTED.

1875. April 9. The Rev. Isaac Van Winkle, into the Rectorship of St Mary's Church, Cold Spring, Putnam County.

" June 6. The Rev. Leon Pons, into the Rectorship of the Frenc Church du St. Esprit, New-York.—2.

CHURCHES CONSECRATED.

Since the last Convention, the following Churches have been consecrated by me:

1874. October 4. The Free Memorial Church of St. John the Evangelist. Barrytown, Red Hook, Dutchess County.

1875. May 6. The Church of the Ascension, West Brighton, Richmond County.

" August 5. St. John's Church, Canterbury, Orange County —3

CHURCH OPENED.

1875. December 25. Trinity Church, Morrisania, New-York.—1.

CLERGYMEN DEPOSED.

Under Canon 6, Title ii., (Digest of Canons of Gen. Conv.,) for causes not affecting their moral character.

1875. July 8. The Rev. William V. Feltwell, Presbyter.

" " " The Rev William T. Sabine, Presbyter

" " " The Rev. Benjamin B Leacock, Presbyter.

" " " The Rev. William W. Sever, Presbyter.

1875. July 8. The Rev. Charles A. Foster, Deacon.
" " " The Rev. J. Eastburn Brown, Presbyter.
" " " The Rev. William M. Postlethwaite, Presbyter.—7.

CORNER-STONES LAID.

1872. October 6. Trinity Church, Morrisania, New-York.
1875. September 9. St. Mary's Church, Mott Haven, New-York.
" " Church at Calicoon.

SUMMARY.

The following is a Summary of Episcopal Acts in the Diocese since the last Convention:

Number of Persons Confirmed,		2,263
Candidates Ordained to the Diaconate,	7	
Candidates Ordained to the Priesthood,	8	
Ordinations, total,		15
Churches Consecrated,		3
Clergymen received from other Dioceses,		28
" transferred to " "		27
" instituted into Rectorships,		2
" deposed,		7

HORATIO POTTER, D. D., LL. D., D. C. L.,
Bishop of New-York.

Appendix:

No. I.

PAROCHIAL, MISSIONARY AND OTHER CLERICAL REPORTS.

The following portions of the Parochial, Missionary and other Clerical Reports, made to the Bishop of the Diocese, are published by his direction, in accordance with the following section, to which attention is respectfully requested, of

CANON 15, TITLE I.,

OF DIGEST OF THE CANONS OF THE GENERAL CONVENTION.

Of the Mode of securing an accurate View of the State of the Church.

§ I. As a full and accurate view of the state of the Church, from time to time, is highly useful and necessary, it is hereby ordered that every Minister of this Church, or, if the Parish be vacant, the Wardens, shall present, or cause to be delivered, on or before the first day of every Annual Convention, to the Bishop of the Diocese, or, when there is no Bishop, to the President of the Convention, a statement of the number of baptisms, confirmations, marriages and funerals, and of the number of Communicants in his Parish or Church; also the state and condition of the Sunday-Schools in his Parish; also the amount of the

Communion alms, the contributions for missions, diocesan, domestic and foreign, for parochial schools, for Church purposes in general, and of all other matters that may throw light on the same. And every Clergyman, not regularly settled in any Parish or Church, shall also report the occasional services he may have performed; and, if he have performed no such services, the causes or reasons which have prevented the same. And these Reports, or such parts of them as the Bishop shall think fit, may be read in Convention, and shall be entered on the Journals thereof.

DUTCHESS COUNTY.

St. Thomas' Church, Amenia; the Rev. AMOS TURNER ASHTON, Deacon and Rector elect.

Families, 44. Individuals, 166. Baptisms, (ad. 12, inf. 2,) 14. Confirmed, 12. Marriages, 2. Burials, 8. Communicants: admitted, 12; removed into the Parish, 2; died, 1; present number, 52. The Holy Communion celebrated monthly and on the chief festivals. Catechists and Sunday-School teachers, 5. Catechumens: total number of young persons instructed, 50. Celebration of Divine Service: Sundays, morning and evening service and sermon; Holy Days, Ash-Wednesday, Good Friday, Christmas; other days, twice each week in Lent.

Contributions.—Episcopal Fund, $2; Diocesan Fund, $8; Missionary Committee of the Diocese, $13 61; Board of Missions P. E. Church, U. S.: Foreign Committee, $3 09; the Poor, (Communion Alms,) $30 25; Church purposes in general, $125 38—total, $182 33.

This Parish has been under the care of the Rev. W. R. Gardner for the most of the year last past.

The present incumbent entered upon his work August 9th, 1875; and, in addition to his Parish work, holds an afternoon mission service at Ameniaville, a village some four miles distant.

Of the official acts in the foregoing report, one baptism was performed, and four funerals attended by him.

The Church has been greatly improved by the addition of a new carpet and lamps.

On the 8th of July an interesting memorial service was held in the Church; the occasion of the service being the setting up of a chancel window, in memory of Rev. Samuel Roosevelt Johnson, Priest and Doctor, the late Rector of the Church. The subject of the window is the aged St. John, carried in his old age into the Church, and uttering his unvarying sermon, which runs as a legend beneath, "Little children, love one another."

Chapel of St. Stephen's College, Annandale; the Rev. R. B. FAIRBAIRN, D. D., the Rev. G. B. HOPSON, the Rev. W. W. OLSSEN, and the Rev. L. L NOBLE, Ministers in charge.

Families, about 35. Individuals, about 150; including College, 225. Baptisms, (ad. 1, inf. 1,) 2. Confirmed, 4. Burial, 1. Marriage, 1. Communicants: added, 18; died, 2; removed, 5; transferred to St. John's Church, 36; present number, about 125. Communion every Sunday in term, and on other important days. Sermons on Sunday, twice during term, once during long vacation. Thirty-five children are taught in the Sunday-School during term. In the long vacation the Warden of the College catechises them each Sunday.

Contributions.—Aged and Infirm Clergy, $35; Society for the Increase of the Ministry, $15; Society for the Promotion of Religion and Learning, $14 50; Episcopal Fund, $7; Diocesan Fund, $20—total, $105 50. College Missionary Society, $14. There has been a weekly offertory for the expense of the Chapel. St. Mark's School, Salt Lake City, $40. Ladies' Sewing Society have again contributed a large amount of clothing for the House of the Good Shepherd, Tompkins' Cove.

St. Peter's Brotherhood continues to render important aid in Parish work.

The Church of St. John the Evangelist, Barrytown.

This Church was consecrated on the 4th of last October. It was erected by Mrs. Aspinwall as a memorial of her late husband, John L. Aspinwall. It is under the charge of the Warden and Professors of St. Stephen's College. The following is the result of the first year's work, which is chiefly due to Professor Hopson, to whom is assigned the morning service and the Parochial work, the Warden and Professors taking their turn in officiating in the evening:

Families, 23. Individuals, 98. Baptisms, (ad. 2, inf. 8.) 10. Confirmed, 9. Married, 1. Burials, 4. Communicants: added, 9; removed into the Parish, 36; died, 2; present number, 43. The Holy Communion, the first Sunday in the month and on the principal Holy Days. Sunday-School teachers, 7. Children instructed, 50. Members of other classes for religious instruction, 12. Young persons instructed, 62. Celebration of Divine Service: Sundays, 104; Holy Days, 4; other days, 25—total, 133.

Contributions.—Episcopal Fund, $3 32; Diocesan Fund, $18 60; Missionary Committee of the Diocese, $44; Education Fund, $15 02; Fund for Aged and Infirm Clergy, $2 40; New-York City Missions, $15 88; Society for Seamen, $11 17; Bible and P. B. Society, $11 60; Protestant Episcopal Tract Society, $18; P. E. Sunday-School Union, $11 82; Board of Missions: Domestic Committee, $23 68; Foreign Committee, $22 05; for Poor of the Parish, $48 47; Parish purposes, $374 91; a Sewing Society also furnished aid to the poor of the neighborhood—total, $620 87.

St. Mark's Church, Carthage Landing; the Rev. FREDERICK W. SHELTON, LL. D., Rector.

Families, 15. Individuals, 60. Baptisms, inf. 5. Marriage, 1. Burials, 2. Communicants: present number, 25. The Holy Communion celebrated on the first Sunday of every month and principal festivals. Catechists and Sunday-School teachers, 8. Catechumens, 30. Celebration of Divine Service: Sundays, every Sunday in the year; Holy Days, Christmas, Ash-Wednesday, Good Friday, Ascension, Thanksgiving; service twice weekly during Lent.

Contributions.—Episcopal Fund, $2; Diocesan Fund, $5; Parish purposes, $500—total, $507.

Trinity Church, Fishkill; the Rev. JOHN R. LIVINGSTON, Rector.

Baptisms, (ad. 1, inf. 1,) 2. Confirmed, 5. Marriages, 2. Communicants: admitted, 4; removed into the Parish, 5; present number, 43. The Holy Communion celebrated on the first Sunday of the month, and upon the chief festivals and several times in private. Catechists and Sunday-School teachers, 4. Catechumens, 12. Celebration of Divine Service: Sundays, morning service; Holy Days, Christmas, Ash-Wednesday, Good Friday, Ascension Day and Thanksgiving; other days, Wednesdays in Lent, and a weekly service during most of the year.

Contributions.—Episcopal Fund, $5; Diocesan Fund, $5; Missionary Committee of the Diocese, $10; Theological Education Fund, $5 50; Fund for Aged and Infirm Clergymen, $21; Sufferers in Osceola, Penna., $10 50; Highland Hospital, Matteawan, N. Y., $17; New-York Bible and Common Prayer-Book Society, $10; Protestant Episcopal Tract Society, $6; Mission to Colored People, $5 50; Dutchess County Convocation, $12 49; Board of Missions P. E. Church, U. S.: Domestic Committee, $32 60; Foreign Committee, $7; for the Indians, $6 25; the Poor, $10; Parish purposes, $82 50; Church purposes in general, $87—total, $333 34.

Free Church of St. John Baptist, Glenham; the Rev. JOHN R. LIVINGSTON, Rector and Missionary.

Baptisms, (ad 2, inf. 10,) 12. Confirmed, 1. Marriages, 5. Burials, 4. Communicants: admitted, 3; died, 2; present number, 30. The Holy Communion celebrated on the third Sunday in the month, Sunday after Christmas, Thursday evening in Passion Week, Sunday after Easter, and on St. John Baptist Day. Catechists and Sunday-School teachers, 6. Catechumens: Children taught the Catechism openly in the Church, 48; times, monthly; total number of young persons instructed, 48. Daily Parish School, free; Scholars, 24. Celebration of Divine Service: Sundays, morning, at 9 o'clock, evening; Holy Days, most of the Saints' Days, Early Service Christmas and Easter; other days, Ember, Rogation Days and Thanksgiving; twice a week during Lent, daily in Passion Week; Evening Prayer daily during the Summer, and weekly throughout the year.

Contributions.—Episcopal Fund, $2; Diocesan Fund, $2; Missionary Committee of the Diocese, $5; Theological Education Fund, $3; Fund for Aged and Infirm Clergymen, $5; New-York Bible and Common Prayer-Book Society, $5; Protestant Episcopal Tract Society, $3; Sufferers in Osceola, Pa., $5; Board of Missions P. E. Church, U. S.: Domestic Committee, $12; Foreign Committee and Indian Mission, $10; Mission to Colored People, $2; Sunday-School offering on St. John Baptist Day, $26 33; the Poor, $20; Parish purposes, $30—total, $128 33.

St. James' Church, Hyde Park; the Rev. J. S. PURDY, D. D., Rector.

Baptisms, (ad. 10, inf. 30,) 40. Confirmed, 24. Burials, 8. Communicants: admitted, 12; removed into the Parish, 2; removed from the Parish, 2; died, 3; present number, about 120. The Holy Communion celebrated on the first Sunday in the month and on all great festivals. Catechists and Sunday-School teachers, 9. Catechumens: Children taught the Catechism openly in the Church, 80; times, every Sunday. Celebration of Divine Service: Sundays, three times, including the Chapel at Staatsburgh; Holy Days, once; other days, from Advent to Easter, as a rule, twice in each week.

Contributions.—Episcopal Fund, $25; Diocesan Fund, $30; Missionary Committee of the Diocese, $30; Theological Fund, $12; Fund for Aged and Infirm Clergymen, $23 22; Christmas Tree, $130 85; County Missions, $73 20; Board of Missions P. E. Church, U. S.: Domestic Committee, $15; Parochial School, Sunday-School Library, &c., $124 76; the Poor, $507 41; Parish purposes, $202 11; Church purposes in general, Library and Reading Room, $200—total, $1,433 55.

St. James' Guild is organized in the Parish. It has about 80 members; and I here record my testimony to the generosity and zeal which the members of the Guild have manifested in all good works; for, through its co-operation, a Reading Room is maintained; a Library of more than 200 volumes has been collected, and during the past two winters courses of lectures have been given. In addition, the Guild has prepared a box of clothing, in value more than $100, to be sent to a Clergyman in Texas.

In the Chapel at Staatsburgh there is an excellent Sunday-School, having more than 70 scholars. Services have been maintained there throughout the year, and this good work is largely due to the Lay-Reading and to the earnest effort of Mr. Leighton Parks, a Student in the General Theological Seminary.

Trinity Church, Madalin; the Rev. JAS. STARR CLARK, D. D., Rector.

Individuals, 200. Baptisms, inf. 5. Marriage, 1. Burials, 8. Communicants: admitted, 2; removed into the Parish, 4; removed from the Parish, 3; died, 1; present number. 50. The Holy Communion celebrated the first and third Sundays in each month and on all high festivals. Catechists and Sunday-School teachers, 6. Catechumens: Children taught the Catechism openly in the Church, 90. Celebration of Divine Service: Sundays. 96; Holy Days, 10; other days, 14—total, 120.

Contributions.—Episcopal Fund, $2; Missionary Committee of the Diocese, $5; Fund for Aged and Infirm Clergymen, $2; County Missions, $9; the Poor, $15; Parish purposes, $250; Church purposes in general, $45—total, $328.

Trinity School—a Church boarding-school for boys, of which the Bishop is Visitor—has been carried on during the past year with greater success than ever before, by the Rector and his Assistants.

It was begun eight years since to meet a want generally and deeply felt, *i. e.*, the combination of home influence with thorough mental, moral and religious training. The School offers special advantages to the sons of the Clergy and to boys looking forward to the Sacred Ministry.

St. Luke's Church, Matteawan; the Rev. EDWARD T. BARTLETT, Rector.

Families, 146. Baptisms, inf. 18. Confirmed, 5. Marriages, 6. Burials, 16. Communicants: admitted, 6; removed into the Parish, 5; removed from the Parish, 4; died, 6; present number, 211. The Holy Communion celebrated on St. Luke's Day, Christmas, Easter, Ascension Day, Whitsun-Day, Trinity Sunday, and first Sunday in each month. Catechists and Sunday-School teachers, 17. Catechumens: about 220; Children taught the Catechism openly in the Church, about 100; times, monthly. Celebration of Divine Service: Sundays, 102; Holy Days, 11; other days, 28—total, 141.

Contributions.—Diocesan Fund, $30; Fund for Aged and Infirm Clergymen, $32 58; Board of Missions P. E. Church, U. S.: Indian Missions, $142 75; Foreign Committee, $124 54; the Poor, $570 65; Parish purposes, $1,433 69; Church purposes in general, $22—total, $2,355 21.

The present Rector took charge of the Parish in October, 1874.

No report having been made for the Conventional year ending Sept., 1874, he begs leave to subjoin the following partial report for that year:

Baptisms, (ad. 7, inf. 38,) 45. Confirmed, 11.

Contributions.—Episcopal Fund, $3 18; Diocesan Fund, $30; Diocesan Missions, $75 70; Education Fund, $14 07; Aged and Infirm Clergy, $10; Domestic Missions, $144 84; Foreign Missions, $34 69: Parish School, $250; the Poor, $203 27; Parish purposes, $346 27—total, $1,117 02.

Grace Church, Millbrook; the Rev. BENJAMIN F. MILLER, Rector and Missionary.

Families, 14. Individuals, 40. Marriages, 3. Burial, 1. Communicants: removed into the Parish, 3; present number, 30. The Holy Communion celebrated on the first Sunday in each month, Christmas, Easter and Whitsun-day. Catechists and Sunday-School teachers, 5. Catechumens, 25. Children taught the Catechism openly in the Church, 25. Celebration of Divine Service: Sundays, 51; Holy Days, 3; other days, 2—total, 56.

Contributions.—Parish purposes, since January 1st, 1875, $15 90.

The Church here is without a debt of so much as even one dollar. Outwardly the building is very attractive, and the Church property is certainly very fine for a small village.

There is a beautiful little union chapel, about two miles from here, surrounded by a dense population for the country. Were I to remain here much longer, I should certainly try to hold Church services there, with the approval of the proper authorities. "Litt rest," together with this burden, presents a field for hard work for my successor here although this place of itself has a sufficient number of people for one laborer, if he can only reach them and gather them into the Church.

Congregation of the Church, Pawling; the Rev. ORSAMUS H. SMITH officiating.

Baptism, ad. 1. Burial, 1. Communicants: admitted, 1; removed into the Parish, 3; present number, 9. The Holy Communion celebrated Christmas, Easter and Midsummer. Celebration of Divine Service: Once in four weeks; Holy Days, Christmas and Easter.

With little variation, I have been enabled to meet my appointments for service at Pawling through the year. A pious and devout lady gives us the use of her rooms, which are large and convenient for Divine Service, and we have a very encouraging attendance of apparently devout worshippers. I think that there is here growing up a strong interest for our Church, which, I trust, will result in something decidedly to her advantage.

St. Paul's Church, Pleasant Valley; the Rev. GEORGE HENRY SMITH, Rector and Missionary.

Baptisms, (ad 5, inf. 5,) 10. Confirmed, 7. Marriages, 2. Burials, 8. Communicants: present number, 34. The Holy Communion celebrated on the first Sunday in the month and high festivals, 16 times. Catechists and Sunday-School teachers, 3. Catechumens, 20. Celebration of Divine Service: Sundays, 55; Holy Days, 8; other days, 17—total, 80.

Contributions.—Missionary Committee of the Diocese, $1 22; Fund for Aged and Infirm Clergymen, $2 10; Mission to Jews, $0 77; Board of Missions P. E. Church, U. S.: Domestic Committee, $3 24; Foreign Committee, $0 77; Parish purposes, $216 40—total, $224 50.

The Rector has resigned his charge, to take effect on the first Sunday in October.

Christ Church, Poughkeepsie; the Rev. PHILANDER K. CADY, Rector, (resigned,) the Rev. HENRY L. ZIEGENFUSS, Minister in charge, and Rector elect.

Baptisms, (ad. 1, inf 26,) 27. Confirmed 29 Marriages, 6 Burials, 27. Communicants, about 300. The Holy Communion is celebrated on the first Sunday in each month, on the great festivals, and weekly from the first Sunday in Advent to Trinity Sunday, inclusive. Catechists and Sunday-School teachers, 35 Catechumens, 250. Daily Parish Schools: 2, free, Scholars, (males, 59, females, 63,) 122. Celebration of Divine Service: Sundays, twice; on all Holy Days, daily during Lent, and five times a week during the rest of the year.

Contributions.—Episcopal Fund, $20 21; Diocesan Fund, $40; Missionary Committee of the Diocese, $50 50, Society for Promoting Religion and Learning, $12 57; St. Barnabas' Hospital, $135; Freedmen, $24 73; New-York Bible and Common Prayer-Book Society, $53 36; Indian Missions, $17 70; Board of Missions P. E. Church, U. S.: Domestic Committee, $176 11, Foreign Committee, $92 83; Parochial Schools, $800; the Poor, $626 97, Parish purposes, $163 70; Dutchess County Convocation, $192 16; Children's offerings, $136 75—total, $2,872 89.

Church of the Holy Comforter, Poughkeepsie; the Rev. ROBERT F. CRARY, Rector.

Baptisms, (ad. 4, inf. 43,) 47 Confirmed, 18. Marriages, 8. Burials, 27. Communicants: admitted, 17; removed into the Parish, 14; removed from the Parish, 21; died,

6; present number, 295. The Holy Communion celebrated on the first Sunday in each month and on the greater festivals, and four times in private. Catechists and Sunday-School teachers, 22. Catechumens, 281. Children taught the Catechism openly in the Church, all the school. Industrial School: Scholars, females, 67. Celebration of Divine Service: twice every Sunday, three times on the first Sunday of each month, and once a Sunday for four months of the year at St. Barnabas' Hospital; Holy Days, all; other days, every Friday throughout the year, daily during Lent, and twice on Wednesdays and Fridays.

Contributions.—Episcopal Fund, $8; Diocesan Fund, $30; Missionary Committee of the Diocese, $26; Dutchess County Convocation, $37 36; Theological Education Fund, $5 50; Fund for Aged and Infirm Clergymen, $5; New-York City Mission to the Jews, $17 05; Bp. Seabury Divinity School, $30 16; Scholarship, Salt Lake City, Bp. Tuttle, $40; Indian Mission, Bp. Hare, $30 11; Pacific Coast Mission, Dr. Breck, $40; Nashotah Mission, Dr. Cole, $40; Board of Missions P. E. Church, U. S.: Domestic Committee, $84 41; Foreign Committee, $25; Church Aid Society, $33 50; Ladies' Association, $44 23; Men's Association, $49 35; Sunday-School, $212 27; Industrial School, $15 05; the Poor, $284 06; St. Barnabas' Hospital, $222 21; Parish purposes, $918 21; Church purposes in general, $36 17—$2,174 64.

St. Paul's Church, Poughkeepsie; the Rev. S. H. Synnott, Rector.

Baptisms, (ad. 4, inf. 36,) 40. Confirmed, 20. Marriages, 10. Burials, 19. Communicants: present number, 215. The Holy Communion celebrated at the usual times. Catechumens: Sunday Scholars, 160. Girls in the Industrial School, 65. Celebration of Divine Service: Sundays, 150; other days, 76—total, 226.

Contributions.—Episcopal Fund, $5; Diocesan Fund, $12; Missionary Committee of the Diocese, $11; Dutchess County Convocation, $67 65; St. Barnabas' Hospital, $356; Board of Missions P. E. Church, U. S.: Domestic Committee, $39; Foreign Committee, $13 24; Indian Committee, $18 50; the Poor, $465; Parish purposes, $2,676; Church purposes in general, $1,342 27—total, $5,005 66.

Through the generosity of a member of the Parish, a peal of three bells has recently been placed in the tower of the Church, at a cost of nearly a thousand dollars.

St. Barnabas' Hospital, Poughkeepsie.

This Institution, under the care of the three Parishes of Poughkeepsie, has been in a prosperous condition during the past year. Divine Service has been celebrated every Sunday afternoon in its wards. The number of patients has been 68, of whom 40 were discharged recovered, 13 improved, 2 unimproved, and 10 have died.

Christ Church, Red Hook; the Rev. John W. Moore, Rector.

Baptisms, (ad. 1, inf. 11,) 12. Marriages, 2. Burial, 1. Communicants: admitted, 6; removed from the Parish, 3; present number, 88. The Holy Communion celebrated monthly, and on the chief festivals. Children taught the Catechism openly in the Church, between 30 and 40; times, every Sunday. Celebration of Divine Service: Sundays, twice; Holy Days, once on all the principal Holy Days; other days, Fridays of Lent, daily during Holy Week, Thanksgiving Day, and Day of Intercession for Missions.

Contributions.—Episcopal Fund, $11; Diocesan Fund, $16; Missionary Committee of the Diocese, $22 75; Theological Education Fund, $13 23; Fund for Aged and Infirm Clergymen, $10; New-York Bible and Common Prayer-Book Society, $9 45; Protestant Episcopal Tract Society, $3 25; Board of Missions P. E. Church, U. S.: Domestic Committee, $43 14; Foreign Committee, $21 32; Indian Commission, $35 86; Home Mission to Colored People, $14 23; Jewish Mission in New-York, $5; Missionary Bishop's

Fund, $7 37; the Poor, Parish purposes and Church purposes in general, $472 24—total, $684 86.

The offerings recorded do not give a full exhibit of what has been contributed for Church purposes, both within and without the Parish. Our Parish Library has been increased, many of the books being the gift of a lady formerly a member of the Parish, and who still continues to take an interest in it.

During the winter, the ladies of the Parish met weekly, to work for our Indian Mission, and about Easter a barrel well filled with articles of considerable value was despatched to Bishop Hare.

I have endeavored also to interest the children in this Mission, and the contributions recorded above, $35 86, comes in great part from them.

Through the liberality of one communicant, the Church has recently been painted within and without, and put in thorough repair, and now looks very pretty.

Still more recently a very handsome cross for the altar has been given to the Church by another member of the same family.

St. Paul's Church, Red Hook; the Rev. G. LEWIS PLATT, (P. O., Tivoli,) Rector.

Families, 25. Baptisms, inf. 4. Marriages, 2. Burials, 3. Communicants; present number, 37. The Holy Communion celebrated once a month. Catechists and Sunday-School teachers, 13. Sunday scholars, 130. Celebration of Divine Service: Sundays every Sunday morning; Holy Days, on Christmas Day, Ash-Wednesday and Good Friday—total, 55.

Contributions.—Diocesan Fund, $15; Fund for Aged and Infirm Clergymen, $10; Communion offerings for charity, $58; Ev. Ed. Soc., (two collections,) $244 60; Ladies' nevolent Society of St. Paul's Church, $51 90; ladies to same Society in addition, $180 for improvement of Church, $200—total, $759 50.

There has been a preliminary purchase of two acres south of the Church as a site for new Rectory. There is considerable interest in carrying out this desirable plan.

The services have been held by the Rector in Clermont Chapel every Sunday afternoon as heretofore, (from May to the middle of November,) with considerable interest in the neighborhood. The Sunday-School has eight teachers and some forty scholars. Contributions for Sunday-School and educational purposes, about twenty dollars.

Church of the Messiah, Rhinebeck; the Rev. A. F. OLMSTED, Rector.

Families, 26. Baptisms, inf. 2. Marriage, 1. Burials, 2. Communicants: present number, 62. The Holy Communion celebrated on the first Sunday of every month, on Easter Day and Christmas. Sunday-School scholars, about 30. Sunday-School teachers 5. Bible Class, instructed by the Rector, 20. Celebration of Divine Service: Sundays 51; times, 101; Holy Days, 8; other days, 11—total, 70 days, 101 times.

Contributions.—Diocesan Fund, $18; Missionary Committee of the Diocese, $7 50 Fund for Aged and Infirm Clergymen, $8; Communion alms and other Sunday collections, $258 49; Parish purposes, including salary of Rector, $2,404 34—total, $2,695 33.

Church of the Ascension, Rhinecliff; the Rev. THOMAS S. SAVAGE, Minister.

Families, 22. Baptisms, inf. and children, 11. Marriage, 1. Communicants: admitted, 3; removed into the Parish, 3; removed from the Parish, 3; present number, 30. The Holy Communion celebrated once every month. Catechists and Sunday-School teachers, 6; scholars, 36. Catechumens, 3. Children taught the Catechism openly in the Church, 36; times, 12; members of other classes for religious instruction, 6; total number of young persons instructed, 42. Daily Parish School: 1, small sum for tuition quired; Scholars, (males, 10, females, 20,) 30. Celebration of Divine Service: 93, on all Sundays and the principal Holy Days.

Contributions.—Episcopal Fund, $2; Fund for Aged and Infirm Clergymen, $4 60; Board of Missions P. E. Church, U. S.: Domestic Committee, $5; Foreign Committee, $19 03; the Poor, (Indian Commission,) $27 16; Parish purposes, $51 19—total, $108 78.

The attendance on Sunday services has been better than in any previous year. The congregation is composed largely of the working class. The year has been one of unusual depression pecuniarily, from which cause the contributions have diminished in amount. The number of communicants is diminished by three by removal, but the condition of the Parish spiritually and pecuniarily in reality is as favorable as it ever has been, and gives ground for hope in the future. The "Rhinebeck and Connecticut Rail-Road" is now in operation, having its commencement here, great benefit from which is expected to be derived to this place, and indirectly, by increased population, to the Church.

Zion Church, Wappinger's Falls; the Rev HENRY Y. SATTERLEE, Rector

Families and parts of families, 349. Individuals, 1,316. Baptisms, (ad. 10, inf. 72,) 82. Confirmed, 45. Marriages, 8. Burials, 28. Communicants: admitted, 53; removed into the Parish, 18; removed from the Parish, 16; died, 4; present number, 326. The Holy Communion celebrated on the first Sunday in the month, and on the greater festivals, sixteen times, and in private, five times; total, 21 times. Catechists and Sunday-School teachers, 29. Catechumens, 486. Children taught the Catechism openly in the Church, all the School; times, 40; members of other classes for religious instruction, 35. Celebration of Divine Service: Sundays, three times every Sunday, except in July, August and part of September, when the afternoon service was omitted; Holy Days and other days, 43 times—total, 194 times.

Contributions.—Episcopal Fund, $10; Diocesan Fund, $40; Missionary Committee of the Diocese, $37 72; Theological Education Fund, $5; Fund for Aged and Infirm Clergymen, $23 44; Society for the Increase of the Ministry, $69 86; New-York Bible and Common Prayer-Book Society, $10; Protestant Episcopal Tract Society, $5; General P. E. S. S. Union and Church Book Society, $5; General Theological Seminary, $5; Board of Missions P. E Church, U. S.: Domestic Committee, $68 50; Foreign Committee, $60 50; the Poor, $698 15; Parish purposes, (including all departments of Parish work,) $1,485 64; Church purposes in general, $125 70—total, $2,619 51.

The Rev. George B. Andrews, S. T. D., the venerable and beloved Rector of Zion Church, entered into rest on the 20th day of last August, in the 90th year of his life and the 57th of his Ministry.

He was the first Rector of the Parish, and held that office for forty-two years.

NEW-YORK COUNTY.

All Angels' Church, New-York; the Rev. CHARLES FREDERICK HOFFMAN, Rector; the Rev. BENJ. WEBB, Rector's Assistant, and Principal of All Angels' Select School.

Families and parts of families, 34. Individuals, 130. Baptisms, (ad 1, inf. 7,) 8. Confirmed, 12. Marriages, 2. Burials, 3. Communicants: admitted, 6; removed from the Parish, 12; present number, 40. The Holy Communion celebrated all Sundays in Advent and Lent, All Saints', Thanksgiving, Christmas, Ash-Wednesday, Holy Thursday, Easter, Ascension, Whitsun-Day, Trinity Sunday, and a number of other days; in all, 37 times. Catechists, the Clergy; Sunday-School teachers, 4. Catechumens, 40. Children taught the Catechism openly at the services, those present at the time; times, 54; one

Bible Class, numbering 11; total number of young persons instructed, 50. Daily Parish School: 1, paid and free, males and females. Celebration of Divine Service: all Sundays and many other days—total, 340.

Contributions.—Episcopal Fund, $2 10; Diocesan Fund, $6; Missionary Committee of the Diocese, $1 50; Theological Education Fund, $1: Fund for Aged and Infirm Clergymen, $15; New-York City Mission Society, $1 52; Church Missionary Society for Seamen, $1; Parochial School, the Poor, Parish purposes and Church purposes in general, $1,500—total, $1,531 12.

This report is more or less approximate, and includes two hundred dollars from Trinity Church and what has been received as rent for the old Parsonage, which is now vacant and to let.

During the year there have been several removals from the Parish and neighborhood, among them Mrs. Pell, the late female Superintendent of New-York Orphan Asylum. Her removal may prove a great loss to All Angels' Church and the Asylum, where she has been for years.

The Rev. Mr. Webb remains with me. The day school has been continued, and is to be re-opened in a few days, at the close of vacation.

An extension to serve for a future western Transept has been added to the Church. It is being arranged for a school and lecture room, and for the use of extra congregations, &c. We are, however, in the midst of much poverty, and have before us a picture which suggests patience and perseverance as the paths, under God, to success.

All Saints' Church, New-York; the Rev. WM. N. DUNNELL, Rector.

Families, 171. Individuals, 855. Baptisms, (ad. 20, inf. 73,) 93. Confirmed, 30. Marriages, 33. Burials, 42. Communicants: admitted, 42; removed into the Parish, 8; removed from the Parish, 29; died, 8; present number, 231. The Holy Communion celebrated monthly and upon greater festivals. Catechists and Sunday-School teachers, 24 Catechumens: times, 57; total number of young persons instructed, 409; Bible and Singing classes, weekly. Celebration of Divine Service: Sundays, twice or thrice; Holy Days, once; other days, every day in Lent—total, 209.

Contributions.—Episcopal Fund, $26; Diocesan Fund, $60; Missionary Committee of the Diocese, $15 36; Fund for Aged and Infirm Clergymen, $5 23; Jews, $1 43; Board of Missions P. E. Church, U. S: Domestic Committee, $13 17; Sunday schools, $212; the Poor, $158; Parish purposes, $831—total, $1,297 19.

Free Church of the Annunciation, New-York; the Rev. WILLIAM J SEABURY, Rector.

Families, 75. Individuals, 291. Baptisms, (ad 2, inf 18,) 20 Confirmed, 8. Marriages, 9 Burials, 17. Communicants: admitted, 12, removed into the Parish, 20; removed from the Parish, 8, died, 3, present number, 146 The Holy Communion celebrated on every Lord's Day and other festival Holy Days, and twice on Christmas, Easter and Whitsun-Day. Catechists and Sunday-School teachers, 11. Catechumens: Children taught the Catechism openly in the Church, about 100, times, 53. Celebration of Divine Service: 51 Sundays, 7½ A. M, 10½ A. M, 3½ P. M, 8 P M; 20 Holy Days, 7 A. M, [illegible] A M, 5 P. M: 238 other days, 9 A. M, 5 P. M.; total number of services actually held under above rule, 789.

Contributions—Episcopal Fund, $15, Diocesan Fund, $40; Missionary Committee of the Diocese, $27 48; Theological Education Fund, $6 01; Fund for Aged and Infirm Clergymen, $165 78; New-York City Mission Society, $23 55, Church Missionary Society for Seamen, $10; Board of Missions P. E Church, U. S.: Domestic Committee, ($59 [illegible] Indian, $59 96; Freedmen, $59 96,) $179 89, Foreign Committee, $59 97; the [illegible] $358 10, Parish purposes, $4,963 75; Church purposes in general, $83 51—total, $5,9[illegible]

Number of individual receptions of the Holy Communion, 1,659.

During the past year the Reverend George Frederick Siegmund, M. A., has become connected with the Parish as Assistant Minister, and has begun to hold regular services in the German language, in accordance with the form sanctioned by the Bishop of the Diocese.

Church of the Atonement, Madison Avenue, New York; the Rev. CHARLES C. TIFFANY, Rector.

Families, 82. Individuals, 280. Baptisms, (ad. 2, inf. 5,) 7. Confirmed, 7. Marriage, 1. Burials, 10. Communicants: present number, 120. The Holy Communion celebrated first Sunday in each month and the greater festivals. Catechists and Sunday-School teachers, 20. Catechumens: Children taught the Catechism openly in the Church, 100; times, monthly. (See report of Mission Chapel of the Atonement.) Celebration of Divine Service: Sundays, twice each Sunday; Holy Days, festivals of our Lord and Ash-Wednesday and All Saints'; other days, Wednesdays, from first Sunday in Advent to Ascension, six week day services in Lent.

Contributions.—Episcopal Fund, $15; Diocesan Fund, $80; Fund for Aged and Infirm Clergymen, $56 98; Board of Missions P. E. Church, U. S.: Domestic Committee, (Mexican Missions,) $63 81; Foreign Committee, $100; Mission Schools and Chapel, $2,500; the Poor, (by Communion alms,) $477 08; Parish purposes, (not including pew rents,) $2,100; Church purposes in general, (Christian work in Societies,) $494 05; Missions to Colored people, $167 10; to St Luke's Hospital, $81 53—total, $6,140 55.

Ladies' Missionary Aid Society sent seven large boxes of clothing to Domestic Missionaries.

The Ladies' Dorcas Society gave out sewing and garments to from 25 to 30 women during the winter.

The Sewing School connected with the Mission gave instruction and presents to 200 cholars.

Mission Chapel of the Church of the Atonement, Madison Avenue, New-York; the Rev. GEORGE HOWELL, A. M., in charge.

Until the third Sunday of the present month during the Diocesan year, I was at the Chapel of the Atonement. The services on Lord's Days were, two sessions of the Sunday-School, and the morning and evening services. During the year one Thursday evening service was held, and, excepting the summer, there were nearly daily assemblies or the interests of the Chapel work. All the summer I have had four regular Church services on Sunday, and one informal service, with four sermons.

Baptisms, including three adults, 27. Marriages, 7. Officiated at burials, 37 times.

None confirmed at the Chapel, but several of its members were confirmed elsewhere.

Church of the Beloved Disciple, New-York; the Rev. ISAAC H. TUTTLE, D. D., Rector; the Rev. T. H. STUBBS, Minister in charge.

Families, 29. Individuals, 153. Baptisms, inf. 12. Confirmed, 11. Marriages, 3. Burials, 10. Communicants: admitted, 12; removed into the Parish, 11; removed from the Parish, 5; died, 7; present number, 106. The Holy Communion celebrated every Sunday and Holy Day. Catechists and Sunday-School teachers, 11. Catechumens, 109. Celebration of Divine Service: Sundays, 106; Holy Days, 64; other days, 542—total, 712.

Contributions.—Missionary Committee of the Diocese, $18; Society for Conversion of the Jews, $9 25; Board of Missions P. E. Church, U. S.: Domestic Committee, $86 71; Sunday-School, $146 42; the Poor, $268 46; Parish purposes, $307 38; Donations to the Church for various purposes, from friends, $583—total, $1,369 22.

Calvary Church, New-York; the Rev. EDWARD A. WASHBURN, D. D., Rector; the Rev. W. D. WALKER, Assistant and Missionary; the Rev. F. A. HENRY, Assistant.

Families, about 300. Baptisms, (ad. 2, inf. 15,) 17. Marriages, 10. Burials, 13. Communicants, 550. The Holy Communion celebrated each fourth Sunday, Christmas, Easter and Trinity Sunday. Catechists and Sunday-School teachers, 10. Catechumens, 80. (See Report of Calvary Free Chapel.) Celebration of Divine Service: Sundays, twice throughout the year, except August; Holy Days, all feasts and fasts, and daily in Lent; other days, Wednesday and Friday mornings.

Contributions.—Episcopal Fund, $140; Diocesan Fund, $120; Aid for Aged and Infirm Clergymen, $700; New-York City Mission Society, $1,675; Church Missionary Society for Seamen, $226 16; New-York Bible and Common Prayer-Book Society, $850; Board of Missions P. E. Church, U. S.: Domestic Missions, $2,590; Foreign Missions, $1,030; the Poor, $2,596 98; Free Mission Chapel, $6,000; City Charities, $2,612; Indian Missions Minnesota and Niobrara, $952; Western Missionary Churches, $2,100; Lent offerin for Missionary Clergy, $300, Legacy to Board of Missions, (Mrs. Van Horne.) $22,246 48 Legacy to St. Luke's Hospital, $80,000; Legacy to Sheltering Arms, $13,333 33; Legacy to St. Barnabas' Home, $11,128 24—$98,175 19.

Calvary Free Chapel, New-York; the Rev. WILLIAM DAVID WALKE Minister.

Families and parts of families, over 300. Individuals, about 1,100. Baptisms, (ad. 4, inf. 43,) 47. Confirmed, 29. Marriages, 27. Burials, 35. Communicants: admitted, 20; removed into the Parish, 24; removed from the Parish, 10; died, 20; present number, about 4 The Holy Communion celebrated every first and third Sunday in the month and on t great feasts. Catechists and Sunday-School teachers, 59. Catechumens: Sunday Scho 600 to 700; Children taught the Catechism openly in the Church, 600 to 700; times, 15; me bers of other classes for religious instruction, 50 or more. Industrial School, 200. Singi School, 500. Daily Parish School: Scholars, about 50. Benevolent Society, 20 membe Free Reading Room Association, 30 members. Young Men's Literary Society, 24 me bers. Celebration of Divine Service: Sundays, twice, except on first in month thre times; Holy Days, once; other days, every Wednesday and Friday evening nearly; als twice daily in Lent.

Contributions.—Mission Work, Salt Lake City, $50; Home Mission, Colored people $10 33; Missionary Committee of the Diocese, $35 08; Theological Education Fund $13 10; Fund for Aged and Infirm Clergymen, $32 61; New York City Mission Society $48 60, Missionary Work of four Boards of the Church, $28 13; New-York Bible and Common Prayer-Book Society, $8 35; Mission to Jews, $19 38; General P. E. S. S. Union and Church Book Society, $15; Indian Missions, $10 93; Seamen's Mission, $10; Domestic Committee, $55 96; Foreign Committee, $75; Weekly offertory, $1,203 31; the Poor, $60; Parish purposes, $625; Sunday-School offerings: Orphan's Home, $50; Sheltering Arms, $25; Mission Work in Haiti, $25; Scholarship in Indian School, $60; Scholarship in Salt Lake City, $40; China Mission, $20; Memorial Font, $150—total $2,670 81.

Grace Church, New-York; the Rev. HENRY C. POTTER, D. D., Rector; the Rev. JOHN C. TEBBETS and the Rev. JOHN W. KRAMER, M. D., Assistant Ministers.

Families, about 350. Individuals, 2,000. Baptisms, (ad. 5, inf. 44,) 49. Confirmed, [illegible] Marriages, 24. Burials, 32. Communicants: present number, 850. The Holy Communion celebrated on the first and second Sundays of the month and on the greater festivals. Catechists and Sunday-School teachers, 30. Catechumens: about 500. Celebration of

Divine Service: Sundays, thrice on all Sundays; Holy Days, on all Holy Days; other days, daily in Lent and semi-weekly in Advent.

Contributions.—Episcopal Fund, $150; Diocesan Fund, $150; Missionary Committee of the Diocese, $1,450; Theological Education Fund, $750; New-York City Mission Society, $2,317 45; Church Missionary Society for Seamen, $200; Board of Missions P. E. Church, U. S.: Domestic Committee, $36,334 89; Foreign Committee, $5,290 02; Parish purposes, $3,636 66; the Poor, $1,840 07; Grace Chapel, $31,201 19; Church purposes in general, $25,095; Home for Incurables, $1,373 32; House of Rest for Consumptives, $635; St. Luke's Hospital, $1,176 96; N. Y. Orphan Asylum, $432 64; Missions to Jews, $260 10; Niobrara, $5,855 65; Home Missions to Colored People, $520; House of the Good Shepherd, $500; Convention Fund, $1,000; St. Luke's Home for Indigent Women, $397 84—total, $126,302 29.

In the absence of the Rector in Europe, the foregoing Report is furnished by the Wardens of the Church.

Grace Chapel, New-York; the Rev. JOHN W. KRAMER, M. D., Minister in charge.

Families, 145. Baptisms, (ad. 2, inf. 35,) 37. Confirmed, 18. Marriages, 12. Burials, 22. Communicants: present number, about 200. The Holy Communion celebrated monthly and on the principal festivals. Catechumens, about 450.

Contributions.—Aged and Infirm Clergymen, $8 05; Missionary Boards P. E. Church, $144 90; St. Luke's Hospital, $21 83; the Poor, $38 78; Parish purposes, $334 45—total, $598 01.

The Congregation under my charge has had the experience of severe trial during the three years succeeding the fire which deprived us of our Church edifice. In a bad location and with a poor building in which to worship, away from the people who composed our old Congregation, and intruders upon the ground of another Parish, but for the courtesy which permitted us to enter it, we have been working with many discouraging facts to contend against. A new Church edifice on our old ground is now being built, and we hope for our success of previous years when we get into it.

Church of the Heavenly Rest, New-York; the Rev. R. S. HOWLAND, D. D., Rector.

Baptisms, (ad. 8, inf. 8,) 16. Confirmed, 28. Marriages, 7. Burials, 7. Communicants: present number, about 250. The Holy Communion celebrated every second Sunday in the month and on all high festivals. Catechists and Sunday-School teachers, 32. Catechumens, 325. Celebration of Divine Service: Sundays, every Sunday, except in August; Holy Days, all Holy Days from All Saints' to 1st June; other days, twice a week in Advent, six times a week in Lent.

Contributions.—Missionary Committee of the Diocese, $20; Church Missionary Society for Seamen, $147 39; Board of Missions P. E. Church, U. S.: Domestic Committee, $480 05; the Poor, $530; Parish purposes, $5,844 20; Church purposes in general, $1,175—total, $8,196 64.

Floating Church of Our Saviour, New-York; the Rev. ROBERT J. WALKER, Missionary.

Families, about 50. Individuals, 500. Baptisms, (ad. 4, inf. 16,) 20. Confirmed, 20. Marriages, 12. Burials, 8 Communicants: admitted, 10; removed into the Parish, 16; removed from the Parish, 4; died, 5; present number, 111. The Holy Communion celebrated on the first Sunday of each month; Christmas and Easter Day. Catechists and

Sunday-School teachers, 7. Catechumens: Children taught the Catechism openly in the Sunday-School, 52. Celebration of Divine Service: Sundays, 104; Holy Days, 3; other days, 81—total, 188.

Contributions.—The Poor, $130 27; For Books, $19 42—total, $149 69.

The attendance of seamen and other persons has been very large during the past year. Every nation of Europe has been represented at the Services, and from every principal port of this continent sailors have found their way to the Floating Church of Our Saviour. This Church is fulfilling the purpose for which it was erected.

Church of the Holy Comforter, New-York; the Rev. HENRY FLOY ROBERTS, Missionary.

Families, 10. Individuals, 25. Baptisms, inf. 7. Burials, 3. Communicants: removed from the Parish, 7; present number, 13. The Holy Communion celebrated first Sunday in each month and at the principal festivals. We have no Sunday-School. Celebration of Divine Service: Sundays, 104; Holy Days, 3; other days, 17—total, 124.

Contributions.—Fund for Aged and Infirm Clergymen, $2 80; the Poor, (Communion offerings, $29 17; box at the door, $21 84,) $51 01; Parish purposes, (for books for men,) $19 88—total, $70 89.

The work of our Mission being entirely among seamen and boatmen, who are constantly changing their position, it is not to be expected that we should be able to give any thing like the ordinary Parochial report. We are exerting ourselves for the spiritual benefit of those who are unable to form Parochial relations; but the work in which we are engaged brings many of these men under the influence of Christian teaching who would otherwise seldom, if ever, hear a Gospel sermon, and eternity alone can reveal the benefits which they have derived through our labors in their behalf. A statistical rep can give no idea of the nature of the work in which we are engaged.

Church of the Holy Apostles, New-York; the Rev. JOHN P. LUNDY, D. D. Rector.

Baptisms, (ad 4, inf. 80,) 84. Confirmed, 26. Marriages, 18. Burials, 43. Communicants: admitted, 20, removed into the Parish, 40; removed from the Parish, 5; died, 4 number reported in 1874, 370. The Holy Communion celebrated monthly, on all the high festivals and on All Saints' Day. Catechists and Sunday-School teachers, 36. Catechumens: total number of young persons instructed, 320. Celebration of Divine Service Sundays, 102; Holy Days, 32; other days, 72—total, 206.

Contributions.—Diocesan Fund, $80; Fund for Aged and Infirm Clergymen, $62 96 New-York City Mission Society, $58 37, Church Missionary Society for Seamen, $38 83 Board of Missions P. E Church, U. S.: Domestic Committee, $166 32; Foreign Committee, $107 23; the Poor, $1,320 52; Parish purposes, $4,922 74; Church purposes in general, $50—total, $6,806 77.

A Woman's Missionary Association, newly organized, auxiliary to the Board of Missions, and the Young People's Association for the Relief of the Poor, have been doing good work during the past year.

Our Industrial School has grown to the full capacity of the building.

The Rector has relinquished five hundred dollars of his salary in behalf of an Assistant Minister The Vestry have passed a resolution to the effect that the financial condition of the Parish precludes any increased appropriations for Clerical services at the present time.

Church of the Holy Communion, New-York; the Rev. F. E. LAWRENCE, D. D., Pastor; the Rev. H. MOTTET, Assistant Minister.

Services: Daily morning and evening prayer. Holy Communion celebrated at least once each Sunday and on the greater festivals. Catechisings: Sermon to children every Sunday; public catechising once a month. Instruction: Parish School, 50; Sunday-School, 530; Womens' Bible Class, 80; Men's Bible Class, 110. Baptisms, 65. Marriages, 81. Burials, 39. Confirmations, 59. Communicants, 550.

Contributions.—About $18,000.

Free Church of the Holy Martyrs, New-York; the Rev. JAMES MILLET, Rector.

Families, 150. Individuals, 450. Baptisms, 75. Confirmed, 20. Marriages, 25. Burials, 50. Communicants, 90. The Holy Communion celebrated on the first Sunday of each month, also Christmas, Easter, Whitsun-Day and Trinity Sunday. Teachers in the Sunday-School, 12; scholars, 80.

Our report this year differs very little, if any, from former ones. Our services are as well attended as can at all be expected, considering the obstacles by which we are surrounded—the large number of lager beer saloons and the tenement houses. Still, even these latter furnish a large amount of Missionary labor.

Church of the Holy Saviour, New-York; the Rev. A. B. CARTER, D. D., Rector.

Baptisms, (ad. 4, inf. 18,) 22. Marriages, 19. Burials, 26. Communicants: present number, about 200. The Holy Communion celebrated the first Sunday in each month and greater festivals. Celebration of Divine Service, 178 times.

The Parish has done nobly in successful struggles against the then hopeless embarrassment in which it was involved, when the present corporation rescued it in its hour of peril. But with so limited a capacity, its resources can never be more than sufficient to defray its own absolutely necessary expenses. The Rector is devoutly thankful that he has been permitted to "labor with his own hands," that he may not be chargeable to the Church, but even with the added results of self-denial, and a liberal offertory, when there are so many past deficiencies to "make up," there can be as yet but little advance toward outside benevolences. We have, however, done what we could, and by contributions of clothing and provisions to western Missionaries, and distribution among the poor and needy at home, endeavored at least to come within the scope of the blessing to "cheerful givers." The Rector has regularly continued his services as acting Chaplain at Ludlow-street prison, always having evening prayer and a sermon on Sundays, and Bible-class instruction on Wednesday afternoons, and as this is without any assistance whatsoever, it has involved a great deal of labor, but which has been more than repaid in the very perceptible influence for good which has been exerted over the unfortunate inmates. He has succeeded, after continued discouragements, in establishing a library and reading-room in the prison, for the free use of all the prisoners. The effect of this was at once clearly apparent, in counteracting agencies always actively at work in such places as our common jails, to make men, as soon as possible, forget even their humanity.

Church of the Holy Sepulchre, New-York; the Rev. J. TUTTLE SMITH, Rector.

Families, 60. Individuals, 275. Baptisms, (ad. 1, inf. 10,) 11. Confirmed, 12. Communicants, present number, 80. The Holy Communion celebrated on all feasts for which there is a Proper Preface, on Epiphany and Maundy-Thursday, on the last Sunday of every month, and weekly during Lent and Advent. Catechumens: Children taught the Catechism openly in the Church, 100; times, 14. Celebration of Divine Service: Sundays, morning and afternoon; Holy Days, all the principal Holy Days; other days, Tuesdays, Wednesdays, Thursdays and Fridays during Lent, and daily during Holy Week.

Contributions.—Episcopal Fund, $3; Parish purposes, $1,048 45—total, $1,053 45.

All the sittings in this Church are free, and the offertory is the sole support.

Church of the Incarnation, New-York; the Rev. ARTHUR BROOKS, Rector.

Families and individuals, same as last report. Baptisms, inf. 16. Confirmed, 11. Marriages, 2. Burials, 9. Communicants: Probably about the same as in former reports, 400. The Holy Communion celebrated the first Sunday in every month. Catechists and Sunday-School teachers, 15. Catechumens, 150. Children taught the Catechism openly in the Church, all; times 8. Celebration of Divine Service: Sundays, morning and afternoon throughout the year; other days, during Lent; occasional services by Minister then in charge.

Contributions.—Diocesan Fund, $80 82; New-York City Mission Society, $722; Board of Missions P. E. Church, U. S.: Foreign Committee, $125; the Poor, $2,763 28; Parish purposes, $892 41; Church purposes in general, $4,426 76—total, $9,009 77.

The present Rector took charge of the Church last April. The Church, therefore, was without a Rector for six months after the death of the late Dr. Montgomery last October. During that time the Rev. Wm. P. Pearce was the Minister in charge of the Parish. These facts will account for any deficiencies in this report, as well as for an apparent falling off in the contributions of the Parish. Many sums hitherto sent through the Rector have, during the past year, been given direct to the beneficiaries. The present Rector has as yet had no opportunity to learn fully the condition of the Parish, as the congregation has been so largely scattered during the summer.

The Mission of the Church, known by the name of the Church of the Reconciliation, has been well sustained during the past year. The report of its work is made by the Minister in charge, Rev. E. S. Widdemer.

Church of the Reconciliation, (Incarnation Mission,) New-York; the Rev. E. S. WIDDEMER, Minister in charge.

Families, 180. Individuals, 500. Baptisms, (ad 2, inf. 37,) 39. Confirmed, 40. Marriages, 16. Burials, 28. Communicants: present number, 250. The Holy Communion celebrated second Sunday in each month. Catechists and Sunday-School teachers, 37. Catechumens: Sunday scholars, 430. Celebration of Divine Service: Sundays, morning and evening.

Church of the Nativity, New-York; the Rev. CALEB CLAPP, Rector.

Families, 145. Individuals, 440. Baptisms, inf. 30. Confirmed, 1. Marriages, 1. Burials, 16. Communicants, 100. The Holy Communion celebrated the first Sunday in each month, on Christmas, Easter, Whitsun-Day and Trinity Sunday. Catechists and Sunday-School teachers, 5. Catechumens: Children taught the Catechism openly in the Church, 150; times, every Sunday; total number of young persons instructed, 1[illegible]. Daily Parish Schools: free; Scholars, males and females, 90. Celebration of Divine Service: Sundays, 11 o'clock, A. M., and during Advent and Lent an evening service. Catechetical service every Sunday, P. M., Holy Days, 9 A. M.; other days, 9 A. M., except on Saturdays.

Contributions.—Episcopal Fund, $2; Diocesan Fund, $24; New-York Bible and Common Prayer-Book Society, $3; Parochial Schools, $400; the Poor, $200; Parish purposes, $100; Church purposes in general, viz: Children, of the Schools, to Charitable objects of the Church, Mission Schools, Orphan Asylums, &c., in sums of $10 each, $13[illegible]—total, $859.

Church of the Redeemer, New-York; the Rev. J. W. SHACKELFORD, A. M., Rector.

Families, about 100. Baptisms, (ad. 15, inf. 47,) 62. Confirmed, 48. Marriages, 12. Burials, 40. Communicants: admitted, 42; removed into the Parish, 14; removed from the Parish, 27: present number, 161. The Holy Communion celebrated every Sunday and Holy Day. Catechists and Sunday-School teachers, 20. Catechumens: Children taught the Catechism openly in the Church, about 125. Celebration of Divine Service: Sundays, three times; Holy Days, once; other days, daily Advent and Lent.

This report covers the Convention years of 1874 and 1875, the absence of the Rector from the country during the session of the Convention of 1874 having prevented any return being made from the Parish.

The extensive works on the railway tracks on the Fourth Avenue have, for two years, rendered the Church almost inaccessible, greatly impeded all Parochial work, and greatly impoverished the Parish.

Church of the Resurrection, New-York; the Rev. EDWARD O. FLAGG, D. D., Rector.

Families, 100. Individuals, 300. Baptisms, (ad. 6, inf. 20,) 26. Confirmed, 9. Marriages, 20. Burials, 21. Communicants: present number, 80. The Holy Communion celebrated first Sunday in the month and greater festivals. Catechists and Sunday-School teachers, 18. Catechumens: total number of young persons instructed, 150. Celebration of Divine Service: Sundays, twice on every Lord's Day; Holy Days, on greater festivals.

Contributions.—Church purposes in general, $5,000.

St. Ambrose' Church, New-York; the Rev. HOWARD T. WIDDEMER, Rector.

Families, about 180. Individuals, about 800. Baptisms, inf. 16. Marriages, 5. Burials, 3. The Holy Communion celebrated first Sunday in the month, All Saints' Day, all days for which a Proper Preface is provided, Ash-Wednesday, Good Friday, and frequently during Lent. Catechists and Sunday-School teachers, 14. Catechumens, 94. Children taught the Catechism openly in the Church, whole school catechised every Sunday afternoon; members of other classes for religious instruction, Bible Class on Friday evening numbers 50 persons. Celebration of Divine Service, (during two months:) Sundays, 33; other days, 6—total, 39.

Contributions.—The Poor, (during two months,) $51 27; Parish purposes, (during two months,) $260—total, $311 27.

I became Rector of St. Ambrose' Church on the 15th of July, 1875. The above, my meagre report, is, therefore, for the two months past only. The sudden death of the late Rector, Mr. Sill, left Parochial matters in a very confused condition, and I am able to make no report of the other ten months' work. The Parish also found itself very seriously involved financially, and there was fear at one time that the Church must be closed; but that danger is now entirely passed, and the outlook was never as bright. We find ourselves burdened, however, with nearly $5,000 *additional* debt, and after earnest consideration have decided that for the present it is our *duty* to deny ourselves the pleasure (for such it certainly is) of contributing to *any* extra Parochial objects. This will account for the absence of any such items in the above report.

As soon as we have been "just" to our creditors, we shall be as "generous" as possible to all Canonical objects in the Church.

Church of Santiago, New-York; the Rev. JOAQUIN DE PALMA, Rector.

Families, 56. Individuals, 280. Baptisms, inf. 16. Confirmed, 60. Marriages, 14. Burials, 4. Communicants: removed from the Parish, 10; died, 2; present number, 40. The Holy Communion celebrated on the first Sunday of the month and Christmas Day. Catechists and Sunday-School teachers, 2. Catechumens, 12; members of other classes for religious instruction, 35; Sunday scholars, 30; total number of young persons instructed, 60. Celebration of Divine Service: Sundays, Service at 12¼, and lectures in the evening; Holy Days, Christmas and Thanksgiving Day; other days, 10th of October and 28th of November.

Contributions.—The Poor, $50.

Being the "Iglesia de Santiago," a Missionary Church to work among the Roman Catholics speaking the Spanish language in this city and Brooklyn, I call the attention of all interested in the increase of our Church to the number of baptisms and marriages that are celebrated in my Church. In the space of seven years I have been officiating at the rate of about 12 yearly; the number amounts to 84 baptisms and 84 marriages, that is equivalent to more than 180 new members, because no Roman Catholic goes to be married by a Protestant Minister or to a Protestant Church, nor will have his children baptized by anybody else but a Roman Catholic priest. I am going to begin next month my evangelical lectures in Brooklyn in the Spanish language.

St. Andrew's Church, New-York; the Rev. GEORGE B. DRAPER, D. D., Rector.

Families, not far from 200. Baptisms, (ad. 5, inf. 44.) 49. Confirmed, 26. Marriages, 20. Burials, 30. Communicants: admitted, 31; removed into the Parish, 48; removed from the Parish, 44; died, 7; present number, 351. The Holy Communion celebrated on the first Sunday of every month, St. Andrew's Day, Christmas Day, Easter, Ascension, Whitsun-Day and Trinity Sunday. Catechists and Sunday-School teachers, 28. Catechumens, 346; Children of S. S. and Parish taught the Catechism openly in the Church, every month. Celebration of Divine Service: Sundays, morning and evening; Children's service on the last Sunday, P. M., of every month; Holy Days, morning; other days, daily in the season of Lent, and evening prayer on Fridays throughout the year.

Contributions.—Episcopal Fund, $15; Diocesan Fund, $72; Missionary Committee of the Diocese, $52 23; Fund for Aged and Infirm Clergymen, $27 64; New-York City Mission Society, $175; City Mission to Jews, $27 02; St. Luke's Hospital, $105; Board of Missions P. E Church, U. S: Domestic Committee, $130 10; Foreign Committee, $89 69; Missions to Colored People of South, $76 94; additional offerings for Missions, $81 25; the Poor, $663 88; Sunday-School of Parish, $614 17; ordinary Sunday offerings for Parish, $1,818 75; offerings and collections for Interest and Sinking Fund, $4,419 01—total, $8,347 68.

Notwithstanding our heavy burden of debt, the discouraging changes wrought by removals, and the very depressing times, our Parish continues to grow and thrive. The new Church building is completely finished and furnished; a bell and alms-chest, given by kind friends in memory of loved ones departed, and a very handsome carpet provided by the young ladies of the Parish, are among the pleasant reminiscences of the year. The cost of these gifts is not reckoned in the above list of contributions. The grounds about the Church have been neatly enclosed and planted. All the floating obligations of the Parish, remaining from the building enterprise, have been discharged. We have also tried not to be altogether selfish in our Parochial work, and trust that the large amount, which we have been compelled to expend of late on our own account, will make us none the less willing, and far more able in future, to contribute liberally to the Missions and Charities of the Diocese and Church at large.

St. Ann's Church for Deaf Mutes, New-York; the Rev. THOMAS GALLAUDET, D. D., Rector; the Rev. EDWARD H. KRANS and the Rev. JOHN CHAMBERLAIN, Assistants.

Families, about 150. Individuals, about 1,000. Baptisms, (ad. 14, (3 deaf mutes,) inf. 52, (2 children of deaf mutes,) 66. Confirmed, 52, (14 deaf mutes.) Marriages, 27, (2 deaf mutes.) Burials, 47, (8 deaf mutes.) Communicants: admitted, 54; removed into the Parish, 13; removed from the Parish, 106; died, 18; present number, 460. The Holy Communion celebrated every Sunday at 7 A. M., on the first Sunday in the month and high festivals at 10.30 A. M., and on other Holy Days at 9 A. M. Catechists and Sunday-School teachers, 25. Catechumens: Children taught the Catechism openly in the Church, about 100; times, 11; members of other classes for religious instruction, 20; Sunday scholars, about 100; total number of young persons instructed, about 200. Daily Parish School: 1, free; Scholars, about 40; Sewing School, about 100; Boys' Thursday evening meeting in the Chapel, about 40. Celebration of Divine Service: Sundays, (including evening service at Chapel,) 6, one being for deaf mutes; Holy Days and other days, twice, and on some days in Lent three times.

Contributions.—Episcopal Fund, $5; Diocesan Fund, $60; Missionary Committee of the Diocese, $41 94; Theological Education Fund, $12 50; Fund for Aged and Infirm Clergymen, $46 36; New-York City Mission Society, (St. Barnabas' House, $11,) $73; Board of Missions P. E. Church, U. S.: Indian Missions, $61; Domestic Committee, $19 54; Foreign Committee, $16 50; Mission to Colored people, $1; Parochial Schools, Sunday-Schools and the Poor, $2,838 19; Parish purposes, ($1,000 from Trinity Church,) $6,894 17; Church purposes in general, $570 69; the Church Mission to Deaf Mutes, $225 70 —total, $10,795 59.

The Rector having been providentially called to increasing work among deaf mutes in other cities, the Rev. Edward H. Krans was called to be his associate as Pastor of the hearing and speaking portion of the Parish. The Rev. John Chamberlain continues his connection with the Parish, giving special attention to deaf mutes, conducting the services for them when the Rector is absent. With its free seats, its Mission Chapel, 18th-treet, near 8th Avenue, and its special work among deaf mutes, it is hoped that St. Ann's Church will receive aid from members of other Parishes.

St. Bartholomew's Church, New-York; the Rev. SAMUEL COOKE, D. D., Rector; Rev. JOSEPH M. WAITE, Assistant Minister.

Families, 250. Individuals, 1,200. Baptisms, 17. Marriages, 9. Burials, 13. Communicants: present number, 450. The Holy Communion celebrated monthly.

St. Clement's Church, New-York; the Rev. THEODORE A. EATON, D. D., Rector.

Baptisms, (ad. 3, inf. 16,) 19. Marriages 8. Burials, 5. Communicants: admitted, 13; removed from the Parish, 8; died, 1; present number, about 160. The Holy Communion celebrated on the first Sunday in each month and on the festivals for which a Special office is provided. Sunday-School teachers, 14; Sunday scholars, 150; members of other classes for religious instruction, 30; public Catechising in Church every month for nine months of the year. Celebration of Divine Service: twice every Sunday, daily in Lent, and every festival and Saints' Day, and every Wednesday and Friday for nine months of the year.

Contributions.—Episcopal Fund, $5; Diocesan Fund, $25; Missionary Committee of the Diocese, $30; St Luke's Home, $70; Fund for Aged and Infirm Clergymen, $76; New-York City Mission Society, (St. Barnabas' House,) $20; admission of a woman to St. Luke's Home, $100; New-York Bible and Common Prayer-Book Society, $20; Mission to Colored people at Petersburg, Va., $25; Thanksgiving Day for the Poor, $50; Christmas Tree, $100; Board of Missions P. E. Church, U. S.: Domestic Committee, $525; Foreign Committee, $78 85; Indian Commission, $70; Home Mission to Colored people, $30; for Bishop Morris, Oregon, $309; Parish Mission, $2,031 75; Burial Fund, $124 30; Flower Fund, $66 85; Mission at Sodus, W. N. Y., $10; Orphans' Home of P. E. Church, $70; St. Mary's Hospital for Children, $46 88; Parish purposes, (Sunday offerings,) $1,496 96; Easter offering, $439 39; the Poor, by Communion Alms, $479 87—total, $6,301 85.

In May last, the house, No. 87 Amity-street, was rented for the accommodation of the "Parish Mission." By the benevolence of individuals it has been modestly furnished, and contains a reading room, an infirmary, and several rooms for the temporary shelter of the homeless wayfarer.

A fine bell of 1,600 lbs. weight has been presented to the Church and placed in the tower by a member of the Parish, a widow, in memory of her deceased husband.

Church Du St. Esprit, New-York; the Rev. LEON PONS, Rector.

Families, about 70. Baptisms, inf. 10. Confirmed, 11. Marriages, 14. Burials, 10. Communicants, 50; admitted, 17; died, 3; present number, 47. The Holy Communion celebrated All Saints', Christmas, Easter, Whitsun-Day and October. Catechists and Sunday-School teachers, 4. Catechumens: Sunday scholars, 30. Celebration of Divine Service: Sundays, every Sunday, 10½ o'clock, A. M.; Holy Days, every Holy Day, one service.

Contributions.—Episcopal Fund, $3; Diocesan Fund, $48; Theological Education Fund, $2; Fund for Aged and Infirm Clergymen, $5; New-York City Mission Society, $10; Board of Missions P. E. Church, U. S.: Domestic Committee, $3; Foreign Committee, $2; the Poor and Parish purposes, $50—total, $123.

Rev. Leon Pons, officiating Minister, was elected Rector of the Church "Du St. Esprit" at a meeting of the Vestry held on May 20th, and instituted by the Right Reverend Bishop Potter on June 6th, 1875.

St. George's Church, New-York; the Rev. STEPHEN H. TYNG, D. D., Rector.

The annual statistics of such a Parish vary but little from year to year. The present being the *Thirtieth* Annual Report, which the present Rector has been permitted to make, he takes the occasion to give a summary of some portion of the results of this whole period of ministry in this station.

The pecuniary dispensations, in the various departments of Christian work for the whole period, have amounted to $962,406 80, giving an average annual dispensation for the whole period of $32,080 28. Dividing this period into its three decades of years, there has been a very remarkable increase in the annual amount of gifts bestowed. The aggregate of the first decade was $77,097, an annual average of $7,709 70. The aggregate of the second decade was $325,024, an annual average of $32,502 40. The aggregate of the third decade has been $560,284, an annual average of $56,028 40.

These amounts include no other funds or expenditures than those which have passed directly through my hands.

During this period, the Ladies' Dorcas Society have clothed 8,124 children with 26,300 garments prepared for this distribution, at a cost of $14,063. They have distributed more than 10,000 pairs of shoes among the children of the poor. Three Mission Chapels and Schools have been maintained for the last fifteen years, at a cost of $15,000 a year. Buildings for these have been erected, or prepared for them, at an additional cost of more than $80,000.

Another important effort during this ministry has been the maintenance of our large and extended Sunday Schools. They have contained an average of 1,500 scholars and teachers; and their gathered contributions to the benevolent fund under their own trol, have exceeded $80,000.

'uring this ministry, I have admitted to the Lord's table over 2,000 Communicants. ive presented 1,500 to the Bishop for Confirmation. I have officiated at 700 marriages. ve admitted to Baptism 1,200, infants and adults.

hese have been some of the outward and statistical results of my ministry in this Die. The present aspect of my Parish is by no means encouraging. The removal of desired residences in the city, and the increase of rents, have combined to reduce the lic attendance upon the worship of the Lord's day, and the effective agency for our ctical parochial work. And thus, in the fifty-fifth year of my ministry, my years and condition unite to remind me, that my work is nearly finished, and my earthly work ts end. The gracious Lord be praised for ever!

urch of St. George the Martyr, New-York; the Rev. HOWARD T. WIDDEMER, Minister in charge.

'he Parish of St George the Martyr worships, by invitation, in St. Ambrose' Church, I elects its Vestry in that Church on Monday in Easter week. The Rector of St. ibrose, the Rev. Mr. Widdemer, is, by election, Minister in charge of St. George the ırtyr, without salary; and as Minister in charge of St. George's, is, *ex-officio*, a Chapn of St. George's Society, with a salary of $250 per annum.

Owing to the decease of the Rev. Mr. Sill, and the appointment and resignation of the ev. Mr. Fair, the present Minister in charge is able to make no detailed report of reipts and disbursements.

. Ignatius' Church, New-York; the Rev. F. C. EWER, D. D., Rector.

Families, on the roll since the Parish was organized, (December, 1871,) 124; after de-rtures and additions, present number, 104. Individuals, 340. Baptisms, total numr from organization, (ad. 27, inf. 62,) 89. Confirmed, total number from organization, 59. arriages, total number from organization, 19. Burials, total number from organization, Communicants: On the roll, 261; after deaths, departures and additions, present mber, 194; total number of Communions made, 7,087; average each year, 1,771. The ly Communion celebrated, on Sundays, at 7 and 11 A. M.; on Saints' Days and Thurs-rs, at 7 A. M.; during Lent, Advent and Octaves, daily, at 7 A. M. Schools, 2; iolars, 180; teachers, 22. Celebration of Divine Service: Sundays, plain celebration, .. M.; morning prayer, 9 A. M.; Litany, 10½ A. M.; Choral celebration, 11 A. M.; ildren's service, 3 P. M.; Evening prayer, 7½ P. M.; other days, Celebration, 7 A. M.; ening prayer, 4½ P. M.

Contributions.—During the four years, (exclusive of pew rents,) $43,389.

During the Conventional year 1873–74, a Guild, (divided into "wards," each ward with special work,) was organized for Parochial work. During the Conventional year '4–75 the Parish purchased from the Reformed Dutch (St. Paul's) Society the land and urch building on 40th-street, between Fifth and Sixth Avenues.

. James' Church, New-York; the Rev. CORNELIUS B. SMITH, Rector.

Baptisms, (ad. 2, inf. 27,) 29. Confirmed, 23. Marriages, 8. Burials, 22. Communiats: present number, 292. The Holy Communion celebrated monthly, and on all high tivals, and on Thursday evening in Holy Week. Catechists and Sunday-School ichers, 32. Catechumens: total number of young persons instructed, 372. Total of ichers and scholars in Church and Chapel, 404. Celebration of Divine Service: on all ndays, with no exception in summer; on all chief Holy Days, daily in Lent, and for ren months on Fridays.

Contributions.—Diocesan Fund, $50; Missionary Committee of the Diocese, $40 07; eological Education, Society Increase of Ministry, $85 27; New-York City Mission

Society, $109 82; St. James' Free Chapel, $1,108 93; the Children's Fold, $60 36; Board of Missions P. E. Church, U. S.: Domestic Committee, (General, $451 72; Indians, $[illegible]; Freedmen, $25 21,) $557 88; Foreign Committee, $108 22; Parochial Sunday-School, $437 71; the Poor, $572 13; Parish purposes, $1,782 28; Church purposes in general, $465 91—total, $5,228 58.

The Church attendance of children has been greatly increased by organizing a Church Society for the purpose, noting the presence of members, indicating the degree of interest by a graduated system of badges, and giving the association a yearly excursion or festival, distinct from that of the Sunday-School.

This plan has been put to the test of a four year's trial, with steadily increasing success, before being thus reported.

Church of St. John Baptist, New-York; the Rev. CORNELIUS ROOSEVELT DUFFIE, D. D., Rector.

Baptisms, (ad. 6, inf. 15,) 21. Confirmed, 13. Marriages, 9. Burials, 10. Communicants: admitted, 16; removed into the Parish, 9; removed from the Parish, 21; died, 2; present number, about 200. The Holy Communion celebrated on the second Sunday of each month and on the chief festivals.

Contributions.—Support of Episcopate, $5; Diocesan Fund, $16; Missionary Committee of the Diocese, $16 85; Board of Missions P. E. Church, U. S.: Domestic Committee, (including Mite Chests, subscriptions and value of articles by Ladies' Missionary Association for Family of a Missionary, and $100 for Bp. Vail's Miss.,) $815 48; Foreign Committee, $23; Freedmen's Commission, $23; Indian Commission, $23; the Poor and Parish purposes, $2,230 03—total, $2,652 34.

The Rev. George W. Bacon, M. D., LL. B., the Assistant Minister of the Parish, after a protracted illness, entered into rest on Christmas Day, 1874.

Lovely in his character as a man and a Christian, learned as a classical scholar, thorough as a teacher, and able and devoted as a Christian Minister while his health lasted, he was early taken from earth, to our great loss, but to his everlasting gain.

Church of St. John the Evangelist, New-York; the Rev. WILLIAM T. EGBERT, Rector.

Families, 425. Individuals, about 1,500. Baptisms, (ad. 15, inf. 53,) 68. Confirmed, 44. Marriages, 14. Burials, 50. Communicants: present number, 500. The Holy Communion celebrated on the first Sunday in every month and on the great festivals. Catechists and Sunday-School teachers, 35. Catechumens: Children taught the Catechism openly in the Church, 300; times, 12; members of other classes for religious instruction, 25, total number of young persons instructed, 325. Celebration of Divine Service: Sundays, 104. Holy Days, 7; other days, 90—total, 201.

Contributions.—Episcopal Fund, $8; Diocesan Fund, $20; Missionary Committee of the Diocese, $10; Theological Education Fund, $3, Fund for Aged and Infirm Clergymen, $31, New-York City Mission Society, $3, Church Missionary Society for Seamen $3; Board of Missions P. E. Church, U. S.: Domestic Committee, $45; Foreign Committee, $45, Rev. Walter More, Mission work in Colorado, $331; the Poor, about $1,500. St. Luke's Hospital, $25; Parish purposes, $7,076 13; Church purposes in general, $250—total, $9,353 13.

St Luke's Church, New-York; the Rev. ISAAC H. TUTTLE, D. D., Rector, the Rev. ARTHUR A. WARNER, Assistant.

Baptisms, (ad. 12, inf. 78,) 90. Confirmed, 40. Marriages, 26. Burials, 41. Communicants, present number, about 350. The Holy Communion celebrated weekly and on all Holy Days. Catechists and Sunday-School teachers and officers, 39. Catechumens.

about 450; the Catechism taught openly in the Church, monthly. Daily Parish School: 1, for girls—paid partly. Celebration of Divine Service: daily; on Sundays, generally three services.

Contributions.—Diocesan Fund, $50; Missionary Committee of the Diocese, $61 40; Rev. S. D. Hinman, through Rev. R. C. Rogers, $48 48; Theological Education, $50; Rt. Rev. Bp. Clarkson, $62 56; Fund for Aged and Infirm Clergymen, $29 31; St. Luke's Hospital, $60; St. Luke's Home, $278; Rt. Rev. Bp. Morris, $21 91; New-York Bible and Common Prayer-Book Society, $56 87; House of Mercy, $51 48; for Church in East Medway, Mass., by a lady, $100; Infant Class, for education of Indian boy, Isaac H. Tuttle, $100; (Miss Elizabeth Pott, Scholarship, $50; A. B. McDonald, Scholarship, $50,) $100; Board of Missions P. E. Church, U. S.: S. School, for Rev. Dr. Breck, $110 10; Domestic Committee, $473 45; Mite Boxes, Foreign Committee, $157 39; after Sermon by Bp. Niles, for Missions, $53 10; Church offerings, $573 77; the Poor, $575 28; for support of S. Schools, $189 87; Ladies' Relief Society, $252 25; Church purposes in general, $60—total, $3,879 24.

Through the assistance of Trinity Church and of our Parishioners, St. Luke's is being greatly enlarged, by a recess Chancel, numerous working rooms and increased sittings, and, when opened, all the seats are to be free and unappropriated. During the last three months Divine Service has been held in the larger Sunday-School room.

St. Mark's Church, New-York; the Rev. J. H. RYLANCE, D. D., Rector; the Rev. S. A. MCNULTY, Assistant.

Families, 270. Individuals, about 850. Baptisms, (ad. 2, inf. 49,) 51. Confirmed, 71. Marriages, 17. Burials, 31. Communicants: admitted, 40; removed into the Parish, 10; removed from the Parish, 12; died, 5; present number, about 435. The Holy Communion celebrated monthly, in both the Church and Chapel, and on all the great festivals. Catechists and Sunday-School teachers, 50. Catechumens, about 800. Daily Parish School: 1, free; Scholars: males, 50; females, 100; teachers, 2. Celebration of Divine Service: Sundays, 52; Holy Days, 25; other days, 26—total, 103.

Contributions.—Episcopal Fund, $60; Diocesan Fund, $120; Aged and Infirm Clergymen, $124 37; New-York City Mission Society, $300 49; New-York Bible and Common Prayer-Book Society, $10; Board of Missions P. E. Church, U. S.: Domestic Committee, about $900; Foreign Committee, $250; Parochial Schools, $1,000; the Poor, $1,632 78; Parish purposes, $2,178 32; Church purposes in general, $1,782 16; Parish Mission, $2,583—total, $10,946 12.

St. Mary's Church, New-York; the Rev. CHARLES COFFIN ADAMS, Rector.

Baptisms, (ad. 1, inf. 18,) 19. Confirmed, 0. Marriages, 3. Burials, 10. Communicants: admitted, 14; removed into the Parish, 4; removed from the Parish, 10; died, 3; present number, 144. The Holy Communion celebrated every Sunday and on the chief Holy Days. Catechists and Sunday-School teachers, 9. Catechumens: Children taught the Catechism openly in the Church, 75; times, 12; total number of young persons instructed, about 90. Celebration of Divine Service: Sundays, morning, 10½ A. M., 7½ P. M.; Holy Days, 10½ A. M., 4 P. M.; other days, daily, 8½ A. M., 4 P. M.—total, 700 daily Prayers.

Contributions.—Episcopal Fund, $5; Diocesan Fund, $12; Missionary Committee of the Diocese, $10; Fund for Aged and Infirm Clergymen, $13; New-York City Mission Society, $5, (Jews, $9,) $14; Board of Missions P. E. Church, U. S.: Domestic Committee, $35; Foreign Committee, $20; the Poor, $10; Parish purposes, $350; Church purposes in general, $646 88—total, $1,115 88.

St. Mary's is a Free Church, in the full meaning of the term, having no pew rents, subscriptions, or envelopes, but the weekly offertory.

Church of St. Mary the Virgin, New-York; the Rev. THOMAS MCKEE BROWN, Minister in charge.

Families, 40. Individuals, about 300. Baptisms, (ad. 6, inf. 7,) 13. Confirmed, 20. Marriages, 4. Burials, 7. Communicants: present number, 195. The Holy Communion celebrated daily throughout the year, and twice each Sunday and chief Holy Day. Catechists and Sunday-School teachers, 12. Catechumens: times, every Sunday; total number of young persons instructed, 100. Celebration of Divine Service: Sundays, 185; Holy Days, 61; other days, 358—total, 604.

Contributions.—Episcopal Fund, $10; Missionary Committee of the Diocese, $10; Fund for Aged and Infirm Clergymen, $27 06; Church purposes in general, $6,000—total, $6,047 06.

The Reverend McWalter Bernard Noyes has rendered valuable assistance on Sundays.

St. Michael's Church, New-York; the Rev. T. M. PETERS, D. D., Rector; the Rev. C. T. WARD, Assistant to Rector.

Families, 88. Individuals, about 900. Baptisms, (ad. 3, inf. 38,) 41. Confirmed, 17. Marriages, 3. Burials, 14. Communicants: admitted, 17; removed into the Parish, 5; removed from the Parish, 28; died, 3; present number, 170. The Holy Communion celebrated monthly on Sunday and on all the great festivals. Catechists and Sunday-School teachers, 16. Catechumens: Sunday scholars, 182; total number of young persons instructed, 162. Celebration of Divine Service: Sundays, always three times, first Sunday in month, four times; on Holy Days generally; other days, daily during Lent.

Contributions.—The Poor, about $900; Parish purposes, about $1,300; all other objects, about $1,100.

Owing to the illness and absence of the Treasurer of the Missionary and Charitable Funds of the Church, the Rector is unable to report the amount and object of offerings. The total of contributions would probably reach $3,300.

The seats in this Church are all free.

St. Peter's Church, New York; the Rev. ALFRED B. BEACH, D. D., Rector; the Rev. A. J. ARNOLD, Assistant.

Baptisms, (ad. 3, inf 108,) 111. Confirmed, 32. Marriages, 35. Burials, 38. Communicants: present number, about 400. The Holy Communion celebrated on the first Sunday in every month and on the great festivals. Catechists and Sunday-School teachers, 76. Catechumens: Children taught the Catechism openly in the Church, all in the Parish who will come, being invited to do so; times, monthly; members of other classes for religious instruction, 66; Sunday scholars, 665; total number of young persons instructed, 731. Celebration of Divine Service: Sundays, 104; on all Holy Days, and daily morning and evening through Lent.

Contributions.—Episcopal Fund, $15; Diocesan Fund, $40; Missionary Committee of the Diocese, $127 28; Fund for Aged and Infirm Clergymen, $58 59; New-York Bible and Common Prayer-Book Society, $42 43; Domestic Missions, $296 57; Foreign Missions, $32 44; African Mission, (from Young Ladies' Bible Class,) $15; Indian Mission, (from the S. S.,) $30 29; Parish Mission, ($245 from S. S.,) $522 63; Orphan's Home, (from S. S.) $52 32; St Luke's Home, $72 54; St Luke's Hospital, $74 18; Sheltering Arms, (from S. S.,) $60 84; Dorcas Society, $128 50; Sewing School, $50; for Sunday-School Library, $138 50; for Sunday-School Christmas festival, $256 90; Collections in Sunday-School for various objects, $307 44; General Fund for Parish purposes, $1,409 83; for the use of the Rector, $802; Young Men's Association, $530 51; Communion Alms and other offerings for the Poor, $325 70—total, $5,359 49.

St. Philip's Church, New-York; the Rev. J. S. Attwell, Rector.

Families, 125 Individuals, 450. Baptisms, (ad. 8, inf. 17.) 25. Confirmed, 21. Marriages, 5. Burials, 17. Communicants: admitted, 27; removed into the Parish, 2; died, 2; present number, 225. The Holy Communion celebrated on the first Sunday of every month and on the great festivals. Catechists and Sunday-School teachers, 11. Catechumens: Children taught the Catechism openly in the Church, 85; times, 47; members of other classes for religious instruction, 21; total number of young persons instructed, 106. Celebration of Divine Service: Sundays, two Services; Holy Days, Christmas, 2, Ash-Wednesday, 2, Good-Friday, 2, Epiphany, 1; other days, 47—total, 150 times.

Contributions.—Diocesan Fund, $30; Fund for Aged and Infirm Clergymen, $8 50; New-York City Mission Society, for the Jews, $10; Board of Missions P. E. Church, U. S.: Domestic Committee, (for Missions in Petersburg, Va., and Savannah, Ga.,) $29 31; Foreign Committee, (for Haiti and Africa,) $134 98: the Poor, (Communion alms and offerings towards a Home) $700 22; Parish purposes, (including repairs to Church,) $3,236 02; Church purposes in general, $2,085—total, $6,234 03.

From the fact that the Parish has been without a Rector for a year, there are deficiencies in the contributions, which otherwise might not have been, and approximations which could not be avoided. The official charge of the present incumbent bears date May 24th, 1875, and it is pleasing to state that his Ministry, so far, is generally acceptable to the congregation, and every thing bids fair for the future increase of the Church. The Rev. John Peterson, Deacon, still renders valuable assistance in the work of the Parish.

From the heavy expenses incurred for repairs to the roof of the Church edifice, and on account of the scarcity of money during the past year, the financial condition of the Parish is not as good as could be desired.

St. Stephen's Church, New-York; the Rev. Joseph H. Price, D. D, Rector; the Rev. A. B. Hart, Associate.

Baptisms, inf. 13. Marriages, 7. Burials, 11. Communicants: admitted, 4; removed into the Parish, 4; removed from the Parish, 10; died, 2; present number, 62. The Holy Communion celebrated the first Sunday in every month and on the high festivals. Catechists and Sunday-School teachers, 9. Catechumens, 52. Celebration of Divine Service: Sundays, 52; Holy Days, all; other days, Thanksgiving, &c.– total, 133.

Contributions.—Fund for Aged and Infirm Clergymen, $65; New-York City Mission Society, $50 83—total, $115 83.

The Rector acknowledges his obligations to the ladies of his Parish for their devotedness to its interests, and especially for their earnest efforts in the cause of Christian charity. The following is a summary of their kind acts in the latter department: Books, pictures, &c., to Missions and Sunday-Schools, $100 36; Indians and their Missionaries, $149 13; (Kansas, $10; Incurables, $5; Africa, $5; India, $4 78,) $24 78; Garments, blankets, muslins, work, $91 47; St. Lazarus, (Blackwell's and Hart's Islands,) $279 90; Box of books, clothing, &c., for Iuka Mission, $22 71; Box for Nebraska, ($57 11, and for Louisiana, $118 90,) $176 01; Missions among city poor, out door relief, &c., $900—total, $1,758 25.

These statistics feebly represent the Christian character of their work. It has been accompanied by a tender sympathy, a delicate regard for the feelings of others, which a cultivated mind, under the influence of Christian principle, understands so well, and is also quite as effective as material aid.

St. Thomas' Church, New-York; the Rev. William F. Morgan, D. D., Rector; the Rev. Mytton Maury, Assistant; the Rev. Robert Lowry, Minister in charge of St. Thomas' Chapel.

Families, 325. Individuals, 1,500. Baptisms, (ad. 3, inf. 23,) 26. Confirmed, 36. Marriages, 16. Burials, 7. Communicants, 800. The Holy Communion celebrated first Sunday in every month, and on all high festivals. Catechists and Sunday-School teachers, 35. Catechumens, 165; Children taught the Catechism openly in the Church, 250; Bible Classes, 50. Celebration of Divine Service: Sundays and Holy Days, all; other days, Wednesdays.

Contributions.—Episcopal Fund, in full; Diocesan Fund, in full; Missionary Committee of the Diocese, $218 36; Fund for Aged and Infirm Clergymen, $161; New-York City Mission Society, $662 32; Church Missionary Society for Seamen, $174 50; New-York Bible and Common Prayer-Book Society, $137 07; Gen. P. E. S. S. Union and Church Book Society, $190 28; Board of Missions P. E. Church, U. S.: Domestic Committee, $1.281; Foreign Committee, $307 07; other offerings for charitable, Missionary and parochial objects, $11,846 96; rental, $40,000—total, $51,846 96.

Nothing has occurred in the history of this Parish during the past year which should vary the tenor of past reports, or require special mention. The Parish Church, as well as St. Thomas' Chapel, have been centres of earnest work, and have enjoyed the Divine favor. The report of the Minister in charge of the Chapel is subjoined.

St. Thomas' Chapel, New-York; the Rev. WILLIAM F. MORGAN, D. D., Rector; the Rev. ROBERT LOWRY, Minister in charge.

Baptisms, (ad. 6, inf. 45,) 51. Confirmed, 31. Marriages, 7. Burials, 28. Families, 122. Communicants: present number, 120. The Holy Communion has been administered on the first Sunday of each month, and also on the occasion of each appointed festival. The average attendance at the Holy Communion has been from 40 to 75.

During the past Conventional year, services have been held at the Chapel every Sunday, and also on all Saints' days, with special services during the season of Lent, and evening lectures from a number of the Clergy of the city.

The Sunday School numbers 355 scholars, with an average attendance of 275. There are 22 female and six male teachers—total 28.

Contributions.—For support of the Chapel services, $745 25; Holy Communion Alms, $169 79, Diocesan Missions, $12 25; Mission to the Jews, $7—total, $934 29.

The Sunday-School continues its prosperous career, and a number of the candidates in the last Confirmation class were from the Bible classes of the school. The congregations attending Divine service have been good, and gradually increasing. The fluctuations arising from removals being more than made up by the incoming of new families.

St. Timothy's Church, New-York; the Rev. GEO. JARVIS GEER, D. D., Rector.

Baptisms, (ad. 2, inf. 22,) 24 Confirmed, 19. Marriages, 16. Burials, 23. Communicants: admitted anew, 14; removed into the Parish, 17; removed from the Parish, 33, died, 1; present number, 272 The Holy Communion celebrated on the first and third Sundays in the month and on the principal Holy Days. Catechists and Sunday-school teachers, 42. Catechumens, total number of young persons instructed, 340. Celebration of Divine Service: Sundays, morning and evening throughout the year; Holy Days, as set forth in the calendar, other days, daily, morning and evening, in Lent, with frequent lectures and readings, Wednesday evening service and lecture from November 1 to May 1.

Contributions.—Episcopal Fund, $5; Diocesan Fund, $28; Missionary Committee of the Diocese, $9; Fund for Aged and Infirm Clergymen, $14; New-York City Mission Society, $6, Board of Missions P E. Church, U. S.: Domestic Committee, $23; Foreign Committee, $13, Indian Commission, $9, Home Missions to Colored persons, $[illegible]. St. Luke's Hospital, $21; Mission to Jews, $ 6 50; Clergymen's Insurance League, (Rector's assessments,) $30; the Poor, $184 73, Parish purposes, (including $2,028 75, Easter offerings,) $6,929 25—total, $7,305 48

Church of the Transfiguration, New-York; the Rev. GEORGE N. HOUGHTON, D. D., Rector; the Rev. EDWARD C. HOUGHTON, M. A., Assistant Minister.

Baptisms, (ad. 9, inf. 31,) 40. Confirmed, 30. Marriages, 46. Communicants: present number, about 450. The Holy Communion celebrated Sundays and other Holy Days. Catechumens: total number of young persons instructed, about 100. Celebration of Divine Service: Daily, morning and evening.

Contributions.—$12,710 17.

Trinity Church, New-York, including St. Paul's, St. John's and Trinity Chapels, the Mission Chapels of St. Chrysostom and St. Augustine, and the Chapel of St. Cornelius, Fort Columbus, on Governor's Island; the Rev. MORGAN DIX, D. D., Rector; the Rev. BENJ. I. HAIGHT, D. D., LL. D., Assistant Rector; the Rev. SULLIVAN H. WESTON, D. D., the Rev. CORNELIUS E. SWOPE, D. D., the Rev. JAMES MULCHAHEY, D. D., the Rev. FREDERICK OGILBY, D. D,, the Rev. WM. H. COOKE, the Rev. CHARLES T. OLMSTED, the Rev. HORACE B. HITCHINGS, the Rev. ALGERNON S. CRAPSEY and the Rev. PHILIP A. H. BROWN, Assistant Ministers; the Rev. THOS. H. SILL, Mission Priest at St. Chrysostom's Chapel; the Rev. ARTHUR C. KIMBER, Mission Priest at St. Augustine's Chapel; the Rev. EDWARD H. C. GOODWIN, Chaplain at Fort Columbus; and the Rev. GEORGE C. HOUGHTON and the Rev. HARRIS C. RUSH, temporarily officiating.

I.—GENERAL STATEMENT.

BAPTISMS: *Adults*, 48; *Infants*, 561—*total*, 609.
CONFIRMED, 317.
MARRIAGES, 138.
BURIALS, 288.
COMMUNICANTS, 2,858.
CATECHISTS AND SUNDAY-SCHOOL TEACHERS, 226.
CATECHUMENS AND SUNDAY SCHOLARS, 3,055.
DAILY PARISH SCHOOLS, free—*Boys*, 481; *Girls*, 267—*total*, 748.
INDUSTRIAL SCHOOLS—
Teachers, ... 123
Scholars, ... 2,190
CONTRIBUTIONS OF THE PEOPLE, $29,632 81.

II.—SPECIFICATIONS.

TRINITY CHURCH—
Baptisms: Adults, 5; *Infants*, 91—*total*, 96.
Marriages, ... 27
Confirmed, ... 58
Burials, ... 43
Communicants—
Added, ... 62
Died or removed, ... 19
Present number, ... 686
Catechumens—
Sunday-School: Teachers, ... 34
Scholars, ... 543
Industrial School: Teachers, ... 21
Scholars, ... 146
Daily School for Boys: Teachers, ... 5
Scholars, ... 283

St. Paul's Chapel—

Baptisms: Adults, 2; *Infants,* 56—*total,* 58.
Marriages,........ 10
Confirmed,........ 35
Burials,........... 18
Communicants—
Added,.................... 28
Died or removed,......... 7
Present number, about..... 400
Catechumens—
Sunday-School: Teachers,.................................... 22
Scholars,.................................... 250
Industrial School: Teachers,............................... 8
Scholars, all in the Parish School.
Daily School for Girls: Teachers,.......................... 3
Scholars,.......................... 185

St. John's Chapel—

Baptisms: Adults, 12; *Infants,* 132—*total,* 144.
Marriages,........ 32
Confirmed,........ 100
Burials,........... 102
Communicants—
Added,.................... 56
Died or removed,.......... 30
Present number,.......... 689
Catechumens—
Sunday-School: Teachers,.................................. 61
Scholars,.................................. 993
Industrial School: Teachers,.............................. 86
Scholars, about.............................. 1,000
Daily School for Boys: Teachers,.......................... 3
Scholars,.......................... 104

Trinity Chapel—

Baptisms: Adults, 16; *Infants,* 55—total, 71.
Marriages,........ 19
Confirmed,........ 44
Burials........... 17
Communicants—
Added,.................... 40
Died or removed,.......... 15
Present number,.......... 692
Catechumens—
Sunday School: Teachers,.................................. 43
Scholars,.................................. 361
Industrial School: Teachers,.............................. 25
Scholars.............................. 250
Daily School for Boys: Teachers,.......................... 2
Scholars,.......................... 94

St. Chrysostom's Free Mission Chapel—

Baptisms: Adults, 9; *Infants,* 96—*total,* 105.
Marriages,........ 41
Confirmed,........ 40
Burials,........... 76
Communicants—
Added,.................... 44
Died or removed,.......... 41
Present number,.......... 267

Catechumens—

Sunday-School: Teachers, ... 48

Scholars, ... 485

Industrial School: Teachers, ... 21

Scholars, ... 274

Daily School for Girls: Teachers, ... 2

Scholars, ... 132

AUGUSTINE'S FREE MISSION CHAPEL—

Baptisms: Adults, 4; *Infants,* 120—*total,* 124.

Marriages, ... 9

Confirmed, ... 33

Burials, ... 21

Communicants—

Added, ... 51

Died or removed, ... 20

Present number, ... 104

Catechumens—

Sunday-School: Teachers, ... 18

Scholars, ... 423

Industrial School: Teachers, ... 12

Scholars, ... 315

CORNELIUS' CHAPEL, *Fort Columbus, Governor's Island—*

Baptisms: Infants, 8

Burials, ... 5

Communicants—

Added, ... 3

Removed, ... 6

Present number, ... 20

TRINITY INFIRMARY, 50 *Varick-street—*

Baptisms, ... 3

Confirmed, ... 7

Burials, ... 11

;ELEBRATION OF DIVINE SERVICE.—*Trinity Church:* Daily, twice, throughout the year. *Paul's Chapel:* Sundays, thrice; also on high feast days and Litany days: and daily in ly Week. *St. John's Chapel:* Sundays, thrice; and daily during Lent. *Trinity Chapel:* ly, throughout the year, twice; Sundays, four times, and from Advent to Easter, five ies; four services daily in Holy Week. *St. Chrysostom's Chapel:* Sundays, five ser- es; week days, two; Holy Days, five. *St. Augustine's Chapel:* Sundays, twice; Holy ys, once; occasional week day services and Wednesday evening lectures. *St. Cor- lius' Chapel:* Sundays, twice; chief Holy Days, once; Wednesdays and Fridays in lvent and Lent, once; on Friday evenings in Lent, short service and lectures for men ily.

THE HOLY COMMUNION—When celebrated:

Trinity Church: Every Sunday and Holy Day, except Good Friday; two celebrations on the greater feasts, at 7 A. M. and 10½ A. M.

St. Paul's Chapel: Every Sunday at 7 A. M., and on the second Sunday in the month, and on the high feast days; also at 10½ A. M. From Advent to Trinity, at 12 M.

St. John's Chapel: Every Sunday and high feast day.

Trinity Chapel: Every Sunday, at 7 A. M.; also on the first and third Sundays a second celebration at 10½ A. M.; also every Saints' Day and Holy Day.

St. Chrysostom's Chapel: Two celebrations every Sunday and Holy Day, excepting Good Friday; on Christmas, Easter Day and Whitsun-Day, four celebrations; during Advent and Lent, daily celebration, and daily throughout the octaves of the greater feasts.

St. Augustine's Chapel: First and third Sundays in each month; weekly during Lent, and on Christmas, All Saints' Day, and other high feast days.

St. Cornelius' Chapel: The first Sunday in every month, and the principal feasts.

COLLECTIONS AND CONTRIBUTIONS IN THE PARISH OF TRINITY CHURCH IN THE CITY OF NEW-YORK.

	Trinity Church.	St. Paul's Chapel.	St. John's Chapel.	Trinity Chapel.	St. Chrysos. Chapel.	St. Augus. Chapel.	St. Corns. Chapel.	Total.
Missionary Committee of the Diocese,..........................	$315 55	$90 77	$32 45	$705 39	$33 94	....	....	$1,176 40
New-York City Mission,..	73 10	38 85	20 00	112 63	5 64	....	....	255 21
Theological Education Fund,..................................	39 72	17 50	....	172 16	5 47	$7 71	....	242 56
Fund for Aged and Infirm Clergymen,..........................	237 42	86 46	20 20	....	8 10	29 60	....	331 78
Church Missionary Society for Seamen,........................	31 87	25 80	8 38	55 50	5 21	....	....	126 76
New-York Bible and Common Prayer-Book Society,..........	69 72	17 50	....	172 16	5 40	....	....	264 78
Board of Missions: Domestic Committee,.....................	582 93	142 00	87 90	1,979 63	31 50	27 27	....	2,801 23
Foreign Committee,......................	95 50	25 00	14 10	803 03	9 99	66 33	....	1,013 95
Home African Mission,...................	65 36	25 00	....	424 11	9 35	....	....	523 82
Indian Missions,..........................	17 17	19 22	8 16	229 84	3 71	....	....	282 60
Orphan's Home,...	141 05	57 21	23 73	83 54	11 15	....	....	316 68
House of Mercy,..	129 58	64 44	23 69	216 31	14 57	....	....	448 59
St. Luke's Home for Aged Women,...........................	56 72	71 22	5 00	249 37	14 72	....	....	397 03
The Poor, including a portion of the Communion Alms,.......	807 57	273 04	116 99	754 86	117 29	60 90	....	2,130 65
Other Contributions for the Poor,..............................	1,517 24	601 66	680 36	1,704 91	919 96	312 74	....	5,736 87
Additional Contributions and Offerings,......................	3,683 04	936 00	1,082 19	7,259 16	....	572 76	$45 75	18,533 90
	$7,873 54	$2,441 67	$2,073 15	$14,922 69	$1,199 80	$1,077 31	$45 75	....

By the Vestry:

Special Contributions to the Salary of the Bishop,		$1,800 00
Diocesan Fund,		1,100 00
Parochial Schools: at Trinity Church,	$4,300 00	
St. Paul's Chapel,	1,800 00	
St. John's Chapel,	2,683 33	
Trinity Chapel,	2,300 00	
St. Chrysostom's Chapel,	1,100 00	
		12,183 33
Industrial Schools: at Trinity Church,	1,000 00	
St. Paul's Chapel,	150 00	
St. John's Chapel,	1,000 00	
St. Augustine's Chapel,	175 00	
		2,325 00
Sunday-School Festivals,		2,425 00
Alms to the Poor: Communion Fund,	3,000 00	
Poor of St. John's Chapel,	900 00	
Funerals of St. John's Poor,	201 60	
Burials of the Poor in St. Michael's Cemetery, Astoria, L. I.,	408 00	
		4,509 60
Trinity Infirmary for the Sick Poor,		7,900 00
Five Beds in St. Luke's Hospital,		2,000 00
Indian Missionary Episcopate,		1,000 00
		$64,175 74

Zion Church, New-York; the Rev. J. N. GALLEHER, S. T. D., Rector.

Families, 89. Baptisms, (ad 1, inf. 9) 10. Confirmed, 10. Marriages, 4. Burials, 3. Communicants: admitted, 13; removed into the Parish, 17; removed from the Parish, 18; present number, 155. The Holy Communion celebrated first Sunday in each month and on greater festivals. Catechists and Sunday-School teachers, 13. Catechumens: Sunday scholars, 65; total number of young persons instructed, 65. Celebration of Divine Service: Sundays, 92; Holy Days, 40; other days, 102—total, 234 times.

Contributions.—Episcopal Fund, $10; Diocesan Fund, $100; Missionary Committee of the Diocese, $356 65; Fund for Aged and Infirm Clergymen, $48 98; New-York City Mission Society, $41 87; Board of Missions P. E. Church, U. S.: Domestic Committee, $524 11; Foreign Committee, $321 42; for Poor, $1,008 84; Parish purposes, $7,279 31; Church purposes in general, $1,755 20—total, $11,446 33.

Church of the Holy Trinity, Harlem, New-York. [Rectorship vacant. Reported by Clerk of the Vestry.]

Owing to the absence from town of the late Rector, the Rev. W. Neilson McVickar, who only is in possession of the information required for this Parochial Report, we are unable to supply the data needed.

Grace Church, Harlem, New-York; the Rev. D. BRAINERD RAY.

Families, 80. Baptisms, (ad. 2, inf. 21,) 23. Confirmed, 6. Marriages, 11. Burials, 13. Communicants: removed from the Parish, 11; present number, 108. The Holy Communion celebrated first Sunday in every month, Christmas, Easter. Catechists and Sunday-School teachers, 28. Catechumens: Children taught the Catechism openly in the Church, entire school; times, 9; Sunday Scholars, 225. Celebration of Divine Service: Sundays, 48; Holy Days, 10; other days, Wednesdays and Fridays during Lent—total, 70.

Contributions.—Episcopal Fund, $2; the Poor, $105; morning and evening collections, exclusive of Communion offerings, $406—total, $513.

Bethlehem Chapel, New York; the Rev. FREDERICK OERTEL, Missionary.

Families, 97. Individuals, 240. Baptisms, inf. 38. Confirmed, 23. Marriages, 5. Burials, 14. Communicants: admitted, 28; removed from the Parish, 16; died, 5; present number, 140. The Holy Communion celebrated on all festivals. Catechists and Sunday-School teachers, 5. Catechumens: Children taught the Catechism openly in the Church, 42; times, 25; members of other classes for religious instruction, 45; Sunday-School scholars, males, 101, females, 127. Daily Parish School: free; Scholars, males, 65, females, 54; Industrial School: females, 80. Celebration of Divine Service: Sundays, morning and evening, 104; Holy Days, 9; other days, 10—total, 123 times.

Contributions.—The Poor, $56 69; Parish purposes, $128; Church purposes in general, $37 27—total, $241 96.

The expenses for the support of the Industrial School, and for providing meals and necessaries for the sick and poor during the winter season, were defrayed by the ladies of the Industrial Society, and are not included in this Report.

Another additional expense was also made by them of two hundred and fifty ($250) dollars towards repairing the Church building and school room.

Chapel of Bellevue Hospital, New York; the Rev. P. T. V. VAN ROOSBROECK, Missionary.

Baptisms, (ad. 9, inf. 23,) 32. Burials, 195. Communicants: present number, 237. The Holy Communion celebrated on the third Sunday of every month, Christmas, St. Luke's

Day and Thanksgiving Day. Celebration of Divine Service: Sundays, every Sunday at 10½ A. M.; Holy Days, Christmas, St. Luke's Day and Thanksgiving Day; other days, Good Friday, all the Fridays in Advent and during Lent—total, 70.

St. James' Church, Fordham, New-York; the Rev. MYTTON MAURY, Rector, until May 28th, 1875.

Families, about 20. Individuals, 150. Baptisms, inf. 6. Marriages, 2. Burials, 6. Communicants: present number, about 80. Catechumens: Sunday scholars, about 60.

St. Ann's Church, Morrisania, New-York; the Rev. WILLIAM HUCKEL, Rector.

Families, 70. Individuals, about 300. Baptisms, 14. Marriages, 2. Burials, 8. Communicants, 105. The Holy Communion celebrated on the first Sunday of each month and on the chief festivals. Sunday-School teachers, 17; Scholars, 225. Celebration of Divine Service: Sundays, 100; other days, 40—total, 140.

Contributions.—Episcopal Fund, $7; Diocesan Fund, $10; Board of Missions: Foreign Committee, $31 20; Domestic Committee, $31 20; Home for Incurables, $35; Education Soc., $25; St. Ann's Sunday Schools, $100; Poor, $123 60; Easter offerings for Parish purposes, $1,200; Church purposes, $350; St. Ann's Benevolent Society, $217; contributions of Sunday Schools for benevolent objects, $145—total, $2,375.

The Ladies' Benevolent Association during the past winter gave weekly employment to thirty-two deserving poor women.

The Rector desires to record with gratitude the kindness of his congregation in supplying his pulpit and giving him the means to enjoy a three months' vacation in Europe.

St. Paul's Church, Morrisania, New-York; the Rev. THOMAS R. HARRIS, Rector.

Families, 61. Individuals, about 250. Baptisms, inf. 17. Marriages, 6. Burials, 12. Communicants: admitted, 7; removed into the Parish, 7; removed from the Parish, 8; died, 1; present number, 95. The Holy Communion celebrated the first Sunday of each month, fortnightly in Advent and Lent, and on all the greater festivals. Catechists and Sunday-School teachers, 15. Catechumens, 135. Celebration of Divine Service: Sundays, three times; other days, 62 times.

Contributions.—Diocesan Fund, $12; the Poor and Sunday-School, $130; Parish purposes, from Offertory, $1,221 30; Parish purposes, from Donation, $362—total, $1,725 30.

Trinity Church, Morrisania, New-York; the Rev. ALBERT S. HULL, Rector.

Families, 50. Individuals, 270. Baptisms, (ad. 5, inf. 30,) 35. Marriages, 3. Burials, 15. Communicants: present number, 125. The Holy Communion celebrated every Lord's Day and Holy Day. Catechists and Sunday-School teachers, 13. Catechumens, 100. Celebration of Divine Service: Sundays, three times; Holy Days, once; other days, Wednesdays and Fridays.

Contributions.—Diocesan Fund, $6; Fund for Aged and Infirm Clergymen, $7; Parish purposes, from Offertory, $1,070 33; Church purposes in general, $3,156—total, $4,249 33.

The new Church was opened for Divine worship on Christmas Day, 1874. Although in still an unfinished condition, it gives great satisfaction to all interested in its erection.

St. Mary's Church, Mott Haven, New-York; the Rev. CHRISTOPHER S. STEPHENSON, Rector.

Families, about 75. Individuals, about 225. Baptisms, (ad. 3, inf. 25,) 28. Confirmed, 10. Marriages, 6. Burials, 18. Communicants: admitted, 3; removed into the Parish, 3; removed from the Parish, 6; died, 3; present number, 115. The Holy Communion celebrated the first Sunday in each month, Christmas, Holy Thursday, Easter Day, Ascension, Whitsun-Day and Trinity Sunday. Catechists and Sunday-School teachers, 19. Catechumens, 45; Children taught the Catechism openly in the Church, 120; times, 12; total number of young persons instructed, 165. Celebration of Divine Service: Sundays, morning and evening; Holy Days, All Saints', Christmas, Epiphany, Ash-Wednesday, Good Friday, Ascension Day, Wednesdays and Fridays in Lent, daily in Holy Week; other days, Thanksgiving Day, Friday evenings, and when directed by the Bishop.

Contributions.—Episcopal Fund, $3; Diocesan Fund, (for 1874,) $15; do. for 1875, $30; Gift to the Rector, $116 50; Fund for Aged and Infirm Clergymen, $6 67; New-York City Mission, to Deaf Mutes, $4 80; Church Missionary Society, for Jews, $9; Sunday-School, $20; the Poor, $148 48; Parish purposes, $621 77; Church purposes in general, $3,624—total, $4,599 22.

The lots upon which the Church stood in Garden-street have been sold, and other lots, on Alexander Avenue, purchased.

The building was removed to the new site last June, and has since been enlarged to more than double its former capacity.

This enterprise, with all that it involves, will incur an expenditure of about eight thousand five hundred dollars, exclusive of the lots.

The Ladies' Association of the Parish have been active in good works during the past year, and volunteered to procure a new organ, and to contribute materially towards furnishing the new Church.

We are greatly indebted to our Junior Warden, Mr. William R. Beal, for liberal advances of money, and other assistance, in carrying on the work.

Christ Church, Riverdale, New-York; the Rev. GEORGE D. WILDES, D.D., Rector.

Families, 60. Individuals, about 300. Baptisms, inf. 12. Confirmed: a class is now ready for Confirmation. Marriages, 3. Burials, 3. Communicants, 120. Holy Communion administered on the first Sunday of every month. Sunday-School scholars, 50; teachers, 6. Celebration of Divine Service: twice on Sundays, the greater festivals and fasts, and in Lent two services with lecture every week until Holy Week, when two services with lecture were held daily; also, service, with lecture, from Easter until Trinity Sunday—total, 146.

Contributions.—Episcopal Fund, $12; Diocesan Fund, $66; Sunday-School, for Indian Commission, $50; City Mission and "Poor Children's Fund," $750; Church Mission in Mexico, (individuals,) $1,500; Society for Increase of the Ministry, $25; Church Congress $100; St. Luke's Hospital, $100; to Bp. Whipple through Domestic Committee, for Minnesota, $225; Bp. Whipple, $200; Ladies' Association, for Bp. Holly, (Hayti,) through Foreign Committee, $250; St. John's Hospital, $100; Communion offerings, $481 01; Parish purposes, (not including pew rents,) $3,150; Church purposes in general, specially Southern Mission, $600—total, $7,569 01.

Grace Church, West Farms, New-York; the Rev. ROBERT SCOTT, Rector.

Families, 29. Individuals, 136. Baptisms, inf. 13. Marriage, 1. Communicants: present number, 63. The Holy Communion celebrated the first Sunday in every month and on principal festivals. Catechists and Sunday-School teachers, 14. Catechumens: Children taught the Catechism openly in the Church, 130; times, 12. Celebration of Divine Service: Sundays, 2.

Contributions.—Episcopal Fund, $3 25; Diocesan Fund, $7 20; Theological Education Fund, $7 80; Board of Missions P. E. Church, U. S.: Domestic Committee, $13 56; Foreign Committee, $20; the Poor, $119 70—total, $171 51.

ORANGE COUNTY.

St. John's Church, Canterbury; the Rev. JOHN F. POTTER, A. M., Rector and Missionary.

Baptisms, inf. 9. Confirmed, 4. Marriages, 3. Burials, 3. Communicants: present number, 53. The Holy Communion celebrated first Sunday in each month, on the great feasts, Thursday before Easter, Thanksgiving Day, and weekly during Advent and Lent. Celebration of Divine Service: Sundays, 117; Holy Days, 30; other days, 10—total, 157.

Contributions.—Episcopal Fund, $2; Diocesan Fund, $1 73; Missionary Committee of the Diocese, $3; Theological Education Fund, $2 50; Fund for Aged and Infirm Clergymen, $4 08; St. Luke's Hospital, $10; New-York Bible and Common Prayer-Book Society, $2 75: Protestant Episcopal Tract Society, $1 50; General P. E. S. S. Union and Church Book Society, $2; General Theological Seminary, $2 25; Sunday-School offerings, $10 46; the Poor, $5 93; Parish purposes, $1,103 69—total, $1,231 96.

During the past year a new furnace has been placed in the Church, parts of the floor relaid, and the interior walls throughout polychromed. The pews, roof and furniture have been oiled and varnished.

On the 5th of August the Church was consecrated by the Bishop of the Diocese.

The Rector has held services during the summer in the Temperance Hall near "The Landing."

St. James' Church, Goshen; the Rev. WM. H. DE L. GRANNIS, Rector.

Baptisms, inf. 10. Marriages, 11. Burials, 11. Communicants: died, 3; present number, 225. The Holy Communion celebrated first Sunday in every month and chief Holy Days. Catechists and Sunday-School teachers, 15. Catechumens: Children taught the Catechism openly in the Church, 120; times, 12. Celebration of Divine Service: Sundays, twice; Holy Days, once; other days, those appointed by Ecclesiastical or civil authority.

Contributions.—Missionary Committee of the Diocese, through Convocation, $200; Theological Education Fund, to St. Stephen's College, $195; Fund for Aged and Infirm Clergymen, $35 75; Sunday-School offering, $50; Mite Chests for Domestic Missions, $19 50; the Jews, $8 45; Board of Missions P. E. Church, U. S.: Domestic Committee, $88 82; Foreign Committee, $77 41; Mission to Colored People, $68 65; Indian Missions, $48 43; the Poor, $129 03: Parish purposes, $226; Church purposes in general, sundry boxes of clothing and other things sent to Missionaries in the West by the Ladies' Society—total, $1,147 09.

St. John's Church, Greenwood Iron Works; the Rev. SAMUEL MORAN, Rector and Missionary.

Families, 36. Individuals, 180. Baptisms, (ad. 8, inf. 35,) 43. Confirmed, 10. Marriages, 3. Burials, 4. Communicants: admitted, 10; died, 3; present number, 80. The Holy Communion celebrated on first Sunday of each month, the greater festivals, Thanksgiving Day, and weekly in Advent and Lent. Catechists and Sunday-School teachers, 6. Catechumens: Children taught the Catechism openly in the Church, 40; times, 5; total number of young persons instructed, 51. Celebration of Divine Service: Sundays, 99; Holy Days, once; other days, every Wednesday and Friday in Lent and Thanksgiving Day.

Contributions.—Episcopal Fund, $3; Diocesan Fund, $5; Missionary Committee of the Diocese, $5; Theological Education Fund, $5; Fund for Aged and Infirm Clergymen, $5; the Poor, $40 80; Parish purposes, including Rector's salary, $1,080; Church purposes in general, $205—total, $1,348 80.

The present Rector entered upon his duties on the 18th day of November, 1874. The above report dates back from the resignation of his predecessor in September, 1874.

Church of the Holy Innocents, Highland Falls, Cornwall; the Rev. WILLIAM REED THOMAS, M. A., Rector.

Families, 55. Individuals, 280. Baptisms, (ad. 6, inf. 27,) 33. Marriages, 9. Burials, 8. Communicants: admitted, 2; removed into the Parish, 4; removed from the Parish, 5; died, 2; present number, 80. The Holy Communion celebrated weekly during Lent, on the first Sunday of every month, and on the chief festivals; four times in private and three times at West Point Chapel. Catechists and Sunday-School teachers, 9. Catechumens: Children taught the Catechism openly in the Church, 80; times, 12; total number of young persons instructed, 100. Celebration of Divine Service: Sundays, 119; Holy Days, 26; other days, 62—total, 207.

Contributions.—Episcopal Fund, $3; Diocesan Fund, $20; Missionary Committee of the Diocese, $16 50; Theological Education Fund, $10; Fund for Aged and Infirm Clergymen, $11 83; Board of Missions P. E. Church, U. S.: Domestic Committee, $5; Foreign Committee, $3 51; the Poor, $273 95; Parish purposes, (including Sunday-School,) about $290; Church purposes in general, (debt on Rectory,) $460 65—total, $1,094 47.

The Mission service was continued during the winter among the soldiers with good success.

Grace Church, Middletown; the Rev. ALEXANDER CAPRON, Rector.

Families, about 200. Baptisms, (ad. 6, inf. 15,) 21. Marriages, 13. Burials, 24. Communicants: admitted, 48; removed into the Parish, 4; removed from the Parish, 21; died, 7; present number, 248. The Holy Communion celebrated on the first Sunday of each month and on all the high festivals. Catechists and Sunday School teachers, 20. Children taught the Catechism openly in the Church, about 200. Total number of young persons instructed, about 200. Celebration of Divine Service: Sundays, on all Sundays in the year; Holy Days, all high festivals; other days, every day in Lent—total, 165.

Contributions.—Episcopal Fund, $2; Diocesan Fund, $30; Fund for Aged and Infirm Clergymen, $14 69; the Poor, $111 07; Parish purposes, say $1,500—total, $1,657 76.

Grace Church, Monroe; the Rev. HENRY A. DOWS, Rector and Missionary.

Families, 17. Individuals, 63. Baptisms, (ad. 2, inf. 2,) 4. Burial, 1. Communicants: removed into the Parish, 6; removed from the Parish, 2; present number, 20. The Holy Communion celebrated monthly and on the high festivals. Catechists and Sunday-School teachers, 4. Catechumens: Children taught the Catechism openly in the Church, 18, times, 11 Total number of young persons instructed, 18. Celebration of Divine Service: Sundays, in the morning and afternoon; Holy Days, in the morning; other days, in the morning on Fridays, throughout nearly the whole of the year, and in the morning and evening on Wednesdays and Fridays in Lent; daily service in Passion Week - total, 136.

Contributions.—Episcopal Fund, $2; Diocesan Fund, $2 50; Missionary Committee of the Diocese, $3 68; Theological Education Fund, $1; Fund for Aged and Infirm Clergymen, $1; New-York Bible and Common Prayer-Book Society, $3 67; Board of Missions P. E. Church, U. S.: Foreign Committee, $3 13; Church purposes in general, $273 73—total, $290 71.

The statistics in this report extend back only to St. Luke's Day, 1874. Before that time, the Church had been closed, except for Sunday-School services, for a year; but it has now recovered from this depression, and the prospects for growth are very bright. The Church building is being repaired and improved by contributions mostly from within the Parish, and without incurring any debt whatever.

Nothing has been given to the poor, for the reason that, after careful inquiry, there have been found no cases of persons needing relief.

St. George's Church, Newburgh; the Rev. JOHN BROWN, D. D., Rector; the Rev. OCTAVIUS APPLEGATE, Assistant Minister.

Families, 200. Individuals, 800. Baptisms, (ad. 9, inf. 92,) 101. Confirmed, 54. Marriages, 18. Burials, 24. Communicants: admitted, 31; removed into the Parish, 21; removed from the Parish, 29; died, 5; present number, 400. The Holy Communion celebrated the first Sunday in the month and principal festivals. Catechists and Sunday-School teachers, 50. Catechumens, 350. Celebration of Divine Service: in the Church, 261; in Mission Chapel, 132—total, 393.

Contributions.—Episcopal Fund, $18; Diocesan Fund, $40; Missionary Committee of the Diocese, $202 62; Theological Education Fund, $55; Fund for Aged and Infirm Clergymen, $118 77; New-York Bible and Common Prayer-Book Society, $66 66; General Theological Seminary, Professorship, $40; Board of Missions P. E. Church, U. S.: Domestic Committee, $130 49; Foreign Committee, $120 69; the Poor, Alms, $447 37; Parish purposes, $1,201 72; Church purposes in general, $1,204 58; Indian Mission, $100 63; Mission to Colored People, $105 48; Mission to the Jews, $28 63; St. Mark's School, Salt Lake City, $110; St. John's Mission, Utah, $10; Bishop Holly, $10; Nebraska, $30; Nashota, $15; Seabury Divinity School, $141 86; Pine Island, (Minn.,) $17; Herndon Mission, (Virginia,) $32; Bishop Garrett, $61; Midnight Mission, $35; St. Barnabas' House, $20; Western Convocation, $328; St. Luke's Home and Hospital, $68 50; S. S. Library, $125 99; Sunday-School expenses, $85 54; St. George's Mission, $1,139 16; Benevolent Association, $148 60; Altar Society, $113 43—total, $6,401 90.

Rev. G. W. Hinkle, ordained Priest in St. George's Church, November 20th, 1874, has charge of St. George's Mission.

St. Paul's Church, Newburgh; the Rev. RUFUS EMERY, Rector.

Families and parts of families, 141. Individuals, about 400. Baptisms, (ad. 1, inf. 8,) 9. Confirmed, 9. Marriages, 3. Burials, 3. Communicants: admitted, 9; removed into the Parish, 8; removed from the Parish, 13; died, 1; present number, 147. The Holy Communion celebrated on the first Sunday in every month and every day with Proper Preface. Catechists and Sunday-School teachers, 14. Catechumens: Children taught the Catechism openly in the Church, 100; times, 10. Celebration of Divine Service: Sundays, twice; Holy Days, once; other days, every Wednesday—total, 170.

Contributions.—Episcopal Fund, $5; Diocesan Fund, $5; Missionary Committee of the Diocese, $1; Fund for Aged and Infirm Clergymen, $5; Sunday-School, $35; Bp. Vail, in clothing, $40; Western Convocation, $25; the Poor, $25; Parish purposes, $1,913 90; Church purposes in general, $235—total, $2,289 90.

During the past year we have united with the Parishes of St. George's, in this city, and St. Thomas', New-Windsor, in establishing and maintaining St. Luke's Home and Hospital, which was opened early in the spring, and is now in successful operation.

By the exertions of the young ladies of the Sunday-School, the Chapel has been repaired and improved. The interior of the Church has also been improved.

St. Luke's Home and Hospital, Newburgh.

This institution was established on November 4th last, by members of the Parishes of Newburgh and New-Windsor, and is under the charge of the Bishop and of the Rectors of St. George's and St. Paul's, Newburgh, and St. Thomas', New-Windsor

The work has been successfully prosecuted since the time of organization.

Grace Church, Port Jervis; the Rev. J. G. ROSENCRANTZ, Rector and Missionary.

Families, 47. Individuals, 174. Baptisms, (ad. 5, inf. 19,) 24. Confirmed, 18. Burials. 11. Communicants: admitted, 11; removed into the Parish, 6; removed from the Parish. 3; died, 3; present number, 72. The Holy Communion celebrated on the first and third Sundays of every month, all festivals for which there is provided a Proper Preface, the first Sunday in Advent and the first Sunday in Lent. Catechumens: Children taught the Catechism openly in the Church, about 70; times, monthly; total number of young persons instructed, 70. Celebration of Divine Service: Sundays, morning, 11 A. M., and evening, 7 P. M.; Holy Days, every Saints' Day, and other days for which there is Collect, Epistle and Gospel provided; other days, Wednesdays during the year, Wednesdays and Fridays during Lent, and daily in Holy Week—total number of services, 143.

Contributions.—Parish purposes, $245 31; Church purposes in general, $204 40—total, $419 71.

There was a vacancy in the Rectorship of this Parish from the beginning of Advent until Ash-Wednesday. The report for the most part is only for work done from February 10th until September 29th. There is a heavy debt upon the Parish incurred in the building of the present Church edifice; but there is a steady increase in the growth of the Parish, and if it was only relieved from the present embarrassment, a permanent and self-supporting Parish would almost immediately come into existence.

St. Thomas' Church, New-Windsor; the Rev. HASLETT MCKIM, Rector.

Families, 36. Individuals, 132. Baptisms, (ad. 1, inf. 10,) 11. Confirmed, 6. Marriages, 2. Burial, 1. Communicants: admitted, 4; removed from the Parish, 1; present number, 46. The Holy Communion celebrated on the first Sunday of each month, Christmas and Whitsun-Day. Catechists and Sunday-School teachers, 6. Catechumens: Sunday scholars, 51. Celebration of Divine Service: Sundays, 62; Holy Days, Christmas, Passion Week, Ash-Wednesday and Ascension; other days, every Friday in Lent and Thanksgiving—total, 78.

Contributions.—Episcopal Fund, $3; Diocesan Fund, $20; Missionary Committee of the Diocese, $16; Theological Education Fund, $9; Fund for Aged and Infirm Clergymen, $21 25, the Poor, $75 73, Church purposes in general, $12 95—total, $157 93.

Other contributions of the Church go towards the Rector's salary

Up to July there was a Ladies' Bible Class, under charge of the Rector, every Sunday afternoon. Since then regular afternoon Service has taken its place.

St. Andrew's Church, Walden; the Rev. WILLIAM E. SNOWDEN, Rector and Missionary.

Families, 53. Individuals, about 200. Baptisms, (ad. 4, inf. 18.) 22 Confirmed, 12 Marriages, 6. Burials, 8. Communicants: admitted, 20; removed from the Parish, 5. deceased, 2; present number, 79.

Sunday-School teachers, 9. S S. children catechised openly in the Church every Sunday, about 50. Holy Communion on the first Sunday in every month and whenever there is a Proper Preface. Services at St. Andrew's Church every Sunday morning and night and on every Friday in Lent and daily in Holy Week.

Contributions.—Episcopal Fund, $2; Missionary Committee of the Diocese, $14; Convocation, $10 47; Aged and Infirm Clergy, $3; Bible and Prayer-Book Society, $3; Parish purposes, $425 31—total, $457 78.

At Montgomery, a Service established nearly a year ago, on the second and last Sunday of every month, at 3 P. M. A few members of the Church there and Services well attended. One Service held at Shawangunk Village.

Christ Church, Warwick; the Rev. ALFRED GOLDSBOROUGH, Rector.

Baptisms, (ad. 5, inf. 6,) 11. Confirmed, 6. Marriages, 4. Burials, 8. Communicants: admitted, 5; removed from the Parish, 1; present number, 50. The Holy Communion celebrated on the first Sunday in each month and on the higher festivals. Catechists and Sunday-School teachers, 6. Catechumens: Children taught the Catechism openly in the Church, 30. Celebration of Divine Service: Sundays, all Sundays in the year, and on the greater festivals and fasts.

Contributions.—Episcopal Fund, $2; Diocesan Fund, $12; Missionary Committee of the Diocese, $5; Convocation, $15; Fund for Aged and Infirm Clergymen, $5; the Poor, $12; Parish purposes, (towards liquidating debt,) $500; Church purposes in general, (not including salary,) $275—total, $826.

PUTNAM COUNTY.

St. Mary's Church in the Highlands, Cold Spring; the Rev. ISAAC VAN WINKLE, Rector.

Families, 114. Individuals, about 500. Baptisms, inf. 16. Confirmed, 4. Marriages, 3. Burials, 15. Communicants: admitted, 4; removed into the Parish, 1; removed from the Parish, 7; died, 4; present number, 124. The Holy Communion celebrated on festivals, Saints' Days, and on first Sunday in the month. Catechists and Sunday-School teachers, 18. Catechumens: Children taught the Catechism openly in the Church, 150; times, 12. Celebration of Divine Service: Sundays, 122; Holy Days, 26; other days, 121—total, 269.

Contributions.—Episcopal Fund, $15; Diocesan Fund, $12; Missionary Committee of the Diocese, $16 08; Theological Education Fund, $5; Fund for Aged and Infirm Clergymen, $33; Missions to the Jews, $2; Board of Missions P. E. Church, U. S.: Domestic Committee, $22 17; Sunday-School, $216 04; the Poor, $210 56; Parish purposes, $1,297 91—total, $1,859 76.

The Honorable Gouverneur Kemble, the senior Warden of this Parish from its first foundation, and to whose personal efforts its origin is due, died on the 16th day of September, ultimo, at the venerable age of 90 years.

The universal respect shown to his memory on the day of his funeral showed how he had deeply rooted himself in the affections of the people among whom he had lived, and to whom he had been a true friend during so many years.

St. Philip's Church in the Highlands, Philipsetown; the Rev. ALBERT ZABRISKIE GRAY, Rector.

Families, about 50. Individuals, about 200. Baptisms, (ad. 1, inf. 5,) 6. Burials, 5. Communicants: died, 2; present number, about 55. The Holy Communion celebrated the first Sunday of the month and festivals generally. Catechists and Sunday-School teachers, 6. Catechumens, about 50; times, monthly. Celebration of Divine Service: Sundays, twice at Church and once at Mission Chapel of St. James; Holy Days, on all Holy Days; other days, generally Wednesdays, Fridays and Saturdays.

Contributions.—Episcopal Fund, $13; Diocesan Fund, $24; Missionary Committee of the Diocese, $15 35; Missions of Convocations, $27 61; Theological Education Fund, $10; special, $37 08; Fund for Aged and Infirm Clergymen, $40, New-York Bible and Common Prayer-Book Society, $19 02; Protestant Episcopal Tract Society, $14 59; Jews, $3 12; "House of Good Shepherd," $105; St. Barnabas' Hospital, Poughkeepsie, $40; Board of Missions P. E. Church, U. S: Mission to Freedmen, $40 37; Domestic Committee, (including $100 special by a member of the Parish.) $508 42; Foreign Committee, $64 50; local Mission work, $375; Indian Missions, (including $50 of yet unpaid pledge,) $194 63; the Poor, $360 66; Sunday-School purposes, $85 44; Parish purposes, about $8,750; Church purposes in general, (St. Paul's Church, Rome, Italy,) $177; "Potter-Selwyn Scholarship," Litchfield, England, by a member of the Parish, $100—total, $11,004 79.

The above liberal contributions for Parish purposes are inclusive of moneys actually raised for alterations and repairs of Rectory, to some subscriptions for which allusion was made in Report of last year.

"Local Mission work" refers to services which have been regularly held in the Mission Chapel of St. James, and also during a good portion of the time at the Chemical Works of Highlands-on-the-Hudson.

The Rector would again express his obligation to the kind assistance of the Rev. James A. Upjohn.

RICHMOND COUNTY.

Church of the Ascension, West Brighton, Castleton; the Rev. JAMES S. BUSH, Rector.

Families, 120. Individuals, 720. Baptisms, (ad. 2, inf. 56,) 58. Confirmed, 11. Marriages, 7. Burials, 19. Communicants: admitted, 17; removed into the Parish, 6; removed from the Parish, 7; died, 6; present number, 298. The Holy Communion celebrated the first Sunday of each month and on the greater festivals. Catechists and Sunday-School teachers, 30. Catechumens, 320; Sunday scholars, 20; total number of young persons instructed, 340. Celebration of Divine Service: Sundays, twice each Sunday; Holy Days, once on the chief festivals; other days, in Lent three times each week.

Contributions.—Diocesan Fund, $52; Fund for Aged and Infirm Clergymen, $30 85; Sunday-School offering to Chinese Mission in San Francisco, $120; Sunday Schools, $727 51; the Poor, $760 92; Parish purposes, $2,047 17; Church Debt, $11,500—total, $15,328 55.

St. Mary's Church, Castleton; the Rev. HORACE L. EDGAR PRATT, Rector.

Families, 26. Individuals, 150. Baptisms, inf. 4. Marriages, 3. Burials, 3. Communicants: admitted, 5; removed into the Parish, 3; died, 1; present number, 54. The Holy Communion celebrated on the first Sunday of each month, and other days for which there is a "Proper Preface." Celebration of Divine Service: Sundays, twice; Holy Days, Wednesdays and Fridays in Lent, and every day in "Passion Week."

Contributions.—Episcopal Fund, $4; Diocesan Fund, $6; the Poor, $71 95; Parish purposes, $359 51—total, $441 46.

The Church has suffered a serious loss since the last report by the death of one of its oldest and most worthy members, Mr. William Wilson, for eighteen years Senior or Junior Warden.

Christ Church, New-Brighton; [No Rector. Reported by L. SATTERLEE, Warden, presiding.]

Families, about 100. Individuals, about 400. Baptisms, (ad. 1, inf. 19,) 20. Confirmed, 14 Marriages, 7. Burials, 20. Communicants: present number, about 125. The Holy Communion celebrated on the first Sunday of every month, Christmas Day, Whitsun-Day, Easter. Catechists and Sunday-School teachers, 16. Catechumens: Sunday scholars, 177. Celebration of Divine Service: Sundays, twice each Sunday; Holy Days, the usual Lent services; other days, full service and sermon Thursday evenings during Lent.

Contributions.—Episcopal Fund, $13; Diocesan Fund, $20; Fund for Aged and Infirm Clergymen, $38 58; Board of Missions P. E. Church, U. S.: Domestic Committee, $156 32;

Foreign Committee, $122 92; the Poor, $58 19; Parish purposes, $1,822 92—total, $2,230 93.

This Parish has had but one Rector, the Rev. P. P. Irving; he was elected on the 17th of July, 1849, and on account of failing health resigned April 1st, 1875. His resignation having been accepted, the Vestry, by unanimous vote, continue to pay him a retired salary of $1,500. He is very much beloved by his late congregation, who deeply regret his inability longer to perform his duties. Our assistant Minister, the Rev. Hamilton Lee, resigned on the 1st of August, 1875, leaving an excellent record. Our Church is free from debt. Nearly every pew rented, except one-fourth part of the whole number, which are free. The Church and Parish are both in a most prosperous condition.

St. Paul's Memorial Church, Edgewater; the Rev. THOMAS W. PUNNETT, Rector; subsequently the Rev. C. B. COFFIN; but now vacant, by death of the latter. Reported by the Wardens.

Families, about 124. Individuals, about 450. Baptisms, (ad. 1, inf. 17,) 18. Marriages. 8. Burials, 15. Communicants: removed from the Parish, 7; present number, 200. The Holy Communion celebrated weekly during Advent, on Christmas Day, Easter Day, Whitsun-Day, Trinity Sunday and first Sunday in each month. Catechists and Sunday-School teachers, 17. Catechumens, 190. Celebration of Divine Service: twice every Sunday and on principal Holy Days.

Contributions.—Episcopal Fund, $8; Diocesan Fund, $12; the Poor, $148; Parish purposes, $2,545 73; Church purposes in general, $864 06—total, $3,577 79.

The Rev. Thomas W. Punnett resigned the Rectorship on 8th February, 1875.

The Rev. Charles B. Coffin was elected Rector, and entered on his duties on Trinity Sunday, 1875.

In tue interim the services were duly performed by various Clergymen.

Mr. Coffin died on 9th July last, since which the services have been conducted by temporary supplies.

The Rev. Albert U. Stanley, (of Trinity Church, Trenton, N. J.,) was elected Rector, and accepted, and will enter on his duties on Sunday, 31st October.

In consequence of the above incidents, a full statement, such as contributions to Missions and other items, received and paid by the Rectors, cannot be included in this report.

St. Andrew's Church, Richmond; the Rev. KINGSTON GODDARD, D. D., Rector.

Families, 80. Individuals, 500. Baptisms, (ad. 4, inf. 5,) 9. Communicants: present number, 100. The Holy Communion celebrated once a month. Catechists and Sunday-School teachers, 10. Catechumens, about 60. Celebration of Divine Service: Sundays, every Sunday; Holy Days, Good Friday, Christmas; other days, Lent.

Contributions.—Not able to state the amount.

Church of the Holy Comforter, Ellingville, Southfield; the Rev. FREDERICK M. GRAY, Rector.

Families, 43. Individuals, 194. Baptisms, (ad. 1, inf. 3,) 4. Marriage, 1. Communicants: admitted, 2; removed into the Parish, 1; removed from the Parish, 7; died, 1; present number, 43. The Holy Communion celebrated the first Sunday in every month, Christmas Day, Easter Day and Whitsun-Day. Sunday-School teachers, 6. Catechumens: Children taught the Catechism openly in the Church, 45; times, 10. Celebration of Divine Service: Sundays, 103; Holy Days, 6; other days, 6—total, 115.

Contributions.—Diocesan Fund, $2; Fund for Aged and Infirm Clergymen, $6 72; Board of Missions P. E. Church, U. S.: Bishop Vail, for Kansas, $20 50; Parish purposes, $1,618 02—total, $1,647 24.

St. Luke's Church, Rossville; the Rev. HENRY H. BEAN, Rector.

Families, 25. Individuals, 75. Baptisms, (ad. 1, inf. 9,) 10. Burials, 3. Communicants: died, 3; present number, 25. The Holy Communion celebrated on the first Sunday of each month and on high festivals. Catechists and Sunday-School teachers, 4. Catechumens: Children taught the Catechism openly in the Church, 25; times, 12.

Contributions.—Board of Missions P. E. Church, U. S.: Domestic Committee, (from the S. School,) $18 55; Foreign Committee, (Miss. boxes,) $10—total, $28 55.

ROCKLAND COUNTY.

St. John's Church, Clarkstown; the Rev. ROMAINE S. MANSFIELD, Rector and Missionary.

Families, 30. Individuals, 150. Baptisms, inf. 5. Burial, 1. Communicants: admitted, 1; present number, 26. Catechists and Sunday-School teachers, 7. Catechumens, 40; total number of young persons instructed, 50. Celebration of Divine Service: Sundays, once each Sunday; Holy Days, high festivals—total, 60.

Contributions.—Missionary Committee of the Diocese, $10; Board of Missions P. E. Church, U. S.: Domestic Committee, $4; Indian Missions, $5 50; House of Good Shepherd, $5; S. Missionary Convocation, $12 42; Parish purposes, (including Rector's salary,) $570 84—total, $607 76.

Trinity Church, Haverstraw; the Rev. CHARLES B. COFFIN, late Rector and Missionary.

Families, 78. Individuals, 379. Baptisms, (ad. 1, inf. 17,) 18. Marriage, 1. Burials, 8. Communicants: removed into the Parish, 9; removed from the Parish, 6; present number, 76. The Holy Communion celebrated on the first Sunday in each month and on all the great festivals. Catechists and Sunday-School teachers, 8. Catechumens: Children taught the Catechism openly in the Church, 80; times, 36; total number of young persons instructed, 80. Daily Parish School: 1; paid; Scholars, males, 2, females, 5. Celebration of Divine Service: Sundays, morning and evening; Holy Days and Saints' Days, on Christmas, twice on Ash-Wednesday and Good-Friday; other days, Thanksgiving Day.

Contributions.—Episcopal Fund, $4 50; Fund for Aged and Infirm Clergymen, $5 85; New-York Bible and Common Prayer-Book Society, $2 21; Board of Missions P. E. Church, U. S.: Domestic Committee, $10 69; Foreign Committee, $12 44; Mission to the Jews, $1 46; St. Mary's Hospital, $12; House of Good Shepherd, $7 50; Church purposes in general, $915 37—total, $972 05.

St. Luke's Church, Haverstraw; the Rev. E. GAY, Jr., Rector.

Families, 22. Individuals, 80. Baptisms, inf. 2. Communicants: present number, 23. The Holy Communion celebrated once a month. Catechists and Sunday-School teachers, 4. Catechumens: Children taught the Catechism openly in the Church, 45. Celebration of Divine Service: Sundays, every Sunday, P. M., and once a month in the A. M.

Contributions.—Parish purposes, about $600, principally for repairs on Church building. As the work is now being done and the account not made up, we cannot give exact figures.

The present Rector took charge of this Parish on the first of October, 1874, and found the Pari-h greatly depressed. The Services have been regularly kept up and the Sunday-School in operation. A new roof has been put on the Church building, the walls having been lowered, and the building otherwise greatly improved.

Grace Church, Nyack; the Rev. FRANKLIN BABBITT, Rector and Missionary

Families, 71. Individuals, about 350. Baptisms, (ad. 3, inf. 13,) 16. Confirmed, 17. Marriages, 5. Burials, 17. Communicants: present number, 130. The Holy Communion celebrated monthly. Sunday-School teachers, 8. Sunday scholars, 60. Celebration of Divine Service: twice each Sunday and on the principal Holy Days.

Contributions.—Diocesan Fund, $5 81; Missionary Committee of the Diocese, $10 80; Fund for Aged and Infirm Clergymen, $20 06; House of Good Shepherd, Rockland County, $32 59; New-York Bible and Common Prayer-Book Society, $7 69; Sunday-School, $80 84; Board of Missions P. E Church, U. S.: Domestic Committee, $41 80; Home Mission for Colored People, $8; the Poor, $16 13; the new Church, $1,897 75; Church purposes in general, (weekly offertory,) $638 90—total, $2,760 37.

Christ Church, Piermont; the Rev. SOL. G. HITCHCOCK, Rector and Missionary.

Families, 40. Baptisms, inf. 15. Confirmed, 7. Marriages, 4. Burials, 20. Communicants: admitted, 3; removed into the Parish, 8; removed from the Parish, 6; died, 3; Present number, 71. The Holy Communion celebrated from Trinity to Advent on the first Sunday of the month, from Advent to Trinity on the festivals commemorative of our Saviour. Sunday-School teachers, 10; scholars, 129; number of young persons instructed, as many as wish to come, every Sunday P. M. Celebration of Divine Service: Sundays, A. M. and P. M., and on Holy Days and other days generally observed.

Contributions.—Episcopal Fund, $2; Diocesan Fund, $5; Missionary Committee of the Diocese, $5; Orphan's Home Asylum, $10; Church Mission to the Jews, $5; Fund for Aged and Infirm Clergymen, $1; Sheltering Arms, $2; Southern Convocation, $11 35; responses to special appeals, $8; New-York Bible and Common Prayer-Book Society, $8; Protestant Episcopal Tract Society, $6 80; General P. E. S S. Union and Church Book Society, $1 80; General Theological Seminary, $1; Board of Missions P. E. Church, U. S.: Indian Commission, $9 31; Domestic Committee, (check $20,) $36 57; Home Mission to Colored, $2; Foreign Committee, (check $20,) $34 75; Sunday-School, (Mrs. S., $25 45; others, $7; Christmas Tree, $100.) $165 38; the Poor, (Mr. H. R. L., $50,) $91 58; Parish purposes, $494 22; Church purposes in general, $9 75; towards salary, $181 35; Ministerial gifts and perquisites, $117—total, $1,208 86.

The unusual number of funerals is partly owing to an unusually large number of deaths, and partly to the constantly increasing calls upon the Minister for his services outside of our own ecclesiastical pale.

Thanksgiving Day was made joyful by its accompaniments of the two preceding years, and a collection for the disabled organist.

The purchase, by Henry E. Lawrence, Esq., of a summer residence near Sneeden's Landing, furnishes an invaluable accession to our congregation.

Christ Church, Ramapo; the Rev. GUSTAV EDM. PURUCKER, Rector and Missionary.

Families and parts of families, 36. Individuals, 157. Baptisms, (ad. 3, inf. 8,) 11. Marriages, 2. Burials, 2. Communicants: admitted, 6; removed into the Parish, 6; removed from the Parish, 8; died, 2; present number, 46. The Holy Communion celebrated on the first Sunday in each month and on the great festivals of the Church. Catechists and Sunday-School teachers, 5, and Librarian, 1. Catechumens: Children taught the Catechism openly in the Church, 47; times, 12; members of other classes for religious instruction, 9; total number of young persons instructed, 56. Celebration of Divine Service: Sundays, twice every Lord's Day; Holy Days, once each Holy Day; other days, on all the Saints' Days and during Lent daily, Wednesdays and Fridays in Lent, twice Thanksgiving Day—total, 172.

Contributions.—Episcopal Fund, $2; Diocesan Fund, $8; Missionary Committee of the Diocese, $2; Fund for Aged and Infirm Clergymen, $13 22; Parochial School and Sunday-School, $185; the Poor, (out of the Communion alms,) $34 50; Parish purposes, (including the rest of the Com. Fund, $1,215 93; Church purposes in general, $9 75—total, $1,770 40.

We would gratefully recognise the merciful hand of God in the spiritual advancement of the few who strive to be earnest, faithful disciples of our blessed Lord and Master. In particular, it deserves mention that much of the Church's success is due to the hearty endeavors and liberality of our Wardens.

The Parish School, which was started a year and a half ago, has been discontinued for the present, with the hope, however, of re-opening the same as soon as expedient.

The Missionary does not cease to minister to the colored portion of the settlers around Suffern.

Our Sunday-School enjoys the benefit of three festivals annually—Christmas Tree, Easter, and a Pic-Nic in summer.

St. Paul's Church, Spring Valley; the Rev. ROMAINE S. MANSFIELD, Rector and Missionary.

Baptism, inf. 1. Confirmed, 3. Marriages, 3. Burials, 6. Communicants: admitted, 6; removed from the Parish, 2; present number, 36. Catechists and Sunday-School teachers, 10. Catechumens. Children taught the Catechism openly in the Church, 50; times, 10.

Contributions.—Board of Missions P. E. Church, U. S.: Bishop Tuttle, $5; Indian Commission, $2 93, House of Good Shepherd, $3 05; Parish purposes, (including Rector's salary,) $530 14; Building Fund, $377 75—total, $918 87.

Church of the Holy Child Jesus, Stony Point; the Rev. E. GAY, Jr., Missionary.

Baptisms, (ad. 3, inf. 11,) 14. Marriages, 2. Burial, 1. Communicants: present number, 15. The Holy Communion celebrated weekly and on the greater festivals. Catechumens: total number of young persons instructed, 60. Celebration of Divine Service: Sundays, twice; Holy Days, twice; other days, daily in Advent and Lent.

Contributions.—Fund for Aged and Infirm Clergymen, $3 81; New-York City Mission Society, to Jews, $2 72; Church Missions, $10 81; to purchase Bible for the Chapel, $10; for Church Building, $140 32—total, $167 66.

SULLIVAN COUNTY.

St. John's Church, Monticello; the Rev. CHARLES F. CANEDY, Rector and Missionary.

Families, 80. Individuals, 345. Baptisms, (ad. 2, inf. 17.) 19. Marriage, 1. Burials, 8. Communicants: present number, 143. The Holy Communion celebrated on the first and third Sundays of every month, on the chief festivals, and twice in private. Catechists and Sunday-School teachers, 20, and 12 at Thompsonville; Catechumens, 156, and 45 at Thompsonville. Children taught the Catechism openly in the Church, 156; times, 26. Total number of young persons instructed, 201. Celebration of Divine Service: Sundays, 116; Holy Days, 28; other days, 58—total, 202.

Contributions.—Episcopal Fund, $2; Diocesan Fund, $16; Missionary Committee of the Diocese, $16 20; Theological Education Fund, $5 50; Fund for Aged and Infirm Clergymen, $10 86; New-York Bible and Common Prayer-Book Society, $4 17; Board of Missions P. E. Church, U. S.: Domestic Committee, $4 18; Parish purposes, $1,243 64; Church purposes in general, $3 44—total, $1,305 99.

The above report includes the celebration of Divine Service by the Rector at St. Mary's Church, Thompsonville, at St. James' Church, Callicoon Depot, and at Long Eddy. During the summer months services have been maintained at these Mission stations by Mr. O. P. Vinton and Mr. V. C. Smith, of the General Theological Seminary. As one result of Mr. Vinton's efforts, the Rector, by the appointment of the Bishop, laid the corner-stone of a Chapel at Callicoon Depot on Tuesday, September 1st, 1875 The Chapel at Thompsonville is slowly approaching completion. The Rev. E. K. Fowler, some time Rector, has completed forty-eight years of residence in the Parish, forty-two of which were occupied in active duty, and is still blessed with such a measure of health that he is enabled to attend Divine service regularly.

ULSTER COUNTY.

Church of the Ascension, Esopus; the Rev. HENRY BEERS SHERMAN, Rector.

Baptisms, inf. 2. Marriages, 2. Burials, 3. Communicants: removed from the Parish, 1; died, 1. The Holy Communion celebrated monthly. Celebration of Divine Service: Sunday morning, during the summer.

The state of the Parish is the same as previously reported. During the summer months, from June to November, the congregations are respectable, and the attendance upon the Holy Communion ranges in numbers from 20 to 30.

The entire support of the Parish is derived from the summer residents.

St. John's Church, Kingston; the Rev. C. WILLIAM CAMP, Rector.

Families, 97. Baptisms, inf. 2. Marriages, 2. Burials, 9. Communicants: admitted, 9; removed from the Parish, 14; died, 7; present number, 174. The Holy Communion celebrated on the first Sunday in every month. Celebration of Divine Service: Sundays, all; Holy Days, all.

Contributions.—Episcopal Fund, $3; Diocesan Fund, $24; Fund for Aged and Infirm Clergymen, $16 41; Board of Missions P. E. Church, U. S.: Domestic Committee, $3; Foreign Committee, $3; Church purposes in general, $2,656 51—total, $2,737 24.

This Parish has been without a Rector for the year ending August 1, 1875. Wise enough to call the Rev. Clarence Buel to the Rectorship, they were so unfortunate as to lose his efficient services after a six months' acquaintance had rendered them very conscious of his worth. During the *interregnum*, the Rev. Dr. Waters has been often called upon, and he has often responded with the performance of clerical duty, for which he has our hearty thanks. I took charge of the Parish August 1st, and the two months' residence has satisfied me that the Parish is united and anxious to go on—willing to serve and to be served—and we hope to present a better report of our work next year. I am sorry to be unable to forward a more complete report than this; but trustworthy records are not at my disposal. We hope to welcome our Bishop among us at an early day, and to present a class for Confirmation.

Christ Church, Marlborough; the Rev. SAMUEL M. AKERLY, Rector.

Families, 22. Individuals, 90. Communicants: admitted, 6; died, 1; present number, 40. Baptisms, (ad. 2, inf. 6,) 8. Marriages, 2. Sunday scholars, 50; teachers, 7. All the scholars catechized in Sunday-School. Services, with sermon, twice on Sunday; Thanksgiving, Christmas, Christmas-Tree festival, Ash-Wednesday; weekly lecture during Lent, daily during Passion Week. Holy Communion celebrated once a month.

The foregoing report embraces the period from Sept. 1st, 1874, to June 19th, 1875, at which time my resignation as Rector took effect. I had been Minister of Christ Church for seventeen years, previous to which I acted as Lay Reader for two years and nine months. During this time the Church edifice, a substantial structure of brick, and a convenient Rectory, were built; the ground for the latter was given, and the whole paid for.

Christ Church, Marlborough. [Without a Rector. Reported by the Wardens.]

Families, 20. Individuals, 70. Baptisms, inf. 2. Confirmations, 6. Marriage, 1. Burials, 2. Communicants, 40. Holy Communion celebrated monthly. Sunday-school children, 30; teachers, 5.

Collections for several Missionary and Church objects cannot be specified, nor the sums given. Ladies' Society have raised $173; sundry collections, $123 36—total, $296 36.

The Rev. Samuel M. Akerly resigned the Rectorship of this Parish in June, and from the 27th of that month it has been under the charge of Rev. Dr. Waters, of Kingston.

All Saints' Church, Milton; the Rev. JOSEPH H. JOHNSON, Missionary.

Families, 22. Individuals, 86. Baptisms, (ad. 7, inf 9,) 16. Confirmed, 14. Marriage, 1. Burials, 6. Communicants: admitted, 11; removed into the Parish, 2; died, 6; present number, 30. The Holy Communion celebrated every Sunday and Holy Day. Catechumens: Children taught the Catechism openly in the Church, 75, times every Sunday; Sunday Scholars, the 75 children above from this Sunday-School; total number of young persons instructed, 75. Celebration of Divine Service: Sundays, four services each Sunday; Holy Days, two services; other days, services each day either at Milton or Highland—total, 215.

Contributions—Church purposes in general, $472 68.

Trinity Church, Saugerties; the Rev. J J. ROBERTSON, D. D., Rector.

Families, about 45. Individuals, about 196. Baptisms, inf. 12. Marriages, 2. Burials, 8. Communicants: admitted, 2, removed into the Parish 7; died, 2; present number, 75. The Holy Communion celebrated the first Lord's Day in each month, and festivals with Preface, except Ascension Day; private Communions, 5 Catechists and Sunday-School teachers, 12 Catechumens, about 100. Children taught the Catechism openly in the Church, the Sunday-School, times, 4 Celebration of Divine Service: Sundays, 99; Holy Days, 14; other days, 42—total, 155.

Contributions.—Bishop's salary, $4; Episcopal Fund, $4 78; Diocesan Fund, $18; Missionary Committee of the Diocese, $127 09; to the Western Convocation, $30; Theological Education Fund, $11 15; Fund for Aged and Infirm Clergymen, $31 54; Church Mission to Jews, $6 47; New-York Bible and Common Prayer-Book Society, $30 10; Protestant Episcopal Tract Society, $11 84; General P. E. S. S. Union and Church Book Society, $3 79; Indian Commission, $31 29; pupils of Sunday-School, for Mission work to Indians, $25; Board of Missions P. E. Church, U. S.: Domestic Committee, $125 92; Foreign Committee, $109 69; Home Missions to Colored People, $34 37; the Poor, $113 52; Parish purposes, $417 55; Church purposes in general, (Mission in Utah of Mr. Gilogly,) $10—total, $1,201 10.

Trinity Church, Saugerties, since last report, has continued the work of improvement of its edifice. Gas pipes have been introduced, and the interior now is beautifully lighted for services at night. This led, a few months since, to a change of the time for evening prayer and preaching, in consequence of which the two services of the day have been more fully attended. For a season the Rector's health has prevented frequent personal Catechetical instruction of the children in the Church. The teachers, meanwhile, led by a devoted female superintendent, have increased in number and zeal, and the number of pupils is much enlarged. The last quarter has given us, also, an earnest and experienced male superintendent, and we are looking forward to have all things in the school soon greatly improved. To accomplish this the better, the female superintendent, with peculiar zeal and personal liberality, exerted herself to procure funds to erect a Chapel in the immediate vicinity of the Church for Sunday-School purposes and other occasional services. This structure is now nearly completed. It is hoped that about the middle of October it will be furnished with all that is requisite for the objects in view. A well-toned organ, the gift of one friend, is among the contributions to it. The entire cost of the Chapel and its furniture will considerably exceed $3,000, a large portion of which is already contributed. Notwithstanding this, it will be seen that the collections for the various Church purposes outside the Parish have been liberal, especially for the missionary departments, Foreign, Domestic and Diocesan. Great credit is due to the Building Committee of the Vestry for the thought, care and time they have devoted to this unpretending, yet graceful edifice they have superintended.

It has pleased our Heavenly Father to visit the Rector and his family with great affliction. A dear daughter, for many years the manager of the household, has been confined to bed with serious illness. This has called forth the warm sympathies and kind and generous aids of friends both in and out of our congregation. May God richly reward them! For some months the Rector has necessarily been less active than usual in out door Parish duties, but is now resuming his customary course. The prospect for the future is cheering, as it is hoped will be manifested, through God's grace, in next year's report.

I have neglected to state that a burial lot in the Church yard has been presented by the Vestry (their own spontaneous act) to the Rector.

St. Peter's Church, Stone Ridge; the Rev. Geo. W. West, Rector and Missionary.

Families, 20. Individuals, 50. Baptisms, (ad. 13, inf. 19,) 32. Confirmed, 12. Burial, 1. Communicants: admitted, 12; removed from the Parish, 4; died 1; present number, 27. The Holy Communion celebrated twice each month and on Holy Days. Catechists and Sunday-School teachers, 5. Catechumens: Children taught the Catechism openly in the Church, 75; times, 52; total number of young persons instructed, 75. Celebration of Divine Service: Sundays, 130; Holy Days, 25—total, 155.

Contributions.—Episcopal Fund, $2; the Poor, $60; Parish purposes, (bell, tower and fence,) $134; Church purposes in general, (salary of Rector,) $500—total, $996

The Rector takes this opportunity to mention the great obligations the Parish is under to H. P. Delafield, Esq., Mrs Young, Mrs. Eliza Delafield and Mrs. L. Robinson.

The Mission at Rosendale is most encouraging. In three or four years it promises to become even more prosperous than the Parish Church at Stone Ridge.

The Sunday-School at High Falls has been carried on through the past year, and five baptisms lately testified to the necessity and utility of the work.

The Rector has also had a day school for the last year, teaching the higher English studies and Latin and Greek. It numbers twelve pupils. A Boarding School was intended, but owing to the inland situation of Stone Ridge, the project has been abandoned.

WESTCHESTER COUNTY.

St. Matthew's Church, Bedford; the Rev. LEA LUQUER, Rector.

Families, 47. Confirmed, 5. Marriage, 1. Burials, 5. Communicants: died, 1; present number, 75. The Holy Communion celebrated on the first Sunday in every month and on great festivals. Sunday scholars, 30.

Contributions.—Episcopal Fund, $4; Fund for Aged and Infirm Clergymen, $25 09; Board of Missions P. E. Church, U. S.: Domestic Committee, (Missionary Bishops,) $56 63; Parish purposes, $208 10—total, $293 82.

All Saints' Church, (Briar Cliff,) Ossining; the Rev. J. BRECKENRIDGE GIBSON, Rector.

Families, 12. Individuals, 50. Burials, 2. Communicants: present number, 20. The Holy Communion celebrated on the first Sunday in each month and on the greater festivals. Catechists and Sunday School teachers, 3 Catechumens, 24. Celebration of Divine Service: Sundays, 104; Holy Days, 11—total, 115.

Contributions.—Episcopal Fund, $2; Diocesan Fund, $9; Missionary Committee of the Diocese, $12 50; New York Bible and Common Prayer-Book Society, $10; Board of Missions P. E. Church, U. S: Domestic Committee, $16 09; House of the Good Shepherd, Tomkins' Cove, $67 76; Parish purposes, $689; Southern Convocation, $25—total, $831 35.

Grace Church, City Island; the Rev. J MORSELL, D. D., Rector and Missionary.

Baptisms, (ad 1, inf 9) 10. Marriages, 2. Burials, 3. Confirmations, 14. Communicants: deceased, 1, added, 3, present number, 45. Those who have been confirmed will make their first Communion next Sabbath. Sunday-School scholars, 90; teachers, 12.

Contributions.—Collection weekly, about $60; Foreign Missions, $7; Diocesan, $5; Sunday-School, $40, for Parochial purposes, $584--total, $596.

I entered upon the charge of this Parish in October, 1874. It is a weak and struggling Parish in its present condition, but gives promise of future growth and expansion A very promising class was confirmed at the recent visitation of the Bishop, and a number remaining who will come forward at an early day.

St. Paul's Church, East Chester; the Rev. WILLIAM SAMUEL COFFEY, Rector.

Families, 80 Individuals, 400. Baptisms, (ad. 3, inf. 26.) 29. Marriages, 5 Burials, 21 Communicants: admitted, 1, removed into the Parish, 7, removed from the Parish, 10, died, 3: present number, 105 The Holy Communion celebrated on the first Sunday in the month and greater festivals Catechists and Sunday-School teachers, 7 Catechumens: total number of young persons instructed, 45. Celebration of Divine Service: twice on Sundays, on Friday mornings, and three times a week in Lent.

Contributions.—Episcopate, $8; Diocesan Fund, $14, Missionary Committee of the

Diocese. $10 78; Theological Education Fund. $14 31; Fund for Aged and Infirm Clergymen. $4 90; Mission to the Jews, $8; Southern Convocation, $9 21; New York Bible and Common Prayer-Book Society, $7 13; Board of Missions P. E. Church, U. S.: Domestic Committee, $11 67; the Poor and Parish purposes, $843 81—total, $983 31.

Zion Church, Greenburgh; the Rev. George B. Reese, Rector.

Baptisms, (ad. 1, inf. 12,) 13. Confirmed, 8. Marriages, 8. Burials, 9. Communicants: present number, 90. The Holy Communion celebrated every first Sunday of the month and on the greater festivals. Catechists and Sunday-School teachers, 15. Catechumens: Children taught the Catechism openly in the Church, 150. Celebration of Divine Service: as reported last year.

Contributions.—Episcopal Fund, $10; Diocesan Fund, $30; Missionary Committee of the Diocese, $10; Fund for Aged and Infirm Clergymen, $35; Board of Missions P. E. Church, U. S.: Domestic Missions, $38; Foreign Committee, $43; the Poor, $208 97; Parish purposes, $1,900; Church purposes in general, $175—total, $2,439 97.

St. Paul's Church, Saw Mill Valley, Greenburg; the Rev. John Drisler, deacon, Missionary.

Families, 10. Individuals, 25. Baptisms, inf. 6. Confirmed. 3. Burials, 4. Communicants: removed from the Parish, 2: present number, 12 Two left the Church. The Holy Communion has been celebrated very irregularly; there has been no celebration since May the present year. Catechists and Sunday-School teachers, 4. Catechumens: Children taught the Catechism openly in the Church, 20; times, 10. Sunday scholars, 20. Daily Parish School: but two pay. Taught by the Missionary. Scholars, males, 3, females, 5. A number have removed to other places to find employment, which has decreased the number both in the Sunday-School and Church Celebration of Divine Service: Sundays, twice generally; during July and August but one service has been held; Holy Days, Ash-Wednesday, Good Friday, Christmas, Epiphany, Ascension.

Contributions.—Episcopal Fund, $2.

The Church was closed on the first and second Sundays of September, on account of painting and cleaning.

St. John's Church, Lewisboro'; the Rev. Robert Bolton, A. M., Rector and Missionary.

Families, 30. Individuals, 90. Baptisms, (ad 1, inf. 2,) 3. Confirmed, 5. Marriages, 5. Burials, 4. Communicants: admitted, 6; removed from the Parish, 2; died, 2; present number, 36. The Holy Communion celebrated the first Sunday in every month, Christmas, Easter, Whitsun-Day and on all great festivals. Catechists and Sunday-School teachers, 1. Catechumens, 12. Daily Parish School: 1, paid; Scholars, males and females, irregular. Celebration of Divine Service: twice every Lord's Day.

Contributions.—Episcopal Fund, $1; Diocesan Fund, 50c.; Missionary Committee of the Diocese, $1; Theological Education Fund, 50c.; Fund for Aged and Infirm Clergymen, 50c.—total, $3 50.

St. Thomas' Church, Mamaroneck; the Rev. William White Montgomery, Rector.

Baptisms, inf. 21. Marriages, 6. Burials, 20. Communicants: present number, 128. The Holy Communion celebrated sixteen times in public, including Christmas, Easter Day, Ascension Day, Whitsun-Day and Trinity Sunday; in private, once. Sunday-School teachers, 9. Sunday scholars, 85. School under the personal supervision of the

Rector. Celebration of Divine Service: Sundays, 95; Holy Days and other days, 34—total, 129.

Contributions.—Episcopal Fund, $9; Diocesan Fund, $30; Missionary Committee of the Diocese, $38; Southern Convocation, $28; Fund for Aged and Infirm Clergymen, $41; New-York Bible and Common Prayer-Book Society, $13; Board of Missions P. E. Church, U. S.: Domestic Committee, $45 15; for Oregon, (from a Parishioner,) $50; Foreign Committee, for China, $26 50; for Africa, (from Sunday-School,) $40; the Poor, $164 74; Parish purposes, (including Sunday-School,) $1,053 50—total, $1,538 89.

At the urgent request of the Rector, the Bishop kindly consented to defer his proposed visitation till later in the season. Hence no Confirmation is reported above.

Church of the Divine Love, Montrose; the Rev. Gouverneur Cruger, Rector and Missionary.

Baptisms, inf. 20. Confirmed, 2. Marriages, 2. Burials, 7. Communicants: admitted, 8; present number, 27. The Holy Communion celebrated on the first Sunday of each month and on the greater festivals. Catechists and Sunday-School teachers, 13. Catechumens: Children taught the Catechism openly in the Church, 166; times, 52; total number of young persons instructed, 166. Celebration of Divine Service: Sundays, all, morning and evening, 104; Holy Days, all, morning, 35; other days, 1—total, 140.

Contributions.—Episcopal Fund, $5; Diocesan Fund, $5; Missionary Committee of the Diocese, $5; Theological Education Fund, $5; Fund for Aged and Infirm Clergymen, $5; New-York Bible and Common Prayer-Book Society, $10 35; Parish purposes, $1,024 46—total, $1,059 81.

Church tower completed, and a Meneely bell of 1,000 lbs. weight placed therein.

St. Mark's Church, Mt. Pleasant, Tarrytown; the Rev. Edmund Guilbert, Rector.

Families, 72. Individuals, 425 Baptisms, (ad. 3, inf. 18,) 21. Confirmed, 16. Marriages, 6. Burials, 11. Communicants: present number, 125. The Holy Communion celebrated weekly on the Lord's Day, on Saints' Days, and on the greater festivals. Catechists and Sunday-School teachers, 15. Catechumens, 125. Daily Parish School: 1, paid; Scholars, males, 15 Celebration of Divine Service: Sundays, 104; Holy Days, 20; other days, 48—total, $172.

Contributions.—Episcopal Fund, $4; Diocesan Fund, $6; Missionary Committee of the Diocese, $15, Fund for Aged and Infirm Clergymen, $9; Sunday-School, $223 68; Board of Missions P. E. Church, U. S.: Domestic Missions, $50; for floating debt on Church, $1,800; the Peor, $203; Parish purposes, $1,051; Church purposes in general, $200—total, $4,471 68.

Trinity Church, Mount Vernon; the Rev. William Berrian Hooper, Rector.

Families, 169. Individuals, 500 Baptisms, (ad. 5, inf. 37,) 42. Confirmed, 19. Marriages, 4. Burials, 13. Communicants: admitted, 20; removed into the Parish, [illegible] moved from the Parish, 13, died, 5; present number, 178 The Holy Communion celebrated on all festivals, the first Sunday in the month, and during Advent and Lent Sunday. Catechists and Sunday-School teachers, 16. Catechumens, 189 Ch[illegible] taught the Catechism openly in the Church, 211; times, 11 Celebration of Divine Service: Sundays, twice on each, first Sunday in month and great festivals, three t[illegible] Holy Days, once, with Holy Communion, other days, Fridays throughout the year, during Holy Week, four times a week during the rest of Lent.

Contributions.—Episcopal Fund, $3; Diocesan Fund, $24; Missionary Committee of the Diocese, $15; Theological Education Fund, $17 31; Fund for Aged and Infirm Clergymen, $27 78; Southern Convocation, $21 85; Church Mission to Jews, $6 68; Church at Dresden, $17; the Poor, $67 69; Parish purposes, $4,014 88—total, $4,216 69.

St. Mark's Church, New Castle; the Rev. JOSEPH H. YOUNG, Deacon and Missionary.

Families, 47. Baptisms, inf. 2. Confirmed, 4. Marriages, 2. Burials, 5.

Having but recently (Sept. 1st) entered upon the charge of St. Mark's Parish, and having but few facts concerning its spiritual condition during the last Convention year in my possession, my report is necessarily meagre.

Trinity Church, New-Rochelle; the Rev. JOHN HENRY WATSON, Rector.

Families, 121. Individuals, 475. Baptisms, (ad. 4, inf. 18,) 22. Confirmed, 25. Marriages, 6. Burials, 19. Communicants: admitted, 28; removed into the Parish, 10; removed from the Parish, 13; died, 5; present number, 155. The Holy Communion celebrated the first Sunday in each month and the great festivals, All Saints' Day, and six times in private. Catechists and Sunday-School teachers, 11. Catechumens, 100. Children taught the Catechism openly in the Church, all; times, 8. Celebration of Divine Service: Sundays, two services; Holy Days, one service generally; other days, every Friday; in Lent, four services weekly; Holy Week, twice daily—total, 216.

Contributions.—Episcopal Fund, $14; Diocesan Fund, $30; Missionary Committee of the Diocese, $12 38; Missions of Southern Convocation, $20 24; Fund for Aged and Infirm Clergymen, $17 55; Church Mission to Jews, $13 40; Church Mission to Deaf Mutes, $58 84; Indian Commission, $61; Women's Auxiliary to Domestic Missions, $450; Board of Missions P. E. Church, U. S.: Domestic Committee, $79 91; Foreign Committee, $5; Sunday-School, $126; Communion Alms, $174 74; Parish purposes, $1,309 28; Church purposes in general, $271 80—total, $2,654 14.

St. Stephen's Church, North Castle; the Rev. CORNELIUS WINTER BOLTON, Rector.

Families, 36. Individuals, 107. Baptisms, (ad. 2, inf. 9,) 11. Marriages, 8. Burials, 8. Communicants: present number, 58. The Holy Communion celebrated first Sunday in the month. Catechists and Sunday-School teachers, 5. Catechumens: Sunday scholars, 57. Celebration of Divine Service: every Sunday; Holy Days, Christmas, Good Friday, Ash-Wednesday; other days, Thanksgiving.

Contributions.—Jewish Mission Society, $5 74; Am. Ch. Missionary Society, $26 49; Foreign Committee, $5 80; Sunday School, $10; the Poor, $42 51—total, $90 54.

St. Peter's Church, (Cortlandt,) Peekskill; the Rev. WILLIAM FISHER LEWIS, Rector.

Families and parts of families, 95. Baptisms, (ad. 4, inf. 27,) 31. Confirmed, 13. Marriages, 2. Burials, 12. Communicants: admitted, 11; removed into the Parish, 2; removed from the Parish, 1; died, 4; present number, 109. The Holy Communion celebrated every Sunday, greater festivals, Christmas, Easter and Whitsun-Day twice. Catechists and Sunday-School teachers, 14. Catechumens: Children taught the Catechism openly in the Church, 100; times, 12. Celebration of Divine Service: Sundays, (Parish Church, 8; St Peter's Chapel, 155,) 163; Holy Days, 13; other days, 141; Advent, Wednesday and Friday; Lent, daily morning and evening—total, 317.

Contributions.—Episcopal Fund, $7; Diocesan Fund, $31; Missionary Committee of the Diocese, $16 37; Theological Education Fund, $10 44; Fund for Aged and Infirm Clergymen, $13 20; Southern Miss. Convocation, $32 54; House of the Good Shepherd, $34 61; St. Mary's Hospital, $15; Board of Missions P. E. Church, U. S.: Domestic Committee, $10; Indian Miss. Committee, $15; Colored Missions, $10; Parochial Schools, $156 89; the Poor, $35 08; Parish purposes, $1,771 68; Jews, $6—total, $2,183 76.

Christ Church, Pelham; the Rev. CHAS. HIGBEE, Rector.

Families, 50. Individuals, about 240. Baptisms, (ad. 3, inf. 7,) 10. Confirmed, 4. Marriages, 2. Communicants: present number, 58. Sunday-School teachers, 4. Catechumens: members of other classes for religious instruction, 21; Sunday scholars, 52. Celebration of Divine Service: Sundays, twice each Sunday; other days, occasional services, about 100.

Contributions.—Diocesan Fund, $20; Fund for Aged and Infirm Clergymen, $13 36; Colored people South, $19; Mission to Jews, $1 08; Kansas, $11; to New-Hampshire, $26; Board of Missions P. E. Church, U. S.: Foreign Committee, $35 21; Sunday-School, $159 27; the Poor, (Communion alms, $103 30; other, $257 53,) $360 83; Parish purposes, $1,479 46; from Ladies' Auxiliary Missionary Society of the Parish, (Foreign Missions, $125 75; Mission to Indians, $153 32,) $279 07—total, $2,406 28.

St. Peter's Church, Portchester; the Rev. BROCKHOLST MORGAN, Rector.

Families, 140. Individuals, 520. Baptisms, (ad. 6, inf. 36,) 42. Confirmed, 28. Marriages, 9. Burials, 23. Communicants: admitted, 10; removed into the Parish, 3; removed from the Parish, 2; died, 8; present number, 177. The Holy Communion celebrated on the first Sunday of every month and on the festivals of Christmas, Easter and Whitsun-Day. Catechists and Sunday-School teachers, 40. Catechumens: Children taught the Catechism openly in the Church, 280; total number of young persons instructed, 280. Celebration of Divine Service: Sundays, 104; other days, 80—total, 184.

Contributions.—Episcopal Fund, $5; Missionary Committee of the Diocese, $9 63; for China Mission, $15; Parochial Schools, $557 35; the Poor, $323 05; Parish purposes, $318 16; Ch. Mission to the Jews, $13 46; Nebraska Divinity School, $27 40, House of the Good Shepherd, $37 95; Mission of Mr. Bonham, $11 43—total, $1,323 49.

The life and vigor of this Parish is constantly on the increase, and year by year it is so widening its influence that soon the Church building will be insufficient to hold the congregation, and the Chapel is already too small for the ever growing Sunday-School.

Christ Church, Rye; the Rev. CHAUNCEY B. BREWSTER, Rector.

Families, about 190. Baptisms, (ad. 2, inf 22,) 24. Confirmed, 13. Marriages, 2. Burials, 9 Communicants: admitted, 16, removed into the Parish, 5; removed from the Parish, 1; died, 1; present number, about 290. The Holy Communion celebrated the first Sunday in every month, the greater festivals and All Saints' Day. Catechists and Sunday-School teachers, 25. Catechumens: in Parish Sunday-School, 116; S. Milton, 30; Children taught the Catechism openly in the Church, 107; times, 11; members of other classes for religious instruction, 9; total number of young persons instructed, 155. Celebration of Divine Service in the Parish Church: Sundays, twice; Holy Days, all; other days, Fridays. In the Chapel at Milton, once every Sunday.

Contributions.—Episcopal Fund, $18; Diocesan Fund, $60; Missionary Committee of the Diocese, $73 93; Southern Missionary Convocation, $46 97; Fund for Aged and Infirm Clergymen, $72 50; House of the Good Shepherd, $07 08; Soc. Increase Mini[illegible] $69 01, New-York Bible and Common Prayer-Book Society, $52 81; Mission to J[illegible] $23, Missions to Freedmen, $35 12; Ch. work in Ogden, Utah, $62 41; Board of Missions P. E. Church, U. S.: Domestic Committee, $122 06; Mite Chests, $11 51: Fo[illegible]

Committee, $122 21; Woman's Missionary Association, $304 37: the Poor, $408 62; Parish purposes, $800 60; raised by Ladies' Sewing Soc., $516 14; Improvement of Ch. grounds, $2,750; Improvements, etc., Chapel at Milton, $863 63—total, $7,220 97.

Mission work at Milton has progressed, through the liberality and devotion of two Laymen especially. The Chapel has been enlarged by the addition of chancel and transept. Services have been maintained regularly on Sunday evenings, and the attendance has been encouraging.

Church of St. James the Less, Scarsdale; the Rev. WILLIAM AUGUSTUS HOLBROOK, Rector.

Families, 52. Individuals, 276. Baptisms, inf. 9. Confirmed, 7. Burials, 3. Communicants: admitted, 7; removed into the Parish, 8; removed from the Parish, 3; died, 1; present number, 91. The Holy Communion celebrated on the first Sunday of each month and greater festivals. Catechists and Sunday-School teachers, 14. Catechumens: Children taught the Catechism openly in the Church, 50; times, 12; members of other classes for religious instruction, 16; total number of young persons instructed, 70. Celebration of Divine Service: Sundays, 2; Holy Days, Morning Service generally; other days, Thanksgiving Day, Confirmation day, and twice a week during Lent—total, 142.

Contributions.—Episcopal Fund, $2; Diocesan Fund, $30; Missionary Committee of the Diocese, $15 50; Theological Education Fund, $9 10; Fund for Aged and Infirm Clergymen, $7 40; New-York Bible and Common Prayer-Book Society, $14 50; Protestant Episcopal Tract Society, $2 06; General P. E. S. S. Union and Church Book Society, $6 36; Board of Missions P. E. Church, U. S.: Domestic Committee, $25; Parochial School, $45; Parish purposes, $2,419 45; Church purposes in general, (Church Mission to the Jews, $3; Indian Department of Board of Missions, $22 56; City poor, $14; Bp. Tuttle, $25 80; two Scholarships in Utah, $80; Indian Scholarship, $60; Sewing Society for School at Utah and for the Shepherd's Fold, $75,) $280 36—total, $2,856 73.

St. Paul's Church, Sing Sing; the Rev. JAMES I. HELM, D. D., Rector.

Baptisms, inf. 15. Confirmed, 8. Marriages, 4. Burials, 16. Communicants: present number, 130. The Holy Communion celebrated on the first Sunday in every month, on great festivals, Midlent, and with the sick in private. Celebration of Divine Service: Sundays, twice; Holy Days, once; in Holy Week, twice; other days, Fridays, once; in Lent, twice; Thanksgiving, once; Wednesdays in Lent, twice—total, 2.0.

Contributions.—Bishop's Salary, $8; Diocesan Fund, $20; Missionary Committee of the Diocese, $24; Fund for Aged and Infirm Clergymen, $35 14; New-York Bible and Common Prayer-Book Society, $10; Board of Missions P. E. Church, U. S.: Domestic Committee, $52 66; Foreign Committee, $15; the Poor, $150; Parish purposes, $1,500; Church purposes in general, $220—total, $1,931 80.

During Lent the ladies of the Parish prepared and forwarded to one of our Missionaries a box of clothing and useful articles valued at $200.

The Ladies' Aid Society has had the walls and ceiling of the Church painted, the doors, woodwork and furniture painted and grained, the Chancel beautifully painted and illuminated, and both Chancel and Church newly carpeted.

A Cabinet Organ has been purchased for the Sunday-School room.

Trinity Church, Sing Sing; the Rev. GEO. W. FERGUSON, Rector.

Baptisms, (ad. 4, inf. 30.) 34. Confirmed, 17. Marriages, 3. Burials, 15. Communicants: admitted, 16; removed into the Parish, 3; removed from the Parish, 4; died, 5; present number, 162. The Holy Communion celebrated on the first Sunday of each month, weekly during Advent and Lent, on the great festivals, and on Ash-Wednesday and Thanksgiving Day. Catechumens: Children taught the Catechism openly in the Church, 114; times, 12. Celebration of Divine Service: Sundays, 104; Holy Days, all, 41; other days, 110—total, 255.

Contributions.—Episcopal Fund, $9; Missionary Committee of the Diocese, $10; Fund for Aged and Infirm Clergymen, $27 15; Mission to the Jews, $14 23; Missionary Box, from the Parish Guild, $361 69; New-York Bible and Common Prayer-Book Society, $20 81; American Chapel at Dresden, Saxony, $250 59; General Theological Seminary, $25; from St. Mary's Guild, for St. Mary's Hospital, N. Y., $58 30; Board of Missions P. E. Church, U. S.: Domestic Committee, $113 68; Indian Missions, $125 83; the Poor, $158 44; Parish purposes, $798 28—total, $2,273 40.

Christ Church, Tarrytown; the Rev. J. SELDEN SPENCER, Rector.

Families, about 80. Individuals, about 400. Baptisms, inf. 19. Marriages, 4. Burials, 5. Communicants: present number, about 120. The Holy Communion celebrated on the first Sunday in every month and on greater festivals. Catechists and Sunday School teachers, 12. Catechumens: Sunday scholars, 90. Celebration of Divine Service: Sundays, morning and evening; Holy Days, great festivals; other days, Wednesday and Friday in Lent, and daily in Holy Week.

Contributions.—Episcopal Fund, (Bishop's salary,) $20; Diocesan Fund, $50; Missionary Committee of the Diocese, $38 48; Southern Missionary Convocation, $24 26; Fund for Aged and Infirm Clergymen, $25 07; New-York Bible and Common Prayer-Book Society, $24 63; Society for Increase of Ministry, $90 34; Board of Missions P. E. Church, U. S.: Domestic Committee, $22 33; Foreign Committee, (for China, $43 65; General, $16 69,) $60 34; Sunday School, Christmas Tree, Books, &c., $181; the Poor, $199 03; Parish purposes, (enlarging Sunday School Room, $550; for Rectory, $5,500,) $6,050—total, $6,736 08.

The Rector gratefully records the completion of a beautiful and commodious Rectory, adjoining the Church, at a cost of about $8,000.

St. John's Church, Tuckahoe; the Rev. ANGUS M. IVES, Minister.

Families and parts of families, 58. Individuals, 195. Baptisms, (ad. 1, inf. 3,) 4. Confirmed, 15, (confirmed last year, but not reported.) Marriage, 1. Burials, 6. Communicants: admitted, 5; removed into the Parish, 4; died, 1; present number, 72. The Holy Communion celebrated monthly and on the principal festivals. Catechists and Sunday School teachers, 7. Catechumens: Children taught the Catechism openly in the Church, 44. Celebration of Divine Service: Sunday mornings throughout the year, and on the greater festivals.

Contributions.—Episcopal Fund, $8; Diocesan Fund, $7; Missionary Committee of the Diocese, $10 48; Fund for Aged and Infirm Clergymen, $3 54; New-York Bible and Common Prayer-Book Society, $10; Board of Missions P. E. Church, U. S.: Domestic Committee, $5; Foreign Committee, $3 17; Mission to the Jews, $5 65; Parish purposes, $979 35—total, $1,032 19.

St. Peter's Church, Westchester; the Rev. CHRISTOPHER B. WYATT, D. D., Rector.

Families, about 120. Baptisms, (ad. 2, inf. 27,) 29. Confirmed, 7. Burials, 23. Communicants, about 125. The Holy Communion celebrated the first Sunday of each month and on chief festivals. Catechists and Sunday-School teachers, 18. Catechumens: members of other classes for religious instruction, 13. Sunday scholars, 160. Celebration of Divine Service: Sundays, twice; Holy Days, once; other days, twice in each week.

Contributions.—Offerings and subscriptions, $2,251 81.

St. John's Church, Wilmot; the Rev. ANGUS M. IVES, Missionary.

Families, 29. Individuals, 106. Baptisms, inf. 3. Confirmed, 6, (confirmed last year, but not reported.) Burials, 2. Communicants: removed from the Parish, 3; died, 1; present number, 22. The Holy Communion celebrated on the third Sunday of every month and on the greater festivals. Catechists and Sunday-School teachers, 5. Catechumens: Children taught the Catechism openly in the Church, 31. Celebration of Divine Service: Sunday afternoons throughout the year, on the greater festivals and on the morning of the third Sunday of every month.

Contributions.—Episcopal Fund, $2; Diocesan Fund, $3 05; Missionary Committee of the Diocese, $3 72: Theological Education Fund, $3; Fund for Aged and Infirm Clergymen, $5; Board of Missions P. E. Church, U. S.: Domestic Committee, $2 04; Foreign Committee, $1 70; Mission to the Jews, $2 75; Church purposes in general, $218 45—total, $241 71.

Grace Church, White Plains; the Rev. FREDERICK B. VAN KLEECK, Rector.

Baptisms, (ad. 5, inf. 24,) 29. Confirmed, 14. Marriages, 11. Burials, 28. Communicants: admitted, 14; removed into the Parish, 2; removed from the Parish, 5; died, 10; present number, 193. The Holy Communion celebrated the first Sunday in the month, weekly in Advent and Lent, and all high festivals. Catechists and Sunday-School teachers, 20. Catechumens: Children taught the Catechism openly in the Church, 180; times, 12; total number of young persons instructed, 180. Celebration of Divine Service: Sundays, morning and night in the Parish Church: in afternoon, every Sunday at Rosedale; Holy Days, morning service; other days, Wednesdays and Fridays all the year; in Lent, every afternoon except Friday, at 5 P. M.; Wednesday, Thursday and Friday mornings, and Friday night, with lecture; Meditations at all afterno on services; last of Lent upon "The Sermon on the Mount."

Contributions.—Episcopal Fund, $10; Diocesan Fund, $40; Missionary Committee of the Diocese, $25 91; Theological Education Fund, $21 42; Southern Missionary Convocation, $40; Mission in Rockland Co., $25; General Theological Seminary, $40; House of the Good Shepherd, Rockland Co., $107 53; Board of Missions P. E. Church, U. S.: Domestic Committee, (Parish Church, $98; Rosedale, $7,) $105; Children's savings in Lent, for Bp. Tuttle, $56 89; Foreign Committee, $31 14; Indian Commission, $33 51; to Grasshopper sufferers, per Rev. Dr. Hoyt, $50; the Poor, $140 75; Parish purposes, $527 21; Church purposes in general, $516 84; Nashotah, $40—$2,151 11.

St. John's Church, Yonkers. [Rectorship vacant. Reported by the Wardens.]

Baptisms, (ad. 8, inf. 59,) 67. Confirmed, 36. Marriages, 4. Burials, 26. Communicants: present number, 350. The Holy Communion celebrated the first Sunday in each month, and Christmas, Good Friday, Easter and Whitsun-Day. Catechists and Sunday-School teachers, 40. Catechumens: total number of young persons instructed, 500. Celebration of Divine Service: Sundays, morning and evening, and a children's service in the afternoon of the third Sunday of each month; Holy Days, service on all Holy Days which refer directly to our Divine Lord; other days, every Wednesday morning, and frequent services during Lent—total, about two hundred.

Contributions.—Episcopal Fund, (to meet deficiency in,) $18; Diocesan Fund, $26 40: Missionary Committee of the Diocese, through Convocation, $25 11; Fund for Aged and Infirm Clergymen, $20; for the Jews, $35 35; Sewing School, $41 26; the Poor, $304 69; Parish purposes, including hospital and other benevolences, $227; Church purposes in general, $1,291 49; towards Church debt, $10,000—total, $12,189 80.

The following Report was received too late for insertion in its proper place:

Anthon Memorial Church, New-York; the Rev. R. HEBER NEWTON, Rector; the Rev. J. W. PAIGE, deacon, Assistant Minister.

Families, about 125. Individuals, about 500. Baptisms, inf. 22. Confirmed, 14. Marriages, 12. Burials, 10. Communicants: admitted, 14; removed into the Parish, 16; removed from the Parish, 4; present number, 339. The Holy Communion celebrated the first Sunday in the month, Christmas, Easter, Holy Thursday. Catechists and Sunday-School teachers, 44. Catechumens, 360. Children taught the Catechism openly in the Church, about 400. Industrial School: females, 120; teachers, 15. Celebration of Divine Service: Sundays, morning and evening, 101; Holy Days, evening prayer and lecture; other days, Fridays, evening prayer and lecture—total, 148.

Contributions.—Missionary Committee of the Diocese, $47 94; New-York City Mission Society, $67 10; miscellaneous charities, $448 41; Bishop Whittaker's work in Nevada, $84 07; Board of Missions P. E. Church, U. S.: Domestic Committee, $237 46; Foreign Committee, $151 54; work among the Indians, $58 48; the Poor, $2,165 25; Parish purposes, $1,790 98—total, $5,066 23.

The Bread and Beef House still remains an adjunct of our Parish work. It has for its object the relief of the sick and starving poor of this section of our city, extending its ministrations to all creeds and nationalities.

In addition to large quantities of provisions and clothing, nearly $3,000 in money has been contributed the past year for the prosecution of this work.

FROM THE FOLLOWING PARISHES NO REPORTS HAVE BEEN RECEIVED.

St. Peter's Church, Lithgow, Dutchess County.

Church of the Regeneration, Pine Plains, Dutchess County.

Church of the Ascension, New-York, the Rev. J. Cotton Smith, D. D., Rector.

Ascension Mission Chapel, New-York.

Christ Church, New-York, the Rev. Hugh Miller Thompson, D. D., Rector.

Church of the Epiphany, New-York, the Rev. U. T. Tracy, Rector.

Church of the Holy Trinity, New-York, the Rev. S. H. Tyng, Jr., D. D., Rector.

Church of the Intercession, New-York.

Church of the Intercessor, New-York.

St. Matthew's Church, New-York, the Rev. N. E. Cornwall, D. D., Rector.

Church of the Mediator, New-York.

Christ Church, Paterson, Putnam County.

St. John's Church, Clifton, Richmond County, the Rev. J. C. Eccleston, M. D., Rector.

St. Paul's Church, Ellenville, Ulster County, the Rev. Obadiah Valentine, Minister.

Church of the Holy Spirit, Rondout, Ulster County

St. Mary's Church, Beechwood, Westchester County, the Rev. Edward N. Mead, D. D., Rector.

St. Augustine's Church, Croton, Westchester County, the Rev. A. Vallete Clarkson, Rector.

St. Barnabas' Church, Irvington, Westchester County, the Rev. W. H. Benjamin, Rector.

St. John's Church, Katonah, Westchester County.

St. Mary's Church, North Castle, Westchester County.

St. James' Church, North Salem, Westchester County, the Rev. R. Condit Russell, Rector.

St. John's Church, Pleasantville, Westchester County.

St. Luke's Church, Somers, Westchester County, the Rev. R. Condit Russell, Rector.

St. Paul's Church, Yonkers, Westchester County, the Rev. David Banks, Rector.

St. Mary's Church, Yorktown, Westchester County.—25.

Also from the following, which have been admitted into unio with the Convention, but which maintain no services:

St. Mary's Church, Beekman, Dutchess County.
Church of the Advent, New-York
Church of the Atonement, New-York.
Church of the Crucifixion, New-York.
Emmanuel Church, New-York.
Free Church of St. George's Chapel, New-York.
Church of the Saviour, New-York.
Church of the Good Shepherd, New-York.
Church of the Holy Evangelists, New-York.
Church of the Holy Innocents, New-York.
Church of the Holy Light, New-York.
Church of the Redemption, New-York.
St. Barnabas' Church, New-York.
St. Jude's Church, New-York.
St. Matthew's Church, New-York.
St. Paul's Church, 12th Ward, New York.
St. Saviour's Church, New-York.
St. Sauveur's Church, New-York.
St. Simon's Church, New-York.—19.

OTHER CLERICAL REPORTS.

The Bishop of the Diocese has also received Reports, according to the Canon, from the following Clergymen of the Diocese, not having Parochial or Missionary charge:

The Rev. GEORGE F. BEHRINGER, deacon, reports as follows:

Since my ordination, July 14th, 1875, I have acted as *Assistant* to the Rev. Jas. S. Bush, of the Church of the Ascension, at West New Brighton, and also as *Chaplain* to the "Child's Nursery and Hospital," (Country Branch,) located here, on Staten Island.

I have assisted in the celebration of the Holy Communion, 2 times; have read service, (Sundays,) in whole or in part, 16 times; preached, 14 times; baptized 10 infants, and read the burial service, 7 times.

I have likewise had sole charge of a Sunday-School, of about 50 young children, belonging to the "Nursery;" held a daily evening service in the Chapel of the institution, and have distributed 200 tracts and 150 religious newspapers among the inmates of the "Hospital."

The Rev. W. M. A. BRODNAX reports as follows:

I have officiated, during the twelve months since my last report, as I have had opportunities.

The Rev. SAMUEL BUEL, D. D., Professor of Systematic Divinity and Dogmatic Theology in the General Theological Seminary, reports as follows:

I respectfully report, that since the last Annual Convention of the Diocese, I have been regularly engaged in the discharge of my duties as Professor of Systematic Divinity and Dogmatic Theology in the General Theological Seminary; and have also acted as Professor of the Evidences of Christianity in the institution. My instructions have been given by lectures, oral and written, and by a diligent use, with the Students, of approved text books. I have taken my alloted part in the services of the Seminary Chapel. I have also officiated--by reading service, administering the Holy Communion, baptizing and preaching—in different churches in the Diocese of New-Jersey, in Northern New-Jersey, and in the City of New-York. The offices which I have performed, will be reported from the Parishes, in which I have officiated.

The General Theological Seminary has been in a healthful condition during the past year; the Students have been faithful and attentive to their duties; and the work which has been done there will not be, I trust and think, without good to the Church and to its mission in the world.

The Rev. EDWARD COWLEY respectfully reports:

That during the Convention year he has officiated as occasion offered, otherwise than in connection with "The Children's Fold," both within and without the Diocese. A short service is held in the Fold, morning and evening, daily, throughout the year. The children take an active part in the service. They learn the Catechism, the Collect for the day, and brief portions of Holy Scripture; nor are they behind others of their age in deportment and week-day studies. The children have long been ranked as among the most healthy in the city. While many of them have been brought up in the Fold from infancy, till they are now ten to twelve years old, thanks to a kind Providence, of those who have been three months in the institution, but one has died. Including those of new members, there have been three deaths during nine years.

Because of the continued "hard times," no special effort has been made to materially increase the Building Fund, so that it remains about as last year. The approximate amount of money raised for current expenses, for the year ending Oct 1st, (not elsewhere reported.) is $4,500. Baptisms, 11; burials, 2; marriage, 1. Total number of children supported during the year, 80; present number, 57; girls, 29; boys, 28.

The Children's Fold has no debt, but it greatly needs a suitable house and chapel of its own. Will Churchmen please remember this want in the disposition of the means with which Providence has favored them?

The Rev. WILLIAM E. EIGENBRODT, D. D., Professor of Pastoral Theology in the General Theological Seminary, respectfully reports:

That during the last year, besides the regular discharge of his duties in the General Theological Seminary, he has officiated in various Parish churches, by saying prayers, preaching, baptizing, (6 infants and 2 adults, total, 8 persons,) several times performing the burial service, and frequently administering the Holy Communion.

The Rev. WALTER RUSSELL GARDNER reports:

I beg to report, that during the greater part of the past year, up to Aug. 1st, I have officiated as Rector of St. Thomas' Church, Amenia, during which time I baptized 9 adults and 4 infants, and presented a class of 13 for confirmation.

Aug. 1st I resigned the Rectorship of the Parish, and since then have officiated occasionally at the Church of the Advent, Boston; have baptized three infants, and have officiated at four funerals.

The Rev. RANDALL C. HALL, Professor of the Hebrew and Greek Languages in the General Theological Seminary, reports:

In addition to my duties in the General Theological Seminary, during the past year, I have officiated nearly every Sunday From May 30th to July 4th I took temporary charge of Trinity Church, Haverstraw. During July and August, assisted at St. Stephen's Church of this city. During the present month assisted at the Anthon Memorial Church, also of this city.

The Rev. ALEXANDER HAMILTON, deacon, respectfully reports:

That during the past year he has been engaged in the duties of his office, in Westchester County, New-York City, and assisted occasionally at St. John's Church, Huntington, Long Island, the past summer.

The Rev. ROBERT HOLDEN, Rector of Trinity School, New-York, respectfully reports:

That in addition to the performance of his duties as Rector of Trinity School, he has assisted in Divine service, during the past year, at Grace Church, New-York, and in the Churches of Morrisania, reading service 38 times, and preaching 13 times.

The Rev. RALPH HOYT respectfully reports:

That he is still in charge of Good Shepherd Parish, at Fort Lee, N. J., under the sanction of Bishop Odenheimer.

The Rev. CHARLES S. KNAPP reports as follows:

That during the past year he has been acting as Chaplain of the Panama Rail-Road Company and as Rector of Christ Church, Aspinwall, Panama.

Has held two services nearly every Sunday, also organized and conducted a Sunday-School for native children, and had occasional week day services.

Administered the Holy Communion monthly and on the principal festival days.

Baptisms, (ad. 2, inf. 50,) 52. Marriages, 6. Funerals, 21.

A large number are ready to be confirmed as soon as the visitation of a Bishop can be secured.

The Rev. R. W. LEWIS respectfully reports:

That he only returned to the country in June last; since that date, (June 4th,) he has been occupied to some extent in supplying the places of Clergymen absent from their Parishes; he has also been looking for a regular and permanent field of labor; thus far, however, without success.

The Rev. CHARLES S. LITTLE reports as follows:

I beg leave to make the following report, in accordance with the Canon:

That owing to a long and severe illness, I have been unable to do any duty for more than two years.

I am now slowly recovering, and trust soon to enter the field again.

The Rev. DAVID H. MACURDY respectfully reports:

That since the last Convention he has resided for nine months in Philadelphia, and for three months in Cornwall, officiating almost every Sunday.

His health being re-established, he holds himself in readiness for duty, whenever he may be called to it.

The Rev. R. U. MORGAN, D. D., in the 54th year of his Ministry, presents this, his 53d consecutive annual report:

I have read prayers and preached six times in Trinity Church, New-Rochelle. Also married 1 couple, baptized 1 infant, and buried 4 adults, all of which I suppose will be included in the report of the Parish.

On other occasions I have said morning and evening prayer, 17 times, and assisted in performing the same, 19 times; preached, 14 times. Celebrated the Holy Communion, 5 times, and assisted in the same, 22 times.

The Rev. EDWIN A. NICHOL reports as follows:

I have officiated quite often, reading, preaching and administering the Holy Communion, both in the Dioceses of New-York and Long Island, assisting the Clergy in charge of Parishes.

The Rev. WILLIAM W. OLSSEN, Professor of the Greek Language and Literature and of the Hebrew Language in St. Stephen's College, Annandale, N. Y., reports as follows:

During the past year I have performed the duties of the above named professorship, and have taken part in the preaching and the daily service in the College Chapel. In addition, I have read service, in whole or in part, 31 times, and preached 23 times in other Churches. I have administered, or assisted in administering the Holy Communion in the College Chapel and elsewhere, 40 times. I have read the burial service twice, and solemnized one marriage.

The Rev. SAMUEL OSGOOD, D. D., residing in New-York, reports as follows:

I take the liberty to say, that I have baptized one child, married three couples, and attended four funerals as minister—all these official acts, except one of the funerals, having been performed in the Diocese of New-York.

I have generally preached on Sundays, and administered the Holy Communion at the usual seasons. I have joined in a course of Sunday evening Sermons at Christ Church, and, by request of the Trustees, visited St. Johnland, and preached there.

I preached at St. Michael's, N. Y., from Advent to Whitsun-Day, and during my stay in Fairfield I have preached at St. Paul's there, and have lately been preaching at Christ Church, Bridgeport, where I now am occupied on Sunday mornings.

It may not be obtrusive for me to say, that I am following seriously and somewhat laboriously the studies of my profession, and trying, in my humble way, to do the work of a Christian scholar, with my voice and pen, in the great field in which we are to discern the vineyard of the Lord. The fact that I have been left very much to work alone, may have sometimes added to the burden, but ought not to lessen the motive of my work, or its dignity.

The Rev. JOHN J. ROBERTS reports:

In accordance with the Canon, I beg leave to report, that since the Convention of 1874 I have, in addition to my professional engagements in Madison Avenue, performed the duties of President of "The Home for the Blind," in 14th-street, and officiated about sixty times in various Parishes, in and out of the Diocese of New-York.

The Rev. CHARLES SEYMOUR, A. M., respectfully reports:

That, from the adjournment of the Diocesan Convention of 1874 to the Wednesday after the ensuing Easter Day, he continued ministering to the small and struggling Parish of Grace Church, Westfield, New-Jersey, until it completed and occupied its neat and furnished edifice for public worship, within which services are now celebrated by a Deacon. That is the third House of Prayer which it has been my privilege to begin and supervise; and one circumstance connected with the efforts in Westfield is so exceptional, that it ought to be recorded, namely, that Christians of all names, laying aside suspicion and jealousy, helped forward the good work, well aware, as they were, of our position and obligations. Since my retirement from that temporary charge, I have constantly, (except on two Sundays, when sickness hindered,) been engaged in priestly duties.

Holy Communion celebrated, or assisted in the celebration, 13 times. Baptisms, 4 infants.

The Rev. GEORGE F. SEYMOUR, S. T. D., Dean of the General Theological Seminary, and Professor of Ecclesiastical History in the same, respectfully reports:

That since the last Convention, in addition to his duties in the General Theological Seminary, he has continued to hold the position of Chaplain of the House of Mercy, New-York, at the foot of West 86th-street

In this institution, which has for its object the reclamation of fallen women, he has officiated on 221 occasions; he has baptized 3 adults, admitted 5 to the Holy Communion, and attended 2 funerals.

The Bishop of New-York visited the House of Mercy on June 2[illegible]th and July 14th, and confirmed, on the two occasions, 7. The Sisters of St Mary are still in charge of the House; twelve years of faithful service in this institution commends them to the Clergy and Laity of the Diocese, as those who have forsaken all to follow Christ in a labor of love for lost souls, that lays a heavier burden of self-denial and severity of endurance upon those who engage in it than any other that can be named.

Outside of the House of Mercy the Dean has baptized 1 infant and 2 adults, preached 53 times, and attended 6 funerals.

Summary.—Baptisms, (ad. 5, inf. 1,) 6. Confirmed, 7. Burials, 8. New Communicants admitted, 5.

The Rev. J. A. SPENCER, S. T. D., reports as follows:

That since the last Convention he has been constantly occupied in the duties of his position as Professor of the Greek Language and Literature in the College of the City of New-York. In addition, he has officiated in the public services of the Church, preaching, administering the Holy Communion, etc., on eleven occasions. He has solemnized one marriage, and buried two adults.

COLLEGE OF THE CITY OF NEW-YORK, cor. Lexington Avenue and 23d-street,
New-York, September 29th, 1875.

The Rev. WALTER STIRLING respectfully reports:

That during the past year he has been engaged in Clerical duty chiefly at the Church of Our Lord, 352 West 35th-street, and elsewhere. That he has assisted in the services, 34 times, preached, 22 times, baptized 3 infants, married, 2, buried, 1, catechised and addressed the Sunday-School, 43 times.

The Rev. H. C. STOWELL reports as follows:

During the last Conventional year, either in or out of the City of New-York, I have officiated every Sunday at least once, generally twice. I have celebrated alone, or assisted in the celebration of the Holy Eucharist, 16 times. I have solemnized two marriages, baptized two children, and officiated at two funerals.

The Rev. EDWARD W. SYLE begs leave to report:

That in the capacity of a Chaplain residing abroad, he continued to officiate in Christ Church, Yokohama, until the end of April of the present year.

Since May 1st he has resided in Yedo, as Professor of Moral Philosophy in the Imperial College.

Yedo, Japan, 23d August, 1875.

The Rev. A. C. TREADWAY reports:

During the year past I have preached, baptized and assisted in the Holy Communion, &c., as opportunities have offered and the state of my health would admit. These labors have been bestowed in Washington City, where I spent the last winter, and in Oswego, my home, (because it is convenient to make it such,) where, especially, I am glad to do what I am able for my brethren and the Church's sake. The special offices are on record where they were performed.

Oswego, N. Y., September 22, 1875.

The Rev. E. H. VAN WINKLE, deacon, respectfully reports:

That since the last Convention, he has performed the following services:

He has read morning or evening service, 40 times, and assisted at the same on 42 occasions. He has preached, 54 times. He has assisted at the Holy Communion on 9 occasions. He has baptized one child.

He has resided at 25 West Ninth-street, New-York City.

The Rev. WILLIAM WALSH reports:

In the past year my services, mainly consisting in acts of assistance to my brethren in the ministry, have been confined mostly to Orange County. Another year may enable me to do more than I have done in the one that is past.

The Rev. GEORGE WATERS, D. D., respectfully reports:

That since his return to this Diocese from that of Albany, when his connection with St. Paul's, Kinderhook, terminated, Jan. 10, he has rendered several services in and for St. John's, Kingston, preaching, administering Holy Communion, and officiating at burials. During Lent he supplied the Church of the Intercession, New York, and from the 27th of June to the present time has officiated regularly in Christ Church, Marlborough, to which he has received a call to be their Rector.

That he has also had a weekly service with the prisoners in Kingston Jail, on Wednesdays throughout the year.

The Rev. JOSHUA WEAVER reports:

The past year has been spent mostly in California, and I have there, and in Colorado—officiated as follows:

Read the service on 32 occasions. Assisted in the service, 82 times. Celebrated the Holy Communion, 12 times, and assisted in the celebration, 27 times. Have preached 3[illegible] Sermons, baptized one child, and attended 4 funerals.

New-York, September 29th, 1875.

The Rev. BENJAMIN WEBB reports as follows;

Besides my duties as assistant at All Angels' Church, New-York, I have rendered a number of other services during the year, having celebrated the Holy Eucharist eighty-four times, and assisted in the same service twenty-one. Officiated at six baptisms, (reported,) at two burials, (reported,) and at morning and evening prayers on three hundred and eighteen occasions, and preached forty times.

I have been engaged in teaching during the usual hours daily throughout the school year.

The Rev. FRED'K W. WEY reports as follows:

Having worked in your Diocese since the 15th of May, but not being able to get any letter Dimissory, I submit the following report of my work to you:

On Whitsun-Day I held the first service in the Church of the Nativity, this being the beginning of a German Mission named "The Mission of the Holy Cross," in conjunction and additional to the work which the Sisters of St John Baptist had already done for some time in this part of the city.

I have baptized 26 children, 1 adult, married two couples, buried, 4, administered the Holy Communion 67 times in public and twice in private, preached 48 sermons, and delivered 8 addresses. 10 families have handed in their names as belonging to the Mission. We have 26 communicants. 108 Sunday-School children are on the roll, with an average attendance of about 65 at each session, 8 teachers are in the Sunday-School. We also have a night school, with 30 pupils and 3 teachers.

The work which is done in this district, and exclusively by the Sisters, will be in their report. The celebrations above mentioned were partly held in the Church and partly in the Chapel of the Sisters. The above number of families and communicants are not by far all that belong to us, but I have only mentioned those who have given their names.

The Rev. C. T. WOODRUFF, Superintendent of the New-York Protestant Episcopal City Mission Society, respectfully reports:

That since the last Convention, in addition to his duties as Superintendent, he has officiated regularly at the "New-York Infant Asylum" on the first and third Sundays of each month, and since March 1st has been the regular Chaplain of the "Midnight Mission," holding services every Sunday P. M., and Wednesday at 12 M. He has officiated at 3 weddings, 33 baptisms, 15 funerals, preached 18 times, and read prayers 16 times in St. Barnabas' Chapel, administered Holy Communion wholly or in part on 28 public occasions. He has also assisted his brethren of the Clergy very often, been frequently called to visit the sick, and has taken the place of the Chaplain in Bellevue while he was away for a fortnight's vacation in August.

His address is 304 Mulberry-street, New-York.

Appendix:

No. II.

ble,—Showing the names of the Churches and Chapels in the of New-York, with the numbers in each, respectively, of BAPTISMS, MATIONS, COMMUNICANTS, MARRIAGES and BURIALS, so far as re- the Bishop, for the year ending September 29, 1873. Prepared and d at the request of the Convention by the Secretary, in compliance Resolution recorded on p. 94 of the Journal of 1866. In those cases ll the columns are blank, there is no Parochial Report from the or the past year.

urches and Chapels.	Baptisms.	Confirmations.	Communicants.	Marriages.	Burials.
utchess County.					
St Thomas',	14	12	52	2	8
e, St. Stephen's College Chap	2	4	125	..	4
n. St John the Evangelist's,	10	9	43	1	4
, St. Mary's,	..	..	..	..	..
Landing, St. Mark's,	5	..	25	1	2
Apostle's,	.	..	..	..	..
Trinity,	2	5	43	2	..
St. John Baptist,	12	1	80	5	4
k, St. James',	40	24	120	..	8
St Peter's,	.	..	..	..	..
Trinity,	5	..	50	1	8
n, St. Luke's,	13	5	211	6	16
, Grace,	..	..	30	3	1
	1	..	9	..	1
s, Regeneration,	..	..	..	..	..
Valley, St. Paul's,	10	7	34	2	8
psie, Christ,	27	29	300	6	27
Holy Comforter,	47	18	295	8	27
St. Paul's,	40	20	215	10	19
, Christ,	12	..	38	2	1
St Paul's,	4	..	37	2	3
c, Messiah,	2	..	62	1	2
, Ascension,	11	..	30	1	..
r's Falls, Zion,	82	45	376	8	23
w-York County.					
, Advent,	..	..	..	..	..
All Angels',	8	..	40	2	3
All Saints',	93	30	231	33	42
Annunciation,	20	8	146	9	17
Anthon Memorial,	22	14	339	12	10
Ascension,	..	..	..	..	..
Ascension Miss. Chapel,	..	..	..	..	..
Atonement,	..	..	..	..	..

Churches and Chapels.	Baptisms.	Confirmations.	Communicants.	Marriages.	Burials.
New-York, Atonement, Madison Av..	7	7	120	1	10
Atonement Chapel,......	27	..	101	7	37
Bellevue, ...	32	..	237	..	193
Beloved Disciple,...... ..	12	11	106	3	10
Bethlehem Chapel, ...	33	23	140	5	14
Calvary..	17	..	550	10	13
Calvary Free Chapel, ...	47	29	460	27	35
Christ Church,..........	..	..	..	..	..
Crucifixion, ...	..	..	..	..	..
Emmanuel, ...	..	..	..	..	..
Epiphany..	..	..	..	..	..
Free Church of Saint George's Chapel, ...	..	..	..	..	..
Our Saviour,.	..	..	..	..	..
Floating Chapel of Our Saviour,.........	20	20	111	12	8
Good Shepherd, ...	..	..	..	.	..
Grace, ...	49	84	850	34	32
Grace Chapel,...........	37	18	200	12	22
Heavenly Rest,..........	16	28	250	7	7
Holy Apostles,.	84	26	370	18	43
Holy Communion,........	65	59	550	31	39
Holy Comforter,.........	7	..	18	..	3
Holy Evangelists,........	..	..	..	..	..
Holy Innocents,...... ...	..	..	..	..	..
Holy Light, ...	..	..	..	..	..
Holy Martyrs,...........	73	20	90	25	50
Holy Saviour,.	22	..	200	19	26
Holy Sepulchre,.........	11	12	80	..	..
Holy Trinity, ...	..	..	..	..	..
House of Mercy,...... ..	7	7	..	..	3
Incarnation, ...	16	11	400	2	9
Intercession, ...	..	..	.	..	..
Intercessor or St. Alban's	..	..	..	..	..
Mediator,...............	..	..	..	..	..
Nativity, ...	30	1	100	17	16
New-York City Mission, (including Bellevue and Bethlehem Chapels,)	341	63	868	..	297
Reconciliation,..........	39	40	250	16	23
Redeemer, Yorkville,...	62	48	161	12	40
Redemption,............	..	..	..	..	..
Reformation,............	..	..	..	..	..
Resurrection, ...	26	9	80	20	21
Santiago,.	16	60	40	14	4
St. Ambrose, ...	16	..	175	5	3
St. Andrew's, ...	49	28	351	20	30
St. Ann's,..........	66	52	460	27	47
St. Barnabas',............	.	..	..	..	..
St. Bartholomew's, ...	17	..	450	9	13
St. Clement's,...........	19	.	160	3	5
St. Esprit,.	10	11	47	14	10
St. George's and Chapels,*	..	..	..	..	..
St. George the Martyr's,.	..	..	..	..	..
St. Ignatius',†..	..	..	..	..	..
St James'.	29	23	292	8	22
St. John Baptist.	21	13	200	9	10
St John Evangelist,....	68	44	500	14	50
St Jude's.	..	..	..	.	.
St. Luke's,..............	90	40	350	26	41
St Mark's, ... St. Mark's Mission,....	57	71	435	17	31
St. Mary's,.	19	9	144	3	10
St. Mary the Virgin,. ...	13	20	193	4	7

* The particulars for this year, not specified in the report, but included in aggregate from several years,

† The report of the Parish gives an aggregate since its organization, without specifying the particulars of the year 1874-75.

Churches and Chapels.	Baptisms.	Confirmations.	Communicants.	Marriages.	Burials.
New-York, St. Matthew's,	..	..	..	..	..
St. Matthias',	..	..	..	..	..
St. Michael's,	41	17	170	3	14
St. Paul's in 12th Ward,	..	..	..	..	..
St. Peter's,	111	32	400	35	38
St. Philip's,	25	21	225	5	17
St. Saviour's,	..	..	..	..	..
St. Sauveur's,	..	..	..	..	..
St. Simon's,	..	..	..	..	..
St. Stephen's,	12	..	60	5	7
St. Thomas',	26	36	800	16	7
St. Thomas' Miss. Chap.,	51	31	180	7	28
St. Timothy's,	24	19	272	16	23
Transfiguration,	40	30	450	46	..
Trinity Church, St Paul's Chapel, St John's Chapel, Trinity Chapel, St. Chrysostom, S. Augustine, St. Cornelius', Governor's Island, (Miss. Cha.)	609	317	2,858	138	288
Zion Church,	10	10	155	4	3
Harlem, Grace,	23	6	108	11	18
Fordham, St. James',	6	..	80	2	6
Morrisania, St. Ann's	14	..	105	2	8
St. Paul's,	17	..	95	6	12
Trinity,	35	..	125	8	15
Mott Haven, St. Mary's,	28	10	115	6	18
Riverdale, Christ,	12	..	120	3	3
Kingsbridge, South Yonkers, Mediator,	..	..	..	..	..
West Farms, Grace,	18	..	63	1	..

Orange County.

Churches and Chapels.	Baptisms.	Confirmations.	Communicants.	Marriages.	Burials.
Canterbury, St. John's,	9	4	55	3	3
Cornwall, Holy Innocents, Highland Falls,	33	..	80	9	8
Goshen, St James',	10		225	11	11
Greenwood Iron Works, St. John's,	43	10	80	8	4
Monroe, Grace,	4	..	20	..	1
Newburgh, St George's,	101	54	400	13	21
St. Paul's,	9	9	147	3	3
New-Windsor, St. Thomas',	11	6	46	2	1
Port Jervis, Grace,	24	18	72	..	11
South Middletown, Grace,	21	..	218	13	24
Walden, St. Andrew's,	22	12	79	6	8
Warwick, Christ,	11	6	50	4	8

Putnam County.

Churches and Chapels.	Baptisms.	Confirmations.	Communicants.	Marriages.	Burials.
Cold Spring, St. Mary's,	16	4	124	13	15
Paterson, Christ,	.	..	..	..	..
Philipsetown, St. Philip's,	6	..	55	..	5

Richmond County.

Churches and Chapels.	Baptisms.	Confirmations.	Communicants.	Marriages.	Burials.
Castleton, West Brighton, Ascension,	58	11	283	7	19
St. Mary's,	4	..	54	3	3
Clifton, St. John's,	..	..	..	..	..
Edgewater, St. Paul's,	18	..	200	8	15
New-Brighton, Christ,	20	14	125	7	20
Richmond, St. Andrew's,	9	..	100	.	..
Rossville, St. Luke's,	10	..	25	..	3
Southfield, Holy Comforter,	4	..	43	1	..

Churches and Chapels.	Baptisms.	Confirmations.	Communicants.	Marriages.	Burials
Rockland County.					
Clarkstown, St. John's,	5	..	26	..	1
Haverstraw, Holy Trinity,	18	..	76	1	8
St. Luke's,	2	..	23	..	..
Nyack, Grace,	16	17	130	5	17
Piermont, Christ,	15	7	71	4	20
Ramapo, Christ,	11	..	46	2	2
Spring Valley, St. Paul's,	1	3	36	3	6
Stony Point, Holy Child Jesus,	14	..	15	2	1
Sullivan County.					
Monticello, St. John's,	19	..	143	1	8
Ulster County.					
Ellenville, St. Paul's,	..	..	..	..	..
Esopus, Ascension,	2	..	6	2	3
Kingston, St. John's,	2	..	174	2	9
(Rondout,) Holy Spirit,	..	..	..	..	..
Marlborough, Christ,	10	..	40	3	2
Milton, All Saints',	16	14	30	1	6
Saugerties, Trinity,	12	..	75	2	8
Stone Ridge, St. Peter's,	32	12	27	..	1
Westchester County.					
Bedford, St. Matthew's,	..	5	75	1	5
Beechwood, St. Mary's,	..	..	..	..	..
Briar Cliff, All Saints',		..	29	..	2
City Island, Grace,	10	14	81	2	3
Cortlandt, Divine Love,	20	2	27	2	7
Croton, St. Augustine's,	..	..	..	..	..
East Chester, St. Paul's,	29	..	105	5	21
Greenburgh, Zion,	13	8	90	3	9
Mission Chapel,	6	3	12	..	4
…vington, St. Barnabas',	..	..	..	..	..
Katonah, St. Mark's,	..	..		..	
Lewisborough, St. John's,	8	5	36	5	4
Mamaroneck, St. Thomas',	21		128	6	20
Mount Pleasant, St. Mark's,	21	16	125	6	16
Mount Vernon, Trinity,	42	19	178	4	13
New-Castle, St. Mark's,	2	4	63	2	5
New-Rochelle, Trinity,	22	25	155	6	19
North Castle, St. Mary's,	..	..	..	..	..
St. Stephen's,	11	..	58	8	8
North Salem, St. James',	..		..	..	..
Peekskill, (Cortlandt,) St. Peter's,	31	13	109	2	12
Pelham, Christ,	10	4	58	2	
Pleasantville, St. John's,	..	..	..	..	
Portchester, St. Peter's,	42	28	177	9	[illegible]
Rye, Christ,	24	13	200	2	9
Scarsdale, St. James the Less,	9	7	91	..	3
Sing Sing, St. Paul's,	15	8	130	4	16
Trinity,	34	17	162	3	15
Somers, St. Luke's,	..	..	..	..	..
Tarrytown, Christ,	19	..	120	4	5
Tuckahoe, St. John's,	4	15	72	1	6
Westchester, St. Peter's,	29	7	125	..	23
White Plains, Grace,	29	14	193	11	25
Wilmot, St. John's,	3	6	22	..	2
Yonkers, St. John's,	67	36	350	4	26
St. Paul's,	..	..	..	..	..
Yorktown, St. Mary's,	..	..	..	..	..

A Table,—Showing the names of the Churches and Chapels of the Diocese of New York, with the sums contributed by each to the EPISCOPAL, DIOCESAN, EDUCATION and MISSIONARY FUNDS, respectively, for the year 1874–75, in compliance with Canons xiii., xiv. and xv.; prepared and published by order of the Convention, by the Secretary of the same, with the aid of the Treasurers of the Funds; to which are added the Contributions to the FUND FOR AGED AND INFIRM CLERGYMEN, required by Canon xvi. The apportionment for the Salary of the Bishop, when paid, appears in the columns of the Episcopal Fund.

Counties.	Churches and Chapels.	Clergymen.	Episcopal.	Diocesan.	Education.	Missionary.	Aged and Inf. Clergy.
Dutchess........	Amenia, St. Thomas'..............	Rev. Amos. T. Ashton.......	$2 00	$8 00	....	$13 61	....
	Annandale, St. Stephen's Chapel....	R. B. Fairbairn, D. D....	7 00	20 00	$14 50	....	$35 00
	Barrytown, St. John's Ev. Memorial.	G. B. Hopson..........	....	18 60	15 02	44 50	2 40
	Beekman, St. Mary's.............	....	....	....	....	....	....
	Carthage Landing, St. Mark's......	F. W. Shelton, D. D. ...	2 00	5 00	....	....	....
	Clinton, Apostles,................	....	....	....	....	....	....
	Fishkill, Trinity..................	J. R. Livingston........	5 00	5 00	5 50	10 00	21 00
	Glenham, St. John Baptist..........	J. R. Livingston........	2 00	2 00	2 50	....	....
	Hyde Park, St. James'............	J. S. Purdy, D. D.......	25 00	30 00	12 00	20 00	23 22
	Lithgow, St. Peter's..............	....	2 00	....	....	....	....
	Madalin, Trinity,.................	J. S. Clark, D. D.......	....	....	....	....	....
	Matteawan, St. Luke's.............	E. T. Bartlett.....	....	....	....	....	32 58
	Millbrook, Grace	B. F. Miller............	....	....	....	....	....
	Pine Plains, Regeneration.........	....	....	....		....	....
	Pleasant Valley, St. Paul's........	G. H. Smith...........	....	....	....	....	2 10
	Poughkeepsie, Christ..............	H. L. Ziegenfuss.......	15 00	40 00	5 50	50 60	....

Churches and Chapels.	Baptisms.	Confirmations.	Communicants.	Marriages.	Burials.
New-York, Atonement, Madison Av.,	7	7	120	1	10
Atonement Chapel,	27	..	101	7	37
Bellevue,	32	..	287	..	193
Beloved Disciple,	12	11	106	3	10
Bethlehem Chapel,	38	23	140	5	14
Calvary,	17	..	550	10	13
Calvary Free Chapel,	47	29	460	27	35
Christ Church,	..	..	..	..	..
Crucifixion,	..	..	..	..	..
Emmanuel,	..	..	..	..	..
Epiphany,	..	..	..	..	..
Free Church of Saint George's Chapel,	..	..	..	..	..
Our Saviour,	..	..	..	..	..
Floating Chapel of Our Saviour,	20	20	111	12	8
Good Shepherd,	..	..	..	..	..
Grace,	49	84	850	34	32
Grace Chapel,	37	18	200	12	21
Heavenly Rest,	16	28	250	7	7
Holy Apostles,	84	26	370	18	43
Holy Communion,	65	59	550	31	39
Holy Comforter,	7	..	18	..	3
Holy Evangelists,	..	..	..	..	..
Holy Innocents,	..	..	..	..	..
Holy Light,	..	..	..	..	..
Holy Martyrs,	73	20	90	25	50
Holy Saviour,	22	..	200	19	26
Holy Sepulchre,	11	12	80	..	..
Holy Trinity,	..	..	..	..	..
House of Mercy,	7	7	..	..	3
Incarnation,	16	11	400	2	9
Intercession,	..	..	.	..	..
Intercessor or St. Alban's	..	..	..	..	..
Mediator,	..	..	..	..	..
Nativity,	30	1	100	17	16
New-York City Mission, (including Bellevue and Bethlehem Chapels,)	341	63	868	..	297
Reconciliation,	39	40	250	16	23
Redeemer, Yorkville,	62	48	161	12	40
Redemption,	..	..	..	..	..
Reformation,		..	..	..	..
Resurrection,	26	9	80	20	21
Santiago,	16	60	40	14	4
St. Ambrose,	16	..	175	5	8
St. Andrew's,	49	26	351	20	30
St. Ann's,	66	52	460	27	47
St. Barnabas',	.	..	..	..	..
St. Bartholomew's,	17	..	450	9	13
St. Clement's,	19	.	160	3	5
St. Esprit,	10	11	47	14	10
St. George's and Chapels,*	..	..	..	..	..
St. George the Martyr's,	..	..	..	..	..
St. Ignatius',†	..	..	..	..	..
St. James'	29	23	292	8	22
St. John Baptist,	21	13	200	9	10
St. John Evangelist,	68	44	500	14	50
St. Jude's,	..		..	.	.
St. Luke's,	90	40	350	26	41
St. Mark's, St. Mark's Mission,	57	71	435	17	31
St. Mary's,	19	9	144	3	10
St. Mary the Virgin,	13	20	195	4	7

* The particulars for this year, not specified in the report, but included in aggregat[e] from several years.

† The report of the Parish gives an aggregate since its organization, without specifyin[g] the particulars of the year 1874-75.

Churches and Chapels.	Baptisms.	Confirmations.	Communicants.	Marriages.	Burials.
New-York, St. Matthew's,	..	..	..	..	..
St. Matthias',	..	..	..	..	..
St. Michael's,	41	17	170	3	14
St. Paul's in 12th Ward,	..	..	..	..	..
St. Peter's,	111	82	400	35	38
St. Philip's,	25	21	225	5	17
St. Saviour's,	..	..	..	..	..
St. Sauveur's,	..	..	..	..	..
St. Simon's,	..	..	..	..	..
St Stephen's,	12	..	60	5	7
St. Thomas',	26	36	800	16	7
St. Thomas' Miss. Chap.,	51	31	180	7	28
St. Timothy's,	24	19	272	16	23
Transfiguration,	40	30	450	46	..
Trinity Church, St. Paul's Chapel, St John's Chapel, Trinity Chapel, St. Chrysostom, St. Augustine, St. Cornelius', Governor's Island, (Miss. Cha.)	609	317	2,858	138	288
Zion Church,	10	10	155	4	3
Harlem, Grace,	23	6	108	11	18
Fordham, St. James',	6	..	80	2	6
Morrisania, St. Ann's,	14	..	105	2	8
St. Paul's,	17	..	95	6	12
Trinity,	35	..	125	8	15
Mott Haven, St. Mary's,	28	10	115	6	18
Riverdale, Christ,	12	..	120	3	3
Kingsbridge, South Yonkers, Mediator,	..	..	..	..	..
West Farms, Grace,	18	..	63	1	..
Orange County.					
Canterbury, St. John's,	9	4	55	3	3
Cornwall, Holy Innocents, Highland Falls,	33	..	80	9	8
Goshen, St James',	10	..	225	11	11
Greenwood Iron Works, St. John's,	43	10	80	3	4
Monroe, Grace,	4	..	20	..	1
Newburgh, St George's,	101	54	400	18	24
St. Paul's,	9	9	147	3	3
New-Windsor, St. Thomas',	11	6	46	2	1
Port Jervis, Grace,	24	18	72	..	11
South Middletown, Grace,	21	..	248	13	24
Walden, St. Andrew's,	22	12	79	6	8
Warwick, Christ,	11	6	50	4	8
Putnam County.					
Cold Spring, St. Mary's,	16	4	124	18	15
Paterson, Christ,	.	..	..	..	..
Philipsetown, St. Philip's,	6	..	55	..	5
Richmond County.					
Castleton, West Brighton, Ascension,	58	11	288	7	19
St. Mary's,	4	..	54	3	3
Clifton, St. John's,	..	..	..	..	..
Edgewater, St Paul's,	18	..	200	8	15
New-Brighton, Christ,	20	14	125	7	20
Richmond, St. Andrew's,	9	..	100	.	..
Rossville, St. Luke's,	10	..	25	..	3
Southfield, Holy Comforter,	4	..	43	1	..

Counties.	Churches and Chapels.	Clergymen.	Episcopal.	Diocesan.	Education.	Missionary.	Aged and Inf. Clergy.
Dutchess........	Poughkeepsie, Holy Comforter......	Rev. R. F. Crary............	$8 00	$30 00	....	$26 00	$5 00
	St. Paul's...........	S. H. Synnott..........	5 00	12 00	....	11 00	....
	Red Hook, Christ.................	J. W. Moore...........	11 00	8 32	$13 23	23 75	10 00
	St. Paul's, Tivoli........	G. L. Platt............	2 00	15 00	....	....	10 00
	Rhinebeck, Messiah...............	A. F. Olmstead.........	....	18 00	....	7 50	8 00
	Rhinecliff, Ascension............	T. S. Savage, M. D.....	2 00	....	....	....	4 40
	Wappinger's Falls, Zion...........	H. Y. Satterlee.........	10 00	40 00	....	37 72	23 44
New-York.......	New-York, Advent..................	....	....	....	....	....	....
	All Angels'............	C. F. Hoffman..........	2 10	6 00	1 00	4 50	15 00
	All Saints'............	W. N. Dunnell..........	2 00	60 00	....	....	....
	Annunciation..........	W. J. Seabury.........	15 00	42 00	6 01	27 48	165 78
	Anthon Memorial.......	R. H. Newton..........	12 00	....	....	....	....
	Ascension	J. Cotton Smith, D. D...	....	110 00	....	....	....
	Atonement............	....	....	....	....	....	....
	Atonement, Madison Av.	C. C. Tiffany...........	15 00	....	....	....	66 18
	Calvary...............	E. A. Washburn, D. D..	....	120 00	....	....	....
	Christ................	H. M. Thompson, D. D..	20 00	....	....	38 09	....
	Crucifixion...........	....	....	....	....	....	....
	Emmanuel	....	....	....	....	....	....
	Epiphany.............	U. T. Tracy...........	....	....	....	....	12 30
	Free Church St. George's Chapel, Beekman-st...	....	....	....	....	....	....
	Good Shepherd........	....	....	....	....	....	....
	Grace	H. C. Potter, D. D......	120 00	150 00	....	....	75 00
	Heavenly Rest.........	R. S. Howland, D. D....	....	....	....	20 00	....
	Holy Apostles.........	J. P. Lundy, D. D......	15 00	80 00	....	....	62 96
	Holy Communion.......	F. E. Lawrence, D. D....	80 00	....	....	200 00	....
	Holy Comforter.........	H. F. Roberts..........	....	....	....	....	2 80
	Holy Evangelists.......	....	....	....	....	....	....
	Holy Innocents........	....	....	....	....	....	....
	Holy [illegible]	....	....	....	....		

A Table,—Showing the mes of the Churches and pels of the Dise of k, with the sums contributed by each to the L, DIOCESAN, EDUCATION and MISSIONARY s, respectively, for the year 1874–75, in compliance with ths xiii., xiv. and xv.; prepared and published by order of the Convention, by the Secretary of the same, with the aid of the e rs of the Funds; to h are d the Contributions to the FUND FOR AGED AND INFIRM CLERGYMEN, required by Canon xvi. The ient for the Salary of the Bishop, when paid, appears in the columns of the Episcopal Fund.

Counties.	Churches and Chapels.	Clergymen.	Episcopal.	Diocesan.	Education.	Missionary.	Aged and Inf. Clergy.
Dutchess........	Amenia, St. Thomas'..............	Rev. Amos. T. Ashton.......	$2 00	$8 00	....	$13 61	....
	Annandale, St. Stephen's Chapel....	R. B. Fairbairn, D. D....	7 00	20 00	$14 50	....	$35 00
	n, St. John's Ev. Memorial.	G. B. Hopson..........	....	18 60	15 02	44 50	2 40
	Beekman, St. Mary's..............	....	....	....	....	....	....
	Carthage g, St. Mark's......	F. W. Shelton, D. D. ...	2 00	5 00	....	....	....
	Clinton, Apostles,................	....	....	....	....	....	....
	Fishkill, ity..................	J. R. Livingston........	5 00	5 00	5 50	10 00	21 00
	Glenham, St. John Baptist.........	J. R. ingston........	2 00	2 00	2 50	....	....
	Hyde Park, St. James'...........	J. S. y, D. D.......	25 00	30 00	12 00	20 00	23 22
	Lithgow, St. Peter's..............	....	2 00	....	....	....	....
	Malin, Trinity,.................	J. S. Clark, D. D.......	....	....	....	....	....
	Matteawan, St. Luke's.............	E. T. Bartlett........	....	....	....	....	32 58
	Millbrook, ce	B. F. Miller...........	....	....	....	....	....
	Pine Plains, Regeneration.........	....	....	....		....	....
	nt Valley, St. Paul's.........	G. H. Smith...........	....	....	....	....	2 10
	Poughkeepsie, Christ..............	H. L. Ziegenfuss.......	15 00	40 00	5 50	50 60	....

Counties.	Churches and Chapels.	Clergymen.	Episcopal.	Diocesan.	Education.	Missionary.	Aged and Inf. Clergy.
Dutchess	Poughkeepsie, Holy Comforter	Rev. R. F. Crary	$8 00	$30 00	....	$26 00	$5 00
	St. Paul's	S. H. Synnott	5 00	12 00	....	11 00	....
	Red Hook, Christ	J. W. Moore	11 00	8 32	$13 23	22 75	10 00
	St. Paul's, Tivoli	G. L. Platt	2 00	15 00	....	....	10 00
	[illegible], Messiah	A. F. Olmstead	....	18 00	....	7 50	8 00
	Rhinecliff, Ascension	T. S. Savage, M. D.	2 00	..	....	....	4 40
	Wap[illegible]s Falls, Zion	H. Y. Satterlee	10 00	40 00	....	37 72	23 44
New-York	New-York, Advent	....	....	..	....	....	....
	All Angels'	C. F. Hoffman	2 10	6 00	1 00	4 50	15 00
	All Saints'	W. N. Dunnell	2 00	60 00	....	....	....
	Annunciation	W. J. Seabury	15 00	42 00	6 01	27 48	165 78
	Antho[illegible] Mmorial	R. H. Newton	12 00	....	....	....	....
	Ascension	J. Cotton Smith, D. D.	....	110 00	....	....	....
	Atonement	....	....	....	....	....	....
	Atonement, Madison Av.	C. C. Tiffany	15 00	....	....	....	66 18
	Cal[illegible]ary	E. A. Washburn, D. D.	....	120 00	....	....	....
	Christ	H. M. Thompson, D. D.	20 00	....	....	38 09	....
	Crucifixion	....	....	....	....	....	....
	Emmanuel	....	....	....	....	....	....
	Epiph[illegible]any	U. T. Tracy	....	....	....	....	12 30
	Free Church St. George's Chapel, Beekman-st.	....	....	....	....	....	....
	Good Shepherd	....	....	....	....	....	....
	Grace	H. C. Potter, D. D.	120 00	150 00	....	....	75 00
	Heavenly Rest	R. S. Howland, D. D.	....	....	....	20 00	....
	Holy Apostles	J. P. Lundy, D. D.	15 00	80 00	....	....	62 96
	Holy Communion	F. E. Lawrence, D. D.	30 00	....	....	200 00	....
	Holy Comforter	H. F. Roberts	....	....	....	....	2 30
	Holy Evangelists	....	....	....	....	....	....
	Holy Innocents	....	....	....	....	....	....
	Holy Light	....	....	....	....	....	....

Counties.	Churches and Chapels.	Clergymen.	Episcopal.	Diocesan.	Education.	Missionary.	Clergy.
New-York.......	New-York, Holy Martyrs..........	Rev. James Millett..........	....	....	....	....	....
	Holy Saviour..........	A. B. Carter, D. D.....	....	....	....	....	....
	Holy Sepulchre........	J. Tuttle Smith........	$3 00	....	....	....	....
	Holy Trinity..........	S. H. Tyng, Jr., D. D...	....	....	....	....	....
	Incarnation............	Arthur Brooks........	45 00	....	....	....	....
	[illegible]ion........	E. W. Donald........	....	....	....	....	....
	[illegible]er, or St. Alban's	C. W. [illegible]rill..........	20 00	....	....	$54 05	....
	Mediator...............	....	....	....	....	....	....
	Nativity...............	Caleb Clapp............	2 00	$24 00	....	....	$3 00
	Reconciliation.........	E. S. [illegible]er........	....	....	....	....	....
	Redeemer..............	J. W. Shackelford......	3 00	....	....	...	25 15
	Redemption............	....	....	....	....	....	....
	Reformation...........	....	....	....	....	....	....
	Resurrection...........	E. O. Flagg, D. D......	....	....	....	....	....
	Santiago..............	J. De Palma,..........	....	....	....	....	....
	St. Ambrose...........	H. T. Widdemer........	....	....	....	....	....
	St. Andrew's...........	G. B. Draper, D. D.....	15 00	....	....	52 23	27 64
	St. Ann's..............	T. Gallaudet, D. D......	5 00	60 00	$12 50	41 94	46 36
	St. Barnabas'..........	....	....	....	....	....	....
	St. Bartholomew's......	Samuel Cooke, D. D.....	80 00	....	....	404 50	335 40
	St. [illegible]t's...........	T. A. Eaton, D. D......	5 00	25 00	....	30 00	76 00
	St. Esprit.	Leo Pons..............	....	48 00	....	....	....
	St. George's...........	S. H. Tyng, D. D..1874,	125 00	80 00	....	....	....
	St. George the Martyr's.	H. T. [illegible]er........	....	....	....	....	....
	St. Ignatius'..........	F. C. Ewer, D. D.......	5 00	....	....	....	....
	St. James'.............	C. B. Smith............	5 00	50 00	....	40 07	....
	St. John Baptist........	C. D. [illegible]e, D. D.......	5 00	16 00	....	16 88	....
	St. John Evangelist.....	W. T. Egbert,.........	5 00 8 00	20 00	8 00	....	24 09
	St. Jude's.............	....	....	....	....	....	....
	St. Luke's.............	I. H. Tuttle, D. D.......	7 00	50 00	....	61 49	....

Counties.	Churches and Chapels.	Clergymen.	Episcopal.	Diocesan.	Education.	Missionary.	Aged and Inf. Clergy.
New-York......	New-York, Beloved Disciple,......	Rev. F. H. Stubbs..........	....	....	....	$18 00	....
	St. Mark's..........	J. H. Rylance, D. D....	$60 00	$120 00	....	....	....
	St. Mary's..........	C. C. Adams..........	4 00	13 00	....	5 00	$13 00
	St. Mary the Virgin....	T. M. Brown..........	10 00	....	....	10 00	27 06
	St. Matthew's..........	....	....	....	....	....	....
	St. Matthias'..........	N. E. Cornwall, D. D...	....	....	....	....	....
	St. Michael's..........	T. M. Peters, D. D.....	20 00	....	$10 24	26 03	6 89
	St. Paul's, 12th Ward...	....	....	....	....	....	....
	St. Peter's..........	A. B. Beach, D. D......	15 00	40 00	....	127 28	58 59
	St. Philip's..........	J. S. Attwell..........	2 00	80 00	....	....	....
	St. Sauveur..........	....	....	....	....	....	....
	St. Saviour's..........	....	....	....	....	....	....
	St. Simon's..........	....	....	....	....	....	....
	St. Stephen's..........	J. H. Price, D. D......	....	20 00	....	....	65 00
	St. Thomas'..........	W. F. Morgan, D. D....	75 00	200 00	....	261 37	....
					Chapel,	12 25	
	St. Timothy's..........	G. J. Geer, D. D........	5 00	28 00	....	9 00	14 00
	Transfiguration........	G. H. Houghton, D. D..	45 00	160 00	....	....	220 00
	Trinity, with	Morgan Dix. D. D....			15 60	370 00	197 42
	St. Paul's, ...	....			17 50	314 55	....
	"	....			24 75	90 77	36 46
	St. John's, ...	....	1 800 00	1,100 00	....	89 19	20 20
	Trinity Chapels, ...	....			160 00	705 84	320 36
	St. Augustine's, ...	....			7 71	12 16	29 60
	St. Chrysostom's, ...	....			5 47	70 24	8 10
	Zion..................	J. N. Gallaher, D. D....		100 00	....	356 65	48 93
	Holy Trinity, Harlem...	....		....	....	....	68 21
	Grace, Harlem........	D. B. Ray..........		....	....	....	....
	St. James', Fordham....	Mytton Maury..........		30 00	7 00	....	15 37
	St. Ann's, Morrisania...	Wm. Huckell..........		10 00	....	....	....

New-York	New-York, Trinity, Morrisania	Rev. A. S. Hull	....	$6 00	....	....	....
	St. Mary's, Mott Haven	C. B. Stephenson	$3 00	30 00	....	....	$6 67
	Christ, Riverdale	G. D. Wildes, D. D.	12 00	66 00	....	....	....
	Mediator, South Yonkers or Kingsbridge	W. T. Wilson	....	....	....	....	30 20
	Grace, West Farms	Robert Scott	3 25	7 20	....	....	....
Orange	Canterbury, St. John's	J. F. Potter	2 00	1 75	$2 50	$3 00	4 08
	Cornwall, (or Highland Falls,) Holy Innocents	W. R. Thomas	3 00	20 00	10 00	16 50	11 68
	Goshen, St. James'	W. H. De L. Grannis	7 00	....	....	....	35 75
	Greenwood Iron Works, St. John's	Samuel Moran	3 00	5 00	5 00	5 00	5 00
	Monroe, Grace	Henry A. Dows	2 00	2 50	1 00	3 68	1 00
	Newburgh, St. George's	John Brown, D. D.	18 00	40 00	55 00	202 60	118 77
	St. Paul's	Rufus Emory	....	....	....	....	....
	New-Windsor, St. Thomas'	H. McKim	3 00	20 00	9 00	16 00	21 25
	Port Jervis, Grace	J. G. Rosencrantz	....	....	....	....	2 75
	South Middletown, Grace	A. Capron	....	....	....	....	....
	St. Andrew's	Wm. E. Snowden	2 00	....	....	14 00	3 00
	Warwick, Christ	Alfred Goldsborough	2 00	12 00	....	5 00	5 00
Putnam	Cold Spring, St. Mary's	Isaac Van Winkle	15 00	42 00	5 00	16 08	33 00
	Paterson, Christ	....	....	....	....	....	3 50
	Philipsetown, St. Philip's	A. Z. Gray	13 00	24 00	10 00	15 35	40 00
Richmond	Castleton, (West Brighton,) Ascension	James S. Bush	....	52 00	....	....	30 85
	St. Mary's	H. L. E. Pratt	4 00	6 50	....	....	....
	Clifton, St. John's	J. C. Eccleston, M. D.	9 00	....	....	....	....
	Edgewater, St. Paul's Memorial	....	8 00	12 00	....	....	23 00
	New-Brighton, Christ	....	13 00	20 00	....	....	38 58
	Richmond, St. Andrew's	Kingston Goddard, D. D.	....	....	....	....	....
	Rossville, St. Luke's	Henry H. Bean	....	....	....	....	....
	Southfield, (Eltingville,) Holy Comforter	Fred. M. Gray	2 00	....	....	....	6 72

Counties.	Churches and Chapels.	Clergymen.	Episcopal.	Diocesan.	Education.	Missionary.	Aged and Inf. Clergy.
Rockland........	Clarkstown, St. John's............	Rev. R. S. Mansfield.........	....	....	....	....	....
	Haverstraw, Holy Trinity..........	Geo. W. West..........	$2 00 2 50	....	....	....	$5 85
	St. Luke's...........	....	....	....	....	....	....
	Nyack, Grace....................	F. Babbitt............	3 00	$20 06	....	$10 80	....
	Piermont, Christ..................	S. G. Hitchcock........	2 00	5 00	....	5 00	1 00
	Ramapo, Christ..................	G. E. Purucker........	2 00	8 00	....	2 00	3 15
	Spring Valley, St. Paul's..........	R. S. Mansfield.........	....	....	....	....	....
	Stony Point, Holy Child Jesus......	E. Gay..................	....	....	....	....	....
Sullivan.........	Monticello, St. John's............	C. F. Canedy...........	2 00	16 00	....	16 10	10 76
	Thompsonville, St. Mary's.........	....	....	....	....	....	....
Ulster....	Ellenville, St. Paul's.............	O. Valentine...........	....	....	....	....	....
	Esopus, Ascension...............	H. B. Sherman..........	....	....	....	....	....
	Highland, Trinity................	J. Horsfall Johnson.....	....	....	....	....	....
	Holy Spirit, Rondout............	....	....	....	....	....	....
	Kingston, St. John's.............	C. W. Camp............	3 00	24 00	....	31 32	16 81
	Marlborough, Christ............	....	....	....	....	6 25	....
	Milton, All Saints'.............	J. Horsfall Johnson.....	....	1 00	....	....	....
	Saugerties, Trinity..............	J. J. Robertson, D. D...	4 00 4 78	18 00	$11 15	127 09	31 54
	Stone Ridge, St. Peter's..........	Geo. W. West..........	....	....	....	....	....
Westchester.....	Bedford, St. Matthew's..........	Lea Luquer............	4 00	....	....	....	25 08
	Beechwood, St. Mary's...........	E. N. Mead, D. D......	....	....	....	....	....
	City Island, Grace..............	J. Morsell, D. D........	....	....	....	....	....
	Croton, St. Augustine's..........	A. V. Clarkson.........	....	....	....	....	....
	Eastchester, St. Paul's..........	W. S. Coffey...........	8 00	14 00	14 31	10 78	4 90
	Greenburgh, Zion..............	Geo. B. Reese..........	10 00	20 00	....	10 00	35 00
	Irvington, St. Barnabas'.........	W. H. Benjamin.......	....	....	....	....	16 61
	Katonah, St. Mark's	....	....	....	....	....	....
	Lewisboro', St. John's...........	Robert Bolton.........	1 00	0 50	0 50	....	0 50
	Mamaroneck, St. Thomas'..........	Wm. W. Montgomery..	9 00	30 00	....	33 00	41 00

Counties.	Churches and Chapels.	Clergymen.	Episcopal.	Diocesan.	Education.	Missionary.	Aged and Inf. Clergy.
Westchester.....	Montrose, [illegible] Love,...........	Rev. G. M. Cruger...........	$5 00	$5 00	$5 00	$8 87	$5 00
	Mount Pleasant, St. Mark's.........	Ed. Guilbert............	....	6 00	....	....	....
	[illegible], Trinity............	W. B. Hooper..........	8 00	24 00	....	15 00	27 78
	[illegible], St. Mark's	J. H. Young...........	....	....	....	....	....
	New-Rochelle, Trinity............	J. H. Watson..........	14 00	30 00	....	12 38	17 55
	North Castle, St. Mary's...........	....	....	....	....	....	....
	St. Stephen's.........	C. W. Bolton...........	....	....	....	....	....
	North [illegible], St. [illegible]'...........	R. C. Russell...........	....	....	....	....	7 13
	Peekskill, (Cortlandt,) St. Peter's....	W. F. Lewis...........	7 00	30 00	10 34	33 46	13 20
	Pelham, Christ.....................	Chas. Higbee..........	....	20 00	....	....	10 36
	Pleasantville, St. John's...........	....	....	....	....	....	....
	Portchester, St. Peter's.............	Brockholst Morgan.....	5 00	....	....	9 69	....
	[illegible], Christ......................	C. B. Brewster..........	18 00	60 00	....	73 93	72 82
	Saw Mill Valley, St. Paul's.........	J. Drisler,.............	2 00	....	....	1 80	3 00
	Scarsdale, St. [illegible] the [illegible].......	W. A. Holbrook........	2 00	30 00	7 40	15 50	9 10
	Sing Sing, All [illegible]', Briar Cliff....	J. B. Gibson, D. D......	2 00	9 00	....	27 86	....
	St. Paul's..............	J. I. Helm, D. D........	8 00	20 00	....	25 00	35 14
	[illegible]..................	G W. Ferguson.........	9 00	....	....	15 00	27 15
	Somers, St. Luke's................	R. C. Russell...........	....	....	....	....	....
	Tarrytown, Christ.................	J. S. [illegible]...........	20 00	50 00	....	38 48	25 67
	Tuckahoe, St. John's..............	A. M. Ives.............	8 00	7 00	4 70	10 48	8 54
	[illegible], St. Peter's............	C. B. Wyatt, D. D.......	22 00	60 00	19 23	188 97	60 42
	[illegible] Plains, Grace..............	Fred. B. Van Kleeck....	8 00	40 00	21 42	25 91	....
	Wilmot, St. John's................	A. M. Ives.............	4 04	3 05	....	3 72	5 00
	Yonkers, St. John's...............	....	18 00	26 40	....	....	20 00
	St. [illegible]................	D. F. Banks............	5 00	50 00	....	25 00	25 00
	[illegible], St. Mary's.............	....	2 00	5 00	....	....	....

SUMMARY

FOR THE YEAR ENDING AT THE CONVENTION, 1875.

*Episcopal Fund, from 102 Churches,			$3,329 81
Diocesan " " 110 "			5,342 24
Education " " 36 "			902 05
Missionary " Collections from — "		$5,480 26	
Interest,		838 25	
Donations,		1,055 00	
			$6,873 54
Aged and Infirm Clergy Fund:			
Contributions from 91 Churches,		$3,384 85	
Interest on investments and rents,		2,026 60	
Donations and Legacy,		5,090 00	
			10,601 45
Total,			$27,049 09

NOTE.—In some instances, contributions sent to the Treasurer immediately after the Convention of 1874, but before the preparation of the Table for 1873–74, being included in that year's Table, are not repeated in the Table which is above. The fact of the contributions will, in such case, appear by reference to such items in the Parochial Reports of this Journal in 1875. In this Table appear some contributions handed to the Treasurer since their official Reports to the Convention. This will account for any seeming discrepancy in a few instances between this Table and Parochial Reports.

* This includes the apportionment for the Salary of the Bishop.

Appendix:

No. IV.

)TE.—According to a Resolution recorded on page 94 of the Journal of , there is included in the following List of Churches of this Diocese the of the admission into its Convention of such Churches as are in union the same. It is to be observed, that such date is not always that of the n or incorporation of the Parish.

Of these Parishes, some existed under Royal Charter, or otherwise, · to the first Convention of the Diocese in 1785. This class is denoted ıe letter A, placed after the date of admission into union.

A few others seem to have been admitted by the Conventions, in which respectively appeared for the first time by their delegates, although tion of the admission seems to have been omitted by the Journal. Such lesignated by the letter B.

The few, incorporated under the law of April 13, 1854, are marked by letter C.

ıt of Churches in the Diocese of New-York.

Counties.	Towns.	Churches.	Admitted.
:hess..........	Amenia,	St. Thomas',	1849
	*Annandale,	*Holy Innocents,	
	*Barrytown,	*St. John Evangelist, Memorial,	
	Beekman,	St. Mary's,	1850
	Carthage Landing,	St. Mark's,	1863
	*Clinton,	*Apostles,	
	Fishkill,	Trinity,	1787 A
	*Glenham,	*St. John Baptist,	
	Hyde Park,	St. James',	1812
	Lithgow,	St. Peter's,	1834 A
	Madalin,	Trinity,	1866
	Matteawan,	St. Luke's,	1833
	*Millbrook,	*Grace,	
	Pine Plains,	Regeneration,	1860
	Pleasant Valley,	St. Paul's,	1837
	Poughkeepsie,	Christ,	1785
		Holy Comforter,]	1866 C
		St. Paul's,]	1835
	*Red Hook,	*Christ,	

		Churches.	Admitted.
....	Red Hook,	St. Paul's,	1817
	Rhinebeck,	Messiah,	1852
	*Rhinecliff,	*Ascension,	
	Wappinger's Falls,	Zion,	1834
....	New-York,	Advent,	1847
		All Angels',	1859
		All Saints',	1824
		Annunciation,	1838
		Anthon Memorial,	1861
		Ascension,	1827
		*Ascen. Miss. Chapel,	
		Atonement,	1860
		Atonement, Madison Avenue,	1867
		*Beloved Disciple,	
		Calvary,	1836
		*Calvary Miss. Chap'l,	
		Christ,	1802
		Crucifixion,	1846
		Emmanuel,	1845
		Epiphany,	1845
		Heavenly Rest,	1870
		*Holy Comforter,	
		*Our Saviour,	
		Free Church of St. George's,	1864 C
		Good Shepherd,	1846
		Grace,	1809
		Holy Apostles,	1845
		*Holy Communion,	
		Holy Evangelists,	1845
		Holy Innocents,	1854
		Holy Light,	1870
		Holy Martyrs,	1847
		Holy Saviour,	1866
		Holy Sepulchre,	1866
		Holy Trinity,	1865
		Holy Trinity of Harlem,	1874
		Incarnation,	1852
		Intercession,	1849
		Intercessor,	1861
		Mediator,	1862
		Nativity,	1834
		Reconciliation,	1863
		Redeemer,	1853
		Redemption,	1843
		*Reformation,	
		Resurrection,	1862
		Santiago,	1867
		St. Ambrose,	1867
		St. Andrew's,	1829
		St. Ann's,	1854
		St. Barnabas',	1846
		St. Bartholomew's,	1835

ies.	Towns.	Churches.	Admitted.
k.........	New-York,	*St. Chrysostom's,	
		St. Clement's,	1830
		*St. Cornelius',	
		St. Esprit,	1804 B
		St. George's,	1812
		St. George the Martyr's,	1845
		St. Ignatius',	1874
		St. James',	1810
		St. John Baptist's,	1848
		St. John Evangelist's	1853
		St. Jude's,	1843
		St. Luke's,	1821
		St. Mark's,	1801
		St. Mary's, *b.*	1824
		St. Mary the Virgin's,	1874 C
		St. Matthew's,	1846
		St. Matthias',	1864
		St. Michael's, *a.*	1807
		St. Paul's, 12th Ward	1862
		St. Peter's,	1831
		St. Philip's,	1853
		St. Sauveur's,	1844
		St. Saviour's,	1864
		St. Simon's,	1844
		St. Stephen's,	1805
		St. Thomas',	1824
		St. Timothy's,	1854
		Transfiguration,	1849
		Trinity,	1785 A
		with St. Paul's, St. John's and Trinity Chapels,	
		Zion,	1810
	*Harlem,	*Grace,	
	Fordham,	St. James',	1855 A
	Morrisania,	St. Ann's,	1841
		St. Paul's,	1853
		Trinity,	1869
	Mott Haven,	St. Mary's,	1857
	Riverdale,	Christ,	1866
	West Farms,	Grace,	1848 B
....	Canterbury,	St. John's,	1858
	Cornwall,	Holy Innocents,	1850
	Goshen,	St. James',	1803
	Greenwood,	St. John's,	1868 C
	*Monroe,	*Grace,	
	Newburgh,	St. George's,	1785 A
		St. Paul's,	1860
	New-Windsor,	St. Thomas',	1818
	Port Jervis,	Grace,	1854

orporated Aug. 17, 1807. (*b.*) Incorporated Dec. 8, 1823.

Counties.	Towns.	Churches.	Admitted.
Orange............	South Middletown,	Grace,	1845
	Walden,	St. Andrew's,	1785 A
	Warwick,	Christ,	1866
Putnam...........	Cold Spring,	St. Mary's,	1840
	Paterson,	Christ,	1831 B
	Philipsetown,	St. Philip's,	1840
Richmond.	Castleton, (W. Brighton,)	Ascension,	1870
	Castleton,	St. Mary's,	1851
	Clifton,	St. John's,	1843
		*St. Simon's Chapel,	
	Edgewater,	St. Paul's Memorial,	1868
	New-Brighton,	Christ,	1851
	Richmond,	St. Andrew's,	1785
	Rossville,	St. Luke's,	1843
	Southfield,	Holy Comforter,	1866
Rockland.........	Clarkstown,	St. John's,	1867
	Haverstraw,	Trinity,	1847
		St. Luke's,	1871
	Nyack,	Grace,	1863
	Piermont,	Christ,	1848
	Ramapo,	Christ,	1866
	*Spring Valley,	*St. Paul's,	
Sullivan...........	Monticello,	St. John's,	1817
	*Thomsonville,	*St. Mary's,	
Ulster............	Ellenville,	St. Paul's,	1868
	Esopus,	Ascension,	1842
	*Highland,	*Holy Trinity,	
	Kingston,	St. John's,	1832
	Marlborough,	Christ,	1837
	Milton,	All Saints',	1850
	Rondout,	Holy Spirit,	1850
	Saugerties,	Trinity,	1831
	Stone Ridge,	St. Peter's,	1846
Westchester.......	Bedford,	St. Matthew's,	1787
	*Beechwood,	*St. Mary's,	
	Briar Cliff,	All Saints',	1869
	*City Island,	*Grace,	
	Cortlandt, (Croton,)	St. Augustine's,	1855
	East Chester,	St Paul's,	1787
	Greenburg,	Zion,	1834
	Irvington,	St. Barnabas',	1859
	Katonah,	St. Mark's,	1853
	Lewisboro',	St. John's,	1853
	Mamaroneck,	St. Thomas',	1817
	*Montrose,	*Divine Love,	
	Mount Pleasant,	St. Mark's,	1864
	Mount Vernon,	Trinity,	1857
	New Castle,	St. Mark's,	1851 A
	New-Rochelle,	Trinity,	1785
	North Castle,	St. Mary's,	1853 A
		St. Stephen's,	1844
	North Salem,	St. James',	1792 A

* Not in Union with the Convention.

Counties.	Towns.	Churches.	Admitted.
Westchester,......	Peekskill,	St. Peter's,	1791 A
	Pelham,	Christ,	1843
	Pleasantville,	St. John's,	1853
	Portchester,	St. Peter's,	1852
	Rye,	Christ,	1786 A
	Scarsdale,	St. James the Less,	1849
	Sing Sing,	St. Paul's,	1834
	Sing Sing,	Trinity,	1869
	Somers,	St. Luke's,	1839
	Tarrytown,	Christ,	1836
	Tuckahoe,	St. John's,	1853
	Westchester,	St. Peter's,	1790 A
	White Plains,	Grace,	1824 A
	Wilmot,	St. John's,	1861
	Yonkers,	Mediator,	1858 B
		St. John's,	1787 A
		St. Paul's,	1859
	Yorktown,	St. Mary's,	1870

Number of Churches and Chapels represented by certificates of Lay Delegates,.. 117

Number of Churches not represented,........................ 49

Number do. entitled to representation,...................... 166

Number do. not in union with the Convention,............. 27

Number of Churches and Chapels in the Diocese,.................. 193

* Not in union with the Convention.

Appendix:

No. V.

Officers of the Diocese.

THE DIOCESAN CONVENTION.

'he Rt. Rev. HORATIO POTTER, D. D., LL. D., D. C. L., *President.*
'he Rev. WILLIAM E. EIGENBRODT, D. D., *Secretary.*
he Rev. THEODORE A. EATON, D. D., *Assistant Secretary.*
DWARD F. DE LANCEY, Esq., *Treasurer.*

THE STANDING COMMITTEE.

The Rev. MORGAN DIX, D. D., *President.*
The Rev. WILLIAM E. EIGENBRODT, D. D., *Secretary.*
The Rev. WILLIAM F. MORGAN, D. D.,
The Rev. ISAAC H. TUTTLE, D. D.,
STEPHEN P. NASH, Esq.,
LLOYD W. WELLS, Esq.,
HENRY DRISLER, LL. D.,
GEORGE MACCULLOCH MILLER, Esq.

THE DEPUTIES TO THE GENERAL CONVENTION.

The Rev. BENJAMIN I. HAIGHT, D. D.,
The Rev. SAMUEL COOKE, D. D.,
The Rev. ALFRED B. BEACH, D. D.,
The Rev. PHILANDER K. CADY, D. D.,
The Hon. SAMUEL B. RUGGLES,
The Hon. HAMILTON FISH,
CAMBRIDGE LIVINGSTON, Esq.,
WILLIAM A. DAVIES, Esq.

THE PROVISIONAL DEPUTIES.

The Rev. GEORGE J. GEER, D. D.,
The Rev. HENRY C. POTTER, D. D.,
The Rev. THEODORE A. EATON, D. D.,
The Rev. CHRISTOPHER B. WYATT, D. D.,
The Hon. JOHN A. DIX,
The Hon. JAMES EMOTT,
Prof. T. ECCLESTON,
Prof. HENRY DRISLER, LL. D.

THE MISSIONARY COMMITTEE.

The Rev. ALFRED B. BEACH, D. D.,
The Rev. CORNELIUS E. SWOPE, D. D.,
The Rev. JAMES STARR CLARK, D. D.,
The Rev. OCTAVIUS APPLEGATE,
The Rev. CHRISTOPHER B. WYATT, D. D.,
HAMILTON [illegible], Esq.,
A. B. [illegible], Esq.,
WILLIAM M. KINGSLAND, Esq.,
JAMES POTT, Esq.,
C. A. HIGGINS, Esq.

TRUSTEES OF THE EPISCOPAL FUND.

GOUVERNEUR M. OGDEN, Esq.,
THOMAS P. CUMMINGS, Esq., *Secretary and Treasurer*,
FREDERICK G. FOSTER, Esq.,
HUGH AUCHINCLOSS, Esq.,
Hon. JOHN A. DIX.

THE TRUSTEES OF THE AGED AND INFIRM CLERGY FUND.

The Rt. Rev. HORATIO POTTER, D. D., LL. D., D. C. L.,
CYRUS CURTISS, Esq.,
WILLIAM BETTS, Esq.,
EDWARD F. DE LANCEY, Esq.

THE TRUSTEES OF THE PAROCHIAL FUND.

The Right Rev. THE BISHOP OF THE DIOCESE, *ex-officio*.
ADAM NORRIE, ROBERT B. PARROTT, } Until October, 1876.
MURRAY HOFFMAN, FREDERICK S. WINSTON, } Until October, 1877.
JOHN JAY, WILLIAM ALEXANDER SMITH, } Until October, 1878.

The Committee

ON THE INCORPORATION AND ADMISSION OF CHURCHES.

CHARLES TRACY, Esq.,
The Rev. ALFRED B. BEACH, D. D.,
The Hon. JOHN A. DIX.

Special Committees of the Convention.

ON THE SALARY OF THE BISHOP.

(See Journal of 1875, p. 45.)

The Rev. Benjamin I. Haight, D. D.; the Rev. Isaac H. Tuttle, D. D.; Cyrus Curtiss, Esq.; Hon. John A. Dix; Frederick G. Foster, Esq.; William Scott, Esq.; Lloyd W. Wells, Esq.; Frederick Prime, Esq.; Thomas P. Cummings, Esq., and George Macculloch Miller, Esq.

ON A CATHEDRAL.

(See Journal of 1872, pp. 89, 111.)

The Rt. Rev. Horatio Potter, D. D., LL. D., D. C. L.; the Rev. Morgan Dix, D. D.; Henry C. Potter, D. D.; John Cotton Smith, D. D.; George H. Houghton, D. D.; Philander K. Cady, D. D.; Hon. Hamilton Fish; Messrs. John J. Cisco, Stephen P. Nash, Mr. Guion, Mr. Duncan; Hon. S. B. Ruggles; Messrs. William Scott, George M. Miller, Howard Potter, Wm. T. Blodgett.*

---

* Deceased since the Convention.

**** The* STANDING COMMITTEE *of the Diocese meets statedly on the* FIRST THURSDAY *of every month. Papers requiring the action of the Committee should be sent prior to this date, and addressed to the Secretary.*

Appendix:

No. VI.

STATISTICS OF THE DIOCESE, 1874-75.

From the Episcopal Address, the Parochial and Missionary Reports, etc.

Clergymen canonically resident in the Diocese,..................	304
Churches and Chapels,..	193
Ordinations: Deacons, 7; Priests, 8, ...	15
Clergymen instituted into Rectorships,..........................	2
" received into the Diocese,............................	28
" transferred to other Dioceses,.........................	27
" died,..	8
" deposed,,..	7
Candidates for Orders,..	33
Churches consecrated,..	3

The following statistics are derived from 146 Parochial Reports:

Baptisms: Adults, 509; Infants, 4,154—total,.		4,663
Confirmed,..		2,263
Marriages,..		1,113
Burials,..		2,641
Catechumens,..		22,764
Catechists, or Sunday-School teachers,..........................		2,020
Communicants: admitted, as reported,...........................		930
present number, as reported from 146 Congregations,....................	27,138	
add as estimated from 25 Parishes not reporting,........................	2,000	
		29,138

CANONICAL COLLECTIONS AND FOR OTHER OBJECTS.

For the Episcopal Fund, Salary of the Bishop, &c., from 102 Churches,..........			$3,329 81
" Education " 36 "			902 05
" Diocesan " 110 "			5,342 24
" Missionary " — "	$5,480 26		
" " Donations,.............	1,055 00		
" " Interest on Investments,	338 28		
			6,873 54
For the Aged and Infirm Clergy, 91 Churches,......	$3,384 85		
" " " Int. on investments and rents,.......	2,026 60		
" Donations and legacy, &c.,.........	5,190 00		
			10,601 45
Total,...................			$27,049 09

TOTAL CONTRIBUTIONS FROM 146 PAROCHIAL REPORTS,......$774,801 33

There being no reports from 25 living and working Churches on the List of this Diocese, these statistics do not present a complete view of the Diocese in these respects during the past year.

Difference in the dates of making the calculations severally will account for any discrepancy between the foregoing statement of the Contributions and those given in the preceding Table.

Appendix:

No. VII.

CATALOGUES OF JOURNALS OF CONVENTIONS

And other Documents belonging to the Diocese of New-York, in charge of the Secretary of the Convention.

NEW-YORK JOURNALS.

BOUND.

Two Sets, complete, from 1785 to 1874, 22 vols.
One Set from 1785 to 1874, with the exception of Journals for 1820 and 1829, 18 vols.
One " from 1765 to 1874, with the exception of Journals for 1821, 1822, 1823, 1824, 1827, 1828, 1829, 1830, 18 vols.
One " from 1785 to 1874, with the exception of Journals from 1820 to 1830, inclusive, 18 vols.
Six Sets from 1847 to 1874, 48 vols.
Four " from 1847 to 1874, with the exception of Journal for 1865, 32 vols.
One Vol. from 1831 to 1840, inclusive, except 1836.
One " from 1839 to 1842, "
Two Vols. from 1839 to 1840, "
Three " from 1850 to 1851, "
One Vol. each for 1839, 1854, 1855, 1856, 1857, 1858, 1859, 1860, 15 vols.

GENERAL CONVENTION JOURNALS.

BOUND AND UNBOUND.

Same as reported in the Journal of 1874.

MISCELLANEOUS.

Same as reported last year, with the addition of a bound vol. of the Obsequies of Bishop Onderdonk.

JOURNALS OF OTHER DIOCESES.

24 vols., containing Journals as follows:

Rhode Island, Western New-York, Louisiana, from 1838 to 1852, inclusive.
Vermont, Connecticut, Kentucky, from 1839 to 1852, inclusive.
Maine, Massachusetts, New-Jersey, Pennsylvania, Virginia, North Carolina, South Carolina, Georgia, Alabama, Tennessee, Indiana, Michigan, Missouri, from 1840 to 1852, inclusive.
New-Hampshire, Delaware, from 1841 to 1852, inclusive.
Easton, from 1840 to 1842, inclusive.
Maryland, 1824, 1837, 1839, and from 1841 to 1852, inclusive.

Mississippi, from 1841 to 1852, inclusive, except 1844.
Florida, from 1840 to 1852, inclusive, except 1843 and 1850.
Ohio, 1821, and from 1839 to 1852, inclusive.
Illinois, from 1841 to 1852, inclusive, except 1846.

Also the following

BOUND AND UNBOUND.

DIOCESE OF	BOUND.	UNBOUND.	WANTED.
Alabama,	1 vol. from 1854 to 1870,	1871 to 1875,	1853.
Albany,	2 " " 1868 " 1872,	1873 " 1875.	....
Arkansas,	....	1871, 1872,	1873, 1874, 1875.
California,	1 " " 1853 " 1867,	1868 to 1874,	1868, 1870.
Central New-York,	1 " " 1868 " 1874,	....	1875.
Central Pennsylvania,	....	1871 to 1874.	....
Connecticut,	3 " " 1854 " 1873,	1853, 1874, 1875.	....
Delaware,	1 " " 1853 " 1868,	1869 to 1875,	1863, 1866.
Easton,	....	1866 " 1875.	....
Florida,	....	1858 " 1875,	1856, 1859, 1868, 1871, 1874, 1875.
Fond du Lac,	....	1875, special and annual.	....
Georgia,	1 " " 1858 " 1870,	1871 to 1875.	....
Illinois,	5 " " 1853 " 1873,	1874, 1875, special.	....
Indiana,	1 " " 1854 " 1869,	1870 to 1875,	1858.
Iowa,	1 " " 1854 " 1869,	1870 " 1874.	....
Kansas.	....	1869 " 1874.	....
Kentucky,	1 " " 1858 " 1873,	1874, 1875.	....
Long Island,	1 " " 1868 " 1872,	1873 to 1875.	....
Louisiana,	1 " " 1858 " 1867,	1868 " 1875.	....
Maine,	1 " " 1858 " 1869,	1870 " 1874.	....
Maryland,	....	1858 " 1875,	1857, 1861.
Massachusetts,	3 " " 1854 " 1873,	1858 " 1874,	1875.
Michigan,	4 " " 1858 " 1873.	1874, 1875.	....
Minnesota,	1 " " 1857 " 1872,	1873, 1874,	1875.
Mississippi,	1 " " 1853 " 1871,	1873 to 1875,	1872.
Missouri,	2 " " 1853 " 1873,	1874, 1875.	....
Nebraska,	....	1868 to 1874,	1869, 1875.
New-Hampshire,	1 " " 1853 " 1874,	1875.	....
New-Jersey,	2 " " 1853 " 1860, 1868 to 1873,	1861 to 1867, 1874, 1875,	1866.
Northern New-Jersey,	....	1874, primary.	....
Ohio,	4 " " 1853 " 1872,	....	1873, 1874, 1875.
Pennsylvania,	1 " " 1853 " 1857,	1858 to 1875,	1858, 1860, 1866, 1867, 1[illegible] 1872.
Pittsburgh,	1 " " 1865 " 1873,	1874.	....
Rhode Island,	2 " " 1853 " 1874,	1875.	....
South Carolina,	2 " " 1853 " 1873,	1874, 1875.	....
Tennessee,	1 " " 1854 " 1873,	1875,	1853, 1874.
Texas,	1 " " 1853 " 1873.	1874.	....
Vermont,	2 " " 1853 " 1874,	....	1875.
Virginia,	2 " " 1854 " 1873,	1874, 1875,	1853.
Western Michigan,	....	1874.	....
Western New-York,	4 " " 1853 " 1873,	1874,	1875.
Wisconsin,	1 " " 1868 " 1874,	1853 to 1867, 1875,	1853, 1861, 1867.
North Carolina,	2 " " 1853 " 1873,	1874, 1875.	....
Confederate States,	....	1861, adjourned 1862, 1865,	1861, 1863, 1864.
Oregon & Washington,	....	1853 to 1874,	1860, 1861, 1863 to 18[illegible] 1868 to 1870.
Dakota,	....	1873.	....
Colorado,	....	1874.	....
Northern California,	....	1875.	....

Total number of bound volumes, 251.

September, 1875.

JOURNAL OF THE CONVENTION:

1875.

CONTENTS.

NOTICE.

It is respectfully requested of

The Reverend the Secretaries of Diocesan Conventions,

that they will be so kind as to examine the column marked

WANTED,

in Appendix VII., p. 196 of this Journal. They will confer a favor, if they will send by mail any Journals there specified, and which they can spare for the purpose, to the Secretary of the Convention of the Diocese of New-York for that Body. The postage will be promptly remitted.

The Journal of the Convention of the Diocese of New-York is regularly sent to the Secretaries of all other Diocesan Conventions for those Bodies. In return, a copy of the Journal of each Convention of other Dioceses is respectfully solicited for the Convention of the Diocese of New-York.

NEW-YORK, *November* 1, 1875.

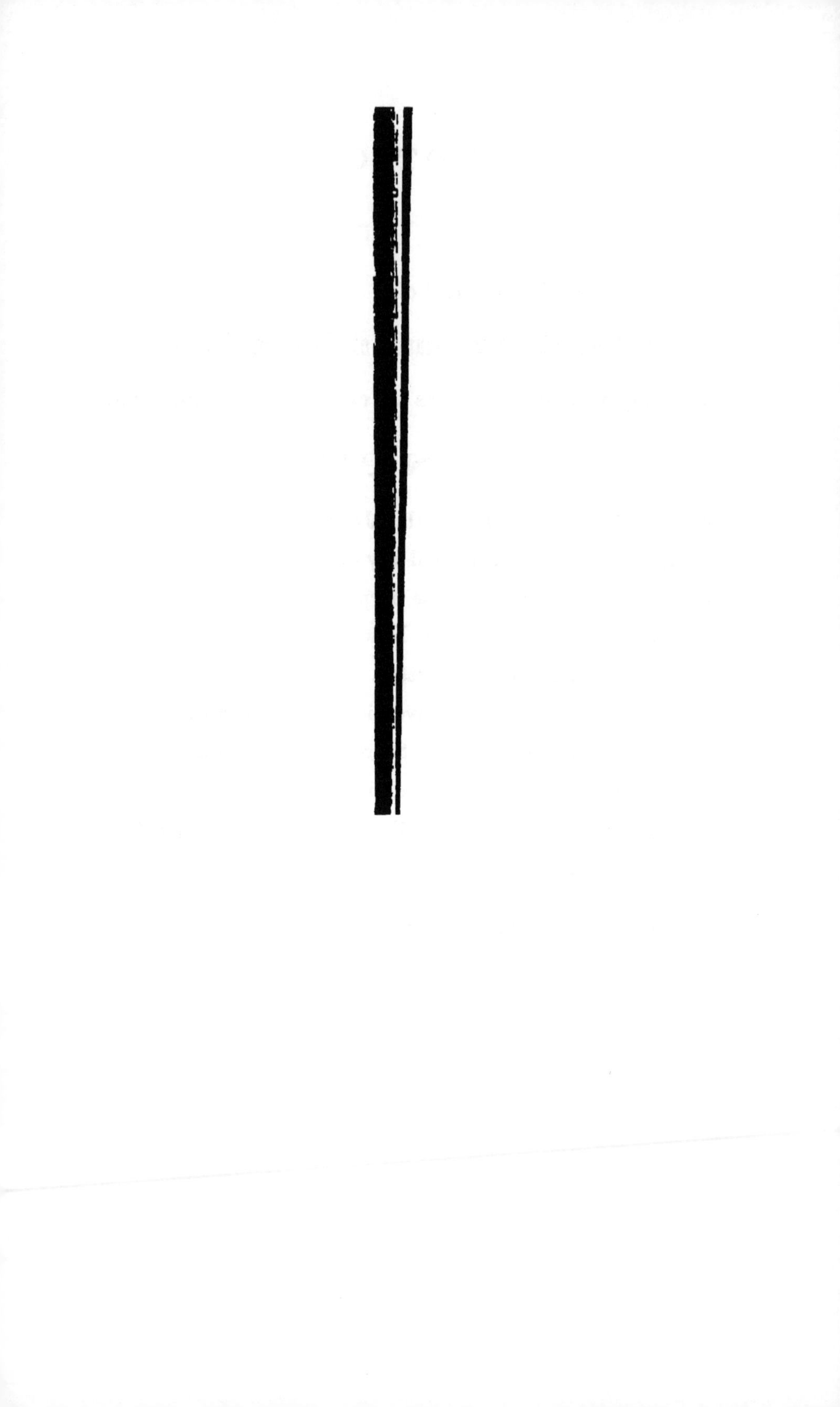

JOURNAL OF THE PROCEEDINGS

OF THE

INETY-THIRD CONVENTION

OF THE

Protestant Episcopal Church

IN THE

DIOCESE OF NEW-YORK,

WHICH ASSEMBLED IN

. JOHN'S CHAPEL IN THE CITY OF NEW-YORK,

ON

WEDNESDAY, SEPTEMBER 27, A. D. 1876.

New-York:
PUBLISHED FOR THE CONVENTION,
BY POTT, YOUNG & CO., COOPER UNION, FOURTH AVENUE.
M.DCCC.LXXVI.

AMERMAN & CO., PRINTERS,
No. 47 Cedar Street, N. Y.

List of the Clergy

OF THE

DIOCESE OF NEW-YORK.

SEPTEMBER 27, 1876.

This List of Clergy, being that presented by the Bishop to the Convention, contains no note of changes which have since taken place.

This mark * designates the Alumni of the General Theological Seminary of the Protestant Episcopal Church in the United States.

THE RIGHT REV. HORATIO POTTER, D. D., LL. D., D. C. L., BISHOP OF THE DIOCESE.

The Rev. Charles C. Adams, rector of St. Mary's Church, Manhattanville, New-York.

The Rev. Samuel M. Akerly, New-York.

The Rev. John G. Ames, a Professor in the House of Evangelists, New-York.

The Rev. John Anketell, A. M., New-York.

The Rev. Edward Anthon, New-York.

*The Rev. Octavius Applegate, assistant minister of St. George's Church, Newburgh, Orange county.

*The Rev. Amos Turner Ashton, rector of St. Thomas' Church, Amenia, Dutchess county, and missionary. P. O., Amenia Union.

*The Rev. George Coutts Athole, deacon, officiating in New-York.

The Rev. Addison B. Atkins, D. D., rector of St. John's Church, Yonkers, Westchester county.

The Rev. Joseph S. Atwell, rector of St. Philip's Church, New-York.

*The Rev. Franklin Babbitt, rector of Grace Church, Nyack, Rockland county, and missionary.

*The Rev. Brady Electus Backus, rector of the Church of the Holy Apostles, New-York.

The Rev. David F. Banks.

The Rev. Frederick A. P. Barnard, D. D., LL. D., President of Columbia College, New-York.

The Rev. James S. Barnes, Brooklyn, Long Island.

The Rev. Edward T. Bartlett, rector of St. Luke's Church, Matteawan, Dutchess county.

The Rev. John G. Barton, LL. D., deacon, Professor of the English Language and Literature in the College of the City of New-York.

*The Rev. Alfred B. Beach, D. D., rector of St. Peter's Church, New-York.

*The Rev. Wm. H. Benjamin, rector of St. Barnabas' Church, Irvington, Westchester county.

The Rev. John Blake, chaplain in U. S. Navy.

The Rev. Joseph N. Blanchard, rector of St. James' Church, Fordham, New-York.

The Rev. Cornelius W. Bolton, rector of St. Stephen's Church, North Castle, Westchester county.

The Rev. Robert Bolton, missionary at Lewisboro', Westchester county.

The Rev. Chauncey B. Brewster, rector of Christ Church, Rye, Westchester county.

The Rev. Wm. M. Atkinson Brodnax, New-York.

The Rev. Arthur Brooks, rector of the Church of the Incarnation, New-York.

The Rev. John Brown, D. D., rector of St. George's Church, Newburgh, Orange county.

*The Rev. Philip A. H. Brown, an assistant minister in the Parish of Trinity Church, New-York.

*The Rev. Thomas McKee Brown, minister of the Church of St. Mary the Virgin, New-York.

The Rev. Anselan Buchanan, St. George's Mission Chapel, New-York.

*The Rev. Samuel Buel, D. D., Professor of Systematic Divinity in the General Theological Seminary, New-York.

The Rev. Edward C. Bull, Tarrytown, Westchester county.

The Rev. James S. Bush, rector of the Church of the Ascension, West Brighton, Richmond county.

*The Rev. Philander K. Cady, D. D, rector of St. James' Church, Hyde Park, Dutchess county.

The Rev. C. William Camp, rector of St. John's Church, Kingston, Ulster county.

*The Rev. Charles Fobes Canedy, Rector of St. John's Church, Monticello, Sullivan county, and missionary.

The Rev. Alexander Capron, rector of Grace Church, South Middletown, Orange county.

The Rev. Abraham Beach Carter, D. D., rector of the Chapel of the Holy Saviour, New-York.

The Rev. John Chamberlain, an assistant minister at St. Ann's Church for Deaf Mutes, New-York.

*The Rev. George Alexander Chambers, officiating in Central New-York.

The Rev. Elie Charlier, New-York.

*The Rev. Caleb Clapp, rector of the Church of the Nativity, New-York.

The Rev. James Starr Clark, D. D., Trinity Church, Madalin, Dutchess county, and missionary.

*The Rev. Augustus Vallete Clarkson, rector of the Church of St. Augustine, Croton, Westchester county. P. O., New-York.

The Rev. Lyman Cobb., Jr., deacon, (Note A.,) at St. John's Church, Yonkers, Westchester county.

*The Rev. William S. Coffey, rector of St. Paul's Church, Eastchester, Westchester county.

*The Rev. Hiram H. Cole, New-York.

*The Rev. Samuel Cooke, D. D., rector of St. Bartholomew's Church, New-York.

*The Rev. William H. Cooke, an assistant minister of Trinity Church, New-York.

*The Rev. Nathaniel E. Cornwall, D. D., rector of St. Matthias' Church, New-York.

The Rev. Nathaniel E. Cornwall, Jr., New-York.

The Rev. Edward Cowley, New-York.

*The Rev. Algernon Sidney Crapsey, an assistant minister in Trinity Parish, New-York.

*The Rev. Robert Fulton Crary, rector of the Church of the Holy Comforter, Poughkeepsie, Dutchess county.

*The Rev. Robert B. Croes, D. D., Yonkers, Westchester county.

*The Rev. Gouverneur Cruger, missionary at Montrose, Westchester county.

The Rev. J. Radcliff Davenport, New-York.

The Rev. A. Sidney Dealey, rector of the Church of the Holy Spirit, Rondout, Kingston, Ulster county.

The Rev. Benjamin F. De Costa, New-York.

The Rev. Joaquim De Palma, rector of the Church of Santiago, New-York.

*The Rev. Morgan Dix, D. D., rector of Trinity Church, New-York.

The Rev. Elijah Winchester Donald, rector of the Church of the Intercession, New-York.

*The Rev. Zina Doty, rector of St. Ambrose' Church, New-York.

*The Rev. George William Douglas, deacon.

*The Rev. Henry A. Dows, missionary at Monroe, Orange county.

The Rev. John Drisler, deacon, (Note A.,) Mission Chapel, Saw Mill Valley, Greenburgh, Westchester county.

*The Rev. Cornelius R. Duffie, D. D., rector of the Church of St. John Baptist, and chaplain of Columbia College, New-York.

*The Rev. Henry E Duncan, D. D., Elizabeth, New-Jersey.

*The Rev. William N. Dunnell, rector of All Saints' Church, New-York.

*The Rev. Heman Dyer, D. D., an assistant minister of the Church of the Ascension, New-York.

*The Rev. Theodore A. Eaton, D. D., rector of St. Clement's Church, New-York.

*The Rev. John C. Eccleston, M. D., rector of St. John's Church, Clifton, Richmond county.

*The Rev. William E. Eigenbrodt, D. D., Professor of Pastoral Theology in the General Theological Seminary, New-York.

*The Rev. William T. Egbert, rector of the Church of St. John the Evangelist, Memorial of Bishop Wainwright, New-York.

The Rev. Rufus Emery, rector of St. Paul's Church, Newburgh, Orange county.

The Rev. Ferdinand C. Ewer, D. D., rector of St. Ignatius' Church, New-York.

*The Rev. Robert B. Fairbairn, D. D., LL. D., Warden of St. Stephen's Training College, Annandale, Dutchess county.

*The Rev. George W. Ferguson, rector of Trinity Church, Sing Sing, Westchester county.

The Rev. Edward O. Flagg, D. D., New-York.

The Rev. John C. Fleischhacker, minister of St. George's German Mission Chapel, New-York.

*The Rev. John Murray Forbes, D. D., Elizabeth, New-Jersey.

The Rev. Edward K. Fowler, Monticello, Sullivan county.

*The Rev. William G. French, officiating for the New-York Protestant Episcopal City Mission Society, on Blackwell's Island.

The Rev. John Fulton, D. D., rector of Christ Church, New-York.

The Rev. Thomas Gallaudet, D. D., Rector of St. Ann's Church for Deaf Mutes, New-York.

The Rev. John N. Galleher, D. D., rector of Zion Church, New-York.

The Rev. Ebenezer Gay, missionary at Stony Point, Rockland county.

*The Rev. G. Jarvis Geer, D. D., rector of St. Timothy's Church, New-York.

*The Rev. J. Breckenridge Gibson, D. D., rector of St. John's School, Sing Sing, and of All Saints' Church, (Briar Cliff,) Ossining, Westchester county. P. O., Sing Sing.

*The Rev. Alfred Goldsborough, rector of Christ Church, Warwick, Orange county, and missionary.

*The Rev. E. H. C Goodwin, an officiating minister of Trinity Parish, New-York, at Fort Columbus, New-York harbor.

*The Rev. George S Gordon, Peekskill, Westchester county.

*The Rev. William H. De L. Grannis, rector of St. James' Church, Goshen, Orange county.

*The Rev. Albert Zabriskie Gray, rector of St. Philip's Church in the Highlands, Philipsetown, Putnam county. P. O., Garrison's.

The Rev. Frederick M. Gray, rector of the Church of the Holy Comforter, (Eltingville,) Southfield, Richmond county

The Rev. Horatio Gray.

*The Rev. Edmund Guilbert.

*The Rev Benjamin I Haight, D D, LL. D, an assistant minister of Trinity Church, New-York.

*The Rev Randall C Hall, Clement C. Moore Professor of the Hebrew and Greek Languages in the General Theological Seminary, New-York.

The Rev. Alexander Hamilton, Jr, deacon, New-York, (Note A.)

*The Rev. Thomas R. Harris, rector of St. Paul's Church, Morrisania, New-York.

*The Rev. A. Bloomer Hart, rector of St. Stephen's Church, New-York

The Rev. John G. B. Heath, officiating for the New-York Protestant Episcopal City Mission Society in the Tombs and other public institutions, New-York.

The Rev. James I. Helm, D. D., rector of St. Paul's Church, Sing Sing, Westchester county.

The Rev. Francis A. Henry.

The Rev. Charles Higbee, rector of Christ Church, Pelham, Westchester county.

*The Rev. George H. Hinkle, Newburgh, Orange county.

*The Rev. Solomon G. Hitchcock, missionary at Piermont, Rockland county.

The Rev. Horace B. Hitchings, an assistant minister of Trinity Church, New-York.

*The Rev. John Henry Hobart, D. D., New-York.

The Rev. Charles Frederick Hoffman, rector of All Angels' Church, New-York.

The Rev. William A. Holbrook, rector of the Church of St. James the Less, Scarsdale, Westchester county.

The Rev. Robert Holden, rector of Trinity School, New-York.

The Rev. Stephen F. Holmes, officiating for the New-York Protestant Episcopal City Mission Society, as chaplain of St. Barnabas' House and Chapel, New-York.

The Rev. Montgomery R. Hooper, an assistant minister of St. Paul's Church, Yonkers, Westchester county.

*The Rev. William Berrian Hooper, rector of Trinity Church, Mount Vernon, Westchester county.

*The Rev. George B. Hopson, Professor of the Latin Language in St. Stephen's Training College, Annandale, Dutchess county.

*The Rev. Frederick H. T. Horsfield, deacon.

*The Rev. Edward C. Houghton, assistant minister of the Church of the Transfiguration, New-York.

*The Rev. George C. Houghton, an officiating minister in the Parish of Trinity Church, New-York.

The Rev. George H. Houghton, D. D., rector of the Church of the Transfiguration, New-York.

The Rev. George Howell.

*The Rev. Robert S. Howland, D. D., rector of the Church of the Heavenly Rest, New-York.

The Rev. Ralph Hoyt.

The Rev. William Huckel, rector of St. Ann's Church, Morrisania, New-York.

*The Rev. Albert S. Hull, rector of Trinity Church, Morrisania, New-York.

The Rev. Pierre P. Irving, New-Brighton, Richmond County.

The Rev. Theodore Irving, LL. D., residing in New-York.

**The Rev. Angus M. Ives, missionary at Tuckahoe and Wilmot, Westchester county.

**The Rev. Alfred Evan Johnson, S. T. B.

The Rev. George D. Johnson, rector of Christ Church, New-Brighton, Richmond county.

*The Rev. Joseph Horsfall Johnson, missionary at Highland and Milton, Ulster county.

*The Rev. J. Copeland Lea Jones.

*The Rev. William Marvin Jones.

*The Rev. Joseph F. Jowitt, New-York.

The Rev. Justin P. Kellog, New-Windsor, Orange county.

The Rev. James E. Kenney, New-York.

The Rev. Arthur Clifford Kimber, an officiating minister in Trinity Parish, New-York.

*The Rev. Charles S. Knapp.

The Rev. John W. Kramer, M. D.

*The Rev. Edward H. Krans, an assistant minister at St. Ann's Church for Deaf Mutes, New-York.

*The Rev. Francis E. Lawrence, D. D., pastor of the Church of the Holy Communion, New-York.

*The Rev. Hamilton Lee.

The Rev. Alexander S. Leonard, D. D , Fordham, New-York

The Rev. Robert W. Lewis, New-York.

The Rev. S. Seymour Lewis.

*The Rev. William Fisher Lewis, rector of St. Peter's Church, Peekskill, Cortlandt, Westchester county.

The Rev. Charles S. Little, New-York.

*The Rev. John R. Livingston, rector of Trinity Church, Fishkill, Dutchess county, and missionary at Glenham. P. O., Glenham.

*The Rev. Robert Lowry, an assistant minister of St. Thomas' Church, in charge of St. Thomas' Free Mission Chapel, New-York.

*The Rev. Nicholas F. Ludlum, missionary and financial agent of the New-York Protestant Episcopal City Mission Society, New-York.

*The Rev. William S. Ludlum, New-York.

The Rev. John P. Lundy, D. D.

The Rev. Lea Luquer, rector of St. Matthew's Church, Bedford, Westchester county.

*The Rev. David H. Macurdy.

The Rev. Isaac Maguire, deacon, (Note A.,) missionary of the Protestant Episcopal Missionary Society for Seamen in the port and city of New-York, New-York.

*The Rev. Romaine S. Mansfield, missionary at Spring Valley, Rockland county, in charge also of St. John's Church, Clarkstown, Rockland county.

The Rev. Dan Marvin, Jr., deacon, Brooklyn, N. Y.

The Rev. Mytton Maury, D. D., New-York.

The Rev. Dominick M. McCaffrey, officiating in New-York.

The Rev. Haslett McKim, Jr., rector of St. Thomas' Church, New-Windsor, Orange county.

The Rev. Randolph H. McKim, D. D., rector of the Church of the Holy Trinity, Harlem, New-York.

*The Rev. William A. McVickar, D. D., officiating at Nice.

The Rev. Alexander McWhorter, deacon.

*The Rev. Edward N. Mead, D. D., minister of St. Mary's Church, Beechwood, Westchester county, P O., Scarborough, Westchester county.

The Rev. J. Austen Merrick, D. D., West Farms, New-York.

The Rev. James Millett, rector of the Church of the Holy Martyrs, New-York.

The Rev. Benjamin F. Miller.

*The Rev. William White Montgomery, rector of St. Thomas' Church, Mamaroneck, Westchester county.

*The Rev. John W. Moore, minister of Christ Church, Red Hook, Dutchess county.

*The Rev. William Moore.

*The Rev. Samuel Moran.

*The Rev. Brockholst Morgan, rector of St. Peter's Church, Port Chester, Westchester county.

The Rev. James Hervey Morgan, New-York.

The Rev. Richard U. Morgan, D. D., residing at Stamford, Connecticut.

*The Rev. William F. Morgan, D. D. rector of St. Thomas' Church, New-York.

*The Rev. Charles W. Morrill, Church of the Intercessor, New-York.

The Rev. Lewis F. Morris, Sing Sing, Westchester county.

The Rev. Joshua Morsell, D. D., rector of Grace Church, City Island, and missionary.

*The Rev. Henry Mottet, Church of the Holy Communion, New-York.

The Rev. William A. Muhlenberg, D. D., Superintendent of St. Luke's Hospital, New-York.

The Rev. James Mulchahey, D. D., an assistant minister of Trinity Church, New-York.

The Rev. James Byron Murray.

The Rev. Chester Newell, chaplain in the United States Navy.

The Rev. R. Heber Newton, rector of the Anthon Memorial Church, New-York.

*The Rev. Edwin A. Nichols.

The Rev. Samuel Nichols, residing at Greenfield, Connecticut.

*The Rev. Louis L. Noble, Professor of History and of the English Language and Literature in St. Stephen's College, Annandale, Dutchess county.

The Rev. McWalter B. Noyes, an assistant minister of the Church of St. Mary the Virgin, New-York.

The Rev. Frederick Oertel, in charge of Bethlehem Mission Chapel, under the direction of the New-York Protestant Episcopal City Mission Society, New-York.

*The Rev. Frederick Ogilby, D. D., an assistant minister of Trinity Church, New-York.

The Rev. Andrew Oliver, D. D., Professor of Biblical Learning and the Interpretation of Scripture in the General Theological Seminary, New-York.

The Rev. A. F. Olmstead, rector of the Church of the Messiah, Rhinebeck, Dutchess county.

*The Rev. Charles Sanford Olmsted, deacon.

The Rev. Charles T. Olmsted, an assistant minister of Trinity Church, New-York.

*The Rev. William W. Olssen, D. D., Professor of the Greek Language and Literature, and of Hebrew, in St. Stephen's College, Annandale.

The Rev. Samuel Osgood, D. D., LL. D., New-York.

The Rev. John William Paige, New-York.

*The Rev. Leighton Parks, deacon.

The Rev. Isaac Peck.

*The Rev. Edward W. Peet, D. D., assisting at St. George's Church, New-York.

*The Rev. Thomas M. Peters, D. D., rector of St. Michael's Church, New-York.

The Rev. John Peterson, deacon, (Note A.,) assisting in St. Philip's Church, New-York.

The Rev. George L. Platt, rector of St. Paul's Church, Red Hook, Dutchess county. P. O., Madalin.

The Rev. Leon Pons, rector of the French Church du St. Esprit, New-York.

The Rev. Henry C. Potter, D. D., rector of Grace Church, New-York.

*The Rev. John F. Potter, St. John's Church, Canterbury, Orange county, and missionary.

The Rev. Horace L. E. Pratt, New-York.

The Rev. Joseph H. Price, D. D., New-York.

*The Rev. Gustav Edmund Purucker, rector of Christ Church, Ramapo, Rockland county, and missionary. P. O., Suffern.

The Rev. D. Brainard Ray, Grace Church, Harlem, New-York.

The Rev. George B. Reese, Jr., rector of Zion Church, Greenburgh, Westchester county.

The Rev. George T. Rider.

The Rev. Henry C. Riley, officiating in Mexico.

The Rev. H. Floy Roberts, missionary of the Church of the Holy Comforter for Seamen, New-York.

The Rev. John J. Roberts, New-York.

The Rev. J. J. Robertson, D. D., rector of Trinity Church, Saugerties, Ulster county.

The Rev. N. Frazier Robinson, deacon, officiating in Trinity Church, New-York.

*The Rev. John Gardner Rosencrantz, Grace Church, Port Jervis, Orange county, and missionary.

The Rev. R. Condit Russell, rector of St. James' Church, North Salem, and of St. Luke's Church, Somers, Westchester county, and missionary.

The Rev. Joseph Hine Rylance, D. D., rector of St. Mark's Church in the Bowerie, New-York.

*The Rev. Henry Y. Satterlee, rector of Zion Church, Wappinger's Falls, Dutchess county.

*The Rev. Erastus Huntington Saunders.

The Rev. Thomas S. Savage, M. D., D. D., officiating at Rhine Cliff, Dutchess county.

The Rev. Charles Schramm, D. D.

*The Rev. John F. Schroeder, deacon.

The Rev. Uriah Scott, New-York.

*The Rev. William J. Seabury, D. D., rector of the Church of the Annunciation, and Ludlow Professor of Ecclesiastical Polity and Law in the General Theological Seminary, New-York.

The Rev. Francis M. Serenbez, missionary among the Germans, Middletown, Orange county.

*The Rev. George F. Seymour, D. D., St. Mark's Church in the Bowerie Professor of Ecclesiastical History in the General Theological Seminary, New-York.

*The Rev. John W. Shackelford, rector of the Church of the Redeemer, New-York.

*The Rev. Frederick W. Shelton, LL. D., rector of St. Mark's Church, Carthage Landing, Dutchess county.

The Rev. Henry Beers Sherman, rector of the Church of the Ascension, Esopus, Ulster county.

*The Rev. Charles L. Short, deacon, officiating at Staatsburgh, Dutchess county.

The Rev. George F. Siegmund, an assistant minister of Grace Church, New-York.

*The Rev. Thomas H. Sill, an officiating minister in Trinity Parish, New-York.

*The Rev. Cornelius B. Smith, rector of St. James' Church, New-York.

*The Rev. George Henry Smith, Middletown, Conn.

*The Rev. James Tuttle Smith, rector of the Church of the Holy Sepulchre, New-York.

*The Rev. John Cotton Smith, D. D., rector of the Church of the Ascension, New-York.

*The Rev. Orsamus H. Smith, officiating at North Paterson, Putnam county.

*The Rev. William E. Snowden, rector of St. Andrew's Church, Walden, Orange county, and missionary.

*The Rev. Jesse A. Spencer, D. D., Professor of the Greek Language and Literature in the College of the City of New-York, New-York.

*The Rev. J. Selden Spencer, rector of Christ Church, Tarrytown, Westchester county.

*The Rev. Albert U. Stanley, rector of St. Paul's Memorial Church, Edgewater, Richmond county.

*The Rev. Constantine Stauder, officiating among Italians in New-York.

*The Rev. William Staunton, D. D., New-York.

*The Rev. John F. Steen, officiating in Missions of the Church of the Ascension, New-York.

*The Rev. Christopher S. Stephenson, rector of St. Mary's Church, Mott Haven, New-York.

*The Rev. Walter A. Stirling, New-York.

*The Rev. Charles Robert Stroh, deacon, St. Clement's Church, New-York.

The Rev. Henry C. Stowell, New-York.

*The Rev. Francis Henry Stricker, deacon.

*The Rev. Francis H. Stubbs, Church of the Beloved Disciple, New-York.

The Rev. Cornelius E. Swope, D. D., an assistant minister of Trinity Church, New-York.

*The Rev. John Sword, deacon.

The Rev. Edward W. Syle, officiating in Japan, and Professor in the Imperial College, Yedo.

*The Rev. Stephen H. Synnott, rector of St. Paul's Church, Poughkeepsie, Dutchess county.

The Rev. John Clough Tebbetts, Jr., an assistant minister of Grace Church, New-York.

The Rev. Charles C. Tiffany, rector of the Church of the Atonement, Madison Avenue, New-York.

The Rev. William B. Thomas, Cleveland, Ohio.

*The Rev. William Reed Thomas, rector of the Church of the Holy Innocents, Highland Falls, Orange county, and missionary.

*The Rev. Wm. Henry Tomlins, deacon, missionary at Stone Ridge and parts adjacent, Ulster county.

*The Rev. Henry Martyn Torbert, assistant minister of St. Peter's Church, Peekskill, Westchester county.

*The Rev. Uriah T. Tracy, rector of the Church of the Epiphany, New-York.

The Rev. Amos C. Treadway, residing in Watertown, New-York.

*The Rev. John W. Trimble, New-York.

*The Rev. Isaac H. Tuttle, D. D., rector of St. Luke's Church, New-York.

The Rev. Alvi T. Twing, D. D., secretary and general agent of the Domestic Committee of the Board of Missions of the Protestant Episcopal Church, New-York.

The Rev. Morris Ashurst Tyng, New-York.

The Rev. Stephen H. Tyng, D. D., rector of St. George's Church, New-York.

The Rev. Stephen H. Tyng, Jr., D. D., rector of the Church of the Holy Trinity, New-York.

*The Rev. Obadiah Valentine, missionary at Ellenville, Ulster county.

*The Rev. Frederick B. Van Kleeck, rector of Grace Church, White Plains, Westchester county.

The Rev. Peter Joseph Victor Van Roosbroeck, officiating for the New-York Protestant Episcopal City Mission Society, as chaplain of Bellevue Hospital, New-York.

*The Rev. Isaac Van Winkle, rector of St. Mary's Church in the Highlands, Cold Spring, Putnam county.

*The Rev. Joseph M. Waite, at St. Bartholomew's Church, New-York.

The Rev. Robert J. Walker, missionary of the Floating Church of our Saviour for sailors in the port and city of New-York.

*The Rev. William D. Walker, assistant minister in charge of the Mission Chapel of Calvary Church, New-York.

*The Rev. William Walsh, Newburgh, Orange county.

*The Rev. Caleb T. Ward, deacon, New-York.

*The Rev. Arthur H. Warner, assistant minister of St. Luke's Church, New-York.

The Rev. Edward A. Washburn, D. D., rector of Calvary Church, New-York.

The Rev. George Waters, D. D., rector of Christ Church, Marlborough, and missionary.

The Rev. John Henry Watson.

*The Rev. Joshua Weaver, New-York.

The Rev. Benjamin Webb, New-York.

The Rev. J. C. S. Weills, missionary at Lithgow and Millbrook, Dutchess county.

The Rev. Wilberforce Wells, missionary at Paterson, Putnam county, and parts adjacent.

*The Rev. George W. West, missionary at Haverstraw, Rockland county.

The Rev. Sullivan H. Weston, D. D., an assistant minister of Trinity Church, New-York.

The Rev. Frederick W. Wey, officiating in New-York.

The Rev. E. S. Widdemer, assistant minister of the Church of the Incarnation, in charge of the Mission Chapel of the Reconciliation, New-York.

The Rev. Howard T. Widdemer, assistant minister of the Church of St. John Baptist, New-York.

The Rev. George D. Wildes, D. D., rector of Christ Church, Riverdale, New-York.

*The Rev. James Henry Williams.

The Rev. Walter W. Williams, D. D., associate rector of St. George's Church, New-York.

*The Rev. William T. Wilson, rector of the Church of the Mediator, South Yonkers, New-York. P. O., Kingsbridge, New-York.

The Rev. C. Maurice Wines, rector of St. Paul's Church, Yonkers, Westchester county.

The Rev. Alvah Wiswall, deacon, New-York.

*The Rev. Curtiss T. Woodruff, Superintendent of the New-York Protestant Episcopal City Mission Society, New-York.

The Rev. D. G. Wright, in charge of the Poughkeepsie Academy, Poughkeepsie, Dutchess county.

*The Rev. Christopher B. Wyatt, D. D., rector of St. Peter's Church, Westchester, Westchester county.

The Rev. Joseph H. Young, at St. Mark's Church, New-Castle, Westchester county, and missionary. P. O., Mount Kisco.

The Rev. Henry L. Ziegenfuss, rector of Christ Church, Poughkeepsie, Dutchess county.

Number of Clergy present at this Convention,................ 151
Number of Clergy absent,.................................. 37

Number on the Roll of Convention,......................... 188
Number not entitled to seats,............................. 117

Number of Clergymen belonging to the Diocese,............. 305

Bishop,.. 1
Priests,... 283
Deacons, with full qualifications,................. 16
" restricted, without full qualifications,... 5
— 21

Whole number of Clergymen,........................ 305

Note A.—This letter (A) designates deacons who have not passed the Examinations required by Canon 7, § II., and Canon 4, § V., Title I., of the Digest of the Canons of the Gen. Conv., and have been admitted to the restricted Diaconate.

A List of the Clergy

PRESENT AT THIS

CONVENTION.

The following Clergy of the Diocese, entitled to seats in the onvention, were present at its sittings:—

The Right Rev. Horatio Potter, D. D., LL. D., D. C. L.

ev. Charles C, Adams,
Octavius Applegate,
Amos T. Ashton,
Addison Atkins, D. D.,
Joseph S. Atwell,
Franklin Babbitt,
Brady E. Backus,
Edward T. Bartlett,
Alfred B. Beach, D. D.,
William H. Benjamin,
Joseph N. Blanchard,
Cornelius W. Bolton,
Robert Bolton,
Chauncey B. Brewster,
Arthur Brooks,
P. A. H. Brown,
T. McKee Brown,

Rev. Samuel Buel, D. D.
James S. Bush,
C. William Camp,
Charles F. Canedy,
Alexander Capron,
A. B. Carter, D. D.,
Caleb Clapp,
A. Vallete Clarkson,
William S. Coffey,
Samuel Cooke, D. D.,
William H. Cooke,
Nath'l E. Cornwall, D. D.,
Algernon S. Crapsey,
Robert F. Crary,
Gouverneur Cruger,
A. Sidney Dealey,
Joaquim De Palma,

Rev. Morgan Dix, D. D.,
E. W. Donald,
H. A. Dows,
William N. Dunnell,
Heman Dyer, D. D.,
Theodore A. Eaton, D. D.,
John C. Eccleston, M. D.,
William T. Egbert,
Wm. E. Eigenbrodt, D. D.,
Ferdinand C. Ewer, D. D.,
George W. Ferguson,
John C. Fleischhacker,
John Fulton, D. D.,
Thomas Gallaudet, D. D,
John N. Galleher, D. D.,
E. Gay,
George Jarvis Geer, D. D.,
J. Breckenridge Gibson, D.D.,
Alfred Goldsborough,
H. C. Goodwin,
William H. De L. Grannis,
Albert Z. Gray,
Frederick M. Gray,
Benjamin I. Haight, D. D.,
Randall C. Hall,
Thomas R. Harris,
A. Bloomer Hart,
James I. Helm, D. D.,
Charles Higbee,
Solomon G. Hitchcock,
Horace B. Hitchings,
Charles F. Hoffman,
William A. Holbrook,
William B. Hooper,
Edward C. Houghton,
George C. Houghton,
George H. Houghton, D.D.,
Robert S. Howland. D. D.,
Albert S. Hull,
Angus M. Ives,

Rev. George D. Johnson,
Joseph H. Johnson,
Edward H. Krans,
William Fisher Lewis,
John R. Livingston,
Lea Luquer,
Haslett McKim,
Randolph H. McKim, D.
Romaine S. Mansfield,
James Millett,
Wm. W. Montgomery,
John W. Moore,
Brockholst Morgan,
Joshua Morsell, D. D.,
James Mulchahey, D. D.,
R. Heber Newton,
Frederick Oertel,
Frederick Ogilby, D. D.,
Andrew Oliver, D. D.,
A. F. Olmstead,
C. T. Olmsted,
William W. Olssen, D. D.
Thomas M. Peters, D. D.,
George L. Platt,
Leon Pons,
Henry C. Potter, D. D.,
John F. Potter,
G. E. Purucker,
George B. Reese,
H. Floy Roberts,
J. J. Robertson, D. D.,
J. G. Rosencrantz,
R. Condit Russell,
Joseph H. Rylance, D. D.,
Henry Y. Satterlee,
William J. Seabury, D. D.,
George F. Seymour, D. D.,
Fred'k W. Shelton, LL. D.,
Henry B. Sherman,
George F. Siegmund,

v. Thomas H. Sill,
Orsamus H. Smith,
William E. Snowden,
Jesse A. Spencer, D. D.,
J. Selden Spencer,
Albert U. Stanley,
Christopher S. Stephenson,
Stephen H. Synnott,
C. E. Swope, D. D.,
John C. Tebbetts, Jr.,
Charles C. Tiffany,
William R. Thomas,
William H. Tomlins,
Uriah T. Tracy,
Isaac H. Tuttle, D. D.,
S. H. Tyng, Jr., D. D.,
Obadiah Valentine,
Frederick B. Van Kleeck,
P. J. V. Van Roosbroeck,

Rev. Isaac Van Winkle,
Robert J. Walker,
William D. Walker,
Arthur H. Warner,
Edw'd A. Washburn, D. D.,
George Waters, D. D.,
J. C. S. Weills,
Wilberforce Wells,
George W. West,
Sullivan H. Weston, D. D.,
E. S. Widdemer,
H. T. Widdemer,
George D. Wildes, D. D.,
William T. Wilson,
C. Maurice Wines,
Curtiss T. Woodruff,
Christopher B. Wyatt, D.D.
Joseph H. Young,
Henry L. Ziegenfuss.

A List of the Lay Delegates

TO THIS

CONVENTION.

THE following Delegates from the Churches of the Diocese, entitled to representation, presented the required certificates. The names of those who were present and sat in the Convention are printed in Roman letters. The names of those who were absent, or were not heard to answer to their names, are printed in Italics.

Counties.	*Churches.*	*Delegates.*
Dutchess,....	St. Thomas', Amenia,	William Nelson, Jr.,
		Edward P. Frost,
		John Knibloe.
	St. Mark's, Carthage Landing,	*John H. Shurter,*
		Robert N. Verplanck,
		Samuel Verplanck.
	Trinity, Fishkill,	*Oliver W. Barnes,*
		John D. Fouquet,
		James W. Andrews.
	St. John Baptist, Glenham,	*Charles G. Bartow,*
		John P. Schack, M. D.,
		Ed. A. Gosalberg.
	St. James', Hyde Park,	*B. B. Dobbs,*
		Miles Hughes.
	St. Luke's, Matteawan,	*Winthrop Sargent,*
		Douglas W. Burnham.
	Christ, Poughkeepsie,	Steph. M. Buckingham,
		Le Grand Dodge,
		Edward H. Parker.

Counties.	*Churches.*	*Delegates.*
Dutchess,....	Holy Comforter,	William A. Davies,
		Samuel K. Rupley,
		William Harloe.
	St. Paul's, Poughkeepsie,	*George B. Lent,*
		Guy C. Bailey, M. D.,
		Robert E. Wilkinson.
	St. Paul's, Red Hook,	*Robert E. Livingston,*
		John H. Livingston,
		Val ntine G. Hall, Jr.
	Messiah, Rhinebeck,	*Edward R. Jones,*
		Walter T. Livingston,
		James H. Fraleigh.
	Zion, Wappinger's Falls,	*Irving Grinnell,*
		Theodore R. Wetmore,
		Samuel W. Johnson.
New-York,..	All Angels', New-York,	*W. C. Wannenberg,*
		T. H. Bainton,
		James M. Smith.
	All Saints',	Wilson Small,
		John H. Betts,
		John Blake.
	Annunciation,	*John D. Jones,*
		George Shea,
		Jacob S. Cronise.
	Anthon Memorial,	William Tracy.
	Ascension,	Frederick De Peyster,
		Fred. G. Foster,
		Francis Leland.
	Atonement, Madison Avenue,	William Graydon,
		Frederick Gallatin.
	Calvary,	Samuel B. Ruggles,
		Frederick S. Winston,
		James Emott.
	Christ,	*Simeon Fitch,*
		E. A. Quintard,
		W. G. Davies.

Counties.	*Churches.*	*Delegates.*
ew-York, . .	Epiphany, New-York,	*Robert Betty,*
		Chas. Treichell,
		Charles E. Woodnosgh.
	Grace,	Adam Norrie,
		Lloyd W. Wells,
		Charles G. Landon.
	Heavenly Rest,	*Benj. A. Willis,*
		Elbridge T. Gerry,
		Charles S. Fisher, Jr.
	Holy Apostles,	Dan'l B. Whitlock,
		Enoch Chamberlin,
		James W. Buckingham.
	Holy Martyrs,	*More Mulligan,*
		George T. Baldwin,
		Samuel Ross.
	Holy Sepulchre,	*Stephen Merrihew,*
		John Pyne,
		John E. Hagler.
	Incarnation,	*William B. Clark,*
		John L. Riker,
		Carlisle Norwood.
	Intercession,	James Monteith,
		B. H. Van Voorhees,
		William Porter.
	Nativity,	*John L. Smith,*
		Thomas Smith,
		William Peacey.
	Redeemer,	Rufus B. Cowing,
		Charles A. Acton,
		George H. Belden.
	Santiago,	*José Joaquin Govantes,*
		Leandro Rodriguez,
		Domingo Ferrer.
	St. Ambrose,	Wm. S. Cutter,
		Joseph H. Buttenheim,
		Wm. W. Crossley.
	St. Andrew's,	*Edward H. Jacot,*
		Alonzo C. Stewart,
		William H. Riblet.

Counties.	*Churches.*	*Delegates.*
New-York,..	St. Ann's, New-York,	D. Colden Murray,
		Pomeroy P. Dickinson,
		Henry I. Haight.
	St. Bartholomew's,	George D. H. Gillespie,
		Stephen A. Main,
		Alfred M. Hoyt.
	St. Clement's,	John Buckley,
		Stephen T. Wygant,
		George H. Romaine.
	St. Esprit,	John P. Schlumpf,
		Lewis H. Pignolet,
		Andrew Gilhooly.
	St. George's,	Charles Tracy,
		J. Pierrepont Morgan,
		Harvey Spencer.
	St. George the Martyr's,	*Robert Waller,*
		Henry E. Pellew,
		John Moulson.
	St. Ignatius',	Christian Zabriskie,
		Ellsworth H. Denslow,
		John Long.
	St. John Baptist's,	*Thomas W. Clerke,*
		John Dewsnap,
		William B. Dixon.
	St. John Evangelist's,	Hamilton R. Searles,
		Thomas G. Pratt,
		Edward Buss.
	St. Luke's,	A. B. McDonald,
		Francis Pott,
		Julian Botts.
	St. Mark's,	William Remsen,
		P. J. Schuyler,
		Allen J. Cuming.
	St. Mary's,	Richard L. Schieffelin,
		Peter C. Tiemann,
		George R. Schieffelin.
	St. Mary the Virgin's,	Bradbury C. Chetwood,
		Benj. W. Winans,
		John E. Atkins.

Counties.	*Churches.*	*Delegates.*
New-York,..	St. Michael's, New-York,	D. Tilden Brown,
		Benj. F. Tieman,
		Wm. F. Chester.
	St. Peter's,	George P. Quackenbos,
		E. H. Cushman,
		Edwin Young.
	St. Philip's,	David Roselle,
		John J. Brown,
		Ezekiel Dias.
	St. Stephen's,	*James Blackhurst,*
		Robert Hewitt,
		Francis C. Hall.
	St. Thomas',	Lyman Denison,
		George M. Miller,
		William H. Lee.
	St. Timothy's,	Elam O. Potter,
		Enos T. Throop,
		Hubbard G. Stone.
	Transfiguration,	Sidney S. Harris,
		John Cary, Jr.,
		William C. Prime.
	Trinity,	John A. Dix,
		Cambridge Livingston,
		Stephen P. Nash.
	Zion,	David Clarkson,
		George H. Byrd,
		John M. Stuart.
	Holy Trinity of Harlem,	*Frederick Tinson,*
		Charles F. Alvord,
		Benjamin P. Paddock.
	St. James', Fordham,	G. L. Dashwood,
		Hugh N. Camp,
		Fordham Morris.
	St. Ann's, Morrisania,	William H. Morris,
		J. Wm. Entz,
		Thomas W. Faile.
	St. Paul's,	*T. J. Potter,*
		Henry C. Tallman,
		S. S. Randall.

Counties.	*Churches.*	*Delegates.*
New-York..	Trinity, Morrisania,	William A. Bedell,
		James P. Fitch,
		James Henry Welsh.
	Christ, Riverdale,	Joseph J. Bicknell,
		Francis M. Bacon,
		Bowie Dashe.
	Mediator, South Yonkers,	Maturin L. Delafield,
		Joseph H. Godwin,
		John L. Berrien.
	Grace, West Farms,	Samuel M. Purdy,
		A. M. Campbell, M. D.,
		James L. Wells.
Orange,.....	St. James', Goshen,	George C. Miller,
		Henry C. Duryea,
		William T. Russell.
	Holy Innocents, Highland Falls,	*Robert W. Weir,*
		Stephen R. Roe,
		Charles Tracy.
	St. George's, Newburgh,	Henry Dudley,
		David B. St. John,
		Henry R. Benkard.
	St. Paul's,	*William E. Warren,*
		John S. Heard,
		John Miller.
	St. Thomas', New-Windsor,	G. J. Appleton.
	Grace, Port Jervis,	*John Dutton,*
		James Hiff,
		Thomas Laidley.
	Grace, South Middletown,	Joseph B. Swalm,
		Oliver B. Vail,
		John Wilkins.
	St. Andrew's, Walden,	George Weller,
		Samuel H. Wait,
		David B. Parshall.
	Christ, Warwick,	Henry C. Weir,
		Samuel B. Dolson,
		John Cowdray.

Counties.	*Churches.*	*Delegates.*
Putnam,.....	St. Mary's, Cold Spring,	Robert P. Parrott,
		Robert B. Hitchcock,
		Fredk. P. James.
	St. Philip's, Philipsetown,	William Moore,
		Henry W. Belcher,
		Hamilton Fish.
Richmond,...	Ascension, Castleton, West Brighton,	Cornelius Dubois,
		Erastus Brooks,
		George H. Wooster.
	St. John's, Clifton,	*John A. Appleton,*
		Dwight Townsend,
		J. Buchanan Henry.
	St. Paul's, Edgewater,	*Albert Ward,*
		Joseph R. Kearney,
		Alex. E. Outerbridge.
	Christ, New-Brighton,	*John Q. Jones,*
		Anson Phelps Stokes,
		H. Eugene Alexander.
	St. Andrew's, Richmond,	Alexander H. Britton,
		Joseph R. Clark,
		Nathaniel Britton.
	St. Luke's, Rossville,	D. A. Edgar,
		H. S. Biddle,
		William P. Wallace.
Rockland,...	Trinity, Haverstraw,	James E. West,
		George W. Burr,
		George Askew.
	Grace, Nyack,	Wm. C. Moore,
		Edwin S. Babcock,
		John H. Tingley.
	Christ, Piermont,	*Henry E. Lawrence,*
		William A. Smith,
		Henry A. Blauvelt.
	Christ, Ramapo,	William G. Hamilton,
		Theodore Haff,
		Henry R. Sloat.

Counties.	*Churches.*	*Delegates.*
Sullivan,.....	St. John's, Monticello,	*Wm. H. Cady,*
		J. L. Hasbrouck,
		Israel P. Tremaine.
Ulster,......	Ascension, Esopus,	*Alexander Holland,*
		Daniel Butterfield,
		E. Bergh Brown.
	St. John's, Kingston,	*William B. Fitch,*
		Charles A. Fowler,
		Daniel T. Van Buren.
	Christ, Marlborough,	John Buckley,
		Edward Jackson,
		Nathaniel H. Dubois.
	Holy Spirit, Rondout,	*John McEntee,*
		Clifford Coddington,
		John C. Romeyn.
	All Saints', Milton,	Charles A. Valentine,
		John Townsend,
		Charles Weston.
	Trinity, Saugerties,	*Aaron E. Vanderpool,*
		Cicero Hawks Ripley.
	St. Peter's, Stone Ridge,	*Henry P. Delafield,*
		Richard Delafield,
		Lorenzo Robinson.
Westchester,.	St. Matthew's, Bedford,	*John Jay,*
		William P. Woodcock,
		James M. Bates.
	Zion, Greenburgh,	Shadrach Taylor,
		Alex. Vanderburgh,
		William A. Ross.
	St. Barnabas', Irvington,	*W. A. Haines,*
		J. C. Fargo,
		D. B. Williamson.
	St. John's, Lewisboro',	*Ebenezer W. Raymond,*
		Stephen L. Hoyt,
		Charles A. Raymond.
	St. Thomas', Mamaroneck,	Charles H. Burney,
		James Stringer,
		Curtis H. Peck.

unties.	*Churches.*	*Delegates.*
tchester,	St. Mark's, Mount Pleasant,	Samuel E. Fisher,
		Charles H. Currier,
		John Webber.
	Trinity, Mount Vernon,	William A. Seaver,
		Gideon D. Pond,
		Samuel A. Howe.
	Trinity, New Rochelle,	Robert C. Fisher,
		Clarkson N. Potter,
		Richard Lathers.
	St. Peter's, Peekskill, Cortlandt,	Calvin Frost,
		Robert P. Fox,
		James H. Robertson.
	Christ, Rye,	John C. Jay,
		Adam T. Sackett,
		Gerritt H. Van Wagenen.
	St. James the Less, Scarsdale,	William S. Popham,
		James Bleecker,
		Lewis C. Popham.
	All Saints', Briar Cliff, Sing Sing,	*Russell Knowlton,*
		Charles C. Clarke,
		Henry M. Brinckerhoff.
	St. Paul's,	M. L. Cobb,
		Charles O. Joline,
		John W. Mulholland.
	Trinity,	*Benjamin Moore,*
		George D. Arthur,
		Robert Mead.
	Christ, Tarrytown,	Nathaniel B. Holmes,
		George W. Morell,
		Ambrose C. Kingsland.
	St. John's, Tuckahoe,	Andrew Findley,
		Samuel M. Raesbreck,
		Alexander Forbes.
	St. Peter's, Westchester,	Robert H. Ludlow,
		John H. Screven,
		Henry A. Costar.

Counties.	*Churches.*	*Delegates.*
Westchester,	Grace, White Plains,	E. T. Prudhom
		William H. Dearman,
		Daniel J. Tri
	St. John's, Wilmot,	Sylvester L.
		Zalmon Bonnett,
		Albert S. Archer.
	St. John's, Yonkers,	Levi P. Rose,
		Henry Anstice,
		Edward P. Baird.
	St. Paul's,	J. Foster Jenkins,
		Henry C. Crane,
		William H. C. Bartlett.
	St. Mary's, Yorktown,	*Henry S. Billings,*
		John C. Nicoll,
		Charles D. Morris.

JOURNAL

OF

THE PROCEEDINGS

OF THE

CONVENTION.

NEW-YORK, WEDNESDAY, SEPTEMBER 27TH, 1876.

THIS being the day fixed by the Constitution of the Protestant Episcopal Church in the Diocese of New-York for the meeting of the Annual Convention of the same, a number of the Clergy and Laity assembled for Divine Service, at ten o'clock in the morning, at St. John's Chapel in the City of New-York, the place appointed by the Bishop for the meeting.

Morning Prayer was said by the Rev. Addison B. Atkins, D. D., Rector of St. John's Church, Yonkers, assisted by the Rev. George D. Johnson, Rector of Christ Church, New-Brighton, and the Rev. Albert U. Stanley, Rector of St. Paul's Memorial Church, Edgewater, who read the Lessons. The Litany was said by the Rev. Randolph H. McKim, D. D., Rector of the Church of the Holy Trinity, Harlem, New-York. The Ante-Communion Service was read by the Right Rev. Horatio Potter, D. D., LL. D., D. C. L., Bishop of the Diocese; the Rev. John C. Eccleston, D. D., Rector of St. John's Church, Clifton, reading the Epistle, and the Rev. Morgan Dix, D. D., Rector of Trinity Church, New-York, reading the Gospel. The Sermon was preached by the Rev. James I. Helm, D. D., Rector of St. Paul's Church, Sing Sing. The Holy Communion was celebrated by the Right Reverend the Bishop of the Diocese, assisted by the Rev. Morgan Dix, D. D., the Rev. Sullivan H. Weston, D. D., the Rev. Robert S. Howland, D. D., the Rev. George D. Wildes, and the Rev. C. Maurice Wines.

The Bishop of the Diocese took the Chair, and called the Convention to order.

The Secretary then proceeded, under the direction of the Bishop, to call the names of the Clergy of the Diocese entitled to seats, when one hundred and twelve* answered to their names, and took their seats as members.

The Churches entitled to representation were then called over, and the Lay Delegates presented their certificates; which were examined by the Secretary and a Committee of two members, appointed by the Presiding Officer, viz.: Hon. Samuel B. Ruggles and Gen. George W. Morell. The names of the Lay Delegates duly appointed were called, when Lay Delegates from eighty-two Parishes appeared and took their seats.†

A constitutional quorum being present, the Right Reverend the President declared the Convention organized for business.

The President announced the Seventh Rule of Order on the admission of persons not members to the sittings of the Convention.

It was moved that the reading of the Rules of Order be dispensed with.

Objection having been made, the Secretary proceeded to read the Rules of Order.

---

* A List of the Clergy who attended this Convention is prefixed to the Journal.

† A List of the Lay Delegates present in this Convention is prefixed to the Journal.

During this reading, the Rev. Henry C. Potter, D. D., moved that the further reading of the Rules of Order be dispensed with.

This motion was adopted.

On motion, the reading of the Rules of Order was unanimously dispensed with.

The Convention then proceeded, according to the Sixth Article of the Constitution, to the appointment of a Secretary and Treasurer.

On motion of William A. Seaver, Esq., the vote by ballot was unanimously dispensed with; and the Rev. William E. Eigenbrodt, D. D., was elected Secretary.

On motion of the same, the vote by ballot was unanimously dispensed with; and Edward F. De Lancey, Esq., was elected Treasurer.

The Secretary announced to the Convention, that he appointed the Rev. Theodore A. Eaton, D. D., the Assistant Secretary.

In compliance with Canon I. of the Diocese, the Bishop laid before the Convention a list of the Clergy of the Diocese.

The following Standing Committees, appointed by the Right Rev. the President, were then announced:

ON THE INCORPORATION AND ADMISSION OF CHURCHES.

Charles Tracy, Esq., the Rev. Alfred B. Beach, D. D., and the Hon. John A. Dix.

ON THE DIOCESAN FUND.

The Rev. Thomas Gallaudet, D. D., the Rev. John N. Galleher, D. D., Francis Pott, Esq., Charles Tracy, Esq., and the Treasurer.

ON THE TREASURER'S REPORT.

David Clarkson, Esq., Frederick S. Winston, Esq., and Robt. H. Ludlow, Esq.

ON THE GENERAL THEOLOGICAL SEMINARY.

The Rev. Morgan Dix, D. D., the Rev. George Jarvis Geer, D. D., John Buckley, Esq., Cambridge Livingston, Esq., and Anthony B. McDonald, Esq.

ON CANONS.

The Rev. Benjamin I. Haight, D. D., LL. D., the Rev. Henry C. Potter, D. D., the Rev. Christopher B. Wyatt, D. D., the Hon. Hamilton Fish, Hon. Samuel B. Ruggles and Frederick Gallatin, Esq.

INSPECTORS OF ELECTION.

For the Standing Committee: For the Clerical Votes—The Rev. William White Montgomery and Mr. Cornelius Dubois. For the Lay Votes—The Rev. Robert F. Crary and Frederick G. Foster.

For the Missionary Committee: For the Clerical Votes—The Rev. Thomas M. Peters, D. D., and Mr. Ambrose C. Kingsland. For the Lay Votes—The Rev. Charles T. Olmsted and Mr. Gerritt H. Van Wagenen.

For Deputies to the General Convention: For the Clerical Votes—The Rev. W. W. Olssen, D. D. and Mr. Tracy. For the Lay Votes—The Rev. Albert Z. Gray and Mr. Robert H. Ludlow.

For the Provisional Deputies to the General Convention: For the Clerical Votes—The Rev. Thomas R. Harris and Mr. A. B. McDonald. For the Lay Votes—The Rev. C. F. Hoffman and Mr. William A. Seaver.

On motion of the Secretary, it was

Resolved, That the Rev. Joseph H. Price, D. D., be invited to a seat in this Convention as an Honorary Member.

The Convention adjourned until ten o'clock to-morrow morning.

THURSDAY, SEPTEMBER 28, TEN O'CLOCK, A. M.

The Convention met pursuant to adjournment.

Morning prayer was said by the Rev. Thomas R. Harris, rector of St. Paul's Church, Morrisania, New-York, assisted by the Rev. William W. Montgomery, rector of St. Thomas' Church, Mamaroneck, and the Rev. Robert Fulton Crary, rector of the Church of the Holy Comforter, Poughkeepsie.

The Right Rev. the Bishop of the Diocese took the Chair.

The Minutes of yesterday's proceedings were read and approved.

Several Clergymen, not present yesterday, appeared and took their seats.*

Lay Delegates from several Parishes, from which no certificates were before received, presented certificates, which were examined by the Committee on the subject. On approval, the Delegates took their seats.†

The Report of the Committee on the Incorporation and Admission of Churches was presented and read, as follows:

Report

ON THE INCORPORATION AND ADMISSION OF CHURCHES.

To the Convention of the Diocese of New-York:

The Committee on the Incorporation and Admission of Churches respectfully report as follows:

The Committee have had under consideration the application of The Society of the Church of the Holy Trinity in Highland, town of Lloyd, county of Ulster.

---

* A List of the Clergy who attended this Convention is prefixed to the Journal.

† A List of the Lay Delegates present in this Convention is prefixed to the Journal.

This application is made on the same papers, upon which this Church applied for admission to the Convention in 1875, and which the Committee then reported to be insufficient, and no amendment or addition has since been made. The defect then pointed out still exists, namely, the certificate of incorporation does not declare on its face that the Society is incorporated as a Protestant Episcopal Church, and is for ever to continue as such in communion with the Protestant Episcopal Church in the State of New-York. The Society was formed under the free Church act of 1854, with a board of trustees, and not under the act of 1818, and the amendments thereof. In all such cases, Section 1 of Canon IV. requires that such declaration shall be contained in the certificate of incorporation, and without it the Church cannot be admitted to the Convention. The Convention of 1875 ordered that these papers be referred back to the applicants for remedy. (*Journal of* 1875, p. 83.)

The Committee have also had under consideration the application of the Rector, Churchwardens and Vestrymen of the Free Church of Saint John Baptist, in the village of Glenham, town of Fishkill, Dutchess county.

This Church was incorporated under the general law of 1813, as amended in 1819. The meeting at which the certificate of incorporation was made took place August 30, 1858. The certificate was properly drawn, acknowledged and recorded, and the other documents required to entitle the Church to admission to the Convention are complete and regular.

The Committee, therefore, recommend that the Free Church of Saint John Baptist, in the village of Glenham, in the town of Fishkill, in the county of Dutchess, be admitted into union with the Convention.

All which is respectfully submitted.

CHARLES TRACY,
ALFRED B. BEACH, } *Committee.*
JOHN A. DIX,

Dated September 27, 1876.

Mr. Elbridge T. Gerry offered the following Resolution :

Resolved, That the Society of the Church of the Holy Trinity, in Highland, town of Lloyd, county of Ulster, be admitted into union with this Convention.

The following was offered as a substitute :

Resolved, That it be referred to the Committee on Canons to consider the expediency of so amending Sec. 1 of Canon IV., that it may provide for the admission of Churches which may have been incorporated under such circumstances as to time, as those reported respecting the Church of the Holy Trinity, Highland, to wit, at a time previous to the last alteration of said Canon in 1872.

The substitute having been lost, the Resolution was passed.

On motion of Mr. Charles Tracy, it was

Resolved, That the free Church of St. John Baptist, in the village of Glenham, town of Fishkill, Dutchess county, be admitted into union with the Convention.

The Bishop of the Diocese then delivered his

ANNUAL ADDRESS.

The Rules of Order having been suspended for the purpose, the Rev. Dr. Peters presented and read the following Testimonial and Resolutions commemorative of the late Reverend Doctor Draper.

On motion of the same, it was

Ordered, That the Testimonial and Resolutions just read be adopted, and placed on the Journal of this Convention, as an expression of its respect for the character of the Rev. Dr. Draper, and its sense of the loss sustained by the Church in his death.

TESTIMONIAL AND RESOLUTIONS.

In Memoriam.

The Committee, appointed to prepare Resolutions commemorative of the late Dr. DRAPER, respectfully recommends the adoption of the following Testimonial:

Whereas It has been made known to this Convention that the Rev. GEO. BARNARD DRAPER, D. D., a Priest in the Church of Christ, and Rector of Saint Andrew's Church, Harlem, in the City of New-York, has been taken from a laborious and useful Ministry upon earth to the rest of the blessed: And inasmuch as the sad circumstances of his death and burial denied to his companions in labor the comforting privilege of gathering for his funeral service, and attending his remains to the grave:

Therefore we, the members of the Convention of the Protestant Episcopal Church in the Diocese of New-York, take this occasion both to open our grief, and to give token of our high esteem for our departed Brother, and of our appreciation of his character and services.

Acknowledging, in all human events, the directing hand of God, we know that the evening and morning of this Christian soldier's day were completed and his warfare accomplished.

He has kept the faith loyal to his Church—her prosperity was his happiness. Well grounded in the doctrines of her Creed, he did not confound the fleeting shadows of the human mind with the changeless articles of a Christian's belief. The garments of transient opinion hung lightly around the body of his Faith; hence he neither feared to accept the truths from time to time brought to light through the investigations of human science, nor hesitated to adapt himself to the conclusions of modern thought. With him the traditions of the past coalesce with the knowledge of this hour, and the Christ Whom he had early learned to love, became daily more and more fully the Way, the Truth, and the Life, until that last moment when, with the words "IN CHRIST" upon his dying lips, he passed from terrestrial darkness into celestial day.

He has fought a good fight. His only parochial charge was St. Andrew's Church, Harlem. Twenty-six years ago he accepted a call to what was then a feeble suburban Parish. Without a thought or ambition beyond the discharge of his duty to the best of his ability, he remained steadfast at his post. Diligent in his pastoral duty, painstaking in his pulpit preparations, faithful and precise in his teachings, he leaves behind a generation of devout and active churchmen.

He bore himself as the good shepherd of his whole flock, during many an exciting controversy, the friend to all, the healer of wounds, and the composer of strife.

As the monuments of that quiet yet persistent zeal, he leaves behind him a beautiful Parish Church, a numerous and united people, a Sunday School large in its membership, and possessing a building perfect in its appointments.

All around revered him, and joined with his own smitten people in sending up one common wail of woe, when that exemplary pastorate came to its sudden termination.

Resolved, That we offer to the congregation of St. Andrew's the assurance of our deep sympathy in their affliction; to his bereaved family, the imperfect consolation of our own sorrow; to the Great Head of the Church, our devout thanksgiving for the good example of this faithful servant.

Resolved, That the Secretary of the Convention be instructed to send copies of this Testimonial to the family and congregation of the deceased, and to cause its insertion in the Church and secular papers of this City, or to make it public in any other manner at his discretion.

NEW-YORK, *Sept.* 28, 1876.

Respectfully submitted.

THOMAS M. PETERS,
ISAAC H. TUTTLE,
ROBERT S. HOWLAND, } *Committee.*

The Convention took a recess for half an hour.

The time of recess having expired,

The Convention proceeded to the election of the Standing Committee, the Missionary Committee of the Diocese, Deputies to the General Convention, and Provisional Deputies.

The names of the Clergy were called by the Secretary, and of the Churches by the Assistant Secretary. The members having deposited their ballots, the Tellers retired to count the votes.

The Convention proceeded to the election of the Trustees of the Fund for the Relief of Aged and Infirm Clergymen.

Ballot was unanimously dispensed with, and the following persons were chosen

TRUSTEES OF THE AGED AND INFIRM CLERGY FUND.

CYRUS CURTISS, Esq.,
WILLIAM BETTS, Esq.,
EDWARD F. DE LANCEY, Esq.,

The Secretary of the Convention presented the following Report:

Report

OF THE SECRETARY OF THE CONVENTION.

The Secretary of the Convention begs leave respectfully to report:

That he has complied with the order of the last Convention respecting the printing and distribution of the Journal of its Proceedings. As required by the Canons, he has recorded the various documents, sent to him for the purpose, including sixteen certificates of the reception of Clergymen into the Diocese, and twenty-four certificates of the settlement of Clergymen in cures. In compliance with the Canons, he has also sent a large number of documents and papers to Clergymen and Parishes, whom they concerned.

He has received from the Right Reverend the Bishop of the Diocese, with his official endorsement of approval, a certificate, which had been sent to the Bishop by the Committee on the Incorporation and Admission of Churches. It declared the satisfaction of the Committee with the evidence presented to it, that a change of name had been legally made, in regard to one of the Churches in the Diocese, to wit: "the Church of the Holy Innocents, town of Cornwall, Orange county." Its name in law has now become "the Church of the Holy Innocents, Highland Falls, Orange county." Under the order of the Convention, recorded on page 61 of the last Journal, he has, therefore, changed accordingly the designation of that Church in the list of the Churches of the Diocese. The certificate referred to is, by the same rule, to be printed in an Appendix to the Journal of this Convention

In due season your Secretary, as instructed, sent to the Right Reverend the Bishop of the Diocese of Albany, as President of its Convention and for that body, a copy of the Report made by the Special Committee of the last Convention of the Diocese of New-York, on a communication from the Diocese of Albany, with a statement of the approval, by the Convention of the Diocese of New-York, of the recommendation contained in the report so forwarded by him.

During the past year, by exchanges and the goodness of personal friends, the Collection of Journals from other Dioceses has been considerably enlarged. By the kind permission of the General Theological Seminary, it remains on deposit in the Library of that Institution.

All of which is respectfully submitted.

WILLIAM E. EIGENBRODT,

Secretary of the Convention of the Protestant Episcopal Church in the Diocese of New-York.

NEW-YORK, *September* 26, 1876.

The report of the Missionary Committee of the Diocese was presented and read by the Rev. Cornelius E. Swope, D. D.:

Report

OF THE MISSIONARY COMMITTEE OF THE DIOCESE OF NEW-YORK.

At the close of another Conventional year, the Missionary Committee of the Diocese have to report, that the work committed to their charge has been prosecuted to the full extent of the means placed at their disposal.

We have 28 Missionaries laboring at various stations, all faithful men, doing the Master's work amid many difficulties and discouragements, and depending mainly for support upon the stipends paid by the Committee.

Most earnestly do we wish that a more general interest was taken in our work, so that we could enlarge our field of operations. Among the many claims pressing upon the Church for Missionary effort, certainly we ought to give the first place to that which comes so near to our own door.

It ought to be borne in mind, that without our aid many places of worship would be closed, and the ministrations of the Church be denied in many portions of our Diocese.

Our Treasurer has received the following sums during the past year:

October 1, 1875, balance on hand,.......	$35 57
Received from Interest,..	835 50
Donations,..	725 00
Church Collections,..	3,872 92
From Estate of the late D. A. Cushman,.................	500 00
	$5,968 99

The payments during the same period have amounted to $5,550 00, leaving a balance of $418 00, towards the stipends due October 1, 1876. There is thus a deficiency of $1,000; this we trust will be speedily received, so that your Committee may commence a new year free from debt, and in good courage to go on with renewed energy in the prosecution of its important work.

Respectfully submitted.

C. E. Swope, *Sec'y.*

The total receipts, including the sum passing through the several Convocations, for Diocesan Missions during the past year, will be about $10,000.

LIST OF MISSIONARIES IN THE DIOCESE OF NEW-YORK.

Counties.	*Stations.*	*Missionaries.*
Dutchess,........	Pleasant Valley,	
	Madalin,	The Rev. J. S. Clark, D. D.
	Glenham,	J. R. Livingston.
	Amenia Union,	A. T. Ashton.
	Pine Plains,	
	Lithgow and Millbrook,	J. C. S. Weills.
Orange, ...	Highland Falls,	W. R. Thomas.
	Greenwood Iron Works,	
	Walden,	W. E. Snowden.
	Canterbury,	J. F. Potter.
	Port Jervis,	J. G. Rosencrantz.
	Monroe,	H. A. Dows.
	Middletown,	F. M. Serenbez.
	Warwick,	A. Goldsborough.
Putnam,.........	Patterson,	W. Wells.
Rockland,.........	Clarkstown,	
	Haverstraw,	G. W. West.
	Nyack,	F. Babbitt.
	Piermont,	S. G. Hitchcock.
	Spring Valley,	R. S. Mansfield.
	Stony Point,	E. Gay, Jr.,
	Suffern,	G. E. Purucker.
Sullivan,.........	Monticello,	C. F. Canedy.
Ulster,..........	Marlboro',	G. Waters, D. D.
	Ellenville,	O. Valentine
	Milton,	J. H. Johnson.
	Stone Ridge,	W. H. Tomlins.
Westchester,......	Lewisboro',	R. Bolton.
	New-Castle, (Mt. Kisco,)	J. H. Young.
	North Castle,	
	Loomis,	
	Wilmot,	A. M. Ives.
	Montrose,	W. M. Cook.
	Pelhamville,	
	City Island,	J. Morsell, D. D.

The Report of the Education Committee was presented a[illegible] read by the Rev. George F. Seymour, D. D.:

Report

OF THE SOCIETY FOR PROMOTING RELIGION AND LEARNING IN THE STATE OF NEW-YORK.

The Superintendent of the Society for Promoting Religion and Learning in the State of New-York, as the Canonical agent of the Diocese of New-York for distributing all funds for Theological Education, respectfully submits the following report:

That during the past Convention year, from October 1, 1875, to October 1, 1876, in discharging the duty with which it has been entrusted by the Convention, the Society has received and distributed the following sums:

Received by the Treasurer from the Diocese of New-York, from October 1, 1875, to October 1, 1876,........................	$744 16
Received from other Dioceses during the same time,............	394 56
Total amounts received,....................................	$1,138 72

This entire sum has been devoted to the objects for which it was bestowed.

The demand for aid on the part of those studying for the Holy Ministry was never greater than at present. Many who are well on in their theological course, and who felt assured that they had enough to carry them through, unexpectedly find their means exhausted, and are obliged to look elsewhere for support; others who are just beginning their studies, and counted with confidence upon relatives and friends for aid, are disappointed in their hopes, and are left entirely or in part dependent. In view of these facts, the Trustees of the Society for Promoting Religion and Learning appeal to the Clergy, and by them to make collections for the Theological Education Fund as speedily as possible, and to urge upon their congregations to contribute liberally; and they would request their Brethren of the Laity, who have the ability to do so, to send in special offerings to meet the present and exceptional distress.

It is worthy of repetition, although it has often been stated before, as an inducement to quicken liberal giving to the Treasury of the Society for Promoting Religion and Learning, that every farthing bestowed goes directly to the object for which it is contributed. There are no salaries or commissions to come between the donor and the recipient to absorb a considerable portion of what is given.

The sudden and distressing death of one of their number, at the beginning of the present week, calls for more than ordinary notice on the part of the Trustees of the Society for Promoting Religion and Learning. The Rev. George B. Draper, D. D., Rector of St. Andrew's Church, Harlem, fell a victim in the discharge of duty to a virulent disease. The precautions which are necessary in such cases, in order to protect the health and lives of others, require interment so speedily after dissolution, that the burial is over before the friends are made aware of the decease. It adds poignancy to the sorrow, therefore, when loving hearts, which reverenced the departed for his exalted worth, are denied the poor privilege of paying the usual tribute of respect to his memory in attending his funeral.

The Trustees may be pardoned in consequence if they extend their report on this occasion beyond its usual scope, by adding a few paragraphs in order to place on permanent record the sense of the great loss which they, in common with the Church at large, have sustained in the death of the Rev. Dr. Draper, and to bear their testimony to his unostentatious life, his blameless character and his many virtues.

The association of the Trustees, with their departed Brother for many years, at certain recurring intervals, revealed to them, what may be known and read of all men in the Parish, which was his only cure, that the more he was known, the more he was respected and loved. His quiet dignity, his calm, gentle manner, his simple, unaffected behaviour, won their way to the hearts of all who were about him; and hearts once secured by him were never alienated or abated their esteem. Those who made his acquaintance found in the man more than they anticipated. Beneath that sweet, placid exterior there dwelt an intellect of more than usual power, and there was added a culture which was refined, elevated and admirable. His sermons were replete with instruction, and were models of a pure, perspicuous style. His care of his Parish was such as to leave no cause for complaint, and in positive results to be an example much needed in this restive age, of what patient continuance in well doing can accomplish. The words of the Trustees must needs be few, and they regret that the necessities of the occasion forbid that they should say more to apprise the Church in this Diocese of the value of the treasure which God has translated, as they humbly trust and believe, to a higher and better estate, in the departure out of this life of their late associate, the Rev. George B. Draper, D. D.

All of which is respectfully submitted.

George F. Seymour,

Superintendent of the Society for Promoting Religion and Learning in the State of New-York.

General Theological Seminary,
Sept. 28, 1876.

The Report of the Trustees of the Episcopal Fund was presented and read :

Report

OF THE TRUSTEES OF THE EPISCOPAL FUND.

The Trustees of the "Episcopal Fund of the Diocese of New-York" report to the Convention as follows:

The capital of the Fund is $110,544 11, of which $36 61 was contributed by three Parishes during the past year. $110,500 is invested in bonds and mortgages on improved City property, and $44 11 cash in Phenix Bank. There is also belonging to the Fund, the Rail-Road stock and scrip mentioned in the report of last year.

During the year a bond and mortgage of William Mason for $3,000 has been paid off, and the amount invested as follows:

$2,000 to Jno. B. Stout, additional, on No. 153 Broadway; $1,000 to Albert Journeay, additional, on No. 76 South 5th Avenue.

The Income Account is as follows:

RECEIPTS.

Balance reported at last Convention,		$45 71
Interest on Bonds and Mortgages,		7,715 72
" on City Stocks and Trust Co.,		393 45
Sundry Parishes—Assessments, viz.:		
On account 1875,	$509 14	
" " 1876,	2,378 37	
		2,887 51
		$11,042 39

PAYMENTS.

To Bishop Potter, to 1st October,		$9,000 00
" City taxes on Episcopal residence for 1875,		705 60
" Croton Water Tax " " 1876,	$19 00	
" Fire Insurance premium "	30 00	
" Painting and repairs, "	455 35	
		504 35
" Circulars for assessing Parishes, Envelopes and Stamps,		24 10
" Invested on bond and mortgage, temporarily,		500 00
" Balance of Cash in Phenix Bank,		308 34
		$11,042 39

Balance, $6,000 New-York City stock.
" 3,000 bond and mortgage, including the above $500.

All of which is respectfully submitted.

THOMAS P. CUMMINGS, *Treasurer*,
G. M. OGDEN,
FRED. G. FOSTER,
JOHN A. DIX,
} *Trustees.*

NEW-YORK, *September 27th*, 1876.

The Report of the Special Committee on the Salary of the Bishop of the Diocese was presented and read:

Report

OF THE SPECIAL COMMITTEE ON THE SALARY OF THE BISHOP.

The Special Committee on the Salary of the Bishop report:

The deficiency of income of the "Episcopal Fund" has been supplied the past year by an apportionment among the Parishes of the Diocese by your Committee.

As the income of the Fund is still insufficient, an additional amount must be raised as heretofore.

Your Committee, therefore, offer the following resolution:

Resolved, That a Committee be appointed to make an equitable apportionment among the Parishes of the Diocese of a sum which, with the income of the "Episcopal Fund," will meet the amount pledged by this Convention for payment to the Bishop.

By order of the Committee.

THOS. P. CUMMINGS,
Secretary.

NEW-YORK, *September* 30, 1875.

The Resolution recommended in this Report was adopted.

The Rev. Benjamin I. Haight, D. D., Rev. Isaac H. Tut[illegible] D. D., Cyrus Curtiss, Esq., Hon. John A. Dix, Frederick Foster, Esq., William Scott, Esq., Lloyd W. Wells, Esq., Fr[illegible]erick Prime, Esq., Thomas P. Cummings, Esq., and George Miller, Esq., were appointed this Committee.

The Report of the Trustees of the Aged and Infirm Cler[illegible] Fund was presented and read:

Report

OF THE TRUSTEES OF THE AGED AND INFIRM CLERGY FUND.

The Trustees of the Fund for the Relief of Aged and Infirm Clergymen of the Protestant Episcopal Church in the Diocese of New-York, respectfully report:

That since their report to the Convention of 1875, there have been received—

Contributions from 92 Churches,	$3,256 81
Interest and rents,	1,833 10
Gift from "X.," through Dr. Ogilby,	10 00
" " "Several well wishers,"	20 00
" " Rev. H. McKim,	25 00
" " "Unknown," through J. J. Benton,	83 00
" " James S. Bogert,	25 00
" " through Dr. Ogilby,	2 50
" " "Z," through Dr. Ogilby,	50 00
By payment on account of principal of a mortgage,	2,500 00
Balance fund at last Convention,	2,664 92
Total,	$10,419 83

There have been paid during the same period—

To beneficiaries,	$4,200 00
To Church of St. Esprit, to refund an erroneous contribution....	10 00
For insurance, putting in water and sewer connections, and repairs to three houses on Madison-street, and one on Broadway, Brooklyn, bought in on foreclosure,	577 15
Principal awaiting re-investment,	2,500 00
Contingent expenses, printing, stationery, stamps, &c.,	26 80
	$7,313 95
Leaving a balance fund of	3,105 88
	$10,419 83

Investments heretofore reported,	$50,235 72
Less payment of part of principal of one mortgage,	2,500 00
	$47,735 72
Add principal awaiting re-investment, above reported,	2,500 00
Total permanent investment,	$50,235 72

The Trustees have been unable, in consequence of the great stagnation and depression in real estate, and in business generally, to sell the three dwelling-houses on Madison-street, Brooklyn, or rent them to any advantage. The store on Broadway, Brooklyn, which produced $650 per annum, was injured by fire, but has been repaired fully by the Company in which it was insured, without expense, except fifty dollars paid to a builder to supervise the repairing on behalf of the Trustees. No rent has been received since the fire, but it is expected that it will shortly be rented to a new tenant.

The number of stipendiaries paid quarterly, during the year, has been twelve.

Special appropriations have been made in seven cases.

One of the stipendiaries has died during the past year, and one has been added to the list.

HORATIO POTTER,
CYRUS CURTISS,
WILLIAM BETTS,
EDWARD F. DE LANCEY, } *Trustees.*

NEW-YORK, *September 27th*, 1876.

On motion of the Secretary, it was

Resolved, That the Clergy of the Diocese in charge of Parishes be and hereby are requested by this Convention to read to their congregations, on the next annual Thanksgiving Day, or on the Sunday preceding, so much of the Bishop's Address as relates to the Fund of the Diocese of New-York for the Relief of Aged and Infirm Clergymen.

Ordered, That a copy of this Resolution and such portion of the Bishop's Address be transmitted, prior to that period, to the Parochial Clergy of the Diocese.

The Report of the Standing Committee on the Treasurer's Report was presented and read:

Report

OF THE TREASURER OF THE CONVENTION.

The Convention of the Diocese of New-York, in account current with EDWARD F. DE LANCEY, *Treasurer.*

September, 1875	DR.
To paid the Rev. Clergy, mileage to Convention of 1875,......	$1[illegible] 40
" " J. W. Amerman, printing blank forms,..............	[illegible] 25
" " [illegible]y's Salary,..............................	6[illegible] 00

'o paid Pott, Young & Co., printing Journal of Convention of 1875,	$972 56
" " J. W. Amerman, printing circulars, certificates, &c.,	14 50
" " Amerman & Co., printing notices for Standing Committee,	5 75
" " Amount retained under Canon XIV. towards expenses of General Convention,	304 00
" " Amerman & Co., printing forms and certificates for Convention,	55 75
" " Contingent expenses, for stamps, envelopes, paper, &c.,	14 80
	$2,154 01
Balance,	8,998 64
	$11,152 65

Cr.

By balance from last year	$6,466 62
" contributions from 96 Parishes,	4,686 03
	$11,152 65

Dated September 27th, 1876.

EDWARD F. DE LANCEY,
Treasurer of the Convention of the Diocese of New-York.

The Committee on the Treasurer's account have examined the same, and compared the payments with the vouchers, and find them to correspond, and that there is now in the hands of the Treasurer eight thousand nine hundred and ninety-eight dollars and sixty-four cents, ($8,998.64.)

ROBERT H. LUDLOW, }
F. S. WINSTON, } *Committee.*

Dated NEW-YORK, *September 28th*, 1876.

The Rev. Dr. Rylance offered the following Resolution, viz.:

Whereas a very considerable surplus has accumulated in the hands of the Treasurer of the Diocesan Fund, therefore,

Resolved, That fifty per cent. of the sums paid by the Parishes upon the assessment of the year 1875–6 be returned, and that hereafter the assessment be one and a half per cent. upon the salaries of the parochial clergy, instead of two per cent., as at present, and that the Committee on Canons be instructed to report the necessary change in the terms of the 14th Canon.

The Rev. Henry C. Potter, D. D., offered the following as a substitute:

Resolved, That it be referred to the Standing Committee on Canons to examine and report, whether it be not expedient to amend Section I. of Canon XIV. of this Diocese, by the addition, after the words "two per cent. on the amount of the salary of the clergymen," of these words, "unless otherwise ordered by the preceding Convention."

This substitute was adopted.

The Report of the Standing Committee on the General Theological Seminary was presented and read:

Report

OF THE STANDING COMMITTEE OF THE GENERAL THEOLOGICAL SEMINARY.

The Standing Committee on the General Theological Seminary, respectfully report:

That nothing has occurred during the past year in connection with the Seminary and its relations to this Diocese, which requires action by this Convention.

The Committee take occasion to congratulate the Convention, and the friends of the Seminary throughout the Diocese, on the prosperous and happy condition of that Institution, which, with its able and learned Dean and Professors, and its large number of students, presents a gratifying scene of tranquillity and good order, while the important way of training our candidates for the ministry of the Lord Jesus Christ is still, as heretofore, pursued with conscientious devotion, and in a spirit befitting that high and sacred duty.

All which is respectfully submitted.

Morgan Dix,
Geo. Jarvis Geer,
Cambridge Livingston,
A. B. McDonald.

The Report of the Standing Committee on the Diocesan Fund was presented and read:

Report

OF THE STANDING COMMITTEE ON THE DIOCESAN FUND.

The Standing Committee on the Diocesan Fund respectfully recommend to the Convention the adoption of the following Resolution, viz.:

Resolved, That there be paid to the Clergy attending the Convention, who reside more than twenty miles from the place of meeting, and whose Parishes have contributed to the fund, as required by the Canon, ten cents per mile for every mile of the distance from their respective Parishes; and that the remainder be appropriated to paying for the printing of the Journal of the Convention, and the Canonical customary and prescribed expenses of the Diocese.

THOMAS GALLAUDET, *Chairman.*
J. N. GALLEHER, S. T. D.,
CHARLES TRACY,
FRANCIS POTT,
EDWARD F. DE LANCEY.

NEW-YORK, *September* 27, 1876.

The Resolution recommended in this Report was adopted.

The Report of the Trustees of the Sands' Fund was presented and read:

Report

OF THE TRUSTEES OF THE SANDS' FUND.

The Trustees of the Sands' Fund respectfully report:

That there has been received since their Report to the last Convention, for interest,..................	$189 25
For principal of bonds and mortgages paid,................	3 000 00
	$3.189 25

That there has been paid during the same period to the Bishop for the purposes of the Fund...............	$182 25
And for a Record book and Seal,...............	7 00
	$189 25

Principal on deposit in the New-York Life and Trust Company, awaiting re-investment on bond and mortgage, pursuant to the will of Mr. Sands,........... $3,000 00

$3,189 25

HORATIO POTTER, *President*,
WM. E. EIGENBRODT, *Secretary of the Convention of the Diocese of New-York*,
EDWARD F. DE LANCEY, *Treasurer of the Convention of the Diocese of New-York*,
THOS. P. CUMMINGS, *Treasurer of the Episcopal Fund*,
} *Trustees.*

Dated NEW-YORK, *September 27th*, 1876.

The Report of the Trustees of St. Stephen's College, Annandale, was presented and read:

Report

OF ST. STEPHEN'S COLLEGE, ANNANDALE.

The following report is submitted to the Convention of the Diocese of New-York, in behalf of the Trustees of St. Stephen's College:

There have been 80 students, members of the College, the past year. Of these, 78 were communicants, and it is the purpose of 70 to study for Holy Orders. The College opened on the 13th of September with 77 students in attendance.

The Trustees, at their late meeting, recognised a scientific and practical knowledge of music, as a necessary part of the education of a clergyman. Mr. William H. Whittingham has charge of this department, and gives instruction to every member of the College. He also conducts the musical part of the service in the daily morning and evening worship in the chapel.

It is now 16 years since the College went into operation. Of those who have received their classical education wholly or in part at Annandale, 80 have received Holy Orders. Of these 5 have died. The remaining 75 are doing faithful service in 18 Dioceses, one Foreign Missionary Diocese, and in two Dioceses in the Dominion of Canada.

For these sixteen years the College has been carried on with less pecuniary trouble than falls to the lot of most of our Church Institutions. It has been due to the liberality of the Society for the Promotion of Religion and Learning, and to a few devoted friends and Trustees. This liberality cannot be expected to continue always. The College has certainly done enough to entitle it to a share in the general liberality of the Church. The present season there have been over 30 applicants for admission Only 14 could be received. These filled our vacant rooms, and more than exhausted the fund for scholarships. Enough names are now recorded for entrance a year hence to fill the places which will then be left vacant by those who will graduate next June. A moderate sum for buildings, and for the endowment of professorships and scholarships, will establish the College on such a foundation as will insure its future usefulness to the Church as a Training College for the ministry.

All which is respectfully submitted.

R. B. Fairbairn, *Warden, &c., &c.*

Annandale, *September 25th*, 1876.

The Inspectors of the Votes for the Missionary Committee presented their Reports.

Whereupon the following persons were declared duly elected by the concurrent votes of the Clergy and Laity, to be

THE MISSIONARY COMMITTEE.

CLERGY.

Rev. Alfred B. Beach, D. D.,
Cornelius E. Swope, D. D.,
James Starr Clark, D. D.,
Octavius Applegate,
Christopher B. Wyatt, D. D.

LAITY.

Hamilton Bruce, Esq.,
William M. Kingsland, Esq.,
James Pott, Esq.,
C. A. Higgins, Esq.,
John Carey, Jr., Esq.

The Inspectors of the Votes for the Standing Committee of the Diocese presented their Reports.

Whereupon the following persons were declared duly elected by the concurrent votes of the Clergy and Laity, to be mem-

THE STANDING COMMITTEE OF THE DIOCESE.

CLERGY.

Rev. Morgan Dix, D. D.,
William E. Eigenbrodt, D. D.,
Isaac H. Tuttle, D. D.

LAITY.

Stephen P. Nash, Esq.,
Lloyd W. Wells, Esq.,
Henry Drisler, LL. D.,
George MacCullough Miller, Esq.

The Rev. Wm. F. Morgan, D. D., and the Rev. Henry C. Potter, D. D., having received each the same number of clerical votes, and the former having been elected by the Laity; on motion of the Rev. Dr. Potter, the ballot was unanimously dispensed with; and the Rev. Wm. F. Morgan, D. D., was, by the concurrent votes of both orders, elected a member of the Standing Committee.

The Inspectors of the Votes for Provisional Deputies to the General Convention presented their Reports.

Whereupon the following persons were declared duly elected by the concurrent votes of the Clergy and Laity, to be the

PROVISIONAL DEPUTIES TO THE GENERAL CONVENTION.

CLERGY.

Rev. George Jarvis Geer, D. D.,
Christopher B. Wyatt, D. D.,
Morgan Dix, D. D.,
Robert S. Howland, D. D.

LAITY.

Henry Drisler, LL. D.,
Hon. John A. Dix,
Hon. James Emott,
Thomas Eggleston, Esq.

The Inspectors of the Votes for Deputies to the General Convention presented their Reports.

Whereupon the following persons were declared duly elected by the concurrent votes of the Clergy and Laity, to be

DEPUTIES TO THE GENERAL CONVENTION.

CLERGY.

Rev. ALFRED B. BEACH, D. D.,
PHILANDER K. CADY, D. D.

LAITY.

Hon. HAMILTON FISH,
CAMBRIDGE LIVINGSTON, Esq.,
WILLIAM A. DAVIES, Esq.

The Convention proceeded to the second ballot for two Clerical Deputies and one Lay Deputy to the General Convention.

The names of the Clergy were called by the Secretary, and of the Churches by the Assistant Secretary. The members having deposited their ballots, the Tellers retired to count the votes.

The Secretary presented a Report from the Treasurer of sundry subscriptions, formerly received by a Committee of this Convention, for aid in enlargement of the Episcopal Fund of the Diocese of Albany:

Report

OF THE TREASURER OF THE SUBSCRIPTIONS FOR THE ENLARGEMENT OF THE ENDOWMENT OF THE EPISCOPATE OF ALBANY.

EDWARD HAIGHT, *Treasurer, in account with the* COMMITTEE ON SUBSCRIPTIONS FOR THE DIOCESE OF ALBANY.

Balance on hand, as per last report, Sept. 29, 1875,		$1,438 72
Invested in receipts of the United States Trust Co.,	$1,433 72	
Cash on hand,	5 00	
		$1,438 72

E. E.

EDWARD HAIGHT,
Treasurer.

NEW-YORK, *Sept.* 27, 1876.

The Rev. Dr. Beach, from the Special Committee on the changes proposed by the last General Convention to be made in the Constitution of the Protestant Episcopal Church in the United States, presented and read the following Report:

Report

ON PROPOSED CHANGES IN THE CONSTITUTION OF THE PROTESTANT EPISCOPAL CHURCH IN THE UNITED STATES.

The Special Committee appointed last year, to which were referred the proposed changes recommended by the General Convention of 1874, to be made in the Constitution of the Protestant Episcopal Church in the United States, with instructions to report to this Convention, respectfully report as follows:

The proposed changes are three in number. The First is an alteration to be made in Article 5 of the Constitution, to wit:

Insert at the end of the Article the words, "The General Convention may, upon the application of the Bishop and Convention of an organized Diocese, setting forth that the territory of the Diocese is too large for due Episcopal supervision by the Bishop of such Diocese, set off a portion of such Diocesan territory, which shall thereupon be placed within, or constitute a missionary jurisdiction, as the House of Bishops may determine.

The Second proposed change is an amendment to Article 8 of the Constitution, to be added at the end of the Article as it now stands, to wit, the words:

"*Provided*, That the General Convention may by Canon arrange and set forth a shortened form of Morning and Evening Prayer, to be compiled wholly from the Book of Common Prayer."

Both these changes appear to your Committee to be inexpedient.

The Third change proposed, and the one to which the attention of the Committee was more especially requested, is the following amendment by way of addition to the Article 8 of the Constitution, to wit:

"*Provided, however*, That the General Convention shall have power, from time to time, to amend the Lectionary; but no act for this purpose shall be valid which is not voted for by a majority of the whole number of Bishops entitled to seats in the House of Bishops, and by a majority of all the Dioceses entitled to representation in the House of Deputies."

Your Committee find that the resolution under which the very important change in the Constitution here proposed was introduced, appears in the Journal of the General Convention as part of the last day's proceedings, and cannot but think that it did not receive that close attention and full consideration which it deserved. It will be well for us correctly to understand the purpose and effect of this proposed change.

The purpose of it is, not directly to amend the Lectionary, but to establish a method by which this may be done. We may all desire a Lectionary different from that now in use; but this change in the Constitution will not, of itself, give us what we desire. If it is made, it will simply declare the way in which a different Lectionary is to be obtained To this proposed way or method of accomplishing the object aimed at, your Committee think there are some serious objections.

The Church, in her Constitution as it now stands, has carefully protected the Book of Common Prayer, by making it impossible to alter any part of it, without long deliberation, a full understanding, and thorough examination, giving notice, and allowing time to those who are chosen to legislate for her interests in the several Dioceses, to weigh well whatsoever may be proposed in this direction, so that when she finally acts, she may act under the guidance of a judgment matured by the most intelligent reflection, and strengthened by the largest possible approbation. The wisdom of this none will question. But in the change here proposed, there is certainly a departure from this most safe and conservative principle. The Lectionary is a part of the Book of Common Prayer, and this change in the Constitution, should it be made, will subject this part of that sacred Book to alteration at the will of any one General Convention, without the approval or even the knowledge of the several Dioceses. It will be liable to alteration every three years; and, considering how fond men are of change, and how many there will be having the right to propose alterations, it is hardly probable that we would have the same Lectionary for any considerable period of time.

It is to be considered, moreover, that such alterations may be proposed at times and under circumstances most unfavorable to an exercise of that care which so important a matter requires. Under existing provisions, abundant opportunity is given for deliberate inquiry and the wisest selection; but under the proposed change, this is impossible.

Influenced by these considerations, your Committee cannot but think that it will be safest and best to let this part of the Article VIII. of the Constitution stand unchanged.

We therefore recommend the adoption of the following resolution:

Resolved, That in the opinion of this Convention, the change proposed to be made in the Article VIII. of the Constitution of the Protestant Episcopal Church in the United States, giving power to the General Convention, from time to time, to amend the Lectionary, is inexpedient.

(Signed,)

ALFRED B. BEACH,
WM. E. EIGENBRODT,
HAMILTON FISH,
SAMUEL B. RUGGLES.

On motion of the Hon. S. B. Ruggles, it was

Ordered, That the consideration of the report be postponed until the next Convention.

The Right Reverend the Bishop presented to the Convention a communication from the Convention of the Diocese of Albany.

Whereupon, on motion of the Rev. Dr. Dix, it was

Ordered, That this communication be received and placed on file.

On motion of Charles Tracy, Esq., it was

Resolved, That it be referred to a Committee of Five, to consider and report upon the expediency of electing, by this Convention, the Bishop and members of the Standing Committee of this Diocese and their successors in office, or others than such members, to be a body corporate, by the name and style of the "Trustees of Estate and Property belonging to the Diocese of New-York," under the Act of the Legislature of the State of New-York, passed April 11, 1876, being Chapter 110 of the Laws of 1876; the term of office of such Trustees to be one year.

Charles Tracy, Esq., Cambridge Livingston, Esq., the Rev. Wm. E. Eigenbrodt, D. D., Frederick S. Winston, Esq., and Hon. Samuel B. Ruggles were appointed this Committee.

The Rev. Henry C. Potter, D. D., from the Committee on Canons, presented and read the following Report:

Report

OF COMMITTEE ON CANONS.

The Standing Committee on Canons, to whom was referred the proposed amendment to Section 1st, of Canon XIV , desire to report, that they have given the subject their best consideration, and beg leave to recommend the adoption, by the Convention, of the following Resolution:

Resolved, That Section 1st of Canon XIV. be amended, by adding after the words " two per cent. on the amount of the salary of the Clergyman," these words, " unless it shall be otherwise ordered by a preceding Convention," so that the whole Section will read: "Whereas, &c., it is hereby required of every congregation in this Diocese to pay to the Treasurer of the Convention, on or before the day of its annual meeting, a contribution of not less than two per cent. on the amount of the salary of the Clergyman, unless it shall be otherwise ordered by a preceding Convention," &c., &c.

All of which is respectfully submitted.

(Signed,) HENRY C. POTTER,
CHRISTOPHER B. WYATT,
SAMUEL B. RUGGLES,
FREDERICK GALLATIN.

Under Canon XIX., "*Concerning Alterations in the Canons, and Additions thereto*," the Resolution recommended by this Committee was laid over.

The Report of the New-York Protestant Episcopal City Mission Society was presented and read:

Report

OF THE NEW-YORK PROTESTANT EPISCOPAL CITY MISSION SOCIETY.

The Executive Committee of the New-York Protestant Episcopal City Mission Society respectfully report:

That in the face of trying financial embarrassments and business difficulties, they have been enabled, by God's blessing, to carry forward the vast work of the Society steadily and successfully, and to retain all the faithful Missionaries at their posts. But this simple statement includes much more than appears on the surface. It will be remembered that one year ago the Society was unable to meet its pecuniary obligations. There was no money in the treasury to pay the Missionaries their salaries on the first of October—no money to meet the wants of St. Barnabas' House—no money for any purpose. The outlook was dark. It seemed as if the work must stop, and, humanly speaking, it would have stopped, had not two members of the Executive Committee generously made a "*call loan*" of $1,000 each. Thus the year began in fear and trembling, yet in faith. The Committee felt assured that this was the Master's work, and that, if they did their duty, He would bless their efforts. Appeals were made setting forth the danger of an utter failure if immediate relief was not had, and there were a few liberal responses; but the *heart* of the Church was not touched. Her children did rise, in the spirit of true loyalty and intense earnestness, and declare that this Society must not stop—must not even reduce its work—must not be perplexed for want of funds. No, they left the Executive Committee to solve the problem alone; thinking, perchance, that what had been done in the past would be done again, and the money needed be somehow obtained to sustain the work.

Other appeals were made, and the Committee waited a reasonable time for responses, but waited almost in vain. Then they resolved to face the fact, hard and sad as it was, and reduce the work and expenses to a level with the probable income. Accordingly, they decided, after long deliberation, to give up Bethlehem Chapel altogether, to discharge the Chaplain of St. Barnabas' Chapel, and to cut down the salaries of all the Missionaries *ten per cent.*, thus reducing the expenses $7,200 at once.

When this was noised abroad, there was no small stir among the people, and some persons charged the Committee with having acted hastily and unadvisedly. But what could they do? To go on as they were, was to run hopelessly and dishonestly into debt. They felt, moreover, that it was not their duty to borrow money to carry on the great mission work of the Church in this rich city, and they determined not to do it. They solemnly resolved that nothing should move them from the fixed policy to bring the expenses clearly within the income, and leave the consequences with God.

That was, providentially, the dawn of a bright day for the Society. This action of the Committee awoke the people as from a stupor, and they were both astonished and glad at the new stand which had been taken. The Clergy commended it—business men commended it, and expressed renewed confidence in the Society, and from all quarters money flowed freely into the treasury, so that the loan was soon paid, and all expenses promptly met. Special funds were also contributed to go on with Bethlehem Chapel, and to retain the Chaplain at St. Barnabas'.

In short, by individual donations, by collections, by offerings in Churches, money enough was obtained to pay all the current expenses up to October 1st, and have a small balance left in the treasury. GLORY BE TO GOD!

The following summary shows what has been done since the last Diocesan Convention: 1,602 public, and 106 private services, with an aggregate attendance of 114,329 persons; 63 persons confirmed; Holy Communion administered to an average of 275 individuals monthly; 315 children and 15 adults baptized; 209 bodies received Christian burial; an average of 148 scholars at the Sunday School in St Barnabas' Chapel, and of 99 in Bethlehem Chapel; an average of 94 children in the Day School of Bethlehem Chapel, and of 34 in St. Barnabas' House and Day Nursery; an average of 165 girls in the Industrial School held in St Barnabas' Chapel and the Free Reading Room, and of 50 at Bethlehem Chapel; an average of 47 women supplied with sewing, weekly, by the Ladies' Industrial Association; and a nightly average of 24 boys and young men in the Free Reading Room; 2,376 families, and 27,873 individuals visited, and more or less relieved, in tenement houses and institutions; books drawn from the "Gilbert Library" in the Tombs, 50 times a week, on an average, and from libraries on Blackwell's Island, 350 times a week, 27,098 magazines and papers distributed on Blackwell's Island, and a very great many in the other institutions. Indeed, the supply of abundant reading matter, in the shape of books, magazines and papers, has become a marked feature of our work among the criminal and unfortunate, and has been attended with the most beneficial results.

From Oct. 1, 1875, to the present time, 1,439 women and children were admitted and cared for in St. Barnabas' House, and 150 children admitted to the Day Nursery, making a total of 1,589. In consequence of extensive repairs, St. Barnabas' House was reduced to one-half its usual capacity for several weeks. But, notwithstanding this, 21,272 free lodgings were furnished, and 140,069 free meals supplied; being an increase of 724 lodgings and of 33,204 meals over the previous year.

Never have St. Barnabas' House and the Sisters in charge been more helpful than the past year, and never has the want of room been more sadly felt than at this moment. It is painful and humiliating to see a work of this kind—so needful, so fruitful in good, so economically conducted, and so favorably situated to do a vast deal more than is now done—crippled from day to day and week to week for want of sufficient room. Yet, so it is, and, as a consequence, hundreds of children are to-day slowly perishing in tenement houses for want of proper food and care, and from the poisonous air of their surroundings, who might be saved to life and usefulness if brought to the Day Nursery of St. Barnabas' House. Not only so, but their mothers would thus be lifted up from a state of desperation to a patient and hopeful condition, and enabled to work to advantage, and make for themselves a comfortable and cheerful home.

What we need is a new and commodious building, in place of the old and unfit one at 306 Mulberry-street; and now, when labor is cheap and material low priced, we earnestly hope the $16,500 required, will be furnished speedily to build it, and thus meet the wants of poor and worthy mothers and their children.

In regard to the whole work of the Society, it should be remembered that notwithstanding the glorious success of the past year, we are just as dependent as ever on the voluntary contributions of the people; and that, unless these are as liberal and prompt for the current year, we shall be compelled to again reduce the salaries and cut down the work.

But we look forward hopefully, and expect liberal things; believing, as has been well said, that "nowhere in the whole range of the Protestant Episcopal Church is there an organization so well adapted to its purposes, or capable of wielding, if rightly conducted, so immense a power for good as this."

And now we ask you, brethren of the Clergy and Laity, to feel that the responsibility of sustaining this Society, and enabling the Committee to use this power, rests upon you—not on us—you, who belong to this city and Diocese—you, who are here present, and can influence those who are absent.

Many of you—we say it with joy and pride—have gladly thrown the whole weight of your social, personal and official influence upon the lever which has lifted this Society from the slough of desponding debt, and placed it on the firm ground of "PAY AS YOU GO." Give us, then, your warm sympathy and cordial support the coming year, and the report of 1877 will be fuller of work for God and His church, and richer in the fruitage of immortal souls.

The Clergy in the employ of the Society are: The Rev. C. T. Woodruff, Superintendent, who is chaplain of the "Midnight Mission," and has charge of the

"New-York Infant Asylum," 24 Clinton Place, and the corner of Sixty-first-street and Tenth Avenue; and has, also, temporary charge of St. Barnabas' Chapel, because of the long-continued illness of the faithful chaplain, Rev. Stephen F. Holmes; the Rev. F. Oertel, pastor of Bethlehem German Chapel, corner of Ninety-third-street and Ninth Avenue; the Rev. V. Van Roosbroeck, chaplain of Bellevue Hospital and Visitor to the Emigrant and Homœopathic Hospitals and the Lunatic Asylum on Ward's Island; the Rev. J. G. B. Heath, missionary to the Tombs, the Jefferson, Essex Market, Harlem and Yorkville Prisons, the Ludlow-street Jail, the Colored Home, the House of Detention and the Nursery and Child's Hospital; the Rev. Wm. G. French, missionary to the Lunatic Asylum, Work House, Penitentiary, Alms House and Charity Hospital on Blackwell's Island; the Rev. N. F. Ludlum, Financial Agent and Visitor to Roosevelt Hospital.

The officers of the Society are: *President*, (*ex-officio*,) the Rt. Rev. Horatio Potter, D. D., LL. D., D. C. L. *Vice-Presidents*, Rev. T. M. Peters, D. D., Rev. William F. Morgan, D. D., Mr. Frederick S. Winston, Mr. Thomas Eggleston. *Secretary*, Mr. Isaac H. Holmes. *Treasurer*, Mr. Robert S. Holt.

Executive Committee.—The Rt. Rev. the Bishop of the Diocese, Rev. T. M. Peters, D. D., Rev. Wm. F. Morgan, D. D., Rev. E. A. Washburn, D. D., Rev. Thomas Gallaudet, D. D., Rev. G. J. Geer, D. D., Rev. Henry C. Potter, D. D., Rev. C. C. Tiffany, Rev. Arthur Brooks, Messrs. Frederick S. Winston, Thomas Eggleston, Wm. Alex. Smith, Robert S. Holt, James W. Elliott, M. D., Geo. R. Schieffelin, Adam T. Sackett, Isaac H. Holmes, Charles Spear, John H. Boynton, Peter G. Tiemann, Alfred M. Hoyt, William Borden, Henry E. Pellew, James Pott.

All of which is respectfully submitted.
By order of Executive Committee.

CURTISS T. WOODRUFF,
Superintendent of the New-York Protestant Episcopal City Mission Society.

NEW-YORK, *September* 28, 1876.

On motion of the Secretary, it was

Resolved, That the thanks of this Convention be given to the Rector, Church Wardens and Vestrymen of Trinity Church, New-York, for the use of this Chapel by the Convention, and for their generous hospitality to its members.

On motion of the Rev. A. Zabriskie Gray, it was

Resolved, That 1,500 copies of the Journal of this Convention be published and distributed under the direction of the Secretary.

On motion of the Rev. William T. Egbert, it was

Resolved, That the thanks of this Convention be given to the Secretary, the Assistant Secretary and the Treasurer, for their labors.

The Inspectors of the Votes for two Clerical and one Lay Deputy to the General Convention presented their Reports.

Whereupon it was declared, that there was not present a Canonical Quorum of the Convention, and consequently that there had been no election.

Whereupon, on motion of Frederick G. Foster, Esq., it was

Resolved, That after the reading of the minutes and the usual devotions, this Convention adjourn *sine die*.

The minutes of this day's proceedings were read and approved.

The Doxology was sung by the members; Prayers were said by the Rev. Morgan Dix, D. D.; the Blessing was pronounced by the Bishop of the Diocese:

And the Convention adjourned *sine die*.

HORATIO POTTER, D. D., LL. D., D. C. L.,
Bishop of New-York and President of the Convention.

Attest:

WILLIAM E. EIGENBRODT, D. D., *Secretary.*

THEODORE A. EATON, D. D., *Assistant Secretary.*

Annual Address

OF

THE BISHOP OF NEW-YORK.

My Brethren of the Clergy and Laity:

After a year, which in temporal things has been a year of great trials and anxieties to multitudes around you, if not to yourselves individually—a period of disappointment and loss and general distress, spreading a sombre hue over the whole country, and awakening serious apprehensions about the future—after such a year in temporal things, I can conceive, my dear Brethren, that you come up to this annual Convention with one anxious question uppermost in your minds: Since failure and loss and distress have characterized the year, so far as secular things are concerned, how has it fared with the Church of our Love? Has there been a depression in spiritual things corresponding to the general depression in temporal things? Has the work of the Church languished in any thing like the same measure in which the secular business of the country has languished? Has there been a lack of good fruit in the Vineyard of the Lord, as there have been drought and barrenness in the recently fertile and abundant fields of secular husbandry?

Ah, my dear Brethren, such queries, such thoughts are natural. It is not entirely without reason that they arise in our minds in the midst of temporal distress. But it is my great happiness to-day to be privileged to give you a comfortable, yea, a glad response to all such questions: Oh no! I say an hundred times, No! The general and severe depression in temporal things has *not* been accompanied by a corresponding depression in spiritual things. The work of the Lord in His Church with the souls of men, has *not* gone backward! Quite the contrary! For ever blessed be His Holy Name! *Light*, the Light of Truth and Grace, has sprung up in the darkness. Good Fruits in the Vineyard of the Lord have abundantly rewarded the labors of the husbandmen. Many and many a parent, while battling with difficulties and harassed with cares about his family, has had the unspeakable comfort of seeing children come forward to seal their devotion to their Lord, and to seek His Grace and Blessing. "Whom the Lord loveth He chasteneth"—a word of everlasting comfort to all who fear and love Him! Yes; and while our Gracious Lord sends chastisement in the taking away of temporal blessings, He often shows His Love by enlarging His spiritual gifts, or by imparting to them a Divine sweetness.

Everywhere among our Parishes I have seen a zeal and unity and love which gave evidence of a Heavenly blessing. And among other tokens of faithful work as well as of gracious influences, have been the abundant and earnest Confirmations—more numerous by far than in any previous year since the division of the Diocese—more than a thousand in excess of the Confirmations of last year.

And here, my dear Brethren, allow me, once for all, to say a word in reference to the frequent giving of statistics in our Episcopal and other reports. There is something in the Sacred History about the "numbering of the people," which, in some minds, excites a prejudice against all reports of spiritual growth and improvement as represented by numbers. No doubt there may be, and often are, abuses, exaggerations, from pride and vanity, and from rash judgments. But here, as in many other cases, everything depends upon the circumstances and the motives. It must be remembered that we have many Canons positively enjoining statistical reports, and that for a very good reason. There must be a basis of *known facts* for much of the work which the Church has to do —in her legislation, in her organization of Dioceses, in her provision for the supply of her own needs. Facts must be made known in regard to her growth, in regard to the zeal and liberality of her children: they need to be known for encouragement or for warning. In short, we must know from year to year what our actual state is, in order that we may know what we have to do, and what we *can* do. And so the Church provides for reports being made of the number of Baptisms, of Confirmations, of new Communicants, of deaths, &c., and of offerings made for our different pious and charitable undertakings. Without such reports, we should often work in the dark, without guidance and without encouragement. Therefore the Church is very particular in insisting on such reports being made by her Bishops and Clergy. Let them be made, as far as human infirmity will allow, without egotism, without pride or envy. Let them be careful and sincere, and they will greatly assist the judgment of the Church, and animate the spirit of her children. Indeed, my dear Brethren, I cannot but indulge the hope that the statement I have just made respecting the life of the Diocese during the past year, at least in one of its manifestations, will have the effect of cheering you, and making you feel, with renewed assurance, that your "labor is not in vain in the Lord."

There are, no doubt, many ways in which the financial troubles of the past year have operated severely upon the life and work of the Church. It has required care and special effort to secure the regular supplies of means necessary to give efficiency and steadiness to the various agencies, pious and charitable, employed in propagating the Gospel of our Lord and Saviour, and in ministering after His example to the poor and suffering of His Church. But I am happy to say, that in almost all cases the desired offerings have been made with a liberality and a cheerful good will most creditable to the givers, and most comforting to those who had the responsibility of watching over and directing the agencies in question.

But before leaving this subject, there is one observation tending to qualify, in some measure, the cheerful views just presented, which I feel bound to make. A few cases have been reported to me of Parishes, chiefly in the rural districts, in which Vestries, under the pressure of the times, have very considerably reduced the salary of the Rector. In some cases this has been done to such an extent as to constrain an able and faithful man, generally acceptable to the people, to remove to a more adequate living. There may be cases in which retrenchment in arranging the expenses of a Parish becomes a matter of necessity. But to *begin* to economize by taking away from the very moderate support of the Spiritual Pastor, is scarcely delicate or just toward him: while it must occasion pain and discouragement where there is the greatest need of tenderness and sympathy. Such measures, which drive away from the Parish a good man, who knows the Parish, who is well known and beloved by the people, creating a vacancy which must be filled by a stranger, perhaps after a long interval, possibly by an inferior person—such measures help to lower the tone and character of the Church, and often result in doing more injury to the temporal and spiritual interests of the flock than they had done to the feelings and character of the departed Pastor. O! my dear Brethren, all those things which tend to chill and depress the spirit of the Pastor, are poor economy. The severe retrenchment may seem to save a little money at the first. But a brief experience will suffice to show that such policies are as unwise as they are unkind and unjust. Leave your minister without sympathy, without cheerful support, and you take the very life out of his work. Warm him with your love, cheer him by your generous and thoughtful provision for his comfort, and you more than double his power of quickening the life and advancing the temporal and spiritual prosperity of your Parish. These observations, I need hardly say, are chiefly applicable to Parishes in the rural districts; and even in those parts of the Diocese, I am happy to say, the cases I have referred to are not numerous.

On Monday of this present week I had very great satisfaction in consecrating to the worship and service of Almighty God the Free Chapel of Grace Church in this city, to replace, aye, more than replace, the previous chapel destroyed by fire. I say it more than replaces the former chapel, because it is superior to the former in appliances to facilitate and enlarge the mission work to which it is to be preëminently devoted. It will no doubt be very largely for the use of the poor, but not exclusively so. Doubtless many persons will be glad to avail themselves of its privileges, who will be both able and willing to contribute to the current expenses of the chapel, and to the general pious and charitable objects of the Church. And only a few weeks previously,—on Saturday, the 2d day of September,— the Rev. Dr. Dix, acting by my request, during my brief absence from the Diocese, laid the corner stone of the Free Chapel of St. Augustine, in Houston-street, near the Bowery, a chapel of Trinity Parish, which is also to be provided with very ample appliances and accommodations for mission work in that quarter of the town, where, indeed, a temporary chapel under that name has for four or five years been doing an excellent mission work in connection with Trinity Parish.

And yet further, it must be added that an enlarged Free Chapel is about to be erected by the Church of the Incarnation, in the eastern part of the city, to take the place of a smaller chapel with inferior accommodations, in which for several years a very useful work has been done under the patronage of that Parish. When we consider, in connection with these, the very admirable

Free Chapels of Calvary Church, of St. George's, of the Ascension, of St. Mark's in the Bowery,—when we think of the number of families which they include and hold under their faithful ministrations; the number of young people which their Pastors annually instruct and bring to Confirmation, and afterwards faithfully watch over,—we cannot but feel a glow of thankfulness that through the goodness of God, through the zeal and liberality of our Brethren, the comforting, healing ministry and care of the Church have been so widely extended among those who most need care, and who, I had almost said, best repay it.

My dear Brethren, I need hardly say that this special attention to enlargement of Christian work among the poor is one of the greatest encouragements and consolations of my Episcopal life. But in addition to all these Free Chapels several churches have been enlarged, or Sunday-school buildings erected with special reference to enlarged work among the poor.

Now, my dear Brethren, one of the many reasons why I rejoice so much in the erection of these Free Churches, these special provisions, not only for the poor, but also for the accommodation of persons of moderate means, deserves to be frankly stated: I sometimes fear that we are leaning too much toward the erection of very expensive churches,—churches apt to be so much encumbered with heavy debt as to make attendance upon them an extravagantly expensive thing. I sometimes fear that some of the most valuable families of the Church may in time be quite driven away from those churches to places less expensive. And so I am sometimes led to indulge the thought, what a blessing it would be if we could have erected a few plain, substantial edifices,—plain but *correct* in the exterior, warm and cheering within,—in which ministrations might be offered at a less extravagant cost; services of which multitudes of sober-minded people would be glad to avail themselves. It seems to me that such free chapels as are now being erected will go far toward supplying that great desideratum: a church thoroughly respectable and comfortable in all its appointments, well conducted, blest with excellent ministrations, and asking in return for its Gospel privileges only such free-will offerings as are within the ability of that great multitude of people who have only modest means. The absolutely poor will have their free, open door, their house of spiritual refreshment, where they may "buy wine and milk without money and without price," where they may find a man of God always ready to listen to their distress, while there will be room and inviting accommodation enough for those who, having more freely received of the good things of this life, are glad to give back a part to the gracious Giver.

I am very far indeed from being inclined to disparage grandeur and magnificence in Holy Places dedicated to the worship of Almighty God, where there are the means for erecting such goodly structures without imposing too severe a burden upon those who in coming years are to use them. There is no estimating the influence of a sublime Temple, which, standing for ages, goes on day after day, year after year, century after century, inspiring awe, commanding reverence, contributing to exalt human conceptions of God's glory and holiness. The words of King David, when collecting material and making preparation for the building of the Temple at Jerusalem, are a lesson for all ages: "The work is great, for the *Palace* is not for man, but for the Lord God." How the great Cathedral, how York Minster, how Westminster Abbey have for ages moved human hearts, filling them even in a single visit with awe-inspiring images and thoughts never to be forgotten! It is not every place of worship that needs to be a Cathedral, or in any way a costly edifice. But in every great metropolis there should be a "Temple to the Lord," which, by its magnitude, its religious expression, its sublime worship, its vast comprehensive Christian work, its visible influence as a centre of unity, would tend to diffuse everywhere around it, to awaken in the millions, ever coming and going, a deep sense of a present Deity, of the sanctity of Religion, of the supreme importance of our duty to God. When once the heart of the faithful in the great congregation is set upon such a House of the Lord, such "a *Palace*, not for man, but for the Lord God," the consummation will be assured. It will come in its time. It is not to be hurried like a frail, perishable structure. If it wait for years, thoughtful Christians will never speak of it as a "failure;" it will grow in secret; its foundations will be laid deep down in the souls of the loving and devout; fervent secret prayer will be offered; first longing wishes and then burning words will pass in secret from one to another, until at length a cry will arise and go forth: "Come, let us arise and build; let us build an House unto the Lord, an Habitation for the mighty God of Jacob." The faithful will rival each other in bringing offerings; and such will be the rising up of a loving zeal, that this great work, instead of absorbing, as some have feared, the treasures needed by ordinary works of piety and charity, will cause the supplies for those works to flow in from every side more abundantly than ever before.

But I return, for a single moment, to the case of the very poor, and to those who, though not very poor, live in the midst of very great temptations. Of *young men*—mechanics or clerks—who are released from their employments every evening at eight o'clock, and then left free to chose for themselves how they will spend the next hour or two, I suppose there must be in this great city from fifty to one hundred thousand. Contemplate for a moment the case of the youth, the young man, who, at eight o'clock on a Winter's night, is turning the key upon his workshop, or his little store, and coming forth into the street to decide what he will do with himself for the next hour or two. His place of rest for the night is probably a cold, dark, solitary room in an attic—not an attractive place to go to before it is absolutely necessary;

while probably at the same moment there are, within the range of his vision, a dozen or twenty brilliant places of resort, rendered attractive at such a season, and after a day of confinement and labor, by the cheerful light and warmth, the gay company and the stimulating beverage. In one case out of twenty the youth may have fixed principles and fixed habits, which will, without fail, turn his feet in a safe direction. But how hard it is that he should have no pure, bright, refreshing resting-place to turn to! How wrong it is that in a Christian city he should be left, at that dark, cheerless, treacherous hour, exposed, in his weakness and inexperience, to so many dazzling, seductive, fiery temptations! What a grievous pity it is that those two daily returning hours, so important to a youth, should not be put to some saving, redeeming use. O how many poor, obscure youths, with no friends and no hopes, have, by a noble use of those two daily hours, taken from labor or from sleep, raised themselves to eminent usefulness and lasting honor! What a *divine Alchemy* would that be which could take something, (that youth) that threatens to grow into a deadly scourge to the community, and transmute it into a saving agency; and in doing so save a soul, yea, save many souls!

Is there any such Alchemy? "Yes," you will say, "there is the Gospel; there is the *Grace* of our Lord Jesus Christ." Yes, my dear Brethren, yes! That is our first, our last, our best hope. That Alchemy is sovereign. It changes the beginnings of Hell into Heaven. It should always be first in our thoughts. But in order that that *sovereign specific* may reach the young man's heart of hearts, we must do what we can to keep him from going night after night to the *gin palace.* We must try with all our might to keep his feet from those deadly paths which lead straight down to Hell.

And how can we do that? By putting something better in their place, something more attractive, more satisfactory to the judgment and conscience; something which will help to educate the judgment and conscience, and arm them against the enemies and perils I have referred to. Suppose when that youth comes forth from his shop or store at eight o'clock on a winter's night, he knows that within easy distance of him there are cheerful, well lighted and warmed apartments—clean, quiet, comfortable,—where he may find pleasant friends, interesting reading, or entertaining and instructive Lectures, and a warm cup of coffee, or other simple refreshment, if he fancy it? If his taste and his moral feelings have not already been perverted and vitiated, he will turn his steps toward the cheerful, friendly apartments, where he can find all needed comfort, pure, social enjoyment, refreshment for the mind as well as for the weary body. He will thus be *withdrawn* from the haunts of intemperance, from temptation to dissolute courses; and in the society of young men who aim at self-improvement, who love reading and instructive lecturing, there may be hope that he will enlarge and elevate his views of life, that the love of knowledge will spring up within him, and that by diligence and self-control he will expand into a noble manhood, a blessing to his family and to the community.

Now, my dear Brethren, I suppose that it is safe to say, that in every half mile square in this city, in every space containing a dozen of our ordinary squares, there are at least *twenty*, if not *fifty*, gin shops, to say nothing of other sinks of iniquity. Would it not be *reasonable*, is it not a duty to open in every such space at least one comfortable resort for the young,—a reading room, a room for conversation, for occasional lectures, for simple refreshments? They need not be very expensive. Place them within such distances of each other all over the city, that every young man would have one or two within his reach. Let them be *made known* to the young and to their friends and employers. Let small committees, consisting of men and women of practical ability, be entrusted with the duty of securing such apartments and supplying them with the requisite furniture, with reading matter, and with simple lectures of an instructive and entertaining character; and let each apartment or set of apartments be placed under the care of a plain, intelligent woman of prudence, firmness and kindly disposition. And it is quite possible that the requiring of a *small payment* for admission to the enjoyment of such privileges might have a beneficial effect. I am quite aware of the magnitude and difficulty of the enterprise proposed; and I am not ignorant that in a few isolated instances such efforts, somewhat feeble and imperfect, have been tried, but, as was thought, without much useful result.

Much, no doubt, would depend upon a *general* feeling of the great importance of such an instrumentality, upon the energy and thoroughness with which it could be undertaken and conducted, upon the disposition of our kindly and thoughtful people to look in occasionally upon such rooms, and leave in them a cheery, encouraging, and, perhaps, *guiding* influence.

These suggestions are commended to the serious consideration of the Clergy and Laity of the city. I may be mistaken as to the practicability of creating and maintaining such an instrumentality. I fear there is no doubt as to its urgent importance. The loss of character among young men in such a city as this is something fearful. I have no wish to see rash and crude undertakings. I earnestly deprecate partial and feeble efforts. First, let the subject be carefully considered by those most competent to deal with it; and then, if action be resolved upon, let it be united and earnest.

Before turning quite away from the subject of free chapels and work among the poor, I wish to say how much I have been struck, on casting my thoughts back over the work of the Diocese during the year, with the large proportion of fruit, say in Confirmations, which has been derived from mission chapels in the city, and from mission churches in the country, which are under the care of our Diocesan missionaries, thus showing two things: *first*, in a general way, how very large a portion of all our Church work is *Mission work*, in the special sense of that word; second, and more particularly, how very large a space in our Diocesan Church work is occupied by the work of our Diocesan missionaries—those who are laboring in the rural portions of the Diocese. I speak of this, in order to bring strongly before you the claims of our City missions and the claims of our Diocesan missions. The City missions have advocates, (the superintendent and collector,) who are always at work in the city; the Diocesan missionaries, who labor in the remote and rough places of the Diocese, have no advocates, no agents, no representatives, to plead their cause, to set forth the important and necessary character of their ministry, unless, indeed, the Bishop be such agent and advocate. His voice is heard in this place, and perhaps once or twice a year in other ways, when there is urgent need—as there too often is. He himself is an itinerating missionary, and he sympathizes with his Brethren. He goes from place to place in the country, and looks upon the very field which is being cultivated by the patient, laborious Diocesan missionary. He considers the work that is being done; the value of it, the necessity of it, the painstaking labor, the hardness and self-denial required for it. He sees the barren field slowly yielding to patient labor, and in time producing an abundant harvest. Surely it is a truth, that "the laborer is worthy of his hire."

A few years since a Canon was passed by the General Convention, as you know, forbidding the Consecration of a church until such time as it could be certified to as being free from debt. It seemed to be a proper and necessary measure, one calculated to secure beneficial and satisfactory results. Before we can have any right to present an edifice as an offering unto the Lord our God, (which is the nature of Consecration,) it should be wholly and entirely ours to give. One consequence of this regulation of the Church has been, that for the present, for a very few years, the number of Consecrations has been diminished. Perhaps quite the usual number of churches have been erected, but being encumbered with some measure of debt, they have been opened for use with some appropriate service, the full Service of Consecration being postponed until the required condition could be complied with. This postponement is indefinite, often for a long season; and when, at length, after many years, the time for a Service of Consecration arrives, the church has been so long in use, has been so hallowed by use, as well as by the opening service of dedication, that this late Service of Consecration seems, so far as the religious effect on the people is concerned, almost nugatory, a mere futile ceremony. A Consecration, it is true, is something real and vital, apart from its present effect upon the feelings of the people. But to put ourselves in the way of having a very solemn service out of time, so that it must needs appear to many as a superfluous ceremony, is certainly undesirable. And besides, it must be added, that the great object sought to be attained by the Canon referred to, is not attained, or attained only in part. The church *is* used as an Holy Place, as the House of the Lord, when, in fact, it is so far private property, that it is liable to be seized upon and sold for debt—a thing, no doubt, very rare and very improbable, but still possible, and so casting over a very high and sacred thing an air of *unreality*, as well as of insecurity.

No doubt the whole object of the Church in this part of her legislation, would be more fully attained by a modification of the Canon in question, so as to forbid the opening of a church for divine service at all, until it should be clear of all encumbrance of debt. This would be regarded by many as a *severe* measure; it might in some cases discourage church building; and though as a religious measure it would admit of easy vindication, yet I have never proposed it, nor have I sufficiently considered it to feel certain whether I could give it my suffrage, were it proposed by another.

Very lately, in visiting a Parish in a country village on duty, I found the Congregation and Rector occupying themselves with a work of church-building, conducted prudently, and, as it seemed to me, on very sound principles. The services of the Church began to be regularly held in that place some fifteen or sixteen years ago. Their first work was to erect a small but churchly wooden edifice, and a good substantial parsonage. It soon began to be seen that a larger church would be required, and it was resolved that it should be of stone. Several years ago, on a beautiful Summer afternoon, and in the presence of most beautiful scenery, I had the pleasure of laying the corner-stone, attended by a very considerable gathering of the people. In the outset they resolved that they would build no faster than the means should come to them. They would have no debt, and they would trouble no distant friends to assist them in doing that religious work which they thought they ought to do for themselves. They were not too proud to accept of offerings which might be voluntarily proffered to them; but they would not leave their work to go in search of outside assistance. They preferred self-denial and patient waiting. The solid, church-like structure is slowly rising toward the skies. Can we doubt, my dear Brethren, that in a work of church-building so prosecuted, in faith and patience and prayer, there is a self-discipline for Pastor and People which must greatly contribute to their moral and religious elevation; and that when at last they enter that goodly house to join in the solemnities of Consecration, they will do it with a fullness of joy and content not often experienced? What heartfelt devotion in that Psalm for the Service of Consecration: "O how amiable are Thy dwellings, Thou Lord of Hosts!" "My soul hath a desire and longing to enter into the courts of the Lord! My heart and my flesh rejoice in the living God!" Or in the Venite: "O come, let us sing unto the Lord; let us heartily rejoice in the strength of our Salvation!" Or, again, in the wondrous

Te Deum: "We praise Thee, O God; we acknowledge Thee to be the Lord. All the earth doth worship Thee, the Father Everlasting!"

There is great joy in the consummation of a good work, when that work has been in faith and patience thoroughly well done.

Speaking of the opening and consecration of places of worship, I am tempted to refer to a pleasing and characteristic incident which occurred at the opening of the Chapel of Keble College, Oxford—a College which, as you know, was erected in memory of the late Rev. John Keble, the author of The Christian Year, and other works of learning and devotion. At the opening service of the Chapel of that College, which seems to have drawn together a large assemblage of the first people of England, with the Archbishop of Canterbury at their head; at that solemn service the two lessons of Holy Scripture were read—by whom do you think? Many of you, doubtless, have noticed that the first lesson was read by the Marquis of Salisbury, one of the first noblemen of England for ability and standing, a prominent member of the present Government of England, and I think the present Chancellor of the University of Oxford; and the second lesson was read by the Right Hon. Gathorne Hardy, also a member of the present Government—a man of high personal character, and one of the very ablest and most eloquent men in the House of Commons. I do not, by any means, speak of this as some persons have vaunted the fact, that men like John Locke and Sir Isaac Newton were Christians, as if the credit, or if you please, the credibility, of Christianity depended upon the patronage of great names. Far from it. But I hold up this incident as one example among many of the spirit, of the love and reverence for the Church in England by laymen of the highest rank, in the highest official positions, and of the most transcendent ability. They lay aside their robes of civil or official rank, and come forward in the great congregation, under the eye and with the sanction of the Archbishop, and perform one of the *subordinate offices*, yet one of the most honorable in the Service of the Church—reading the lessons from God's Holy Word! And so, on other public occasions, at meetings in support of pious and charitable objects, they frankly and freely come forward with their advocacy and with their munificent offerings. Such examples are calculated not only to strengthen and animate the Church in her great work, but also to elevate the tone and spirit of the whole country.

And something of the same kind we have to acknowledge and express our gratitude for in this country. In our Diocesan and in our General Conventions there are always to be found eminent men, men in high and responsible civil positions involving great labor, who cordially give their time and attention to duties in the Councils of the Church. And to their sagacity and caution the Church has often been indebted for successful resistance to short-sighted schemes and unwise legislation. For myself, personally speaking, after an attendance upon the sittings of this Convention for upwards of forty years, and upon the sittings of the General Convention for upwards of a quarter of a century, I must acknowledge that I feel what I may venture to call *a just* pride in looking back over the eminent men—men eminent for worth no less than for station—who year after year have adorned, and many of whom do now adorn, the Councils of the Church. And while we gratefully acknowledge the good Providence of God which has vouchsafed to us such valuable countenance and aid, we humbly trust that the presence and services of those distinguished persons in our Councils have for the most part been good for them, as well as good for the Church. It certainly is to be hoped that something of the moderate and conservative spirit of the Church has been spread abroad in the country through the eminent men of our Communion who have been employed in important civil affairs. Our numbers may have been too limited to exert a commanding influence in restraining excesses of opinion or of action; but such a religious education as comes from the Prayer Book, such elements of character as the Church, fairly administered, tends to form—calm, sober, reflective, charitable—must have been in some degree healthful to the country at large.

And here, my dear Brethren, we cannot but remember that the present is the first Centennial of this nation. The late Fourth of July completed one hundred years since we began our independent existence. One hundred years ago our population consisted of a *scanty fringe* of settlements, extending along the Atlantic Coast, and for some little distance up along the banks of the chief rivers; while everywhere else in the interior was an unbroken wilderness. We counted thirteen feeble States. Facilities for internal communication, there were next to none. At certain seasons of the year a journey from Philadelphia to Washington required a space of time and involved an amount of peril and discomfort which now seem to us incredible. I will not so far trifle with your patience as to enlarge this picture of rude weakness and destitution, which has been of late quite sufficiently dwelt upon.

Well, the first century of national existence has passed away, and what do we behold? This picture, too, has been, perhaps, abundantly exhibited. The wilderness and the solitary places have been peopled with busy, thriving populations—with a vast multitude, consisting of a fusion of all nations. In place of those impracticable highways once to be found even between the leading cities of the nation, we travel in what are called "palace cars," "drawing-room" cars, over metallic roads, not merely between the chief towns in the central portions of the country, but from the shores of the Atlantic to the borders of the Pacific, from the further extremity of Maine to the remotest borders of Texas and Mexico, from the Lakes to the Gulf of Mexico. Everywhere the luxurious accommodation spares us fatigue, and multiplies tenfold our power to labor. The once inaccessible mountains yield up their treasures; the vast Western plains send their immense golden harvests to the populous cities on the borders of the sea, or across the sea to the needy nations of the Old World; vast populations, which in foreign countries had for ages lived in grinding poverty, with no hope of change for their children, having bid adieu to their native land, having braved unknown seas and strange climates, and having trusted themselves to an untried government and nation, are now seen dwelling together in peace and competence, admitted to the privileges of a free people, and many of them rising to positions of wealth and honor. Suddenly, (for what is a *century* in the history of a nation?)—suddenly, as if by a miracle, a mighty nation has sprung up—mighty for multitude, for material power and energy, notable for a quick, sharp intelligence, brave and resolute in prosecuting worldly enterprises, and not altogether insensible, I hope, to spiritual interests at home and abroad.

My dear Brethren, if we look at what *Divine Providence* has done for us—the magnificent country assigned to us, the many and extraordinary deliverances vouchsafed to us, the wise, virtuous and magnanimous patriots raised up to enlighten and guide us in the early and difficult periods of our history—we can only say, as for the Lord our God, the Supreme Creator and Governor of the World, He hath done *His* part toward us most graciously, most munificently, most mercifully! He might say of *us*, as He said of His chosen people, Israel, so wonderfully delivered, guided, succored by him: "What could have been done more to My vineyard that I have not done in it?" Yes! The Lord most High hath done *His part* toward this land with a lavish goodness. He hath dispensed His favors to us most liberally. If we turn to consider our history and our condition on the side of *human agency*, and inquire how *man* has played *his* part toward securing the honor and true welfare of the nation, we feel bound to recognise great services, great acrifices given for the conservation of all that we hold lear in civil life. We cannot but pay a tribute of admi- ation and respect to the wonderful *energy*, courage, en- erprise of this people in surmounting obstacles, in naking rough places smooth, in binding together far- distant States and oceans, in causing beauty and abun- dance to spring up in the wilderness and the desert.

And if we are constrained to acknowledge that these extraordinary energies, this brave spirit of enterprise, have sometimes run into frenzied excitements, impelling to most extravagant undertakings, which could not but endanger private fortunes, troubling the peace of families and the public credit; if high character has sometimes yielded to great temptations; if the service of the country has sometimes turned into corruption, through ambition and the love of *pelf;* what are all these sad blemishes on the surface of the nation's life but melancholy proofs of the infirmity of our nature—a stern *reminder* of the great lesson, applicable to nations (whatever their form of government) as to individuals: "Let him that thinketh he standeth take heed lest he fall?"

And so, my dear Brethren, if we have abundant cause for thankfulness to the Giver of all Good for His manifold and great gifts to us; if we have just reason to felicitate ourselves upon the privilege of belonging to a family endowed with many distinguished qualities, yet we have, at the same time, reason to humble ourselves at the view of our short-comings in the past, and to seriously consider what we can do in the future to guard against our besetting weaknesses and sins; how we can pour into the religious and social atmosphere elements that will make the national life more pure and healthful, more temperate, more inflexibly faithful to all the requirements of truth and duty toward God and toward man.

We can all do something, the feeblest as well as the strongest, toward making our *Religion* more than it is among us—a great and all-pervading *reality*, a reality tested not by feelings and excitements, but by an entire, loving, cheerful conformity to the whole will of God, seen in our business, our social relations, our relaxations, our political concerns, our care for God's Church and for His poor.

And then the *Education* of the young in the family and in the school. I confess I wish there were more marked approbation and more rewards bestowed upon faithful, loving *dutifulness*, transparent truth, self-denying kindness, and fewer stimulating premiums offered for mere intellectual sharpness, for *victory* in a competitive examination. Education, in the case of the young, is not the mere receiving and storing up of facts and principles. It is the *formation of habits*—moral, intellectual, religious. Habits of emulation—living and striving to pass others in the race of life, and to establish a superior position among men for wealth, power, rank—such habits make a poor life and a poor character open to great temptations; such habits of feeling and acting open the way, if they do not lead directly on to, chicanery and corruption. Teach the boys and girls in your families and in your schools that the supreme aim should be not so much to rise to true excellence in knowledge and in moral conduct, as to be the *first* among equals, to surpass others in the competitions of life, and you educate a nation of boys and girls, soon to be a nation of men and women, who will be restless, aspiring, excitable, prone to envy and jealousy, ready to seize upon every possible means of gaining the first place. Innocence, true goodness, a noble manhood or womanhood, cannot result from such training.

And if it must be admitted, as I fear it must, that our form of government, with all its excellencies, does favor high excitements, passionate competitions, then it seems to me there is the more reason why our children, our *young America*, should be habituated in the family and in the school, to live and labor not with a view to *success* in the field of competition, but from a deep sense of the value of knowledge in itself, and for its own sake, and from a love of the good, the true, the inherent beauty of excellence, apart from all outward rewards, gains or losses.

But, my dear Brethren, I must break off from this most momentous subject, which is altogether too complex and great a subject to be adequately dealt with in the closing portions of such an address as this.

Ah, my dear Brethren, little did I dream three days ago that I should come to this hour so oppressed with grief as I now find myself. Death has rushed into our circle in his most appalling form, and has struck down one of the best and dearest and most valuable of our number. The Rev. George B. Draper, D. D., for many years Rector of St. Andrew's Church, Harlem—one of our ablest, most faithful, and highly valued clergymen—died on Sunday morning last, the 24th of September, of small-pox; and owing to the nature of the disease, his mortal remains were on the same day laid in the grave, before any but a very few of his friends knew any thing of his illness. And to add to the harrowing features of the visitation, when he was taken away, he left behind him in his earthly home the frightful malady which had been the instrument in removing him from this present scene of labor. I am sure the afflicted widow and interesting family of children will have your sympathy and your earnest prayers. God comfort them! God help them! A few years ago Dr. Draper's character was subjected to a severe ordeal. His church was laid in ashes; and to keep his congregation together, and to prudently and energetically conduct the work of erecting a new edifice worthy of the congregation, and of the position, churchly and becoming, without extravagance, without ruinous debt, the attachment of the People to the Pastor all the time increasing, that was to make a history which could leave no doubt as to the qualities of mind and heart of the Rector. Every year by his transparent integrity, his devotion to his work, his modesty and independence, his truth and loyalty, he won upon my respect and love more and more; and to-day I feel his removal as a great personal loss. While we lovingly cherish his memory, let us try to imitate his virtues.

The past season, on account of the excessive and long continued heat, has been a trying one, but the mortality among the Clergy, compared with that of other years, has not been great.

I have to record the death of the Rev. Kingston Goddard, D. D., Rector of St. Andrew's, Richmond, S. I.

The Rev. William Morris, LL. D., formerly for many years Rector of Trinity School, New-York, but in later years long in failing health.

The Rev. Charles F. Rodenstein, M. D., of West Farms; and

The Rev. Henry H. Bean, Rector of St. Luke's, Rossville, Staten Island.

And during the past year the Church has lost that lovely Christian gentleman and fervent preacher of the Gospel, the Right Reverend John Johns, D. D., Bishop of Virginia. He had attained to a good old age, and continued to exercise his winning, persuasive ministry, up to very near the close of his life.

Having referred to the excessive and long continued heat of the past Summer, which, when accompanied by severe drought, makes the daily exercise of the episcopal office a severe duty, I cannot but return my thanks to the Clergy, and to the Laity also, for the kind and considerate ways in which they sought to lessen inconveniences and fatigue, and to facilitate my movements. Nor can I be insensible to the gracious Providence which through such a season has watched over me, and preserved me from every accident and indisposition which could unfit me for the work I had to do.

My dear Brethren, last year I closed my address to the Convention with a few words in reference to the Fund for the relief of the Aged and Infirm Clergy—*Aged and Infirm!* Do we need any other words to touch our feelings, and move us to an earnest, energetic discharge of the duty which we owe to our faithful, our suffering Brethren? Can we be willing to allow the cheerful day of our annual Thanksgiving, the appropriate day recommended by the Church for making an offering to the Fund for the Relief of our Aged and Infirm Brethren; can we allow such a day to come and go without remembering the Aged and Infirm?

During the Conventional year preceding the one just closed, *payments* more than $1,000 in excess of the receipts were made to the Clergy having claims on that fund; and there were no expenses for management. I believe something like the same state of facts is repeated this year.

My dear Brethren, I think I am safe in saying, that among our Clergy and Laity also, not only in this Diocese but in all our Dioceses, there is an universal conviction that in no one thing is our Church more lacking than in *an adequate provision for the Aged and Infirm Clergy*. Whether we think of the young who are just considering the question of embracing the ministry as their life-long work, and who, as well as their friends, may very naturally ask what is the prospect of sympathy and support, should they survive until through age and infirmity they shall become incapable of further labor, and who may not feel able to embrace a career of severe duty which is to close with an old age of neglect, poverty, and suffering; or whether we look simply to the claims of common humanity, to Christian obligation to our aged, worn-out Pastors, we must feel that there is no claim upon us as Churchmen, as Christians, so sacred as is the claim of our Aged and Infirm Pastors. And yet, my dear Brethren, the Journal of our last Convention seems to show, that out of all our Parishes only about ninety reported any contribution to that most sacred of all our Funds. I do not believe that the omission was intentional. I do not believe that it resulted from deliberate design. I rather think that in many cases it occurred through inadvertence, or through the distracting pressure of many claims and objects. And I have faith to believe that at the approaching Thanksgiving you will unite with one heart in giving even out of your poverty, if it must be so, before you give to any thing else, before you taste one of God's bounties,—unite in giving something to help brighten the last days of the worn Laborers in the Vineyard of the Lord your God. *So may it be!*

DETAILED ACCOUNT OF VISITATIONS AND ACTS.

The following is an account of the places visited and the Episcopal Acts performed by me since the last Convention:

1875. *Oct.* 4, *Monday.*—In Calvary Church, New York, I solemnized a marriage.

Oct. 10, *Twentieth Sunday after Trinity*, A. M.—In St. Philip's Church, New-York, I instituted the Rev. Joseph S. Atwell, the Rev. Dr. Gallaudet preaching.

Oct. 11, *Monday*, P. M.—I presided at a meeting of the Standing Committee of the General Theological Seminary, New York.

Oct. 17, *Twenty-first Sunday after Trinity*, A. M.—In the Church of the Ascension, New-York, at a special ordination, the Rector preaching, I advanced to the Priesthood the Rev. Elijah Winchester Donald, late assistant minister of said Church, and now Rector of the Church of the Intercession, New-York.

Oct. 22, *Friday*, Evening.—In St. John's Church, Kingston, I preached, confirmed *five*, and briefly addressed them.

Oct. 23, *Saturday.*—I addressed the students of St. Stephen's College, Annandale.

Oct. 24, *Twenty-second Sunday after Trinity*, A. M.—In the Church of the Messiah, Rhinebeck, I preached, confirmed *eight*, and addressed them.

Oct. 25, 26, 27, 28, 29.—Portions of these days I was occupied with a meeting of the Board of Missions, New-York, and afterwards with the meeting of the House of Bishops.

Oct. 31, *Twenty-third Sunday after Trinity*, A. M.—In St. Mary's Church, Castleton, Staten Island, I confirmed *fourteen*, and addressed them.

P. M.—In St. Ambrose Church, New-York, after an interesting service in Italian, I confirmed *eighty-five*, and addressed them. This is an interesting and encouraging Italian Mission.

Nov. 1, *All Saints.*—I gave my Canonical consent to the consecration of the Rev. W. E. McLaren, D. D., as Bishop of Illinois, and to the consecration of the Rev. James H. Eccleston, D. D., as Bishop of Iowa.

Nov. 2, *Tuesday*, P. M.—In Christ Church, Sufferns, I confirmed *eight*, and addressed them.

Nov. 7, *Twenty-fourth Sunday after Trinity*, Evening.—In the Church of Transfiguration, New-York, I presided at a meeting in behalf of the Mission

Work of the Western Convocation, and made a few remarks. Addresses by the Rev. M. Capron, Dean of the Western Convocation, and by Bishop Talbot, of Indiana.

On same day, *six* persons were confirmed in Christ Church, Riverdale, by the Bishop of Rhode Island.

Nov. 14, *Twenty-fifth Sunday after Trinity,* A. M.—In Trinity Church, St. Louis, I preached.

Nov. 21, *Twenty-sixth Sunday after Trinity,* A. M.—In the Cathedral Church, Chicago, I assisted in the service, celebrating the Holy Eucharist.

Nov. 27, *Saturday,* A. M.—In Trinity Chapel, New-York, I took part in the funeral service of Mr. Wm. B. Astor.

Nov. 28, *Advent Sunday,* Evening.—I presided at a service in behalf of the Sunday School Association. Sermon by the Right Rev. the Bishop of Central New-York.

Nov. 30, *Tuesday,* Evening.—In the Mission Chapel, at Kent Cliffs, I preached, and confirmed *sixteen,* and addressed them, *eight* had, during the service, been baptized. This work has largely been done by the members of one or two earnest Christian families.

Dec. 6, *Monday.*—I presided at a meeting of the Trustees of Columbia College, New-York.

Dec. 7, *Tuesday,* Evening.—In Trinity Church, Haverstraw, I preached, confirmed *fifteen,* (*five* of them from St. Luke's Church, Haverstraw,) and addressed them.

Dec. 8, *Wednesday.*—At the House of the Good Shepherd, New-York, I confirmed *nine,* and addressed them.

Dec. 9, *Thursday,* A. M.—In Christ Church, Poughkeepsie, I met the Dutchess County Convocation, the Rev. Mr. Platt preaching. I celebrated the Holy Eucharist, and presided at a business meeting of the Convocation.

Dec. 10, *Friday,* Evening.—In Grace Church, Port Jervis, I preached, confirmed *thirty-one,* and addressed them.

Dec. 12, *Third Sunday in Advent,* Evening.—In the Church of the Nativity, New-York, devoted at that hour to the German service, I confirmed *thirty-one,* and briefly addressed them. This German work, in which the Clergyman has been assisted by the Sisters of St. John Baptist, is a most gratifying and encouraging one.

Dec. 13, *Monday,* P. M.—In the Chapel of St. Mary's School, (the Sisters,) New-York, I confirmed *one* person.

Dec. 15, *Wednesday.*—In St. John's Church, Cohoes, I officiated as Consecrator, at the consecration of the Rev. John Henry Hobart Brown, S. T. D., as Bishop of the Diocese of Fond Du Lac, the Right Rev. the Bishop of Wisconsin preaching.

Dec. 19, *Fourth Sunday in Advent,* A. M.—In the Chapel of St. Chrysostom, New-York, I preached, and advanced to the Priesthood the Rev Alfred Evan Johnson, the Rev. Moses Turner Ashton, the Rev. Joseph H. Young, the Rev. Edward H. Van Winkle, and, acting for the Bishop of Long Island, the Rev. Spencer S. Roche, of that Diocese.

Dec. 21, *St. Thomas' Day*, P. M.—In West Farms, in Grace Church, I confirmed *twenty-one*, and addressed them.

Jan. 2, *Second Sunday after Christmas*, A. M.—In St. Peter's Church, Philadelphia, I took part in the service, celebrating the Holy Eucharist, assisted by the Rector.

Jan. 9, *First Sunday after the Epiphany*, A. M.—In St. Mark's Church, Philadelphia, I took part in the service, celebrating the Holy Eucharist, assisted by the Rector.

Jan. 16, *Second Sunday after the Epiphany*, A. M.—In St. Mary's Church, Mott Haven, I preached.

Jan. 23, *Third Sunday after Epiphany*.—In St. Mary's Church, Manhattanville, I said a few words to the congregation, confirmed *eight*, and addressed them.

Jan. 24, *Monday*, A. M.—In the Church of the Transfiguration, New-York, I officiated at a funeral.

Jan. 29, *Saturday*.—In Albany, I took part in the funeral services for an old friend and parishioner.

Jan. 30, *Fourth Sunday after the Epiphany*, A. M.—In the Church of the Transfiguration, New-York, I assisted in the services, celebrating the Holy Eucharist.

Feb. 4, *Friday*, P. M.—I met the Foreign Committee.

Feb. 6, *Fifth Sunday after the Epiphany*, A. M.—I took part in the services in Grace Church, New-York, celebrating the Holy Eucharist.

Evening.—In St. Barnabas' Chapel, New-York, at a special confirmation, I confirmed *one* person, and preached. I also confirmed, in private, *two* persons connected with St. Barnabas'.

Feb. 7, *Monday*, P. M.—I met the Trustees of Columbia College.

Feb. 13, *Septuagesima Sunday*, P. M.—In Zion Church, New-York, I presided at a service in the interest of Mission Work in this Diocese, and made a brief address to the congregation. Addresses were also made by the Rector of the Church, and by the Rev. Mr. Valentine, of Ellenville.

Feb. 17, *Thursday*, P. M.—In the Chapel of the Alms House, on Blackwell's Island, I confirmed *nineteen*, and addressed them.

Feb. 18, *Thursday*, A. M.—In the Church of the Ascension, New-York, I officiated in the last offices for an aged and highly valued member of the Church.

Feb. 27, *Quinquagesima Sunday*, P. M.—In the Seamen's Floating Chapel of our Saviour, I confirmed *thirty-four*, and addressed them.

Feb. 29, *Tuesday*—I confirmed *one* person in private.

March 6, *Monday*.—I attended a meeting of the Trustees of Columbia College, New-York.

March 9, *Thursday*.—I met in St. Paul's Church, Poughkeepsie, the Dutchess County Convocation, the Rev. Dr. Purdy, of Hyde Park, preaching.

March 12, *Second Sunday in Lent*, A. M.—In Calvary Free Mission Chapel, New-York, the Rev. Dr. Eigenbrodt preaching, I admitted to the Diaconate Dan Marvin, of this Diocese, and William White Wilson and Robert Bayard

Snowden, of Long Island, at the request of the Standing Committee of that Diocese, in the absence of the Bishop.

P. M.—In St. Stephen's Church, New-York, I preached, confirmed *nineteen*, and addressed them.

March 13, *Monday*, P. M.—I confirmed a sick person in private.

March 14, *Tuesday*, P. M.—In Grace Church, New-York, I solemnized a marriage.

March 19, *Third Sunday in Lent*, A. M.—In St. Clement's Church, New-York, I preached, confirmed *thirty-two*, and addressed them, and visited the Infirmary of the Parish.

P. M., *at two o'clock*.—I officiated at a funeral at Grace Church, New-York.

At four P. M.—In the Church of the Annunciation, New-York, I confirmed *eighteen*, and addressed them.

March 25, *Saturday*, *Feast of the Annunciation*, A. M.—In the Chapel of St. Mary's School, New-York, I received *three* probationers into the Sisterhood of St. Mary, and celebrated the Holy Eucharist.

March 26, *Fourth Sunday in Lent*, A. M.—In St. Paul's Church, Morrisania, I preached, confirmed *seventeen*, and addressed them.

Evening.—In the Church of the Redeemer, New-York, I confirmed *twenty-two*, and addressed them.

March 28, *Tuesday*, Evening.—In St. Peter's Church, Westchester, I confirmed *twenty*, and addressed them.

March 29, *Wednesday*, Evening.—In St. Paul's Church, Edgewater, Staten Island, I confirmed *forty-four*, (*two* of them in private,) and addressed them.

March 30, *Thursday*, Evening.—In the Church of our Saviour, New-York, I confirmed *thirteen*, and addressed them.

March 31, *Friday*, Evening.—In the Church of St. John Baptist, Glenham, I preached, confirmed *thirteen*, (*one* of them in private,) and addressed them.

April 2, *Fifth Sunday in Lent*, A. M.—In the Church of the Holy Apostles, New-York, I confirmed *nineteen*, (*one* of them from the Church of the Holy Trinity, New-York,) and addressed them.

P. M.—In the Church of St. John Baptist, New-York, I confirmed *six*, (*one* of them from the Church of the Redeemer, New-York,) and addressed them.

Evening.—In St Peter's Church, New-York, I confirmed *sixty-two*, and addressed them.

April 4, *Tuesday*, Evening.—In St. George's English Mission Chapel, New-York, I confirmed *twenty-three*, and addressed them, and, at my request, they were also addressed by the Rev. Dr. Tyng, Rector of the Parent Church.

April 5, *Wednesday*, Evening.—In the Church of the Heavenly Rest, New-York, I confirmed *nineteen*, and addressed them.

April 6, *Thursday*, P. M—In the Church of the Intercession, New-York, I confirmed *seventeen*, and addressed them.

Evening.—In St. George's German Mission Chapel, New-York, I confirmed *forty-four*, and briefly addressed them, and, at my request, they were addressed by the Rev. Dr. Tyng, the Rector of the Parent Parish.

April 7, *Friday*, Evening.—In St. Peter's Church, Peekskill, I confirmed *forty four*, (*one* of them from Grace Church, White Plains,) and addressed them.

April 8, *Saturday*, A. M.—In Trinity Chapel, New-York, I officiated at a funeral.

P. M.—At the Midnight Mission, New-York, I confirmed *seven*, and addressed them.

April 9, *Sunday before Easter*, A. M.—In St. Thomas' Church, New-York, I confirmed *fifty-six*, and addressed them.

P. M.—In Calvary Church, New-York, I confirmed *twenty*, and addressed them.

Evening.—In the Church of the Messiah, Brooklyn, at the request of the Standing Committee of Long Island, (in the absence of the Bishop,) I preached, confirmed *forty seven*, and addressed them.

April 10, *Monday*, P. M.—In Trinity Church, Sing Sing, I confirmed *twenty-one*, and addressed them.

Evening.—In St. Paul's Church, Sing Sing, I confirmed *ten*, and briefly addressed them.

April 11, *Tuesday*, Evening.—In St. Luke's Church, New-York, I confirmed *forty six*, and addressed them. The church has been enlarged and much improved, and is now in admirable order.

April 12, *Wednesday*, A. M.—In St. Bartholomew's Church, New-York, I confirmed *twenty-one*, (*one* of them from the Church of the Holy Innocents, Highland Falls,) and addressed them briefly.

Evening.—In St. Timothy's Church, New-York, I preached, confirmed *twenty-one*, and addressed them.

April 13, *Thursday*, A. M.—I officiated at a funeral.

P. M.—In the Church of the Atonement, New-York, I confirmed *twenty-three*.

Evening.—In St. Paul's Chapel, New-York, I confirmed *fifty-three*.

April 14, *Good Friday*, A. M.—In St. George's Church, New-York, the Rector preaching, I confirmed *fifty*, (some of whom were from St. George's English Chapel of " The Bread of Life,") and briefly addressed them.

P. M.—In St. John's Church, Clifton, Staten Island, I confirmed *twenty-three*, and briefly addressed them.

Evening.—In the Church of the Holy Trinity, New-York, I confirmed *two hundred and seventy-three*, and addressed them; and, at my request, they were also addressed by the Rev. Dr. Tyng, Sen.

April 15, *Easter Even*, A. M.—In the Church of the Holy Communion, New-York, I confirmed *fifty one*, and addressed them.

P. M.—In Trinity Church, New-York, I confirmed *seventy-four*, and briefly addressed them.

Evening.—In St. John's Church, Yonkers, I confirmed *sixty-four*, and addressed them.

April 16, *Easter Day*, A. M.—In All Saints' Church, New-York, I confirmed *twenty-eight*, and addressed them, and celebrated the Holy Eucharist, assisted by the Rector.

P. M.—In Christ Church, New-York, at a special confirmation, I confirmed *fourteen*, and addressed them.

Evening.—In the Wainwright Memorial Church of St. John the Evangelist, I confirmed *forty-four*, and addressed them.

April 17, *Easter Monday*, A. M.—In the Church of the Ascension, New-York, I confirmed *twenty-four*, and addressed them briefly.

April 18, *Easter Tuesday*, Evening.—In St. Mary's Church, Mott Haven, I preached, confirmed *twelve*, and addressed them.

April 19, *Wednesday*, Evening.—In St. Philip's Church, New-York, I confirmed *forty-two*, and addressed them.

April 20, *Thursday*, Evening.—In Grace Church Chapel, New-York, I confirmed *twenty-two*, and addressed them.

April 21, *Friday*, Evening.—In the Chapel of the Shepherd's Flock, New-York, I confirmed *fifty-nine*, and addressed them.

April 23, *First Sunday after Easter*, A. M.—In St. John's Chapel, (Trinity Parish,) New-York, I confirmed *one hundred and fourteen*, and addressed them.

P. M.—In the Church of the Holy Innocents, (a new Mission at 141st-street and Eighth Avenue,) New-York, I confirmed *twelve*, and addressed them

Evening.—In Trinity Chapel, New-York, I confirmed *sixty-one*, (*one* of them from Trinity Church,) and addressed them.

April 24, *Monday*, Evening.—In the Church of the Epiphany, New-York, I confirmed *nine*, and addressed them.

April 26, *Wednesday*, Evening.—In the Chapel of St. Chrysostom, (Trinity Parish,) New-York, I confirmed *fifty-one*, and addressed them.

April 27, *Thursday*, P. M.—In the Trinity Infirmary, New-York, I confirmed *five* sick persons.

Evening.—In St. James' Church, New-York, I confirmed *twenty-two*, and addressed them.

April 28, *Friday*.—In the Church of the Holy Innocents, Highland Falls, (West Point,) I confirmed *twenty-three*, and addressed them.

April 30, *Second Sunday after Easter*, A. M.—In Christ Church, Poughkeepsie, I preached, confirmed *thirty-six*, and addressed them.

P. M.—In St. Paul's Church, Poughkeepsie, I preached, confirmed *twelve*, and addressed them.

Evening.—In the Church of the Holy Comforter, Poughkeepsie, I confirmed *twenty-five*, and addressed them.

May 1, *Monday*, A. M.—In Poughkeepsie, I confirmed, separately, *two* sick persons connected with the Church of the Holy Comforter.

May 2, *Tuesday*, P. M.—In St. Mark's Church, Carthage Landing, I confirmed *twenty*, and briefly addressed them.

Evening.—In Zion Church, Wappinger's Falls, I confirmed *sixty-six*, and addressed them.

May 3, *Wednesday*, P. M.—In St. Luke's Church, Matteawan, I confirmed *nine*, and briefly addressed them.

May 4, *Thursday*, A. M.—In the Church of the Transfiguration, New-York, I baptized an infant.

Evening.—In St. Thomas' Mission Chapel, New-York, I confirmed *thirty-eight*, (*one* of them from St. Thomas' Church,) and addressed them.

May 7, Third Sunday after Easter, A. M.—In the Church of the Holy Sepulchre, New-York, I confirmed *eleven*, and addressed them.

P. M.—In St. Ann's Church, New-York, I confirmed *fifty-two*, (*twenty-three* of them deaf mutes,) and addressed them.

P. M., later.—In St. Ambrose Church, New-York, the Italian Mission, I confirmed *thirteen*.

Evening.—In Calvary Free Mission Chapel, New-York, I confirmed *thirty*, and addressed them.

May 9, Tuesday, Evening.—In the Anthon Memorial Church, New-York, I confirmed *twenty*, and briefly addressed them.

May 10, Wednesday, P. M.—I attended, as Pall Bearer, the funeral of the Rev. Dr. Sprague.

Evening.—In the Church of St. Ignatius, New-York, I confirmed *forty-eight*, and addressed them.

May 12, Friday, Evening.—In the Chapel of St. Augustine, (Trinity Parish,) New-York, I confirmed *thirty-one*, (*one* of them in private, and *nine* of them from St. Paul's Chapel,) and addressed them.

May 14, Fourth Sunday after Easter, A. M.—In St. Mark's Church in the Bowery, New-York, I confirmed *seventy-one*, (*forty* of them from the Mission Chapel,) and addressed them.

P. M.—In the Church of the Holy Trinity, Harlem, I confirmed *twenty-nine*, and addressed them.

Evening, 7 o'clock.—In the Church of the Nativity, New-York, I confirmed *fifteen*.

At 8 o'clock, in the same Church, after a German Service, I confirmed *seventeen*, and briefly addressed them.

May 16, Tuesday, Evening.—In Christ Church, Tarrytown, I preached, confirmed *thirty-two*, and addressed them.

May 17, Wednesday, Evening.—In Grace Church, White Plains, I preached, confirmed *fifteen*, and addressed them.

May 18, Thursday, Evening.—In the Church of St Ambrose, New-York, I confirmed *twenty*, and addressed them.

May 19, Friday, Evening.—In Grace Church, City Island, I confirmed *ten*, and addressed them.

May 21, Fifth Sunday after Trinity, A. M.—In the Church of the Transfiguration, New-York, I confirmed *twenty-seven*, and addressed them.

In Grace Church, Harlem, I preached, confirmed *ten*, and briefly addressed them

In St. Andrew's Church, Harlem, I confirmed *twenty-one*, (*one* from Holy Trinity Church, Harlem, and *one* from Grace Church, Harlem, *two* belonging to St. Andrew's Church, separately, in private,) and addressed them.

May 24, Wednesday, Evening.—In St. Barnabas' Chapel, New-York, I confirmed *twenty-two*, and addressed them.

May 25, Ascension Day, A. M.—In Zion Church, New-York, I confirmed *twelve*, addressed them, and celebrated the Holy Eucharist, assisted by the Rector.

Evening.—In the Church of the Incarnation, I confirmed *twenty-six*, and addressed them.

May 26, *Friday*, Evening.—In St. Mark's Church, Tarrytown, I confirmed *twelve*, and addressed them.

May 27, *Saturday*, A. M.—In Christ Church, Pelham, I preached, confirmed and addressed them.

May 28, *Sunday after the Ascension*, A. M.—In Christ Church, Rye, I preached, confirmed *twenty three*, (*one* of them in private,) and addressed them.

P. M.—In St. Thomas' Church, Mamaroneck, I preached, confirmed *eight*, and addressed them.

May 29, *Monday*, Evening.—In St. Mark's Church, Brooklyn, E. D., (officiating at the request of the Standing Committee of Long Island, in the absence of the Bishop,) I confirmed *twenty-three*, (*four* of them from St. Mary's Church, Brooklyn, *one* from St. Luke's Church, Brooklyn, and addressed them.

May 30, *Tuesday*, Evening.—In the Bethlehem Mission Chapel, (German,) New-York, I confirmed *eleven*, and addressed them.

May 31, *Wednesday*, Evening.—In St. James' Church, Fordham, I confirmed *twenty-one*, and addressed them.

June 1, *Thursday*, Evening.—In the Church of St. Mary the Virgin, New-York, I confirmed *twenty-five*, (*three*, from the Chapel of the Holy Saviour, and *one* from the Church of the Redeemer,) and addressed them.

June 2, *Friday*, Evening.—In the Chapel of the Reconciliation, (of the Church of the Incarnation,) New-York, I confirmed *twenty-two*, and addressed them.

June 4, *Whitsun-Day*, A. M.—In Christ Church, New-Brighton, Staten Island, I confirmed *fourteen*, and addressed them, and celebrated the Holy Eucharist, assisted by the Rector.

P. M.—In the Church of the Ascension, West New-Brighton, I confirmed *eighteen*, and addressed them.

June 6, *Tuesday*, Evening —In the Church of the Holy Trinity, New-York, I confirmed (at a second visitation) *one hundred and seventy-five*, and briefly addressed them.

June 7, *Wednesday*, P. M.—In Grace Church, Monroe, I preached, confirmed *five*, and addressed them.

Evening —In Christ Church, Warwick, I preached, confirmed *five*, and addressed them.

June 8, *Thursday*, P. M.—In St. James' Church, Goshen, I confirmed *fifteen*, and addressed them.

Evening.—In Grace Church, Middletown, after a few words to the congregation, I confirmed *forty*, and addressed them.

June 9, *Friday*, Evening.—In Grace Church, Walden, I preached, confirmed *eight*, and addressed them.

June 11, *Trinity Sunday*, A M —In St. Ann's Church, Morrisania, I confirmed *fourteen*, and addressed them.

P. M.—In St. Barnabas' Church, Brooklyn, (acting at the request of the Standing Committee of Long Island, in the absence of the Bishop,) I confirmed *twenty-nine*, (*one* of them from St. George's Church, Brooklyn,) and addressed them.

Evening.—In St. Luke's Church, Brooklyn, in the presence of the United Congregations of St. Luke's and St. Mary's Churches, I confirmed a large class, (St. George's, *eighteen*, St. Mary's, *twenty-six*, St. Luke's, *twenty-six*, —total, *seventy*,) and addressed them—a very interesting occasion.

June 18, *First Sunday after Trinity*, A. M.—In Trinity Church, Saugerties, I preached, confirmed *thirty-three*, and addressed them.

Evening.—In the Church of the Holy Spirit, Rondout, I preached, confirmed *thirty one*, and addressed them.

June 19, *Monday*, A. M.—In St John's Church, Kingston, I confirmed *twelve*, and addressed them.

4 P. M.—In the Church of the Ascension, Rhinecliff, I confirmed *two*.

June 20, *Tuesday*, Evening.—In Trinity Church, Tivoli, I confirmed *six*, and addressed them.

June 21, 22, *Wednesday and Thursday*.—St. Stephen's College.

June 22, *Thursday*, Evening.—In the Memorial Chapel of St. John Baptist, Barrytown, I confirmed *nine*, and addressed them.

June 25, *Second Sunday after Trinity*, A. M.—In St. Matthew's Church, Bedford, I preached, confirmed *twelve*, and addressed them.

Evening.—In St. Stephen's Church, Armonck, I confirmed *eight*, and addressed them.

June 27, *Tuesday*, Evening.—In Trinity Church, Mount Vernon, I confirmed *eight*, and addressed them.

July 2, *Third Sunday after Trinity*.—In the Church of the Transfiguration, New-York, I admitted to the Diaconate Oliver Perry Vinton, A B., Leighton Parks, Charles Lancaster Short, A. M., Gustav Arnold Carstensen, A. B, Frederick Henry Townsend Horsfield, A. B., Charles Robert Stroh, A. B., Charles Sandford Olmsted, John Sword, George Coutts Athole, William Henry Tomlins, A. B, and I advanced to the Priesthood the Rev. Julius W. Paige. Sermon by the Rev. Dr. Geer.

P. M—In the Church of the Beloved Disciple, New-York, I confirmed *nine*, and addressed them.

Evening.—In the Mission Chapel of the Church of the Atonement, New-York, I made a visit of inspection, and delivered a brief address.

July 9, *Fourth Sunday after Trinity*, A. M.—In St. Michael's Church, New York, I confirmed *twenty-two*, addressed them, and celebrated the Holy Eucharist, assisted by the Rector.

July 11, *Tuesday*, A. M.—In the Church of the Holy Comforter, Southfield, Staten Island, I preached, confirmed *fifteen*, and addressed them.

P. M.—I visited the Parish of St. Luke's, Rossville, but owing to a misapprehension, there was no service.

July 16, *Sunday*, A. M.—In St. Philip's Church in the Highlands, I preached, confirmed *fourteen*, and addressed them.

July 17, *Monday*, Evening.—In Trinity Church, Haverstraw, I preached, confirmed *seventeen*, and addressed them.

July 18, *Tuesday*, Evening.—In Grace Church, Port Jervis, I confirmed *eleven*, and addressed them.

July 20, *Thursday*, Evening.—In St. John's Church, Monticello, I preached, confirmed *twenty-nine*, and addressed them.

July 21, *Friday*, P. M.—On my way from Monticello to Ellenville, I confirmed *two* persons, (*one* of them sick,) belonging to St. John's Church, Monticello.

July 21, *Friday*, Evening.—In St. Paul's Church, Ellenville, I preached, confirmed *twenty-four*, and addressed them.

July 23, *Sixth Sunday after Trinity*, A. M.—In All Saints' Church, Milton, Ulster county, I preached, confirmed *two*, and celebrated the Holy Eucharist, assisted by the Rector.

P. M.—In the Holy Trinity Church, Highland, I confirmed *twelve*, and addressed them.

July 25, *Tuesday*, P. M.—In Christ Church, Red Hook, I confirmed *twelve*, and addressed them.

July 29, *Saturday*.—I certified my Canonical consent to the consecration of the Rev. William Stevens Perry, D. D., Bishop elect of Iowa.

August 13, *Ninth Sunday after Trinity*, A. M.—I preached in the newly erected Church at Rye Beach.

P. M.—I took part in the service in the same Church.

September 2, *Saturday*, P. M.—The Rev. Dr. Dix, at my request, laid the corner-stone of the Chapel of St. Augustine, (Trinity Parish,) New-York.

September 3, *Twelfth Sunday after Trinity*, A. M.—I preached in Rye Beach, and officiated at the P. M. service.

September 10, *Thirteenth Sunday after Trinity*, A. M.—In Zion Church, Greenburgh, I preached, confirmed *six*, and briefly addressed them.

September 14, *Thursday*, A. M.—In the Chapel of St. Mary's School, New-York, I received *two* probationers into the Sisterhood of St. Mary, and celebrated the Holy Eucharist, assisted by the Rev. Dr. Houghton.

Evening.—In St. Paul's Church, Newburgh, I confirmed *fourteen*, and addressed them.

September 15, *Friday*, P. M.—In St. James' Church, Hyde Park, I confirmed *twenty-two*, and addressed them. This was a very interesting class of young persons, and the service was all the more touching, as being nearly the last before the removal of the Rector to another Diocese.

September 18, *Monday*, Evening.—In Grace Church, Nyack, I confirmed *ten*, and addressed them.

September 25, *Monday*, A. M.—I consecrated Grace Chapel, Mission Chapel of Grace Church, New-York, a very admirable structure, with appliance and convenience for Mission work. Sermon by the Rev. Dr. Potter, Rector of Grace Church.

P. M.—I presided at a meeting of the Foreign Committee.

Evening.—I presided at a meeting of the Society for Promoting Religion and Learning.

CANDIDATES FOR HOLY ORDERS.

he following is a complete List of the Candidates for Holy Orders in this ese, with the dates of their admission respectively; being in all, 40.

I.—CANDIDATES FOR DEACON'S AND PRIEST'S ORDERS.

George B. Johnson, A. B., June 1, 1871.
William Henry Conover, A. B., August 3, 1871.
Henry Stoughton Tracy, A. B., { C. D. O., September 27, 1871. C. P. O., November 2, 1871. }
Edgar Snyder, A. B., December 5, 1872.
John Punnett Peters, A. B., September 4, 1873.
Henry Van Rensselaer, September 18, 1873.
William Oliver Embury, November 6, 1873.
Henry Townsend Scudder, A. B., June 4, 1874.
George H. Wilson, A. B., September 30, 1874.
Victor C. Smith, A. B , September 30, 1874.
Edwin C. Alcorn, A. B., November 5, 1874.
John Quick Archdeacon, A. B., November 5, 1874.
Richard Hamilton, A. B. February 4, 1875.
Le Grand Randall, May 6, 1875.
Harry J. Bodley, A. B., July 1, 1875.
Benjamin M. Bradin, A. B., September 24, 1875.
William Montague Geer, A. B., October 8, 1875.
Henry Robert Percival, A. B., October 8, 1875.
William Westover, November 4, 1875.
Charles Tunder Middlebrook, November 4, 1875.
Josephus Tragitt, December 2, 1875.
Albert Eugene George, A. B., January 6, 1876.
Charles James Wood, A. B., February 3, 1876.
Robert Spear Gross, A. B., March 3, 1876.
John Franklin Herrlich, April 6, 1876.
John Brazer Draper, A. B., August 8, 1876.
George Newton Eastman, A. B , September 7, 1876.
William Cuff Maguire, A. B., September 7, 1876.
Joseph Dunkley Herron, A. B., September 23, 1876.—29.

II.—CANDIDATES FOR DEACON'S ORDERS.

Not having passed any Literary Examination:

John Pickavant Crawford, November 5, 1868.
Henry Homer Washburn, June 5, 1873.
Benjamin Haight, May 7, 1874.

Charles Tileston Whittemore, September 30, 1874.
Charles Philip Augustus Burnett, December 2, 1875.
John George Fawcett, January 6, 1876.
Matthew A. Bailey, M. D., February 3, 1876.
William Lucas Mott, March 3, 1876.
Julius Ungar, March 15, 1876.
J. Newton Perkins, June 1, 1876.
Manuel Graeter, April 6, 1876.—11.

CANDIDATES FOR HOLY ORDERS ORDAINED DEACONS.

I. The Candidates for Deacon's and Priest's Orders, named below, have passed the examination required by Canon VIII., Section 3, and Section 7, Title I., of the Digest of the Canons of the General Convention, and have been ordained to the Diaconate:

1876.	March	12.	Dan Marvin, Jr., A. M.,	For the Bishop of Long Island.
"	"	"	William White Wilson,	
"	"	"	Robert Bayard Snowden,	
"	July	2,	George Coutts Athole.	
"	"	"	Gustav Arnold Carstensen, A. B.	
"	"	"	Frederick Henry Townsend Horsfield, A. B.	
"	"	"	Charles Sanford Olmsted.	
"	"	"	Leighton Parks.	
"	"	"	John Sword.	
"	"	"	Charles Lancaster Short, A. M.	
"	"	"	Charles Robert Stroh.	
"	"	"	William Henry Tomlins, A. B.	
"	"	"	Oliver Perry Vinton, A. B.—13.	

DEACONS ADVANCED TO THE PRIESTHOOD.

The Deacons named below have been ordained to the Holy Order of Priests:

1875.	October	17.	The Rev. E. Winchester Donald.
"	December	19.	The Rev. Alfred Evan Johnson.
"	"	"	The Rev. Amos Turner Ashton.
	"	"	The Rev. Joseph H. Young.
	"	"	The Rev. Edward H. Van Winkle.
	"	"	The Rev. Spencer H. Roche, for the Bishop of Long Island.
1876.	July	2.	The Rev. Julius W. Paige.—7.

RESIGNATION OF PARISHES.

I have received Notice of the Resignation, by the Clergymen named below, of the Parishes or Cures respectively mentioned:

The Rev. David Banks, of the Rectorship of St. Paul's Church, Yonkers.

The Rev. Edward O. Flagg, D. D., of the Rectorship of the Church of the Resurrection, New-York.

The Rev. Alfred Evan Johnson, S. T. B., of the Rectorship of St. Peter's Church, Stone Ridge.

The Rev. John W. Kramer, M. D., as an Assistant Minister of Grace Church, in charge of Grace Chapel, New-York.

The Rev. John P. Lundy, D. D., of the Rectorship of the Church of the Holy Apostles, New-York.

The Rev. Stephen A. McNulty, as an Officiating Minister of St. Mark's Church, New-York.

The Rev. Benjamin F. Miller, of the Rectorship of Grace Church, Millbrook.

The Rev. Samuel Moran, of the Rectorship of St. John's Church, Greenwood Iron Works, Orange county.

The Rev. Horace L. Edgar Pratt, of the Rectorship of St. Mary's Church, Castleton, Richmond county.

The Rev. Joseph H. Price, D. D., of the Rectorship of St. Stephen's Church, New-York.

The Rev. Robert Scott, of the Rectorship of Grace Church, West Farms, New-York.

The Rev. George Henry Smith, of the Rectorship of St. Paul's Church, Pleasant Valley.

The Rev. Hugh Miller Thompson, D. D., of the Rectorship of Christ Church, New-York.

The Rev. Allan Sheldon Woodle, as Assistant Minister of Christ Church, New-York.

The Rev. George F. Siegmund, as Assistant Minister of the Church of the Annunciation, New York.

The Rev. James F. Purdy, D. D., of the Rectorship of St. James' Church, Hyde Park.—16.

CLERGYMEN APPOINTED TO CURES.

In behalf of the Clergymen named below, I have received the Canonical Certificate of the election or appointment to the Cures or offices respectively mentioned. In each case I have certified that the person so chosen is a qualified Minister of this Church, and transmitted the certificate to the Secretary of the Convention for record by him, according to the requirements of the Canon.

The Rev. Addison B. Atkins, D. D., to the Rectorship of St. John's Church, Yonkers.

The Rev. Brady Electus Backus, to the Rectorship of the Church of the Holy Apostles, New-York.

The Rev. Joseph N. Blanchard, to the Rectorship of St. James' Church Fordham, New-York.

The Rev. A. Sidney Dealey, to the Rectorship of the Church of the Holy Spirit, Rondout, Kingston.

The Rev. Zina Doty, to the Rectorship of St. Ambrose Church, New-York.

The Rev. Ferdinand C. Ewer, D. D., to the Rectorship of St. Ignatius' Church, New-York.

The Rev. A. B. Hart, to the Rectorship of St. Stephen's Church, New-York.

The Rev. George D. Johnson, to the Rectorship of Christ Church, New-Brighton.

The Rev. Albert U. Stanley, to the Rectorship of St. Paul's Memorial Church, Edgewater.

The Rev. Walter W. Williams, D. D., as Associate Rector of St. George's Church, New-York.

The Rev. C. Maurice Wines, to the Rectorship of St. Paul's Church Yonkers.

The Rev. E. S. Widdemer, as an Assistant Minister of the Church of the Incarnation, New-York.

The Rev. Howard T. Widdemer, as an Assistant Minister of the Church of St. John Baptist, New-York

The Rev. George Waters, D. D., to the Rectorship of Christ Church, Marlborough.

The Rev Randolph H. McKim, D. D , to the Rectorship of the Church of the Holy Trinity, Harlem, New-York.

The Rev. John Clough Tebbetts, Jr., as an Assistant Minister of Grace Church, New-York.

The Rev. George F. Siegmund, as an Assistant Minister of Grace Church, New York.

The Rev. Philander K. Cady, D. D., to the Rectorship of St. James' Church, Hyde Park.

The Rev. Thomas S. Yocom, to the Rectorship of St. Andrew's Church, Richmond.

The Rev. McWalter B. Noyes, as Assistant Minister of the Church of St. Mary the Virgin, New-York.

The Rev. H. M. Torbert, as Assistant Minister of St. Peter's Church, Peekskill.

The Rev. N. Frazier Robinson, Deacon, officiating at Trinity Church, New York.

The Rev. John Fulton, D. D., to the Rectorship of Christ Church, New York.

The Rev. Robert Lowry, as an Assistant Minister of St. Thomas' Church, New-York.—24.

CLERGYMEN RECEIVED INTO THE DIOCESE.

The Clergymen named below have been received into the Diocese upon Letters Dimissory of the Ecclesiastical Authority of the Dioceses respectively mentioned. I have given to them the Canonical Certificate of their reception.

The Rev. Frederick W. Wey, from the Diocese of Northern New-Jersey.
The Rev. Albert U. Stanley, from the Diocese of New-Jersey.
The Rev. Addison B. Atkins, D. D., from the Diocese of Maryland.
The Rev. Randall H. McKim, D. D., from the Diocese of Virginia.
The Rev. Joseph N. Blanchard, from the Diocese of Albany.
The Rev. A. Sidney Dealey, from the Diocese of New-Jersey.
The Rev. George D Johnson, from the Diocese of Massachusetts.
The Rev. Anselan Buchanan, from the Diocese of Northern New-Jersey.
The Rev. John Anketell, A. M., from the Diocese of Connecticut.
The Rev. Zina Doty, from the Diocese of Northern New-Jersey.
The Rev. Brady Electus Backus, from the Diocese of Albany.
The Rev. Wilberforce Wells, from the Diocese of Pennsylvania.
The Rev. Walter W. Williams, D. D., from the Diocese of Maryland.
The Rev. J. C. S. Weills, from the Diocese of New-Jersey.
The Rev. C. Maurice Wines, from the Diocese of Ohio.
The Rev. Thomas S. Yocom, from the Diocese of Southern Ohio.
Also, John Coutts Athole, candidate for Holy Orders from the Diocese of Pennsylvania.—17.

LETTERS DIMISSORY GRANTED.

I have granted Letters Dimissory, at their request, to the Clergymen named below, and have received notice of the acceptance of the same from the respective Ecclesiastical Authorities, viz.:

The Rev. William N. McVickar, to the Diocese of Pennsylvania.
The Rev. Walter Russell Gardner, to the Diocese of Massachusetts.
The Rev. Robert George Hamilton, deacon, to the Diocese of Albany.
The Rev. Charles R. Hale, to the Diocese of Maryland.
The Rev. Hugh Miller Thompson, D. D., to the Diocese of Louisiana.
The Rev. George T. Kaye, to the jurisdiction of the Bishop of Oregon.
The Rev. Charles Seymour, to the Diocese of Central New-York.
The Rev. Richard Temple, to the Diocese of Albany.
The Rev. George Love, deacon, to the Diocese of New-Jersey.
The Rev. Robert Scott, to the Diocese of California.
The Rev. George F. Behringer, deacon, to the Diocese of Long Island.
The Rev. Edward H. Van Winkle, to the Diocese of Northern New-Jersey.
The Rev. Allan S. Woodle, to the Diocese of Central Pennsylvania.

The Rev. G. Arnold Carstensen, deacon, to the Diocese of Indiana.
The Rev. James A. Upjohn, to the Diocese of Fond du Lac.
The Rev. Stephen A. McNulty, to the Diocese of Pittsburgh.
The Rev. James S. Purdy, D. D., to the Diocese of Maine.—17.

ALSO, THE CANDIDATE FOR DEACON'S AND PRIEST'S ORDERS NAMED BELOW.

Samuel M. C. Orpen, to the Diocese of Indiana.

ALSO, THE CANDIDATE FOR DEACON'S ORDERS NAMED BELOW.

James R. F. Nisbett, to the Diocese of Albany.

CLERGYMEN DECEASED.

Since the last Convention, the following Clergymen of the Diocese have departed this life:

The Rev. Kingston Goddard, D. D., Rector of St. Andrew's Church, Richmond, at Richmond, on the 22d Sunday after Trinity, October 24, 1875.
The Rev. Charles F. Rodenstein, M. D., at West Farms, March 18, 1876.
The Rev. Henry H. Bean, Rector of St. Luke's Church, Rossville, at Rossville, April 8, 1876.
The Rev. William Morris, LL. D., at Fordham, July 15, 1876. Aet. 68.
The Rev. George Barnard Draper, D. D., Rector of St. Andrew's Church, Harlem, New-York, 15th Sunday after Trinity, September 24, 1876.—5.

RECTORS INSTITUTED.

October 10, 1875. The Rev. Joseph S. Atwell, into the Rectorship of St. Philip's Church, New-York.
The Rev. Thomas S. Yocom, into the Rectorship of St. Andrew's Church, Richmond, the Rev. Heman Dyer, D. D, officiating in my place as Institutor by my appointment.—2.

CHAPEL CONSECRATED.

Since the last Convention, the following Chapel has been consecrated by me:

September 25, 1876. Grace Chapel, New-York.—1.

CORNER-STONE LAID.

September 16, 1876. St. Augustine's Chapel, New-York, the Rev. Dr. Dix officiating on the occasion.—1.

SUMMARY.

The following is a Summary of Episcopal Acts in the Diocese since the last Convention:

Number of Persons Confirmed, ...		3,612
Candidates Ordained to the Diaconate, . . .	13	
Candidates Ordained to the Priesthood, . .	7	
Ordinations, total, ...		20
Church Consecrated, ...		1
Clergymen received from other Dioceses, . . .		16
" transferred to " "		17
" instituted into Rectorships, ...		2

HORATIO POTTER, D. D., LL. D., D. C. L.,
Bishop of New-York.

Appendix:

No. I.

A.

CERTIFICATE OF APPROVAL OF PROCEEDINGS IN MATTER OF THE CHANGE OF NAME OF THE CHURCH OF THE HOLY INNOCENTS, HIGHLAND FALLS, ORANGE COUNTY.

THE RT. REV. HORATIO POTTER, D. D.,
Bishop of the Diocese of New-York.

The Standing Committee on the Incorporation and Admission of Churches, in pursuance of the resolution adopted by the Diocesan Convention, September 29, 1875, as contained on page 61 of the Journal of that year, respectfully certify as follows:

The incorporated Parish in union with the Convention, known as the Church of the Holy Innocents, Cornwall, Orange County, has laid before this Committee documentary evidence, showing that the corporate name given to said Church by its legal organization in 1850, was, " The Rector, Churchwardens and Vestrymen of the Church of the Holy Innocents, Township of Cornwall, Orange County," and that by legal proceedings for that purpose in the County Court of Orange County, and by the order of said court, duly published, the name of said corporation has been changed to and now is " The Church of the Holy Innocents, Highland Falls, Orange County;" and this Committee having examined said evidence, do hereby certify that the same is satisfactory.

All which is respectfully submitted.

CHARLES TRACY,
ALFRED B. BEACH,
JOHN A DIX,
} *Committee.*

NEW-YORK, *April* 4, 1876.

Approved:

HORATIO POTTER,
Bishop of New-York.

B.

Report

OF THE TRUSTEES OF THE PAROCHIAL FUND.

(This Report having been put into the Box of Parochial Reports, was not presented; and is here printed by order of the Bishop.)

To the Convention of the Diocese of New-York:

The Trustees of the Parochial Fund of the Diocese of New-York respectfully report:

That the accompanying account of the Treasurer shows the receipts and disbursements of the past year, and the securities and funds now on hand.

All which is respectfully submitted.

MURRAY HOFFMAN, *President,*
WM. ALEX. SMITH, *Secretary,* } *Trustees.*
A. NORRIE,

NEW-YORK, *September* 27, 1876.

The Parochial Fund of the Diocese of New-York in account with WM. ALEX. SMITH, *Treasurer.*

	DR.	
1875.		
Dec. 15.	To cash, St. Philip's Church, amount of appropriation,	$290 50
1876.		
July 11.	" " " " " " "	290 50
19.	" $500 U. S. 5-20's of 1867, reg'd, @ 119⅞,.....	599 38
Sept. 26.	" Balance,..................................	43 25
		$1,222 63

	CR.	
1875.		
Sept. 30.	By balance account rendered,......................	$291 27
Oct. 16.	" cash, int. due July, 1874, on $2,600 U. S. 5-20's of 1867, reg'd, (not collected by former Treasurer,) $78, gold, at 116¾,..........................	91 06
Nov. 30.	" " interest on mortgage of D. Maguire,.........	290 50
Dec. 29.	" " " on $2,600 U. S. 5-20's of 1867, reg'd, $78, gold, @ 113,..........................	88 14

1876.

March 1.	To cash, three U. S. 10-40 coupons, $37 50, gold, @ 114¼,	$42 84
June 3.	" " interest on mortgage of D. Maguire,........	290 50
July 7.	" " " on $2,600 U. S. 5-20's of 1867, reg'd, $78, gold, @ 111¾,....................	87 26
Sept 2.	" " three U. S. 10-40 coupons, $37 50, gold, @ 109½.	41 06
		$1,222 63
Sept 26.	By Balance,......................................	$42 25

Memorandum of securities on hand:

$1,500 U. S. 10-40 coupons.
$3,100 U. S. 5-20's of 1867, registered.
$8,300 bond and mortgage of D. Maguire.

E. & O. E.

WM. ALEX. SMITH,
Treasurer.

NEW-YORK, *September* 26, 1876.

C.

(The following Acts of the last Legislature of the State of New-York are printed here for the information of the Diocese.)

CHAP. 176.

AN ACT SUPPLEMENTARY TO CHAPTER SIXTY OF THE LAWS OF EIGHTEEN HUNDRED AND THIRTEEN, ENTITLED "AN ACT TO PROVIDE FOR THE INCORPORATION OF RELIGIOUS SOCIETIES, AND THE ACTS SUPPLEMENTARY THERETO."

PASSED April 26, 1876.

The People of the State of New-York, represented in Senate and Assembly, do enact as follows:

SECTION 1. The rector, wardens and vestrymen, or the trustees, consistory or session of any church, congregation or religious society, incorporated under any of the laws of this State, shall administer the temporalities thereof and hold and apply the estate and property belonging thereto, and the revenues of the same, for the benefit of such corporation, according to the rules and usages of the church or denomination to which said corporation shall belong; and it shall not be lawful to divert such estate, property or revenue to any purpose, except the support and maintenance of any church or religious or benevolent institution or object connected with the church or denomination to which such corporation shall belong.

§ 2. Each and every of the corporations aforesaid may receive, use and apply all rents and income derived from pews of their respective churches, in addition to the annual income limited by any statute now in force relating thereto.

§ 3. Any two or more of the corporations aforesaid, are hereby authorised to unite and consolidate themselves into a single corporation of the denomination to which at least one of such corporations shall belong, in the manner following: The said corporations may enter into an agreement under their respective corporate seals for the union and consolidation of the said corporations, setting forth the terms and conditions thereof, the name of the proposed new corporation, the church or denomination to which it shall belong, the names of the persons who shall be the church wardens and vestrymen, or elders and deacons, or trustees or other officers, as the case may be, until the first annual election of the proposed new corporation, and fixing the day of such election. But in the case of Protestant Episcopal churches, no such agreement shall be valid unless approved by the bishop and standing committee of the diocese in which such churches are situated. Each of the said corporations may make its separate petition to the Supreme Court, in the judicial district in which such corporations are situated, for an order for such union and consolidation, setting forth in such petition the reasons for such union and consolidation, the agreement made as hereinbefore provided, and a statement of all of its property, real and personal, all its debts and liabilities, and the amount and sources of its annual income. Upon such petition from each of such corporations so proposing to be united and consolidated, and upon the said agreement, satisfactorily proved or certified, the Supreme Court may, in case it shall deem it proper, make an order for the union and consolidation of such corporations, determining all the terms, conditions and provisions thereof. All parties interested therein may be heard on such petition. When such order is made and entered, according to the practice of the court, the said corporations shall be united and consolidated into one corporation, by the name designated in the order; and it shall have all the rights and powers, and be subject to all the obligations of religious corporations under the act to which this is supplementary, and the acts amendatory thereof and supplementary thereto.

§ 4. And thereupon all the estate, rights and property, of whatsoever nature, belonging to either of said corporations, shall, without further act or deed, be vested in and transferred to the new corporation as effectually as they were vested in or belonged to the former corporations, and the said new corporation shall be liable for all the debts and liabilities of the former corporations, in the same manner and as effectually as if said debts or liabilities had been contracted or incurred by it.

§ 5. This act shall take effect immediately.

CHAP. 110.

AN ACT SUPPLEMENTAL TO CHAPTER SIXTY OF THE LAWS OF EIGHTEEN HUNDRED AND THIRTEEN, ENTITLED "AN ACT TO PROVIDE FOR THE INCORPORATION OF RELIGIOUS SOCIETIES," AND OF THE SEVERAL ACTS AMENDATORY THEREOF.

PASSED April 11, 1876.

The People of the State of New-York, represented in Senate and Assembly, do enact as follows:

SECTION 1. It shall be lawful for any diocesan convention, presbytery classis, synod, annual conference, or other governing body having jurisdiction over a number of churches, congregations or societies of any church or religious denomination in this State, now or hereafter to be constituted or established, and not already incorporated, at any stated meeting thereof, by a plurality of voices, to elect any number of discreet persons, not less than three nor exceeding nine in number, as trustees to take charge of the estate and property belonging thereto, and to transact all affairs relating to the temporalities thereof. The presiding officer and clerk of such governing body shall immediately thereafter certify, under their hands and seals, the names of the persons elected as trustees as aforesaid, in which certificate the name or title by which the said trustees and their successors shall be known shall be particularly mentioned, which said certificate, being duly acknowledged by the said presiding officer and clerk, shall be recorded, by the clerk of one of the counties, situated in whole or in part within the bounds of the jurisdiction of such governing body, or in the book kept for the record of religious corporations; and such trustees and their successors shall thereupon, by virtue of this act, be a body corporate, by the name or title expressed in such certificate.

§ 2. Such trustees shall be capable of taking for religious, educational and charitable purposes, by gift, devise, bequest, grant or purchase, and of holding and disposing of the same, any real and personal estate held for the benefit of any such governing body, or of any parish, congregation, society, church, chapel, mission, religious, benevolent, charitable or educational institution, existing or acting under such governing body at the time of their election, or which had then or may thereafter be given for any such purposes, provided that the net yearly income received from the said property shall not at such time exceed the sum of twenty-five thousand dollars.

§ 3. Whenever any parish, church, congregation or religious society in connection with any such governing body, shall become extinct by reason of the death or removal of its members, it shall be lawful for the trustees, elected by such body as aforesaid, to take possession of the temporalities and property belonging to such extinct church or organization, and manage and dispose of the same, and apply the proceeds thereof to any of the objects mentioned in the second section of this act.

§ 4. The trustees elected by virtue of this act shall hold their offices at the pleasure of the governing body by whom they are elected, and all vacancies shall be filled by such body as they occur.

Appendix:

No. II.

PAROCHIAL, MISSIONARY AND OTHER CLERICAL REPORTS.

The following portions of the Parochial, Missionary and other Clerical Reports, made to the Bishop of the Diocese, are published by his direction, in accordance with the following section, to which attention is respectfully requested, of

CANON 15, TITLE I.,

OF DIGEST OF THE CANONS OF THE GENERAL CONVENTION.

Of the Mode of securing an accurate View of the State of the Church.

§ I. As a full and accurate view of the State of the Church, from time to time, is highly useful and necessary, it is hereby ordered that every Minister of this Church, or, if the Parish be vacant, the Wardens, shall present, or cause to be delivered, on or before the first day of every Annual Convention, to the Bishop of the Diocese, or, when there is no Bishop, to the President of the Convention, a statement of the number of baptisms, confirmations, marriages and funerals, and of the number of Communicants in his Parish or Church; also the state and condition of the Sunday-Schools in his Parish; also the amount of the

Communion alms, the contributions for missions, diocesan, domestic and foreign, for parochial schools, for church purposes in general, and of all other matters that may throw light on the same. And every Clergyman, not regularly settled in any Parish or Church, shall also report the occasional services he may have performed; and, if he have performed no such services, the causes or reasons which have prevented the same. And these Reports, or such parts of them as the Bishop shall think fit, may be read in Convention, and shall be entered on the Journals thereof.

DUTCHESS COUNTY.

St. Thomas' Church, Amenia; the Rev. AMOS TURNER ASHTON, Rector and Missionary.

Families, 43. Individuals, 152. Baptisms, (ad. 3, inf. 7,) 10. Marriages, 5. Burials, 8. Communicants: removed from the Parish, 1; died, 1; present number, 59. The Holy Communion celebrated twice every month, on the higher festivals, and twice in private. Catechists and Sunday-School Teachers, 6. Catechumens: Children taught the Catechism openly in the Church, 35; total number of young persons instructed, 35. Celebration of Divine Service: Sundays, morning and evening prayer, with sermon; Holy Days, Christmas, Ash-Wednesday, Good Friday and Ascension; other days, daily through Holy Week, and on Thanksgiving Day.

Contributions.—Episcopal Fund, $2; Diocesan Fund, $8; Missionary Committee of the Diocese, $6 85; Theological Education Fund, $3 69; Fund for Aged and Infirm Clergymen, $3 60; for the Jews, $7 84; Board of Missions P. E. Church U. S: Domestic Committee, $3 19; Foreign Committee, $3 20; Salary of the late Dr. Johnson, (returned,) $588; the Poor, (Communion Alms,) $27 71; Parish purposes, $79 93; Church purposes in general, $437—total, $1,171 01.

In addition to his services already reported, the Rector has to make note of an afternoon service, (held at the request of Bishop Williams, of Connecticut, and with the consent of the Bishop of New-York,) in the neighboring Parish of Christ Church, Sharon, Connecticut.

Last year St. Thomas' Church had to report the erection of a chancel window to the memory of the late Dr. Johnson, at a cost of $1,035 88, of which the sum of $556 35 was drawn from funds within the Parish, the balance being made up from other sources.

This year a long cherished hope of the Parish has been realized. The late Rector (Dr. Johnson) returned his salary to the Church, to be devoted to the purchase of a Rectory. To that sum, $437 has been added, and a very suitable house has been procured for a very small sum. The Parish is entirely free from debt.

Chapel of St. Stephen's College, Annandale; the Rev. R. B. FAIRBAIRN, D. D., the Rev. G. B. HOPSON, the Rev. W. W. OLSSEN, D. D., and the Rev. L. L. NOBLE, Ministers in charge.

Families, about 35. Individuals, about 150; including College, 225. Baptisms, (ad. 1, inf. 16,) 17. Burials, 6. Communicants, about 125. Communion, every Sunday in term, and on other important festivals and days. Morning and evening service every day in term; on Sundays, in the long vacation, Sermons twice on Sunday in term; once in the long vacation. Thirty-five children are taught in the Sunday-School.

Contributions.—Aged and Infirm Clergy, $26 06; Episcopal Fund, $7; Diocesan Fund, 0; School at Ogden, $17 95; Diocesan Missions, $10 65; Dutchess County Convoca- on, $10; St. Peter's Brotherhood, $10 36; Society for the Promotion of Religion and arning, $14 57; new Furnace for Chapel, $216 97. The Ladies' Sewing Society have ntinued to contribute clothing for the House of the Good Shepherd, Tompkins' Cove— tal, $323 56.

The St. Peter's Brotherhood continues to render aid in Parish work, and to maintain a rvice in a School House, two miles from the College.

hurch of St. John the Evangelist, Barrytown.

This Church continues under the charge of the Warden and clerical Professors of St. ephen's College. The morning service and the Parish work are under direction of the ev. Prof. Hopson. During the year, Mrs. Aspinwall has built, for the use of the Parish, very neat School House, which serves for Sunday-School and the meetings of an Indus- ial Society, which has afforded great assistance to the neighborhood, and also for rvices in Lent.

Families, 23. Individuals, 101. Baptisms, (ad. 3, inf 6,) 9. Confirmed, 9. Marriage, 1 urials, 2. Communicants: admitted, 9, removed into the Parish, 1; removed from the arish, 1, present number, 52. The Holy Communion administered the first Sunday of ich month, and on principal Holy Days. Sunday-School teachers, 9. Catechumens: umber of children taught the Catechism openly in the Church, 56; members of other asses for religious instruction, 9; total number of young persons instructed, 65. Cele- ation of Divine Service: Sundays, 104; Holy Days, 5; other days, 36—total, 145.

Contributions.—Episcopal Fund, $2: Diocesan Fund, $6 65; Missionary Committee of e Diocese, $16; Education Fund, $11 18; Aged and Infirm Clergy, $12 95; New-York ity Missions, $11 45; Mission to Seamen in New-York, $12 10; Bible and P. B. Society, 12 60; Tract Society, $13 85; Sunday-School Union, $11 96: Missions: Domestic Com- ittee, $100 05; Foreign Committee, $8 50; Poor, $77 07; Parish purposes, $369 24; ashotah, $87; Indian Missions, $22 87; Mission to Freedmen, $16 07; Jews, $6 56; chool in Ogden, $9 58; Dutchess County Convocation, $103 17—total, $910 85.

t. Mark's Church, Carthage Landing; the Rev. F. W. SHELTON, LL. D., Rector.

Families, 15. Individuals, 51 Baptisms, (ad 8, inf 7,) 15 Confirmed, 20. Marriage, Communicants: present number, 30 The Holy Communion celebrated on the first unday of the month and on the principal festivals Catechists and Sunday-School achers, 6. Catechumens, 30; total number of young persons instructed, 30. Celebra- on of Divine Service: Sundays 52, Holy Days, 6. other days, 12—total, 70.

Contributions.—Episcopal Fund, $2; Diocesan Fund, $4; Parish purposes, $155—total, 161.

Trinity Church, Fishkill; the Rev. JOHN R. LIVINGSTON, Rector.

Baptisms, inf 3. Marriage, 1. Burial, 1. Communicants. removed from the Parish, ; died, 1; present number, 37. The Holy Communion celebrated upon the first Sunday f the month and on the chief festivals Catechists and Sunday-School teachers, 4 atechumens, 12. Celebration of Divine Service: Sundays, morning service; Holy Days, hanksgiving, Christmas, Ash-Wednesday and Good Friday; other days, Wednesdays in ent, and a weekly service during a large portion of the year.

Contributions.—Episcopal Fund, $5: Diocesan Fund, $6 25; Missionary Committee of e Diocese, $19 05; Theological Education Fund, $10; Fund for Aged and Infirm lergymen, $23 31; New-York City Mission Society, (Fresh Air Fund,) $5 30; New-York ible and Common Prayer-Book Society, $7 75; Protestant Episcopal Tract Society, $4; lission to Jews, $1 50; Dutchess County Missionary Convocation, $3 77; Board of

Missions: Colored people, $6 10; Domestic Committee, $25 80; Foreign Committee, $5; Indian, $3 88; Highland Hospital, Matteawan, $11; Parish purposes, (Hymnal, $18; Christmas gift to Sexton, $13 86,) $31 86; Church purposes in general, $75—total, $2[illegible].

Free Church of St. John Baptist, Glenham; the Rev. JOHN R. LIVINGSTON, Rector and Missionary.

Baptisms, (ad. 1, inf. 34,) 35. Confirmed, 13. Marriages, 5. Burials, 10. Communicants: admitted, 14; removed into the Parish, 20; removed from the Parish, 3; died, 1; present number, 61. The Holy Communion celebrated on the third Sunday of the month, Sunday after Christmas, Thursday evening in Passion Week, Sunday after Easter, and on the Rector's Birthday. Catechists and Sunday-School teachers, 12. Catechumens, 97. Daily Parish School, free; Scholars, 35. Celebration of Divine Service: Sundays, morning (9 o'clock) and evening; Holy Days, most of the Saints' Days; other days, early service Christmas and Easter, midnight service New Year's Eve, Ember and Thanksgiving Days, twice a week in Lent, daily in Passion Week, and generally weekly throughout the year.

Contributions.—Episcopal Fund, $2; Diocesan Fund, $3 98; Missionary Committee of the Diocese, $12; Fund for the Jews, $2 50; Fund for Aged and Infirm Clergymen, $5; New-York City Mission Society, (Fresh Air Fund,) $6 10; Highland Hospital, Matteawan, $6 50; New-York Bible and Common Prayer-Book Society, $8 00; Protestant Episcopal Tract Society, $4 50; General P. E. S. S. Union and Church Book Society, $2; General Theological Seminary, $2; Sunday-School, "Daisy Bed," $1 75; Sunday-School, Florida, $6; Indian Mission, $2 50; Sunday-School, $1 80; Colored Mission, $4 11; Parish purposes and for the Poor, $40 10; Church purposes in general, (Sunday-School offerings,) $32 25—total, $143 89.

Our season of adversity has given way to a time of blessing, and brighter days dawn on this juvenile Parish. A Parish and Sunday-School room is being built, and other plans are in progress for the benefit of Christ's redeemed people. During the past year the Rector has been greatly assisted by the Rev. Dr. Shelton, of St. Mark's, Carthage Landing, a noble servant in the household of faith and its firm defender, true in the home and in the Church, and my good people appreciate and are very thankful for his many and willing services in this portion of the vineyard of the Lord. His books are worthy of frequent perusal, and his life of earnest imitation. God bless the Free Church of St. John Baptist.

St. James' Church, Hyde Park; the Rev. JAMES S. PURDY, D. D., late Rector.

Baptisms, (ad. 15, inf. 29,) 44. Confirmations, 22. Marriage, 1. Communicants, 128. Burials, 11. Sunday-School, 1; No. of children, 100; teachers, 9. Services: twice Sunday, twice a week during Lent, and on all great Holy Days. Holy Communion celebrated 21 times; once a month, and on all great feasts. Sermons, 130.

Contributions.—Total of Offering, $939 67; Diocesan Fund, $16; Domestic Missions, $26 18; Aged and Infirm Clergy, $23 22; Missions in the Diocese, $24 31; Bishop's salary, $25. The rest for the poor and general Parish purposes.

The Parish is in a very flourishing condition. The Staatsburgh Chapel now supports a Deacon for its own especial work. The Parish Church and Hyde Park Chapel are in good repair, and both well attended.

St. Peter's Church, Lithgow; the Rev. J. C. S. WEILLS, Rector and Missionary.

Families, 15. Individuals, 52. Baptisms, inf. 2. Communicants: present number, 17. The Holy Communion celebrated on the first Sunday of the month and high festivals. Catechumens: Children taught the Catechism openly in the Church, 15; times, 6; Sunday Scholars, 10; total number of young persons instructed, 25. Celebration of Divine Service: every Sunday morning.

Contributions.—The Poor, $10 43; Parish purposes, $75 total, $85 43.

This Parish was vacant for a length of time previous to April of this year, and it seems as if greater love and warmer attachment for the Church has resulted from having experienced what it is to be without her services. While there is but a limited number who attend our services, yet the average attendance is very encouraging.

I have occasionally held services in the Church of the Regeneration at Pine Plains, and baptized one infant.

Trinity Church, Madalin; the Rev. JAMES STARR CLARK, D. D., Rector.

Individuals, 200. Baptisms, (ad. 1, inf. 14,) 15. Confirmed, 6. Marriage, 1. Burials, 6. Communicants: admitted, 7; removed into the Parish, 5; removed from the Parish, 4; present number, 58. The Holy Communion celebrated the first and third Sundays in each month and on all high festivals. Catechists and Sunday-School teachers, 6. Catechumens: Sunday scholars, 85. Celebration of Divine Service: Sundays, 95; Holy Days, 10; other days, 13—total, 118.

Contributions.—Episcopal Fund, $2; Missionary Committee of the Diocese, $5: Board of Missions P. E. Church U. S.: Domestic Committee, $10; County Missions, $15; the Poor, $12; Parish purposes, $200; Church purposes in general, $20—total, $264.

Trinity School—a Church boarding-school for boys, of which the Bishop is Visitor—has been carried on during the past year with greater success than ever before, by the Rector and his Assistants.

It was begun nine years since to meet a want generally and deeply felt, *i. e.*, the combination of home influence with thorough mental, moral and religious training. The School offers special advantages to the sons of the Clergy and to boys looking forward to the Sacred Ministry.

St. Luke's Church, Matteawan; the Rev. EDWARD T. BARTLETT, Rector.

Families, 150. Baptisms, (ad. 1, inf. 17,) 18. Confirmed, 8. Marriages, 4. Burials, 19. Communicants: admitted, 5; removed into the Parish, 7; removed from the Parish, 1; died, 5; present number 217. The Holy Communion celebrated on the first Sunday in each month, St. Luke's Day, Easter, Christmas, Ascension Day, Whitsun-Day and Trinity Sunday. Catechists and Sunday-School teachers, 28. Catechumens, about 220. Children taught the Catechism openly in the Church, about 100; times, monthly; members of other classes for religious instruction, 6. Celebration of Divine Service: Sundays, 102; Holy Days, 10; other days, 36—total, 148.

Contributions.—Diocesan Fund, $30; Fund for Aged and Infirm Clergymen, $35 45; Board of Missions P. E. Church U. S.: Domestic Committee, $202 30; Foreign Committee, $247 15; the Poor, $305 80; Parish purposes, $1,592 30; Church purposes in general, $300 55—total, $2,713 55.

Grace Church, Millbrook; the Rev. J. C. S. WEILLS, Rector and Missionary.

Families, 34. Individuals, 95. Baptisms, inf. 2. Communicants: admitted, 4; removed from the Parish, 4; present number, 42. The Holy Communion celebrated on the second Sunday of the month and on some of the minor festivals. Catechumens: Sunday Scholars, 21; total number of young persons instructed, 21. Celebration of Divine Service: Every Sunday afternoon; Holy Days, 6; other days, 2—total, 37.

Contributions.—The Poor, $5 91; Parish purposes, $100—total $105 91.

This report covers the period of time from April to September 24th.
A very large attendance at our services, and every indication of future prosperity.

Congregation of the Church at Pawling; the Rev. ORSAMUS H. SMITH, officiating.

Families and parts of families, 6. Baptisms, inf. 1. Communicants: present number, 5. Holy Communion celebrated Christmas and Easter. Celebration of Divine Service: Once in four weeks.

I am very thankful that I have been enabled to carry on my work in Pawling on the same plan as formerly, through the year, with a good degree of punctuality. The large room, kindly lent to us by a pious lady, in which to hold service, is often well filled with apparently devout people.

Christ Church, Poughkeepsie; the Rev. HENRY L. ZIEGENFUSS, Rector.

Baptisms, (ad. 10, inf. 47,) 57. Confirmed, 36. Marriages, 12. Burials, 28. Communicants: present number, about 400. The Holy Communion celebrated on the first Sunday in each month, on the greater festivals, and weekly during Advent and Lent. Catechists and Sunday-School teachers, 31. Catechumens, 250. Daily Parish School: 1, free; Scholars, (males, 71; females, 67,) 138. Celebration of Divine Service: Sundays, twice; on all Holy Days, daily during Lent, and five times a week during the rest of the year.

Contributions.—Episcopal Fund, $15; Diocesan Fund, $40; Children's offerings for Missions, $94 14; Missionary Committee of the Diocese, $87 71; Theological Education Fund, $14 86; Fund for Aged and Infirm Clergymen, $32 18; Dutchess County Convocation, $102 66; St. Luke's, Atlanta, Ga., $25; New-York Bible and Common Prayer-Book Society, $40 31; St. Barnabas' Hospital, $407 03; White Earth Reservation, $27 83; Pleasant Valley, N Y, $26, Board of Missions P. E. Church U. S.: Domestic Committee, $206 53; Foreign Committee, $116 06; Parochial Schools, $550; the Poor, $705 09, Parish purposes, $438 50; Church purposes in general, $25—total, $3,253 90.

Church of the Holy Comforter, Poughkeepsie; the Rev. ROBERT F. CRARY, Rector.

Baptisms, (ad 11, inf. 50,) 61. Confirmed, 27. Marriages, 13. Burials, 17. Communicants: admitted, 25, removed into the Parish, 1, removed from the Parish, 19; died, 5; present number, 297. The Holy Communion celebrated on the first Sunday in each month, and on the greater festivals, and eight times in private. Catechists and Sunday-School teachers, 23. Catechumens, 256; number of children taught the Catechism openly in the Church, all the school; times, 12. Industrial School: Scholars, females, 68; teachers, 7. Celebration of Divine Service: twice every Sunday, three times on the first Sunday of each month, and once a Sunday for four months of the year at St. Barnabas' Hospital; Holy Days, all; other days, every Friday throughout the year, daily during Lent, and twice on Wednesdays and Fridays during that season.

Contributions—Episcopal Fund, $8; Diocesan Fund, $30; Missionary Committee of the Diocese, $30, Convocation of Dutchess County, $30; Theological Education Fund, $10 87; Fund for Aged and Infirm Clergymen, $2; New-York City Mission to the Jews, $10 19; Church Missionary Society for Seamen, (Nashotah Mission,) $50; Men's Association, $43 84; Ladies' Association, $19 05; Pacific Coast Mission, $30; Faribault Mission, $25; Scholarship, Salt Lake City, $10; Churchman's Cot, St. Luke's Hospital, from Sunday-School, $20; St Barnabas' Hospital, Poughkeepsie, $147 28; Board of Missions P. E Church U. S.: Domestic Committee, $182 06; Foreign Committee, $42; Indian Missions, $20; Sunday-School, $150 20; the Poor, $220 24; Industrial School, $12; Church Aid Society, $31 99; Parish purposes, $901 22; Church purposes in general, $202 20—total, $2,211 14.

St. Paul's Church, Poughkeepsie; the Rev. S. H. SYNNOTT, Rector.

Baptisms, (ad. 1, inf. 28,) 29. Confirmed, 12 Marriage, 1. Burials, 20. Communicants: admitted, 16; removed into the Parish, 10; removed from the Parish, 11; died, 5; present number, 221. The Holy Communion celebrated on the first Sunday of each month and at other times, 18 times in public and many times in private. Catechists and Sunday-School teachers, 25. Catechumens: Sunday Scholars, about 160. Girls in Industrial School, 80.

Contributions.—Episcopal Fund, $5; Diocesan Fund, $15; Dutchess County Missions, $65 66; St. Barnabas' Hospital, $264 55; for Bishop Spaulding, $68 85; Board of Missions P. E. Church U. S.: Domestic Committee, $23 97; Foreign Committee, $27 80; Indian Committee, $23 97; the Poor, (special contributions:) $229; Parish purposes, $2,486 64; Church purposes in general, $549 72—total, $3,760 16.

St. Barnabas' Hospital, Poughkeepsie.

This useful Church institution, under the care of the three Parishes of the City, continues to be as popular and successful as ever. Its history and working might well furnish a precedent for similar undertakings in many other places.

The building has accommodations for only sixteen patients, yet owing to the remarkable healthiness of Poughkeepsie and its environs, it has never been taxed to its utmost capacity.

During the past Convention year, sixty, mostly of the poorer class, have been cared for within its wards, of whom three have died, 53 have been discharged, and four remain at the present date. Divine Service has been regularly celebrated every Sunday afternoon in the Hospital.

Christ Church, Red Hook; the Rev. JOHN W. MOORE, Rector.

Baptisms, (ad. 3, inf. 4,) 7. Confirmed, 12. Marriage, 1. Burials, 4. Communicants: admitted, 8; removed into the Parish, 1; removed from the Parish, 7; died, 2; present number, 38. The Holy Communion celebrated monthly and on the chief festivals. Catechumens: Children taught the Catechism openly in the Church, between 30 and 40; times, every Sunday after evening prayer. Celebration of Divine Service: Sundays, twice; Holy Days, once on the chief Holy Days; other days, Fridays of Lent, daily during Holy Week, Fourth of July, Thanksgiving Day, Day of Intercession for Missions, and several times in the month of July, with lectures on Confirmation preparatory to the Bishop's Visitation.

Contributions.—Episcopal Fund, $6; Diocesan Fund, $10 19; Missionary Committee of the Diocese, $15 89; Theological Education Fund, $14 15; Fund for Aged and Infirm Clergymen, $10; New-York Bible and Common Prayer Book Society, $11 30; P. E. Tract Society, $3 40; Church Mission to the Jews, $4 17; Board of Missions P. E. Church U. S.: Domestic Committee, $25 34; Foreign Committee, $17 53; Indian Commission, $12; Home Mission to Colored People, $7 72; Centennial Offering for Missions, $12 50; towards Current Expenses of the Church, through Weekly Offertory, $109 92, Contributions from individuals (not all of them connected with the Parish) towards the support of the Rector, $375—total, $665 11.

This Parish has sustained a severe loss during the past Conventional year in the death of Mr. William B. Astor, which occurred Nov. 24th, 1875.

We have adopted, since January 1st, the plan of having monthly collections on the third Sunday in each month for specific objects. The Offertory on the other Sundays, goes as heretofore towards defraying the current expenses of the Church.

St. Paul's Church, Red Hook (Tivoli); the Rev. G. LEWIS PLATT, Rector. (Tivoli P. O.)

Families, 25. Baptisms, inf. 4. Marriages, 3. Burials, 6. Communicants: admitted, 1; died, 1; present number, 37. The Holy Communion celebrated every month on the first Sunday, and at Christmas. Catechists and Sunday-School teachers, 10. Total number of young persons instructed, about 130. Celebration of Divine Service: every Lord's Day, on Ash-Wednesday, Good Friday and Thanksgiving Day—total, 55.

Contributions.—Diocesan Fund, $15; Fund for Aged and Infirm Clergymen, $13; Evangelical Educational Soc., $80; Offerings for the Sunday-School, $240; Episcopal Fund, $3; Communion offerings for charity, $48 31; Ladies' Benevolent Soc., St. Paul's Ch. $120—total, $621 31.

The Rector continues to hold the services at the Clermont Chapel, three miles or more to the north of the Church, every Sunday afternoon, from May to the middle of November, with a fair attendance and with some considerable interest. The Sunday-School, with eight teachers and about thirty scholars, is doing a good work.

Church of the Messiah, Rhinebeck; the Rev. A. F. OLMSTED, Rector.

Families, 26. Baptisms, (ad. 5, inf. 3,) 8. Confirmed 8. Marriage, 1. Burials, 9. Communicants: admitted, 8; removed into the Parish, 4; removed from the Parish, 10; died, 4; present number, 53. The Holy Communion celebrated monthly, and on Christmas Day and Whitsun-Day. Sunday-School scholars, 30; Bible Class by the Rector, 20—total, 50. Celebration of Divine Service: Sundays, 51; 101 times; Holy Days, 9; 10 times, other days, 10; 10 times—total, 170 days; 121 times.

Contributions.—Diocesan Fund, $18; Missionary Committee of the Diocese, $10; Fund for Aged and Infirm Clergymen, $7 50; Board of Missions P. E. Church U S: Domestic Committee, $53 48; Communion Alms and other Sunday Collections, $241 07; Church purposes in general, including Pew Rents and Salary of Rector, $2,057 80—total, $2,3[illegible] 85

Church of the Ascension, Rhinecliff; the Rev. THOMAS S. SAVAGE, D. D., Minister.

Families, 21. Individuals, about 65. Baptisms, (ad 2, inf. 7,) 9. Confirmed, 2. Communicants: admitted, 6; removed into the Parish, 4; removed from the Parish, 1. present number, 36. The Holy Communion celebrated every first Sunday in the month and other principal feast days. Catechumens: Number of Children taught the Catechism openly in the Church, 35; Daily Parish School: small sum for tuition required, 1; Scholars, (males, 10; females, 20,) 30. Celebration of Divine Service: on Sundays, once, and service for the Sunday-School; other days, Friday evenings—total 192.

Contributions.—Episcopal Fund, $2; Missionary Committee of the Diocese, for Missions in the County, $3; Fund for Aged and Infirm Clergymen, $3 03; Board of Missions P. E. Church U. S.: Domestic Committee, $8 40; Foreign Committee, $14 20. the Poor, $21 22; Parish purposes, $45 03; Mission to Mexico, $30; Centennial offering, $20—total, $146 88.

The condition of the Parish is encouraging—gradually improving, though not very marked; the attendance on Sunday services increasing.

Zion Church, Wappinger's Falls; the Rev. HENRY Y. SATTERLEE, Rector.

Families and parts of families, 421. Individuals, about 1,300. Baptisms, (ad. 23, inf. 54,) 77. Confirmed, 66. Marriages, 10. Burials, 19. Communicants: admitted, 78; removed into the Parish, 38; removed from the Parish, 21; died, 5; present number, 407. The Holy Communion celebrated on the first Sunday of each month and on the greater festivals, sixteen times, and in private, five times—total, twenty one times. Catechists and Sunday-School teachers, 32. Catechumens: Children taught the Catechism openly in the Church, 456; times, 52; members of other classes for religious instruction, 191; total number of young persons instructed, 646. Celebration of Divine Service: Sundays, three times every Sunday, excepting July, August and part of September, when the afternoon service was omitted; Holy Days and other days, 46 times—total, 191 times.

Contributions.—Episcopal Fund, $10; Diocesan Fund, $110; Missionary Committee of the Diocese, $37 54; Theological Education Fund, $10; Fund for Aged and Infirm Clergymen, $22 23; Church Mission to the Jews, $26 20; Sheltering Arms, $102 57; Christ Church, Dyersville, Iowa, $25; St. Mary's Hospital, New-York, $40 08; Board of Missions P. E. Church U. S.: Domestic Committee, $80; Foreign Committee, $78 56; Dutchess County Convocation, $66 46; the Poor, $111 79; Parish purposes, (including all departments of Parish work and benevolence,) $3,412 90—total, $4,133 88.

NEW-YORK COUNTY.

All Angels' Church, New-York; the Rev. CHAS. F. HOFFMAN, Rector; the Rev. BENJAMIN WEBB, Rector's Assistant and Principal of All Angels' School.

Families and parts of families, 40. Individuals, 130. Baptisms, inf. 5. Marriages, 3. Burials, 2. Communicants: admitted, 1; removed into the Parish, 6; removed from the Parish, 3; present number, 40. The Holy Communion celebrated the first and third Sundays in the month, All Saints', Thanksgiving, Sundays in Advent, Christmas, Ash-Wednesday, Sundays in Lent, Thursday before Easter, Easter Day, Ascension Day, Whitsun-Day and Trinity Sunday. Catechists and Sunday-School teachers, 6. Catechumens: times children catechised openly in the Church and School-Room Chapel, 60; Bible Class, 13. Daily Parish School: 1, paid and free; Scholars: males, 14, females, 2; total number of young persons instructed, 50. Celebration of Divine Service: Sundays, twice three-quarters of the year; Holy Days, often twice; the majority of other days, once and often twice—total, 370.

Contributions.—Episcopal Fund, $2 37; Diocesan Fund, $6; Missionary Committee of the Diocese, $1; Theological Education Fund, $2 37; Fund for Aged and Infirm Clergymen, $6 50; New-York City Mission Society, $2 52, Church Missionary Society for Seamen, $2 52; Missions: Mexico, $2 06; Niobrara League, $18 12; Jews, $1 66; Parochial School, the Poor, Parish purposes and Church purposes in general, $1,925—total, $1,970 12.

The above is more or less approximate, and includes $200 from Trinity Church, rent collected for Rectory, and receipts of a fair.

The Church is a free Church.

The extension mentioned in my last report is designed, if need be, for a future northern Transept, and not a western Transept, as was last year stated.

All Saints' Church, New-York; the Rev. WILLIAM N. DUNNELL, Rector.

Families, 168. Individuals, 852. Baptisms, (ad. 12, inf. 87,) 99. Confirmed, 27. Marriages, 33. Burials, 43. Communicants: admitted, 36, removed into the Parish, 7; removed from the Parish, 84; died, 2, present number, 238. The Holy Communion celebrated monthly and on greater festivals. Catechists and Sunday-School teachers, 25.

Catechumens: Children taught the Catechism openly in the Church, 414: times, [illegible]; members of other classes for religious instruction, Bible and singing classes, twice a week; total number of young persons instructed, 439. Celebration of Divine Service: Sundays, twice or thrice; Holy Days, once; other days, every day in Lent—total, 213.

Contributions.—Episcopal Fund, $4; Diocesan Fund, $60; Fund for Aged and Infirm Clergymen, $5 28; Jews, $4 38; Parochial Schools, $231; the Poor, $230; Parish purposes, $904 00—total, $1,489 19.

Church of the Annunciation, New-York; the Rev. WILLIAM J. SEABURY, D. D., Rector.

Families, 111. Individuals, 408. Baptisms, (ad. 4, inf. 16,) 20. Confirmed, 17. Marriages, 4. Burials, 16. Communicants: admitted, 11; removed into the Parish, 11; removed from the Parish, 8; died, 4; present number, 166. The Holy Communion celebrated on every Lord's Day and other festival Holy Days, and twice on Christmas, Easter and Whitsun-Day. Catechists and Sunday-School teachers, 10. Catechumens: Children taught the Catechism openly in the Church, about 80; times, 46; members of other classes for religious instruction, 17. Celebration of Divine Service; 52 Sundays, 7½ A. M., 10½ A. M., 4 P. M., and during part of the year, 8 P. M.; 28 Holy Days, 7 A. M., 9 A. M., 5 P. M.; 216 other days, 9 A. M. and 5 P. M.; total number of services held under above rule, 706.

Contributions.—Episcopal Fund, $15; Diocesan Fund, $42; Missionary Committee of the Diocese, $5 85; Fund for Aged and Infirm Clergymen, $10 90; the Poor, $314 48; Parish purposes, $6,659 66; Church purposes in general, (St. Luke's Hospital, $7; St. Mary's Hospital, $35 56,) $42 56—total, $7,120 45.

Number of individual receptions of Holy Communion, 1,639.

In consequence of the absence from the city of the Rev. Mr. Siegmund, it became necessary to discontinue the German services in this Parish in the spring. The return of Mr. Siegmund and the renewal of the services is expected in the present autumn.

Anthon Memorial Church, New-York; the Rev. R. HEBER NEWTON, Rector

Families, (pew renting.) 102. Baptisms, (ad. 5, inf. 23,) 28. Confirmed, 18. Marriages, 7. Burials, 13. Communicants: admitted, 18; removed into the Parish, 34; died, 1; present number, 368. The Holy Communion celebrated first Sunday each month, Christmas, Easter, Holy Thursday, Trinity Sunday. Catechists and Sunday-School teachers, 40 Catechumens, 350. Industrial School: Scholars, 140. Celebration of Divine Service: Sundays, 94; Holy Days, &c., 95—total, 189.

Contributions.—Parish Expenses, $1,767 47; Parish Works: Poor Communicants, $729 92; Bread and Beef House, $1,913 62; Fresh Air Fund, $180 12; Workingmen's Club, $300; Employment Society, $328 06; Industrial School, $78 63; Parish Library, $74 28; Sunday-School, $505 73; Sunday-School Improvements, $506 95; Young Ladies' Sewing Society, $82 67; Extra Parochial: P. E. City Mission Soc., $87 10; N. Y. Bible Society, $59 42; Aged Clergy Fund, $54 58; St. Luke's Hospital, $152 48; Children's Aid Soc., $25; Diocesan Fund, $43 91; Evangelical Education Soc., $84 07; Board of Missions: Domestic Committee, $127; Foreign Committee, $64 17; Mission to Colored people, $13 12; Indian Committee, $21 48; Evangelical Knowledge Soc., $200; Miscellaneous, $432 52—total, $7,832 15.

Church of the Atonement, Madison Avenue, New-York; the Rev. C. C. TIFFANY, Rector.

Families, 80. Individuals, 230. Baptisms, (ad. 1, inf. 5.) 6. Confirmed, 21. Marriages, 6. Burials, 3. Communicants, 135. The Holy Communion celebrated first Sunday in each month, and at the festivals of our Lord. Catechists and Sunday-School teachers, 20. Catechumens, 100. Children taught the Catechism openly in the Church, 100; times, 8. Members of other classes for religious instruction: Bible Class, 40. Total number of young persons instructed, (see Report of Atonement Chapel) Celebration of Divine Service: Sundays, twice each Sunday; Holy Days, festivals of our Lord, All Saints' and Ash-Wednesday; other days, Fridays, from Advent to Ascension, four days weekly in Lent, twice daily in Holy Week.

Contributions.—Episcopal Fund, $15; Diocesan Fund, $80; Fund for Aged and Infirm Clergymen, $50; New-York City Mission Society, $200; Board of Missions P. E Church U. S.: Domestic Committee, $62 87; Foreign Committee, $91 88; Mexican Mission, $19 87; the Poor, $780 75; Parish purposes, $600; Church purposes in general, (various Societies,) $1,200; Indian Mission, $50; Jews, $35; Freedmen, $200; St. Luke's Hospital, $150; to Mission Chapel of the Atonement, $2,000—total, $5,574 37.

The Ladies' Societies sent six boxes of clothing to various Mission Stations; furnished work and clothes to from 30 to 40 women during the winter, and taught 200 children to sew, furnishing them with garments.

The Mission Chapel of the Atonement, Forty-first-street, New-York.

The Chapel has been under the charge of the Rev. Wm. Foster Morrison, Deacon and Student in the General Theological Seminary. The services and Sunday-School are held every Sunday, and two night services during the week. The Holy Communion is administered once a month. There have been, Baptisms, (ad. 2, inf 18,) 20; Marriages, 2; Burials, 7; Confirmed, 13, included in those confirmed at the Church.

Church of the Beloved Disciple, New-York; the Rev. ISAAC H. TUTTLE, D. D., Rector; the Rev. F. H. STUBBS, Minister in Charge.

Families, 32. Individuals, about 180. Baptisms, (ad. 5, inf. 19,) 24. Confirmed, 9. Marriages, 2. Burials, 14. Churchings, 2. Communicants: admitted, 12; removed into the Parish, 19; removed from the Parish, 13; died, 6; present number, 119. The Holy Communion celebrated every Sunday and Holy Day, except Ash-Wednesday and Good Friday. Catechists and Sunday-School teachers, 11. Catechumens: Children taught the Catechism openly in the Church, about 40: times, 13. Sunday scholars, 103. Total number of young persons instructed, 143. Celebration of Divine Service: Sundays, 104; Holy Days, 63; other days, 472—total, 639.

Contributions.—Missionary Committee of the Diocese, $8 12; Church Mission to the Jews, $8 57; for the Charitable Work of the Guild of the Holy Cross, $129 56; for the Sheltering Arms, $28 87; Board of Missions P. E. Church U. S.: Domestic Committee, $11 52; Centennial Offering for General Missions, $11 66; for Sunday-School purposes, $95 70; the Poor, $142 63; Parish purposes, $634 12; Donated by the Foundress for various Parish objects, $509—total, $1,579 75.

In the spring a box was sent by the Guild of the Holy Cross to Yankton Agency, estimated worth of which was about $30.

Calvary Church, New-York; the Rev. EDWARD A. WASHBURN, D. D., Rector; the Rev. WM. D. WALKER, Assistant and Missionary.

Families, 300. Baptisms, 14. Confirmed, 20. Marriages, 7. Burials, 11. Communicants, 580. The Holy Communion celebrated on the fourth Sunday of each month, Christmas, Easter and Trinity Sunday. Catechists and Sunday-School teachers, 10. Catechumens, 80. (See, for full statistics, Report of Calvary Free Chapel.) Celebration of Divine Service: Sundays, twice throughout the year; Holy Days, all feasts and fasts and daily in Lent; other days, Wednesday and Friday mornings.

Contributions.—Episcopal Fund, $140; Diocesan Fund, $120; Aid for Aged and Infirm Clergymen, $500; New-York City Mission Society, $905 74; Church Missionary Society for Seamen, $184 30; New-York Bible and Common Prayer-Book Society, $[illegible]; Board of Missions P. E. Church U. S: Domestic Committee, $2,115; Foreign Committee, $[illegible]; the Poor, $2,241 46; Free Mission Chapel, $6,000; Church Charities in the City, $3,257 10; Indian Missions, $930; Western Missionary Churches, $1,120 25; Lent offerings for Missionary Clergy, $300; Legacy to Seamen's Mission, $10,000; to Home for Incurables, $7,000; to St. Luke's Home, $5,000; to New-York Orphan Asylum, $10,000; to the Orphans' Home, $10,000; to Widow's Relief Society, $7,500—total, $78,017 85.

Calvary Free Chapel, New-York; the Rev. WILLIAM DAVID WALKER, Minister in charge.

Families, about 300. Individuals, over 1,030. Baptisms, (ad. 4, inf. 53,) 57. Confirmed, 81. Marriages, 18. Burials, 46. Communicants: admitted, 39; removed into the Parish, 35; died, 10; present number, about 450. The Holy Communion celebrated twice each month and on all the great festivals. Catechumens, 54. Children taught the Catechism openly in the Church, 500 to 600; times, 15; members of other classes for religious instruction, 50; total number of young persons instructed, upwards of 600. Daily Parish School: free; Scholars, 45 to 55. Celebration of Divine Service: Sundays, twice; on first Sunday in month, three times; Holy Days, morning, sometimes in the evening; other days, all the days of Lent, nearly, two services; every Wednesday night in the year; nearly all Friday evenings.

Contributions.—Offerings from Women's Foreign Missionary Society of the Parish, $233 85; Offerings from Women's Domestic Missionary Society of the Parish, $159 78; Missionary Committee of the Diocese, $28 97; Theological Education Fund, $8 36; Fund for Aged and Infirm Clergymen, $30 24; New-York Bible and Common Prayer-Book Society, $5 74; Special Collection for Missions, $9; Indian Missions, $6 26; Board of Missions P. E. Church U. S: Domestic Committee, $28 28; Foreign Committee, collection, $28 97; Freedmen, $5 54; Mission to Jews, $10 17; Parish purposes, $96 65; Church purposes in general, $550; Weekly offertory, $1,118 01; Sunday-School Offerings: St. Mark's School, Utah, $40; Support of Indian child at Santee Agency, $60; Scholarship in Hayti, $25; Orphan's Home, $50; Sheltering Arms, $25—total, $2,596 26.

Christ Church, New-York; the Rev. JOHN FULTON, D. D., Rector.

Families, quite unknown. Baptisms, inf. 2. Confirmed, 12. Communicants: present number, very uncertain. Catechists and Sunday-School teachers, hardly any. Catechumens, very few.

This Parish has been without a Rector for nine months past. The present Rector has been in actual charge for less than a week. The Clerk of the Vestry is absent. For these reasons it is impossible to make any accurate statistical report.

Church of the Epiphany, New-York; the Rev. U. T. TRACY, Rector.

I find it impossible, this year, to make an exact report of my Parish. In the removal, from Stanton-street to the present site of the Church in East 50th-street, the records have become confused. I have not yet been able to sift them, and to complete a record of the present membership.

There is promise of a good work this winter by the company of devout people who form the active force of the Parish.

Last year, the financial support of this Parish was mainly in the Church of the Holy Trinity. On January 1st, of the current year, that support was withdrawn. The Church of the Epiphany became, and is now, independent.

It is established as a free Church.

Through judicious management of property owned by the corporation an endowment has been secured, which will bring to the Church, at the rate of rental now coming in, an annual income of about three thousand dollars over and above interest on the debt, current expenses and taxes.

After this year, with the present promise, the Church of the Epiphany will be able to discharge with more regularity its Canonical obligation to the Diocese and to the Church at large.

Grace Church, New-York; the Rev. HENRY C. POTTER, D. D., Rector.

Families, 268. Individuals, 2,000. Baptisms, (ad. 2, inf. 31,) 33. Confirmed, 23. Marriages, 19. Burials, 36. Communicants: admitted, 40; died, 22; present number, 812. The Holy Communion celebrated on the first and second Sundays of the month and on the greater festivals. Catechumens: Children taught the Catechism openly in the Church, 650; times, weekly; members of other classes for religious instruction, 75; total number of young persons instructed, 725. Celebration of Divine Service: Sundays, all Sundays; Holy Days, all Holy Days; other days, daily in Lent and semi-weekly in Advent season.

Contributions.—Diocesan Fund, $175; Diocesan Missions, $675; Theological Education, $3,750; Fund for Aged and Infirm Clergymen, $452 95; New-York City Mission Society, $1,060 54; Mission to the Jews, $203 05; St. Luke's Home, $293 80; Home for Incurables, $862 50; St. Luke's Hospital, $31,075 71; St. Johnland, $6,000; Orphans' Home, $325; Home Missions to Colored People, $429 75; Domestic Missions, $27,514 90; Foreign Missions, $10,124 54; Parochial Schools, $618 97; the Poor, $14,575 24; Parish purposes, $4,594 51; Church purposes in general, $10,675—total, $112,406 48.

Of the above statistics, the following belong to Grace Chapel: Families, 139. Communicants, 196. Baptisms, 19. Confirmed, 21. Burials, 19. Marriages, 11. Offerings, $498 33.

The new buildings connected with Grace Chapel were completed in June, Grace Hall being occupied by the Sunday-School on the first Sunday in July, and Grace Chapel having been consecrated by the Bishop on the 25th of September. The total cost of the buildings is nearly $100,000, and they are freed from all lien or incumbrance.

The Rev. W. T. Egbert, Rector of the Church of St. John the Evangelist, has been called to the charge of Grace Chapel, and enters upon his duties on the first of October, proximo.

I cannot conclude this report without expressing my grateful sense of the singular wisdom and fidelity of the Assistant Minister, the Rev. John C. Tebbets, Jr., who had charge of the Parish during my recent absence abroad for a year. To him, and to Lloyd W. Wells, Esq., a warden of Grace Church, I owe a large debt of gratitude for their constant devotion to the interests and their untiring labors for the welfare of the Church and congregation.

Church of the Heavenly Rest, New-York; the Rev. R. S. HOWLAND, D. D., Rector.

Baptisms, (ad. 4, inf. 12,) 16. Confirmed, 19. Marriages, 9. Burials, 11. Communicants, about 225. The Holy Communion celebrated every second Sunday of the month and on chief Holy Days. Catechists and Sunday-School teachers, 37. Catechumens, 286. Celebration of Divine Service: Sundays, every Sunday except in August and last half of July; Holy Days, every Holy Day except in the summer months; other days, twice a week in Advent, ten times a week in Lent.

Contributions.—Missionary Committee of the Diocese, $85; New-York Bible and Common Prayer-Book Society, $50; Board of Missions P. E. Church U. S.: Domestic Committee, $800; the Poor, $670 55; Parish purposes, $4,319; Church purposes in general, $751 16—total, $6,675 71.

Church of the Holy Apostles, New-York; the Rev. BRADY E. BACKUS, Rector.

Baptisms, (ad. 2, inf. 75,) 77. Confirmed, 19. Marriages, 10 Burials, 35. Communicants: present number, (revised list,) 250. The Holy Communion celebrated monthly, on all high festivals and on All Saints' Day. Catechists and Sunday-School teachers, 32 Catechumens, 250; Children taught the Catechism openly in the Church, 250; times, 14. Celebration of Divine Service: Sundays, 102; Holy Days, 35—total, 137.

Contributions.—Episcopal Fund, $15; Fund for Aged and Infirm Clergymen, $40 65; New-York City Mission Society, $75 17; Board of Missions P. E. Church U. S.: Domestic Committee, $108 09; Foreign Committee, $101 91; Sunday-School offerings, $175 19; the Poor, (Dorcas Society, $50; Industrial School, $100; Young People's Association, $489; Communion Alms, $352 38, and Coal, $97 63,) $1,089 01; Parish purposes, $4,732 25; Mission Building Improvement Fund, $785; Church purposes in general, $240—total, $7,334 19.

The present Rector of the Parish entered upon the discharge of his duties March 19th, 1876. The Women's Missionary Association, auxiliary to the Board of Missions and the Young People's Association for the Relief of the Poor, have been doing a good work during the past year. Our Industrial School has grown to the full capacity of the accommodations at present afforded. The Sunday-School and Mission Building has been thoroughly refitted and refurnished during the summer at a cost of $1,400, by the offerings and subscriptions of the people and children.

Church of the Holy Comforter, New-York; the Rev. HENRY FLOY ROBERTS, Missionary.

Families, 10. Individuals, 25. Baptisms, inf. 6. Marriage, 1. Burials, 5. Communicants: died, 1; present number, 14. The Holy Communion celebrated thirteen times. Celebration of Divine Service: Sundays, 104; Holy Days, 3; other days, 20—total, 127.

Contributions.—Fund for Aged and Infirm Clergymen, $3 42; the Poor, $43 70; Parish purposes, (books for seamen,) $14 34—total, $61 46.

There have been the following books distributed among seamen: Bibles, 18; Testaments, (in seven languages,) 349; Miscellaneous Books, 1,830; Pages of tracts on board of vessels and in the Chapel, 4,681.

Floating Church of Our Saviour, New-York; the Rev. ROBERT J. WALKER, Missionary.

Families, 50. Individuals, 500. Baptisms, (ad. 2, inf. 15,) 17. Confirmed 34. Marriages, 15. Burials, 8. Communicants: admitted, 37; removed into the Parish, 21; removed from the Parish, 25; died, 4; present number, 140. The Holy Communion celebrated on the first Sunday of each month, Christmas and Easter Day. Catechists and Sunday-School teachers, 11. Catechumens, 78. Children taught the Catechism openly in the Sunday-School, 78. Celebration of Divine Service: Sundays, 104; Holy Days, 3; other days, 87—total, 194.

Contributions.—The Poor, $161 85; for books, $12 32—total, $174 17.

The attendance of seamen at the Floating Church, during the past year, has been over five thousand, including natives of nearly every maritime country of the globe. One thousand one hundred sailors have been supplied with Bibles, testaments, books, tracts, &c., in ten languages. Several families residing in the neighborhood, whose male members are connected with the shipping, make the Floating Church their spiritual home.

Free Church of the Holy Martyrs, New-York; the Rev. JAMES MILLETT, Rector.

Families, 170. Individuals, 400. Baptisms, 90. Marriages, 30. Burials, 70. Communicants, 100. The Holy Communion celebrated on the first Sunday of each month, also Christmas, Easter, Whitsun-Day and Trinity Sunday. Teachers in the Sunday-School, 12. Scholars, 100.

We are not able to collect any thing except for the current expenses of the Church: very many are suffering for want of work, to whose spiritual and temporal wants we strive humbly to minister. We draw as many as we can into the fold, by baptism, and administer the Holy Communion to those who, from sickness or other cause, cannot come to the Sanctuary. May God bless our feeble efforts, done in His name, and for the promotion of His glory.

Church of the Holy Saviour, New-York; the Rev. ABRAHAM BEACH CARTER, D. D., Rector.

Baptisms, (ad. 1, inf. 15,) 16. Marriages, 13. Burials, 25. Communicants: present number, 200. The Holy Communion celebrated first Sunday of each month and greater festivals. Celebration of Divine Service: The Church is never closed on any Sunday throughout the year, and the greater festivals are regularly observed.

The Church has been generally filled to its utmost capacity, and were it not for the depressing influences of an overpowering indebtedness, we should have every thing to encourage from the past year's experiences. The Missionary Work of our Parish, at Ludlow street Jail, has been regularly carried on, and with an increased interest; while the results afford good ground to hope that our labor is very far from being "in vain in the Lord."

Church of the Holy Sepulchre, New-York; the Rev. J. TUTTLE SMITH, Rector.

Families, 60. Individuals, 280. Baptisms, (ad. 3, inf. 6,) 9. Confirmed, 11. Marriage, 1. Burials, 7. Communicants: present number, 80. The Holy Communion celebrated on all feasts for which there is a Proper Preface, on Epiphany and Maundy Thursday, on the last Sunday of every month, and weekly during Lent and Advent. Catechists and Sunday-School teachers, 12. Catechumens: Children taught the Catechism openly in the Church, 100; times, 16. Celebration of Divine Service: Sundays, morning and afternoon; Holy Days, all the principal Holy Days; other days, Tuesdays, Wednesdays, Thursdays and Fridays during Lent, and daily during Holy Week.

Contributions.—Episcopal Fund, $3.

All the sittings in this Church are free, and the offertory is the sole support.

Church of the Incarnation, New-York; the Rev. ARTHUR BROOKS, Rector.

Families, 200. Individuals, 1,100. Baptisms, (ad. 2, inf. 16,) 18. Confirmed, 26. Marriages, 11. Burials, 17. Communicants: present number, 425. The Holy Communion celebrated on the first Sunday of every month, on Christmas Day and on Easter Sunday. Catechists and Sunday-School teachers, 15. Catechumens, 175. Children taught the Catechism openly in the Church, all; times, 10. Celebration of Divine Service: Sundays, morning and afternoon, except during July; Holy Days, Ash-Wednesday, Christmas, Epiphany and Ascension; other days, every Wednesday evening and Saturday preceding Communion, from November to June, four services every week during Lent, and daily during Passion Week.

Contributions.—Episcopal Fund, $45; Diocesan Fund, $60; New-York City Mission Society, $1,562 96; Church Missionary Society for Seamen, $100; New-York Bible and Common Prayer-Book Society, $25; Board of Missions P. E. Church U. S.: Domestic Committee, $405; Foreign Committee, $788 33; Parochial Schools, $1,023 42; the Poor, $2,475; Parish purposes, $6,500; Mission Chapel, $3,861 95; Church purposes in general, $5,344 87—total, $23,206 53.

Church of the Intercession, New-York; the Rev. E. W. DONALD, Rector.

Families, 92. Individuals, 575. Baptisms, (ad. 2, inf. 21,) 23. Confirmed, 16. Marriages, 3. Burials, 19. Communicants, 185; admitted, 24; removed into the Parish, 8; removed from the Parish, 11; died, 2; present number, 185. The Holy Communion celebrated first Sunday in each month, Christmas, Maundy Thursday, Easter, Whitsun-Day, Trinity Sunday. Catechists and Sunday-School teachers, 15. Catechumens, 110. Children taught the Catechism openly in the Church, 110. Total number of young persons instructed, 110. Celebration of Divine Service: Sundays, morning and afternoon, or 96 times; other days, Fridays, or with Lenten services, 67 times.

Contributions.—Mission for Deaf and Dumb, $19 51; Board of Missions P. E. Church U. S.: Domestic Missions, $918 95; Foreign Work, $85 54; Sewing School of Parish, $36 45; the Poor, $409 53; Parish purposes, $3,128 51—total, $3,598 46.

Church of the Nativity, New-York; the Rev. CALEB CLAPP, Rector.

Families, 140. Individuals, 875. Baptisms, inf. 27. Confirmed, 18. Marriages, 14. Burials, 15. Communicants, 100. The Holy Communion celebrated on the first Sunday of each month, and on the festivals of Christmas, Easter, Whitsun-Day and Trinity Sunday. Catechists and Sunday-School teachers, 8. Catechumens, 150; total number of young persons instructed, 150. Daily Parish Schools: free; Scholars, males and females, 90. Celebration of Divine Service: Sundays, at 11 A. M.; Catechetical Service at 2 P. M.; Holy Days, at 9 A. M.; other days, at 9 A. M., and Fridays, at half past 7 P. M.

Contributions.—Diocesan Fund, $28; Fund for Aged and Infirm Clergymen, $2; New-York Bible and Common Prayer-Book Society, $35; Parochial Schools, $250; the Poor, $200; Parish purposes, (children's offerings,) $102—total, $637. Offerings of the children of the schools: Indian Missions, $12; Seabury Mission, $10; Orphans' Home, 49th-street, N. Y., $10; Freedmen of the South, $10; Bible and Prayer Book Society, $10; Nashotah, $20; Oregon, Bishop's P. School, $10; St. Johnland, $10; St. Mary's Hospital for Children, $10—total, 102.

Church of the Reconciliation, (Mission of the Church of the Incarnation,) New-York; the Rev. E. S. WIDDEMER, Minister in charge.

Families, 183. Individuals, about 500. Baptisms, (ad. 2, inf. 29.) 31. Confirmed, 22. Marriages, 8. Burials, 12. Communicants, about 200; died, 12. The Holy Communion celebrated second Sunday each month. Catechists and Sunday-School teachers, 25. Catechumens, 470.

Church of the Redeemer, New-York; the Rev. J. W. SHACKELFORD, A. M., Rector.

Families, 100. Baptisms, (ad. 6, inf. 40,) 46. Confirmed, 24. Marriages, 11. Burials, 32. Communicants: admitted, 36; removed into the Parish, 15; removed from the Parish, 16; died, 5; present number, 191. The Holy Communion celebrated every Sunday and Holy Day. Catechumens: Children taught the Catechism openly in the Church, 150. Celebration of Divine Service: Sundays, three times; Holy Days, twice; other days, Advent and Lent daily.

Spanish Church of Santiago, New-York; the Rev. JOAQUIM DE PALMA, Rector.

Families, 57. Individuals, 284. Baptisms, inf. 12. Confirmed, 60. Marriages, 12. Burials, 3. Communicants: removed from the Parish, 6; died, 3; present number, 35. The Holy Communion celebrated monthly. Catechists and Sunday-School teachers, 2. Catechumens, 10; Sunday scholars, 30; total number of young persons instructed, 62. Celebration of Divine Service: Sundays, service at 12½, and evening lectures; Holy Days, Christmas and Thanksgiving; other days, 10th October and 25th November.

Contributions.—The Poor, $60.

I keep the Church of Santiago open always during the summer, this being specially the season when many Cubans and South Americans come to the United States; and this year, on account of the Centennial, greater numbers have arrived in our City. I have had many Sundays, during the months of July and August, more than one hundred and twenty persons present at our services in the Spanish language. In this way the seed of Gospel truth has been scattered among these new comers.

St. Ambrose' Church, New-York; the Rev. ZINA DOTY, Rector.

Baptisms, 55. Confirmed, 20. Marriages, 17. Burials, 20. Communicants, at each celebration, about 40. Holy Communion celebrated on the first Sunday of every month, and on each of the high festivals Celebration of Divine Service· Sundays, twice, every Wednesday evening throughout the year, and on most of the Holy Days.

The debt of $609 15, reported by the Rector (now deceased) at the close of 1864, has been paid; new doors (to open outwards) have been put up in compliance with orders from the Building Department, and a new vestry room built; many bills of long standing have been paid, and no bills remain unpaid, "except for the current month," while a considerable sum is still in hand towards further reducing the debt on the Church property.

This has been accomplished by means of a handsome donation of $1,000, the kind assistance of several "up town Churches," and the generous contributions of many formerly connected with the Church. Another lady friend of the Church has also presented the interest on nearly $800, (over $53 per year,) towards current expenses.

An excellent work has lately been commenced in this district by ladies from the "Mission," who hold a "Mother's meeting" in the Church every Friday afternoon. Much good will no doubt be the result; it will also, it is hoped, lessen the labors of the Rector, who would otherwise often have to climb the high tenement houses which abound in this neighborhood, only to find the poverty he would not have the means of relieving.

This Church having been a portion of the year without a Rector, its limited means, and the necessity which exists for paying off (or greatly reducing) its debt, "without which it cannot continue," are reasons offered for omitting to report contributions, etc.

St. Ann's Church for Deaf Mutes, New-York; the Rev. THOMAS GALLAUDET, D. D., Rector; the Rev. EDWARD H. KRANS and the Rev. JOHN CHAMBERLAIN, Assistants.

Families, about 150. Individuals, about 1,000. Baptisms, (ad. 18, (9 deaf mutes,) inf. 60,) (2 of deaf mutes,) 78. Confirmed, 52, (23 deaf mutes.) Marriages, 29, (1 deaf mute.) Burials, 44, (3 deaf mutes, and 3 children of deaf mutes.) Communicants: admitted, 52; removed into the Parish, 9; removed from the Parish, 51; died, 10; present number, 460, (about 60 deaf mutes.) The Holy Communion celebrated every Sunday at 7 A. M., on the first Sunday of the month and high festivals at 10½ A. M., and on other Holy Days at 9 A. M. Catechists and Sunday-School teachers, 25. Catechumens: Children taught the Catechism openly in the Church, 100; times, 12; members of other classes for religious instruction, 35; Sunday Scholars, 100; total number of young persons instructed, 225. Daily Parish School: one, free; Scholars, about 40; Sewing School, about 100. Boys' weekly evening meeting in Chapel, about 40. Celebration of Divine Service: Sundays, (including evening service at the Chapel,) 6, one for deaf mutes; Holy Days and other days, twice, and on some days in Advent and Lent three times.

Contributions.—Episcopal Fund, $5; Diocesan Fund, $60; Missionary Committee of the Diocese, $30; Theological Education Fund, $6; Fund for Aged and Infirm Clergymen, $42 25; New-York City Mission Society, (St. Barnabas' House, $31,) $184; Board of Missions P. E. Church U. S.: Domestic Committee, $60 84; Indian, $17 70; Colored People, $17—$95 04; Foreign Committee, $30; Parochial Schools, Sunday-Schools and the Poor, $2,777 78; Parish purposes, ($1,000 from Trinity Church,) $7,621 09; Church purposes in general, $476 25; the Church Mission to Deaf Mutes, $290 71—total, $11,621 05.

To sustain the Church work among Deaf Mutes in New-York and throughout the country, St. Ann's is obliged to have three Clergymen. Its own income is not sufficient to support them. On account of the work which it is doing for all the Churches among Deaf Mutes, it hopes to be remembered by brethren of other Parishes.

St. Bartholomew's Church, New-York; the Rev. SAMUEL COOKE, D. D., Rector.

Families, 200. Individuals, 1,200. Baptisms, (ad. 6, inf. 14,) 20. Confirmed, 21. Marriages, 10. Burials, 10. Communicants: present number, 400.

St. Clement's Church, New-York; the Rev. THEODORE A. EATON, D. D, Rector; the Rev. CHARLES R. STROH, Deacon, assistant to the Rector.

Baptisms, (ad. 4, inf. 15,) 19. Confirmed, 32. Marriages, 8. Burials, 10. Communicants: admitted, 18; died, 8; present number, about 150. The Holy Communion celebrated on the first Sunday of each month, and on the festivals for which a Special Preface is provided. Sunday-School teachers, 14. Sunday scholars, 150. Members of other classes for religious instruction, 35. Public Catechising in Church every month, for nine months of the year. Celebration of Divine Service: twice every Sunday, daily in Lent, and on every festival and Saint's Day, and every Wednesday and Friday for nine months in the year.

Contributions.—Episcopal Fund, $5; Diocesan Fund, $25; Missionary Committee of the Diocese, $20; Society for Increase of the Ministry, $20; Fund for Aged and Infirm Clergymen, $120; New-York City Mission Society, (St. Barnabas' Home,) $20; Orphans' Home, $90; New-York Bible and Common Prayer-Book Society, $10; St. Luke's Home, $108; Thanksgiving Day for the Poor, $100; Christmas Tree, $60; Board of Missions P. E. Church U. S.: Domestic Committee, $300; Foreign Committee, $50; Indian Commission, $30; Home Mission to Colored People, $25 25; Nashotah Seminary, $25; Church at Atlanta, Ga., $10; Burial Fund, $93 09; Garment Fund, $75; Sunday offerings for Parish purposes, $1,397 23; Easter offerings, $785 27; for "Parish Mission," $2,170 04; for the Poor, by Communion Alms, $463 10; St. Mary's Hospital for Children, by subscriptions and Sunday-School offerings, $120 73; Memorial offerings for St. Mary's Hospital, $100—total, $6,222 71.

The "Parish Mission," now in its fourth year, has continued its work, steadily and unostentatiously, among the sick and the destitute, and has been instrumental, it is believed, in doing good to souls as well as bodies. It is sustained by the voluntary offerings of the congregation, and has enlisted the personal services of several of its members.

Church Du St. Esprit, New-York; the Rev. LEON PONS, Rector.

Families, 53. Individuals, 188. Baptisms, inf. 11. Confirmed, 53. Marriages, 15. Burials, 9. Communicants: admitted, 7; removed into the Parish, 2; died, 9; present number, 20. The Holy Communion celebrated Ember Days of September, Christmas Day, Easter Sunday. Catechists and Sunday-School teachers, 5. Catechumens, 15; Children taught the Catechism openly in the Church, 30; times, 45. Total number of young persons instructed, 30. Celebration of Divine Service: Sundays, 45; (morning and evening services;) Holy Days, 3—total, 48.

Contributions.—Episcopal Fund, $1; Diocesan Fund, $18; Theological Education Fund, $2; Fund for Aged and Infirm Clergymen, $5; New-York City Mission Society, $6; Board of Missions P. E. Church U. S.: Domestic Committee, $3; Foreign Committee, $2; the Poor and Parish purposes, $90—total, $158.

My Parish is composed of people living in Long Island, Hoboken, Jersey. Most of them are members of my Church, by joint agreement, and come to me for Christening, marriages and burials, but cannot possibly attend my Church regularly. Many American people attend my Church without being members of it.

It is my earnest desire to open a Mission and a Sunday-School amidst French people who live too far away from my Church and are not able to pay the cars for their children, in order that they might attend my Sunday-School. The French speaking population is agglomerated between Washington Park and Canal-street, Bowery and Greenwich-street. In order that we might do some good to those people, it is urgent that I might preach, every Sunday afternoon, in a place near them, and establish a Sunday-School in that locality. My Church on Twenty-second-street is out of reach for the French, who are the most in need of religious instruction. May God and the Church help me in that undertaking!

Church of St. George the Martyr, New-York; the Rev. ZINA DOTY, Minister in charge.

Contributions.—Diocesan Fund, $5; the Poor, $9 74; Parish purposes, (including six months' salary to Minister in charge,) $209 36—total, $224 10.

On the resignation of the Rev. Howard T. Widdemer, the Rev. Zina Doty accepted the position of Minister in charge. The congregation worshipped, by invitation, in the Church of St. Ambrose, Thompson, corner of Prince-street. On the third Sunday of each month the offertory at the morning service was taken for the benefit of this Parish.

Church of St. Ignatius, New-York; the Rev. FERDINAND C. EWER, S. T. D., Rector.

Families, 114. Individuals, 358. Baptisms, (ad. 14, inf. 31,) 45 Confirmed, 48 Marriages, 3. Burials, 11. Communicants: added, 63; removed from the Parish, 19; died, 3; present number, 285. The Holy Communion celebrated on Sundays, twice; on Saints' Days, Ember and Rogation Days, and Thursdays, once; in Advent, Lent and through Octaves, daily; number of Communions made, 2,329 Catechists and Sunday-School teachers, 22. Catechumens, 140. Industrial School: Scholars, 125; Teachers, 22. Celebration of Divine Service: Sundays, five services, two being celebrations; Holy Days, two services; other days, two services—total, 498. Number of sermons, 148.

Contributions.—Total, (exclusive of pew rents,) $6,500.

The Parochial Guild, consisting of 120 members, accomplished a large amount of charitable work during last winter and spring, in visiting and aiding the sick and needy, and in gathering the poor into the Church and instructing them. The work has been chiefly among our German fellow citizens. Four classes were formed (chiefly of adults) for religious instruction, each meeting on some week-day evening or afternoon.

Church of St. John Baptist, New-York; the Rev. Cornelius Roosevelt Duffie, D. D., Rector; the Rev. Howard T. Widdemer, Assistant Minister.

Baptisms, (ad. 4, inf. 25,) 29. Confirmed, 5. Marriages, 6. Burials, 9. Communicants: admitted, 7; removed into the Parish, 39; removed from the Parish, 28; died, 2; present number, about 208. The Holy Communion celebrated monthly and on the chief festivals.

Total Contributions, (including a bequest of $1,712 25, from the late Miss Maria E. Duffie, being one-tenth of her estate,) $4,251 35.

Church of St. John the Evangelist, (Wainwright Memorial,) New-York; the Rev. William T. Egbert, Rector.

Families, about 400. Individuals, 1,300. Baptisms, (ad. 19, inf. 36,) 55. Confirmed, 44. Marriages, 23. Burials, 37. Communicants: admitted, 75; removed from the Parish, [illegible]; died, 10; present number, [illegible]. The Holy Communion celebrated the first Sunday in every month and on the greater festivals, 7 times in private. Catechists and Sunday-School teachers, 30. Catechumens: Children taught the Catechism openly in the Church, 250; times, 26. Celebration of Divine Service: Sundays, 104; Holy Days, 7; other days, 98—total, 209.

Contributions.—Episcopal Fund, $8; Diocesan Fund, $30; Missionary Committee of the Diocese, $10; Theological Education Fund, $3; Fund for Aged and Infirm Clergymen, $71 09; New-York City Mission Society, $3; Church Missionary Society for Seamen, $8; St. Luke's Hospital, $58 29; St. Luke's Home, $29 57; Board of Missions P. E. Church U. S., $54; the Poor, $1,161 99; Parish purposes, $[illegible],554 99; Church purposes in general, $675—total, $8,251 98.

The Rector of this Parish has resigned, his resignation to take effect on the 1st of October. Last spring the Vestry purchased a good Rectory in a good locality near the Church. This will be left in perfect repair, and nearly free from debt. During the past summer the Church building has been put in thorough repair. The Parish is at unity in itself, and strong in that strength which comes with a union blessed from above.

St. Luke's Church, New-York; the Rev. Isaac H. Tuttle, D. D., Rector.

Baptisms, (ad. 14, inf. 103,) 117. Confirmed, 45. Marriages, 50. Burials, 71. Communicants, about 360. The Holy Communion celebrated every Sunday and festivals. Catechists and Sunday-School teachers, 34. Catechumens, about 475; taught the Catechism openly in the Church, once a month; members of other classes for religious instruction, 18; total number of young persons instructed, 493. Daily Parish School, paid in part, one, for girls. Celebration of Divine Service, daily throughout the year; Sundays, three services each Sunday from October to July.

Contributions.—Diocesan Fund, $50; Missionary Committee of the Diocese, $55 73; Theological Education Fund, (student at Annandale College,) $50; Fund for Aged and Infirm Clergymen, $29 26; New-York City Mission Society, $80 42; Church Missionary Society for Jews, $29 53; for support of Sunday-School, $177 04; St. Luke's Home for Indigent Christian Females, $236 30; New-York Bible and Common Prayer-Book Society, $38 71; Penny Collections, $483 82; through aid of the ladies for Church enlargement, $701; paid subscriptions towards Church enlargement, $1,802 57; envelope subscriptions, $1,563 97; Domestic Committee of Board of Missions, $439 38; Foreign Committee, $137 56; Infant Class, for support of Indian boy, Isaac H. Tuttle, $100; Sunday-School Missionary collections, $151, Easter offerings, $67 54; the Poor, Communion and other offerings, $826 94; flowers for higher festivals, $75; Church purposes in general, $50; Ladies' Relief Society, $280 75—total, $7,426 86.

Trinity Church has liberally aided this Parish the better to do the Mission work in this section of the city. After enlargement and improvement, St. Luke's opened on the latter part of October last with its seats all free and unappropriated, and, judging from its statistics, this has been its most successful year.

St. Mark's Church and Mission, New-York; the Rev. J. H. RYLANCE, D. D., Rector.

Families, 360. Individuals, about 1,080 Baptisms, (ad. 5, inf. 42,) 47. Confirmed, 71, (40 from the Mission Chapel.) Marriages, 12. Burials, 47. Communicants: present number, about 580. The Holy Communion celebrated monthly in the Church and Mission Chapel. and on all great festivals. Catechists and Sunday-School teachers, 51. Catechumens: Sunday Scholars, about 700. Daily Parish School: 1, free; Scholars, (males, 48, females, 87,) 135. Celebration of Divine Service: Sundays, 200; Holy Days, 25; other days, 26—total, 251.

Contributions.—Episcopal Fund, $60; Diocesan Fund, $120; Fund for Aged and Infirm Clergymen, $116 56; New-York City Mission Society, $345; New-York Bible and Common Prayer-Book Society, $10; Board of Missions P. E. Church U. S.: Domestic Committee, $771 07; Foreign Committee, $372 90; Parochial Mission and Schools, $3,550 50; the Poor, $1,996 63; Parish purposes, $1,031 24; Church purposes in general, $1,096 21; Church in Mexico, $200; Indian Commission, $271 74; Missions to Colored People, $194; American Missionary Society, $400—total, $10,574 40.

St. Mary's Church, New-York; the Rev. CHARLES C. ADAMS, Rector.

Families, 53. Individuals, 100. Baptisms, (ad. 7, inf. 22,) 29. Confirmed, 8. Marriages, 8. Burials, 7. Communicants: admitted, 18; removed into the Parish, 2; removed from the Parish, 8; died, 4; present number, 153. The Holy Communion celebrated every Sunday and on the principal Holy Days. Catechists and Sunday-School teachers, 9. Catechumens, 60 to 70; Children taught the Catechism openly in the Church, 60. The above include Sunday-School Children. Total number of young persons instructed, 66. Celebration of Divine Service: Sundays, 10½ A. M., 7½ P. M.; Holy Days, 10½ A. M.; other days, daily morning service all the year at 8½ A. M., and 4 P. M.

Contributions.—Episcopal Fund, $4; Diocesan Fund, $12; Missionary Committee of the Diocese, $5; Fund for Aged and Infirm Clergymen, $14; New-York City Mission Society, (Jews,) $10; Board of Missions P. E. Church U. S., Domestic Committee, $45; Foreign Committee, $25; the Poor, $25; Parish purposes, $380; Church purposes in general, $893 72—total, $1,413 72.

St. Mary's Church has free sittings; neither pew rents, subscriptions nor envelopes are resorted to.

Eleven of the baptisms were at the Eighth Avenue Mission, in charge of Mr. George C. Athole, who has since been ordained Deacon, and three were from the Colored Ophan Asylum.

The 100 individuals are persons not included in the families.

Church of St. Mary the Virgin, New-York; the Rev. THOMAS McKEE BROWN, Minister in charge; the Rev. McWALTER BERNARD NOYES, Assistant Minister.

Families, 55. Individuals, about 350. Baptisms, (ad. 6, inf. 23,) 29. Confirmed, 21. Marriages, 7. Burials, 4. Communicants: admitted, 19; removed into the Parish, 22; removed from the Parish, 4; died, 2; present number, 200. The Holy Communion celebrated daily, except Good Friday. Catechists and Sunday-School teachers, 12.

Catechumens: total number of young persons instructed, [illegible]. Celebration of Divine Service: Sundays, 142; Holy Days, 78; other days, [illegible]—total, [illegible].

Contributions.—Episcopal Fund, $10; Diocesan Fund, $45, due last year, $[illegible]; Missionary Committee of the Diocese, $10; Theological Education Fund, $5; Fund for Aged and Infirm Clergymen, $25; New-York City Mission Society, $5; Church purposes in general, $6,[illegible]—total, $6,[illegible]00.

St. Michael's Church, New-York; **the Rev. T. M. PETERS, D. D., Rector; the Rev. C. T. WARD, Deacon, Assistant to the Rector.**

Families, 118. Individuals, about 900. Baptisms, (ad. 6, inf. 24,) 30. Confirmed, [illegible]. Marriages, 3. Burials, 26. Communicants: admitted, 22; removed into the Parish, [illegible]; removed from the Parish, 10; present number, 192. The Holy Communion celebrated on the first and third Sundays of the month and on all high festivals. Catechists and Sunday-School teachers, 17. Catechumens: Sunday Scholars, 182; total number of young persons instructed, about 500. Celebration of Divine Service: Sundays, first and third Sundays in the month, four times, other Sundays three times; a morning service on all other days; more frequent services during Holy Week.

Contributions.—Missionary Committee of the Diocese, $9 60; Theological Education Fund, $4 34; Fund for Aged and Infirm Clergymen, $9 15; New-York City Mission Society, $81 54; New-York Bible and Common Prayer-Book Society, $[illegible]; Board of Missions P. E. Church U. S.: Freedmen's Mission, $9 60; Domestic Committee, $[illegible]; Foreign Committee, $10 63; Indian Mission, $11 60; the Poor, $634 22; Parish purposes, $1,197 04; Church purposes in general, $1,111 32—total, $3,099 91.

The seats in this Church are all free.

St Peter's Church, New York; **the Rev. ALFRED B. BEACH, D. D., Rector; the Rev. A. J. ARNOLD, Assistant.**

Baptisms, (ad. 7, inf. 122,) 129. Confirmed, 62. Marriages, 18. Burials, 46. Communicants: present number, about 450. The Holy Communion celebrated on the first Sunday in every month and on the great festivals. Catechists and Sunday-School teachers, 72. Children taught the Catechism openly in the Church, all in the Parish who will come, being invited to do so; times, monthly. Members of other classes for religious instruction, 69. Sunday scholars, 700. Total number of young persons instructed, 769. Celebration of Divine Service: Sundays, 104; on all Holy Days, and daily, morning and evening, through Lent.

Contributions.—Episcopal Fund, $15; Diocesan Fund, $40; Missionary Committee of the Diocese, $96 09; Fund for Aged and Infirm Clergymen, $56 88; New-York Bible and Common Prayer-Book Society, ($25 from S. S.,) $66 96; Domestic Missions, $133 83, Nashotah, (from S. S.,) $24 24; African Mission, (from young ladies' Bible Class,) $15; Orphan's Home, (from S. S.,) $68; Sheltering Arms, (from S. S.,) $60 41; Parish Mission, ($235 from S. S.,) $1,200; Fund for relief of Sick Poor, $178 65; Young Men's Association, $381 94; for Sunday-School, (Christmas Festival, $271 50,) $521 50; in Sunday-School for various purposes, $168 73; Dorcas Society, $81 49; Sewing School, $45 03; Communion Alms and other offerings for the Poor, $336 74; General Fund, $2,676 94—total, $6,168 03.

St. Philip's Church, New-York; **the Rev. J. S. ATTWELL, Rector.**

Families, 130. Individuals, 500. Baptisms, (ad. 5, inf. 11,) 16. Confirmed, 42. Marriages, 11. Burials, 19 Communicants: admitted, 23; removed into the Parish, 2; removed from the Parish, 8; died, 7; present number, 240. The Holy Communion celebrated on the first Sunday of every month and on the great festivals. Catechists and Sunday-School teachers,

12. Catechumens: Children taught the Catechism openly in the Church, 80; times, monthly; members of other classes for religious instruction, 42; total number of young persons instructed, 122. Celebration of Divine Service: Sundays, two services; Holy Days, two services—during Lent, on Wednesday and Friday; other days, Missionary service once per quarter, and on Wednesday, from Advent to July—total, 165 times.

Contributions.—Episcopal Fund, $2; Diocesan Fund, $30; Missionary Committee of the Diocese, $4; Fund for Aged and Infirm Clergymen, $6; New-York City Mission Society, (for the Jews,) $4; Board of Missions P. E. Church U. S.: Domestic and Foreign Committees, Centennial offerings, $24; for Freedmen, $40; the Poor, (including current expenses of "The Home,") $761 24; Parish purposes, $2,086 68; Church purposes in general, $2,196 29—total, $5,154 16.

Since the last Parochial Report the Rector has been duly instituted in accordance with the Institution Service, by the Bishop, assisted by other brethren of the Clergy. This took place on the 20th Sunday after Trinity, Oct. 10, 1875.

The attendance at Divine Service has steadily increased, and was remarkably large during the Lenten season, at which time the Rector was assisted by several of the leading Clergy of the city; for which he feels very grateful. These increased services, during Lent, were not without fruit; this is verified from the large class confirmed.

There has been progress, also, in other directions: A lease has been purchased, whereby a "Home" has at last been procured for aged and infirm members. This has been accomplished by the persistent efforts of a few members, who, for several years, have been struggling against adverse circumstances—about $800 is needed to meet indebtedness. The Parish Missionary Society has kept up slowly, but it is to be hoped surely. Another society has been organized, consisting chiefly of the recently confirmed. It is called "The Christian Workers," which title indicates the object of its formation. The Rev. Mr. Peterson, Deacon, continues to render valuable services, and it is to be regretted that he has been cut off the list of Public School Teachers, for this leaves him without a salary.

St. Stephen's Church, New-York; the Rev. A. B. HART, Rector; the Rev. Prof. R. C. HALL, Assistant.

Baptisms, inf. 2. Confirmed, 19. Marriages, 2. Burials, 5. Communicants, 70. The Holy Communion celebrated on the first Sunday in each month and on the five chief festivals. Catechists and Sunday-School teachers, 8. Catechumens, 87. Children taught the Catechism openly in the Church, every Sunday. Celebration of Divine Service: on Sundays, twice; on all Holy Days and other days.

Contributions.—Bishop's salary, $5; Diocesan Fund, $36; Missionary Committee of the Diocese, $50; Theological Educational Fund, $54 76; Fund for Aged and Infirm Clergymen, $45; New-York City Mission Society, $53; New-York Bible and Common Prayer-Book Society, $38; Jewish Mission, $22 46; Nashotah, $25; by the Ladies' Aid Society, to Indian Missions, $275 32; and Missions in different Dioceses, $369 21; and to the Cuban Mission, $25 50; the Poor, (by the offertory, $101 31; Ladies' Aid Society, $587 19,) $688 50; Parish purposes, $3,240 15—total, $4,929 90.

St. Thomas' Church, New-York; the Rev. W. F. MORGAN, D. D., Rector; the Rev. FREDERICK COURTNEY, Assistant Minister; the Rev. ROBERT LOWRY, Minister in charge of St Thomas' Chapel.

Families, 300. Individuals, 1,500. Baptisms, (ad. 8, inf. 18,) 26. Confirmed, 56. Marriages, 12. Burials, 14. Communicants, about 800. The Holy Communion celebrated first Sunday in every month, and on all high festivals. Catechists and Sunday-Schoo teachers, 35. Catechumens: Children taught the Catechism openly in the Church, about 250 Bible Classes, 50. Celebration of Divine Service: on all Sundays and Holy Days; other days, every Wednesday.

Contributions.—Episcopal Fund, in full; Diocesan Fund, in full; Missionary Committee of the Diocese, $[illegible]; Theological Education, $130 [illegible]; Fund for Aged and Infirm Clergymen, $[illegible] 40; New-York City Mission Society, $[illegible]; Church Missionary Society for Seamen, $214 76; New-York Bible and Common Prayer-Book Society, $[illegible]; Board of Missions P. E. Church U. S.: Domestic Committee, $[illegible]; Foreign Committee, $[illegible] 94; large additional amount through Societies; the Poor, $1,[illegible] 90; Parish purposes, $2,0[illegible] 85; St. Thomas' Chapel, $2,10[illegible] 90; House of Rest for Consumptives, $1[illegible]; Mission at Athens, $150 [illegible]; St. Luke's Hospital, $462 70; Commission to Colored people, $1[illegible]; Good Friday Collection for Jewish Mission, $[illegible]; Home for Incurables, $140 17; St. Luke's Home, $1[illegible] 24; Sunday-School Books, $[illegible]; House of Mercy, $[illegible] 15; Sunday-School, $1[illegible]; Parish Library, $[illegible]; Thanksgiving, $[illegible]; Christmas offerings, $[illegible] 52; Employment Society, $15[illegible] 90; Diocesan Missions, $[illegible]; Easter offerings, $[illegible] 30; Rental, $40,000—total, $51,[illegible].

St. Thomas' Parish, although sharing in the effects of a depressed and disastrous period, has, by the blessing of God, maintained its ground in temporal matters, while in spiritual, there has been much occasion for encouragement and thankfulness. More extended and efficient parochial work in the future is likely to result from the appointment of the Rev. Frederick Courtney, an accomplished Presbyter from England, as an Assistant to the Rector. Mr. Courtney entered upon his duties in June last. The Charitable and Missionary Societies of the Parish have been zealous and fruitful in their work. Appended to this will be found the Report of the Rev. the Minister in charge of St. Thomas' Free Chapel. Under his earnest and faithful ministrations, there has been a constant addition to the flock, and a very marked increase of spiritual life and interest. An excellent lady of the congregation has supplied the Chapel with an organ of superior size and quality, upon very advantageous terms.

St. Thomas' Chapel, New-York; the Rev. ROBERT LOWRY, Minister in charge.

Families, 127. Individuals, 593. Baptisms, (ad. 6, inf. 34,) 40. Confirmed, 37. Marriages, 7. Burials, 23. Communicants: admitted, 25; removed into the Parish, 4; removed from the Parish, 3; died, 3; present number, 146. The Holy Communion celebrated the first Sunday of each month, Christmas Day, Thursday in Holy Week, Easter Day and Trinity Sunday. Catechists and Sunday-School teachers: males, 7; females, 18. Catechumens, 223; Children taught the Catechism openly in the Church, 223; times, 10; Sunday scholars: infant class, 101; total number of young persons instructed, 324 Celebration of Divine Service: Sundays, 100; Holy Days, 18; other days, 74—total, 192

Contributions.—Missionary Committee of the Diocese, $11 09; Fund for Aged and Infirm Clergymen, $9; New-York City Mission to the Jews, $4; the Poor, $171 52; Parish purposes, $747 85—total, $943 46.

St Thomas' Chapel is the centre of a very large population, and the Church work in baptisms, visitation of the sick, and burials, occupies the engrossed care of the Minister in charge. The attendance at the regular services on Sunday steadily increases from month to month. The Sunday-School is very prosperous, and each Sunday morning session is an index of the solid and useful work being accomplished in the sacred culture of nearly four hundred youthful minds. A fine organ has lately been placed in the Chapel, the cost of which has been assumed by the parishioners attending our services.

St. Timothy's Church, New-York; the Rev. GEO. JARVIS GEER, D. D., Rector.

Baptisms, (ad. 5, inf. 30,) 35. Confirmed, 21. Marriages, 7. Burials, 29. Communicants: admitted anew, 26; removed into the Parish, 41; removed from the Parish, 15; died, 5; present number, 283. The Holy Communion celebrated the first and third Sundays of each month (the early Communion on the third Sunday being suspended in July and

August) and on the great festivals. Catechists and Sunday-School teachers, 40. Catechumens: Bible Class, 12; Sunday scholars, 330; total number of young persons instructed, 342. Celebration of Divine Service: Sundays, morning and evening, throughout the year, (the Church being never closed on the Lord's Day in the Summer;) Holy Days, as set forth in the Calendar, except in the Summer months; other days, daily, morning and evening, in Lent, (with two weekly evening Lectures and two morning readings; a Wednesday evening service, with Pastoral Lecture, is maintained from Nov. 1 to May 1.

Contributions.—Missionary Committee of the Diocese, $12; Theological Education Fund, $9; Fund for Aged and Infirm Clergymen, $12; New-York City Mission Society, $11; Board of Missions P. E. Church U. S.: Domestic Committee, $29 60; Foreign Committee, $13 75; Mission to Jews, $11; the Poor, $146 91; Parish purposes, $6,640 23; Church purposes in general, $38; St. Luke's Hospital, $18—total, $6,938 89.

Trinity Church, New-York, including St. Paul's, St. John's and Trinity Chapels, the Mission Chapels of St. Chrysostom and St. Augustine, and the Chapel of St. Cornelius, Fort Columbus, on Governor's Island; the Rev. MORGAN DIX, D. D., Rector; the Rev. BENJAMIN I. HAIGHT, D. D., LL. D., the Rev. SULLIVAN H. WESTON, D. D., the Rev. CORNELIUS E. SWOPE, D. D., the Rev. JAMES MULCHAHEY, D. D., the Rev. FREDERICK OGILBY, D. D., the Rev. W. H. COOKE, the Rev. CHARLES T. OLMSTED, the Rev HORACE B. HITCHINGS, the Rev. ALGERNON S. CRAPSEY, and the Rev. PHILIP A. H. BROWN, Assistant Ministers; the Rev. THOMAS H. SILL, Mission Priest at St. Chrysostom's; the Rev. ARTHUR C. KIMBER, Mission Priest at St. Augustine's; the Rev. EDWARD H. C. GOODWIN, Chaplain at Fort Columbus, and the Rev. GEORGE C. HOUGHTON, and the Rev. N. FRAZIER ROBINSON, Deacon, temporarily officiating.

I.—GENERAL STATEMENT.

BAPTISMS: *Adults*, 66; *Infants*, 637—*total*, 703.
CONFIRMED, 390.
MARRIAGES, 132.
BURIALS, 272.
COMMUNICANTS, 3,083.
CATECHISTS AND SUNDAY-SCHOOL TEACHERS, 246.
CATECHUMENS AND SUNDAY SCHOLARS, 3,363.
DAILY PARISH SCHOOLS, free—*Boys*, 414; *Girls*, 180—*total*, 594.
INDUSTRIAL SCHOOLS—
Teachers, ... 146
Scholars, ... 2,160
CONTRIBUTIONS OF THE PEOPLE, $36,887 34.

II.—SPECIFICATIONS.

TRINITY CHURCH—
Baptisms: Adults, 12; *Infants*, 104—*total*, 116.
Marriages, ... 18
Confirmed, ... 74
Burials, ... 61
Communicants—
Added, ... 68
Died or removed, ... 20
Present number, ... 734

Catechumens—

Sunday School: Teachers,.................................... 33
Scholars, ... 525
Industrial School: Teachers,.................................... 11
Scholars, ... 107
Daily School for Boys: Teachers,.................................... 5
Scholars, average attendance,........ 223

ST. PAUL'S CHAPEL—

Baptisms: Adults, 4; *Infants,* 86—*total,* 90.
Marriages,............ 22
Confirmed,............ 64
Burials,.............. 30
Communicants—
Added, ... 75
Died or removed,... 17
Present number, about........ 600
Catechumens—
Sunday-School: Teachers,.................................... 23
Scholars,.................................... 300
Industrial School: Teachers,.................................... 7
Scholars, ... 135
Daily School for Girls: Teachers,.................................... 3
Scholars, average attendance,........ 64

ST. JOHN'S CHAPEL—

Baptisms: Adults, 12; *Infants,* 150—*total,* 162.
Marriages, ... 31
Confirmed,.......... 114
Burials,............. 61
Communicants—
Added,.............................. 65
Died and removed,............. 33
Present number,............... 721
Catechumens—
Sunday-School: Teachers,.................................... 78
Scholars, ... 982
Industrial School: Teachers,.................................... 55
Scholars, about 1,000
Daily School for Boys and Girls: Teachers,........... 3
Scholars, av. attendance, 132

TRINITY CHAPEL—

Baptisms: Adults, 14; *Infants,* 52—*total,* 66.
Marriages, ... 19
Confirmed,....... 60
Burials,........... 21
Communicants—
Added,........ 38
Died or removed,............ 42
Present number, ... 688
Catechumens—
Sunday-School: Teachers,.................................... 42
Scholars, ... 390
Industrial School: Teachers,.... 30
Scholars,.................. 290
Daily School for Boys: Teachers,........ 2
Scholars, ... 79

ST. CHRYSOSTOM'S FREE MISSION CHAPEL—

Baptisms: Adults, 9; *Infants,* 115—*total,* 124.
Marriages,........ 35
Confirmed,........ 51
Burials,.......... 69

Communicants—
- Added, ... 68
- Died or removed,.......... ... 49
- Present number, ... 286

Catechumens—
- Sunday-School: Teachers,........... 55
  - Scholars, ... 545
- Industrial School: Teachers, ... 19
  - Scholars,.... 240
- Daily School for Girls: Teachers,........................... 2
  - Scholars, average,.................. 76

ST. AUGUSTINE'S FREE MISSION CHAPEL—

Baptisms: Adults, 15; *Infants*, 118—*total*, 133.
Marriages,........ 6
Confirmed,........ 22
Burials,........... 16

Communicants—
- Added,........................ 32
- Died or removed,.............. 9
- Present number,.............. 129

Catechumens—
- Sunday-School: Teachers,............................. ... 16
  - Scholars,................................. 548
- Industrial School: Teachers,............................ 22
  - Scholars,............................. 298

ST. CORNELIUS' CHAPEL, *Fort Columbus, Governor's Island*—

Baptisms: Infants, 5
Marriages,......... 1
Burials,............ 3
Communicants,...... 23
Sunday Scholars,... 25

AT TRINITY INFIRMARY—

Baptisms, ... 7
Confirmed,......... 5
Burials,........... 11

CELEBRATION OF DIVINE SERVICE.—*Trinity Church:* Daily, twice, throughout the year. *St. Paul's Chapel:* Sundays, four services; on high feast days and Litany days; daily in Holy Week. *St. John's Chapel:* Sundays, three services; daily during Lent. *Trinity Chapel:* Daily, twice, throughout the year; Sundays, three services, and from Advent to Easter Day, four; four services daily in Holy Week. *St. Chrysostom's Chapel:* Sundays, five services; week days, two; Holy Days, five; and during Lent, daily. *St. Augustine's Chapel:* Sundays, twice; chief Holy Days, once; Wednesdays and Fridays in Advent and Lent. *St. Cornelius' Chapel:* Sundays, twice; on the greater Holy Days, once; and on Wednesdays and Fridays in Lent.

THE HOLY COMMUNION—When celebrated:

Trinity Church: Every Sunday and Holy Day, except Good Friday; two celebrations on the greater feasts, at 7 A. M. and 10½ A. M.

St. Paul's Chapel: Every Sunday at 7 A. M.; second celebration on the second Sunday of the month and high feast days: Thursdays, from Advent to Trinity.

St. John's Chapel: Every Sunday and high feast day.

Trinity Chapel: Every Sunday, at 7 A. M.; second celebration on the first and third Sundays in the month, and on all Holy Days and Saint's Days.

St. Chrysostom's Chapel: Every Sunday and Holy Day; on high feasts, three celebrations.

St. Augustine's Chapel: Twice every month, and on the chief Holy Days.

St. Cornelius' Chapel: The first Sunday of every month, and on the greater feast days.

COLLECTIONS AND CONTRIBUTIONS IN THE PARISH OF TRINITY CHURCH IN THE CITY OF NEW-YORK.

	Trinity Church.	*St. Paul's Chapel.*	*St. John's Chapel.*	*Trinity Chapel.*	*St. Chrysos. Chapel.*	*St. Augus. Chapel.*	*St. Corns. Chapel.*	*Total.*
Missionary Committee of the Diocese, ...	$237 02	$77 03	$48 61	$[illegible] 73	$118 91	...	....	$[illegible] 31
New-York City Mission, ...	483 70	87 00	.. .	435 98	13 75	....	....	960 73
Theological Education Fund, ...	15 30	24 60	....	160 01	3 87	....	....	203 78
Fund for Aged and Infirm Clergymen, ...	154 77	86 00	24 75	335 06	9 09	$79 00	....	689 37
Church Missionary Society for Seamen, ...	36 35	17 98	8 43	74 34	7 88	....	....	144 96
New-York Bible and Common Prayer-Book Society, ...	15 80	24 60	8 60	160 01	5 00	....	....	213 51
Board of Missions: Domestic Committee, ...	619 37	189 70	86 02	1,715 09	53 00	19 34	....	2,655 39
Foreign Committee, ...	123 90	44 67	16 88	872 46	6 97	8 56	....	1,072 81
Home African Mission, ...	16 58	11 00	13 14	390 65	....	....	....	490 87
Indian Mission, ...	16 58	11 00	....	240 63	....	....	....	[illegible] 21
Church Orphan's Home, ...	162 41	166 17	100 46	436 61	30 19	....	....	895 84
House of Mercy, ...	108 27	30 00	57 78	345 63	20 73	....	...	562 41
The Poor, including Communion Alms, ...	2,790 70	1,307 59	692 96	2,846 44	892 03	840 94	$22 20	8,791 16
Other Offerings and Contributions, ...	8,815 70	1,457 81	2,168 57	9,410 08	1,982 05	45 96	...	18,881 47
	$8,595 03	$3,305 39	$3,289 73	$17,741 55	$2,986 93	$992 40	$[illegible]	

COLLECTIONS AND CONTRIBUTIONS IN THE PARISH OF TRINITY CHURCH IN THE CITY OF NEW-YORK.

By the Vestry:

Special Contribution to the Salary of the Bishop,		$1,600 00
Diocesan Fund,		1,100 00
Parochial Schools: at Trinity Church,	$5,250 00	
St Paul's Chapel,	2,250 00	
St John's Chapel,	3,300 00	
Trinity Chapel,	2,800 00	
St. Chrysostom's Chapel,	1,500 00	
		15,100 00
Industrial Schools: at Trinity Church,	1,000 00	
St. Paul's Chapel,	400 00	
St. John's Chapel,	1,000 00	
St. Augustine's Chapel,	350 00	
		2,750 00
Sunday-School Festivals,		2,475 00
Alms to the Poor: Communion Fund,	3,000 00	
Poor of St. John's Chapel,	1,200 00	
Funerals of St. John's Poor,	217 00	
Burials of the Poor in St. Michael's Cemetery, Astoria, L. I.,	441 00	
		4,858 00
Trinity Infirmary for the Sick Poor,		7,200 00
Five Beds in St. Luke's Hospital,	....	2,000 00
Indian Missionary Episcopate,	....	1,000 00
		$74,970 34

Zion Church, New-York; the Rev. J. N. GALLEHER, D. D., Rector.

Baptisms, inf. 6. Confirmed, 12. Marriages, 4. Burials, 8. Communicants: admitted, 46; removed into the Parish, 26; removed from the Parish, 10; died, 3; present number, 200. The Holy Communion celebrated first Sunday in each month and chief Holy Days. Catechists and Sunday-School teachers, 12. Catechumens: Sunday scholars, 60; total number of young persons instructed, 60. Celebration of Divine Service: Sundays, 94 times; Holy Days, 37 times; other days, 86 times—total, 217.

Contributions.—Diocesan Fund, $100; Missionary Committee of the Diocese, $168 50; Fund for Aged and Infirm Clergymen, $55 15; New-York City Mission Society, $401 76; Board of Missions P. E. Church U. S.: Domestic Committee, $413 27; Foreign Committee, $50; the Poor, $672 21; Parish purposes, $4,421 11; Church purposes in general, $1,732 20—total, $8,009 23.

St. James' Church, Fordham, New-York; the Rev. JOSEPH N. BLANCHARD, Rector.

Families, 71. Individuals, 300. Baptisms, (ad 2, inf. 9.) 11. Confirmed, 20. Marriages, 2. Burials, 11. Communicants: admitted, 20; removed into the Parish, 19; removed from the Parish, 4; died, 1; present number, 132. The Holy Communion celebrated the first Sunday in the month, Christmas, Maundy Thursday, Easter, Ascension Day, Whitsun-Day and Trinity Sunday. Catechists and Sunday-School teachers, 11. Catechumens, 114. Children taught the Catechism openly in the Church, 114; times, 6. Celebration of Divine Service; Sundays, 102; Holy Days, 15; other days, 29—total, 146.

Contributions.—Episcopal Fund, $8; Diocesan Fund, $30; Missionary Committee of the Diocese, $29 29; Fund for Aged and Infirm Clergymen, $26 30; New-York City Mission Society, $13; Board of Missions P. E. Church U. S.: Domestic Committee, $72 65; Foreign Committee, $25 56; St. Luke's Hospital, $183 78; Communion Alms, $179 05; Parish purposes, $3,607 10; Mission to Jews, $8 15; Mission to Freedmen, $20 71, Society for Increase of the Ministry, $39—total, $4,212 59.

During the winter a society was organized by the ladies of the Parish, which proved of great benefit in giving aid to Domestic Missions. Three large boxes of clothing were sent to different missionaries, and great interest was taken in the work. It is hoped to do much more in the same direction this year Several of the Parish have become actively interested in the work of the House of Rest for Consumptives, Tremont. The Rector has celebrated the Holy Communion at that institution, five times; and at the Home for Incurables, Fordham, three times He has also read service and preached at the House of Rest, four times The Holy Communion has been administered to the sick in St James' Parish, in private, twice The Sunday-School has gained greatly from the efficient superintendence of Mr Victory E. Wetmore A large Bible-class for young ladies has been formed, and is doing great good. The sum of $654 26 has been raised for the improvement of the Chapel, in which the Sunday-School is held.

Church of the Holy Trinity, Harlem, New York; the Rev. RANDOLPH H. MCKIM, D D., Rector.

Families 150 Baptisms, (ad 6, inf 7) 13 Marriages, 2. Burials, 14. Communicants: admitted, 30; removed into the Parish, 16, removed from the Parish, 7; died, 3, present number, 251 The Holy Communion celebrated on the first Sunday in every month, and on Christmas, Holy Thursday, Easter and at Confirmation season Catechists and Sunday-School teachers 25 Catechumens Children taught the Catechism, monthly, Sunday scholars 269 Celebration of Divine Service Sundays, 97; Holy Days, 7, other days, 60—total 164

Contributions.--Episcopal Fund, $5; Diocesan Fund, $71; Fund for Aged and Infirm lergymen, $60 60; Mission to the Jews, $20; Missionary work in Harlem, $83 72; Board of Missions P. E. Church U. S.: Foreign Committee, $50 04; Mexican Mission, 114 21; Dakota Mission, $87; the Poor, $126 57; aid to the needy through Parochial ocieties, $1,111 72; Church debt and Parish purposes in general, $9,906 29—total, 11,636 19.

The present Rector assumed charge Nov. 21st, 1875. The spirit of the congregation is ood, and its prospects hopeful. The bonded debt of the Church has been reduced in he sum of $8,500 since January 1st.

St. Ann's Church, Morrisania, New-York; the Rev. William Huckel, Rector.

Families, 65. Individuals, about 260. Baptisms, 6. Marriages, 2. Burials, 15. Communicants, 85. The Holy Communion celebrated on the first Sunday of each month and on the chief festivals. Sunday-School teachers, 15. Scholars, 200. Celebration of Divine Service: Sundays, twice; other days, 40—total, 140.

Contributions.—Episcopal Fund, $7; Diocesan Fund, $10; Fund for Aged and Infirm Clergymen, $20; Foreign Missions, $26; Home Missions to Colored People, $15; Education Soc. for the Ministry, $36 50; St. Luke's Hospital, $20; Home for Incurables, $30 50: St. Ann's Sunday Schools, $150; the Poor, $125; Easter offerings, $372; St. Ann's Benevolent Society, $294; Church purposes, $1,200; Contributions of Sunday Schools for benevolent objects, $140 78—total, $2,476 78.

The Ladies' Benevolent Association, during the past winter, gave weekly employment to thirty-three deserving poor women. Number of garments made and sold at cost, 584.

St. Paul's Church, Morrisania, New-York; the Rev. Thomas R. Harris, Rector.

Families, 84. Individuals, about 300. Baptisms, (ad. 4, inf. 14,) 18. Confirmed, 17. Marriages, 4. Burials, 12. Communicants: admitted, 23; removed into the Parish, 22; removed from the Parish, 5; died, 2; present number, 133. The Holy Communion celebrated the first Sunday in each month, fortnightly in Advent and Lent on Sundays, and every Thursday in Lent, on all the greater festivals and on many of the Holy Days. Catechists and Sunday-School teachers, 14. Catechumens, 140. Children taught the Catechism openly in the Church, monthly. Celebration of Divine Service: Sundays, twice, and part of the year three times; Holy Days, as the rule—total, 168 times.

Contributions.—Diocesan Fund, $12; Board of Missions P. E. Church U. S.: Domestic and Foreign Committees, $25 48; the Poor and Sunday School, $88 35; Parish purposes, from Offertory, $440; Donations, &c., $1,304 72—total, $1,870 50.

The Parish has been slowly recovering from the severe losses of former years, and during the past twelve months the number of Communicants has increased nearly fifty per cent.

St. Mary's Church, Mott Haven, New-York; the Rev. Christopher S. Stephenson, Rector.

Families, 112. Individuals, about 300. Baptisms, (ad. 3, inf. 29,) 32. Confirmed, 12. Marriages, 12. Burials, 17. Communicants: admitted, 12; removed into the Parish, 30; removed from the Parish, 18; died, 4; present number, 189, of which number 23, although confirmed, do not attend. The Holy Communion celebrated the first Sunday in each month, Christmas Day, Holy Thursday, (P. M.,) Easter Day, Ascension, Whitsun-Day and Trinity Sunday. Catechists and Sunday-School teachers, 20. Catechumens, 60. Children taught the Catechism openly in the Church, 130; total number of young persons instructed, 180. Celebration of Divine Service: Sundays, morning and evening; Holy Days, All Saints', Christmas, Epiphany, Ash Wednesday, Good Friday, Ascension Day, Wednesdays and Fridays in Lent, daily in Holy Week; other days, Thanksgiving Day, Wednesday or Friday evenings, and when directed by the Bishop.

Contributions.—Episcopal Fund, $3; Diocesan Fund, $20; Southern Missionary Convocation, $27; Mission to Deaf Mutes, $6 18; Fund for Aged and Infirm Clergymen, $15; New-York City Mission to the Jews, $10 50; Mission to Colored People, $1 14; St. Luke's Hospital, $6 12; Donation to Rector, $167; Board of Missions P. E. Church U. S.: Domestic Committee, $5 12; Foreign Committee, $7 50; Sunday-School, [illegible]; the Poor, (Communion Alms,) $163 87; Parish purposes, $504 07; Church purposes in general, $3,859 78—total, $5,285 14.

The new Church edifice was opened for Divine Service on Sunday, October 24th, 1875, being the twenty-second Sunday after Trinity. The opening sermon was preached by the Rt. Rev. R. W. B. Elliott, D. D., Missionary Bishop of Western Texas. The Church is not yet consecrated, as there is a small amount of debt still resting upon it, which we hope to remove at no very distant day.

Christ Church, Riverdale, New-York; the Rev. GEORGE D. WILDES, D. D., Rector.

Families, 60. Individuals, about 300. Baptisms, inf. 5. Confirmed, 6. Burials, 8. Communicants: admitted, 6; removed from the Parish, 6; died, 3; present number, 120. Catechumens, 50; teachers, 5. Celebration of Divine Service: Sundays, twice; Holy Days, the greater festivals and fasts; other days, in Lent, two services, with lecture every week until Holy Week, when two services, with lecture, are held daily; also, service, weekly, from Easter until Trinity Sunday—146.

Contributions.—Episcopal Fund, $10; Diocesan Fund, $15; St. John's Hospital, $125; Fund for Aged and Infirm Clergymen, $64 75; New-York City Missions, approximate, $300; Sewing Circle for Poor, $50 60; Mexican Work, $1,500; Employment Society, $20; Fair for St. Luke's Hospital, (approximate,) $300; Indian Commission, $50; Sunday-School, for Hayti, $50; Alms Chest, for Parish Tracts, $15; the Poor, (Offerings at Holy Communion,) $518 85; Parish purposes, not including Pew Rents, about $3,750; Church purposes in general, individuals and collections, about $2,000—total, $10,028 60.

Grace Church, West Farms, New-York; the Rev. EDWARD O. FLAGG, D. D, Minister in charge. Reported by SAMUEL M. PURDY, *Warden.*

Families, 45. Individuals, 135. Baptisms, (ad. 6, inf. 10,) 16. Confirmed, 20. Marriage, 1. Burials, 6. Communicants: removed from the Parish, 1; present number, 55. The Holy Communion celebrated the first Sunday in each month, Christmas, Easter and other Holy Days. Catechists and Sunday-School teachers, 12. Catechumens. Children taught the Catechism openly in the Church, 120; times, 12. Celebration of Divine Service: Sundays, 52, twice each Sunday, Holy Days, 3; other days, 1—total, 56 times.

Contributions.—Diocesan Fund, $24, Church purposes in general, $1,200—total, $1,224.

Collections were taken up for several other purposes mentioned in this list, but I am unable to state the various amounts, as the Rector of our Church, who had charge of the collections, has resigned, and gone to California.

Chapel of Bellevue Hospital, New-York; the Rev. P. JOSEPH V. VAN ROOSBROECK, Missionary.

Baptisms, (ad. 17, inf. 10,) 27. Marriage, 1. Burials, 193. Communicants, 506. The Holy Communion celebrated on the third Sunday in each month, St. Luke's Day, Christmas Day, Easter and Whitsun-Day. Celebration of Divine Service: Sundays, every Sunday at 10½ A. M.; Holy Days, Christmas, St. Luke's Day and Thanksgiving Day; other days, Ash-Wednesday, Good Friday and all the Fridays in Lent—total, 70.

Bethlehem Chapel, New-York; the Rev. FREDERICK OERTEL, M. D., Missionary.

Families, 91. Individuals, 225. Baptisms, inf. 52. Confirmed, 18. Marriages, 12. Burials, 20. Communicants: admitted, 25; removed from the Parish, 12; died, 6; present number, 141. The Holy Communion celebrated on all festivals. Catechists and Sunday-School teachers, 9. Catechumens: Children taught the Catechism openly in the Church, 69; times, 28; members of other classes for religious instruction, 64; Sunday scholars, 160. Daily Parish School: free; Scholars, males, 65, females, 56; Industrial School: females, 75. Celebration of Divine Service: Sunday, morning and evening, 107; Holy Days, 8; other days, 10—total, 125.

Contributions.—The Poor, $48 25; Parish purposes, $60; Church purposes in general, $54 16—total, $162 41.

Holy Cross Mission, New-York; the Rev. FREDERICK W. WEY, officiating.

Families, 54. Individuals, 129. Baptisms, (ad. 44, inf. 62,) 106. Confirmed, 48. Marriages, 7. Burials, 13. Communicants: present number, 80. The Holy Communion celebrated every Sunday in the Church, and several times in each week in the Chapel of the Sisters; number of times in public, 219; in private, 10—total, 229. Catechists and Sunday-School teachers, 10 Catechumens: Children taught the Catechism, 205; times, 52. Celebration of Divine Service: Sundays, 104; Holy Days, 23; other days, 135—total, 262.

Besides the above, we have a night school of about 50 pupils; during the winter we have a sewing school for girls, and an employment society for women. In connection with our German Mission work, the Sisters conduct a daily infant school, which is well attended. The Sisters work, besides the above mentioned, very faithfully, in visiting the whole district and relieving and comforting the sick and poor.

ORANGE COUNTY.

St. John's Church, Canterbury; the Rev. JOHN F. POTTER, A. M., Rector and Missionary.

Baptisms, (ad. 1, inf. 16,) 17. Marriage, 1. Burials, 4. Communicants: removed into the Parish, 1; removed from the Parish, 5; died, 1; present number, 50. The Holy Communion celebrated on the first Sunday in each month, Thanksgiving Day, Thursday before Easter Day, on the great feasts, and weekly during Advent and Lent, 28 times; in private, 3 times—total, 31. Celebration of Divine Service: Sundays, 106; Holy Days, 30; other days, 27—total, 163.

Contributions—Episcopal Fund, $2; Diocesan Fund, $2; Missionary Committee of the Diocese, $8; Theological Education Fund, $3; Fund for Aged and Infirm Clergymen, $5 60; Western Convocation, $3; New-York Bible and Common Prayer-Book Society, $5; Protestant Episcopal Tract Society, $2; General P. E. S. S. Union and Church Book Society, $2 50; General Theological Seminary, $3 50; St. Luke's Hospital, $5; for the Jews, $1 50; for the Sunday-School, $33 26; the Poor and other alms, $52 43; collections for current expenses, $281 24; subscriptions for current expenses, $326; interest on Legacy, &c., $274 70—total, $1,010 73.

St. James' Church, Goshen; the Rev. WILLIAM H. DE L. GRANNIS, Rector.

Baptisms, (ad. 2, inf. 17,) 19. Confirmed, 15. Marriages, 5. Burials, 16. Communicants; present number, 225. The Holy Communion celebrated the first Sunday in every month, and Holy Days for which there is a Special Preface. Catechists and Sunday-School teachers, 15. Catechumens, 120. Members of other classes for religious instruction, 5. Total number of young persons instructed, 125. Celebration of Divine Service: Sundays, twice; Holy Days, once; other days, once a month at Orange County Alms House.

Contributions.—Episcopal Fund, $7; Diocesan Fund, $15; for the Western Convocation, $228 21; Theological Education Fund, (to a Student at St. Stephen's College,) $120; Fund for Aged and Infirm Clergymen, $36 53; Mission to the Jews, $9 97; Barrel of clothing for Nashotah, (value,) $75; Sunday-School, (Christmas offering for Bishop Tuttle and Mr. Hinman,) $70; the Poor, and for various Church purposes, $129 73; Parish purposes, $122 37; for Sunday-School, $126; Disbursed by "St. James' Guild," $221; incidentals, about $250—total, $1,481 84.

Church of the Holy Innocents, Highland Falls; the Rev. WILLIAM REED THOMAS, M. A., Rector.

Families, 57. Individuals, 240. Baptisms, (ad. 5, inf. 52,) 57. Confirmed, 23. Marriages, 6. Burials, 16. Communicants: admitted, 23; removed from the Parish, 18; died, 2; present number, 88. The Holy Communion celebrated weekly during Lent, on the first Sunday of every month, and on the chief festivals. Catechists and Sunday-School teachers, 11. Catechumens: Children taught the Catechism openly in the Church, 120; times, 12; total number of young persons instructed, 123. Celebration of Divine Service: Sundays, 104; Holy Days, 26; other days, 30—total, 160.

Contributions.—Episcopal Fund, $3; Diocesan Fund, $20; Missionary Committee of the Diocese, $11 67; Missionary Committee of the Western Convocation, $56; Theological Education Fund, $5; Fund for Aged and Infirm Clergymen, $29 12; New-York Bible and Common Prayer-Book Society, $2 10; Board of Missions P. E. Church U. S.: Domestic Committee, $5; Foreign Committee, $5; Indian Commission, $4 05; Home for Old Men and Aged Couples, $1; the Poor, $245 87; Parish purposes, (including Sunday-School,) $637 82; Church purposes in general, $25 13—total, $1,050 76.

During the winter a series of cottage lectures (mothers' meetings) was held with encouraging results. Throughout the Lenten season weekly mission services were continued among the soldiers at West Point. These services have now been maintained for three years, and the attendance has been almost uniformly excellent. Three soldiers were confirmed at the Bishop's visitation, on April 28th last.

Grace Church, Monroe; the Rev. HENRY A. DOWS, Rector and Missionary.

Families, 15. Individuals, 44. Baptisms, (ad. 3, inf. 7,) 10. Confirmed, 4. Marriage, 1. Burials, 2. Communicants: admitted, 5; removed from the Parish, 2; present number, 24. The Holy Communion celebrated monthly and on every day with Proper Preface; once in private. Catechumens: Children taught the Catechism openly in the Church, 19; times, 12; total number of young persons instructed, 19. Celebration of Divine Service: Sundays, 56 times; Holy Days, 18 times; daily service in Passion Week—total, 74.

Contributions.—Episcopal Fund, $2; Diocesan Fund, $2; Missionary Committee of the Diocese, $2 41; Theological Education Fund, $1; Fund for Aged and Infirm Clergymen, $2; Western Convocation, $2 23; Board of Missions P. E. Church U. S.: Foreign Committee, $54 57; the Poor, $6; Parish purposes, $253 62—total, $325 86.

Especial attention has been paid, during the past year, to the work of the Church in the Sunday-School; and though the number of scholars is very small, the progress of the children in the knowledge of the Church Catechism and of Church teachings generally, is very encouraging.

St. George's Church, Newburgh; the Rev. JOHN BROWN, Rector; the Rev. OCTAVIUS APPLEGATE, Assistant Minister; the Rev. GEORGE D. SILLIMAN, officiating in St. George's Mission.

Families, 200. Individuals, 700. Baptisms, (ad. 8, inf. 65,) 73. Marriages, 2. Burials, 36. Communicants: admitted, 21; removed into the Parish, 15; removed from the Parish, 30; died 14; present number, 392. The Holy Communion celebrated on the first Sunday of every month and principal feasts, etc.; in public at the Church, 26, at the Chapel, 26—total, 52; in private, 10. Catechists and Sunday-School teachers, 50. Catechumens: members of classes for religious instruction, 25; Sunday Scholars, 380; total number of young persons instructed, 405. Celebration of Divine Service: Sundays, (at the Church, 110, at the Mission, 123,) 233; Holy Days, (at the Church, 34, at the Mission, 6,) 40; other days, (at the Church, 125, at the Mission, 5,) 130—total, 408.

Contributions.—Episcopal Fund, $18; Diocesan Fund, $40; Missionary Committee of the Diocese, $50; Theological Education Fund, $50 17; Fund for Aged and Infirm Clergymen, $52 42; New-York City Mission Society, $21 30; New-York Bible and Common Prayer-Book Society, $39 16; General Theological Seminary Professorship, $20; Board of Missions P. E. Church U. S.: Domestic Committee, $760 99; Foreign Committee, $113 13; the Poor, alms, $512 35; Parish purposes, $930 29; Church purposes in general, $8; Indian Missions, $163 13; Mission to Colored People, $113 13; Mission to the Jews, $151 75; St. Mark's School, Salt Lake City, $93; Midnight Mission, $50; Western Convocation, $465; Irvington Church Debt, $36 88; Sunday-School Expenses, $50 56; St. George's Mission, (of which by itself the sum of $425 85,) $1,211 30; Benevolent Association, say $125; Altar Society, $129 09; St. Luke's Home and Hospital, Newburgh, $210 60; St. Mary's Hospital, New-York, $16; Church of Jesus, Mexico, $25; Church of the Prince of Peace, Gettysburgh, $10; Bishop Lay's Cathedral, $25; Faribault, $40; Bishop Spalding, $25; Atlanta, Georgia, $85—total, $5,669 65.

In addition to the above amounts, given through the offertory, members of the Parish have contributed liberally to the maintainance of St. Luke's Home and Hospital, which is supported by the gifts of the Church people of Newburgh and New-Windsor.

St. Paul's Church, Newburgh; the Rev. RUFUS EMERY, Rector.

Families, 94. Parts of families, 89. Individuals, 380. Baptisms, (ad. 2, inf. 25,) 27. Confirmed, 14. Marriages, 3. Burials, 13. Communicants: admitted, 4; removed into the Parish, 4; removed from the Parish, 12; died, 3; present number, 141. The Holy Communion celebrated on the first Sunday in every month and every day with Proper Preface. Catechists and Sunday-School teachers, 10. Catechumens: Children taught the Catechism openly in the Church, 95; times, 12. Celebration of Divine Service: Sundays, twice; Holy Days, once; other days, every Wednesday—total, 170.

Contributions.—Episcopal Fund, $5; Diocesan Fund, $5; Missionary Committee of the Diocese, $2; Fund for Aged and Infirm Clergymen, $2; Western Convocation, $8; Sunday-School, $100; the Poor, $50; Parish purposes, $1,272 39; Church purposes in general, $350—total, $1,794 39.

St Thomas' Church, New-Windsor; the Rev. HASLETT MCKIM, Rector.

Families, 37. Individuals, 136. Baptisms, inf. 6. Marriage, 1. Burials, 2. Communicants: removed into the Parish, 4; removed from the Parish, 2; present number, 53. The Holy Communion celebrated on the first Sunday of each month, Christmas and

Whitsun-Day. Catechists and Sunday-School teachers, 6. Catechumens, 51; Children taught the Catechism openly in the Church, monthly. Celebration of Divine Service: Sundays, 92; Holy Days, Christmas, Passion Week, Ash-Wednesday and Ascension; other days, every Friday in Lent and Thanksgiving—total, 108.

The Rector having been delayed in Europe longer than was anticipated, a report of the contributions cannot be given.

In the Rector's absence the Parish has been under the charge of the Rev. Dr. R. H. McKim, Rector of the Church of the Holy Trinity, Harlem.

Grace Church, Port Jervis; the Rev. J. GARDNER ROSENCRANTZ, Rector and Missionary.

Families, 49. Individuals, 204. Baptisms, (ad. 16, inf. 16,) 32. Confirmed, (December 10, 31; July 18, 11,) 42. Marriages, 2. Burials, 9. Communicants: admitted, by Confirmation and from other Parishes, 48; removed into the Parish, 1; removed from the Parish, 5; died, 2; present number, 141. The Holy Communion celebrated on the first and third Sundays of the month, on all festivals for which there is a Proper Preface, and on the first Sundays in Advent and Lent. Catechists and Sunday-School teachers, 8. Catechumens: Children taught the Catechism openly in the Church, about 60; times, 12; members of other classes for religious instruction, about 25, (adults;) Sunday scholars, 70; total number of young persons instructed, 70. Celebration of Divine Service: Sundays, morning and evening; Holy Days, daily in Lent and on festivals; other days, Wednesdays and Fridays during Advent and Wednesdays during the year.

Contributions.—Episcopal Fund, $2; Missionary Committee of the Diocese, $[illegible]; Fund for Aged and Infirm Clergymen, $5; Parish purposes, (including Clergyman's salary, etc.,) $849 91; Church purposes in general, offerings, $450 08—total, $1,[illegible] 14.

Grace Church, Middletown; the Rev. ALEX. CAPRON, Rector.

Baptisms, (ad. 8, inf. and children, 12,) 20. Confirmed, 40. Marriages, 9. Burials, 16. Communicants: admitted, 20; removed into the Parish, 3; removed from the Parish, 8; died, 1; present number, about 240. The Holy Communion celebrated once every month and on high festivals. Catechists and Sunday-School teachers, 24. Catechumens, about 200. Children taught the Catechism openly in the Church, about 200; times, twice a month. Total number of young persons instructed, about 200. Celebration of Divine Service: Sundays, all Sundays of the year; other days, Mission of two weeks in January, every day, and every day in Lent—about 175.

Contributions.—Episcopal Fund, $2; the Poor, $25; Parish purposes, say $600; Church purposes in general, about $2,400—total, $3,025.

This Parish has experienced a sore loss this year in the decease of its long-tried and faithful friend—for thirty years, and from the organization of the Parish, to the time of his death, the Senior Warden, honored, beloved, and now lamented by all—Elisha P. Wheeler. Few men in Orange County have done more for the extension of the Church in this portion of the Diocese, and few men would be more missed or lamented than Mr. Wheeler is.

St. Andrew's Church, Walden; the Rev. WILLIAM EDWARD SNOWDEN, Minister and Missionary.

Baptisms, (ad. 1, inf. 10,) 11. Confirmed, 9. Marriage, 1. Burials, 2. Communicants: present number, 78. The Holy Communion celebrated the first Sunday in every month and on all days for which there is a Special Preface. Catechists and Sunday-School teachers, 10. Catechumens, 50. Children taught the Catechism openly in the Church, 50; times, every Sunday. Members of other classes for religious instruction, a Confirmation class. Total number of young persons instructed, 60. Celebration of Divine Service: Full Morning Prayer, Litany and Ante-Communion, with Sermon and full Evening Prayer with Sermon on all Sundays. Full Morning Prayer and Sermon on the chief Holy Days, and full Evening Prayer and Historical Lecture on the Life of our Lord, on all the week days of Lent.

Contributions.—Episcopal Fund, $2; Diocesan Fund, $9; Missionary Committee of the Diocese, $10; Fund for Aged and Infirm Clergymen, $3; New-York Bible and Common Prayer-Book Society, $4—total, $28.

Christ Church, Warwick; the Rev. ALFRED GOLDSBOROUGH, Rector.

Families, about 35. Individuals, about 100. Baptisms, (ad. 3, inf. 10,) 13. Confirmed, 5. Marriage, 1. Burials, 4. Communicants: admitted, 8; removed into the Parish, 3; removed from the Parish, 8; died, 1; present number, 50. The Holy Communion celebrated the first Sunday in each month and on the higher festivals. Catechists and Sunday-School teachers, 6. Catechumens: Children taught the Catechism openly in the Church, 30. Celebration of Divine Service: Sundays, all Sundays in the year, and on the greater festivals and feasts.

Contributions.—Episcopal Fund, $2; Diocesan Fund, $12; Missionary Committee of the Diocese, $10; Convocation, $20; Fund for Aged and Infirm Clergymen, $5; Board of Missions P. E. Church U. S.: Domestic Committee, (including Indian and Colored,) $6; Foreign Committee, $2; Parish purposes, (interest on Rectory debt,) $105; Church purposes in general, (not including salary,) $210—total, $372.

PUTNAM COUNTY.

St. Mary's Church in the Highlands, Cold Spring; the Rev. ISAAC VAN WINKLE, Rector.

Families, 96. Individuals, about 450. Baptisms, inf. 12. Marriages, 4. Burials, 12. Communicants: admitted, 1; removed from the Parish, 7; died, 6; present number, 66. The Holy Communion celebrated on the first Sunday in the month; during Advent and Lent, every Sunday; on all Holy Days; in private, 8 times. Catechists and Sunday-School teachers, 17. Catechumens: Children taught the Catechism openly in the Church, 140; times, 10; total number of young persons instructed, 140. Celebration of Divine Service: Sundays, 112; Holy Days, 20; other days, 115—total, $247.

Contributions.—Episcopal Fund, $15; Diocesan Fund, $35; Missionary Committee of the Diocese, $11 62; Theological Education Fund, $6 68; Fund for Aged and Infirm Clergymen, $17 70; Church Mission to the Jews, $4 75; Italian Mission in New-York City, $10; Southern Convocation Missions, $77 72; Sunday-School, $273 81; the Poor, $163 40; Parish purposes, $1,720 33—total, $2,336 01.

Christ Church and Mission, Patterson; the Rev. WILBERFORCE WELLS, Missionary.

Families, 33. Individuals, 100. Baptisms, (ad. 14, inf. 8,) 22. Communicants: admitted, 19; removed from the Parish, 3; died, 1; present number, 45. The Holy Communion celebrated at Patterson one service out of every three; in the rest of the Mission less than half as often, there being no Church building except in the former place; service at each place, every other Sunday. Catechists and Sunday-School teachers, 16. Catechumens, 9; Sunday scholars, 150. Celebration of Divine Service: Sundays, 39; Holy Days, 2; other days, 22—total 63.

Contributions.—Missionary Committee of the Diocese, $2 50; the Poor, $9 16; Parish purposes, $250—total, $261 66.

There is one old wooden Church at Patterson. This is the best of the three stations in a financial point of view, and most of the money raised has been for repairing the aforesaid building. At the other two stations, Brewsters and Kent Cliffe, there are no Churches. We meet in unconsecrated buildings. At Patterson there is almost no Sunday-School, at the others, quite flourishing ones.

During three months of this year the present Missionary had not been appointed and there was no service.

St. Philip's Church in the Highlands, Philipsetown; the Rev. Albert Zabriskie Gray, Rector.

Families, about 60. Individuals, about 250. Baptisms, (ad. 2, inf. 14,) 16. Confirmed, 14. Burials, 8. Communicants: present number, about 70. The Holy Communion celebrated on the first Sunday of the month and festivals generally. Catechists and Sunday-School teachers, 10. Catechumens, about 60; Children taught the Catechism openly in the Church, monthly. Celebration of Divine Service: Sundays, twice in Parish Church and once in Mission Chapel of St. James'; Holy Days, all Holy Days; other days, Wednesdays, Fridays and Saturdays, and more frequently in special seasons.

Contributions.—Episcopal Fund, $15; Diocesan Fund, $24; Missionary Committee of the Diocese, $45 75; Missions of Convocation, $60; Theological Education Fund, $19 21; Fund for Aged and Infirm Clergymen, $41 75; Mission to Freedmen, $14 50; St. Mary's Hospital for Children, $15; New-York Bible and Common Prayer-Book Society, $8 84; Protestant Episcopal Tract Society, $7 61; Mission to the Jews, $13 35; "House of Good Shepherd," $36 29; Board of Missions P. E. Church U. S.: Domestic Committee, $388 74; Foreign Committee, $41 85; for "Church of Jesus," in Mexico, $221; Indian Missions, $98 06; Local Mission work, $300; the Poor, $254 80; Sunday-School purposes, $124 45; Parish purposes, including pew rents, offerings, etc., for Parish support, $2,831 45—total, $4,514 05.

Services have been regularly held during the past year in the Mission Chapel of St. James' with increasing and encouraging interest, thanks very much to the generous, Christian aid rendered by a family not immediately connected with this Parish.

The repairs and improvements to the Chapel property, as well as much of the satisfactory results among the poor themselves, are due to the above mentioned and untiring zeal.

RICHMOND COUNTY.

Church of the Ascension, (West-Brighton,) Castleton; the Rev. James S. Bush, Rector.

Families, 133. Individuals, 720. Baptisms, (ad. 3, inf. 40,) 43. Confirmed, 18. Marriages, 5. Burials, 22. Communicants: admitted, 18; removed into the Parish, 5, removed from the Parish, 8; died, 5; present number, 280. The Holy Communion celebrated on the first Sunday in each month and on the greater festivals. Catechists and Sunday-School teachers, 34. Catechumens, 400; Children taught the Catechism openly in the Church, all in the Sunday-School. Celebration of Divine Service: Sundays, twice each Sunday; Holy Days, the greater festivals; other days, three times a week in Lent.

Contributions.—Fund for Aged and Infirm Clergymen, $35 15; Chinese Mission, San Francisco, $119 57; the Poor, $451 83; Church purposes in general, $2,357 80—total, $2,964 35.

St. John's Church, Clifton; the Rev. John C. Eccleston, D. D, Rector.

Individuals, 700. Baptisms, (ad. 2, inf. 45,) 47, Confirmed, 39. Marriages, 11. Burials, 20. Communicants: present number, 300. Catechists and Sunday-School teachers, 20. Catechumens, 300; members of other classes for religious instruction, 100.

Contributions.—Episcopal Fund, $10; Diocesan Fund, $10; Theological Education, $91; Missions: Foreign, Domestic and Diocesan, $438 94; American Bible Society, $75 48; the Poor, $558 17; Parish purposes, including Sunday-School and Mission work, $1,476 23; Church purposes in general, $15,000—total, $17,659 82.

This report covers a period of two Conventional years. Within the past year the new Church debt has been liquidated. The labor of faith and love, on which the Parish entered six years ago, (which has cost $120,000,) is ended.

St. Paul's Memorial Church, Edgewater; the Rev. ALBERT U. STANLEY, Rector.

Families, 200, or more. Individuals, about 1,000. Baptisms, (ad. 6, inf. 44,) 50. Confirmed, 44. Marriages, 7. Burials, 21. Communicants: admitted, 45; removed into the Parish, 2; removed from the Parish, 8; died, 1; present number, about 300. The Holy Communion celebrated every Sunday and upon the greater Holy Days. Catechists and Sunday-School teachers, 21. Catechumens: Children taught the Catechism openly in the Church, 260; times, 11; Sunday scholars, 260. Celebration of Divine Service: Sundays, 128; Holy Days, 31; other days, 118—total, 277.

Contributions.—Episcopal Fund, $8; Diocesan Fund, $15; Fund for Aged and Infirm Clergymen, $23; New-York Bible and Common Prayer-Book Society, $6 79; Board of Missions P. E. Church U. S.: Domestic Committee, $284 18; Foreign Committee, $15 89; the Poor, $159 59; Parish purposes, $2,901 59; Church purposes in general, $118 48—total, $3,532 52.

The present Rector took charge the 25th of October, 1875. The above report, therefore, is in the main particulars for the period of eleven months only.

Christ Church, New-Brighton; the Rev. GEO. D. JOHNSON, Rector.

Baptisms, inf. 25. Confirmed, 15. Marriages, 7. Burials, 19. Communicants: present number, 175. The Holy Communion celebrated on all the greater festivals and on the first Sunday of each month. Catechists and Sunday-School teachers, 20. Catechumens: Children taught the Catechism openly in the Church, 150.

Contributions.—Fund for Aged and Infirm Clergymen, $48 13; Board of Missions P. E. Church U. S.: Domestic Committee, (Indian Commission,) $130 77; Foreign Committee, $348 65; the Poor, $246; Parish purposes, &c., $1,931 74—total, $2,705 29.

St Luke's Church, Rossville; (no Rector.)

Families, 43. Individuals, 129. Baptisms, inf. 3. Burials, 4. Communicants, 50; removed into the Parish, 3; died, 4. The Holy Communion celebrated on the first Sunday of the month. Catechists and Sunday-School teachers, 8. Catechumens: Sunday scholars, 50; total number of young persons instructed, 50.

Contributions.—Fund for Aged and Infirm Clergymen, $20; Board of Missions P. E. Church U. S.: Domestic Committee, $9 53; Foreign Committee, $13 40; Parish purposes, $861—total, $903 93.

Church of the Holy Comforter, (Eltingville,) Southfield, and Mission at Tottenville; the Rev. FREDERICK M. GRAY, Rector.

Families, 62. Individuals, 228. Baptisms, (ad. 2, inf. 14,) 16. Confirmed, 15. Marriages, 2. Burials, 6. Communicants: present number, 60. The Holy Communion celebrated the first Sunday in every month in the Parish Church, and on Christmas Day, Easter Day and Whitsun-Day. The second Sunday in the month at Tottenville, also on Christmas Day and Whitsun-Day. Catechumens: Children taught the Catechism openly in the Church, 40; times, 8; Sunday scholars, 25; total number of young persons instructed, 65. Celebration of Divine Service: Sundays, 134; Holy Days, 7; other days, 9—total, 150.

Contributions.—Fund for Aged and Infirm Clergymen, $5 60; Board of Missions P. E. Church U. S.: Domestic Committee, $38; Parish purposes, $966; Church purposes in general, $24—total, $1,083 60.

Since December I have held services at Tottenville on Sunday afternoons. This point has never been fairly occupied by the Church, although the village is the largest centre of population on this part of the Island. I have found twenty Church families, and baptized 2 adults and 10 infants. Nine persons were confirmed at the Parish Church in July, (all included in above report.) The attendance at the service averages about forty.

ROCKLAND COUNTY.

St. John's Church, Clarkstown; the Rev. ROMAINE S. MANSFIELD, Rector and Missionary.

Families, 32. Individuals, about 160. Baptisms, inf. 1. Marriage, 1. Burial, 1. Communicants: present number, 26. Celebration of Divine Service: once each Sunday; Holy Days, high festivals; other days and total, 65.

Contributions.—Diocesan Fund, $2; Missionary Committee of the Diocese, $1 60; House of the Good Shepherd, $6 05; Parish purposes, (including Rector's salary,) $[illegible]—total, $500 28.

Trinity Church, Haverstraw; the Rev. GEO. W. WEST, M. A., Rector and Missionary.

Families, 81. Individuals, 418. Baptisms, (ad. 19, inf. 25,) 44. Confirmed, 32. Marriage, 1 Burials, 8. Communicants: admitted, 36; removed into the Parish, 4; removed from the Parish, 15; died, 1; present number, 105. The Holy Communion celebrated every Sunday, Christmas, Ascension Day and Thanksgiving Day. Catechists and Sunday-School teachers, 12. Catechumens: Children taught the Catechism openly in the Church, 120; times, 50; total number of young persons instructed, 120. Daily Parish School, 1; paid. Scholars: males, 6; females, 15. Night School, 1. Celebration of Divine Service: Sundays, 130; Holy Days, 3; other days, 14—total, 147.

Contributions.—Episcopal Fund, $2; Diocesan Fund, $5; Missionary Committee of the Diocese, $5; the Poor, $15 88; Parish purposes, $299 60; Church purposes in general, $205; Rector's salary, $800—total, $1,332 48.

The Rector takes this opportunity of adding, among other indications of prosperity, that the land has been given for the erection of a Parsonage, and it is expected that the building will be completed by spring.

The Sunday-School has been graded so that pupils who enter the lowest class, the Calvary Catechism, will be taken through a complete course of Church instruction, and end with the Confirmation class.

A night school, in addition to the daily Parish School, has been started—a want long felt among the men and boys engaged in the Print Works.

In memory of the Rev. C. B. Coffin, who died six weeks after resigning this Parish, and who was greatly endeared to all his people, a solid floriated brass Altar Cross was presented to the Church on Easter Day, by the members of the Choir.

Grace Church, Nyack; the Rev. FRANKLIN BABBITT, Rector.

Families, 85. Baptisms, (ad. 6, inf. 14,) 20. Confirmed, 10. Marriages, 4. Burials, 14. Communicants: present number, 141. The Holy Communion celebrated monthly. Sunday-School teachers, 7. Catechumens: Sunday scholars, 60. Celebration of Divine Service: Sundays, twice, and principal Holy Days.

Contributions.—Episcopal Fund, $3; Diocesan Fund, $5 81; Missionary Committee of the Diocese, $20 69; Weekly offertory, $604 43; Fund for Aged and Infirm Clergymen, $18 45; New Church, about $2,300; Board of Missions P. E. Church U. S.: Domestic Committee, $22 63; House of Good Shepherd, Rockland County, $17 06; the Poor, $68 64; Parish purposes, $45 10; Sunday-School, $59 05—total, $3,158 97.

Christ Church, Piermont; the Rev. SOL. G. HITCHCOCK, Rector and Missionary.

Families, 46. Baptisms, (ad. 1, inf. and children, 16,) 17. Marriages, 7. Burials, 19. Communicants: admitted, 8; removed into the Parish, 7; removed from the Parish, 7; died, 4; present number, 75. The Holy Communion celebrated from Trinity to Advent on the first Sunday of each month, from Advent to Trinity in accordance with the ecclesiastical year. Sunday-School teachers, 9; Scholars, 121. Celebration of Divine Service: Sundays, A. M. and P. M., or evening; Holy Days, such as are of general observance; other days, as occasion may require.

Contributions.—Episcopal Fund, $2; Diocesan Fund, $5; Missionary Committee of the Diocese, $7; Southern Convocation, $10; Church Mission to Jews, $5; Fund for Aged and Infirm Clergymen, $3 65; Orphans' Home Asylum, $10; House of Good Shepherd, $10; Sheltering Arms, $2; New-York Bible and Common Prayer-Book Society, $7; Protestant Episcopal Tract Society, $10; General P. E. S. S. Union and Church Book Society, $4 33; Board of Missions P. E. Church U. S.: Domestic Committee, (Mr. and Mrs. S., $20,) $25; Foreign Committee, (Mr. and Mrs. S., $20,) $46 23; Indian Commission, $4 13; Home Missions to Colored People, $2; the Poor, $24 39; Sunday-School, (Mrs. S., $25; Christmas Tree, $100,) $153 12; Parish purposes, $461 45; towards Salary, $52 11; Church purposes in general, $1; Ministerial gifts and perquisites, $130—total, $998 41.

The family of the late James F. De Peyster, Esq., though no longer resident in the place, have shown a very gratifying interest in the minister and his work, by the presentation to him of a check for $100.

The liberality of the congregation, too, as evinced by the ordinary Sunday collection, has exceeded that of previous years.

Our A. M. service has been attended by a goodly number, including such as Henry E. Lawrence, Esq., and family from New-York city, and the attendance at the P. M. or evening service has been better than usual.

The blessing of peace is enjoyed by both minister and people.

Christ Church, Ramapo; the Rev. GUSTAV EDMUND PURUCKER, Rector and Missionary.

Families and parts of families, 36. Individuals, 159. Baptisms, (ad. 1, inf. 4,) 5. Confirmed, 8. Marriages, 5. Burials, 3. Communicants: admitted, 8; removed into the Parish, 8; removed from the Parish, 5; died, 1; present number, 51. The Holy Communion celebrated on the first Sunday of every month, and on the great Church festivals noted with a Preface in the Communion Office. Catechists and Sunday-School teachers, 3; Librarian, 1. Catechumens, 47; Children taught the Catechism openly in the Church, 47; times, 12; total number of young persons instructed, 47. Celebration of Divine Service: twice every Lord's Day; Holy Days, once each Holy Day; other days, all through Lent, once daily, and twice on Wednesdays and Fridays throughout; Thanksgiving Day, 1—total, 172.

Contributions.—Episcopal Fund, $3; Missionary Committee of the Diocese, $3; Theological Education Fund, $1; Fund for Aged and Infirm Clergymen, $4; the Sunday-School's Christmas Tree, Easter Party, Pic-nic and books, $39; the Poor, (from the Communion Alms.) $19 41; Parish purposes, (including the balance of Communion Alms.) $1,022 87; Church purposes in general, $6 60—total, $1,106 58.

The above statistics as to the number of families and individuals do not include the colored portion of Church members, of whom there are about one hundred baptised souls.

The Pastor of this Parish, about to leave it, deems it but proper and just, as well as a slight tribute of grateful acknowledgment, to mention that during the past two years the Church and her ministering servant here have indeed had a staunch and faithful friend in their Senior Warden, Mr. Wm. G. Hamilton, who, despite discouraging trials, has stood forth with a real, self-sacrificing generosity and liberality.

Christ Church, Suffern, though ever slowly progressing in regard to numerical strength, has yet of late years gained, at least, in point of Churchliness, and a marked appreciation on the part of some for our beautiful Liturgy and services. May the wing of time, by the Eternal Spirit, fan this appreciation into a flame of love, which shall truly magnify the Lord our Saviour!

St. Paul's Church, Spring Valley; the Rev. ROMAINE S. MANSFIELD, Rector and Missionary.

Baptisms, inf. 13. Marriage, 1. Burials, 4. Communicants: removed into the Parish, 3; removed from the Parish, 3; present number, 86. Catechumens, 10; Children taught the Catechism openly in the Church, 60; times, 4; total number of young persons instructed, 60. Celebration of Divine Service: Sundays, twice; Holy Days, Fridays in Lent; other days, high festivals—total, 125.

Contributions.—For Parish purposes, including Rector's Salary, $460; from all sources, for the Building Fund, $613 41—total, $1,073 41.

SULLIVAN COUNTY.

St. John's Church, Monticello; the Rev. CHARLES F. CANEDY, Rector and Missionary.

Families, 104. Individuals, 418. Baptisms, (ad. 15, inf. 9,) 24. Confirmed, 32. Marriages, 5. Burials, 11. Communicants: admitted, 22; removed into the Parish, 6, removed from the Parish, 4; died, 1; present number, 166. The Holy Communion celebrated on the first and third Sundays of every month and on the chief festivals. Catechists and Sunday-School teachers, 25. Catechumens: Children taught the Catechism openly in the Church, 179; times, 15; total number of young persons instructed, 179. Celebration of Divine Service: Sundays, 116; Holy Days, 24; other days, 50—total, 190.

Contributions.—Episcopal Fund, $2; Diocesan Fund, $16; Missionary Committee of the Diocese, $10 74; Fund for Aged and Infirm Clergymen, $10 57; Centennial Fund, $5; the Poor, $1 45; Parish purposes, (Monticello, including Rector's Salary, $1,395 81; Thompsonville, $406 60; Callicoon Depot, $1,100,) $2,902 41; Church purposes in general, $7 55—total, $2,955 72.

The above report includes the ministrations of the Rector at three Mission Stations outside of Monticello. During the year two Chapels have been finished and opened for Divine Service. St. James', at Callicoon Depot, was opened in January, and was entirely freed from debt in May last. The building is delightfully situated upon a valuable plot of ground given by the Hon. James C. Curtis. St. Mary's, at Thompsonville, begun during the rectorship of the Rev. G. D. Silliman, was opened on St. Matthew's Day, 1876. This Chapel has accommodations for seating one hundred and sixty people, and has an unusually neat and attractive interior. The Rector has been assisted during the past summer by Mr. Francis J. Clayton as Lay Reader.

It is our painful duty to mention that the Rev. E. K. Fowler, for forty-two years Rector of this Parish, has so far failed in health that he is no longer able to leave his room, and that his many infirmities are fast increasing.

ULSTER COUNTY.

St. John's Memorial Church, Ellenville; the Rev. O. VALENTINE, Rector and Missionary.

Families, 63. Individuals, about 175. Baptisms, (ad. 21, inf. 42,) 63. Confirmed, 24. Marriage, 1. Burials, 14. Communicants: admitted, 19; removed from the Parish, 17; present number, 65. The Holy Communion celebrated first Sunday of the month. Catechumens, 75; Children taught the Catechism openly in the Church, 75; times, 14. Celebration of Divine Service: Sundays, all; Holy Days, chief festivals and Saints' days; other days, Lent, Wednesday and Friday evenings; Passion Week, daily, morning and evening; every Friday evening throughout the year.

Contributions.—Episcopal Fund, $2; Missionary Committee of the Diocese, $3; Church purposes in general, $668 68—total, $673 68.

The present Rector and Missionary entered upon his duties Aug. 1, 1875. During the past year, besides his regular duties at E., he has held weekly missionary services at Oak Ridge, three miles from E. He has had much to encourage him in his labors, and hopes to see the Church planted firmly in these parts.

Church of the Ascension, Esopus; the Rev. HENRY BEERS SHERMAN, Rector.

Marriage, 1. Burials, 3. Communicants: admitted, 1; died, 1. The Holy Communion celebrated monthly. Catechumens: Sunday scholars, 30.

The congregation, which is composed of summer residents, is much the same as formerly reported, and there is no present likelihood of either diminution or growth.

St. John's Church, Kingston; the Rev. C. WILLIAM CAMP, Rector.

Families, 117. Baptisms, (ad. 3, inf. 14,) 17. Confirmed, 19. Marriages, 4. Burials, 10. Communicants: admitted, 18; removed into the Parish, 7; removed from the Parish, 22; died, 5; present number, 173. The Holy Communion celebrated first Sunday in every month, also Holy Days having Proper Preface. Children taught the Catechism openly in the Church, weekly. Celebration of Divine Service: Sundays, 147; Holy Days, 49; other days, 84—total, 280.

Contributions.—Episcopal Fund, $3 31; Diocesan Fund, $24; Missionary Committee of the Diocese, $5 45; Fund for Aged and Infirm Clergymen, $22 70; the Poor, $121 87; Parish purposes, $2,560 17—total, $2,737 50.

Church of the Holy Spirit, Rondout; the Rev. A. SIDNEY DEALEY, Rector.

Families, 104. Individuals, 426. Baptisms, (ad. 1, inf. 15,) 16. Confirmed, 32, (*one* at St. Luke's, Catskill.) Burials, 10. Communicants: present number, 102. The Holy Communion celebrated the first Sunday in each month, the principal festivals, and four times in private. Catechists and Sunday-School teachers, 12. Catechumens: Sunday scholars, 110. Celebration of Divine Service, *from Jan.* [illegible], 1876: Sundays, [illegible]; Holy Days, 15; other days, 23—total, 105.

Contributions.—Board of Missions P. E. Church U. S.: Domestic Committee, $[illegible]; the Poor, (Communion Alms,) $19 56; Parish purposes, $1,350 [illegible]—total, $1,[illegible].

The congregation is largely composed of mechanics and laboring people. The financial condition of the Parish—partly in consequence of the hard times—is very much depressed. This must account for the failure to make the Canonical and other offerings. We are not meeting the running expenses.

Christ Church, Marlborough; the Rev. GEORGE WATERS, D. D., Rector.

Families, 20. Individuals, 80. Baptisms, (ad. 1, inf. 2,) 3. Marriages, 2. Burials, 1. Communicants: present number, 45. The Holy Communion celebrated monthly. Sunday-School teachers, 5; Scholars, 40. Bible Class, in all, 57. Total number taught the Catechism openly in the Church, 55; generally on Sunday afternoons. Celebration of Divine Service: Twice on Sundays, and on the principal festivals and fasts, and on the Fridays and Saturdays of Lent; also Thanksgiving Day.

Contributions.—Diocesan Fund, $4; Missionary Committee of the Diocese, $11 [illegible]; Board of Missions P. E. Church U. S.: Foreign Committee, $5; Weekly offertory, $118 67; Parish purposes, (Ladies' Festival and Fair,) $155; other contributions, $[illegible]—total, $349 37.

This Parish, though small, is in a sound and healthy condition. It has made progress for the year, and good opportunity is afforded for its appropriate work.

The present Rector, being about to retire from the charge, would cordially commend it to the attention of some earnest Pastor. The beautiful Church and commodious Parsonage, situated on the Hudson, and amidst the finest rural scenery, await some faithful occupant.

No visitation of the Bishop has been enjoyed, but a few candidates for Confirmation anticipate his next coming.

All Saints' Church, Milton; the Rev. JOSEPH H. JOHNSON, Rector and Missionary.

Families, 22 Individuals, 103. Baptisms, (ad. 17, inf. 24,) 41. Confirmed, 14. Marriages, 2. Burials, 6. Communicants: admitted, 14; removed from the Parish, 3; present number, 50. The Holy Communion celebrated Sundays and Holy Days. Catechists and Sunday-School teachers, 6. Catechumens, 60. Celebration of Divine Service: Sundays, Holy Communion at 7, at Highland; Morning Prayer and Sermon at 10.30, at Milton; Evening Prayer and Sermon at 3 P. M., at Highland; Litany and Sermon at Brownville, 7 P. M.; Holy Days, Holy Communion; other days, Communicants' Class, Monday evening; Evening Prayer and Sermon at Clintondale—total, 325.

Contributions.—Total, $1,500.

Trinity Church, Saugerties; the Rev. J. J. ROBERTSON, D. D., Rector.

Families, about 53. Individuals, about 219. Baptisms, (ad. 5, inf. 9,) 14. Confir[illegible] 32 Marriages, 5. Burials, 8. Communicants; admitted, 27; removed into the Pa[illegible] 1; died, 4; present number, 99. The Holy Communion celebrated the first Lord's D[illegible] each month, and festivals with Preface, except Ascension Day; private Communion[illegible] Catechists and Sunday-School teachers, 25. Catechumens, 157. Children taught the [illegible]chism openly in the Church, pupils of Sunday School and a few others; times, 5. [illegible]bration of Divine Service: Sundays, 99; Holy Days, 12; other days, 107—total, 218.

Contributions.—Bishop's salary, $4; Episcopal Fund, $3 62; Diocesan Fund, $18; for Western Convocation of N. Y. Diocese, $60; Missionary Committee of the Diocese, $118 28; Theological Education Fund, $12 71; Fund for Aged and Infirm Clergymen, $32 63; Church Mission to Jews, $17 58; Indian Commission, $29 17; Pupils of Sunday-School, for Indian Commission, $25; New-York Bible and Common Prayer-Book Society, $44 15; Protestant Episcopal Tract Society, $39 22; General P. E. S. S. Union and Church Book Society, $8 86; Home Mission to Colored People, $27 68; Board of Missions P. E. Church U. S.: Domestic Committee, $97 90; Foreign Committee, $102 85; the Poor, (Communion Alms,) $119 07; Parish purposes, $117 30; from Sewing Soc. of Trinity Church, Saugerties, box for Rev. Jacob Welch, Charleston, S. C., box valued at $90; to aid a Rector in Donaldsonville, Louisiana, $65; (To be added to Report for 1875, received too late for insertion then,) box to Parish at Camden, S. C., $70; box to St. Mark's Hospital, Salt Lake City, $78 25; box to Bp. Whittle's Hospital, White Earth, Minn., $110—total, $1,157 25.

The Report of Trinity Church, Saugerties, shows, that notwithstanding the pressure of the times, its usual liberality towards the charities of the Church continues. In spiritual things, through the grace of God, the Church is improving. The number confirmed, on a late occasion, is 32, and there is a large addition to the communicants. Both these are greatly owing, under God, to the earnest and intelligent zeal of the male and female Superintendents of the Sunday Schools. Both have been unwearied in their devotion to the schools, and also to visitations to the poor and others. The teachers, too, are giving fresh indications of their interest in the work of instruction. The Rector cannot be too thankful for this aid, as his own energies have been lessened by the painful condition of his family, interfering much with his repose at night. Still he has been able to continue regularly his duties twice each Lord's Day in Church, and to hold two services in the Chapel in the week. One of these has lately been transferred to a large Hall in a distant part of the town, where, in addition to the regular evening service, a Lecture is given. Here, also, a second flourishing Sunday-School has been organized by the male Superintendent. The expense of rent, &c., for this is considerable, and is assumed by a few liberal members of the Church. During domestic trials, the Rector and his family feel grateful for the kind sympathy and benefactions, still continued, of the congregation.

St. Peter's Church, Stone Ridge; the Rev. Wm. H. Tomlins, Deacon, Minister in charge and Missionary. (P. O. Address, High Falls, Ulster County.)

Families, 39. Individuals, 159. Baptisms, (ad. 6, inf 20,) 26. Confirmed: a Class in preparation. Burials, 2. Communicants: removed from the Parish, 6; present number, 16. The Holy Communion celebrated first Sunday in each month, also once a month in the Mission at Rosendale. Catechists and Sunday-School teachers, 4. Catechumens, 34; Children taught the Catechism openly in the Church, 34; times, 5. Celebration of Divine Service: Sundays, morning and afternoon; Holy Days, morning service.

Contributions.—Episcopal Fund, $2; Diocesan Fund, $10; Missionary Committee of the Diocese, $2; Fund for Aged and Infirm Clergymen, $2; New-York City Mission Society, $2; Board of Missions P. E. Church U. S.: Domestic Committee, $5; Foreign Committee, $6; Church purposes in general, $5—total, $34.

The present Clergyman has had charge of the Church work in this part of Ulster County less than two months Some of the details cannot be given in the Report.

The building of a Church has just been begun in the village of Rosendale. It is hoped it will be finished before winter.

Baptisms, celebration of Holy Communion, Burials, &c., by Rev. Alfred E. Johnson, who resigned the Parish Aug. 15, 1876.

WESTCHESTER COUNTY

St. Matthew's Church, Bedford; the Rev. LEA LUQUER, Rector.

Families, 47. Baptisms, (ad. 7, inf. 6,) 13. Confirmed, 12. Marriage, 1. Burials, 14. Communicants: died, 3; present number, 84. The Holy Communion celebrated on the first Sunday of each month and on the greater festivals. Catechumens, 80.

Contributions.—Episcopal Fund, $4; Fund for Aged and Infirm Clergymen, $[illegible]; Board of Missions P. E. Church U. S.: Centennial collection, $47 77; Foreign Committee, $19 10; Am. Ch. Miss. Soc., $18 51; Parish purposes, Repairs, &c., about $[illegible]; Church purposes, $154 11—total, $856 97.

Grace Church, City Island; the Rev. JOSHUA MORSELL, D. D., Rector and Missionary.

Families, 41. Individuals, 150. Baptisms, (ad. 1, inf. 6,) 7. Confirmed, 10. Marriages, 5. Burials, 4. Communicants: admitted, 3; removed from the Parish, 2; present number, 40. The Holy Communion celebrated on the first Sabbath in every month. Catechists and Sunday-School teachers, 14. Catechumens: Sunday scholars, about 90. Celebration of Divine Service: Sundays, morning and evening service; Holy Days, festivals of the Church and season of Lent, three services weekly; other days, Wednesdays and Fridays.

Contributions.—Church collections, $81 83; Sunday-School collections, $[illegible]; Communion Alms, $21 08; Debt on Parsonage, $70; Board of Missions P. E. Church U. S.: Domestic Committee, $10; Foreign Committee, (Missionary Boxes,) $10; Sunday-School Festival, $100; Parish purposes, $331; Church purposes in general, (St. Luke's Hospital,) $2—total, $655 86.

In addition to my regular parochial duties, I have been preaching, by permission of Rev. Mr. Higbee, Rector of Christ Church, at the Town Hall in Pelham, for the past three months. The congregation has numbered about forty attendants. A Sunday-School of fifteen or twenty children are in attendance each Sabbath.

Church of the Divine Love, Cortlandt; the Rev. GOUVERNEUR CRUGER, Rector and Missionary.

Baptisms, (ad. 2, inf. 22,) 24. Burials, 3. Communicants: present number, 27. The Holy Communion celebrated on the first Sunday of each month and greater festivals. Catechists and Sunday-School teachers, 13. Catechumens: Children taught the Catechism openly in the Church, about 160; times, 52; total number of young persons instructed, 160. Celebration of Divine Service: Sundays, all, 103; Holy Days, 13; other days, 1—total, 117.

Contributions.—Episcopal Fund, $3 85; Diocesan Fund, $3 85; Missionary Committee of the Diocese, $3 85; Theological Education Fund, $3 85; Fund for Aged and Infirm Clergymen, $3 85; Parish purposes, $368 31—total, $387 56.

A class of more than ordinary numbers is prepared for Confirmation, and awaits the early visitation of the Bishop.

For the last eight months, during the absence of the Rector, the Rev. Wm. M. Cook has been in charge of this Parish, and has carried on the Church work with much success.

The Rector re-assumes charge the 16th Sunday after Trinity.

All Saints' Church, Briar Cliff; the Rev. J. BRECKENRIDGE GIBSON, D. D., Rector.

Families, 10. Individuals, about 50. Confirmed, 2. Marriage, 1. Burial, 1. Communicants: present number, 25. The Holy Communion celebrated on all greater festivals and the first Sunday of every month. Celebration of Divine Service: Sundays, 104; Holy Days, 9—total, 113.

Contributions.—Episcopal Fund, $4; Diocesan Fund, $4; Missionary Committee of the Diocese, $12 17; New-York Mission to Jews, $8 26; New-York Bible and Common Prayer-Book Society, $14 52; Board of Missions P. E. Church U. S.: Domestic Committee, $15 25; Foreign Committee, $14 03; the Poor, $29 40; Parish purposes, $561 95—total, $663 58.

St. Paul's Chapel, Saw-Mill Valley, Greenburgh; the Rev. JOHN DRISLER, Deacon, Missionary.

Families, 8. Individuals, 25. Baptisms, inf. 1. Communicants: removed from the Parish, 1; present number, 12. The Holy Communion celebrated as often as a Priest can be obtained to administer it. Catechists and Sunday-School teachers, 2. Catechumens, 16. Celebration of Divine Service: Sundays, twice; Holy Days, all principal Holy Days; other days, every Friday during Lent.

Contributions.—Episcopal Fund, $2; Fund for Aged and Infirm Clergymen, $2 60; New-York Bible and Common Prayer Book Society, $2 94; Board of Missions P. E. Church U. S.: Domestic Committee, $3 10; Foreign Committee, $2—total, $12 64.

The report about the same as last year—no improvement in the state of the mission.

Zion Church, Greenburgh; the Rev. GEORGE B. REESE, Rector.

Baptisms, inf. 12. Marriages, 2. Burials, 9. Communicants: present number, 100. The Holy Communion celebrated on the first Sunday of every month, and on the greater festivals. Catechumens: Children taught the Catechism openly in the Church, 150; total number of young persons instructed, 150. Celebration of Divine Service, as heretofore reported.

Contributions.—Episcopal Fund, $10; Diocesan Fund, $25; Missionary Committee of the Diocese, $10; Fund for Aged and Infirm Clergymen, $20 75; Board of Missions P. E. Church U. S.: Foreign Committee, $34; Parochial Schools, $29; the Poor, $173 54; Parish purposes, $1,471 20; Mexico, "Church of Jesus," $26 25—total, $1,799 74.

During the past year the ladies of the Church have organized a Missionary Association, which has made up and sent away two boxes of valuable clothing; one having been sent to a Domestic, and the other to a Foreign Missionary station.

St. John's Church, Lewisboro'; the Rev. ROBERT BOLTON, A. M., Rector.

Families, 30. Individuals, 90. Baptisms, (ad. 1, inf. 2,) 3. Marriages, 3. Burial, 1. Communicants, 35; removed from the Parish, 1; present number, 35. The Holy Communion celebrated the first Sunday in every month and on the greater festivals. Catechist and Sunday-School teacher, 1. Catechumens, 10; members of other classes for religious instruction, 5; total number of young persons instructed, 15. Daily Parish schools: one, paid; Scholars, males 8, females, 9. Celebration of Divine Service: every Lord's Day, A. M. and P. M.

Contributions.—Episcopal Fund, $1; Diocesan Fund, 50 cts.; Missionary Committee of the Diocese, $3; Theological Education Fund, 50 cts.; Fund for Aged and Infirm Clergymen, 50 cts.—total, $5 50.

St. Thomas' Church, Mamaroneck; the Rev. William White Montgomery, Rector.

Baptisms, (ad. 5, inf. 14,) 19. Confirmed, 8. Marriages, 5. Burials, 16. Communicants: admitted, 6; removed from the Parish, 6; died, 2; present number, [illegible]. The Holy Communion celebrated in public seventeen times, including Christmas Day, first Sunday in Lent, Easter Day, Ascension Day, Whitsun-Day and Trinity Sunday; and three times in private. Catechists and Sunday-School teachers, 8. Catechumens, [illegible]. Celebration of Divine Service: Sundays, [illegible]; Holy Days and other days, [illegible]—total, [illegible].

Contributions.—Episcopal Fund, $9; Diocesan Fund, $[illegible]; Missionary Committee of the Diocese, $32; Fund for Aged and Infirm Clergymen, $61 [illegible]; New-York Bible and Common Prayer-Book Society, $19; Society for the Jews, $10 25; Board of Missions P. E. Church U. S.: Domestic Committee, $23; Foreign Committee, (for Africa, from Sunday-School,) $40; Parochial Schools, (for Sunday-School festivals,) $[illegible]; the Poor, $168 43; Parish purposes, $1,108 06—total, $1,511 99.

St. Mark's Church, Mount Pleasant; the Rev. Edmund Guilbert, (resigned in June, 1876,) late Rector. Reported by the Clerk of the Vestry.

Families, 68. Individuals, 256. Baptisms, inf. 24. Confirmed, 12. Marriages, 2. Burials, 12. Communicants: present number, 134. The Holy Communion celebrated on the first Sunday in the month and on the high festivals. Catechists and Sunday-School teachers, 19. Catechumens, 80. Celebration of Divine Service: Sundays, regularly morning and evening; Holy Days, on all high festivals, and Wednesdays and Fridays during Lent, and usually on Saints' Days.

The Rev. Edmund Guilbert, the Rector, tendered his resignation in June, owing to illness in his family, and sailed for Europe on the 19th of July. For this reason no definite statement can be given of the "Contributions" for the past year, as the Vestry find no record of the same.

Trinity Church, Mount Vernon; the Rev. Wm. B. Hooper, Rector.

Families, 108. Individuals, 500. Baptisms, (ad. 1, inf. 11,) 12. Confirmed, 8. Marriages, 6. Burials, 9. Communicants: admitted, 10; removed into the Parish, 9; removed from the Parish, 11; died, 2; present number, 184. The Holy Communion celebrated in Advent and Lent, every Sunday; the first Sunday of the month during the remainder of the year, and on all festivals. Catechists and Sunday-School teachers, 14. Catechumens, 145; Children taught the Catechism openly in the Church, 145; times, 9; members of other classes for religious instruction, 8; total number of young persons instructed, 153. Celebration of Divine Service: Sundays, twice; Holy Days, once with Holy Communion; other days, Fridays throughout the year, daily during Holy Week, four times a week during the rest of Lent.

Contributions.—Episcopal Fund, $3; Diocesan Fund, $24; Missionary Committee of the Diocese, $3 64; Fund for Aged and Infirm Clergymen, $6 50; Church Mission to the Jews, $3 85; Board of Missions P. E. Church U. S.: Domestic Committee, $25 22; the Poor, $50 24; Church purposes in general, (exclusive of pew rents,) $2,134 68—total, $2,255 53.

During the past Conventional year we have paid off the entire floating indebtedness of the Parish, and reduced the mortgage debt.

St. Mark's Church, New-Castle; the Rev. Joseph H. Young, Rector.

Families, 29. Baptisms, (ad. 5, inf. 14.) 19. Burials, 4. Communicants, 32; died, 2. The Holy Communion celebrated on the first Sunday in the month and high festivals.

Catechists and Sunday-School teachers, 6. Catechumens, 40; Children taught the Catechism openly in the Church, 40.

Contributions.—Board of Missions P. E. Church U. S.: Domestic Committee, $25; Parish purposes, $900—total, $925.

St. Stephen's Church, North Castle; the Rev. C. W. BOLTON, Rector.

Families, 41. Individuals, 108. Baptisms, (ad. 1, inf. 11,) 12. Confirmed, 7. Marriages, 6. Burials, 6. Communicants, 62; admitted, 10; removed into the Parish, 2; died, 1; present number, 62. The Holy Communion celebrated first Sunday in the month. Catechists and Sunday-School teachers, 4. Catechumens: Sunday Scholars, 86. Celebration of Divine Service: Sundays, every Sunday; Holy Days, Christmas, Ash-Wednesday, Good Friday and Thanksgiving.

Contributions.—Fund for Aged and Infirm Clergymen, $6 32; Indian Mission, $58 92; Jews Mission, $2 01; Board of Missions P. E. Church U. S.: American Church Missionary Society, $8 60; Foreign Committee, $12 48; Sunday-Schools, $17 30; the Poor, $36 95—total, $142 58.

St. Peter's Church, (Cortlandt,) Peekskill; the Rev. WM. FISHER LEWIS, Rector; the Rev. H. M. TORBERT, Assistant Minister and Chaplain at St. Gabriel's School.

Families, 110. Baptisms, (ad. 10, inf. 38,) 48. Confirmed, 43. Marriage, 1. Burials, 19. Communicants: admitted, 16; removed into the Parish, 6; removed from the Parish, 3; died, 2; present number, 126. The Holy Communion celebrated every Sunday, Christmas, Easter and Whitsun-Day, two celebrations; private Communions, 6. Catechists and Sunday-School teachers, 14. Catechumens, 134; Children taught the Catechism openly in the Church, 134; times, 12. Celebration of Divine Service: Sundays, Parish Church once a month, St. Peter's Chapel three services; Holy Days, morning service; other days, Advent, Wednesday and Friday, morning service, Lent, daily Morning and Evening Prayer.

Contributions.—Episcopal Fund, $7; Diocesan Fund, $30; Missionary Committee of the Diocese, $15; Theological Education Fund, $3 45; Fund for Aged and Infirm Clergymen, $16 16; New-York City Mission Society for Jews, $9 47; Southern Missionary Convocation, $50 52; House of the Good Shepherd, $33 50; St. Mary's Hospital, $30 55; Board of Missions P. E. Church U. S.: Domestic Committee, $10; Indian Committee, $15; Colored Missionary Committee, $10; Parochial Schools, $249 33; the Poor, $92 86; Parish purposes, $821 49; Church purposes in general, (St. Peter's Guild,) $101 12—total, $1,510 35.

St. Peter's Church, Port Chester; the Rev. BROCKHOLST MORGAN, Rector.

Families, 150. Individuals, 600. Baptisms, (ad. 2, inf. 24,) 26. Marriages, 8. Burials, 16. Communicants: admitted, 13; removed from the Parish, 11; died, 2; present number, 161. The Holy Communion celebrated on the first Sunday in every month, and at Easter, Whitsun-Day and Christmas. Catechists and Sunday-School teachers, 30. Catechumens: Children taught the Catechism openly in the Church, 250. Celebration of Divine Service: Sundays, 100; other days, 60—total, 160.

Contributions.—American Church Missionary Society, $51 92; Nebraska, $12 02; Bishop Tuttle's School, Salt Lake, $40; Home for Aged Deaf Mutes, $10 58; Diocesan Missions, $8 65; Jewish Mission, $10 31; Sunday-School, $246 84; the Poor, $200; Parish purposes, $1,230; Church purposes in general, $4 83—total, $1,815 15.

This Parish is in a highly prosperous condition, and full of earnest, vigorous life. During this year it has steadily maintained its past reputation, and has grown really beyond expectation.

Christ Church, Rye; the Rev. CHAUNCEY B. BREWSTER, Rector.

Families, 168. Baptisms, (ad. 4, inf. 26,) 30. Confirmed, 21. Marriages, 5. Burials, 12. Communicants: admitted, 23; removed into the Parish, 9; removed from the Parish, 1; died, 2; present number, 248. The Holy Communion celebrated on the first Sunday in the month, the chief festivals, Thursday before Easter, and All Saints' Day; in private, three times. Catechists and Sunday-School teachers, 25. Catechumens: in Parish Sunday-School, 130; in Sunday-School at Milton, 45; Children taught the Catechism openly in the Church, 130; times, 12; total number of young persons instructed, 175. Celebration of Divine Service: Sundays, twice in the Parish Church; every Sunday evening in the Chapel at Milton; Holy Days, morning service; other days, Fridays; during Lent, frequently in the Parish Church, and at Milton.

Contributions.—Episcopal Fund, $18; Diocesan Fund, $60; Missionary Committee of the Diocese, $41 87; Theological Education Fund, $14 74; Fund for Aged and Infirm Clergymen, $48 66; Mission to Jews, $21 93; Bishop Garrett, $80 48; Bishop Holly, $40; New-York Bible and Common Prayer-Book Society, $36 13; Society for Increase of Ministry, $100; Southern Missionary Convocation, $18 85; Women's Missionary Association, $943 10; Board of Missions P. E. Church U. S.: Domestic Committee, (Centennial offering,) $110 15; Foreign Committee, $117 08; Sewing Society, $1,650; the Poor, $427 55; Parish purposes, (Chancel, Sunday-School, work at Milton, etc.,) $1,340 66; Church purposes in general, (Indian Missions, Nebraska, Spring Valley, House of Good Shepherd and sundry offerings,) $236 22—total, $5,318 79.

Church of St. James the Less, Scarsdale; the Rev. WILLIAM AUGUSTUS HOLBROOK, Rector.

Families, 75. Individuals, 205. Baptisms, (ad. 1, inf. 7,) 8. Burials, 6. Communicants: removed into the Parish, 3; removed from the Parish, 11; died, 1; present number, 79. The Holy Communion celebrated monthly. Catechists and Sunday-School teachers, 9. Catechumens, 50; Children taught the Catechism openly in the Church, 50; times, 52; Sunday scholars, 6. Celebration of Divine Service: Sundays, morning and afternoo ; Holy Days, morning; other days, forty days in Lent, A. M. or P. M., 25th Anniversary—total, 160.

Contributions.—Episcopal Fund, $2; Diocesan Fund, $30; Board of Missions P. E. Church U. S.: Domestic Committee, $18 91; Parochial School, $70; the Poor, $45; Parish purposes, $2,599 24; Church purposes in general, $100—total, $2,865 15.

It is the intention of the Rector to receive an offering for every canonical charity when the Parish is free from all arrears in its internal economy. Church purposes in general includes the gift of two boxes of clothing made by the Women's Auxiliary of the Parish, one for St Barnabas' House and one for St. Mark's School, Salt Lake City.

St. Paul's Church, Sing Sing; the Rev. JAMES I. HELM, D. D., Rector.

Baptisms, (ad. 5, inf. 16.) 21. Confirmed, 10. Marriages, 7. Burials, 7. Communicants: present number, about 120. The Holy Communion celebrated the first Sunday in every month, on greater festivals, and on All Saints'. Celebration of Divine Service: Sundays, twice; Holy Days, all one service; other days, ordinarily, Friday; in Lent, Wednesday and Friday, twice; every day in Holy Week, twice.

Contributions.—Bishop's salary, $8; Diocesan Fund, $20; Missionary Committee of the Diocese, $22; Fund for Aged and Infirm Clergymen, $16 25; New-York Bible and Common Prayer-Book Society, $10; Board of Missions P. E. Church U. S.: Domestic Committee, $21; Foreign Committee, $20; the Poor, $300; Parish purposes, $995 05; Church purposes in general, $12—total, $1,154 30.

This year has been one of great depression. Families, thrown out of employment, have not been able to contribute. Some have needed help who have heretofore helped others; and those needing help at other times have been more necessitous. Demands have been far greater, and the ability to aid much diminished.

Trinity Church, Sing Sing; the Rev. GEORGE W. FERGUSON, Rector.

Baptisms, inf. 19. Confirmed, 21. Marriages, 4. Burials, 7. Communicants: present number, about 163 The Holy Communion celebrated monthly, except during Advent and Lent, then weekly, and on the chief festivals, Ash Wednesday and Thanksgiving Day. Catechumens: Children taught the Catechism openly in the Church, about 150. Celebration of Divine Service: Sundays, 104; Holy Days, all, 41; other days, 80—total, 225.

Contributions.—Episcopal Fund, $8; Diocesan Fund, $31 31; Missionary Committee of the Diocese, $23 46; Southern Missionary Convocation, $28 72; Fund for Aged and Infirm Clergymen, $32 40; Mission to the Jews, $15 07; Children's Easter Offerings, (to Bishop Hare, $60; Faribault, $52 98; St. Mary's Hospital for Children, $28 70,) $141 68; Indian Missions, $26 47; New-York Bible and Common Prayer-Book Society, $21 27; Sunday-School Offerings to St. Mary's Hospital for Children, $27 50, and Box of Clothing, $40—$67 50; Board of Missions P. E Church U. S.: Domestic Committee, $45 65; Missionary Box from the Parish Guild, $216 32; the Poor, $237 87; Parish purposes, $1,398 68—total, $2,291 40.

Christ Church, Tarrytown; the Rev. J. SELDEN SPENCER, Rector.

Families, about 80. Individuals, about 400. Baptisms, (ad 8, inf. 12,) 20 Confirmed, 32. Marriage, 1. Burials, 9. Communicants: present number, about 120. The Holy Communion celebrated first Sunday in every month and on greater festivals. Catechists and Sunday-School teachers, 16. Catechumens: Sunday scholars, 125. Celebration of Divine Service: Sundays, twice; also service in German language every Sunday for eight months; Holy Days, great festivals and Holy Week; other days, Wednesdays and Fridays in Lent, and Wednesday evenings, with lecture, all the year.

Contributions.—Episcopal Fund, (Bishop's salary assessment,) $20; Diocesan Fund, $50; Missionary Committee of the Diocese, $11 81; Society for Increase of Ministry, $42 69; Fund for Aged and Infirm Clergymen, $20 40; House of Good Shepherd, Haverstraw, $100; Chapel German Mission in Christ Church, Tarrytown, $69 22; Board of Missions P E. Church U. S.: Domestic Committee, $131 36; Sunday School, (Christmas tree, books, &c.,) $133 50; the Poor, $179 47; Parish purposes, (carpeting and refurnishing Sunday-School room,) $360; Church purposes in general, (to meet floating debt,) $1,200—total, $2,327 45.

St. John's Church, Tuckahoe; the Rev. ANGUS M. IVES, Minister.

Families and parts of families, 60. Individuals, 180. Baptisms, (ad. 1, inf. 4,) 5. Marriages, 2. Burials, 3. Communicants: admitted, 5; removed into the Parish, 1; present number, 77. The Holy Communion celebrated monthly and on the principal festivals. Catechists and Sunday-School teachers, 5. Catechumens, 43. Celebration of Divine Service: Sunday mornings throughout the year and on the greater festivals.

Contributions.—Episcopal Fund, $9 83; Diocesan Fund, $8; Missionary Committee of the Diocese, $10; Fund for Aged and Infirm Clergymen, $8 80; New-York Bible and Common Prayer-Book Society, $12; Board of Missions P. E Church U. S.: Domestic Committee, $11; Foreign Committee, $6 55; Mission to the Jews, $2 25; Parish purposes, $791 83—total, $860 36.

A class for Confirmation awaits the Bishop's visitation.

St. Peter's Church, Westchester; the Rev. CHRISTOPHER B. WYATT, Rector.

Families, 120. Baptisms, (ad. 3, inf. 15,) 18. Confirmed, 20. Marriage, 1. Burials, [illegible]. Communicants, 125. The Holy Communion celebrated first Sunday of each month and on chief festivals. Sunday-School teachers, 18. Catechumens: members of other classes for religious instruction, 12; Sunday Scholars, 170. Celebration of Divine Service: Sundays, twice; Holy Days, once; other days, two in each week.

Contributions.—Episcopal Fund, $[illegible]; Diocesan Fund, $[illegible]; Missionary Committee of the Diocese, $165 48; Diocesan Missions, (through Southern Missionary Convocation,) $164 11; Theological Education Fund, $37 95; Fund for Aged and Infirm Clergymen, $72 06; Mission to Jews, $21 45; New-York Bible and Common Prayer-Book Society, $28 18; Board of Missions P. E. Church U. S.: Domestic and Foreign Committees, (Centennial Thanksgiving offering,) $127 94; Domestic and Foreign Missions, (through Ladies' Auxiliary Association,) $500; "House of Good Shepherd," Rockland County, $300; the Poor, offerings in Church, $296 78; the Poor, special gift, $[illegible]; Parish purposes, $165—total, $2,180 20.

The Church has recently received a handsome gift from relations of the late Mistress Catharine Wilkins, who maintained, to the closing days of her life on earth, the consistent course of charitable and pious works by which, during a long membership in this Parish, her faith was illustrated, abundantly and substantially, yet altogether without ostentation.

The gift is a window of stained glass, designed and manufactured in England, with medallions representing the Six Works of Mercy.—St. Matthew, xxv. 35 and 36.

As a window, it greatly improves the light and enhances the beauty of the Church; as a work of fine art, it is excellent; as a memorial, set up by grateful and loving relations, of one gone before in peace and hope to await the judgment, when shall be said, "Inasmuch as ye have done it unto one of the least of these, my brethren," its propriety impressive, and its suggestions hortatory. By happy coincident, altogether fortuitous, the window was seen in its place by the congregation, for the first time, at morning service on the fourteenth Sunday after Trinity, when the XXVth chapter of St. Matthew is the appointed second lesson.

Grace Church, White Plains; the Rev. FREDERICK B. VAN KLEECK, Rector.

Families, 190. Individuals, 800. Baptisms, (ad. 9, inf. 18,) 27. Confirmed, 15. Marriages, 7. Burials, 19. Communicants: admitted, 18; removed into the Parish, 2; removed from the Parish, 11; died, 5; present number, 186. The Holy Communion celebrated on all high festivals, and monthly, with weekly celebrations during Advent and Lent. Catechists and Sunday-School teachers, 21. Catechumens, 200; Children taught the Catechism openly in the Church, 200; times, monthly. Celebration of Divine Service: Sundays, morning and night; Children's Service and Catechizing, monthly, and every other Sunday afternoon, at Rosedale Mission; Holy Days, morning service; other days, Wednesdays and Fridays; in Lent, daily Evening Prayer, with meditation; Wednesdays, Thursdays and Fridays, twice a day.

Contributions.—Episcopal Fund, $8; Diocesan Fund, $40; Missionary Committee of the Diocese, $25; Theological Education Fund, $31 55; Fund for Aged and Infirm Clergymen, $44 28; New-York City Mission Society, to the Jews, $16 60; New-York Bible and Common Prayer-Book Society, $19 53; House of Good Shepherd, Rockland County, $62 60; Indian Commission, $25; Home Missions to Colored People, $13 74; Children's Whitsun-Day Offerings, (Bishop Tuttle,) $231 50; Board of Missions P. E. Church U. S.: Domestic Committee, $63 50; Foreign Committee, $33 35; Southern Missionary Convocation, $40; the Poor, $214 36; Parish purposes, $600; Parish Purposes in general, (Christmas Tree, Guild, &c.) $178 67—total, $1,647 67.

St. *John's Church, Wilmot,* (*New-Rochelle;*) the Rev. ANGUS M. IVES, Missionary.

Families and parts of families, 29. Individuals, 106. Baptism, inf. 1. Marriage, 1. Communicants: admitted, 1; present number, 28. The Holy Communion celebrated on the third Sunday in every month and on the principal festivals. Catechists and Sunday School teachers, 5. Catechumens, 30. Celebration of Divine Service: Sunday afternoons throughout the year, on the greater festivals, and on the morning of the third Sunday of every month.

Contributions.—Episcopal Fund, $3 58; Diocesan Fund, $2; Missionary Committee of the Diocese, $3 18; Fund for Aged and Infirm Clergymen, $1; New-York Bible and Common Prayer-Book Society, $1 81; Board of Missions P. E. Church U. S.: Domestic Committee, $6; Foreign Committee, $3 84; Parish purposes, $340 66—total, $362 07.

St. *John's Church, Yonkers;* the Rev. ADDISON BUTLER ATKINS, D. D., Rector.

Baptisms, (ad. 3, inf. 52,) 55. Confirmed, 63. Marriages, 7. Burials, 36. Communicants, 477. The Holy Communion celebrated the first Sunday in each month, Christmas, Holy Thursday evening, Easter and Whitsun-Day. Sunday-School officers and teachers, 45; Scholars, 520. Children catechized openly in the Church, last Sunday afternoon of month. Divine Service: Sundays, twice, and on the last Sunday in each month, three times; Holy Days, principal; other days, except Summer months, Thursday, and Rector's Bible Class, Fridays; in Lent, three times in the week, and in Passion Week, daily.

Contributions.—Episcopal Fund, $64 40; Missionary Committee of the Diocese, $20; Aged and Infirm Clergy, $32 37; Board of Missions P. E. Church U. S.: Domestic Committee, $60; Foreign Committee, $65; Mexico, $59 25; Indian Department, $15; Society for the Conversion of the Jews, $31 40; the Poor, $745 48; Parish purposes, $2,109 74; St. John's Hospital, $1,669 30; S. S. for Hospital and Missions, $478 22; by Brotherhood for the Poor and for charitable objects, $101 80; for Choir and Parish indebtedness, $1,117—total, $6,568 96.

FROM THE FOLLOWING PARISHES NO REPORTS HAVE BEEN RECEIVED.

Church of the Regeneration, Pine Plains, Dutchess County.

St. Paul's Church, Pleasant Valley, Dutchess County.

Church of the Ascension, New-York, the Rev. J. Cotton Smith, D. D., Rector.

Mission Chapel of the Church of the Ascension, New-York.

Church of the Holy Trinity, New-York, the Rev. S. H. Tyng, Jr., D. D., Rector.

Church of the Intercessor, commonly called St. Alban's, New-York, the Rev. C. W. Morrill, Rector.

Church of the Mediator, New-York.

Church of the Resurrection, New-York.

St. Andrew's Church, New-York.

St. George's Church and Chapels, New-York, the Rev. S. H. Tyng, D. D., Rector.

St. James' Church, New-York, the Rev. C. B. Smith, Rector.

St. Matthias' Church, New-York, the Rev. N. E. Cornwall, D. D., Rector.

Church of the Transfiguration, New-York, the Rev. G. H. Houghton, D. D., Rector.

Grace Church, Harlem, New-York, the Rev. D. B. Ray, Rector.

Church of the Mediator, South Yonkers, Kingsbridge, the Rev. W. T. Wilson, Rector.

St. John's Church, Greenwood Iron Works, Orange County.

St. Andrew's Church, Richmond, Richmond County, the Rev. T. S. Yocom, Rector.

St. Luke's Church, Haverstraw, Rockland County.

Church of the Holy Child Jesus, Stony Point, Rockland County, the Rev. E. Gay, Missionary.

Trinity Church, Highland, Ulster County, the Rev. J. H. Johnson, Minister.

St. Mary's Church, Beechwood, Westchester County, the Rev. E. N. Mead, D. D., Minister.

St. Augustine's Church, Croton, Westchester County, the Rev. A. V. Clarkson, Rector.

St. Paul's Church, Eastchester, Westchester County, the Rev. W. S. Coffey, Rector.

St. Barnabas' Church, Irvington, Westchester County, the Rev. W. H. Benjamin, Rector.

St. Mark's Church, Katonah, Westchester County.

Trinity Church, New-Rochelle, Westchester County.

St. Mary's Church, North Castle, Westchester County.

St. Luke's Church, Somers, Westchester County, the Rev. R. C. Russell, Rector.

St. James' Church, North Salem, Westchester County, the Rev. R. C. Russell, Rector.

St. Paul's Church, Yonkers, Westchester County, the Rev. C. M. Wines, Rector.

St. Mary's Church, Yorktown, Westchester County.—31.

Also from the following, which have been incorporated and admitted into union with the Convention, but which maintain no services, viz.:

St. Mary's Church, Beekman, Dutchess County.
Church of the Advent, New-York.
Church of the Atonement, New-York. (Not that on Madison Avenue.)
Church of the Crucifixion, New-York.
Emmanuel Church, New-York.
Free Church of St. George's Chapel, New-York.
Church of the Good Shepherd, New-York.
Church of the Holy Evangelists, New-York.
Church of the Holy Innocents, New-York.
Church of the Holy Light, New-York.
Church of the Redemption, New-York.
St. Barnabas' Church, New-York.
St. Jude's Church, New-York.
St. Matthew's Church, New-York.
St. Paul's Church, 12th Ward, New-York.
St. Saviour's Church, New-York.
St. Sauveur's Church, New-York.
St. Simon's Church, New-York.—18.

OTHER CLERICAL REPORTS.

The Bishop of the Diocese has also received Reports, according to the Canon, from the following Clergymen of the Diocese, not having Parochial or Missionary charge:

The Rev. JOHN ANKETELL reports as follows:

I beg leave respectfully to report, that for seven months, (from All Saints' Day to Trinity Sunday last,) I acted as assistant to the Rev. Dr. Morgan, of St. Thomas' Church.

Since the latter date I have officiated and preached in various Churches in and about New-York City, having temporary charge of St. Thomas' Chapel during the month of August.

I also report two (2) infant baptisms, one of which was for St. Thomas' Chapel, and two (2) burials for St. Thomas' Church.

The Rev. W. M. A. BRODNAX reports as follows:

I have officiated during the year, since my last report, as I had opportunity, in New-York and adjoining Dioceses.

Statistics of my acts are included in returns from the Parishes in which they were done.

The Rev. SAMUEL BUEL, D. D., Professor of Systematic Divinity and Dogmatic Theology in the General Theological Seminary, respectfully reports:

That during the past year he has discharged the duties of his Professorship in the General Seminary. He has also officiated in Churches in the City of New-York, reading the service, preaching and administering the Holy Communion. He has solemnized one marriage. He has performed one private baptism.

The Rev. EDWARD COWLEY reports as follows:

In reporting the work of "The Children's Fold," during the past Conventional year, I am happy to state that it has gone steadily forward, in hard as in prosperous times. Fifty-four new children have been admitted; total for the year, 109. Average number, 55, viz.: 51 in the Fold, and 4 in private. This is our limit. Until the Church shall furnish the means of a larger house, better adapted to our uses, 55 must remain our limit, compelling us to say, "the Fold is full," and so to refuse more than twice as many applicants as we admit. Total number received and supported during the ten years since our organization, 317 different children. Seven of them have been in our care the whole time, and about a dozen for one-half of that period, while the time of the larger portion has varied from five years to as many days.

Thanks to the gracious Providence who has watched over these little ones, the general health has been excellent. Even the torrid heat of the past summer did not occasion the loss of a single meal to any of them, and the voice of joy and song has resounded through the Fold from all. Their moral and mental training has been careful and thorough. Five of the boys have sung very acceptably the last year in the choir of a neighboring Church. Two girls have been confirmed.

In addition to the various duties in connection with the Fold, I have assisted occasionally several of the clergy. I also report 3 burials, not elsewhere recorded.

The amount received by our treasurer, not otherwise reported to this Convention, is about $5,600.

The Rev. HENRY E. DUNCAN respectfully reports:

That during the last year he has officiated in the four Churches in Elizabeth as follows: Assisted at Holy Communion, 10; assisted at Baptism, 1; performed Baptism, 1; Catechized or addressed Children, 3; assisted at Funerals, 2; Preached, 19; performed Marriage Service, 1; read Prayers, 28; assisted in Prayers, 81 times.

The Rev. WILLIAM E. EIGENBRODT, D. D., Professor of Pastoral Theology in the General Theological Seminary, respectfully reports:

That throughout the last year, besides the regular discharge of his duties in the General Theological Seminary, he has been officiating in various Parish Churches in the Diocese of New-York and elsewhere, by saying prayers, preaching, baptizing, performing the burial service and administering the Holy Communion.

The Rev. RANDALL C. HALL, Professor of the Hebrew Language in the General Theological Seminary, reports as follows:

During the past year, in addition to my duties as Professor in the General Theological Seminary, I have assisted in the services of St. Stephen's Church of this city.

The Rev. ALEXANDER HAMILTON, deacon, respectfully reports:

That from the second Sunday in October, 1875, until the 6th of April last, he assisted in 64 services and performed one burial for the Rector of St. Mark's Memorial Church, Tarrytown, New-York, also assisting the Rector, Rev. Edmund Guilbert, in Parish School of St. Mark's Church. During the past summer I have performed the duties of my office wherever offered.

The Rev. ROBERT HOLDEN respectfully reports:

That in addition to his duties as Rector of Trinity School, he has assisted at St. Paul's Church, Morrisania, and officiated occasionally in other Parishes; has read service in whole or in part, 48 times; preached, 23 times, and officiated at one funeral.

The Rev. ALFRED EVAN JOHNSON reports as follows:

Since the last session of the Diocesan Convention, I have celebrated the Holy Communion seventeen times, and have baptized twenty-eight persons, of whom six were adults. I have officiated at least twice nearly every Sunday. The greater part of these services above mentioned were performed in the fulfilment of my duty as Rector of St. Peter's Church, Stone Ridge, the charge of which Parish I held from October 15th, 1875, to August 15th, 1876.

The Rev. CHARLES S. KNAPP respectfully reports:

That he has continued to act as Chaplain of the Panama Rail-Road Company, and Rector of Christ Church, Aspinwall, Panama. Has officiated at the usual Sunday services, conducted the Sunday-School reported last year, and held week day services during the season of Lent. Celebrated the Holy Communion monthly and on the principal festivals.

Has also been engaged in some Mission work among the Jamaicans, at a place called Monkey Hill, one of the stations on the line of the rail-road.

March 22d, laid the corner-stone of a Chapel here, to be known as St. Andrew's Chapel. July 6th, opened the same for the worship of Almighty God This Chapel is a neat frame building, and was paid for mostly by the Jamaicans. A flourishing Day and Sunday School is also established at this place.

Other official acts: Baptisms, 37; Marriages, 9; funerals, 15—one at sea.

The Rev. ROBERT W. LEWIS respectfully reports:

That during the past Conventional year he has officiated and preached from time to time in various Churches in the City of New-York as he has found opportunity, and in a few instances in country Parishes.

Having recently received an appointment as assistant Missionary in connection with the Church of the Holy Innocents, Hoboken, N. J., and having received a license to this end from the Bishop of Northern New-Jersey, he has entered upon his duties in that position.

The Rev. JOHN P. LUNDY, D. D., reports as follows:

Since my resignation of the Church of the Holy Apostles, New-York, on St. Andrew's Day last, November 30th, I have attended one funeral, solemnized one marriage, and baptized one infant.

I have also read Morning Prayer and sermons on several occasions, at Paul Smith's, Adirondacks, during the past summer.

The Rev. D. MARVIN, Jr., deacon, reports as follows:

Since my ordination in March last, I have been principally engaged in teaching, rendering occasional services in Churches in the City of Brooklyn. I have officiated at 45 services, preached 19 times, baptized one infant, and attended one funeral.

The Rev. R. U. MORGAN, D. D., reports as follows:

By request, I have read prayers and preached on six Sundays in Trinity Church, New-Rochelle; also, on Ascension Day, and the evening of St. John the Baptist. I have also, in the same Church, celebrated the Holy Communion twice, solemnized four marriages, and buried three adults.

On other occasions, either in officiating for my brethren in the ministry, or assisting them in their services, I have read morning and evening Prayers 15 times, assisted in the same 34 times, and preached on ten occasions; have administered the Holy Communion six times, and assisted in its celebration 27 times.

The Rev. EDWIN A. NICHOLS reports as follows:

I have officiated, as called upon, very often during the year past, both in public and private duties of the clerical office, relieving the neighboring clergy, but without any stated or permanent engagement, which would be preferable.

The Rev. SAMUEL OSGOOD, D. D., reports:

One baptism, infant; two marriages; five funerals. Of the above, the baptism was recorded with one of the marriages in Trinity Parish, Mount Vernon.

The funeral services were in the families of old parishioners.

I have generally preached on Sundays, often assisted in Holy Communion and have rendered various services in the Lent season, and in offices of instruction, piety and charity.

The Rev. JOSEPH H. PRICE, D. D., reports as follows:

After thirty-eight years and four months of service, I resigned the Rectorship of St. Stephen's Church, New-York, on the 2d of November, 1875. I did not resign because of insufficient support, nor for the mere purpose of obtaining rest, but for reasons too many and too vital to be embraced in this report.

Since November 2d, I have officiated on thirty-four occasions of public worship, and preached on fourteen of them.

I have officiated at five funerals.

I have presided at the Anniversary of the Bible and Common Prayer-Book Society, held at the Church of the Heavenly Rest, on the evening of the 9th of January last, and, by the appointment of the Bishop of New-Jersey, took part in the interesting Matriculation Services at the General Theological Seminary on St. Andrew's Day.

I desire to record my thankfulness to Almighty God for preserving my life from a burglar, threatening assassination. I ascribe my marvelous escape to that Grace which enabled me to present divine truth to him coolly, fearlessly and affectionately.

The Rev. John J. Roberts reports:

That, during the past year, he has held eighty (80) services in the Dioceses of New-York, New-Jersey and Massachusetts, in addition to the regular discharge of his duties as teacher and lecturer, at his residence 148 Madison Avenue, and as President of the Home for the Blind, 219 West Fourteenth-street.

The Rev. N. Frazier Robinson, deacon, reports as follows:

Having been received into this Diocese by letter dimissory from the Diocese of Pennsylvania, I have, since the 1st of September, 1875, been officiating as deacon at Trinity Church, in this city, and occasionally elsewhere. Baptisms, (ad. 2, child. 13,) 15. Burials, (assisted at 13, officiated alone at 6,) 19. These are recorded in the registers of Trinity Church. I have assisted in the celebration of the Holy Communion, 81 times. I have also, on several occasions, preached and catechized the youth of the Sunday and Parish Schools, visited the poor and sick, &c.

The Rev. George F. Seymour, S. T. D., Dean of the General Theological Seminary, and Professor of Ecclesiastical History in the same, respectfully reports:

That since the last Convention, in addition to his duties in the General Theological Seminary, he has continued to fill the position of Chaplain in the House of Mercy, New-York, at the foot of West Eighty-sixth-street.

In this institution, which has for its object the reclamation of fallen women, he has officiated on 223 occasions; he has baptized 1 adult, admitted 3 to the Holy Communion, and attended 1 funeral.

Outside of the House of Mercy the Dean has baptized 5 adults and 1 infant, preached 55 times for his brethren, celebrated the Holy Communion 5 times, attended 4 funerals, and married one couple.

Summary.—Baptisms, (ad. 6, inf. 1,) 7. Burials, 5. Marriage, 1. New Communicants: admitted, 3. Preached 109 sermons. Celebrations of Holy Communion, 110.

The Rev. George Henry Smith reports as follows:

Since I resigned my Parish in Pleasant Valley, N. Y., in October, 1875, on account of ill-health, I have resided in Middletown, Conn., and have, during that time, performed no official acts, excepting that I have assisted thrice in the administration of the Lord's Supper, and have preached once.

The Rev. J. A. Spencer, S. T. D., reports as follows:

That since the last Convention he has been constantly occupied in the duties of his position as Professor of the Greek Language and Literature in the College of the City of New-York. In addition he has officiated in the public services of the Church on about ten occasions, and buried one adult.

The Rev. H. C. STOWELL reports as follows:

My work in the Church during the last Conventional year has been about the same as the year previous, with the exception of a severe attack of sickness, which disabled me about six weeks. I have baptized three children, solemnized two marriages, and officiated at three funerals.

The Rev. EDWARD W. SYLE, Professor in the Imperial University of Yedo, Japan, respectfully reports:

That since the first of May, 1875, he has resided in Yedo, and has been engaged in the regular discharge of his duties as Professor of History and Philosophy in the *Kaisei Gakko*. He has also maintained a Sunday morning service in his own residence, and officiated occasionally at Christ Church, Yokohama, at H. B. M. Legation, Yedo, and at Bp. Williams' Mission Chapel in the Foreign Concession, *Tskidji*.

The Rev. H. M. TORBERT reports as follows:

Since my arrival in this country, the 1st of July, I have celebrated the Holy Communion about 27 times; preached, 9 times; made 1 address, and baptized 6.

The Rev. A. C. TREADWAY reports as follows:

The state of my health has not admitted of my doing much the year past. During the last winter, I suffered greatly from my old complaints, and was really disabled from doing any thing. And yet it has afforded me great satisfaction to assist my brethren, both here in Oswego, and in Washington City, (where I have spent a considerable part of the year,) in reading, preaching, and other duties, as occasions offered and my physical condition would allow. I have also rendered similar services in Potsdam, Lawrence County, and for my former parishioners in Malone, Franklin County, New-York.

The Rev. EDWARD H. VAN WINKLE reports as follows:

That he has performed the following services between the meeting of the last Convention and May 15th, 1876, the date of his transfer to the Diocese of Northern New-Jersey:

He has read service 22 times, and assisted thereat 82 times.

He has celebrated the Holy Communion twice, and assisted thereat 10 times.

He has preached 28 times.

He has attended one funeral and baptized one infant.

He has performed the above services since December 15th, 1875, as Assistant Minister of St. Matthew's Church, Jersey City.

He has resided at No. 25 West Ninth-street, New-York City.

The Rev. C. T. WOODRUFF, Superintendent of the New-York Protestant Episcopal City Mission Society, respectfully reports:

That in addition to his duties as Superintendent, he has officiated in the "New-York Infant Asylum," corner of 61st-street and 10th Avenue, on the first and third Sundays of the month, and at No. 24 Clinton Place on the second and fourth Sundays; he has also sustained a Sunday service at 4.15 P. M., and a noon service on Wednesdays at the "Midnight Mission."

He has officiated at 4 weddings; 79 baptisms; 21 funerals; taken the daily service, 62 times, and preached 30 times in St. Barnabas' Chapel, and administered Holy Communion wholly or in part on 46 public occasions, besides frequently assisting his brethren of the Clergy, and often visiting and relieving the sick and needy.

His office is at 306 Mulberry-street, New-York City.

The Rev. WILLIAM WALSH reports as follows:

I have not kept a regular list of the services in which I have been engaged the past Conventional year; perhaps it will be sufficient to state that I have been occupied in clerical offices on almost every Sunday, as I have had opportunity.

Appendix:

No. III.

A Table,—Showing the names of the Churches and Chapels in the Diocese of New-York, with the numbers in each, respectively, of Baptisms, Confirmations, Communicants, Marriages and Burials, so far as reported to the Bishop, for the year ending September 27, 1876. Prepared and published at the request of the Convention by the Secretary, in compliance with a Resolution recorded on p. 94 of the Journal of 1866. In those cases, where all the columns are blank, there is no Parochial Report from the Parish for the past year.

Churches and Chapels.	Baptisms.	Confirmations.	Communicants.	Marriages.	Burials.
Dutchess County.					
Amenia, St. Thomas's,	10	..	50	5	8
Annandale, St. Stephen's Coll. Chapel,	17	..	125	..	6
Barrytown, St. John the Evangelist's,	9	9	52	1	2
Beekman, St. Mary's,	..	..	..	..	..
Carthage Landing, St. Mark's,	15	20	30	1	..
Clinton, Apostle's,	..	..	..	..	..
Fishkill, Trinity,	3	..	37	1	1
Glenham, St. John Baptist,	35	18	61	5	10
Hyde Park. St. James',	44	22	128	1	11
Lithgow, St. Peter's,	2	..	17	..	..
Madalin, Trinity,	15	6	58	1	5
Matteawan, St. Luke's,	18	8	217	4	19
Millbrook, Grace,	2	..	42	..	..
Pawling,	1	..	5	..	..
Pine Plains, Regeneration,	..	..	..	..	..
Pleasant Valley, St. Paul's,	..	..	..	..	..
Poughkeepsie, Christ,	57	36	400	12	28
Holy Comforter,	61	27	297	18	17
St. Paul's,	29	12	221	1	20
Red Hook, Christ,	7	12	33	1	4
St. Paul's,	4	..	37	3	6
Rhinebeck, Messiah,	8	8	58	1	9
Rhinecliff, Ascension,	9	..	36	..	..
Wappinger's Falls, Zion,	77	66	407	10	19
New-York County.					
New-York, Advent,	..	..	..	..	..
All Angels',	5	..	40	8	2
All Saints',	99	27	233	33	43
Annunciation,	20	17	166	4	16
Anthon Memorial,	28	18	368	7	18
Ascension,	..	..	..	..	..
Ascension Miss. Chapel,	..	..	..	..	..
Atonement,	..	..	..	..	..

		Baptisms.	Confirmations.	Communicants.	Marriages.	Burials.
New-York,	Atonement, Madison Av.,					8
	Atonement Chapel,					7
	Bellevue,					[illegible]
	Beloved Disciple,					14
	Bethlehem Chapel,					20
	Calvary,					11
	Calvary Free Chapel,					46
	Christ Church,					..
	Crucifixion,					..
	Emmanuel,					..
	Epiphany,					..
	Free Church of Sain George's Chapel,					..
	Our Saviour,				..	..
	Floating Chapel Saviour,				15	8
	Good Shepherd,					..
	Grace,					28
	Grace Chapel,					10
	Heavenly Rest,					11
	Holy Apostles,					28
	Holy Communion,					..
	Holy Comforter,					5
	Holy Evangelists,					..
	Holy Innocents,					..
	Holy Light,					..
	Holy Martyrs,					70
	Holy Saviour,					25
	Holy Sepulchre,					7
	Holy Trinity,					..
	House of Mercy,					1
	Incarnation,					17
	Intercession,					19
	Intercessor,					..
	Mediator,					..
	Nativity,					15
	New-York City Mission, (including Bellevue and Bethlehem Chapels,)					209
	Reconciliation,	31	22			12
	Redeemer,	46	24			22
	Redemption,	..	..			..
	Reformation,	..	..			..
	Resurrection,	..	..		..	..
	Santiago,	12	60		12	3
	St. Ambrose,	53	20			20
	St. Andrew's,	..	..			..
	St. Ann's,	78	52			44
	St. Barnabas',	..	.	..		..
	St. Bartholomew's,	20	21	400		10
	St. Clement's,	19	22	150		10
	St. Esprit,	11	53	29		9
	St. George's and Chapels,	..	..	..		..
	St. George the Martyr's,	..	..	..		..
	St. Ignatius',	45	48	235		11
	St. James',	..	..	..	..	..
	St. John Baptist,	29	5	208	6	9
	St. John Evangelist,	55	44	500	23	37
	St. Jude's	..	..	..	..	.
	St. Luke's,	117	45	860	50	71
	St. Mark's, St. Mark's Mission,	47	71	580	12	47
	St. Mary's,	29	8	158	8	7
	St. Mary the Virgin,	29	21	200	7	4
	St. Matthew's,	..	..	..	..	..
	St. Matthias',	..	..	..	..	..

Churches and Chapels.	Baptisms.	Confirmations.	Communicants.	Marriages.	Burials.
New-York, St. Michael's,	30	23	192	3	26
St. Paul's in 12th Ward,	..	..	..	..	..
St. Peter's,	129	62	450	18	46
St. Philip's,	16	42	240	11	19
St. Saviour's,	..	..	..	..	..
St. Sauveur's,	..	..	..	..	..
St. Simon's,	..	..	..	..	..
St. Stephen's,	2	19	70	2	5
St. Thomas',	26	56	800	12	14
St. Thomas' Miss. Chap.,	40	37	146	7	23
St. Timothy's,	35	21	283	7	29
Transfiguration,	..	..	..	..	..
Trinity Church, St. Paul's Chapel, St. John's Chapel, Trinity Chapel, St. Chrysostom, St. Augustine, St. Cornelius', Governor's Island, } Miss. Cha.,	703	390	3,083	132	272
Zion Church,	6	12	200	4	8
Harlem, Grace,	.	..	..	.	..
Holy Trinity,	13	..	251	2	14
Fordham, St. James',	11	20	182	2	11
Morrisania, St. Ann's,	6	..	85	2	15
St. Paul's,	38	17	138	4	12
Trinity,	.	.	.	..	..
Mott Haven, St. Mary's,	32	12	189	12	17
Riverdale, Christ,	5	6	120	..	8
Kingsbridge, South Yonkers, Mediator,	..	..	..	..	..
West Farms, Grace,	16	20	55	1	6
Holy Cross Mission,	106	48	80	7	18
Orange County.					
Canterbury, St. John's,	17	.	50	1	4
Goshen, St. James',	19	15	235	5	16
Greenwood Iron Works, St. John's,	..	.	..	.	.
Highland Falls, Holy Innocents,	57	23	88	6	16
Monroe, Grace,	10	4	24	1	2
Newburgh, St. George's,	78	.	302	2	36
St. Paul's,	27	14	141	3	13
New-Windsor, St. Thomas',	6		53	1	3
Port Jervis, Grace,	32	42	101	2	9
South Middletown, Grace,	20	40	240	9	16
Walden, St. Andrew's,	11	9	78	1	3
Warwick, Christ,	13	5	50	1	4
Putnam County.					
Cold Spring, St. Mary's,	12	..	140	4	13
Patterson, Christ,	22	.	45	..	..
Philipsetown, St. Philip's,	16	14	70	..	8
Richmond County.					
Castleton, West Brighton, Ascension,	43	18	280	5	23
St. Mary's,	..		..	..	..
Clifton, St. John's,	47	30	300	11	20
Edgewater, St. Paul's,	50	44	300	7	21
New-Brighton, Christ,	25	15	175	7	19
Richmond, St. Andrew's,	..	..	..	..	..
Rossville, St. Luke's,	3	..	50	..	4
Southfield, Holy Comforter,	16	15	60	2	16

Churches and Chapels.	Baptisms.	Confirmations.	Communicants.	Marriages.	Burials.
Rockland County.					
Clarkstown, St. John's,	1	..	26	1	1
Haverstraw, Holy Trinity,	44	32	105	1	8
St. Luke's,	..	.	..	..	.
Nyack, Grace,	20	10	141	4	14
Piermont, Christ,	17	..	75	7	19
Ramapo, Christ,	5	8	50	5	3
Spring Valley, St. Paul's,	18	..	36	1	4
Stony Point, Holy Child Jesus,	..	..	..	..	..
Sullivan County.					
Monticello, St. John's,	24	32	166	5	11
Ulster County.					
Ellenville, St. Paul's,	63	24	65	1	14
Esopus, Ascension,	..	..	6	1	3
Highland, Trinity,	..	..	..	..	
Kingston, St. John's,	17	19	178	4	10
(Rondout,) Holy Spirit,	16	32	102	..	10
Marlborough, Christ,	8	..	45	2	2
Milton, All Saints',	41	14	50	2	6
Saugerties, Trinity,	14	32	99	5	8
Stone Ridge, St. Peter's,	26	..	18	..	2
Westchester County.					
Bedford, St. Matthew's,	18	12	84	1	14
Beechwood, St Mary's,	..		..	.	.
Briar Cliff All Saints',	.	2	25	1	1
City Island, Grace,	7	10	40	5	4
Cortlandt, Divine Love,	24	..	27	..	3
Croton, St Augustine's,	..	..	..	..	..
East Chester, St. Paul's,	.	..	..	..	
Greenburgh, Zion,	12	..	100	2	6
Mission Chapel,	1	..	12	..	
Irvington, St Barnabas,	..	..	..	..	..
Katonah, St Mark's,	..	..	..	.	
Lewisborough, St John's,	3		25	3	1
Mamaroneck, St Thomas',	19	8	123	5	13
Mount Pleasant, St Mark's,	24	12	134	2	18
Mount Vernon, Trinity,	12	8	184	6	9
New-Castle St Mark's,	19	..	52	..	4
New-Rochelle, Trinity	..	..	..	..	..
North Castle, St Mary's,	..	..	..	.	..
St Stephen's,	12	7	62	6	6
North Salem, St James',	..	..		..	.
Peekskill (Cortlandt,) St Peter's,	48	43	126		19
Pelham, Christ,	..	..	..	..	..
Pleasantville, St John's,	..	..	.	.	
Portchester, St Peter's,	26	..	161	7	16
Rye, Christ,	30	23	248	5	12
Scarsdale, St James the Less,	7	6	79	..	6
Sing Sing, St Paul's,	21	10	120	7	7
Trinity,	19	21	163	4	7
Somers, St Luke's,	..	..	..	..	..
Tarrytown, Christ,	20	32	120	1	9
Tuckahoe, St John's,	5	.	77	2	3
Westchester, St Peter's,	18	20	125	1	18
White Plains, Grace,	27	15	186	7	19
Wilmot, St John's,	1	..	23	1	.
Yonkers, St John's,	55	63	477	7	26
St Paul's,	..	..	..	..	..
Yorktown, St Mary's,	..	..	..	..	..

A Table,—Showing the names of the Churches and Chapels of the Diocese of New-York, with the sums contributed by each to the EPISCOPAL, D[illegible]SAN, EDUCATION and [illegible]NARY FUNDS, respectively, for the year 1875–76, in compl[illegible]ance with Canons xiii , xiv. and xv. ; prepared and publ[illegible]hed by [illegible]rder of the Convention, by the Secretary of the [illegible], with the aid of the Treasurers of the Funds ; to [illegible] are [illegible]dd, the Contributions to the FUND FOR AGED AND INFIRM CLERGYMEN, required by [illegible] xvi. The apportionment for the Salary of the Bishop, when paid, appears in the [illegible] of the Episcopal Fund.

Counties.	Churches and Chapels.	Clergymen.	Episcopal.	Diocesan.	Education.	Missionary.	Aged and Inf. Clergy.
Dutchess........	Amenia, St Thomas'...............	Rev. Amos T. Ashton........	$2 00	$8 00	$3 75	$6 85	$3 60
	Annandale, St. Stephen's Chapel....	R. B. Fairbairn, D. D...	7 00	10 00	14 57	10 65	26 06
	Barrytown, St. John's	....	2 00	....	11 18	16 00	12 95
	Beekman, St. Mary's	....	....	....	....	....	....
	Carthage [illegible], St. Mark's......	F. W. Shelton, D. D....	2 00	4 00	....	....	....
	Clinton, Apostles..................	....	....	....	....	....	....
	Fishkill, Trinity...................	J. R. Livingston........	6 00	6 25	10 00	19 05	23 31
	Gl[illegible], St. John Baptist.........	J. R. Livingston	2 00	3 98	....	14 00	5 00
	Hyde Park, St. James'...	P K. [illegible], D. D......	25 00	16 00	....	24 31	15 00
	Lithgow, St. Peter's..............	J. C. S. Weills	....	....	....	....	....
	[illegible], Trinity................	J. S. [illegible], D. D.......	....	....	....	....	....
	Matteawan, St Luke's.............	E. T. Bartlett..........	....	....	....	....	35 45
	[illegible]................	J. C. S. Weills.........	....	....	....	....	....
	Pine Plains, Regeneration..........	....	....	....	....	....	....
	Pl[illegible] Valley, St. Paul's.........	....	....	....	....	....	....
	Poughkeepsie, Christ............ }	H. L Ziegenfuss.......	15 00 20 21	40 00	14 86	87 77	32 18
	Holy Comforter.....	R. F. Crary	8 00	30 00	10 87	30 00	....

Counties.	Churches and Chapels.	Clergymen.	Episcopal.	Diocesan.	Education.	Missionary.	Aged and Inf. Clergy.
Dutchess	Poughkeepsie, St. Paul's	Rev. S. H. Synnott	$5 00	$15 00	....	....	....
	Red Hook, Christ	J. W. Moore	6 00	2 00	$14 15	$15 30	$10 00
	St. Paul's, Tivoli	G. L. Platt	3 00	15 00	....	....	....
	Rhinebeck, Messiah	A. F. Olmstead	....	18 00	....	10 00	....
	Rhinecliff, Ascension	T. S. Savage, D. D.	3 00	....	....	....	3 25
	Wappinger's Falls, Zion	H. Y. Satterlee	10 00	40 00	10 00	37 54	....
New-York	New-York, Advent	....	....	....	....	....	....
	All Angels'	C. F. Hoffman	3 37	6 00	4 77	3 00	6 50
	All Saints'	W. N. Dunnell	3 00	60 00	....	12 17	....
	Annunciation	W. J. Seabury, D. D.	15 00	48 00	....	5 85	40 90
	Anthon Memorial	R. H. Newton	12 00	....	....	....	....
	Ascension	J. Cotton Smith, D. D.	....	110 00	....	....	....
	Atonement	....	....	....	....	....	....
	Atonement, Madison Av.	C. C. Tiffany	15 00	....	....	....	....
	Beloved Disciple	F. H. Stubbs	....	....	....	3 12	....
	Calvary	E. A. Washburn, D. D.	'75, $100	120 00	....	....	....
	Christ	J. Fulton, D. D.	20 00	....	....	....	....
	Crucifixion	....	....	....	....	....	....
	Emmanuel	....	....	....	....	....	....
	Epiphany	U. T. Tracy	....	10 00	....	....	5 00
	Free Church St. George's Chapel, Beekman St.	....	....	....	....	....	....
	Good Shepherd	....	....	....	....	....	....
	Grace	Henry C. Potter, D. D.	120 00	....	....	225 00	422 95
	Heavenly Rest	R. S. Howland, D. D.	....	....	....	25 00	....
	Holy Apostles	B. E. Backus	....	....	....	....	60 65
	Holy Communion	F. E. Lawrence, D. D.	60 40	....	....	100 00	....
	Holy Comforter	H. F. Roberts	....	....	....	....	3 50
	Holy Innocents	....	....	....	....	....	....
	Holy Light	....	....	....	....	....	....
	Holy Martyrs	James Millett	....	....	....	....	....

Counties.	Churches and Chapels.	Clergymen.	Episcopal.	Diocesan.	Education.	Missionary.	Aged and Inf. Clergy.
New-York.......	New-York, Holy Saviour............	Rev. A. B. Carter, D. D......	....	....	....	....	....
	Holy Sepulchre.........	J. Tuttle Smith.........	$3 00	....	....	....	....
	Holy Trinity...........	S. H. Tyng, Jr., D. D...	25 00	....	....	....	....
	Incarnation	Arthur Brooks.........	40 00	$63 75	....	....	....
	Intercession............	E. W. Donald.........	....	....	....	....	....
	Intercessor, or St. Alban's	C. W. Morrill..........	20 00	....	....	....	....
	Mediator...............	....	....	....	....	....	....
	Nativity................	Caleb Clapp...........	....	28 00	....	....	....
	Reconciliation..........	E. S. Widdemer........	....	....	....	....	....
	Redeemer..............	J. W. Shackelford......	8 00	....	....	$27 05	....
	Redemption	....	....	....	....	....	....
	Reformation...........	....	....	....	....	....	....
	Resurrection...........	J. W. Trimble.........	....	....	....	....	....
	Santiago	J. De Palma..........	....	....	....	....	....
	St. Ambrose...........	Z. Doty................	....	12 00	....	....	....
	St. Andrew's..........	....	....	....	....	84 72	$28 58
	St. Ann's..............	Thomas Gallaudet, D. D.	5 00	60 00	$6 00	30 00	42 95
	St. Barnabas'..........	....	....	....	....	....	....
	Miss. Chap.	....	....	....	....	....	6 51
	St. Bartholomew's......	S. Cooke, D. D.........	80 00	....	....	245 60	198 65
	St. Clement's...	T. A. Eaton, D. D......	5 00	27 50	....	20 00	120 00
	St. Esprit..............	Leon Pons...........	'75, 3 00 '76, 2 00	48 00	....	....	5 00
	St. George's...........	S. H. Tyng, D. D.......	'75 $100	....	....	....	....
	St. George the Martyr's.	....	....	....	....	....	....
	St. Ignatius'...........	F. C. Ewer, D. D.......	5 00	....	....	....	....
	St. James'.............	C. B. Smith...........	....	....	....	....	....
	St. John Baptist........	C. R. Duffie, D. D......	5 00	5 00	5 00	5 00	....
	St. John Evangelist.....	W. T. Egbert..........	8 00	20 00	3 00	20 00	50 00
	St. Jude's.............	....	....	....	....	....	....
	St. Luke's.............	I. H. Tuttle, D. D......	7 00	50 00	....	34 53	29 26

Counties.	Churches and Chapels.		
New-York.......	New-York, St. Mark's..............	Rev.	J. H.
	St. Mary's..............		C. C.
	St. Mary the Virgin		T. M.
	St. Matthew's..........		......
	St. Matthias'...........		N. E.
	St. Michael's		T. M.
	St. Paul's, 12th Ward...		......
	St. Peter's..............		A B.
	St. Philip's............		J. S.
	St. Sauveur's...........		......
	St. Saviour's...........		......
	St. Simon's............		......
	St. Stephen's...........		A. B.
	St. Thomas'............		W. F.
	" Chapel......		R. W.
	St. Timothy's..........		G. J.
	Transfiguration.........		G. H.
	Trinity, with		Morg
	St. Paul's, ...		......
	St. John's, ...		......
	Trinity Chapels, ...		.....
	St. Augustine's, ...		......
	St. Chrysostom's, ...		......
	Zion....................		J. N.
	Holy Trinity, Harlem....		R. H.
	Grace, Harlem..........		D. B.
	St. James', Fordham....		J. N.
	St. Ann's, Morrisania....		Wm.
	St. Paul's, Morrisania....		T. R.
	Trinity, Morrisania......		A. S.
	St. Mary's, Mott Haven,..		C. B.

Counties.	Churches and Chapels.	Clergymen.	Episcopal.	Diocesan.	Education.	Missionary.	Aged and Inf. Clergy.
New-York.......	New-York, Christ, Riverdale........	Rev. G. D. Wildes, D. D.....	$12 00	$12 00	....	....	$50 00
	Mediator, South Yonkers or Kingsbridge.......	W. T. Wilson..........	....	....	....	....	....
	Grace, West Farms......	....	....	24 00	....	....	32 00
Orange..........	[illegible]ry, St. John's.............	J. F. Pottter..........	2 00	....	$3 00	$8 00	5 60
	Go[illegible]n, St. James'..............	W. H. De L. Grannis...	7 00	15 00	....	....	36 53
	Greenwood Iron Works, St. John's..	....	3 00	....	....	....	....
	Highland Falls, Holy Innocents.....	W. R. Thomas.........	3 00	20 00	5 00	11 67	29 12
	Monroe, Grace................	Henry A. [illegible]s........	2 00	2 00	1 00	2 22	....
	Newburgh, St. George's...........	John [illegible]n, D. D......	18 00	40 00	59 17	50 00	....
	St. Paul's..............	Rufus Emory..........	....	....	....	....	....
	New-Windsor, St. Thomas'.........	H. McKim,...........	3 00	....	....	....	12 70
	Port [illegible]is, [illegible]ce,...............	J. G. Rosencrantz......	2 00	....	....	15 20	5 00
	South Middletown, Grace..........	A. Capron,............	2 00	....	....	....	....
	[illegible]n, St. Andrew's............	W. E. Snowden,.......	2 00	9 00	....	20 00	....
	Warwick, Christ.................	Alfred Goldsborough...	2 00	12 00	....	10 00	5 00
Putnam..........	Cold Spring, St. Mary's.	Isaac Van Winkle......	15 00	35 00	6 08	11 62	17 70
	Patterson, Christ	Wilberforce Wells......	....	....	....	....	....
	Philipsetown, St. Philip's	A. Z. Gray...........	13 00	24 00	19 21	45 85	41 75
Richmond.......	Castl[illegible]ton,(West Brighton,) Ascension	J. S. Bush...........	....	....	....	....	35 15
	St. Mary's..............	....	....	....	....	....	....
	Clifton, St. John's................	J. C. Eccleston, M. D..	9 00 / 10 00	10 00	....	....	26 67
	[illegible]r, St. Paul's..............	A. U. Stanley.........	....	....	....	....	23 00
	New-Brighton, Christ............	G. D. Johnson........	13 00	....	....	....	48 13
	Richmond, St. Andrew's...........	T. S. Yocom..........	5 00	....	....	....	....
	Rossville, St. Luke's.	....	....	....	....	....	....
	[illegible]d, (Eltingville,) Holy Comforter...........	F. M Gray............	....	....	....	....	5 60
Rockland.......	Clar[illegible]ton, St John's..	R. S. Mansfield........	....	2 00	....	....	....
	Haverstraw, [illegible]ly Trinity.........	Geo. W. West........	2 00	....	....	5 00	....

Counties.	Churches and Chapels.	Clergymen.	Episcopal.	Diocesan.	Education.	Missionary.	Aged and Inf. Clergy.
Rockland........	Haverstraw St. Luke's..............	....	....	....	....	....	....
	Nyack, Grace.....................	Rev. Franklin Babbitt......	$3 00	$5 81	....	$20 63	....
	Piermont, Christ..................	S. G. Hitchcock........	2 00	5 00	....	12 00	3 65
	Ramapo, Christ....................	G. E. Purucker........	....	....	$1 00	2 00	4 00
	Spring Valley, St. Paul's..........	R. S. Mansfield........	....	....	....	....	....
	Stony Point, Holy Child Jesus......	E. Gay................	....	....	....	....	....
Sullivan.........	Monticello, St. John's.............	C. F. Canedy..........	2 00	16 00	....	10 64	10 47
	Thompsonville, St. Mary's..........	....	....	....	....	....	....
Ulster.....	Ellenville, St. Paul's.............	O. Valentine..........	....	....	....	3 00	2 24
	Esopus, Ascension..................	H. B. Sherman..........	....	....	....	....	....
	Highland, Trinity..................	J. Horsfall Johnson....	....	....	....	1 00	....
	Kingston, St John's................	C. W. Camp............	6 00	24 00	....	5 76	22 70
	Rondout, Holy Spirit.....	A. S. Dealey..........	....	....	....	....	....
	Marlborough, Christ................	Geo Waters, D. D......	....	4 00	....	11 70	....
	Milton, All Saints'................	J. Horsfall Johnson....	....	....	....	....	....
	Saugerties, Trinity................	J. J Robertson, D. D.. }	3 62 4 00	}	12 71	118 23	82 63
	Stone Ridge, St. Peter's...........	W T Tomlins........	2 00	10 00	....	2 00	3 00
Westchester......	Bedford, St. Matthew's.............	Lea Luquer............	....	4 00	....	....	28 48
	Beechwood, St. Mary's..............	E. N. Mead, D. D......	....	....	....	....	....
	City Island, Grace.................	J. Morsell, D. D......	....	....	....	5 00	....
	Croton, St. Augustine's............	A. V. Clarkson........	....	....	....	....	97
	Eastchester St Paul'	W. S. Coffey..........	....	7 80	....	15 50	....
	Greenburgh, Zion...................	Geo. B. Reese..........	10 00	25 00	....	10 00	20 75
	Irvington, St. Barnabas'...........	W. H. Benjamin......	....	....	....	100 00	17 05
	Katonah, St. Mark's................	....	....	....	....	....	....
	Lewisboro' St. John's..............	Robert Bolton..........	....	50	....	2 00	50
	Mamaroneck, St Thomas'	W W. Montgomery...	9 00	80 00	....	33 00	31 25
	Montrose, Divine Love..............	G. M. Cruger..........	....	....	....	....	....
	Mount Pleasant, St. Mark's	....	....	....	....	....	....
	Mount Vernon, Trinity....	W. B. Hooper..........	....	17 00	....	8 64	6 50

Counties.	Churches and Chapels.	Clergymen.	Episcopal.	Diocesan.	Education.	Missionary.	Aged and Inf. Clergy.
Westchester.....	New-Castle, St. Mark's............	Rev. J. H. Young...........	....	....	....	....	$3 34
	New-Rochelle, Trinity............	....	$14 00	$30 00	....	....	22 50
	North Castle, St. Mary's..........	....	....	....	....	....	....
	St. Stephen's.........	C. W. Bolton..........	....	....	....	....	6 32
	North Salem, St. James'........ ...	R. C. Russell..........	2 00	12 00	....	....	....
	Peekskill, (Cortlandt,) St. Peter's....	W. F. Lewis...........	7 00	30 00	$8 45	$38 46	16 16
	Pelham, Christ.....................	Chas. Higbee..........	....	....	....	9 40	18 65
	Pleasantville, St. John's...........	....	....	....	....	....	....
	Port Chester, St. Peter's...........	Brockholst Morgan.....	....	....	....	....	....
	Rye, Christ........................	C. B. Brewster.........	18 00	60 00	14 74	41 37	43 56
	Saw Mill Valley, St. Paul's.........	J. Drisler..............	2 00	2 60	....	3 10	....
	Scarsdale, St. James the Less.......	W. A. Holbrook.......	2 00	30 00	....	....	....
	Sing Sing, Briar Cliff, All Saints'....	J. B. Gibson, D. D.....	4 00	4 00	....	13 17	....
	St. Paul's....	J. I. Helm, D. D........	8 00	....	....	22 00	16 75
	Trinity.......	G. W. Ferguson........	8 00	....	....	23 46	32 50
	Somers, St. Luke's................	R. C. Russell..........	....	2 00	....	....	...
	Tarrytown, Christ.................	J. S. Spencer..........	20 00	50 00	....	11 81	....
	Tuckahoe, St. John's..............	A. M. Ives............	9 38	8 00	....	10 00	8 90
	Westchester, St. Peter's...........	C. B. Wyatt, D. D.....	....	60 00	37 90	164 76	76 06
	White Plains, Grace..............	F. B. Van Kleeck......	8 00	40 00	....	35 00	44 28
	Wilmot, St. John's................	A. M. Ives............	3 58	2 00	....	3 14	....
	Yonkers, St. John's...............	A. B. Atkins, D. D.....	18 00	....	....	20 00	33 37
	St. Paul's...............	C. M. Wines..........	....	....	....	....	18 43
	Yorktown, St. Mary's..............	....	....	....	....	....	....

SUMMARY

FOR THE YEAR ENDING AT THE CONVENTION,

*Episcopal Fund, from	95 Churches,	60
Diocesan "	96 "	03
Education "	27 "	98
Missionary	Church Collections, 65 Churches,	
	Interest,	
	Donations and Legacies,	
Aged and Infirm Clergy Fund:		
	Contributions, from 92 Churches,	81
	Interest on investments,	10
	Donations,	50
	Total,	

NOTE.—In some instances, contributions sent to the Treasurer immediately after the
paration of the Table for 1874–75, being included in that year's Table, are not repeated in
the contribution will, in such case, appear by reference to such items in the Parochial Reports of this
Table appear some contributions handed to the Treasurer since their official Reports the Convention.
seeming discrepancy in a few instances between this Table and Parochial Reports.

* This includes the apportionment for the Salary of the

Appendix:

No. V.

NOTE.—According to a Resolution recorded on page 94 of the Journal of 1866, there is included in the following List of Churches of this Diocese the date of the admission into its Convention of such Churches as are in union with the same. It is to be observed, that such date is not always that of the origin or incorporation of the Parish.

A. Of these Parishes, some existed under Royal Charter, or otherwise, prior to the first Convention of the Diocese in 1785. This class is denoted by the letter A, placed after the date of admission into union.

B. A few others seem to have been admitted by the Conventions, in which they respectively appeared for the first time by their delegates, although mention of the admission seems to have been omitted by the Journal. Such are designated by the letter B.

C. The few, incorporated under the law of April 13, 1854, are marked by the letter C.

List of Churches in the Diocese of New-York.

Counties.	Towns.	Churches.	Admitted.
Dutchess.	Amenia,	St. Thomas',	1849
	*Annandale,	*Holy Innocents,	
	*Barrytown,	*St. John Evangelist, Memorial,	
	Beekman,	St. Mary's,	1850
	Carthage Landing,	St. Mark's,	1868
	*Clinton,	*Apostles,	
	Fishkill,	Trinity,	1787 A
	†Glenham,	†St. John Baptist,	1876
	Hyde Park,	St. James',	1812
	Lithgow,	St. Peter's,	1834 A
	Madalin,	Trinity,	1866
	Matteawan,	St. Luke's,	1833
	*Millbrook,	*Grace,	
	Pine Plains,	Regeneration,	1860
	Pleasant Valley,	St. Paul's,	1837
	Poughkeepsie,	Christ,	1785 A
		Holy Comforter,	1866 C
		St. Paul's,	1835
	*Red Hook,	*Christ,	

Counties.		Churches.	Admitted.
Dutchess..........	Red Hook,	St. Paul's,	
	Rhinebeck,	Messiah,	
	*Rhinecliff,	*Ascension,	
	Wappinger's	Zion,	
	New-York,	Advent,	
		All Angels',	
		All Saints',	
		Annunciation,	
		Anthon Memorial,	
		Ascension,	
		*Ascen. Miss. Chapel,	
		Atonement,	
		Atonement, Madison Avenue,	
		*Beloved Disciple,	
		Calvary,	
		*Calvary Miss. Chap'l,	
		Christ,	
		Crucifixion,	
		Emmanuel,	
		Epiphany,	
		Heavenly Rest,	
		*Holy Comforter,	
		*Our Saviour,	
		Free Church of St. George's,	
		Good Shepherd,	
		Grace,	1809
		Holy Apostles,	1845
		*Holy Communion,	
		Holy Evangelists,	1845
		Holy Innocents,	1854
		Holy Light,	1870
		Holy Martyrs,	1847
		Holy Saviour,	1866
		Holy Sepulchre,	1868
		Holy Trinity,	1865
		Holy Trinity of Harlem,	1874
		Incarnation,	1852
		Intercession,	1849
		Intercessor,	1861
		Mediator,	1863
		Nativity,	1834
		Reconciliation,	1863
		Redeemer,	1853
		Redemption,	1843
		*Reformation,	
		Resurrection,	1869
		Santiago,	1867
		St. Ambrose,	1867
		St. Andrew's,	1829
		St. Ann's,	1854
		St. Barnabas',	1846
		St. Bartholomew's,	1835

Counties.	Towns.	Churches.	Admitted.
New-York.........	New-York,	*St. Chrysostom's,	
		St. Clement's,	1830
		*St. Cornelius',	
		St. Esprit,	1804 B
		St. George's,	1812
		St. George the Martyr's,	1845
		St. Ignatius',	1874
		St. James',	1810
		St. John Baptist's,	1848
		St. John Evangelist's	1853
		St. Jude's,	1843
		St. Luke's,	1821
		St. Mark's,	1801
		St. Mary's, *b.*	1824
		St. Mary the Virgin's,	1874 C
		St. Matthew's,	1846
		St. Matthias',	1864
		St. Michael's, *a.*	1807
		St. Paul's, 12th Ward	1862
		St. Peter's,	1831
		St. Philip's,	1853
		St. Sauveur's,	1844
		St. Saviour's,	1864
		St. Simon's,	1844
		St. Stephen's,	1805
		St. Thomas',	1824
		St. Timothy's,	1854
		Transfiguration,	1849
		Trinity, with St. Paul's, St. John's and Trinity Chapels,	1785 A
		Zion,	1810
	*Harlem,	*Grace,	
	Fordham,	St. James',	1855
	Morrisania,	St. Ann's,	1841
		St. Paul's,	1853
		Trinity,	1869
	Mott Haven,	St. Mary's,	1857
	Riverdale,	Christ,	1866
	West Farms,	Grace,	1848 B
Orange.............	Canterbury,	St. John's,	1858
	Goshen,	St. James',	1803
	Greenwood,	St. John's,	1868
	Highland Falls,	Holy Innocents,	1850
	*Monroe,	*Grace,	
	Newburgh,	St. George's,	1785 A
		St. Paul's,	1860
	New-Windsor,	St. Thomas',	1818
	Port Jervis,	Grace,	1854

(*a.*) Incorporated Aug. 17, 1807.

(*b.*) Incorporated Dec. 8, 1823.

C ties.		Churches.	Admitted.
	South Middletown,	Grace,	
	Walden,	St. Andrew's,	
	Warwick,	Christ,	
	Cold Spring,	St. Mary's,	
	Patterson,	Christ,	
	Philipsetown,	St. Philip's,	
Richmond .	Castleton, (W. ,)	Ascension,	
	Castleton,	St. Mary's,	
	Clifton,	St. John's,	
		*St. Simon's Chapel,	
	Edgewater,	St. Paul's Memorial,	
	New-Brighton	Christ,	
	Richmond,	St. Andrew's,	
	Rossville,	St. Luke's,	
	Southfield,	Holy Comforter,	
Rockland..	Clarkstown,	St. John's,	
	Haverstraw,	Trinity,	
		St. Luke's,	
	Nyack,	Grace,	1863
	Piermont,	Christ,	1848
	Ramapo,	Christ,	1860
	*Spring Valley,	*St. Paul's,	
Sullivan..........	*Callicoon Depot,	*St. James',	
	Monticello,	St. John's,	1817
	*Thomsonville,	*St. Mary's,	
Ulster.....	Ellenville,	St. Paul's,	1853
	Esopus,	Ascension,	1842
	†Highland,	†Holy Trinity,	1876 C
	Kingston,	St. John's,	1833
	Marlborough,	Christ,	1837
	Milton,	All Saints',	1850
	Rondout,	Holy Spirit,	1850
	Saugerties,	Trinity,	1831
	Stone Ridge,	St. Peter's,	1846
Westchester.......	Bedford,	St. Matthew's,	1787 A
	*Beechwood,	*St. Mary's,	
	Briar Cliff,	All Saints',	1869
	*City Island,	*Grace,	
	Cortlandt, (Croton,)	Augustine's,	1855
	East Chester,	Paul's,	1787
	Greenburg,	Zion,	1834
	Irvington,	St. Barnabas',	1859
	Katonah,	St. Mark's,	1853
	Lewisboro',	St. John's,	1853
	Mamaroneck,	St. Thomas',	1817
	*Montrose,	*Divine Love,	
	Mount Pleasant,	St. Mark's,	1864
	Mount Vernon,	Trinity,	1857
	New Castle,	St. Mark's,	1861 A
	New-Rochelle,	Trinity,	1785
	North Castle,	St. Mary's,	1853 A
		St. Stephen's,	1844

* Not in union with the Convention.

Counties.	Towns.	Churches.	Admitted.
Westchester.	North Salem,	St. James',	1792 A
	Peekskill,	St. Peter's,	1791 A
	Pelham,	Christ,	1843
	Pleasantville,	St. John's,	1853
	Portchester,	St. Peter's,	1852
	Rye,	Christ,	1786 A
	Scarsdale,	St. James the Less,	1849
	Sing Sing,	St. Paul's,	1834
		Trinity,	1869
	Somers,	St. Luke's,	1839
	Tarrytown,	Christ,	1836
	Tuckahoe,	St. John's,	1853
	Westchester,	St. Peter's,	1790 A
	White Plains,	Grace,	1824 A
	Wilmot,	St. John's,	1861
	Yonkers,	Mediator,	1858 B
		St. John's,	1787 A
		St. Paul's,	1859
	Yorktown,	St. Mary's,	1870

Number of Churches and Chapels represented by certificates of Lay Delegates, ... 117
Number of Churches not represented, ... 51

Number do. entitled to representation, ... 168
Number do. not in union with the Convention, ... 26

Number of Churches and Chapels in the Diocese, ... 194
Two Churches admitted into union this year.

* Not in union with the Convention.
† Admitted at this Convention.

Appendix:

No. VI.

Officers of the Diocese.

THE DIOCESAN CONVENTION.

The Rt. Rev. HORATIO POTTER, D. D., LL. D., D. C. L., *President.*
The Rev. WILLIAM E. EIGENBRODT, D. D., *Secretary.*
The Rev. THEODORE A. EATON, D. D., *Assistant Secretary.*
EDWARD F. DE LANCEY, Esq., *Treasurer.*

THE STANDING COMMITTEE.

The Rev. MORGAN DIX, D. D., *President.*
The Rev. WILLIAM E. EIGENBRODT, D. D., *Secretary.*
The Rev. WILLIAM F. MORGAN, D. D.,
The Rev. ISAAC H. TUTTLE, D. D.,
STEPHEN P. NASH, Esq.,
LLOYD W. WELLS, Esq.,
HENRY DRISLER, LL. D.,
GEORGE MACCULLOCH MILLER, Esq.

THE DEPUTIES TO THE GENERAL CONVENTION.

The Rev. ALFRED B. BEACH, D. D.,
The Rev. PHILANDER K. CADY, D. D.,
The Hon. HAMILTON FISH,
CAMBRIDGE LIVINGSTON, Esq.,
WILLIAM A. DAVIES, Esq.

THE PROVISIONAL DEPUTIES.

The Rev. GEORGE J. GEER, D. D.,
The Rev. CHRISTOPHER B. WYATT, D. D.,
The Rev. MORGAN DIX, D. D.,
The Rev. ROBERT S. HOWLAND, D. D.,
Prof. HENRY DRISLER, LL. D.,
The Hon. JOHN A. DIX,
The Hon JAMES EMOTT,
Prof. THOMAS EGGLESTON.

THE MISSIONARY COMMITTEE.

The Rev. ALFRED B. BEACH, D. D.,
The Rev. CORNELIUS E. SWOPE, D. D.,
The Rev. JAMES STARR CLARK, D. D.,
The Rev. OCTAVIUS APPLEGATE,
The Rev. CHRISTOPHER B. WYATT, D. D.,
HAMILTON BRUCE, Esq.,
WILLIAM M. KINGSLAND, Esq.,
JAMES POTT, Esq.,
C. A. HIGGINS, Esq.,
JOHN CAREY, Jr., Esq.

THE TRUSTEES OF THE EPISCOPAL FUND.

GOUVERNEUR M. OGDEN, Esq.,
THOMAS P. CUMMINGS, Esq., *Secretary and Treasurer,*
FREDERICK G. FOSTER, Esq,
HUGH AUCHINCLOSS, Esq.,
Hon. JOHN A. DIX.

THE TRUSTEES OF THE AGED AND INFIRM CLERGY FUND.

The Rt Rev. HORATIO POTTER, D. D., LL. D., D. C. L.,
CYRUS CURTISS, Esq.,
WILLIAM BETTS, Esq.,
EDWARD F. DE LANCEY, Esq.

THE TRUSTEES OF THE PAROCHIAL FUND.

The Right Rev. THE BISHOP OF THE DIOCESE, *ex-officio.*
ADAM NORRIE, ROBERT B. PARROTT, } Until October, 1876.
MURRAY HOFFMAN, FREDERICK S. WINSTON, } Until October, 1877.
JOHN JAY, WILLIAM ALEXANDER SMITH, } Until October, 1878.

The Committee

ON THE INCORPORATION AND ADMISSION OF CHURCHES.

CHARLES TRACY, Esq.,
The Rev. ALFRED B. BEACH, D. D.,
The Hon. JOHN A. DIX.

Special Committees of the Convention.

ON THE SALARY OF THE BISHOP.

(See Journal of 1876, p. 44.)

The Rev. Benjamin I. Haight, D. D.; the Rev. Isaac H. Tuttle, D. D.; Cyrus Curtiss, Esq.; Hon. John A. Dix; Frederick G. Foster, Esq.; William Scott, Esq.; Lloyd W. Wells, Esq.; Frederick Prime, Esq.; Thomas P. Cummings, Esq., and George Macculloch Miller, Esq.

ON A CATHEDRAL.

(See Journal of 1872, pp. 89, 111.)

The Rt. Rev. Horatio Potter, D. D., LL. D., D. C. L.; the Rev. Morgan Dix, D. D.; Henry C. Potter, D. D.; John Cotton Smith, D. D.; George H. Houghton, D. D.; Philander K. Cady, D. D.; Hon. Hamilton Fish; Messrs. John J. Cisco, Stephen P. Nash, Mr. Guion, Mr. Duncan; Hon. S. B. Ruggles; Messrs. William Scott, George M. Miller, Howard Potter.

ON FORMING A CORPORATION UNDER THE ACT OF THE LEGISLATURE OF THE STATE OF NEW-YORK, PASSED APRIL 11TH, 1876, BEING CHAPTER 110 OF THE LAWS OF 1876.

(See Journal of 1876, pp. 56, 105.)

Charles Tracy, Esq.; Cambridge Livingston, Esq.; Rev. William E. Eigenbrodt, D. D.; Frederick S. Winston, Esq.; Hon. Samuel B. Ruggles.

*** *The* STANDING COMMITTEE *of the Diocese meets statedly on the* FIRST THURSDAY *of every month. Papers requiring the action of the Committee should be sent prior to this date, and addressed to the Secretary.*

Appendix:

No. VII.

STATISTICS OF THE DIOCESE, 1875-76.

From the Episcopal Address, the Parochial and Missionary Reports, etc.

Clergymen canonically resident in the Diocese,..................		305
Churches and Chapels,....................................		193
Ordinations: Deacons, 13; Priests, 7,.........................		20
Clergymen instituted into Rectorships,........		2
" received into the Diocese,..........................		16
" transferred to other Dioceses,.......................		17
" died,..		5
Candidates for Orders,....................................		40
Church consecrated,.......................................		1

The following statistics are derived from 141 Parochial Reports:

Baptisms: Adults, 744; Infants, 3,707—total,....................		4,451
Confirmed,..		3,612
Marriages,..		896
Burials,.........		2,415
Catechumens,..		23,183
Catechists, or Sunday-School teachers,.........................		1,926
Communicants: admitted, as reported,.........................		1,298
present number, as reported from 141 Congregations,....................	24,884	
add as estimated from 31 Parishes not reporting, including some of the largest in the Diocese,..............	5,000	
	———	29,884

a complete view of the Diocese in these respects during the past year.

Difference in the dates of making the calculations severally will account for any discrepancy between the foregoing statement of the Contributions and those given in the preceding Table.

JOURNAL OF THE CONVENTION:

1876.

CONTENTS.

Lightning Source UK Ltd.
Milton Keynes UK
UKHW011426231118
332790UK00011B/1622/P